CRUISING THE
FLORIDA KEYS

CRUISING THE
FLORIDA KEYS

By Claiborne S. Young
and Morgan Stinemetz

PELICAN PUBLISHING COMPANY
GRETNA 2002

*The word "Pelican" and the depiction of a pelican are trademarks
of Pelican Publishing Company, Inc., and are registered
in the U.S. Patent and Trademark Office.*

Maps provided courtesy of Claiborne S. Young
All photographs by Claiborne S. Young, Karen A. Young, and Morgan Stinemetz

ISBN 1-56554-026-3

Information in this guidebook is based on authoritative data available at the time of printing. Prices and hours of operation of businesses listed are subject to change without notice. Readers are asked to take this into account when consulting this guide.

Printed in the United States of America

Published by Pelican Publishing Company, Inc.
1000 Burmaster Street, Gretna, Louisiana 70053

Contents

Foreword

I will never forget my first "get acquainted" trip to the Florida Keys as part of the preparation for writing this guide. My first-rate, first mate, Karen Ann, and I flew into the Fort Lauderdale International Airport, picked up a rental car, and headed for Key Largo with a song in our hearts. That didn't last long.

Having never really driven to the Keys before, we proceeded merrily south down Interstate 95, until it dead-ended into Highway U.S. 1. We thought (so much for thinking) that we then could easily follow this major road to Key Largo.

We arrived at the southerly terminus of I-95 about 5:00 P.M., and you can guess the rest. It was bumper-to-bumper traffic, with legions of stoplights and enough honking cars (plus angry drivers) to make the Long Island Expressway seem like a picnic. By the time Florida City at last topped the horizon, we were both thoroughly frazzled and had begun to entertain deep misgivings as to the wisdom of this new project that I had dreamed up.

Then, we broke off from Florida City, drove across the desolate stretch of U.S. 1, which leads to the Jewfish Creek Bridge, and passed across that span into upper Key Largo. It was as if someone had thrown a very dramatic switch. While, to be sure, there was still automobile traffic, gone were the honking horns and the frenzied, high-energy pace that had so dogged us as we made our stop-and-go way south from Miami to Florida City. Suddenly, things were moving at a far slower and more comfortable pace. The motel clerk in Key Largo was solicitous of our comfort and very helpful with info about where to go and

what to see. Over the next several days, time after time, we encountered Keys citizens who went out of their way to point us in the right direction. We felt like people who wandered in a desert, only to suddenly find an oasis bathed in the shimmering drops of a cool waterfall. In the space of only a few days, it was crystal clear that we were onto something good, and that something was—and is—the Florida Keys.

By the way, under that category of "don't do this," if you ever drive to Key Largo from Miami or Fort Lauderdale, do NOT take the I-95-U.S. 1 route. Instead, fork over a few bucks and follow the wide, stoplightless Florida State Sunshine Parkway all the way south to Florida City. Your nerves will be ever so much happier.

Welcome Morgan

For the first time in this series of guidebooks, this writer is being joined by a coauthor. Morgan Stinemetz is not only a dear friend but also a writer of no mean talent. He has previously helped me with updates to my *Cruising Guide to Western Florida,* as those of you who have that particular volume may have noticed. Morgan pens a weekly sailing column, which has appeared in the *Sarasota Herald-Tribune* for the past decade and more. Additionally, Morgan writes feature nautical pieces for the *Tampa Tribune.* He is also the creator of the popular episodic adventures of a live-alone, live-aboard sailor by the name of Bubba Whartz. Bubba's adventures—some say misadventures—appear monthly in *Southwinds,* a southeastern sailing magazine. Additionally,

Morgan's work has appeared in *Sailing World, Cruising World, Sail, Southern Boating, Sailors' Gazette, Regatta, Gulf Coast Life, Small Boat Journal,* plus a number of other publications. Morgan has a 1973 Ericson 27 sloop, *Reefer,* which he has owned since 1976. He says it is the ideal boat for him, small enough to sail solo and big enough to enjoy staying aboard for days at a time. Morgan has a Coast Guard Master's License and is the recipient of U.S. Sailing's Arthur B. Hanson Rescue Medal for saving a life at sea. In a sailboat race, one of Morgan's crew fell over the side of his vessel. Morgan recovered the man, under sail alone, in forty-five seconds, and *Reefer* went on to win the race.

Morgan brings his keen observer's eye and dry (sometimes wicked) sense of humor to this guide, just as he does to all his other writings. It is my sincere belief that his contributions added immeasurably to this book's appeal and readability.

All readers should be advised that Morgan and I are coequal authors in every sense of the word in regards to this *Cruising the Florida Keys.* We share equally in this book's appeal or lack thereof.

It has been one of the greatest pleasures in my writing career to share responsibility for this book with Morgan. Who knows what the future might bring in regards to other joint projects?

Before pushing on, allow me to announce that Pelican Publishing Company will soon be releasing a collection of Bubba Whartz's exploits. I have no doubt that this book, when available, will sell like proverbial hot cakes.

Well, so much for the "word from Claiborne." The remainder of this introduction, as well as the rest of this guidebook, has been written jointly by both yours truly and Morgan. In fact, most of the introduction you will read below was penned by my worthy coauthor. Enjoy!

Acknowledgments

First and foremost, I want to thank my first-rate, first mate, Karen Ann, without whose help as an experienced navigator, photographer, and research assistant this book would not have been possible. A very special thanks goes to my ace research assistant, Bob Horne. Without his many selfless hours spent with this writer during on-the-water research, this book would have been ever so much more difficult. A most welcome nod also goes to my coauthor, Morgan Stinemetz. This is my first time collaborating with another writer in the composition of a guidebook, and Morgan's good humor and wit have made this association a most pleasant experience, indeed. I would also like to thank Captain Don and Ms. Susan Sorrenson of Tavernier, Florida for looking after our research craft and its associated landside vehicle for many months. Additionally, Captain Don's on-the-water advice has proven to be invaluable. Their contribution to this book cannot be overstated. I would additionally like to recognize the contributions of Ms. Carrie Duvall, who worked on the many grayscale chart snippets that appear in this guidebook. I gratefully acknowledge the assistance of the many dockmasters and marina managers throughout the Florida Keys who gave so much of their time and wisdom to us during our research. While they are too numerous to mention, their input was invaluable. Finally, I would like to thank Dr. Milburn Calhoun, Nancy Calhoun, Kathleen Calhoun Nettleton, Nina Kooij, Cynthia Williams, Tracey Clements, and the rest of the staff at Pelican Publishing Company. Once again, it has been a genuine pleasure to work with the "Pelican Bunch," and we hope our relationship will continue for many years to come.

Claiborne

My coauthor, Claiborne Young, is the first person on my side of this arrangement who gets my thanks. We had done some work together before, on a contract basis. From that experience, Claiborne liked my writing enough to dial me in on this project. He has done it all before, of course. So he was able to keep me on track, on task, and happy. I learned some things about writing from Claiborne—he is very thorough—and I also learned some things about how to get along with other people while working on this book.

I give my thanks, too, to Thorn Trainer, a lady of exceptional charm and good taste. She runs a bed and breakfast on Plantation Key, and I had the great good luck to be referred her way when I was looking for a place to stay while working in the Upper Keys. Casa Thorn is reason enough to go to the Keys, even if you don't cruise. Also, Thorn was my local set of eyes and ears. She corrected, tactfully, my mistakes and helped me pick up little pieces of research that I misplaced here and there, like ashes in the wind.

My thanks, too, goes to Dan Mobley, who provided me with a place to rack out in Key West while there. Dan knows his way around town. He took me out to the nether reaches of Geiger Key, where we ran into some of the Key West "unexpected."

Additional thanks go to Billy Johnson and Norm Hale, my shipmates in the excursion to the Dry Tortugas. Johnson, who is in his late seventies as I am writing this, is the most accomplished mariner I have ever met. He has sailed oceans, lakes, bays, and rivers too many to count. If it were possible to sail to Hell, and Billy asked me to go, I'd go. I know I could count on him to bring me back. Norm Hale and I have sailed together for years. He is a good friend, and he shoulders the extra loads of going to sea in small boats with a willing cheerfulness.

Morgan

Introduction

The Florida Keys, strung, as they are, like a jeweled necklace southwestward from mainland Florida, could arguably be called the precious stones of Florida cruising. They are serenely tropical. Ubiquitous coconut palms dot the islands. The water is clear as gin. The weather picture is nearly always perfect, with vistas that stretch away to the horizon. The fishing is just this side of a sure thing, every time. And the anchorages you find off the beaten path will make you want to linger on until your holding tank is full and your water tank is empty.

Dawdling could get to be a habit down here, because the Florida Keys can be—and probably should be—explored at a leisurely pace. You will quickly discover that most of your fellow cruisers have already adapted to this languid lifestyle.

The Keys themselves are as diverse as opinions from the Supreme Court. However, the one aspect they all share is that they are low-lying islands. Some of the Keys have an exciting array of flora and fauna, while others are not much more than rock, marl, and mangrove. Where facilities that cruisers need—grocery stores, marine repair yards, restaurants, etc.—are plentiful, it is a sure sign that the islands have long-held allure for human habitation. You will note this in particular from Key Biscayne to Marathon. From Marathon to Key West, the number of stopping-off places with amenities thins out considerably. It is a function of landscape, not of economics. Key West, of course, has everything any cruiser might need . . . and a slew of things most cruisers have never thought of or seen before.

Florida Keys Geography

For many years now, fellow cruisers have noted that when they are (for instance) traveling south to north on the Atlantic ICW, the coverage in our guides often runs in the contrary direction, north to south. Thus, they must, in a sense, read backwards. There is really no help for this in a typical coastal setting, unless we had one version of a particular guide running north to south, and another south to north—an impractical suggestion at best.

In this guidebook, however, we have made an extra effort to overcome this problem, at least in regards to those readily navigable routes that connect the outside, Hawk Channel passage with the inside, Florida Bay-ICW route. By the way, "readily navigable route," as used here, is defined as a reasonably well-marked channel, either crossed by no bridge at all or spanned by a high-rise bridge or an opening bridge. Thus, if a passage is crossed by a 12-foot fixed bridge, it does NOT fit our criteria.

What we have done (again, for instance) is to cover such routes as Snake Creek in our ICW section, from its northern inception, hard by the Waterway's track, to its terminus in the offshore waters near Hawk Channel. Then, in our Hawk Channel section, we AGAIN cover Snake Creek, except this time, our account follows Snake Creek from Hawk Channel to the ICW.

Gentle reader, you will appreciate that this two-way coverage means that you will note some sections repeated (in some cases word for word) in both the ICW and Hawk Channel accounts of these waters. Don't worry, we haven't lost our minds. We did not want to force you to have to refer back to a previous section to find ALL the information you might need about any of these important links between the Keys' inland and offshore waters.

As referred to briefly above, the Keys have a unique geography, both from the land and water. For one thing, by the time you reach Islamorada, the Keys begin to run on an east-to-west, instead of a north-to-south, axis. Thus, southbound becomes westbound, and northbound becomes eastbound. It can be a bit confusing at times, but we'll do our best to play the part of interpreters as we make our way through this guide.

There are two fundamentally different routes that one might choose to cruise from Miami to Key West: the ICW or Hawk Channel. The inside–Intracoastal Waterway (ICW or "the Waterway") passage runs south down Biscayne Bay, skips through Little Card Sound, then Card Sound, and finally passes through Jewfish Creek, and under the one and only bridge that crosses the ICW's direct path between Coconut Grove and Key West.

South of Jewfish Creek, the Waterway cuts south and eventually west along the inner face of the Florida Keys. To the east and north, the shoal waters of Florida Bay seem to stretch away endlessly into the sunset and call longingly to the heart of any explorer. Just remember that these waters are very, very shallow, and as we shall learn below, running aground in the Florida Keys can be a very expensive proposition indeed.

A host of streams connect the ICW and the offshore Hawk Channel route, beginning on southerly Biscayne Bay and running all the way to the Moser Channel, just west of Marathon. Many of these passages are shallow, while others are crossed by low-level, fixed bridges that bar passage for all but small craft. Between Key Largo and Big Pine Key, only Angelfish Creek, Snake Creek, Channel Five, and the Moser Channel offer a reliable means for large cruising craft to move from one route to the other.

West (and you might want to think of that as "south") of Marathon, many believe that the ICW ends at Moser Channel. Not so! In fact, one of the most fascinating cruising possibilities in all of the Florida Keys can be accessed by following the Waterway north through Big Spanish Channel, and then west as the ICW skips along the northerly tips of a series of wholly undeveloped Keys all the way to Key West. Some of the best backwater anchorages you will ever enjoy are found along this stretch, though none are without at least a bit of a navigational challenge.

The Florida Keys version of the ICW is well-marked and fairly simple to navigate during daylight and in fair weather. Shallow water certainly abuts the channel here and there, but navigators who pay attention to business should be able to keep to the good water. At night, or with foul weather in the offing, things aren't so easy.

The number one disadvantage of the ICW passage between Key Largo and Key West will be felt most keenly by deep-draft vessels. At times, low-water depths of as little as 5 feet can be experienced, even when following the centerline of the channel directly between the various markers. Clearly, this route is best situated for mariners who pilot vessels 45 feet and smaller, and most importantly, which draw 4½ feet or less.

Another drawback of the ICW route is the relative absence of marinas that cater to cruising-sized craft. To be sure, there are plenty of pleasure-craft facilities along this watery ribbon, but most are geared towards smaller, power vessels. Fortunately, there are a few exceptions.

Conversely, the ICW teems with anchorages of all descriptions. If you are one of those cruisers who prefer to spend your evenings swinging on the hook, rather than tucked snugly into a slip, then by all means consider following the Waterway as opposed to Hawk Channel. Just remember the size and draft requirements outlined above.

The other approach is Hawk Channel. This wide passage runs the gap between the Keys' eastern (and eventually southern) face and a series of offshore reefs. These shallows do tend to shelter Hawk Channel from the very worst of the offshore swells, but when the wind gets its dander up, this can be a very dusty crossing from time to time.

The Hawk Channel passage boasts the best marinas by far for cruising craft in the Florida Keys. While the gaps between Key Biscayne and Key Largo, and between Bahia Honda Key and Stock Island are exceptions, cruisers will otherwise find reliable pleasure-craft facilities within an hour's run, at the most.

In a mirror image of the ICW route, anchorages are few and far between off Hawk Channel. There are a few good stops between Bahia Honda Key and Key West; otherwise, don't count on being able to drop the hook very often while following the Hawk.

Successful navigation of Hawk Channel can be a bit of a challenge. The various aids to navigation along the way are mostly skeletal, steel structures, but they are widely spaced—at times, VERY widely spaced. And it's important to pick up all these various aids to navigation and pass them on the proper side. More than a few of these markers denote shallow water, sometimes stretched over coral reefs, and to repeat ourselves, running aground in the Keys can be a quick study in dollar disposal.

For the most part, depths along the course of Hawk Channel run in the 15+-foot range. For this reason, coupled with the presence of so many pleasure-craft-oriented marinas, captains of most larger vessels choose this passage over its ICW counterpart. That's not a bad plan of action, particularly if your vessel exceeds 45 feet in length and draws 5 feet or more.

Let's now pause for a moment to take a look at the geography of the Florida Keys from the land side. For general purposes of orientation, the Florida Keys start with Key Largo, a large island that hasn't quite decided if it's mainland or more gnarly Keys. Close enough to Miami and Fort Lauderdale to be influenced (but NOT dominated) by the urban milieu, Key Largo carries some vestiges of big-city life. Several large hotel chains are represented on this island, and you can avail yourself of the amenities there and never feel that you have broken with your past . . . or the mainland.

For auto travelers, there are two ways onto Key Largo. The Card Sound Road and (toll) bridge is the northern and less-traveled route. The other route, U.S. 1, cuts into Key Largo a few miles further south and west. It crosses over Jewfish Creek as a two-lane road and doesn't become four lanes until one gets to Key Largo proper.

Also part of Key Largo, but at the southern end, is Tavernier, which has its own community identity and an array of shops and services. Aesthetically different from Key Largo proper, Tavernier is newer and not quite as commercial.

When one crosses the Tavernier Creek Bridge from Tavernier to Plantation Key, things become even more laid back. Plantation Key is mostly residential, and many of those residents are out of sight. There is a great deal of money on Plantation Key, we have been told; but it is old money and not in any way flashy. The best homes are somewhat off the beaten track and do not attract attention.

After Plantation Key comes Windley Key, which is actually several small islands that have been conjoined to make one bigger one—which is still not very big. Windley Key has a geological site that will be of interest to visitors who want to see how the rock that has been used in various Keys construction projects was quarried locally.

Whale Harbor Channel constitutes the dividing line between Windley Key and Upper Matecumbe Key. Both Upper Matecumbe Key and its next of kin, Lower Matecumbe Key, are parts of the municipality of Islamorada. In fact, Plantation Key and Windley Key are also part of this melange. Islamorada ends with the very lower extremity of Lower Matecumbe Key. Between the two islands are Lignumvitae Key and Indian Key, both state sites without any extras, except mosquitoes. The former is botanical and the latter is historical.

Once off Lower Matecumbe Key, you'll be on a bridge over what is called Channel Five. This is one of the main transition points from Hawk Channel to the ICW for boats that need substantial vertical clearance. Continuing west, you'll touch briefly on Fiesta Key and then go over another bridge and be on Long Key for a short while. Then the Long Key Viaduct will carry you over more water. Feet dry at Conch Keys for a half-minute or so, you then go on to Duck Key. Duck Key will show up on your left. It's both commercial and private, the commercial part being the luxurious Hawk's Cay Resort.

A short bridge connects Duck Key to Grassy Key, and then the highway continues onto Vaca Key and into Marathon. Marathon is commercial in the real sense of the word. It's mid-Keys and not much different from the mainland, particularly close to the highway. Marathon is not without its unique charm, but much of it does not come easily to view. You have to look for it.

After Marathon comes the Seven Mile Bridge, which spans Moser Channel and is another cut-through place for sailing vessels that can fit underneath its 63-foot vertical clearance. This bridge perches briefly on Pigeon Key along its lengthy transit. This isle is a lovely historical site (and sight). It has been left pretty much as it was when Henry Flagler was building his railroad through here.

The Seven Mile Bridge ends on Little Duck Key; then the roadway touches on Missouri and Ohio Keys before setting down for a spell on Bahia Honda Key and passing Bahia Honda State Park. This is *the* place in the Florida Keys for beaching it. There's real sand here and the setting is just plain lovely, picture-book-like.

Pressing onward, we come next to Spanish Harbor Keys (which include West Summerland Key, which is miles *east* of Summerland Key) and then to Big Pine Key, one of the larger islands. The road jogs to the northwest here, then straightens itself out again, and heads west.

Big Pine Key is home to many of the endangered Key deer, and the speed limits lower smartly. Woe betide the motorist who runs down a Key deer.

Next to Big Pine Key is No Name Key,

which was once the western terminus for ferry boats that connected Marathon with the Lower Keys before the highway was completed in 1938.

In the back country, to the north and west of Big Pine Key, are some outlying Keys, probably known to skiff fisherman more than to others. They are Annette Key, Howe Key, Cutoe Key (now, how do you think this island got its name?), Content Keys, Big Spanish Key, Water Keys, and more.

On the highway again, you'll pass over Little Torch Key—Middle Torch and Big Torch are further north—then Ramrod Key, Summerland Key, and Cudjoe Key. At Cudjoe Key the government maintains a couple of blimps that they let up into the air on tethers to (a) broadcast TV Marti signals to Cuba and (b) keep an eye over the horizon for smugglers of both narcotics and people. If the weather is good, you may see the blimp(s) off to your north. When the weather turns nasty, the personnel at this secure base bring the blimp(s) down to keep them from blowing away. They are not always successful.

Across the bridge from Cudjoe Key, heading west, is Sugarloaf Key, home to a lasting monument to man's folly and resourcefulness, the Bat Tower. See other references in this tome to the Bat Tower; it is a great tale.

In the back country to the north lie Johnston Key, Snipe Keys, Sawyer Key, Riding Key, Raccoon Key, Budd Keys, Tarpon Belly Keys, Barracuda Keys, Marvin Keys, and many others.

The road crosses Saddlebunch Keys next and then connects with Boca Chica Key, home of the Key West Naval Air Station. Most of this island is not open to the public, but you can see some exotic military aircraft coming and going from this area at most any time of day.

Upon arriving on the shores of Stock Island, you are nearly to Key West. Stock Island is industrial, for the most part, and colorful beyond measure. Exploring the nether reaches of Stock Island is worth the time, but do it in the daylight. That way, you will be able to remember the faces and names of the interesting characters you come across. After dark, it could get a little scary.

The end of the line is Key West. This city is a carnival ride that never stops. You hop on, hold on, and take a deep breath. It will be over when it is over, cost you what it costs, and leave you with memories that, in your dotage, you can resuscitate in living color and smile at all over again. Nothing in the Florida Keys is quite like Key West. Come to think of it, nothing in the WORLD is quite like Key West. For so many, it is the end of the trip and the beginning of an adventure that may last for days or weeks or years. You never know how it will actually go down in Key West, but it will be an experience you will always remember.

Finally, for those intrepid cruisers who are ready to cross many miles of open waters, there are the Dry Tortugas. These remote, desolate isles offer two good anchorages, a historic fort, and the opportunity to visit what was once the most feared federal prison in America.

Florida Keys' Natural and Man-made History
The Florida Keys are far more than bridges and islands and gas stations and T-shirt shops, though the hordes of tourists who regularly descend upon the Keys for relaxation and recreation via U.S. 1 (the principal vehicular avenue of arrival) may believe that the 43 bridges which link 38 of the major islands in the Keys are the most significant structures. They are not.

The most imposing structures in the Florida Keys are the microscopic skeletal remains of coral. Without them and the associated skeletons of other inhabitants of the shallow marine environment that once existed here, there would be no Florida Keys. Geologically, the Florida Platform is made up of 20,000 feet of sedimentary rock that was formed, geologists tell us, 100,000 years ago. At that time, much of peninsular Florida was under 25 feet of seawater. Real-estate agents had not yet arrived to tout an unobstructed waterfront view and sandy beaches. What is now Orlando was above the water, as were parts of Hillsborough and Polk counties to the east of Tampa Bay. The rest of what is now southern Florida was inundated. What much later became Miami, Palm Beach, and Fort Lauderdale was covered with ooze and slime.

The waters covering Florida disappeared during the last large glaciation period, the Wisconsin, when the sea level dropped 350 feet lower than it is today. To get a feeling of how far the Florida coastline stretched out laterally, particularly to the west, find a chart where the water depths show 350 feet and you'll get an idea. A long, long way from anything that we quickly envision today as waterfront property, it was faaaarrrr out. The shoreline in the Keys was about 10 miles south of where one finds it today. Florida Bay was dry land.

The sea level remained low until 15,000 years ago, when it began to rise as the climate warmed. As the warming trend continued, water captured by the polar icecaps was released and the rise in the water levels continued, sometimes amounting to as much as a foot every fourteen years. Were that to happen today, many of the residents of south Florida would find real estate in, say, the Superstition Mountains of Arizona very attractive.

The geology of the Upper Keys is comprised of Key Largo limestone. You can identify Key Largo limestone from the presence of fossil corals in the rock. The Islamorada Hurricane Monument is built of this limestone; it was also used in the facade of the St. Louis Post Office, the Miami Post Office, and the Key West Post Office. The Vizcaya Estate in Miami is faced with Key Largo limestone. Surprisingly, the limestone was still being quarried in the Keys into the 1960s.

In the Lower Keys, west of and including Big Pine Key, the limestone is overlain by Miami oolite, a sand formed by the precipitation of dissolved calcium carbonate out of water. The carbonate accumulates on the sand particle in layers—as the secretion of lubricants accumulate onto an irritating grain of sand inside an oyster, causing the grain of sand to develop into a pearl.

Human habitation began in the Florida Keys about 800 A.D. by aboriginal Indians. There is no record of the Indians opening dive shops or selling souvenirs to Europeans, though Indians did kill or take captive crew members of Spanish ships that wrecked on the off-lying reefs in the Keys. The Native Americans also helped themselves to whatever they could salvage from the wrecks. The Spanish ships that foundered here were often full of plundered wealth from the Incas and Aztecs. It was an example of early trickle-down economics. Hundreds of years later, when the Keys began filling up with citizens of the newly-minted United States, salvaging wrecks became a profession and a way of life in the Keys.

Contacts between the Indians in the Keys and the white newcomers had the same devastating effect on Indian life as similar contacts in colder climes. Some Indians ended up as slaves. Others died from diseases the whites had brought with them—influenza, smallpox, measles—diseases to which the Indians carried no immunity.

The Indians lived off the sea and what they could kill on land. There is no evidence of prehistoric agriculture in the Keys, so the Indians here were hunter/gatherers. If one thinks about how abundant edible fish are today in the Florida Keys, then imagine what it was like when the population in the Keys numbered only a few hundred. There must have been a Florida lobster under every rock, in every crack. Turtles, crabs, clams, and conchs were part of the diet, too. Now, the conch is protected after being fished out, and the conch fritters that one gets in the Keys are made with imported conch from other places.

There are identified former Indian village sites on Key Largo, Upper Matecumbe Key, Indian Key, Windley Key, Big Pine Key, Sugarloaf Key, and Stock Island.

When Europeans moved into the Keys in the early 1800s, it was by boat, and Key West was the main lure which brought them. Also high on their list was the abundance of sea life. They ate what they needed and sold the rest. It was not an easy life, though. The heat, the mosquitoes, lack of fresh water, little sanitation, isolation, and hurricanes put their lives in peril. There were no cheeseburgers. It was not paradise.

As Key West grew because of its proximity to the reefs and to Cuba, the other Keys lagged far behind. For example, in 1950 Key West had a measured population of 26,433. The remainder of the Keys boasted only 3,524 souls. And this is after the building of Henry Flagler's Florida East Coast Railway Extension and the opening of U.S. Highway 1 to Key West (see below).

Today, of course, the Keys are modern and up-to-date. Fresh water is piped down from Dade County, so cisterns are not needed for water catchment now. Electricity runs air-conditioning systems. The highway brings in streams of tourists. Huge cruise ships dock at Key West and disgorge passengers by the thousands. There is scheduled air service in Key West and Marathon. But the interesting past of the Florida Keys is still there for examination, off the beaten path, at a quiet, unhurried pace, by boat.

The Indians and the original settlers came here via the water, and even today there is no better way to enjoy the Florida Keys than by pleasure craft.

One person, more than any other influence, was responsible for the opening up of the Florida Keys. That person was Henry Morrison Flagler, and without his vision—some say greed—the Florida Keys might have languished in the backwater of time for decades, caught up in an eddy of indifference.

Flagler, who built the Florida East Coast Railway Extension—the line that ran from Miami to Key West—had guts and drive and smarts. He also had a pile of money; he had been in on the ground floor of what became Standard Oil, and he was in partnership with John D. Rockefeller. When Flagler was fifty-four years old, he was one of the richest men in the world.

It was at this stage of his life, in 1884, that he turned to building railroads. The state of Florida was offering generous incentives to railroad builders then, huge concessions in the form of land along the railroad right-of-way. It was sort of a "you build it and we'll grant you what you need" kind of deal. The state needed railroads, so incentive to build them was easily conveyed. Swamp land? Who wants it? You just build right on through there. Build one and you'd also get a whole bunch of land along the right-of-way, free.

Flagler knew he was onto something, and—because other tycoons couldn't see the sense of building railroads in Florida—he had the field to himself. Flagler got his start when he purchased the Jacksonville, St. Augustine, and Halifax River Railroad.

Henry Flagler had briefly been in St. Augustine before with his ailing wife, Mary, in hopes that the warmer weather would help her health. It did not. And the local amenities were so tawdry that the Flaglers returned to New York, where the first Mrs. Flagler (there were two subsequent wives) passed away in 1881.

Flagler married her nurse, Ida Alice Shrouds. Ida Alice never lived up to the promises of life that awaited her. She went bonkers and became certain that she would eventually marry the Czar of Russia. Flagler had her committed. Later, the New York Supreme Court adjudicated her insane.

At the age of seventy, Flagler met Mary Lily Kenan, twenty-four years old and a singer and pianist. They wanted to get married, but Henry already had a wife. She was nuts, but she was still legally his wife. Ever the innovator, Flagler changed his residence from New York to St. Augustine and had friends in the Florida legislature draft a new law that permitted divorce on the grounds of insanity. With pesky legal details conveniently taken care of, Flagler married Mary Lily Kenan in 1901.

All during this period, he had been busy pushing his railroad ever farther to the south. After standardizing the track, Flagler extended his railroad to St. Augustine. In 1888, he completed the opulent Hotel Ponce de Leon in St. Augustine. Flagler had a certain genius, because he also built destination resorts to give people majestic places to go when they used his railroad. By 1892 he had extended the tracks south to Palm Beach. Four years later, at the instigation of Julia Tuttle of Miami, who offered him half her real-estate holdings if he would build his railroad down to Miami, Flagler had laid tracks to Miami, a hotel was being built, and surveyors were at work laying out streets.

Flagler already had his sights on Key West. The technological wherewithal, however, was beyond his grasp at the time. The Spanish-American War had come and gone, with Tampa getting the lion's share of the military-shipping business, something that Flagler coveted.

By 1903, however, technology had caught up with Flagler's vision. The Panama Canal was a work in progress. Key West had a deep harbor and was close to Cuba and the Caribbean. All that was needed to link it to the rest of the country was a railroad.

If he had the only rail line between Miami and Key West, Flagler surmised he would also gain access to all the shipping of goods over his rail line to the rest of the United States and back again. It was a staggering thought, almost monopolistic.

Henry Flagler took the step, and even though the setbacks were legion, and building a railroad through inhospitable locations and over water was a daunting undertaking—especially since it was private capital that paved the way—Flagler never wavered. The money went out in buckets. Lives were lost along the way. The engineering feats surpassed the believable. Storms caused long setbacks. But the railroad stretched out toward Key West with unrelenting purpose, mile after tortuous mile. And then it was done.

In 1912, twenty days after his eighty-second birthday, Henry Flagler rode in his private railway car, Rambler, to Key West on the very first train to reach that island city. He received a hero's welcome. He deserved one.

Flagler didn't have much time left, and he knew it. He died in May of 1913 and is buried in the St. Augustine Memorial Presbyterian Church. Mary remarried but died shortly after. She is buried with Henry Flagler in St. Augustine.

Flagler's second wife, Ida Alice, was left with $2 million from Flagler's will. Though Ida Alice never got back in touch with reality, she lived comfortably until 1930, ready to inform anyone with a few minutes extra time about how she was going to marry the Czar of Russia. It is possible no one had the heart to tell her that she had outlived the Czar of Russia, who was killed during the Russian Revolution.

Flagler's railroad, while a marvel of engineering, tenacity, and foresight, never made money. Having so many miles of track over water took a great deal of upkeep. Maintenance men walked the entire one-hundred-fifty-six-mile route, inspecting every aspect of the system—ties, rails, spikes, and bolts. Hard-hat divers checked the bridges' foundations every two years.

Neither was the railroad particularly fast nor did it run on time. Trains ran the bridges at fifteen miles an hour. When the winds blew hard in the Keys, the trains stopped and waited for them to subside. For these and other reasons, a Florida East Coast Railway Extension timetable wasn't worth the paper it was printed on.

The Great Depression and the Labor Day Hurricane of 1935 finished off the railroad that went to sea. During the Depression, what remained of the Key West Extension was sold to the state of Florida for $640,000. The extension had been appraised for more than $27 million when it was operating. It could have been repaired for $1.5 million. Had he been alive, Henry Flagler undoubtedly would have repaired it.

Florida Keys Lighthouses

The lighthouses, which even today warn mariners of the perils of the jagged reefs in the Florida Keys, are an integral part of the beauty of this region. From shore, where they are easily seen, they stand like sentinels against the dark, blinking out their lighted messages: "There is danger here."

In olden days, the reefs along the Atlantic side of the Keys seemed to attract ships like a magnet. There are tricky currents here, and a storm from the south makes the entire Keys chain a lee shore, a one-hundred-fifty-mile-long trap. Some vessels were laden with treasure when they hit the reef, and the treasure went down with the boat. Spanish pieces of eight, emeralds, and gold doubloons went to the bottom only to be recovered later by enterprising, and smart, treasure salvagers, Mel Fisher of Key West being the most notable. Interestingly, some old ships were salvaged by their owners shortly after wrecking, and the salvagers recovered more gold and silver than had been recorded on the ship's manifest. That meant that some smuggling was going on or that the waters of the Florida Keys had created treasure on their own. You can easily figure the conundrum out, unless you are a believer in alchemy.

The reefs, and the fact that shipping blundered onto them, created an industry of opportunity in Key West in the 1800s. It was called "wrecking," and it made Key West one of the most prosperous cities in the state for some time. Wrecking, as practiced in Key West, was a licensed occupation with strict rules and protocols. Though the appellation itself may remind one of synonyms like "plunder," "pillage", "ravage" and "theft," wrecking was, basically, an attempt to help ships that had grounded on reefs save their crew and cargo—and even the vessel itself. The rewards could be large or small, depending on the value of the service rendered and the risk that the wreckers faced when assisting stricken vessels.

It wasn't only sailing ships that were snagged by the reefs when the navigation on board was poor; steamers, too, hit the coral. Today the reefs continue to trap unwary vessels, even though lighthouses are stationed to warn shipping away and satellites circle the earth to help give ships an exact fix on their position. Navigational incompetence knows no era, no season, no locale, no nationality.

The first lighthouses in the Keys were constructed beginning in 1825. They were positioned on Key Biscayne, Key West, Sands Key, and on Garden Key in the Dry Tortugas. The original lighthouses were built of brick and mortar, like the lighthouses of New England, which usually stood on high ground. The Keys lighthouses had no such promontories to perch upon, so when large storms hit the area—most particularly the hurricane of 1846, which raged ashore at Key West—the lighthouses could not endure the pounding waves. Both the Sands Key Light and the Key West Light fell during this storm.

Realizing that the current lighthouse design did not work in the Keys because of differing conditions and low terrain, the U.S. Lighthouse Service rebuilt the Key West Light but located it several blocks further inland.

However, at Sands Key, which was in an exposed location west of Key West, the Lighthouse Service came up with a brilliant new concept called an "iron screw pile" lighthouse design.

The "iron screw pile" was a threaded piece of steel piling that was actually screwed down into the coral reef. After the main support piles had been put into the reef, cross bracing was added for stability and support, and the structure was built tall enough so that a light keeper could live on it. The steel pilings allowed waves to flow under the structure and presented little resistance for storms to batter with their power.

The plan of the Sands Key Light proved to be so effective that other lights of like design were added at points along the reef where shipping had proved most vulnerable to grounding.

The Key Biscayne Light (Cape Florida) and the Key West Light have been abandoned. Garden Key Light is also no longer in operation, but Loggerhead Key Light exists close by in the Dry Tortugas.

From Miami southward and westward the lights that mark the reefs now are (in order)

- Fowey Rocks Light—
  25 35.42 North/080 05.77 West
- Carysfort Reef Light—
  25 13.34 North/080 12.71 West
- Molasses Reef Light—
  25 00.79 North/080 22.59 West
- Alligator Reef Light—
  24 51.15 North/080 37.08 West
- Sombrero Key Light—
  24 37.67 North/081 06.66 West
- American Shoal Light—
  24 31.50 North/081 31.14 West
- Sands Key Light—
  24 27.24 North/081 52.52 West

- Cosgrove Shoal Light—
  24 27.45 North/082 11.07 West
- Rebecca Shoal Light—
  24 34.74 North/082 35.13 West
- Loggerhead Key Light—
  24 38.00 North/082 55.21 West
  All the lights have different characteristics, so each is unique and identifiable.

The United States Coast Guard and the Florida Keys

We talked with CWO3 Stephen Craddock, who is the commanding officer of the Coast Guard station in Islamorada. This base of operations is located on the northeast side of Snake Creek, which separates Windley Key from Plantation Key. Islamorada, Craddock said, is one of the best duty stations in all of the Coast Guard.

The Coast Guard's mission in the Florida Keys crosses a lot of different boundaries. The officers and enlisted men and women run SAR (search and rescue) cases, pluck Cuban immigrants from the water, help out the United States Border Patrol—which keeps a small helicopter at the Islamorada station—plus provide assistance to the DEA and U.S. Customs. The assets at Islamorada consist of a 41-footer, a 24-foot patrol boat, and a 21-foot inflatable with a hard bottom.

Cubans are still being smuggled into the United States by professional people smugglers. The fee for the ninety-mile ride is $5,000 to $10,000 a head, Craddock said. The Coast Guard works hard to keep the Cubans out, but the irony of their mission is not lost on those whose job it is to enforce it. Cubans get special treatment from the United States government, treatment not afforded Haitians or other nationalities attempting to cross United States borders illegally.

Craddock said that his station gets many calls to help people whose boats are taking on water. Some divers anchor their boats by the stern, and when they come up, they find that the boat has been hit by waves and seawater has flooded out the engine, Craddock explained. He said that they handle SAR cases on both sides of the Keys, but they get far more on the ocean side than the bay side.

"We work a lot of overdues, which are most often matters of poor communication between the boater and his family. If we can't find them by phone, then we send out a chopper from Opa Locka (Miami)," Craddock said.

The Coast Guard also has a 110-foot cutter patrolling the Straits of Florida, between Cuba and the United States.

Running aground in the Florida Keys can get expensive. If you hit a reef and do damage to it, then you will get fined. It is a fact of life. On the other side, in Florida Bay, if you run your boat aground in a grass flat and destroy sea grass, you will also lose some money. Craddock said that fines for Florida Bay goofs are predicated by how many lateral feet of sea grass is destroyed. The Coast Guard does not pull grounded vessels off the flats. That honor goes to commercial towing operations like Sea Tow or Tow Boat U.S. It is a given, too, that you will be hearing from the NOAA and the Florida Keys National Marine Sanctuary.

Craddock said that if cruisers come across people in rafts, they need to let the Coast Guard handle the matter. A call in the clear on Channel 16 will garner the instant attention of the closest Coast Guard station. There are four of them, located in Miami, Islamorada, Marathon, and Key West. Getting directly involved with illegal immigrants could lead to complications that would obviously impact negatively on what is supposed to be a relaxing cruise.

Florida Keys Anchoring and Navigational Considerations

In this guide we have endeavored to include all the information waterborne visitors may need to take full advantage of the Florida Keys' tremendous cruising potential. We have paid particular attention to anchorages, marina facilities, and danger areas. All the navigational information necessary for a successful cruise has been included. These data have been set apart in their own subsections and screened in gray for ready identification.

Each body of water has been personally visited and sounded for the latest depth information. However, remember that bottom configurations do change. Dockside depths at marinas seem to be particularly subject to rapid variation. Cruising navigators should always be equipped with the latest charts and "Notice to Mariners" before leaving the dock.

This guide is not a navigational primer and it assumes that you have a working knowledge of piloting, coastal navigation, and electronic navigation. If you don't, you should acquire these skills before tackling the Keys' waters.

All navigators should have a well-functioning depth sounder on board before leaving the dock. This is one of the most basic safety instruments in any navigator's arsenal of aids. The cruiser who does not take this elementary precaution is asking for trouble.

The modern miracle of satellite-controlled GPS (Global Positioning System), particularly when interfaced with a laptop computer loaded with the latest digitized nautical charts, is yet another powerful navigational aid. As we will discover below, these electronic marvels can be of immense value when cruising the complicated waters of the Florida Keys.

Florida Keys navigators will find it most advantageous to keep the current chart and a pair of good binoculars in the cockpit or on the fly bridge at all times. With these aids on hand, problems can be quickly resolved before you have a close encounter of the grounding kind.

In this guide, lighted daybeacons are always called "flashing daybeacons." We believe this is a more descriptive term than the officially correct designation, "light," or the more colloquial expression, "flasher." Also, to avoid confusion, daybeacons without lights are always referred to as "unlighted daybeacons." Similarly, lighted buoys are called "flashing buoys."

The sketch maps contained within this guide have been included to help locate anchorages, marinas, and other points of interest. They are NOT intended for, and should NOT be used for, navigation!

Cruising and navigating the Florida Keys brings on some unique challenges. The first two that come to mind are the challenges of staying off the bottom and anchoring properly. If you do run aground, it's not just a matter of paying for a tow and then replacing underwater hardware. Oh no, the state of Florida and the federal government have something a little more affluent in mind.

The Florida Keys are, for the most part, a national marine sanctuary, so designated by the United States Congress in 1990. One of the catalysts to making the Keys a sanctuary was the frequent grounding of vessels along the offshore reefs, despite modern navigational equipment and a series of large and easily identifiable lights on the reef itself, which is 150 miles long and extends from Key Biscayne to the Dry Tortugas. The Florida Keys National Marine Sanctuary abuts Everglades National Park on peninsular Florida, so almost every square mile of both Hawk Channel and Florida Bay is included in this sanctuary.

This is an ecologically diverse part of our country, but it is also fragile. Sea grass flats bear the scars of intrusion by motor craft for years after the craft have gone. A living coral reef can die if even so much as touched, so you can imagine the impact of an anchor landing on it, much less the keel of a boat.

The beauty of the Keys can be enjoyed by you because others who were here before you took the extra precautions necessary to leave no trace of their presence. Careful consideration of your surroundings and your obligations will make the Keys a better place to luxuriate for those who come after you.

There are many Keys caveats that might not make much difference to you back in your home waters, but they are taken very seriously here.

• Where you can tie up to a mooring buoy, do so. Mooring buoys are available in many locations in the Keys. Reef mooring buoys are distinctively marked, white with a blue horizontal stripe. The yellow buoys are sanctuary-preservation-area boundary buoys and are not to be used for mooring. Anchoring over coral is just not allowed and can bring you some major unhappiness and loss of money, should your doing so come to the attention of people who can do something about it. Need to anchor? Drop the hook into sand.

• Tossing trash overboard cannot be condoned for any reason. With waters so crystalline that they allow a clear view of the bottom almost anywhere in the Keys, what you leave behind will mar the view for years to come.

• Running aground on sea grass beds because of poor judgement or inattention to where you are going will leave scars for a long, long time. Trying to get off immediately in a powerboat will cause additional scarring and damage, primarily a prop-dredged hole and depositing damaging silt over the grass bed. If you find yourself in water shallow enough that your props are stirring up mud behind your boat, stop. If you attempt to power off, you'll just do more damage. Trim your motor

up, turn your boat around by walking it, and then hand push it to deeper water, where you can get going again. If you stick it so hard that you cannot turn it around by hand, you'll have to wait for a higher tide to float you off.

• Running aground happens to most cruisers at one time or another. When it happens in the Keys, the penalties are severe, and notification of the proper authorities is just a VHF radio call away. You might not make the call, but it is a good bet that a number of other people will have no compunction about doing so. If you are not serious about taking care of the landscape, you will meet others who are. Some carry badges and write expensive tickets.

• Because the Keys are a marine sanctuary, you may not even pick up coral from the sea floor and take it home with you. Breaking off pieces of living coral for souvenirs is against the law and the penalties for doing so are severe.

There are sliding scales of penalties/fines for destroying habitat in the Florida Keys, and you should know what you might be in for when it comes to paying for any misdeeds for which you are responsible.

For scarring up the sea grass beds with your prop(s) or your boat's keel, there are three scales of retribution, and they are dependent on whether your transgression was an honest accident or just outright stupidity. In the least-damaging category, fines range up to $850. The middle category of damage can take the perpetrator upward into fines of $50,000, but most average around $1,500 to $2,000. The "granddaddy of them all" is what is called the damage action. The amount of fine that is assessed depends on the amount of damage a vessel has done. Damage actions have reached as much as $5 million, with fines on top of that. Pleasure vessels that get into this area of serious infractions average about $100,000 per incident. This is most certainly an infringement category you want to stay far away from by exercising rigorous vigilance.

Well, wasn't that fun? Do you feel like taking your lawyer along when cruising the Florida Keys? Well, believe us, we have felt the same way at times. Our best advice is to practice the very best, eyeball, DR, and electronic navigation possible, and do everything in your power to avoid keel meeting with bottom

What is "eyeball navigation?" you may ask. Well, while there are most certainly limitations, this may actually be one of the best ways to stay off the bottom of the Florida Keys, at least during the fair weather. Eyeball navigation is made possible in the keys, courtesy of the crystal-clear water. On a sunny day, when you see a light-colored patch of water, chances are that this coloration denotes shoal depths. What you are actually seeing is the sandy bottom reflecting the sunlight. On a contrary note, darker-colored water often means deeper soundings. However, there is a major caveat to this rule. Be advised that sometimes a grassy bottom can appear darker that a lighter patch, but depths over the grass are really just a few feet. It takes practice to distinguish deeper (darker-colored) water from a grassy bottom. So, eyeball navigation can be a powerful tool in the Florida Keys, BUT even the veterans are careful to supplement this inexact science with electronic and DR navigation!

And speaking of navigation, that brings us to the third, real, on-the-water, Florida Keys challenge, finding your way successfully. You won't be cruising long in the Keys before it occurs to you that, at least from the water, one key looks pretty much like the next key. While the ICW sports a fine collection of aids to navigation, markers are far more widely-spaced along Hawk Channel, and those who explore the Florida Bay back country will find nothing but a few sticks rearing their heads above the water. Wonder if these mark good water or shoals? We've asked ourselves that question more than once.

So, what's a captain and navigator to do? Well, we have an answer for you, though it make take a few shekels to implement.

Several years ago, Claiborne was urged to try what was then the new navigational toy on the block, namely, a GPS interfaced with a laptop computer by way of a simple serial cable. The laptop was pre-loaded with digitized versions of the NOAA charts and navigational software that not only displayed the charts but also actually placed a moving icon (representing your vessel's position) on the screen, superimposed over the chart display.

Claiborne admits to being skeptical. Having cut his teeth on DR navigation, his thoughts were something to the effect of "What do I need all this fancy gadgetry for?" Well, fortunately, Milt Baker, former owner of Bluewater Books and Charts in Fort Lauderdale, prevailed upon him to give this system a try.

So the very next week, Claiborne and his trusty research assistant Bob Horne launched one of his smaller, research power crafts at Panama City, Florida and soon proceeded to a remote body of water known as California Bayou. This has always been one of his favorite anchorages in the Florida Panhandle, but the unmarked entry channel is a twisting snake. Heretofore, it had always taken Claiborne fifteen tense minutes to cruise into the bayou's sheltered, interior reaches. Now, watching his position on the screen, he was able to adjust course immediately when his craft began to get a little too close to one side of the channel or the other. In FIVE minutes, he and Bob were comfortably ensconced at anchor on California Bayou.

Later in the trip, it became apparent that

another huge advantage of this sort of navigation was the ability, at a glance, to tell how one's vessel's position corresponded to an intended location. No more wondering if that daybeacon on the horizon was really the outermost marker of the approach channel for one's intended marina. One look at the screen quickly answered the question. To make what is already a long story short, we were sold on electronic navigation thereafter.

And there is perhaps no place in the continental USA that can benefit more from GPS-laptop-computer-style navigation than the Florida Keys. The good news is that if you already own a laptop computer and a GPS, it will only take about $600 to be up and running. This fee will buy you navigational software (we recommend "The Cap'n" or Nobeltec's "Visual Navigation Suite"), a serial cord to connect the GPS to your computer, and a CD of digitized NOAA charts. Incidentally, one CD contains ALL the charts one would ever need to cover the waters of the Florida Keys.

The bad news is that if you don't already own a GPS and a laptop, the price tag goes up to about $3,000. Oh well, the best never comes cheaply.

One word of warning before leaving this subject: DON'T become so dependent on these electronic marvels that you can no longer plot a compass course or keep a good DR track. What are you going to do if (as once happened to us) a wave comes over the bow and drowns the laptop? Those who don't know how to undertake sound, coastal navigation at times like this are in a world of trouble.

Since we have been talking about electronic navigation, this would seem a good time to announce a NEW feature in this guide. For the first time in our series of guidebooks, approximate latitude and longitude positions

of marinas, anchorages, and certain channels have been included within the body of this volume. The latitude and longitude of these locations are strictly for informational purposes; they must NOT be used as GPS or Loran way points!

With the phenomenal increase in popularity of computer navigational software, we thought it important to provide lat/lon information. This data can be plugged into (for instance) Nobeltec's "Visual Navigational Suite" or "The Cap'n" software, and the program will immediately place an icon on the digitized image of the appropriate nautical chart, almost exactly where the marina or anchorage you are making for is located. That's a real, on-the-water advantage, but to be repetitive, PLEASE don't use this data as simple way points. There are several reasons why. Loran C and GPS readings give a mariner a straight-line distance or bearing to the intended way point destination. Straight-line tracks do NOT take into account such vagaries as shoals you will need to avoid, peninsulas you will be unable to cross, or islands that just seem to get in the way.

"Myrtle," a captain might say to his first mate, "will you please check that marvelous cruising guide we just purchased and enter the latitude and longitude for the XYZ Marina into the GPS so we can tell how far, generally, we are from our destination?"

"It's seven miles away and you need to turn right to 190 degrees to go directly to it," Myrtle might respond.

"No way, Sugar," the prudent and wary captain might reply. "I still have to navigate around shoals, rocks, several islands, and then go down a narrow channel before we get to the XYZ Marina."

He knows that a straight line is the shortest

distance between two points only when there is nothing in between. In the Keys—fortunately or unfortunately, it is your call—there are things all over the place that make boats go bump in the night, or even bump in the daytime. So, when using the lat/lons provided in this tome, keep your head on straight and your eyes on where you are going. A GPS or Loran C is an aid to navigation, to be sure, but good headwork is always the order of the day, just as it has been since men first went down to sea in small ships.

Florida Keys cruising visitors can be excused for wondering why things sometimes seem reversed from the characteristics of their home waters. "Why," a curious mariner might ask, "are the depths for many approach channels so skinny when the dockside depths at the marina served by the same cut are far more than I'll ever need?"

In many cases you can thank Henry Flagler's railroad for that. The railroad needed lots of rock for fill and ballast. On the way down, as the railroad lengthened, engineers quarried rock as they went. It was coral rock, from geological early times, and it worked. So, as the railroad line moved along down toward Marathon, the men who built the Overseas Railroad pulled more and more rock from the ground and smashed it into bits big enough to support a railroad. The engineers didn't think about it then, but in the process, they made for some nifty harbors with plenty of water for boats and, usually, a sheltered way to get in and out.

Florida Keys Waste Disposal Regulations

The very day the manuscript for this guide was set to be shipped to Pelican Publishing Company, we heard from Rick Eyerdam, publisher of *The Boating News*. There are few

(if any) people in the world that know more about the Florida Keys.

Rick related to us that a proposal is ongoing to make all waters contained within the borders of Monroe County an official "no discharge zone." He went on to give his opinion that the eventual implementation of this plan was "unstoppable." If passed, this new prohibition will impact all of the Florida Keys waters south of Card Sound.

For those of you who don't already know, a "no discharge zone" is exactly what its name implies. No human waste products can be pumped (or dumped) into the surrounding waters, **even if this waste has been processed by an on-board waste treatment system such as a "Lectra-San."**

This means that cruising craft plying the waters of the Florida Keys with a Lectra-San or equivalent aboard, but no holding tank, are in imminent danger of prodigious fines once these regulations are implemented. If this description matches your vessel, we suggest calling the Marathon office of the Florida Department of Environmental Protection (305-289-2310), the Monroe County Department of Health (Marathon office: 305-289-2365), and/or the Marine Industries Association of South Florida (954-524-2733). Inquire as to whether the proposed "no discharge" regulations have been implemented for Monroe County waters. If you discover that they have, better have your vessels retrofitted with a holding tank before venturing south of Biscayne Bay.

Florida Keys Weather

The weather in the Florida Keys is one of the reasons this string of islands is so attractive to cruisers. The vast amount of water surrounding the Keys takes the sting and heat out of the Florida summers and moderates the cold fronts, which come down from the north in the winter. The summers in the Keys are long and warm and sometimes wet. The winters are short and dry and mild.

Keys residents shiver in rare forty-degree weather, something that would feel like a heat wave up North in the winter. But there is no record of snow ever having fallen in the Keys. Miami and Nassau cannot make that claim. They both received snow in 1977, a fact that is not discussed in their tourism brochures. In the summers, the warmest month is July in Key West and August in Tavernier on Key Largo. But the hot months and the cold months don't vary that much in temperature. Fifteen degrees is the average difference between the two.

Because of its tropical climate, the Keys historically get more rain in the summer (May through October) than winter. The months with the largest overall rainfall are September and October. This is due in part to hurricanes and tropical storms, which are most prevalent in those two months, and also to the movement of the Bermuda High in an easterly direction.

In the wet season, rainfall comes from brief but strong thunderstorms and showers, which usually occur early in the day. As always, strong showers and thunderstorms generate a good bit of local wind and should be regarded with suspicion and caution.

The storms that get the most attention, hurricanes, vary from one chance in one hundred in Jacksonville to one chance in seven in Key West and Miami. The average number of tropical storms to hit Florida annually is 1.7, but the Florida Keys are an unfavorable place to be when bad weather comes calling. The holding ground isn't always good and places to hide are few.

In the early part of the hurricane season, prior to mid-September, hurricanes and named storms usually come from an easterly or southeasterly direction. In later September and into October the direction of tropical storms shifts into the Caribbean, so storms come from a westerly or southwesterly direction at that time.

However, trying to put absolutes onto the path or probable strike area of a hurricane is an exercise in abstract math, as inconclusive as trying to pick a surefire winning number in the Florida Lottery.

Other Publications

Longtime readers of our series of guidebooks will notice that the title of this volume, *Cruising the Florida Keys,* is a bit different from other titles in this series. We have altered our naming practices to avoid any misidentification between our book and *Cruising Guide to the Florida Keys,* written and published by Capt. Frank Papy. Captain Papy's book has been around for many years, and it has a long and enduring reputation. We do not want to have our book confused with Captain Papy's publication. To be clear, these are two entirely different books, and they are not tied together in any way.

The single, most important companion publication to this book is, in our opinion, Joy Williams' wonderful, land-oriented guidebook, *The Florida Keys: A History & Guide* (Random House, New York). Ms. Williams' droll sense of humor, combined with her keen observer's eye, make for an in-depth look at the Florida Keys that this guide's writers could not begin to imitate. There is more information about land attractions contained in Ms. Williams' book than in any other single source we know about.

Sailors will also want to pick up copies of *Southwinds* (www.southwindssailing.com). This wonderful, monthly publication is available free of charge at West Marine, Boater's World, and many other private ship's stores and yacht clubs throughout the Keys. The subtitle of this publication, *Local News for Southern Sailors,* tells all (for both racing and cruising). If it's of interest to sailors, you'll find it in *Southwinds.* Call (727) 825-0433 for more information or to subscribe by mail.

Southern Boating magazine is also an excellent (www.southernboating.com) source of information about cruising the waters of the Florida Keys. While this monthly magazine covers other waters in the southeastern USA, you will find many articles specific to the Keys.

A new kid on the block is *The Boating News* (http://www.theboatingnews.com). This recently revamped and expanded tabloid publication is published by Rick Eyerdam, one of the most knowledgeable Florida Keys cruisers in the world.

Things Change

If there is one constant in the world of cruising guides, it's that things change, sometimes before the ink is dry on the paper. We encourage our fellow cruisers to send us information about what comes to light as being new and different during their time on the waters of the Florida Keys. Have you discovered a new marina? We want to hear about it. Has there been a recent change in aids to navigation? Please let us hear from you. Are the regulations in a particular anchorage different than those we quote in the guide? Send this data our way.

Perhaps the easiest way to send us this info is via e-mail. We can be reached at the following addresses:

C. S. Young—opcom@cruisingguide.com

M. Stinemetz—mstine7611@earthlink.net

May we also extend an invitation to visit our Web site at www.CruisingGuide.com. Here you will find not only information about our guidebooks, but also several photo galleries and, perhaps most importantly, a set of annotated links to EVERY marina from North Carolina to New Orleans that has a Web site. Please check us out!

We also publish an on-line newsletter, the *Salty Southeast,* which helps to keep our readers updated on recent changes, modifications, and additions to the waters we cover in our guidebooks. This is a FREE service. All you need do to subscribe is send an e-mail to opcom@cruisingguide.com containing the word, "subscribe".

And Finally

It is our sincere wish that the information contained within this guidebook will allow our fellow cruisers to take full advantage of the many and varied cruising grounds encompassed in the Florida Keys. We do not know of any other waters, anywhere, which offer so many varied cruising possibilities.

We envy those who have not yet experienced the charms and delights of Florida Keys cruising. You still have one of life's great experiences before you.

Finally, share this thought with us. If you find yourself, one calm and clear night, swinging at anchor off Big Spanish Channel and looking at the starlight gleaming off the undisturbed waters, with nary a sign of human occupation in sight, don't become alarmed. You really have not died and gone to cruising heaven. It just feels that way!

Good luck and good cruising!

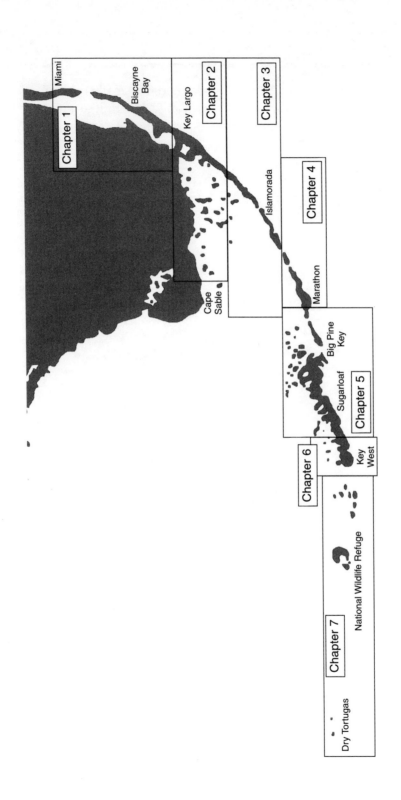

CRUISING THE
FLORIDA KEYS

Rickenbacker Marina Mooring Field (Miami skyline in background)

CHAPTER 1

Biscayne Bay to Jewfish Creek and Largo Sound

Many veteran cruisers argue that a cruise of the Florida Keys does not actually begin until you reach the waters of Jewfish Creek, or, if you choose the outside Hawk Channel route, the sumptuous Ocean Reef complex. We would not really argue with that sentiment. The laid-back, laissez-faire lifestyle that so defines the Florida Keys does not really make itself felt until the waters of Key Largo are slipping past your hull. The marinas and even the anchorages of Biscayne Bay seem to have more of a kinship with the fast-paced atmosphere of the Miami megalopolis than the likes of languid Islamorada or Grassy Key.

So, perhaps, it is best to think of Biscayne Bay as a watery transition between these two very different cruising grounds. Certainly, many cruisers feel their hectic troubles fading into the sunset as the Miami skyline sinks below the stern. May you, too, experience this seemingly magical metamorphosis to the Florida Keys state of mind as you wend your way south.

A watery transition it may be, but Biscayne Bay is a very impressive body of water in its own right. Stretching for better than 22 nautical miles from Rickenbacker Causeway to the northern headwaters of Card Sound, the bay's breadth reaches 8.2 nautical miles at its widest point. Biscayne Bay is bounded by a here-and-there-developed portion of the Florida mainland to the west, while the eastern banks (south of Key Biscayne) are composed of narrow, barrier islands, which have (fortunately) known very little development.

Biscayne Bay anchorages are numerous, though most call for a ready ear to the forecasted wind direction. Some are found hard

by the most virgin of shores, while others lie within sight of the Miami City Hall.

Marina facilities are pocked, here and there, along the bay's mainland banks, with a heavy concentration just south of downtown Miami in the Dinner Key-Coconut Grove community. South of Coconut Grove, there is another collection of mainland facilities lining the bay's westerly banks. All but one of these marinas are owned by Dade County, and transient slips can be as hard to come by as the needle in the proverbial haystack.

Only two overnight pleasure-craft facilities make their homes on Biscayne Bay's oceanside barrier islands, south of Key Biscayne. The first of these lies on Boca Chita Key, while the second (southerly) perches on the westerly banks of Elliott Key. Both are managed by the Biscayne National Park staff. The Boca Chita basin is run in a rather informal manner, and the marina on Elliott Key has very shallow entrance and dockside soundings.

As little as fifteen years ago, the waters of Biscayne Bay were anything but appetizing. Since that time, the bay has been declared a national park and much work has been accomplished to clean up the once pollution-plagued waters. Pollution control efforts by the city of Miami, the state of Florida, and the National Park Service are ongoing, but we are more than pleased to report that cruisers can now look forward to clear, pristine blue waters on the wide breadth of Biscayne Bay.

South of Key Biscayne, captains must make a decision that they will have to live with for many watery miles. Here, for the first—but not the last—time, cruisers have the opportunity to choose between the inside passage (also known as the Intracoastal Waterway) or the outside (Hawk Channel) route. If you have not read our account of Hawk Channel in this guide's introduction, now is the time. For the moment, we need only note that Hawk Channel is buffered to the west by the irregular barrier islands that comprise the easterly shores of Biscayne Bay, and a long series of underwater reefs to the east. While these reefs do tend to shelter Hawk Channel from some of the worst ocean swells, this passage can still become more than a little dusty from time to time, particularly for craft under thirty-five feet.

Farther to the south, there are several streams that connect Hawk Channel to the ICW route. Only one of these is really reliable enough for cruising-sized craft. This passage, known as Angelfish Creek, sits hard by the spectacular Ocean Reef development. It provides good depths (though strong currents are very much in evidence), and most importantly, a bridgeless route to and from the briny blue.

Finally, Hawk Channel cruisers can follow the well-marked (but poorly-charted) channel into the southerly reaches of Largo Sound. The Florida Park Service operates an adequate marina and mooring field on these waters, which are associated with the offshore John Pennekamp Coral Reef State Park.

Turning back to the Biscayne Bay-ICW route, this passage eventually leads south to the northern headwaters of Card Sound near Standard Mile 1119. The Card is also a large body of water that can spawn quite a chop when the fickle wind has its dander up.

A quick scoot under the fixed, high-rise Card Sound Bridge brings cruisers to equally broad Barnes Sound. The ICW tracks its way south down the midwidth of Barnes Sound for slightly better than 4.8 nautical miles into the northerly mouth of narrow, but deep, Jewfish Creek. A passage of just less than 1 nautical mile down this sheltered stream will bring cruisers face-to-face with the Jewfish Creek bascule bridge. This span denotes the southerly extent of this chapter's inside route coverage. The ICW passage south and the adjacent waters of Florida Bay will be outlined in chapter 2.

Before shoving off for a detailed cruise of Biscayne Bay and the adjacent portion of Hawk Channel, let's pause for just a moment to say a word to northbound skippers. If you have successfully tracked your way north to the Rickenbacker Causeway and would like in-depth information about Miami and the watery ribbon stretching on to the north, please consult *Cruising Guide to Eastern Florida*. Well, so much for that. Let's get started.

Telephone numbers to know in southern Miami and Coconut Grove include:

Best Yellow Taxi Service—305-444-7777
Yellow Cab—305-444-4444
Central Cab—305-532-5555
Metro Cab—305-888-8888
Budget Car Rentals—305-447-9706
Alamo Car Rentals—305-633-6076
Avis Car Rentals—305-932-2350
Hertz Car Rentals—305-466-1596
West Marine, 8687 Coral Way—305-263-7465
West Marine, 19407 Dixie Highway—305-232-0811
West Marine, 3635 Dixie Highway—305-444-5520

Charts

Happy days! Cruisers will only need to purchase one NOAA chart for complete coverage of the Key Biscayne and Hawk Channel waters covered in this chapter.

11451—covers both the inside, ICW route and Hawk Channel passage from Miami to Key Largo; this chart also provides many insets, which provide a detailed look at several of the side waters and anchorages along the way.

Bridges

Rickenbacker Causeway—crosses the combined paths of upper Biscayne Bay and the ICW at Standard Mile 1092, south of flashing daybeacon #67—Fixed—76 feet of vertical clearance

Virginia Key/Key Biscayne Bridge—crosses shallow Bear Cut inlet northeast of the entrance to Crandon Park Marina—Fixed—16 feet of vertical clearance

Card Sound Bridge—crosses the ICW and the passage between Little Card Sound and Card Sound at Standard Mile 1126.5, southwest of flashing daybeacon #22—Fixed—65 feet of vertical clearance

Jewfish Creek Bridge—crosses the ICW and Jewfish Creek at Standard Mile 1134, south of unlighted daybeacon #34—Bascule—11 feet (closed) vertical clearance—open on the hour and half-hour Thursday through Sundays; year round from 10:00 A.M. 'til sunset

Marvin D. Adams Waterway Bridge—crosses the narrow waterway connecting Largo and Blackwater Sounds near the westerly ⅓ of its length—Fixed—14 feet of vertical clearance

Virginia Key, Coconut Grove, and Key Biscayne

The northernmost section of Biscayne Bay can be accurately thought of as "southern Miami." These are heavily-traveled waters, with the impressive downtown Miami skyline quite visible just to the north.

Marina facilities abound. One Miami-owned, city marina makes its home on Virginia Key, while another, larger municipal facility and a yacht club have some services available for visiting cruisers on Key Biscayne. The mainland, Miami-Coconut Grove section features a huge city marina, the Biscayne Yacht Club, and several other private marinas. While transient wet slips are certainly available on these waters, there are not nearly so many as this impressive lineup of marinas would lead you to believe.

Surprisingly enough, there are also good spots for those who prefer to spend the evening tranquilly swinging on the hook. One haven resides just off Virginia Key, while Key Biscayne features two good anchorages. The region's most popular anchor-down spot resides on the waters just off Coconut Grove, hard by the shores of Dinner Key.

While none of these northerly Key Biscayne waters will ever be confused with a quiet anchorage off Islamorada, or even a laid-back marina in Key Largo, there is much to interest visiting mariners here. With plentiful anchorages and a plethora of marina facilities, this is a great spot for captains and crew to rest, refit, and prepare for this voyage south into "paradise."

Miami skyline

Virginia Key-Marine Stadium
(Standard Mile 1091.5)

South of the ICW-Miami River intersection, where our coverage of these waters ends in *Cruising Guide to Eastern Florida,* the ICW rushes on toward the fixed, high-rise Rickenbacker Causeway bridge, south of flashing daybeacon #67. Just short of this impressive span, an oblong cove cuts into Virginia Key's northwesterly shores. This body of water is known locally as the "Marine Stadium," and for good reason. Visitors to this cove will quickly note a huge bank of stadium seats flanking the southwesterly shores. The "Stadium" occasionally plays host to speedboat races and concerts. The band usually performs on a large floating stage set just in front of the seats. Hope the winds don't get up too much during the concert!

This cove used to be available for overnight stops by pleasure craft, but we were informed by the dockmaster at nearby Rickenbacker Marina in August of 2001 that pleasure craft trying to drop the hook in the Marine Stadium are now warned to move on by local water cops. The excuse given to us was that "the city doesn't want another colony forming like the anchorage community at Coconut Grove." These words make our collective bloods boil! We regret to inform the cruising community of the loss of this once-popular anchorage. Of course, the city of Miami is ignoring the fact that these prohibitions are completely contrary to Florida state law, but hey, who has the resources to take the city on?

Should you decide to visit Marine Stadium anyway, just for a look around, be advised that the entrance channel is a little tricky for first-timers. Be sure to read the navigational info in the next section of this chapter before attempting an initial entry.

Rickenbacker Marina
(Standard Mile 1091.5)
(25 44.739 North/080 10.442 West)

The first marina available to pleasure craft south of the ICW-Miami River intersection comes up along the Waterway's easterly flank, immediately north of the Rickenbacker Causeway bridge. This facility is known as Rickenbacker Marina, and it is owned and operated by the city of Miami. The marina's entrance is wide, easily-navigated, and carries minimum 8-foot depths. Cruisers entering this

Rickenbacker Marina Mooring Field (Miami skyline in background)

facility will note a new fuel pier flanking the starboard side of the harbor. Gasoline is dispensed at this pier. The dockmaster can arrange for diesel deliveries, via a fuel truck, for larger vessels, which need a good quantity of fuel.

The marina's wet slips will come up to port. These consist of fixed, wooden pilings with a concrete deck perched above. Depths alongside are at least 6 to 7 feet. Open-air dry-stack storage for smaller powercraft is also available.

Transients are accepted on a space-available basis at Rickenbacker Marina. The city dockmaster has informed us that only a few spaces are now available for visitors. He suggests calling ahead of time to make sure there are unoccupied slips.

If you are lucky enough to obtain a berth, expect to find 30- to 50-amp power hookups, plush fresh water connections. Waste tanks can be pumped out with a portable unit. Showers and a semi-open-air Laundromat are found in a building flanking the harbor's northeasterly shores. These are in fair condition and could be a bit cleaner. There is also a small, on-site variety store located in the dockmaster's building. Twenty-four-hour security is provided, and all patrons must leave and return to the dockage basin through locked gates.

Rickenbacker Marina also manages a mooring field, which fronts the marina to the northwest. These mooring buoys can be rented on a daily, weekly, or monthly basis. They are set aside for sailcraft ONLY, and there is a maximum size limit of 40 feet. Again, we suggest calling the dockmaster to check on availability BEFORE the time of your arrival.

The Rickenbacker mooring field sports shelter to the southeast and the east. There is also some lee to the northeast and the west.

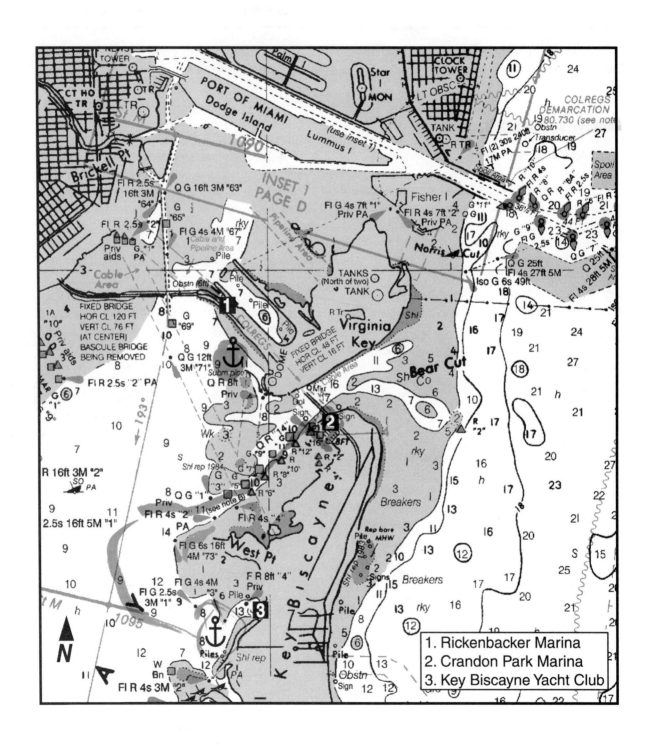

This is NOT a good spot to ride out heavy blows from the north or northwest.

There are two on-site restaurants, the Rusty Pelican (305-361-3818) and the Mad Fish House (305-365-9391). We have not had a chance to sample the bill of fare at this latter dining attraction, but the Rusty Pelican serves some very fresh seafood, even if it is a bit pricey. Some tables look out onto the waters of Biscayne Bay, with the Miami skyline in the background. It's one of the best views in town.

Rickenbacker Marina (305) 361-1900
http://www.rickenbackermarina.com

Approach depth—8 feet (minimum)
Dockside depth—6-7 feet (low water)
Accepts transients—space-available basis
(wet slips)/yes (mooring buoys)
Type of docking—fixed concrete piers
Dockside power connections—30-50 amp
Dockside water connections—yes
Gasoline—yes
Diesel fuel—larger quantities from fuel truck
Waste pump-out—yes
Showers—yes
Laundromat—yes
Variety store—yes
Restaurant—2 on site

Virginia Key Anchorage
(Standard Mile 1092.5)
(25 44.245 North/080 10.337 West)

With moderate winds blowing from the northeast or the north, some cruising craft have been known to anchor off the southwesterly shores of Virginia Key, east of flashing daybeacon #71. This portion of the isle is actually a long causeway leading to the Rickenbacker Causeway bridge. Minimum 7- to 10- foot depths can be held to within 250 yards (no closer) of the shoreline lying to the northeast, but take care not to stray too far to the southeast into the correctly charted, constricted portion

of this channel. Instead, drop anchor several hundred yards to the northwest of this shoal-plagued region.

This anchorage is wide open to winds from the northwest, south, west, and southwest. It is clearly not a foul weather hidey-hole.

The adjacent Virginia Key shoreline borders the huge Miami Seaquarium complex. Unfortunately, there are no docks that readily allow for shoreside landing by cruising craft or dinghies. Your best bet to visit this bright Miami attraction is by way of motorized transportation from one of Miami's many marinas.

No-go Channel

Study chart 11451 for a moment and notice the "Dome" perched on the southwestern tip of Virginia Key. This structure is actually the performing stadium for the Miami Seaquarium. Chart 11451 pictures a narrow channel running south, and then east, from this point (south of the charted, 8-foot, private light) across the breadth of Bear Cut inlet. Cruisers unfamiliar with these waters might think this passage could serve as a shortcut from the above-discussed anchorage to Crandon Park Marina on Key Biscayne (see below). In a word or three, don't try it. This channel is no longer accurately portrayed on 11451, and the surrounding shoals are quite likely to find your keel. We would be more than reluctant to send anything larger that a small, outboard-powered craft through this cut, and even then, a bent prop is a very real possibility.

Vizcaya Channel
(Standard Mile 1093.5)

Turning our attention to the mainland shores of Biscayne Bay, captains and crews have the opportunity to do a bit of historic

Villa Vizcaya

cruising. Notice the correctly charted channel striking northwest, to the west-southwest of flashing daybeacon #71 (near 25 43.985 North/080 12.088 West). The outermost aid to navigation on this well-marked cut is flashing daybeacon #2, and the channel carries minimum 7-foot soundings.

As you make your way between the various markers, an unforgettable sight will meet your eyes. Dead ahead, a dreamlike mansion, known as Villa Vizcaya (meaning "high place"), will rise up before you. No, your craft has not really found its way into the canals of Venice, Italy; it just feels that way.

Believe it or else, the multimillionaire James Deering (founder of International Harvester) built Vizcaya as his winter home in 1916, at a cost of $26 million. He employed better than a thousand workers to complete the showplace's three-year-construction project, and it is been said that this mammoth undertaking was a real boon to what was then the tiny Miami economy.

Your best view of the mansion will come up immediately after passing between unlighted daybeacons #9 and #10. During our last perusal of these waters, we spotted a large barge floating just in front of the mansion. It was being outfitted with several hundred floodlights for some sort of multimedia show.

Villa Vizcaya is now owned by the city of Miami, and it is open for public tours. Unfortunately, there are no provisions for docking pleasure craft or even tying up a dinghy. Instead, visit Vizcaya from one of Miami or Coconut Grove's marinas by way of a taxi or the public transportation system.

This landside trip is highly recommended. Visitors to the Italian Renaissance mansion will be amazed by its seventy luxurious rooms, myriad statues, and many peacefully-dripping fountains. Don't miss the sweeping, grand staircase and the beautifully-landscaped grounds. All in all, a visit to Villa Vizcaya can only be described as an otherworldly experience whose memory is sure to remain undimmed through the years.

Return your attention to chart 11451 for a moment and notice that a series of markers denotes a side channel leaving Vizcaya and rounding the point to the southwest. By keeping all the various unlighted, green daybeacons off our port side, we were able to maintain minimum 6-foot depths around the point. Soon, this cut begins to border the lands set about a large hospital, which will be prominent to starboard. The charted "Hospital Pier" is but a small, fixed, concrete and wooden structure that is only appropriate for emergency medical purposes.

Eventually, this side channel leads into a rectangular cove, which lies southwest of the hospital. Here a condo-dockage-complex, known as the Grove Isle Club, lines the southeasterly shoreline. While the basin's 8- to 11-foot depths are impressive, there are no provisions for visitors at Grove Isle.

Coconut Grove-Dinner Key Channels, Anchorages, and Marinas (Standard Mile 1094.5)

If there is a more concentrated collection of pleasure-craft facilities anywhere in southeastern Florida than the one guarding the shores of Dinner Key (in the community of

Coconut Grove anchorage

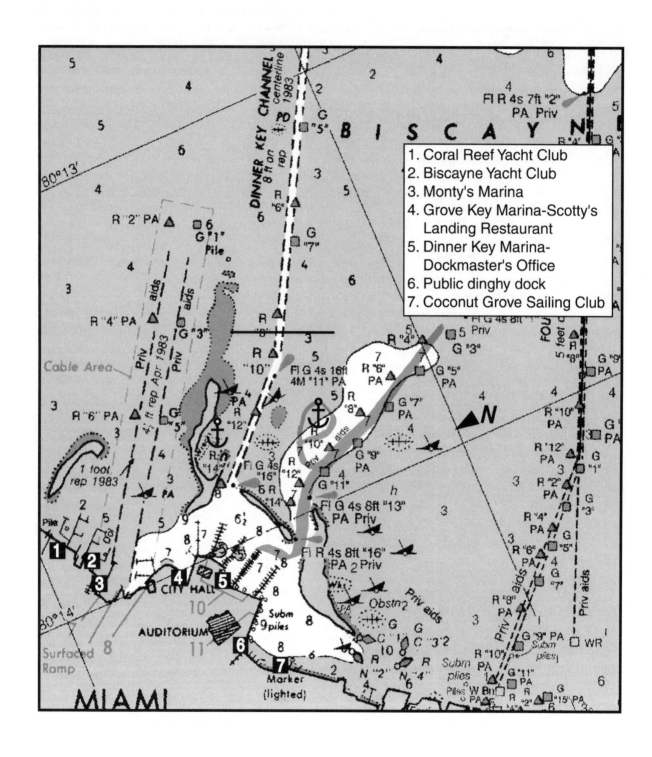

1. Coral Reef Yacht Club
2. Biscayne Yacht Club
3. Monty's Marina
4. Grove Key Marina-Scotty's Landing Restaurant
5. Dinner Key Marina-Dockmaster's Office
6. Public dinghy dock
7. Coconut Grove Sailing Club

Coconut Grove), we do not know of it. Add to this mix a very popular anchorage, an interesting shoreside community, plus a smattering of yacht clubs, and you have good reason to understand why many captains set their course for the waters lying about Dinner Key-Coconut Grove time and time again.

The entire Coconut Grove scene is very much a part of Miami. In fact, just where you would least expect it, the large dome-shaped Miami City Hall overlooks the marinas that line the northwesterly banks. This notable structure once served as the Pan American Airlines headquarters for their transatlantic sea planes. Some of the regional marinas are making use of the old hangar buildings for dry-stack storage.

Marinas are crowded, and the adjacent anchorage is always teeming with visiting craft. We were told by the dockmaster at Dinner Key Marina that better than 1,200 pleasure craft can usually be found at the docks and in the anchorage at Dinner Key. Obviously, this isn't exactly a quiet marina in Bahia Honda, but then again, you will most likely find anything and everything here that a cruising craft or its occupants might ever desire.

Coconut Grove and Dinner Key are served by four (all charted) channels. Three are reliable enough, but the southernmost passage should be avoided by all but those with sure, local knowledge.

We were surprised to learn that the northernmost, unnamed Coconut Grove cut, carries 5½ to 6 feet of depth at low water. Reports from other cruisers had placed these soundings at lesser levels, so we checked the entire channel twice, just to make sure. It should also be noted that the current configuration of aids to navigation runs much farther to the southeast (towards the ICW channel) than

chart 11451 would lead you to believe. This seems to indicate that this northernmost passage has been recently improved, possibly following the wholesale destruction of Hurricane Andrew.

The northern channel provides entry to the marina and yacht club facilities occupying the northerly section of the Dinner Key waterfront. There is NO ready access from this cut to the Coconut Grove anchorages. Those who depart this marked track while trying to reach the anchored craft that will be spotted to the south will undoubtedly hear that sad sound of keel meeting mud.

The primary "Dinner Key" channel is the next passage to the south. It's outermost markers, flashing daybeacon #1 and unlighted daybeacon #2, lie near 25 42.834 North/080 12.645 West. This well-marked route holds at least 8 feet of water, and it's a simple matter to track your way northwest into the inner dockage basin.

Many cruisers make the mistake of trying to cruise directly from the Dinner Key Channel into the large anchorage, which is so readily apparent to the southwest. Sad to say, this seemingly-direct approach will most likely lead you into 3-foot depths. Check out our discussion of the Dinner Key-Coconut Grove anchorage below for tips on successful entry into this haven.

The next channel, moving to the south, is also unnamed. It carries minimum 7-foot soundings and eventually cuts between the southerly pair of spoil islands, which protect the inner harbor. The outermost marker, flashing daybeacon #1, can be found near 25 42.881 North/080 13.710 West. While this cut also provides reliable access to the local marina facilities, its main claim to fame is easy entry into the adjacent anchorage (see below).

Finally, the Four-Way Channel comprises the southernmost of the four Coconut Grove marked passages. It's also the least useful. Low-water depths of only 4 feet in several spots lead off a list of unfortunate qualities. It is theoretically possible to break off from the westerly foot of the Four-Way Channel and track north into the southerly tier of the Coconut Grove inner basin. However, as the commodore of the Coconut Grove Sailing Club put it to us, "There's some good water out there somewhere, but I don't know where." If even the locals have trouble with this route, it's best to leave it strictly alone.

There are actually two anchorages available to pleasure craft on the waters surrounding Dinner Key, though most cruisers will find one far more desirable than the other. What we shall term the primary anchorage begins just to the northeast of the third (counting north to south) Coconut Grove entrance channel and extends for quite some distance to the north-northwest, towards the long, thin spoil island that fronts the Coconut Grove waterfront. The heart of this anchorage lies at about 25 43.286 North/080 13.805 West. Good depths of 7 to 10 feet carry well north-northwest, almost to the shores of the thin isle mentioned above. Some shoal water does lie to the east and northeast, so be sure to read the navigational account of this anchorage in the next section of this chapter.

This haven is well-sheltered from northern, northwestern, and northeasterly breezes, but it is pretty open to all other blows. In strong winds from the north, it might be possible to squeeze to within 50 yards of the thin, spoil island for additional protection.

Be advised that this primary anchorage is almost always crowded. Skippers may find it advisable to make use of a Bahamian-style mooring (two anchors set almost 180 degrees from each other) to minimize swing room and to prevent an unhappy meeting with your neighboring craft during the night.

There are two ways to enter the primary Coconut Grove-Dinner Key anchorage. The simplest approach is to make use of the unnamed third channel (again, counting north to south). You can depart this marked cut at unlighted daybeacon #10 and easily cruise into the heart of the overnight haven.

The primary anchorage can also be accessed from the Dinner Key Channel but ONLY by departing the marked cut just short of flashing daybeacon #15. A small patch of good water lies just south of #15 and allows entry into the haven. Again, check the next section of this chapter for additional details.

The secondary anchorage occupies the waters of the charted cove, north-northwest of Dinner Key Channel's unlighted daybeacon #12 (approximately 25 43.519 North/080 13.738 West). So, why do we call this a secondary anchorage? Well, there are three reasons. First, we found some depths as thin as 4 feet upon entering the protecting cove. Farther to the northwest, soundings deteriorated even more. Secondly, the cove is actually not at all as it appears on chart 11451. The rear portion of the surrounding island has washed away, leaving the impression of two keys instead of one. This can render correct on-the-water identification a bit difficult for first-timers. Finally, our last visit to this anchorage revealed a host of what could only be described as derelict craft. Some were sunken or semisunken. So say what you will, but you will find our craft swinging on the hook in the primary anchorage, rather than this secondary haven, every time.

No matter what anchorage you choose,

cruisers lying on the hook can make use of a most-welcome public dinghy dock. This useful structure guards Coconut Grove's northwesterly banks (west of the charted "Auditorium") between huge Dinner Key Marina (see below) and the Coconut Grove Sailing Club. It is located near 25 43.642 North/080 14.240 West.

In August of 2001, we had an in-depth conversation with one of the most influential members of the Dinner Key-Coconut Grove anchorage community. This helpful individual told us to warn all cruisers who make use of the public dinghy dock NOT to leave anything aboard their dinks after departing for landside destinations. Apparently, even fuel cans and oars can be targets for theft. Take heed of this word to the wise. Take everything with you.

Some dinghies can also be temporarily moored on the concrete sea wall just north of Grove Key Marina (see below). This is apparently a more secure location that seems to lack some of the public dinghy dock's reputation for theft. The same helpful individual who warned us of these problems at the public pier indicated that this second dinghy berth was a more or less invitation-only arrangement. We were never able to determine to whom one applied for admission to this select group, so first-timers may want to use the public dinghy dock to begin with and then apply to their on-the-water neighbors for information as to how to make use of this more secure location.

Let's now turn our attention to the multiple Coconut Grove facilities. We will learn that most of the available dockage on these waters

Dinner Key Marina (Coconut Grove)

is found at the huge, Miami-city-owned Dinner Key Marina. A few other slips can sometimes be found at the other area marinas and yacht clubs. We shall move north to south in our overview of the waterfront facilities.

The northernmost is the Coral Reef Yacht Club. This opulent organization is a member of the Florida Council of Yacht Clubs. Visitors who are members of other clubs with appropriate reciprocal agreements are accepted. Advance arrangements are required, and a three-day-maximum stay is imposed. Berths are provided at fixed concrete piers with 30- to 50-amp power and fresh water connections. Depths alongside run around 7 feet. Vessels as large as 47 feet can be accommodated.

While Coral Reef does not have a fuel dock, diesel deliveries via a tanker truck can be arranged for large yachts that need a prodigious volume of fuel.

The adjacent clubhouse features a most-refreshing swimming pool, and its own dining room. Luncheon is served from 12 noon to 2:00 P.M., Tuesday through Friday, while the evening meal is offered from 6:30 P.M. to 9:00 P.M., Tuesday through Sunday. Coral Reef Yacht Club and its dockage basin are closed Mondays.

Shoreside showers are provided hard by the swimming pool, but there is no Laundromat. Gasoline must also be purchased elsewhere.

The Coral Reef Yacht Club has been around since 1955, and it is one of the most respected organizations of its type in southeastern Florida. If you are lucky enough to secure a visitor's berth here, we suspect you won't soon forget the pleasure of a stay at this club.

Anchored forever (Coconut Grove anchorage)

Coral Reef Yacht Club (305) 858-1733
http://www.coralreefyachtclub.org

Approach depth—5½ feet (via the northernmost
Coconut Grove channel) 8 feet (via the
Dinner Key Channel)
Dockside depth—7 feet
Accepts transients—only members of other
yacht clubs with reciprocal arrangements
(advance reservations required)
Type of docking—fixed concrete piers
Dockside power and water connections—30-50
amp
Dockside water connections—yes
Showers—yes
Restaurant—dining room on site (members and
accredited guests only)

Just to the south of Coral Reef, cruisers will sight the piers of the Biscayne Bay Yacht Club (305-858-6303). As far as we have been able to determine, no dockage or other services for visitors are available at this facility.

Another hop to the south will bring your vessel abeam of Monty's Marina (near 25 43.909 North/080 13.949 West). Monty's is a large complex with two on-site restaurants and numerous yacht brokerage offices. Unfortunately, transient slips are usually not to be found amidst this marina's many, fixed, wooden wet slips. The dockmaster firmly informed us that over seventy percent of the available berths are taken up by brokerage boats. Sometimes, visitors are accepted strictly on a space-available basis, but this practice is clearly more the exception than the rule.

Monty's dockage is composed of fixed wooden slips with 30- to 50-amp power and fresh water hookups. Depths alongside run around 7 feet. Waste pump-out is also offered, but there is no fuel pier. The shoreside showers and Laundromat are first-class, and they are air-conditioned (a real rarity in these climes).

Monty's Seafood Restaurant, Coconut Grove

(305-858-1431) is located on the second floor of the large building just behind the dockage complex. Its large, plate-glass windows look out over the Coconut Grove waterfront and provide a wonderful view, particularly at the end of the day. Reportedly, the seafood here is wonderful, though we have not tried it yet.

Monty's Raw Bar (305-856-3992) is an open-air combination bar and restaurant located on the ground floor, and slightly closer to the dockage basin. We watched a seemingly satisfied lunch crowd go about their arduous tasks of eating and drinking. Everyone seemed happy, but we did not have a chance to participate.

Monty's Marina (305) 854-7997
Approach depth—5½ feet (via the
northernmost Coconut Grove channel) 8 feet
(via the Dinner Key Channel)
Dockside depth—7 feet
Accepts transients—limited
Type of docking—fixed wooden piers
Dockside power connections—30-50 amp
Dockside water connections—yes
Showers—yes
Laundromat—yes
Waste pump-out—yes
Restaurant—two on site

Shake-A-Leg Marina (305-858-5550) occupies a short section of the Coconut Grove waterfront, just south of Monty's. This is a watersports-oriented facility, and there is nothing here to interest cruising-sized craft.

Next up is Grove Key Marina (305-858-6527). This facility guards the shoreline near 25 43.725 North/080 14.024 West. Grove Key is a dry-stack storage marina. Many, many craft are comfortably housed in two converted aircraft hangars left over from the Pan-Am days of glory. Some craft are also stored on racks in the open air.

Gasoline and diesel can be purchased at

Grove Key Marina, though yachts over 50 feet in length may feel a bit cramped at the fuel pier. Take note that Grove Key is the ONLY facility along the Coconut Grove waterfront to offer dockside fuel.

There is no wet slip dockage available at Grove Key Marina, but cruisers might want to check out the on-site ship store, which goes under the name of Alhambra Marine (305-858-1830). This operation claims to offer "over 150,000 items from 1000 manufacturers."

Scotty's Landing Restaurant (305-854-2626) is also located on the grounds of Grove Key Marina. This simply wonderful dining spot is yet another semi-open-air operation. Tables are grouped under shade umbrellas and look directly out over the Coconut Grove waterfront. Additional seating is available at a large bar, just behind the tables.

The food at Scotty's Landing is casual, but wonderful. The "Triple Cheese Cheeseburger" receives our unqualified vote as the best burger in Miami!

When you first cruise through the westerly end of the Dinner Key Channel, into the inner Coconut Grove-Dinner Key basin, it looks as if you are face-to-face with about a dozen different marinas. The fixed wooden docks just seem to go on and on. Surprise, surprise, all these piers are really part of the huge, city-of-Miami-owned Dinner Key Marina. This facility overlooks the waterfront south of Grove Key Marina and north of the Coconut Grove Sailing Club, within sight of the huge Miami City Hall (once the Pan-Am seaplane headquarters). It encompasses 582 slips (that's right, 582), of which a full twenty percent are set aside for transients.

Be advised that the dockmaster's office sits on shore, in the heart of the dockage complex, near 25 43.605 North/080 14.106 West. The marina's showers and Laundromat are also located in this building.

Of course, as the dockmaster told us, "transients" include those who stay for a week, a few weeks, or several months. So, if you are just in the market for an overnight stop, you should call ahead to check on available space, even given this marina's huge proportions.

Dinner Key Marina's seven ranks of piers all consist of fixed wooden docks. All berths feature 30- to 50-amp power hookups, plus fresh water connections. Telephone and cable television hookups are also provided, but there is an extra charge for these services, and arrangements must be made with the local telephone company and cable television supplier.

Dinner Key Marina features a waste pump-out connection at just about every slip. How's that for full service? A few of the smaller slips (geared to boats 30 feet and smaller) do not have a waste connection. Smaller craft at these berths can take advantage of a central waste pump-out at the southeasterly end of pier 3.

The on-site showers consist of four stalls for each sex. We found them in fair condition, but a bit more thorough cleaning would certainly be in order. The shower rooms are NOT climate-controlled. The Laundromat is open to the weather on one side, but it is sheltered under a roof. Frankly, for a marina of this size, we expected a bit nicer showers and Laundromat (this facility could take a lesson from the St. Petersburg municipal marina on Florida's western coast), but they are adequate and certainly no reason for you not to patronize Dinner Key Marina.

The nearest Publix supermarket is two miles away. This can be quite a hike, particularly during hot weather with groceries in hand. We suggest a quick taxi ride under these circumstances.

All the restaurants reviewed above are

within walking distance, as is the Coconut Grove version of the venerable Chart House restaurants (51 Chart House Drive, 305-856-9741). The Chart House overlooks the waterfront north of Grove Key Marina. It is open evenings only, from 5:30 P.M. to 11:00 P.M.

A five-minute walk to the southwest will lead to the many delights and restaurants of the Coconut Grove community. We will detail some of this community's individual attractions below. After dark, you may want to take a taxi to and from the marina.

Dinner Key Marina is *the* transient-oriented pleasure-craft facility in Coconut Grove. Wet slips available to visiting craft south of Coconut Grove become few and far between short of Jewfish Creek. Captains should think long and hard before passing this marina by

and continuing their voyage south, particularly if its late in the day.

Dinner Key Marina (305) 579-6980
http://www.ci.miami.fl.us

Approach depth—8 feet (via Dinner Key
   Channel)
Dockside depth—61/2-8 feet
Accepts transients—yes
Type of docking—fixed wooden piers
Dockside power connections—30 to 50 amp
Dockside water connections—yes
Waste pump-out—yes
Cable television connections—yes (extra charge)
Telephone connections—yes (extra charge)
Showers—yes
Laundromat—yes
Restaurant—many within walking distance

The southernmost of the Coconut Grove

Coconut Grove Sailing Club Mooring Field

waterfront facilities is friendly Coconut Grove Sailing Club (also known as CGSC, 305-444-4571). This cruiser-friendly organization maintains a city-sanctioned mooring field just south of Dinner Key Marina. The heart of the mooring field lies near 25 43.515 North/080 14.228 West. Typical depths in the field are 6 to 7 feet, but some buoys are founded in shallower water. Guest moorings are available for cruisers who are members of other yacht clubs with appropriate reciprocal privileges. Advance reservations must be made at least ninety days in advance. There is a $15 per day charge, and a maximum stay of seven days is imposed. As of August 2001, we were told that the mooring field is very full, and only a few shallow-water moorings were available. Of course, this situation will change, one way or the other, as time goes forward. Call (305) 444-4571 for more information.

Coconut Grove Ashore

A five-minute walk leads visiting cruisers from the waterfront to the colorful community of Coconut Grove. It is a most pleasant stroll to and through this artsy community during the day, but at night, we have heard rumors of less-than-savory happenings. We suggest taking a taxi to and from the marina after dark.

Between Dinner Key Marina and the Coconut Grove shopping district, you will pass a branch of the Miami Public Library (2875 McFarlene Road, 305-442-8695). This facility is convenient to all the nearby transient slips and within a very few steps of the public dinghy dock.

The heart of Coconut Grove lies just a few blocks away, grouped along Grand Avenue and its various cross streets. Here visitors will find a mind-boggling array of vibrant specialty shops, plus lots and lots of restaurants. You can wander happily for hours and easily find a spot to slake your thirst and appetite when ready. The word that comes to mind in describing the Coconut Grove shopping district is "neat."

It would probably require a small book of its own to even begin to cover all the dining attractions Coconut Grove has to offer. We only have time to mention a few that caught our collective attention.

First up is the Barracuda Raw Bar and Grill (3035 Fuller Street, 305-448-1144). We found the seafood as fresh as it could be. Then, there's Green Street Café (3105 Commodore Street, 305-444-0244). This spot's open-air, sidewalk dining is nothing short of charming. If you're up for Cuban-style cuisine, don't miss the Mambo Café (3105 Commodore Street, 305-448-2768). It also features sidewalk dining. The staff at Dinner Key Marina recommended the Taurus Grill (3540 Main Highway, 305-648-1525). While we were not able to sample the fare here, it's always a good idea to take the advice of locals when it comes to good eating places.

On a less happy note, we could not help but observe that the residential districts along the southwestern fringes of Coconut Grove did not seem to be in the best of repair. We strongly recommend against casual strolling through this area.

Before leaving Coconut Grove, we would like to note the one-time presence of a historic night club in this village-like community, which was known as "The Barnacle." Claiborne's Mom has told him about many a wild time there, back in the "good old days."

Currently, the Barnacle is being redeveloped as an "exclusive" condominium complex that will be known as the Cloisters Luxury Villas on the Bay. We were amused to observe a sign on Main Highway that advertised individual units in this complex as "starting at only

$1.5 million." Needless to say, we didn't rush to place an order for one in each color.

Bear Cut

Bear Cut is a shallow inlet that separates Virginia Key and Key Biscayne. The channel, such as it is, lies southeast of the ICW's flashing daybeacon #71. While the southwesterly portion of this cut is deep and well-marked, this passage leads only to well-outfitted Crandon Park Marina on the inner shores of Key Biscayne (see below). The seaward portion of the cut, on the other hand, is very shallow, mostly unmarked, and it is spanned by a fixed bridge with only 16 feet of vertical clearance. Clearly this errant inlet is best left to our outboard and I/O brethren, and even then, the captains of these vessels had better be equipped with the latest local knowledge.

Key Biscayne Facilities and Anchorages

Key Biscayne is a fortunate island for cruising skippers and crews. Meld a city-owned marina with a notable yacht club, plus several good anchorages, and you have a recipe that will bring many a mariner calling time and again. To our way of thinking, Key Biscayne is one of the best parts of Miami cruising!

Key Biscayne is also pleasing to the eye. On calm days, the isle's many elegant homes are mirrored against the bay's clear waters. An evening spent on one of the nearby anchorages is likely to be a memorable experience.

As if all that were not enough, the southerly, Cape Florida portion of Key Biscayne plays host to the Bill Baggs Cape Florida State Recreations Area. This is a wonderful state park and features one of the most historic lighthouses in the Sunshine State.

Cape Florida Lighthouse (Key Biscayne)

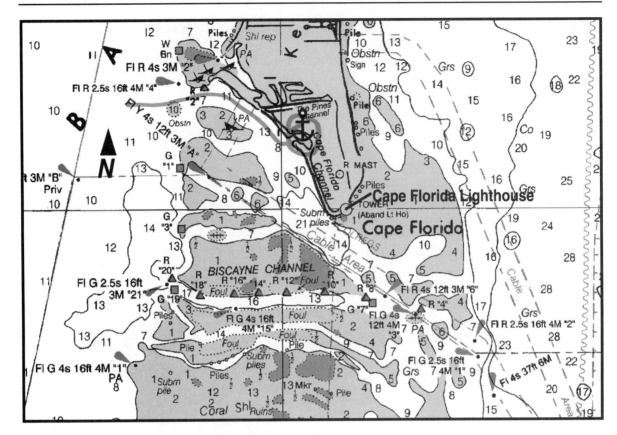

Key Biscayne's north-to-south axis spans some 3.8 nautical miles from Bear Cut to Cape Florida. It lines the easterly limits of the ICW on the long run south from flashing daybeacon #71 to flashing daybeacon #B.

Moving north to south, the key's first pleasure boating attraction sits perched on the northeasterly head of the long, well-marked, and thoroughly-charted channel that follows the initial reaches of Bear Cut (Standard Mile 1094). The entrance to this passage makes into the Waterway's easterly flank, well south of flashing daybeacon #71, near 25 42.886 North/080 10.595 West.

This entrance channel carries 12+ feet of water at low tide, and it eventually leads to Crandon Park Marina. There is one interesting twist in the channel. First-timers should consult the navigational account in the next section of this chapter before attempting entry.

Crandon Park Marina (25 43.560 North/080 09.276 West) is owned and operated by Dade County. In years past, this facility boasted plenty of transient dockage, but that situation has now changed for the worse.

In August of 2001, we were informed by the Crandon Park dockmaster that most of his slips were now leased on a long-term basis. This even includes a whole collection of new docks that were slated to be ready for occupation, shortly after our departure. We were amazed to learn these new spaces were already spoken for.

Again, according to the dockmaster, some

Crandon Park Marina (Key Biscayne)

nights find 3 or 4 berths available for overnighters, while other evenings find the marina completely full. It seems to depend on how many of the resident craft are out cruising at any particular time. Clearly, transient dockage at Crandon Park Marina is now pretty much on a space-available basis.

Those who do secure a berth at Crandon Park will tie their lines securely to ultramodern, concrete-decked floating docks. Dockside depths are an impressive 12 feet or better, and there is excellent protection from foul weather. Dockside connections include 30- to 50-amp power and fresh water hookups.

Gasoline and diesel can be purchased at a fuel pier, just off the harbor's southeasterly entrance point. A small variety store (305-361-8446) sits just behind the pumps.

Patrons of this small shop will find mostly bait-and-tackle items. Waste pump-out is also available.

There are no longer any showers or a Laundromat at Crandon Park Marina. There are some rest rooms, but after taking one look at these facilities, all hands voted to use our on-board head.

The on-site Sundays on the Bay Restaurant (305-361-6777) is as good (and expensive) as ever. During the winter season, it's a wise idea to call ahead for reservations, particularly on weekends.

Crandon Park Marina also features its own mooring field, a short hop southwest of the dockage basin. While you would never guess it from chart 11451, a few small mangroves provide fairly good shelter for this field.

Soundings run 9 feet or better. While this haven cannot be considered a hurricane hole, it does provide enough shelter from moderate breezes.

These moorings can be rented by the day, week, or month. They are reserved for sail-craft, with a maximum size restriction of 50 feet. Call the Crandon Park Marina dockmaster at (305) 361-1281 to check on availability.

Crandon Park Marina (305) 361-1281
http://www.metro-dade.com/parks

Approach depth—12+ feet
Dockside depth—12 feet
Accepts transients—space-available basis
Type of docking—floating concrete docks
Dockside power—30 to 50 amp
Dockside water connections—yes
Waste pump-out—yes

Gasoline—yes
Diesel fuel—yes
Variety store—yes
Restaurant—on site

Next up is a good anchorage (approximately 25 41.736 North/080 10.515 West—Standard Mile 1095) when easterly breezes are wafting. Consult chart 11451 and note the large patch of deep water south of West Point. Good depths of 10+ feet extend to within 250 yards of the easterly shore. There is little in the way of shelter here when the fickle winds are blowing from the west, southwest, or northwest. During fair weather, however, this haven boasts some real eye candy. The adjacent shoreline is heavily dotted with sumptuous, almost dreamlike, homes that are clearly the property of the "rich and famous."

Key Biscayne Yacht Club

Let us now turn our attention to the nearby Key Biscayne Yacht Club (approximately 25 41.966 North/080 10.165 West—Standard Mile 1095). This club's headquarters and dockage basin reside just to the northeast of the anchorage reviewed above (southeast of charted West Point). Three flashing daybeacons help members and guests keep to the good water, but again, newcomers would be well-advised to read the navigational sketch of this channel in the next portion of this chapter. Entrance and alongside depths are an impressive 10+ feet at low water. While a portion of the harbor is protected by a rock breakwater, this is not the most sheltered harbor you will ever come upon. Strong winds from the west, and particularly the northwest, could make your evening a bit uncomfortable.

The Key Biscayne Yacht Club offers limited guest dockage for members of other yacht clubs with appropriate reciprocal privileges. Due to space limitations, advance reservations are mandatory. Call (305) 361-8229 to reserve your slip. The club dockmaster can be found on the dock or in his office Tuesday through Sunday from 8:00 A.M. to 5:15 P.M., and Monday from 8:00 A.M. to 4:30 P.M.

Berths consist of both fixed wooden and fixed concrete slips. Dockside power (30 to 50 amp) and fresh water hookups are in the offing. There is even a club fuel dock, but be advised that gasoline and diesel fuel are sold ONLY to club members and properly registered guests.

Shoreside, visitors will discover excellent showers in the clubhouse and a refreshing swimming pool. The Key Biscayne Yacht Club's dining room is open (only) to members and accredited visitors daily, except Mondays, from 12 noon to 3:00 P.M. and 6:00 P.M. to 9:30 P.M. Reservations are requested.

Alternatively, there is also an excellent lounge and a snack bar on site.

Key Biscayne Yacht Club (Dockmaster: 305-361-8229) (Clubhouse: 305-361-9171)

Approach depth—10-14 feet
Dockside depth—10-13 feet
Accepts transients—members of yacht clubs with appropriate reciprocal privileges
Type of docking—fixed wooden and fixed concrete piers
Dockside power connections—30 to 50 amp
Dockside water connections—yes
Gasoline—yes (members and accredited guests only)
Diesel fuel—yes (members and accredited guests only)
Showers—yes
Restaurant—on site (members and accredited guests only)

Finally, cruisers have the opportunity to drop anchor in the tadpole-shaped harbor, which indents the westerly banks of south Key Biscayne, near Cape Florida (approximately 25 40.611 North/080 09.769 West—Standard Mile 1096). This haven is actually known as No Name Harbor and is a part of the Bill Baggs Cape Florida State Park (see below). Overnight anchorage is allowed on these waters for a daily fee of $11.25. Boats can also anchor just for the day (without an overnight stay) for $2.00.

The approach to No Name Harbor from the ICW and the main body of Biscayne Bay is by way of the charted Cape Florida Channel. This cut does border on two patches of shoaly water, but fortunately, one new but uncharted marker helps navigators to avoid these obstructions. Of course, an on-board GPS interfaced with a laptop computer (containing digitized NOAA charts and navigational software) would make this process ever so much easier and safer. Nevertheless, careful skippers should be able to maintain minimum 7-foot depths to the harbor's entrance.

No Name Harbor boasts superb shelter from all winds and 10+-foot depths at low water. There are no docks provided for cruising-sized craft anywhere along the harbor's shores.

The shores of No Name Harbor are almost completely in their natural state, not surprising since the basin is part of the recreation area. These undeveloped conditions are in marked contrast to virtually every other anchorage north of Key Biscayne. Coupled with the good depths and excellent shelter, we can only conclude that this anchorage is a real winner, always supposing you can cough up that $11.25 anchorage fee.

After cruising into the inner reaches of No Name Harbor, look towards the bay's southerly tip. Here you will spy a two-story building with an adjoining dinghy dock. Just beside the building, cruisers will discover a receptacle for depositing their anchoring fee. Don't be a cheapskate and try to short-circuit this honor-system approach. Someone may very well check up on whether you've paid your fee. Doesn't it make sense to fork over a measly $11.25, rather than pay a stiff fine?

The second floor of the building just behind the fee collecting station plays host to the screen-porch-style, Boater's Grill. This is apparently a leased operation, as the food is quite good and lunches are well-attended, even during high summer. The seafood sandwiches are wonderful! The café is open from 9:00 A.M. to 6:00 P.M. daily.

No Name Harbor (Key Biscayne)

Bill Baggs Cape Florida State Park

The southern tip of Key Biscayne is guarded by the venerable Cape Florida Lighthouse. A state recreation area surrounding this old sentinel of the sea is a great stop for visiting cruisers and landlubber tourists alike. Waterborne visitors are within walking distance of all the park's attractions from the waters of No Name Harbor (see above).

After Florida joined the Union in the 1800s, one of the federal government's first projects in the new Sunshine State was the establishment of a series of lighthouses along the eastern coastline from Fernandina Beach to Miami. The Cape Florida Lighthouse was first lit in 1825 as part of this program. It is now the oldest surviving building in south Florida.

The tragic conflict known as the Second Seminole Indian War broke out in 1835. On July 23, 1836, the Cape Florida Lighthouse was attacked and burned by Native Americans. Miraculously, the lighthouse keeper escaped unharmed, but his assistant was killed. Congress appropriated $23,000 for the rehabilitation of the lighthouse, and it was once again proudly lit on April 30, 1847.

During the War Between the States, Confederates removed the lens and burners so the light could not be used to aid Union naval forces. The lighthouse was repaired and once again lit in 1866.

From 1878 to 1978, the lighthouse was dark. It was thought that the nearby Fowey Rocks Light was sufficient for navigational purposes. The people of Miami were not convinced. Through vigorous and vocal local support and petitions, the Cape Florida Lighthouse once again shone over the waters of Hawk Channel and Biscayne Bay on July 4, 1978.

The surrounding state recreation area is named for Bill Baggs, a local journalist who worked tirelessly to promote the park's establishment. The recreation area today boasts "one of the top 10 beaches in the U.S." Eight fishing platforms allow anglers to try their luck in the surf. The on-site Lighthouse Café (305-361-8487) offers casual, open-air dining and rents bicycles, hydrobikes, beach chairs, and umbrellas.

Guided tours of the historic lighthouse are conducted Thursday through Monday at 10:00 A.M. and 1:00 P.M. The park authorities suggest that patrons arrive early, as space for these tours is limited.

As related above, the park maintains the Boater's Grill on the banks of No Name Harbor. Dockside dining, showers, and a few variety store items are available.

For more information, contact the Bill Baggs Cape Florida State Park, 1200 South Crandon Boulevard, Key Biscayne, Florida, (305) 361-5811.

VIRGINIA KEY, COCONUT GROVE, AND KEY BISCAYNE NAVIGATION

The waters between the Miami River-ICW intersection and the Waterway channel opposite Virginia Key are dotted with an almost dizzying array of aids to navigation. This is certainly not the place to go charging ahead at full bore, navigating by eye. For one thing, most of the ICW channel between the Miami River intersection and the Rickenbacker Causeway is an official no-wake zone. The local water cops and the new incarnation of the Florida Marine Patrol are eagerly waiting to nab violators of this prohibition. Rather, take your time, keep chart 11451 ready-to-hand, and sort out all the various markers along the way. You'll come through much the better for a little caution, not to mention sans speeding tickets.

Conversely, south of flashing daybeacon #71, aids to navigation along the ICW are rather few and far between. Have your compass/GPS courses preplotted for this section of the Waterway. Fortunately, all the various side channels in this region still retain copious markers.

South of the Rickenbacker Causeway, the waters of northerly Biscayne Bay are more than broad enough to foster a healthy chop, particularly when fresh winds are blowing from the south. Small-craft skippers should be aware of this long wind fetch and keep a ready ear to the latest NOAA weather forecast before beginning their cruise.

South to Rickenbacker Causeway Unlighted daybeacon #57 marks the intersection of the ICW and the entrance to Miami River. Southbound Waterway cruisers should come abeam and pass #57 to its southwesterly side and continue on a more or less southeasterly heading, pointing to come abeam of flashing daybeacon #59 to its westerly quarter. Be sure to use inset #1, Page D, on chart 11451 while navigating these waters.

At #59, the ICW turns sharply to the south-southwest and soon begins to border commercial Claughton Island to the west. Flashing daybeacon #63 marks a turn to the south. Past #63, the Waterway hurries on toward a meeting with the tall Rickenbacker Causeway bridge, south of flashing daybeacon #67. Switch back to the main panel of chart 11451 for details of the ICW and adjacent waters south of #63.

Just short of the Rickenbacker span, cruisers have the opportunity to break off to the east and visit either the Marine Stadium Cove or Rickenbacker Marina.

Marine Stadium Cove and Rickenbacker Marina For best depths, depart the Waterway some 50 yards north of the Rickenbacker Causeway and turn sharply to the east. Those unfortunate souls who cut east a bit farther to the north will likely run afoul of the charted shallows east of flashing daybeacon #67.

As you leave the Waterway in your wake, point for the midwidth of the cove, which will be spied immediately north of the bridge's easterly tip. This small body of water is home to Rickenbacker Marina. If this facility is your goal, simply cruise straight into the harbor.

If, on the other hand, you have a mind to visit the Marine Stadium, break off to the north about 40 yards short of the marina entrance. Cruise north at idle speed, favoring the easterly banks, and soon the wide entrance to the cove that hosts the Marine Stadium will open out to the southeast. Be mindful of the correctly charted shallow water to the northwest as you are making this run.

Along the way, you may very well spy a few craft in the Rickenbacker Marina mooring field to the east. This field has little in the way of shelter for any, save easterly, blows.

Cut to the southeast and cruise into the Marine Stadium cove, while favoring the entrance's southwesterly banks. As chart 11451 suggests, there is some less-than-deep water to the northeast.

South on the ICW South of flashing day-beacon #67, the Waterway soon exchanges greetings with the fixed, high-rise Rickenbacker Causeway Bridge. With an impressive vertical clearance of 76 feet, even large sailcraft should not have a problem.

Immediately south of the high-rise, the channel is bordered to the east and west by portions of the old, low-level Rickenbacker bridge that have been left in place for sport fishing purposes. The center span has been removed, so passage is not a problem.

Once the old and new Rickenbacker spans are in your wake, southbound navigators should set course to bring unlighted daybeacon #69 abeam to its westerly side. The channel now swings just a bit to the south-southwest and hurries on to flashing daybeacon #71. Come abeam of #71 to its westerly quarter.

Daybeacons #69 and #71 are fairly close together, as is true of almost all other aids to navigation north of the Rickenbacker Causeway. Well, south of this point, things change in a big way. It is an impressive run of slightly better than 4 nautical miles from #71 to flashing daybeacon #B, the next southerly aid to navigation.

Between #71 and #B, there are many side trips that cruisers might choose. To the west, the Vizcaya Channel and the Dinner Key-Coconut Grove communities beckon.

Meanwhile, Crandon Park Marina, the Key Biscayne Yacht Club, and the various Key Biscayne anchorages lie to the southeast. Let's now take a look at the navigational characteristics of these destinations in the order listed above.

Alternate Virginia Key Anchorage Track your way southeast from unlighted daybeacon #69, pointing for the midsection of the Virginia Key shoreline that comprises the long causeway leading to the Rickenbacker Causeway bridge. Carefully note the correctly charted band of shallows making out from these banks. Don't approach to within less than 250 yards of the northeasterly shores.

Also, don't attempt the passage around the southwesterly tip of Virginia Key that is overlooked by the charted "Dome." This treacherous channel is not correctly charted, and there is almost every reason to believe that should you attempt this passage, Sea Tow will be getting some more business.

Vizcaya Cha]nnel The outermost marker on the channel leading northwest to the Vizcaya mansion is flashing daybeacon #2. This cut is exceedingly well-marked. All you need do is pass between the various unlighted daybeacons until you make a close approach to the Vizcaya harbor. If you run aground here, better line up a few classes at Chapmans.

After cruising between the innermost pair of daybeacons on the primary Vizcaya Channel, the mansion will be quite obvious dead-ahead. Cruisers can, should they so choose, follow another intersecting channel to the southwest. This passage is outlined by a series of green, unlighted daybeacons. Keep all these various markers off your port side as you follow the land round the adjacent point. Soon the large hospital mentioned earlier will come abeam to starboard, followed shortly by the small hospital pier.

Skippers bound for the private Grove Isle Club can continue following this cut around as it curves to the west and enters a sheltered cove. Stick to the centerline for best depths. Soon, Grove Isle's docks will be spotted along the southeasterly banks.

Dinner Key-Coconut Grove Channels and Anchorages The four channels serving the many facilities and anchorages of Dinner Key-Coconut Grove make out from Biscayne's westerly banks, a short hop south of the Vizcaya Channel. As mentioned earlier, the southernmost passage, known as the Four-Way Channel, is shallow, treacherous, and not appropriate for cruising-sized vessels. As such, it is not detailed further in this section. With that said, let's begin our review of the other Dinner Key cuts, moving north to south.

The northernmost (unnamed) channel is easy to run and allows simple access to the facilities along the northern end of the Dinner Key waterfront. About the only other thing navigators need know about this cut (which does not become immediately apparent after a quick perusal of Inset 2 of chart 11451) is that the outermost markers now extend much farther to the southeast than the scheme of aids to navigation

pictured on 11451. The presence of these new markers only makes things simpler. Once you identify the eastern end of the passage, denoted by unlighted daybeacons #1 and #2, simply continue on a straight course to the west-northwest, cruising directly between the various pairs of unlighted daybeacons. Eventually, the track will lead you hard by the north side Dinner Key marinas.

Captains are strictly warned against trying to reach any of the Coconut Grove anchorages from this cut. Check out our account of the two channels below for access to these havens.

Next up is the Dinner Key Channel. This is the best marked of the four area passages, and the easiest to run. Pass between the cut's outermost markers, flashing daybeacon #1 and unlighted daybeacon #2, and continue cruising to the west-northwest, passing all subsequent red, even-numbered markers to your starboard side, and take green markers to port. At unlighted daybeacon #10, the channel cuts a bit farther to the northwest. Come abeam of #10 to its southerly side and then point to pass flashing daybeacon #11 to its northeasterly quarter. Eventually, the channel passes between unlighted daybeacon #14 and flashing daybeacon #15. Soon thereafter, it slips between two of the spoil islands that protect the Coconut Grove waterfront. Huge Dinner Key marina lies in deep water directly ahead.

Cruisers bound for the larger, primary Dinner Key anchorage should resist the temptation to cut off the Dinner Key Channel into this haven. From the water, it looks ever so simple to simply abandon the marked track at flashing daybeacon #11 and cruise between the dozens of boats you will undoubtedly find swinging tranquilly on these waters. Such a move will, however, land you in 3-foot depths. The easiest access to this anchorage is from the next (moving south) channel (see below).

There is one safe way to enter the primary anchorage from the Dinner Key Channel, though you would never guess this passage from the water. We spent almost a half-day sounding all these depths, and we now know where the good water is and where it is not. Anyway, you can depart the Dinner Key cut some 25 yards east-southeast of flashing daybeacon #15 and cut southwest into the primary haven. This passage will run you fairly close to the long, thin, spoil island that borders the northwesterly tip of the anchorage. Fortunately, good depths run almost to shore from this isle. Be sure to leave the Dinner Key Channel well in your wake before turning south or southeast into the heart of the anchorage.

The only access to what we are calling in this account the secondary Dinner Key Anchorage is gained by veering off from the Dinner Key Channel at unlighted daybeacon #12. Set course for the midwidth of the cove, which will open out to the north-northwest. Watch out for sunken and partially sunken vessels as you enter this haven.

Be advised that this cove is now very different from what is pictured on chart 11451 (Page B, Inset 2). The rear portion of the irregular spoil island, which once bordered this anchorage, has now washed away entirely. Now, on the water it appears as if

the cove is nestled between two isles. In any case, depths deteriorate rapidly as you cruise farther to the north-northwest towards the eroded shoreline. Unless you can stand 3-foot soundings, set your hook near the cove's southerly mouth.

The next channel to the south is unnamed, but it is also deep and well-marked. It is a much shorter cut than the Dinner Key Channel, and cruisers heading for this passage will need to travel much farther from the ICW before meeting up with the outermost markers, flashing daybeacon #1 and unlighted daybeacon #2. As you would have most likely guessed without us telling you, pass between #1 and #2 and simply take all subsequent red markers to your starboard side and green beacons to port. West of the gap between flashing daybeacon #13 and unlighted daybeacon #14, this channel slips between two of the spoil islands and enters the primary Coconut Grove waterfront basin. Flashing daybeacon #16 marks the southwesterly tip of the spoil island that will be passed to your starboard side as you make good your entry into the deeper waters abutting Dinner Key Marina and the mooring field associated with Coconut Grove Sailing Club.

As alluded to above, the primary Dinner Key anchorage is easily accessible from this cut. While there are many ways you might go about this, one good plan is to depart the marked channel at unlighted daybeacon #10. Cruise to the east into the heart of the anchorage. Don't approach the Dinner Key Channel side of the anchorage too closely, as depths start to rise. Good water continues well on to the north-northwest, almost to the shores of the long, thin, spoil island, which denotes this anchorage's northwesterly limits.

When making your exit from the Coconut Grove waterfront, depart by one of the three channels reviewed above. Even though chart 11451 shows several floating markers southwest of the Coconut Grove Sailing Club mooring field, which eventually leads to the charted Four-Way channel, this passage is shallow and fraught with peril. We strongly advise you to keep clear.

Crandon Park Marina Channel Carefully identify the outermost aids to navigation on this channel, flashing daybeacons #1 and #2. As you cruise to the northeast, take all subsequent red, even-numbered aids to navigation to your starboard side and pass green markers to port. Be mindful of the correctly charted shallows to the north, northwest, and southeast.

The entire Crandon Park Channel is now an official manatee no-wake zone. All craft should proceed strictly at idle speed.

Daybeacon #14 is charted as an unlighted aid to navigation. It has recently been lighted.

After passing between flashing daybeacon #14 and unlighted daybeacon #12, continue on the same course. Soon both unlighted daybeacons #15 and #16 will come abeam to starboard. These aids mark a sharp turn to the southeast in the channel. Make this turn and pass between #15 and #16. Soon the dockage basin will come abeam to port, while the mooring field will lie to starboard.

Key Biscayne Anchorage and Key Biscayne Yacht Club The sharp promontory of land known as West Point thrusts into the waters of Biscayne Bay from the western shores of Key Biscayne, about halfway along its north-to-south axis. This point is surrounded by extensive shallows. Cruisers making for the Key Biscayne Yacht Club or the adjacent anchorage must be very sure to bypass this hazard, as well as a smaller patch of shoals to the south.

Fortunately, several aids to navigation make this process ever so much simpler. To make good your entry, pass at least 100 yards south of flashing daybeacon #1. Also, be sure to stay well west of flashing daybeacon #73. This aid to navigation marks the western extreme of the West Point shoals.

Once past #1, point to come abeam of flashing daybeacon #3 well to its southerly side. If you are bent on dropping the hook, the correctly-charted deep water south of #3 is ideal. Just be sure to anchor far enough from shore to avoid swinging into the band of shallow water that abuts the banks. Also, don't stray onto the charted shoals, which flank this haven to the south.

Skippers bound for the Key Biscayne Yacht Club should curl around #3 and cut to the northeast. Eventually, you will need to swing almost due east and bring flashing daybeacon #4 abeam to its immediate northerly side. Don't stray too far from #4. Shallow water lies just to the north. Once abeam of #4, the entrance into the breakwater-protected harbor of the yacht club will be spotted immediately to the southeast.

In times past, some cruising craft used to

anchor on the charted bay just south of the anchorage reviewed above. The entrance to this cove is still marked by a flashing daybeacon #2, but shoaling at the entrance has now so constricted this channel that we no longer recommend that any cruising-sized craft attempt to enter these waters.

No Name Harbor Anchorage To make good your entry into No Name Harbor, you must first traverse a portion of the channel that lies just south of Cape Florida. This cut is actually one of four passages that connects Biscayne Bay with Hawk Channel. All these channels will be covered later in this chapter.

For the moment, cruisers bound for No Name Harbor should set course to pass some 25 yards south of flashing daybeacon #4. Then, point for the gap between unlighted daybeacon #2 and (uncharted) unlighted daybeacon #1. It is fortunate that #1 has been added, even if NOAA has not caught on yet. This aid to navigation warns navigators away from the correctly charted 2- and 3-foot waters that lie just to the south.

Continue cruising to the southeast, keeping the Key Biscayne shoreline some 200 yards off your port side. Eventually, the entrance to No Name Harbor will come up to the northeast. Cruise into the harbor's mid-width and drop anchor at any likely place.

ICW—Biscayne Bay to Card Sound

South of Key Biscayne, the wide waters of Biscayne Bay stretch out before the southbound cruiser. Soon, the frenzied reaches of Miami are left behind, and a far more relaxed brand of cruising sets in. That sighing sound you will hear are your nerves slowing uncoiling.

Marina facilities become far more widely spaced, and transient spaces become scarce. Most of the mainland facilities along the lower reaches of Biscayne Bay (south of Coconut Grove) are owned and managed by Dade County. Apparently, the county has recently decided that visiting craft are no longer a priority.

Three Biscayne National Park Service visitor centers, with adjacent low-key marinas, guard the eastern shores of Biscayne Bay south of Key Biscayne. All suffer from shallow depths and/or fierce tidal currents. Nevertheless, two offer interesting overnight stops for captains and crews piloting shallow-draft vessels.

Anchorages range from the challenging to the sublime. None of these overnight havens make for good foul-weather hidey-holes. Be sure to consult the latest forecast for wind direction and speed before committing to an overnight stay.

South of the Biscayne Channel, the only real link north of Card Sound from the ICW-inside route to Hawk Channel is Caesar Creek. Some low-water soundings of a mere 4 feet, not to mention strong tidal currents, could prove to be a problem for many cruising craft.

All in all, we almost always enjoy our cruises of lower Biscayne Bay, unless the wind has its dander up. Don't be in such a hurry to find your way south to "paradise" that you offhandedly overlook the many cruising possibilities these waters can boast. Take your time, consult the latest weather forecast, and watch out if you decide to venture toward Soldier Key!

Matheson Beach Marina (Standard Mile 1097) (25 40.720 North/080 15.534 West)

The prolifically marked entrance to Dade County-owned Matheson Beach Marina (305-665-5475) lies almost 3 nautical miles west of the ICW's flashing daybeacon #B. The outermost marker on the primary channel is flashing daybeacon #2. Minimum depths in this entrance cut run around 7 feet, with at least 6½ to 7 feet of water dockside.

Notice that we said "primary" channel in the above paragraph. That's because this marina actually has two entrance cuts. The main passage cuts north-northwest from flashing daybeacon #2. This is the deeper of the two, and the route that most larger cruising craft should use.

There is also, however, a north-to-south flowing channel that begins with unlighted daybeacons #1 and #2. This passage intersects the primary channel at unlighted daybeacons #7 and #8. Depths are a bit skinnier here, about 5 to 5½ feet at mean low water.

Whatever way you choose to get there, watch to the north as you make your approach for a good view of attractive Matheson Hammock Park. This facility lines the north side entrance point.

Unfortunately, not only are there no transient spaces available at this facility, but overnight stays aboard are not allowed at Matheson Park Marina, even for resident captains and crews. We find this an almost surreal prohibition, particularly in light of the marina's modern, metal-decked piers and the harbor's excellent shelter from foul weather. Go figure!

The Matheson Park wet slips will come up along the northerly banks as the entrance channel slips into a sheltered stream. Dockside soundings run 6½ to 7 feet at low

Matheson Beach Marina (Biscayne Bay)

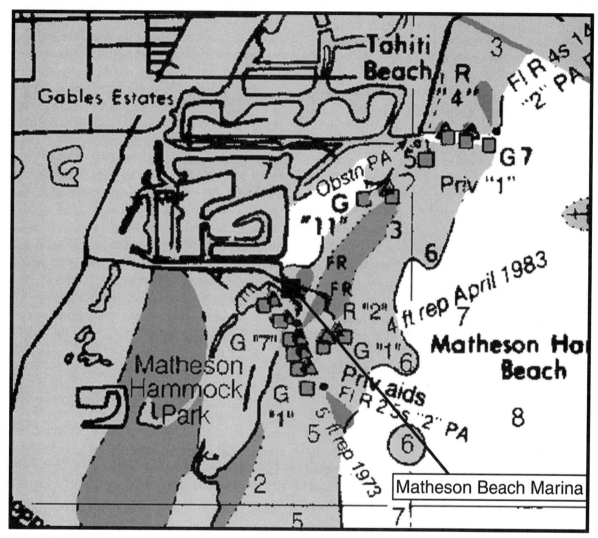

Matheson Beach Marina

water. Resident vessels can make use of 30- to 50-amp dockside power and fresh water hookups. The fuel dock (gasoline and diesel fuel are available) and dockmaster's office will be spotted dead ahead.

Kings Bay Yacht Club
(Standard Mile 1101.5)
(25 38.127 North/080 17.644 West)

Cruisers bound for Kings Bay Yacht Club (305-256-2510) must undertake a lengthy trek

of slightly better than 1.8 nautical miles up its entrance channel and the adjoining canal to the dockage basin. Tack that on to a 3 nautical mile trip from the ICW's flashing daybeacon #C to the yacht club channel's outermost marker, flashing daybeacon #2, and you can quickly discern that it's a bit of a cruise to get here.

And even if you do find your way to the harbor, there are no transient spaces available. In fact, this is a completely private club, and the only visiting craft ever allowed are guests of a member. The dockmaster has informed us that even this circumstance is rare.

That's too bad, as King Bay's harbor is extremely well sheltered. This would be a good spot to ride out anything short of a full-blown hurricane. The entrance channel maintains impressive 7- to 7½-foot minimum depths, coupled with dockside soundings of 9 to 11 feet at the facility's fixed concrete piers. Anyone got a keel deeper than that?

With things as they are, however, the only reason that the vast majority of vessels need undertake a cruise to the club's dockage basin is for sightseeing purposes. Oh well, we can always look in awe.

Soldier Key Anchorage
(Standard Mile 1102)
(25 35.529 North/080 09.864 West)

Okay, listen up all you cruisers out there with wanderlust in your heart. If, and only if, you are willing to risk finding the bottom (and a rocky bottom it may be), then it is possible to follow a completely unmarked track east from flashing daybeacon #C to a fair-weather anchorage behind (west of) Soldier Key. This indistinctly charted, small, low-laying island guards Biscayne Bay's easterly flank, some 3 nautical miles east-southeast of flashing daybeacon #C.

Optimum depths run as thin as 4 (possibly 3½) feet in one spot, though if you can find the channel, typical soundings range in the 4½- to 6-foot range. It doesn't take a rocket scientist to discern that this entire undertaking is meant only for skippers whose craft does not exceed 34 feet and draw 3½ feet or less. Even then, don't come complaining to us if you end up with a bent shaft or rudder.

So, you may be asking by now, why would any cruiser want to wander through such a perilous channel to anchor behind a small island?

The key to understanding Soldier Key's appeal is the off-the-beaten-path, isolated feeling that these waters instantly command if you do drop the hook behind this isle. It's truly amazing to find such a backwater, overnight haven, almost within sight of Miami. Of course, considering what it takes to get here, you may already have a good clue as to why it is so isolated.

If you do make it to Soldier Key, anchor some 100 yards off the westerly shores, abeam of the northerly ⅓ of the island. The waters just to the south are quite shallow!

Once the anchor is out and well-set, break out the dinghy. It's an interesting trip ashore to this remote isle. There is a white-sand beach on which you can temporarily pull up your dink. Just watch out for sharp rocks.

We probably don't need to say this, but let's say it anyway. If you should decide that a visit to Soldier Key is in your cruising future, be SURE to read the navigational account of these waters presented in the next section of this chapter. Even then, proceed with the greatest caution. Good luck!

Ragged Keys Anchorage
(Standard Mile 1106)
(25 31.966 North/080 10.538 West)

Anybody up for, what we can only accurately describe as, a pretty anchorage? Well, if your vessel can stand some 5-foot depths and does not exceed 38 feet in length, then the somewhat open haven behind the second (moving south to north) Ragged Keys, north of Boca Chita Key, may just be for you. During fair weather, this is an idyllic overnight stop. The undeveloped keys just to the east are often reflected perfectly in the intensely blue water. A night spent swinging on the hook in this anchorage could lead one to believe that this is what cruising is really all about.

Lighthouse at Boca Chita Key

On the other hand, no one will ever mistake the Ragged Keys as a foul-weather haven. This anchorage offers protection only from eastern, northeastern and southeastern breezes. Even with breezes blowing from these quarters, don't expect a comfortable night if wind speeds exceed 15 knots. There is no protection whatsoever from any other direction.

It can also be a bit of a navigational challenge to safely reach this anchor down spot without finding the bottom. First, you must negotiate a passage between the northeasterly reaches of ultrashallow Featherbed Bank and another two-foot shoal, which lies just to the east. Fortunately, there are two aids to navigation, unlighted daybeacon #1 and flashing daybeacon #2, to help show you the way.

As soon as these obstacles are successfully in your wake, angle to the east, giving the large 1- and 2-foot shallows lying to the north your greatest respect. Point to drop the hook some 400 yards off the second Ragged Keys,

north of Boca Chita Key. Depths of 5 feet can be expected here, but a closer approach to this Ragged Keys or the small pass just to the north can land you in only 3 feet of water. Don't let this dissuade you from dinghy exploration, however. We always enjoy exploring the Ragged Keys from one of these ultra-shallow-draft vessels. May you, too, be so fortunate!

Boca Chita Key Marina and Visitors' Center (Standard Mile 1106) (25 31.501 North/080 10.527 West)

How would you like to own your own island in paradise, with the shimmering waters of Biscayne Bay on one side and the crashing surf of Hawk Channel on the other? Well, that's exactly what Mark Honeywell, of Honeywell Computers and other early high-tech products, did when he purchased Boca Chita Key in the 1930s. Subsequently, this island passed through ownership of the Baruch and Emmerman families until it was

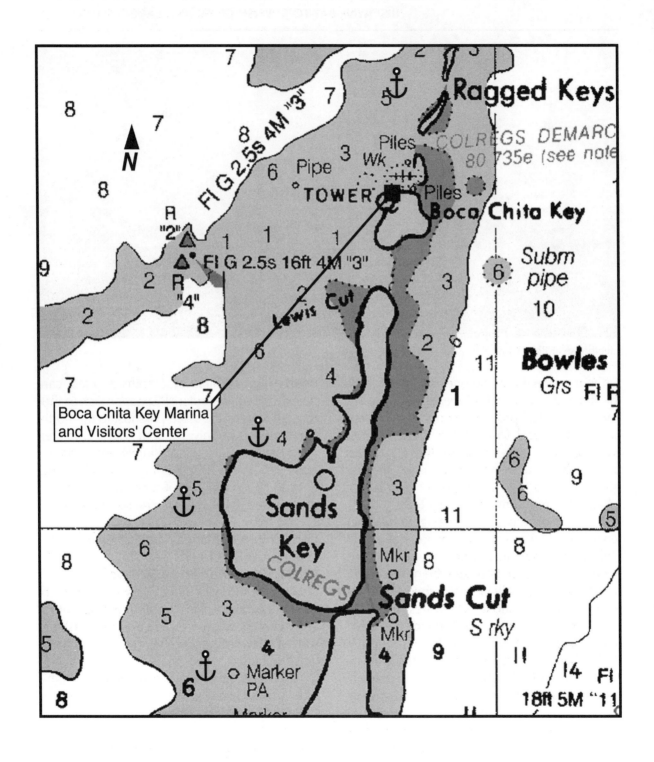

Boca Chita Key Marina and Visitors' Center

finally purchased by the U.S. government in 1985. Since that time, this fair isle has become a part of the Biscayne Bay National Park and remains essentially in its natural state.

The Park Service maintains a visitors' center and a semiround, well-sheltered dockage basin on Boca Chita's westerly shores. Minimum approach depths run around 5 feet, with a surprising 6 to 7 feet of water in the harbor. Considering the harbor and approach channel's size, I would not particularly recommend this side trip to skippers whose craft exceeds 38 feet.

You can't miss the Boca Chita Marina, courtesy of the "ornamental" lighthouse (circa 1937) that overlooks the harbor's westerly shoreline. This attractive sentinel of the seas was, according to Gary Bremman, historian for the Biscayne National Park, never lit. There is a story, which may or may not be true, to the effect that Honeywell meant to bring the lighthouse fully on-line with a beacon but never received permission to do so.

There are actually two routes that cruisers may use to find Boca Chita harbor. Southbound skippers can follow the marked cut past the northerly reaches of the Featherbed Bank, as reviewed above in our discussion of the Ragged Keys anchorages. After skirting south of the correctly charted shallows to the north, the westerly genesis of the Boca Chita approach channel will come up at approximately 25 31.626 North/080 11.323 West. The remainder of the cut is outlined by small, floating, nun and can buoys. Be SURE to observe ALL these markers, even if some do not appear on chart 11451.

Northbound mariners can alternately cut to the northeast at Standard Mile 1110 and follow the marked channel that lies west of ultrashallow Lewis Cut. Three unlighted daybeacons lead navigators north through 5-foot depths, past the shallow easterly reaches of the Featherbed Bank. It's then just a short hop northeast to the westerly genesis of the Boca Chita approach channel.

However you finally make your way into the harbor at Boca Chita Key, visiting craft will be greeted by a whole series of fixed wooden face docks set about the basin's shoreline. Overnight dockage is allowed for a $15 fee. The marina and visitors' center are staffed only sporadically by Park Service personnel, so there is an automated machine where you can pay your overnight dockage fee. By the way, should you have the urge to camp out under the stars, on dry ground, the nightly charge also includes a site at the adjacent campground. Rest rooms (no showers), picnic tables, charcoal grills, and a short hiking trail are available, but there are no dockside power or water connections, nor are fuel or any other marine services available.

In spite of the minimalist nature of the overnight pleasure-craft facilities at Boca Chita Key, we always enjoy spending a night here. (As long as the wind doesn't die during the summer months—if this happens, watch out for a horde of nighttime, winged pests.) The island is absolutely enchanting, and a stroll along its shores is sure to remain with you always as the fondest of memories. After all, it's OK, at least in our book, to spend a night or two from time to time sans the shore-power umbilical cord, or even without the generator. Just bring plenty of fresh water and a well-supplied galley.

Boca Chita Key Marina and Visitors' Center
   (305) 230-7275
http://www.nps.go/eisc

Approach depth—5 feet (low water)

Cruising Black Point Marina entrance channel

Dockside depth—6-7 feet (low water)
Accepts transients—yes ($15 per night dockage fee)
Type of docking—fixed wooden docks

Black Point Marina
(Standard Mile 1108.5)
(25 32.307 North/080 19.617 West)

The long, partially breakwater-protected approach channel leading to Black Point Marina (305-258-4092) cuts in from Biscayne Bay's westerly banks some 3.2 nautical miles south and west of the ICW's flashing daybeacon #6. Cruisers must take extra caution to stay south of the shallows associated with the Featherbed Bank on the initial portion of this run. Also, take note that the entire entrance channel and the approach canal are official no-wake zones. It can seem like a long cruise for faster powercraft used to zipping along at planing speed.

This marina's location is marked in a rather unusual fashion. Cruisers making their approach to the entrance canal will sight what appears to be a small mountain just to the west. This is actually a huge landfill that has been covered over and is now crowned with some of the greenest grass you will ever see. As the late comedian/writer Lewis Grizzard once aptly observed, "The grass is always greenest over the septic tank."

Minimum depths of 8 feet can be expected in the entrance cut, with at least 6 to 7 feet of water dockside. West-northwest of unlighted daybeacon #29, the channel seems to split. Be sure to take the northwesterly fork. Eventually the fuel pier and on-site restaurant

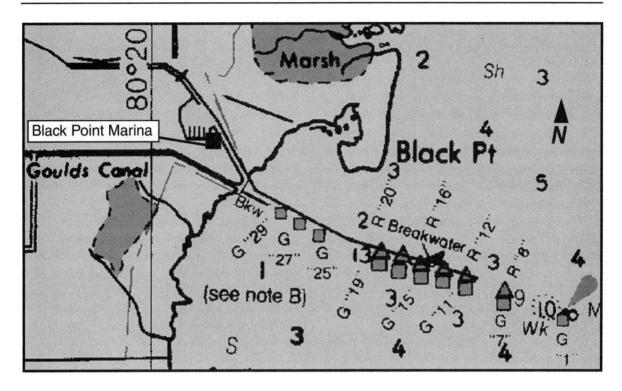

will come abeam to your port side. The very well-protected dockage basin will open out along the southerly banks shortly thereafter.

Black Point Marina is another one of the Dade County-owned facilities that guard the westerly banks of lower Biscayne Bay. We were politely, but firmly, informed by the dockmaster that her marina is "full and has been full for two years." Furthermore, she stated that Black Point is "not in the transient business." Do you get the idea? Finding a slip for visitors at this facility is somewhat akin to the possibility of finding an intact snowball in the nether regions.

Resident vessels at Black Point Marina are moored to fixed concrete piers. There are also a few metal-decked floating docks for small craft. Power connections of the 20-, 30-, and 50-amp persuasions are provided, as are fresh water hookups. There are no shoreside showers nor a Laundromat, which befits this marina's nontransient status.

All vessels can purchase both gasoline and diesel at the fuel pier. Just behind this dock, captains will discover a small variety—bait and tackle—store. Also on site is the Pirate's Den restaurant (305-258-3918). We were impressed with the number of patrons drawn to this dining spot during lunch hour, particularly considering how out-in-the-middle-of-nowhere it happens to be (when approaching the marina by land that is).

South of Black Point Marina's fuel dock, a huge, metal, dry-stack storage building overlooks the approach canal's southwesterly banks. This facility is privately leased from the county. Cruisers looking to dry-store smaller powercraft can call (305) 258-3918 for more information.

Sands Key-Elliott Key Anchorages
(Standard Mile 1109.5)
(Multiple Lat/Lons—see below)

Sands Key is a large body of land that flanks the easterly shores of Biscayne Bay, south of Boca Chita Key and just north of Elliott Key. The waters lying about both Sands Key and the northerly extreme of Elliott Key offer some interesting anchorage possibilities if winds are blowing from the east, northeast, or southeast, and in one case, the south.

All these potential overnight havens lie some 2.5 nautical miles east of the ICW's course line. Some have depths as skinny as 4½ to 5 feet, while others afford 6 feet of water. None is well sheltered from all wind directions, and this is not the place that we would choose to ride out a heavy blow.

With that out of the way, allow me to relate my personal fondness for these anchorages. Like the overnight stop at Ragged Keys, these havens are a visual feast and have a real backwater feeling. Also, swinging room is unlimited. Just be SURE to check out the latest weather forecast before committing to an overnight stay.

Moving south to north, the first anchorage to consider is found almost due west of the charted "Tide Sta" (Tide Station), itself north of Coon Point (approximately 25 28.847 North/080 11.720 West). This is one of the most open anchorages in this section, but it does boast good 6 to 7-foot soundings. Protection is only adequate with moderate winds blowing from the east or southeast.

Vessels that are comfortable with 5 feet of water can cruise a bit further to the east-northeast and drop the hook at 25 28.937 North/080 11.509 West. Protection here is pretty good for eastern, southeastern and northeastern breezes up to 15 knots.

Some cruisers like to anchor off ultrashallow Sands Cut. This narrow pass separates the northern tip of Elliott Key from Sands Key. If you stay at least 400 yards west of the charted "Marker PA" (which is actually noting more than a series of white PVC pipes stuck in the water), 5-foot depths can be maintained. Try dropping the hook near 25 29.371 North/080 11.556 West. This is also an open overnight haven and will only be comfortable in calm conditions.

An attractive anchorage lies some 350 yards off the westerly shores of Sands Key— almost at the midpoint of its north-south axis. Low-water depths seem to run about 5 feet. We suggest anchoring near 25 30.136 North/080 11.628 West. There is good shelter from blows coming from the east, southeast, or northeast.

Finally, mariners whose vessel draws 4 feet or less should consider the waters off the northwesterly point of Sands Key. Depths of 4½ to (more typically) 5 feet can be held, if you stay 150 yards north of the point and drop the hook just as you come under the lee of this point, south of your position. Cruising any closer to the eastern or southern shores invites soundings of 4 feet or less. We suggest 25 30.414 North/080 11.215 West. This haven has the distinct advantage of being well sheltered from all but western, northwestern and northern winds.

Herbert Hoover Marina
(Standard Mile 1111.5)
(25 27.744 North/080 20.340 West)

The canal serving both the Biscayne National Park Headquarters (305-230-7275) and Herbert Hoover Marina bisects the mainland (western) shores of Biscayne Bay, north of the hard-to-miss power plant at Turkey

Herbert Hoover Marina (Dockmaster's office)

Point (some 4.8 nautical miles west-southwest of the ICW channel). Study chart 11451 for a moment and you will quickly note the marked channel that leads to the power-generating facility. Pleasure craft are advised to keep clear of this cut.

The Park Service-marina channel is best approached from the northeast. Generally, minimum approach depths run in the 5½-foot range, with soundings improving to between 6 and 9 feet in the canal and the adjacent dockage basin. Check out our navigational account of these waters in the next section of this chapter before making your first approach.

Immediately upon entering the canal, the park headquarters will come up on the northern shore. It's easy to identify this facility, courtesy of all the docked Park Service boats, which are festooned with an incredible array of blue lights. Sigghh! Some of us remember when the Park Service's primary responsibility was to "welcome" visitors.

Farther along, Herbert Hoover Marina's fuel dock and dockmaster's office will come abeam to the south, followed shortly thereafter by the well-sheltered dockage basin, also indenting the southerly banks. About the only foul-weather problem you might ever encounter here would be a full, gale-force easterly wind that would blow straight up the canal.

By the way, Herbert Hoover Marina is named not for the past United States president of that name, but for the founder of the

Hoover Vacuum Cleaner Company. As we will see during our brief review of the Biscayne National Park below, the private citizen Mr. Hoover was instrumental in preserving the natural character of the barrier islands that line the easterly flank of Biscayne Bay.

Herbert Hoover Marina is the southernmost of the Dade County-owned, pleasure-craft facilities overlooking Biscayne Bay's mainland shoreline. And it is the only one to offer anything in the way of transient space. Even so, this marina remains at about ninety percent capacity. The dockmaster told us that she usually has a few transient slips available each evening, but again, it would be a good idea to call ahead and check on availability.

Berths are provided at fixed concrete piers with fresh water and 30- to 50-amp power connections. There are no shoreside showers nor a Laundromat on the premises, but gasoline and diesel fuel can be purchased at the fuel dock on the approach canal. There is a small bait-and-tackle shop just behind the fuel

pier. Waste pump-out service is also available. There are no restaurants or provisioning facilities anywhere nearby, so be sure to bring all your galley needs with you.

The land immediately adjacent to Herbert Hoover Marina is part of the Homestead Bayfront Park. There is a nice swimming lagoon (with adjacent bathrooms), picnic tables, barbeque grills, and some well-landscaped grounds. During the winter season, the park attracts quite a host of visitors during weekends.

The Biscayne National Park Visitors' Center is within walking distance of the Herbert Hoover dockage basin. As we will see just below, the associated visitors' center is well worth a visit.

Herbert Hoover Marina (305) 230-3033

Approach depth—51/2-9 feet
Dockside depth—6-9 feet
Accepts transients—yes
Type of docking—fixed concrete piers
Dockside power connections—30-50 amp

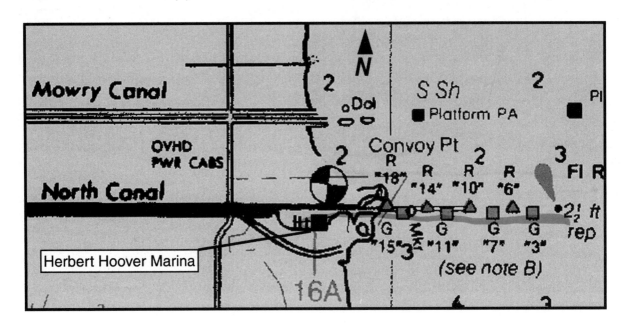

Dockside water connections—yes
Gasoline—yes
Diesel fuel—yes
Waste pump-out—yes
Variety store—yes

Biscayne National Park

By the early 1960s, the heretofore untouched barrier islands lining the easterly shores of lower Biscayne Bay were rapidly on their way to development. An "on paper" community of "Islandia" had been formed, complete with mayor and city council. Plans were drawn up to connect Boca Chita Key, the Ragged Keyss, Elliott Key, and several other pristine islands to the mainland by way of a huge causeway.

It is to every modern day cruiser's good fortune that there were some who foresaw the great natural value of these untouched keys and their neighboring waters. Principal among these early conservation pioneers was Herbert Hoover—no, not the past president of the United States, but rather the founder of the Hoover Vacuum Cleaner Company.

Mr. Hoover was a great sportsman and loved to fish the waters of Biscayne Bay, but as time went on, he began to notice that the bay's waters were becoming cloudier and ever more polluted. Thus began his decade-long effort to preserve the natural character of Biscayne Bay and its barrier islands for all to enjoy.

After many, many years of effort, and after enlisting the aid of several Florida congresspersons, the bill creating Biscayne Bay National Monument was finally signed into law by President Lyndon Johnson in 1968, over the heated objections of a whole army of developers. Perhaps our government really does do something right now and then!

Biscayne National Park Headquarters and Visitors' Center (near Herbert Hoover Marina)

Since Biscayne Bay came under federal protection, there has been tremendous progress in cleaning up the bay's waters and curbing future sources of pollution. Once again, cruisers who make their way through the shallow passages leading to these fascinating islands will discover gin-clear water, a voluminous array of colorful fish life, and lands that look as if they have barely ever known the hand of mankind. Visitor centers have been established on Boca Chita Key, Elliott Key, and Adams Key.

The national monument was upgraded to Biscayne Bay National Park in 1980, and a visitors' center was built on the shores of Biscayne Bay just north of the present location of Herbert Hoover Marina. Fortunately, this center is within walking distance of the marina dockage basin.

We urge all cruisers to visit the park headquarters and check out its three excellent video presentations. Our favorite outlines the history of the park and the titanic struggle to wrest the lands and waters from the clutches of greedy developers.

Here, you can also check out the gift shop and a display that samples the park's flora and fauna. We found the park personnel at the visitors' center to be friendly and helpful. Call (305) 230-7275 for more information.

Elliott Key Harbor
(Standard Mile 1112)
(25 27.223 North/080 11.804 West)

Take a perusal of chart 11451 and notice the notation "Elliott Key Harbor" opposite Point Adelle. (The point is on the ocean side of Elliott Key; the harbor is on the key's westerly banks.) This is the location of the largest visitors' center and marina associated with Biscayne National Park. Unfortunately, you must cruise 2.7 nautical miles from the Waterway, often through 3-foot depths, to reach the 5- to 6-foot waters in the twin dockage basins. Only small craft drawing LESS THAN 3 feet need apply.

If you do manage to get there, visiting

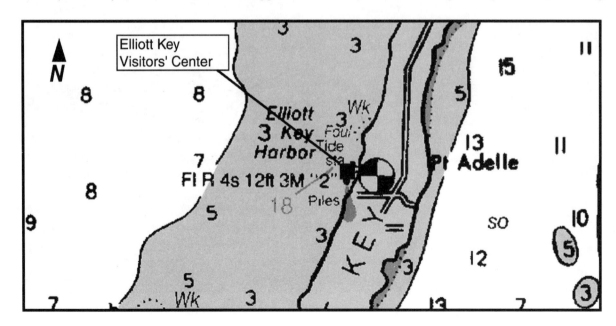

cruisers will discover that the visitors' center lies off the southerly basin. This facility is only staffed on and off, so there is an automated machine on the shores of both harbors that allows you to pay your $15 nightly dockage fee. A shoreside campsite is included with this fee, should you have an irresistible urge to spend a night with solid ground under your feet.

Berths consist of fixed concrete pilings with fixed wooden finger piers. All these slips are relatively narrow, and they did not appear to us to be appropriate for vessels larger than 26 feet. Drinking water is provided at the visitors' center, but there are no dockside power or water connections. There are some cold-water showers available, but no fuel or marine services are to be had.

Elliott Key is seven miles in length and almost entirely in its natural state. In fact, the isle is a one-time, ancient coral reef that is now covered with sand and tropical hardwoods. It is well worthy of foot exploration if you're up to a long hike. The Park Service provides rest rooms, picnic tables, charcoal grills, drinking water, and hiking trails that run the length of the island.

It's a real shame that the approach depths are so skinny. Otherwise, this harbor would deserve a red circle on any cruiser's chart. However, with things as they are, this side trip is pretty much relegated to our outboard and I/O brethren.

Elliott Key-Biscayne National Park Marina (305) 230-7275
http://www.nps.gov/bisc

Approach depth—3 feet (low water)
Dockside depth—5-6 feet
Accepts transients—yes (nightly $15 fee)
Type of docking—fixed wooden piers—yes
Showers—cold water only

Caesar Creek
(Standard Mile 1115.5)
(Visitors' Center dock at approximately 25 23.851 North/080 14.081 West)

The westerly tip of the marked channel leading to Caesar Creek comes up east-northeast of the Waterway's flashing daybeacon #8, at approximately 25 24.234 North/080 14.530 West. Both the creek's entrance from Biscayne Bay and its counterpart, leading to Hawk Channel, are well outlined by aids to navigation. However, minimum low-tide soundings of 4 feet on the connector to Biscayne Bay and low-water depths of 5 feet on the Hawk Channel portion of the cut render these waters unfit for vessels larger than 36 feet or (more importantly) those boats drawing 4 feet or better. Be advised tidal currents run fiercely on Caesar Creek.

That's the bad news. On the other hand, if your boat fits the somewhat rigorous size and draft requirements outlined above, then Caesar Creek offers interesting scenery and access to the Biscayne National Park Adams Key Visitors' Center, a backwater anchorage, and to Hawk Channel.

After traversing the initial portion of the entrance passage, the channel splits at unlighted daybeacon #25. The cut running off to the north-northeast leads to a shallow-water anchorage. Let's first take a quick look at this potential overnight haven.

Several markers outline this northern-running portion of the channel. After cruising between unlighted daybeacons #5 and #6, you can turn to the east-southeast and anchor at approximately 25 24.358 North/080 13.724 West. While the initial section of this cut holds at least 6 feet, depths drop to low-water soundings of about 4 feet as you cruise east into the anchorage. Obviously, this haven is ONLY meant for

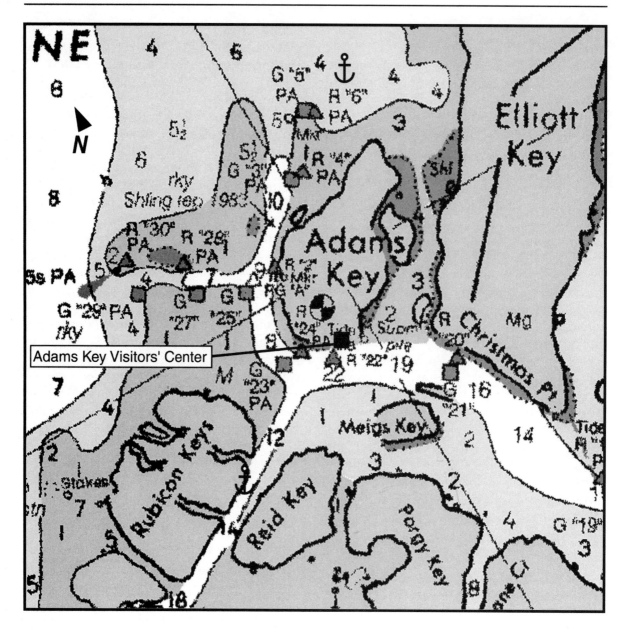

Adams Key Visitors' Center

boats drawing 3½ feet or (preferably) less. There is good shelter to the south, southeast, and east. There is no protection from northern or northwesterly winds. The surrounding shores of both Adams and Elliott keys are about as beautiful as any cruiser has a right to expect.

The main southerly branch of the Caesar Creek channel turns sharply to the southeast as it passes between unlighted daybeacons #23 and #24. Very shortly thereafter, cruisers looking to anchor off on Caesar Creek can cut southwest off the main channel, some 30 yards southeast of #23, and follow a narrow, unmarked track to the sheltered waters lying between beautifully undeveloped Reid and Rubicon Keys. Be warned that this unbuoyed track is surrounded by 1-foot shallows. On a clear, sunny day, or with a GPS interfaced with a laptop computer (plus a digitized version of chart 11451 and appropriate navigational software), you can probably follow this passage with relative ease. Caution should still be your watchword. In low light or stormy conditions, this task may be all but impossible.

If you persevere, this side channel eventually leads to a creeklike patch of good water, lying between Reid and Rubicon Keys. Here, you can anchor a vessel as large as 36 feet amidst at least 8 feet of water (near 25 23.701 North/080 14.441 West). There is excellent shelter from all but strong southwesterly winds. Once the tricky entrance channel is left behind, this stream is an idyllic overnight haven. During September of 2000, we dropped the hook here and watched the sun slowly sink into the waters of Biscayne Bay to the west. We could have sworn we heard it sizzle as it disappeared into the mirror-smooth waters.

Next up is the Adams Key Park Service dock, which overlooks Caesar Creek's northerly shores, hard by unlighted daybeacon #22 (approximately 25 23.851 North/080 14.081 West). While no overnight stays are allowed, visitors can tie temporarily (during daylight hours) to the outer edge of the 125-foot face pier in 6-foot minimum depths. It's then an elementary matter to step ashore and make use of the visitors' center's shaded picnic ground, public bathrooms, and charcoal grills. There is also an adjacent ½-mile hiking trail. The Park Service has informed us that the Adams Key facility is the least frequented of its centers. During our three visits, we have never seen another boat and only once observed anyone making use of the picnic tables. Call the Biscayne National Park Headquarters at (305) 230-7275 for more information.

Have your largest fenders ready when approaching the Adams Key Park dock. The strong tidal currents can sometimes make for a brusque meeting between your boat's rub rail and the pier's pilings.

The seaward portion of the Caesar Creek channel is extremely well marked and carries typical soundings of 6 to 9 feet. However, its easterly tip is plagued by 5-foot depths. The channel does wander quite a bit, so be SURE to take your time so as to and pick out the correct path. Those who land outside of the channel are almost sure to give Sea Tow some business.

Be SURE to read the navigational narrative of Caesar Creek in the following section. It contains mandatory information for first-timers.

BISCAYNE BAY TO CARD SOUND NAVIGATION

There is only one word that accurately describes runs between aids to navigation along the ICW from Key Biscayne to Card Sound. That word would be "long"! Markers are separated by 4 to 5 nautical miles of often choppy water. This is definitely the sort of place to keep a good DR track and have your GPS up and running.

Fair-weather passage of southerly Biscayne Bay is a thoroughly pleasurable experience. As stated several times in this chapter already, this is a fair body of water with the sun gaily dancing on its surface and the east side barrier islands beckoning cruisers to explore by dinghy.

The story can be very different when winds exceed 15 knots, particularly from the south or north. Cruisers bashing their way through the bay's chop on these occasions usually can't wait to sight the northern mouth of Jewfish Creek. The moral to this story is, if at all possible, time your passage to coincide with fair weather. The fillings in your teeth will be ever so happy you took this precaution.

Side trips to marinas or anchorages off this section of the ICW also call for a "long" cruise. You must usually eat up 2 to 3 nautical miles of water before the particular entrance channel you are making for slips behind your stern. Again, good navigation is a must, not just a nicety.

So, stay alert! After all, the world needs all the "lerts" it has. Seriously though, take the time to preplot courses before hand, keep chart 11451 plus your binoculars and GPS at hand, and before long, the Boca Chita Lighthouse will certainly top the horizon. Have a good cruise!

Matheson Hammock Park Marina
Remember what we just said about long treks from the Waterway to this region's marinas. Well, here is a perfect example. You must cover slightly better than 3 nautical miles of water from flashing daybeacon #B to the outermost marker, flashing daybeacon #2, on the primary entrance channel serving Matheson Hammock Park Marina.

Most cruisers should come abeam of #2 to its westerly side, and then follow the well-marked channel north, keeping red aids to navigation on your starboard side and taking green markers to port. Eventually, the channel will carry you into the marina's sheltered dockage basin, with the wet slips quite obvious to the north.

A second channel allows access for shallower draft vessels coming in from points north. This cut carries only 5 to 5½ feet of water at low tide. Larger cruising craft would do better to make exclusive use of the primary passage, outlined above.

For those who do choose to run the northerly channel, pass between the outermost markers, unlighted daybeacons #1 and #2. Keep all subsequent red aids off your starboard side and green markers to port. Soon, this secondary channel intersects the primary passage near the latter cut's unlighted daybeacons #7 and #8. At this point, cruisers should swing sharply to starboard and follow the principal cut into the harbor.

On the ICW Moving south from flashing daybeacon #B, captains can look forward to a cruise of some 4.3 nautical miles before meeting up with the next aid to navigation, flashing daybeacon #C. Along the way, you will pass many markers east of your course line. The first set belongs to the Biscayne Channel, which was reviewed earlier in this chapter. Then, south of this cut, there is a flashing daybeacon #1, and later, a flashing daybeacon #1A, which warns mariners away from the extensive shelf of shallows that jut out from the easterly reaches of Biscayne Bay along this stretch. Ignore flashing daybeacons #1 and #1A, except for being SURE to stay well west of their positions.

From flashing daybeacon #C, cruisers can contemplate two side trips. A turn to the west leads to Kings Bay Yacht Club, while a far riskier, easterly route may lead you to an anchorage behind tiny Soldier Key.

Kings Bay Yacht Club To access the Kings Bay Yacht Club approach channel, cut west-northwest from flashing daybeacon #C and track your way through slightly better than 3 nautical miles of water to the yacht club's outermost marker, flashing daybeacon #2.

Along the way, another flashing daybeacon #2 will be sighted south of your course. Do NOT confuse this aid to navigation with the flashing daybeacon #2 on the Kings Bay Yacht Club channel. Be sure to stay north of the first #2 (the one nearest flashing daybeacon #C). This first (southerly) #2 warns of shallower water to the south and southwest of its position.

From the yacht club channel's #2, the passage cuts to the northwest and continues on its well-marked way. Slow to idle speed. As you approach the gap between unlighted daybeacons #7 and #8, the channel comes under the lee of a mangrove shore to the north. This was ever so nice during a stiff northerly blow that was brewing during the time of our last visit.

After passing between unlighted daybeacons #11 and #12, the channel swings sharply west and enters a sheltered canal. Look ahead for an awesome view of a large, sky-blue power plant.

Soon, this stream splits. Take the northwesterly fork. Several uncharted markers help you keep to the good water along this stretch. Continue to pass all red markers to your starboard side and take green beacons to port. Soon, the yacht club will come up on the northeasterly banks.

Soldier Key Anchorage Please remember that a safe passage to the anchorage west of tiny Soldier Key is tricky at best. There is a very REAL possibility of finding a rocky bottom here.

The course plan outlined below is almost certainly NOT the only route to Soldier Key, but it is the way we found the best depths. Even so, 4-foot sounding will almost certainly be making a visit to your depth-finder display.

Set course from #C for a position just south of the charted "Subm pipe" (approximately 25 35.509 North/080 10.487 West). We did not see the submerged pipe, and we didn't find it with our prop either, but low-tide depths in this section definitely run to 4 feet.

Once abeam of the "Subm Pipe," look to the east and identify Soldier Key. Set course for the midpoint of its north-to-south axis. When you are within some 500 yards of the island, alter course and point for the northern ⅓ of Soldier Key. You can cruise to within 100 yards of this shoreline and hold 5 to 6 feet of water (hopefully).

As you cruise into this anchorage, look south and you may spot what appears to be several trees sticking out of the waters. These denote a shallow patch, which apparently sits astride the midpoint of the isle's north-to-south axis. This is why we suggest that you alter course to the northern 1/3 of the island when you are within 500 yards of the shoreline.

Good luck, you will almost certainly need it.

On the ICW South of flashing daybeacon #C, cruisers face a run of some 4.9 nautical miles to the next pair of aids to navigation, unlighted daybeacon #4 and flashing daybeacon #3. You DON'T want to miss these two markers. They identify a dredged cut leading through otherwise ultrashallow Featherbed Bank. Depths of 0 to 3 feet are all too common outside of the ICW, on the banks.

From a position between #3 and #4, point to pass between the next southerly pair of markers, flashing daybeacon #6 and unlighted daybeacon #5. Watch for lateral current on this run, and don't let leeway ease you out of the channel.

North of Featherbed Bank, cruisers can cut to the southeast and visit either the anchorage near Ragged Keys or the Park Service visitors' center on Boca Chita Key. Similarly, south of #5 and #6, Black Point Marina beckons to the west, while the various anchorages associated with Coon Point and Sands Key beckon to the southeast. Let's first take a look at the Ragged Keys, followed by Boca Chita Key, and then Black Point Marina and the Sands Key anchorages, in that order.

Ragged Keys Anchorage The trick to successfully making your way to both the anchorage that lies off Ragged Keys and the Boca Chita Key entrance channel is to avoid the long arm of shoal water running northeast from Featherbed Bank and an equally menacing offshoot of 2-foot shallows making in from the east. Fortunately, our good friends at the United States Coast Guard have seen fit to mark both these obstructions with two welcome aids to navigation.

Point your vessel to pass between flashing daybeacon #2 and unlighted daybeacon #1 and continue cruising southeast into the wide pool of deep water, which will open out before you.

Identify Boca Chita Key, courtesy of its "ornamental" lighthouse, and then count off the Ragged Keyss to the north of Boca Chita. Point for the midwidth of the second Ragged Keys (moving south to north). Drop anchor at least 400 yards west of this Ragged Keys. A closer approach will land you in 3 feet (or less) of water. Try dropping the hook near 25 31.966 North/080 10.538 West. We found this to be a superior spot.

Boca Chita Key Southbound craft can use the approach described above for the Ragged Keys anchorage until they are well past unlighted flashing daybeacon #1 and flashing daybeacon #2. Instead of swinging east to the second Ragged Keys, use your binoculars to pick out the small, floating, nun and can buoys that outline the Boca Chita Key approach channel. The westerly tip of this marked passage lies near 25 31.626 North/080 11.323 West.

Once you have the entrance cut identified, simply cruise between the various buoys, keeping red to starboard and green to port. Soon, the harbor's entrance will be sighted dead ahead, overlooked by its handsome lighthouse.

There is also an approach south of Boca Chita Key, which is useful for northbound skippers and crew. This route is a bit trickier, as the initial approach is unmarked. Good DR or GPS navigation should see you through.

To access the southerly cut, leave the ICW 1.7 nautical miles south of flashing daybeacon #6 (near Standard Mile 1110). Cut to the northeast, pointing carefully to avoid the shallows striking south and southeast from Featherbed Bank. Along the way, you will pass the anchorages near Sands Key, which will be detailed below. You may also sight several of the charted "W Bn's" (warning beacons), which denote the southerly reaches of the Featherbed Bank's shallows to the north and northwest. Stay south and southeast of these haphazard markers.

Eventually, you should ease your craft to a more northerly heading and pick up flashing daybeacon #3 and unlighted daybeacon #4. Slow to idle speed and pass between these two beacons. Immediately set a new course designed to bring your craft abeam of unlighted daybeacon #2 by some 20 yards to its easterly side. Expect low-water depths of 5 feet between #4 and #2. Watch for leeway—depths outside of the channel are quite shallow.

From unlighted daybeacon #2, a short hop to the northeast will bring you face to face with the westerly genesis of the Boca Chita channel.

Black Point Marina The real trick to reaching Black Point Marina involves the, now rather familiar, problem of avoiding the shallows of Featherbed Bank. We suggest departing the ICW some .5 nautical miles south of flashing daybeacon #6. Only then should you leave the Waterway by making a sharp turn to the east-northeast, pointing for flashing daybeacon #2 (3.3 nautical miles away), the easternmost aid to navigation on the Black Point Marina approach channel. This plan of attack will help you to stay well south of Featherbed Bank, a rather good idea considering that depths over this huge shoal run from 3 feet to nil.

With all of that behind you, pass between flashing daybeacon #2 and unlighted daybeacon #1. Slow to idle speed. The loooong approach channel and the adjoining canal are official no-wake zones. The county sheriff's department keeps a fleet of patrol boats docked just downstream from Black Point Marina. The presence of these craft and their operators should make you think more than once about violating this cut's speed prohibitions.

West of unlighted daybeacons #9 and #10, the channel comes under the protection of a semicharted rock breakwater to the north. Keep clear.

West-northwest of unlighted daybeacon #29, the channel cruises into a protected canal that soon splits. The docks you will spot at the apex of the split are NOT the marina. This is apparently some sort of commercial fishing operation, with nothing to interest visiting cruisers with the possible exception of purchasing some very fresh catch of the day.

Take the northwesterly fork. Soon the previously mentioned dry-stack storage facility will come abeam or port, followed a bit farther upstream by the large Black Point Marina dockage basin.

Sands Key-Elliott Key Anchorages At last we can say, it's not terribly difficult to access these overnight stops, particularly the more southern havens. If you plan to drop the hook at one of the anchorages near Elliott Key's northerly tip, depart the Waterway near Standard Mile 1110 and cut almost due east. Point for the position of the charted "Tide Sta" (Tide Station), north of Coon Point. Drop anchor some .4 of a nautical mile west of the shore adjacent to the "Tide Sta." Don't make a closer approach. We suggest anchoring near 25 28.847 North/080 11.720 West.

For a bit more shelter, captains whose craft aren't bothered by 5-foot depths can work their way a short hop farther to the east-northeast and pitch out the old hook near 25 28.937 North/080 11.509 West.

As observed above, Sands Cut is a tiny, very shallow inlet that separates Elliott Key and Sands Key. Even though you may very well spy some white PVC pipes outlining a supposed channel through this cut, don't even think about venturing into these waters. Depths of 2 to 3 feet are the norm.

It is possible, however, to anchor in 5 feet of water well west of Sands Cut. Try dropping the hook several hundred yards west of the white PVC (so-called) Sands Cut channel markers, near 25 29.371 North/080 11.556 West.

To make good your entry into the anchorage west of Sands Key, keep 500 yards offshore and track your way north to the waters 350 yards off the westerly shores of Sands Key's north-to-south axis. Drop anchor near 25 30.136 North/080 11.628 West.

As you begin your approach to a position abeam of Sands Key, and particularly the anchorage just to the north, reviewed below, the southeasterly edge of Featherbed Bank's shallows begin to come into play. Be SURE to stay southeast of this huge shoal, and any of the "W Bn's" (warning beacons) that denote these shallows.

The final anchorage lies some 100 yards off Sands Key's northwesterly tip. Keep a good 100 yards north of the key's shoreline and drop the hook as soon as this point comes abeam south of your course. Farther to the east, soundings rise dramatically. Try anchoring near 25 30.414 North/080 11.215 West.

Herbert Hoover Marina and the Biscayne National Park Headquarters Cruisers bound for the canal that serves both Herbert Hoover Marina and the Biscayne National Park Headquarters should turn west near Standard Mile 1111 and track their way for 2.1 miles to flashing daybeacon #2. This aid to navigation is the outermost marker on the prolifically outlined channel, which cuts southwest to the huge power plant that you will see in the distance.

The rest of this cut can be ignored by pleasure craft, but #2 makes a nice midroute correction point. From flashing daybeacon #2, swing a bit to the west-southwest and set course for (yet another) flashing daybeacon #2 at the easterly genesis of the marina (and Park Service) approach channel. Don't let the similar numbering of both these #2's confuse you. They are part of very different channels. The two #2's are separated by some 1.9 nautical miles.

Once abeam of the second (western-most) flashing daybeacon #2, it should be a simple matter to pick up the remainder of the entrance channel moving west to the canal's entrance. At unlighted daybeacon #10, a rock breakwater provides a buffer to the north. Be sure to stay well south of this rocky protector.

West of unlighted daybeacon #10, slow to idle speed. The remainder of the channel and the subsequent canal are official no-wake zones. And remember, all those blue, light-equipped boats we mentioned earlier at the Park Service Headquarters. We highly suggest that speed demons not try their luck on these waters.

Shortly after entering the canal, the Park Service Headquarters will be obvious to starboard. Most cruisers will want to continue straight ahead. The dockage basin will be sighted near the stream's westerly tip, with the slips and the dockmaster's office flanking the southerly banks.

On the ICW Okay, we're all beginning to get tired of hearing about "long" runs between aids to navigation on southerly Biscayne Bay, but how about this one? Southbound cruisers must ply just over 7 nautical miles of the ICW between flashing daybeacon #6 (marking the southern side of Featherbed Bank) and the next southerly aid to navigation, flashing daybeacon #8. If you don't have a working GPS aboard, this would be a very good time to practice your DR navigating skills.

Fortunately, this lengthy cruise does not stray near any really shallow water, but best depths can be held by passing #8 by some 50 yards to its easterly side. Another side-water possibility comes up .4 of a nautical mile short of (north of) #8.

Caesar Creek Please remember that minimum depths of 4 feet can be expected on the marked channel from Biscayne Bay into Caesar Creek's interior reaches. Also, soundings on the seaward approach channel to Caesar Creek run as thin as 5 feet at mean low water. This passage is NOT recommended for boats larger than 36 feet or those vessels drawing 4 feet or more.

Note that ALL the aids to navigation on this passage are of the unlighted variety. While fair-weather, daylight entries are relatively routine, you will never catch us truly trying to enter this channel at night or in low-light conditions. May you, too, heed this advice.

Also, it would be advisable to remember our earlier admonition about the strong tidal currents that regularly race in and out of Caesar Creek. This is a really good spot to watch the track over your stern, as well as your course ahead, to make sure a lateral current is not easing you out of the channel.

To make good your entry into Caesar Creek, point for the gap between unlighted daybeacons #29 and #30. While approaching #30, you will note the correctly charted, unnumbered flashing daybeacon to the north of your course line. Then, point for the gap between unlighted daybeacons #27 and #28. Continue cruising to the east-southeast. Watch for unlighted daybeacon #25 and an unlighted junction daybeacon #A. Pass between #25 and #A.

Slow down; you must now make an immediate choice as to your next course of action. Unlighted junction daybeacon #A denotes a split in the channel (as do most junction markers). The main southerly tier goes on to the interior reaches of Caesar Creek, while the northerly branch provides access to a shallow anchorage. Let's first take a look at the northerly passage.

Cruisers bound for the shallow anchorage to the north should round #A, and then cut north-northeast passing #A to its easterly side. Soon thereafter, you should come abeam and pass unlighted daybeacon #2 fairly close to its western quarter. Look to the northeast and pick out unlighted daybeacons #3 and #4. Point for the gap between these two markers. Be mindful of the very shallow water on both sides of the channel. Take your time and pay strict attention to business.

Next, set course for the gap between unlighted daybeacons #5 and #6, the northeasternmost aids to navigation on this side channel. Continue cruising north-northeast of #5 and #6 for some 25 to 40 yards, then cut to the east-southeast and feel your way carefully along for a hundred yards or so with the sounder. Low-water depths of 4 feet are VERY common in this anchorage, so don't even think about going here if these sorts of soundings are a problem for your vessel. Drop the hook before coming abeam of Adams Key's northeasterly tip. East and southeast of this point, depths deteriorate further.

Let's now return our attention to the principal southerly branch of the approach channel and the interior reaches of Caesar Creek.

Cruisers bound for these waters should cut south after passing between #25 and #A and point to eventually pass between unlighted daybeacons #23 and #24. Shortly thereafter, captains might choose to make use of the enchanting, but navigationally challenging, anchorage between Rubicon and Reid keys.

To access this haven, depart the main channel some 30 yards southeast of unlighted daybeacon #23. Swing sharply to the southwest and point for the (more or less) centerline of the passage, which you will spy ahead between the two keys. It is essential to practice eyeball navigation to pick out this unmarked approach channel. Generally, a darker color means deeper water, and a lighter shade denotes a shoal. We suggest that you attempt this side cut only on a clear, sunny day when it is relatively easy to pick out the good water from the bad.

Once between the two keys, favor the northwestern (Rubicon Keys) shores slightly. By the time you reach the second charted offshoot running to the northwest, good depths of 8 feet or better stretch out almost from shore to shore.

To continue seaward on Caesar Creek, you must follow a significant easterly bend in the passage. Set course to come abeam of unlighted daybeacon #22 to its fairly immediate southern side. The Adams Key visitors' center dock lies just north of #22. If you decide to tie up here temporarily, approach with caution, pay the most respectful attention to the tidal currents, and have your largest fenders ready.

From #22, next up are unlighted daybeacons #20 and #21. Pass between these two markers. After leaving #20 and #21, the channel swings to the south-southeast.

It's a bit of a long run to the next set of aids to navigation, unlighted daybeacons #18 and #19. Fortunately, the channel is rather broad along this stretch. Just point to stay some 100 yards southwest of charted Christmas Point and its adjacent shoreline. Do notice the correctly charted 2-foot waters to the west and southwest. It would obviously behoove you to stay well away from these shallows.

At #18 and #19, the cut turns again, this time to the southeast. Point to pass north of unlighted daybeacon #17 and south of unlighted daybeacon #16.

Continuing seaward, the Caesar Creek channel cuts this way and that, but the passage remains exceedingly well marked. Just be sure to observe all aids to navigation carefully. Depths outside of the channel run to 1 foot or less!

The shallowest portion of the seaward channel is found hard by the outermost aids to navigation, unlighted daybeacons #1 and #2. Here, during low tide, don't be surprised if your depth sounder reveals a mere 5 feet of water.

The easternmost marker on the Caesar Creek channel is flashing daybeacon #20. Pass south of #20. The deep waters of Hawk Channel now lie before you.

ICW to Card Sound At flashing daybeacon #8, the ICW cuts to the southwest and soon approaches a dredged cut. This man-made passage allows cruisers to safely transit the very shallow water that separates southern Biscayne Bay and the northern section of Card Sound. We have observed low-water depths of 8 feet from time to time on this portion of the Waterway.

After the rather open and generally deep waters of Biscayne Bay, you may have become a bit cavalier about Waterway navigation. We strongly suggest that you quickly lose that attitude on these waters.

Use your binoculars to pick out unlighted daybeacon #8A and flashing daybeacon #9. These two aids to navigation denote the northerly entrance into the dredged cut described above. For the next 1.5 nautical miles, observe all markers very carefully. Southbound cruisers should continue to pass to the west side of green, odd-numbered aids to navigation and to the east of red markers.

Flashing daybeacon #14 is the second-to-last aid on the dredged passage (moving north to south). Northbound cruisers may mistake an uncharted sign just to the south of the daybeacon's position as #14. Use your binoculars to distinguish between the sign (which is a national park boundary sign) and the daymarker.

Unlighted daybeacon #15 marks the southerly exodus from the dredged cut. Continue on the same course to the (generally) southwest past #15 for several hundred yards. From this point, the channel swings just a bit farther to the southwest and enters the wide and mostly deep waters of Card Sound.

Card Sound to Jewfish Creek

South of Biscayne Bay, the ICW traverses Card Sound, Little Card Sound, and Barnes Sound (in that order, moving north to south) on its way to Jewfish Creek. These are pretty open waters, with the now all-too-familiar long runs between aids to navigation. Once again, if you can time your cruise to coincide with fair winds and sunny skies, so much the better.

Angelfish Creek sits astride the easterly shores of Card Sound and provides reliable access to Hawk Channel, as well as several current-strewn anchorage opportunities of its own.

And speaking of anchorages, there are some interesting overnight stops available along this stretch of the Waterway. All these potential havens are widely spaced, however, so be sure to include enough time to reach your intended destination before the light of day fades.

Marina facilities are few and far between north of Jewfish Creek. One repair yard on the waters of southwestern Barnes Sound does offer some services for visiting cruisers, but mostly skippers must keep on trucking south to Jewfish Creek to find reliable pleasure-craft facilities.

The ICW's trek across Card Sound to Card Bank traverses slightly better than 4.6 nautical miles. This entire passage is unmarked, hence it is rather difficult to locate the side trips below by reference to navigational aids. So, we will instead refer to charted geographic locations and lat/lon coordinates. Let's get started.

Broad Creek
(Standard Mile 1120)

The indistinct and very hard to navigate entrance to Broad Creek flanks the easterly shores of Card Sound between Broad and Swan Keys (well southeast of unlighted day-beacon #15). In a word or two, this is one of those passages between the inside route and Hawk Channel that should be strictly relegated to our outboard and I/O brethren.

On a calm, sunny day in August 2000, fearless research assistant, Bob Horne, and Claiborne actually did make it through Broad Creek in a shallow draft, 25-foot, outboard-powered craft. It is not an experience that we would want to quickly repeat. The channel, such as it is, is completely unmarked, and the only possible way to proceed is by eyeball navigation. Even with these perfect conditions, we would never even consider taking a cruising-sized vessel through this cut. Depths outside of the channel run to a half-foot, and the entrance from Card Sound is a "take your best guess" situation. Our advice: keep on trucking!

Angelfish Creek
(Standard Mile 1121.5)
(Various Lat/Lons—see below)

Angelfish Creek makes into the easterly banks of Card Sound, south of Middle and Linderman Creeks, near 25 20.152 North/080 16.821 West. This fortunate body of water (at last) provides a reliable means to cruise from the ICW-inside route to Hawk Channel and vice versa. Minimum MLW depths run about 6 feet, with the vast majority of the stream exhibiting much deeper soundings. There are also, thankfully, no bridges spanning Angelfish to worry with. If it weren't for the presence of some prodigious tidal currents, this channel would be a breeze.

Angelfish Creek boasts marked entrance channels running into its interior reaches from

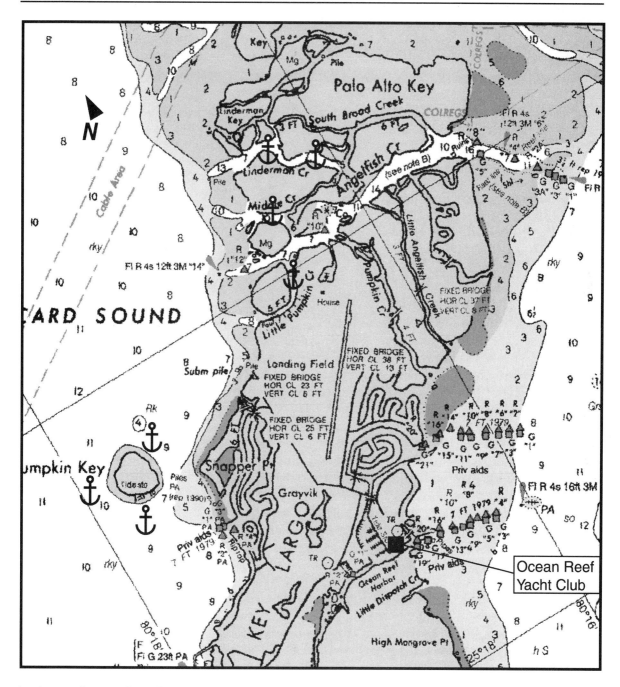

both Card Sound and Hawk Channel. The shallowest portions of the entire Angelfish Creek passage are found at the western and eastern ends of these two approach cuts.

Entering Angelfish Creek from Hawk Channel

Here, captains can expect their depth sounders to show some 6-foot readings, but once into the stream's interior reaches, don't be surprised to find yourself in 7 to 15 feet of water.

A small portion of the sumptuous Ocean Reef development is visible to the south, but for the most part, the shores of Angelfish Creek are delightfully undeveloped. Quite simply, this is a beautiful stream whose passage will undoubtedly engender more than its share of eye candy for nature lovers.

Now, as if all that weren't enough, Angelfish Creek offers overnight anchorage for vessels as large as a 38-footer. All are set in completely natural surroundings, and most boast good shelter, even in really foul weather. Before reviewing these havens, however, allow us to once again call your attention to the strong tidal currents, which regularly scour these waters. Be SURE the

anchor is well set before heading below to begin a memorable evening meal.

Moving west to east, first up are two anchorages that lie west of unlighted daybeacon #10. Here, a southerly offshoot of Middle Creek cuts into the northern shores. It's a relatively simple proposition to cruise north into the main body of Middle Creek. Cut to the west and drop anchor near the point where chart 11451 (Page B, Inset 3) shows a 10-foot sounding (approximately 25 20.253 North/080 16.422 West). Minimum depths are 6 feet, and there should be enough elbowroom for a 36-footer.

Captains who pilot boats 34 feet and smaller, and whose craft can cruise through 5-foot (low-water) depths without finding the bottom, might consider charming Little Pumpkin Creek. This stream cuts the southern banks of Angelfish Creek, some .2 nautical miles west of unlighted daybeacon #10. The mouth of the creek carries only 5 feet of water, and these depths continue upstream for a short stretch. Then, soundings improve to 6 and 7 feet. Drop anchor near 25. 20.018 North/080 16.493 West before cruising into the correctly charted, lazy turn to the west. Some light residential development associated with Ocean Reef is visible from Little Pumpkin Creek, but the presence of the palatial homes adds to, rather than detracts from, the visual appeal of this anchorage.

Now, study chart 11451, Page B, Inset 3 and notice the combined mouths of Middle and Linderman Creeks making into the northerly flank of Angelfish Creek, east of unlighted daybeacon #10. If you can stand the initial 4½-foot depths, Linderman Creek can lead to two potential havens. Good depths of 6 feet or better are in the offing northwest of the intersection with Middle Creek.

The first anchor-down spot to consider is found on the widening body of Linderman Creek, abeam of the unnamed offshoot, which makes off from the northeasterly banks some .14 nautical miles north-northwest of the juncture with Middle Creek (near 25 20.385 North/080 16.085 West). Here, amidst 7-foot depths, cruisers will find plenty of swinging room for a 38-footer.

Those who are up for a bit more exploration can continue tracking their way upstream to the waters abeam of the first two of the three small, unnamed islands south of charted Linderman Key (near 25 20.556 North/080 16.266 West). Here minimum depths also run around 7 feet, and there should be enough elbowroom for a boat as large as 38 feet (at least). Particularly strong winds from the west blowing up the mouth of Linderman Creek could be a bit of a problem.

The buoyed passage leading from the easterly mouth of Angelfish Creek to Hawk Channel has one turn that you would never expect even after a thorough perusal of chart 11451. We heartily suggest that you consult the navigational account of this stream below BEFORE your first-time passage of these waters.

Pumpkin Key Anchorages
(Standard Mile 1122.5)
(Various Lat/Lons—see below)

Pumpkin Key is an attractive, privately owned island that raises its head over the eastern shores of Card Sound, west of Snapper Point and south of Angelfish Creek. The owners must have spent the entire budget on "No Trespassing" signs. An incredible array of these warning placards ring this small body of land. All this apparently protects the palatial homeplace perched on Pumpkin Key. This edifice is visible to all but the blind while cruising anywhere near the key.

Fortunately, anchoring off Pumpkin Key is not restricted. Visiting cruisers can pick and choose their overnight haven, depending on from which direction the wind is blowing.

It is a relatively simple matter to drop the hook a few hundred yards off the western, southern and northeastern shores of Pumpkin Key in at least 7 feet of water. The approach to the northeasterly haven is a bit trickier, as navigators must avoid the correctly charted, but unmarked 4-foot rock. Swinging room is completely unrestricted on all of these havens.

The adjoining shoreline to the east exhibits some rather impressive residential development associated with the nearby Ocean Reef Yacht Club. You may even spot some navigational markers. These daybeacons serve some very private docks, and visiting cruisers should keep clear of these proprietary channels.

We do not recommend that cruising-sized craft attempt to circumnavigate Pumpkin Key. The waters east of the isle are pinched between a shelf of shallows making out from the island shoreline and a broad bank of 4- to 5-foot waters stretching from the easterly, Key Largo banks. We sounded definite low-water depths of 4 and 5 feet along this stretch.

If winds are wafting from the north, try anchoring some 175 yards off the southern banks of Pumpkin Key, near 25 19.398 North/080 17.759 West. Closer to Pumpkin Key, depths rise dramatically.

Easterly breezes call for an anchorage off the key's westerly banks. Again, stay at least 200 yards off the banks. Try near 25 19.620 North/080 17.918 West.

With western or southwestern blows up and coming, cruisers can also choose to anchor off Pumpkin Key's northeasterly shoreline. The trick to this haven is to successfully avoid the correctly charted 4-foot rock. If you can get past this obstruction, try dropping the hook 200 yards offshore near 25 19.665 North/080 17.559 West.

Card Sound Anchorages
(Standard Mile 1124)
(25 17.674 North/080 19.655 West)
(25 18.142 North/080 18.563 West)

After making its long, markerless run across the length of Card Sound, the ICW leaves this body of water via a dredged cut through ultra-shallow Card Bank. Just before entering the Card Bank cut, cruisers can find their way to two anchorages that make for superior overnight stops when winds are blowing from the east or southeast.

The most easily accessed of these two lies in the correctly charted 9-foot waters north of Jew Point. This point of land occupies the

extreme southern corner of Card Sound. Mariners approaching this anchorage can help identify their position by way of the bridge that crosses Steamboat Creek just to the south. This small span shows up nicely from the waters of Card Sound on a sunny day.

We suggest setting the anchor near 25 17.674 North/080 19.655 West, amidst 6-foot minimum depths. A closer approach to Steamboat Creek could land you in the broad shelf of charted 2-foot waters to the southwest.

Swinging room is unlimited in this haven, and the adjacent shoreline is in a virgin state. There can be some lights and faint automobile noise from traffic passing over the Steamboat Creek Bridge, but we have never found this to be much of a problem.

If you seek a bit more shelter and a closer approach to the southeasterly shoreline, check out the cove southwest of Wednesday Point. Depths on this haven can run to as little as 5 feet, however, if you approach to within 100 yards of the shoreline. If that's not a problem for your vessel, anchor anywhere near 25 18.142 North/080 18.563 West. Shelter is great for eastern and southeasterly breezes, but this overnight stop, like the one reviewed above, is wide open to any other wind direction. Check the NOAA forecast and plan accordingly.

This cove's shoreline is all that anyone could ask for. Not only is it undeveloped, but the vegetation could be described accurately as "lush." If the weather cooperates and you do get to spend a night here, don't forget we sent you!

Little Card Sound Anchorage
(Standard Mile 1126)
(25 17.242 North/080 21.405 West)

After a quick hop across Little Card Sound, the Waterway soon approaches the high-rise

Card Sound Bridge (see below). North of this impressive span, captains might choose to cut east and visit the charted 7-foot waters east-southeast of flashing daybeacon #22. Protection is only adequate for southerly, southeasterly and, to a lesser extent, easterly breezes. This anchorage is particularly wide open to blows from the north and northwest. Don't even think about dropping anchor here if the forecast calls for blows of 10 knots or better from these quarters.

While this is what our ace research assistant, Bob Horne, termed an "OK anchorage," it does suffer from two problems. First, in spite of the soundings pictured on chart 11451, water depths can creep up to the 5-foot mark at low tide. More importantly, automobile traffic passing over the Card Sound Bridge can be a bit annoying at night. On the other hand, swinging room is unlimited, and the shoreline is again virtually untouched. And, usually, there is not nearly as much auto traffic passing over the Card Sound Bridge as the rolling armada served by the Jewfish Creek span (see

below). So, we guess Bob is right, this is an "OK anchorage," even if it will never make our highlight reel.

Card Sound Bridge and Alabama Jack's (Standard Mile 1126.5) (25 17.480 North/080 22.728 West)

Southwest of flashing daybeacon #22, the Waterway bids a fond farewell to Little Card Sound and soon passes under the only bridge to cross its path short of Jewfish Creek. The Card Sound span is a towering structure that seems taller than its official 65-foot clearance. That's probably because after running the long bridgeless section of the ICW from Miami to this point, the span looks ever more impressive.

South of the Card Sound Bridge, the Waterway follows a few interesting twists and turns through a dredged cut. Soundings outside of this man-made channel run to 2- and 3-foot levels. Check out the navigational account presented below before transiting this section of the ICW.

South of the Card Sound span, cruisers who

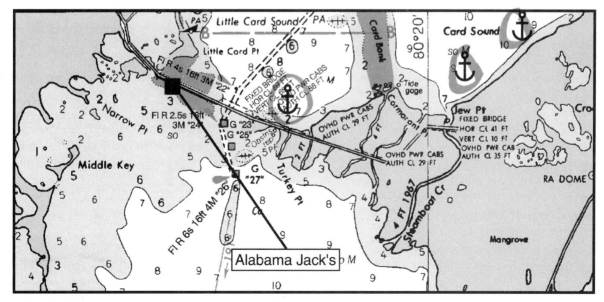

can stand some 5-foot depths might choose to follow an unmarked channel that cuts northwest to legendary Alabama Jack's.

Alabama Jack's (305-248-8741) is a great spot to take a break. This is an outdoor restaurant that is long on color, popularity, and good food but very short on amenities. This doesn't seem to bother Jimmy Buffett or Kathie Lee Gifford, who frequent this place when they are around. It is close to the Ocean Reef Club, out on Key Largo.

Alabama Jack's is just shy of the tollgate on the Card Sound Bridge, but that is of little use to cruisers. Put another way, it is a trip of almost a mile up the channel that runs northwest from the ICW on the south side of the Card Sound Bridge. The channel is not marked, but one can see it from the ICW. Depths in the approach channel run as thin as 5 feet, while generally, dockside soundings run 4½ to 8 feet. Don't even *think* about coming up this channel at night.

The restaurant serves only beer and wine to quench thirsts, and docking space is limited, because most of the restaurant's business comes from highway traffic. There are wooden finger piers just past the restaurant, which are for people to tie up when dining at Alabama Jack's. There are no overnight transient docking facilities.

Alabama Jack's prides itself on being the kind of place that attracts people "who have left the mainstream behind." One could also say that it is popular with people who never knew or will know what the mainstream is all about. A nice ride from the metro haunts of Miami and Fort Lauderdale, Alabama Jack's has a loyal biker clientele. However, given the wide popularity of motorcycles these days, the guy sitting next to you in an outfit that would make Sonny Barger's eyes shine with

pride might, in the light of the 9-5 work week, actually be an accountant.

The food here is mostly a sandwich menu and seafood platters, but it is safe to say that if the food wasn't good, there wouldn't be so many people coming here.

Entertainment on weekends comes from the Card Sound Machine, and Sundays are when the place really jumps. People exiting the Keys seem to have to stop for just one more slice of Florida Key life.

No guarantees that Mr. Buffett or Ms. Gifford will be there when you are, but then you could always view that as *their* loss.

Glades Canal and South Dade Marina (Standard Mile 1131) (25 16.048 North/080 26.342 West)

After leaving the dredged channel south of Card Sound Bridge in their wake, cruisers will soon be skimming across the wide and unsheltered reaches of huge Barnes Sound. It is a run of some 4.8 nautical miles across the sound to the northern mouth of Jewfish Creek. Short of this stream, cruisers might pick from several anchorages and two minimal marina facilities.

First up is South Dade Marina. This small place is accessed by the marked (and only partially charted) channel that leads from the western shores of Barnes Sound, past Manatee Bay, and into the southeasterly mouth of deep Glades Canal. The cut has some markings, but they are not correctly depicted on the present edition of chart 11451. Check out our navigational account below for a more up-to-date scheme of aids to navigation.

The entrance channel, running from Barnes Sound to the southeasterly mouth of the Glades Canal, usually carries 5 feet of water at low tide. We did notice an occasional 4½-foot sounding on one or two occasions during our last visit.

Glades Canal itself is very well sheltered and carries at least 10 feet of water. Depths of 15 feet are not at all uncommon between the southeasterly entrance and the cutoff to South Dade Marina.

And speaking of South Dade Marina, the canal running up to this little facility comes up along the Glade Canal's westerly banks some .6 nautical miles upstream. Entrance and dockside depths are in the 5- to 6-foot range at low water. Unfortunately, there are NO services for visiting cruisers to be found here, and the docks have always been unattended during our several visits.

Anchorage would seem to be a possibility on Glades Canal itself, north of the entrance to South Dade Marina. As far was we have been able to determine, there is no commercial traffic on this stream, but be SURE to show a bright anchor light anyway. The shoreline is absolutely beautiful, overlooked by tall trees and lush vegetation. Shelter is excellent from all winds, but be advised there is a good bit of current running through this canal. The 15+-foot depths, coupled with the relatively narrow width of the canal, would probably not leave enough elbowroom for vessels larger than 36 feet.

Manatee Bay Anchorage
(Standard Mile 1131)
(25 15.412 North/080 24.567 West)

Skippers whose boat requires 3½ feet or less to stay off the bottom may consider dropping anchor in Manatee Bay. This body of water lies just east of the Glades Canal approach channel reviewed above. Depths running as thin as 4 feet can be expected,

though most soundings are in the 5- to 5½-foot range. Don't approach to within less than 300 yards of any of the bay's shorelines. Closer in, depths rise to 3 feet or less.

Shelter is only fair for eastern, southeastern, northern, and northeastern breezes. There is no real protection to the south and southwest. As usual, the shores are lovely and beg for a closer inspection by dinghy.

Cormorant Rookeries Anchorage
(Standard Mile 1131)
(25 13.466 North/080 24.676 West)

With light to moderate westerly winds (ONLY) in the offing, mariners can find an interesting anchorage some 250 to 300 yards east of the southernmost of the two keys, noted on chart 11451 as "Cormorant Rookeries." These isles flank the western side of Barnes Sound, a short hop south of the southeasterly genesis of the Glades Canal approach channel and just northeast of Manatee Creek's unlighted daybeacon #2 (see below for more on Manatee Creek). Depths of 5 to 6 feet run to within 250 yards (no closer) of the isles' easterly shoreline. Swing room is virtually without limit.

The Cormorant Rookeries are aptly named. During our last visit, the two isles and the surrounding waters teemed with waterfowl. Landing is NOT permitted, so do your observations by way of binoculars and dinghy.

Manatee Creek Facilities
(Standard Mile 1131)
(25 14.232 North/080 26.002 West)

The westerly extreme of Barnes Sound plays host to a few facilities on Manatee Creek. The scantily marked entrance channel to this stream lies a short hop southwest of the Cormorant Rookeries anchorage detailed

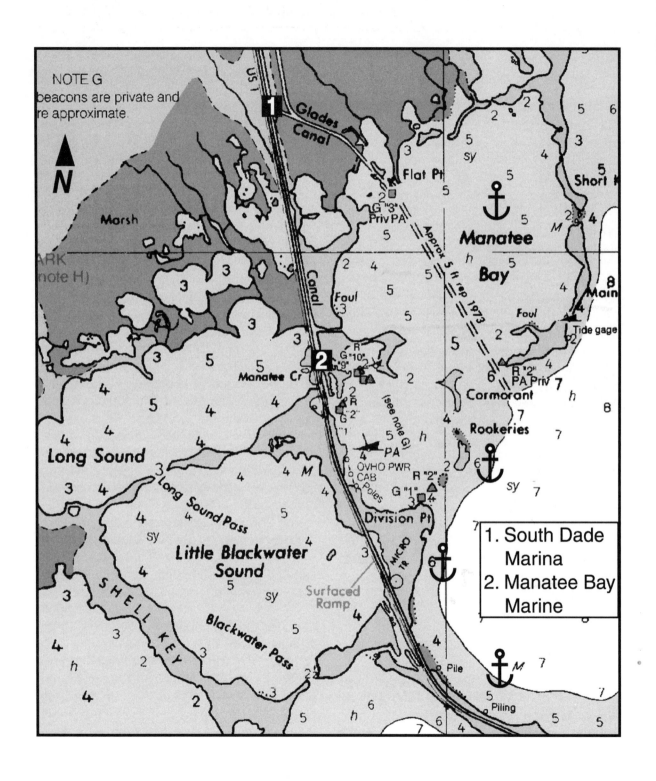

Manatee Creek

above. Entrance depths run to 4½ feet at low tide, even in the best of circumstances. This is a tricky passage. In particular, it is all too easy to mistake a set of private markers just west of the main cut as the correct aids to navigation. Please be SURE to read the navigational account presented below before making the attempt.

Once on the interior reaches of Manatee Creek, depths vary, typically from 4½ to 6 feet. This stream is the dividing line between Dade and Monroe counties. It is not really a place to stop, but you can, if you really must. Located on Cross Key, the creek plays host to a boat yard of serious dimensions and is also the first one in the Florida Keys.

Manatee Bay Marine occupies the extreme upstream reaches of Manatee Creek. This yard does not usually accept transients; however, if you are having work done on your boat, you will be permitted to stay aboard in the yard. While approach depth is 4½ feet at MLW, the place could be accessed on higher tides. The piers are fixed wooden finger piers. There is a marine store that is long on the practical and very short on the fancy. It is not a place to pick up beer and ice and snacks.

The yard is fenced and open from 8:00 A.M. to 4:30 P.M., Mondays through Fridays, and 8:00A.M.-3:00 P.M. on weekends. The shower—there is only one—is spotless and so are the toilet facilities. In fact, there is no trash whatsoever on the ground at this yard, so it shows that the owners and the people who work there have a sense of duty when it comes to keeping things clean.

Keep in mind that if you are here, you must be in the market for a purpose more demanding that relaxation. As a transient, a major problem would have to bring you in. No stores are nearby. You are out in the boonies, but you are also in competent hands.

Additionally, this yard is so protected that it would take a storm of cataclysmic proportions to make you want to cut and run. When tied up at Manatee Bay Marine, you are back in the womb.

Manatee Bay Marine (305) 451-3332

Approach depth—4^1/$_2$-6 feet
Dockside depth—4^1/$_2$-5 feet
Accepts transients—under limited circumstances
Type of docking—fixed wooden finger piers
Dockside power connections—15 amp only
Dockside water connections—yes
Showers—yes (one)
Mechanical repairs—yes, extensive
Below-waterline repairs—yes, 60-ton Travelift and 50-ton crane (the latter suitable for launching big catamarans)
Ship's and variety store—professional boatyard store—no frills
Restaurant—The closest is in Largo. Walking is not an option.

Another facility on Manatee Creek was (is?) known as Key Largo Marina. It has been through receivership and was closed down when we were there. There are apparently a lot of complications in regards to resuming business.

Southwestern Barnes Sound Anchorages
(Standard Mile 1132)
(25 12.134 North/080 24.490 West)
(25 12.870 North/080 25.055 West)

To the west of Jewfish Creek's northerly mouth, a large lobe of deep water extends almost to the extreme southwesterly shores of

Barnes Sound. This is a popular overnight stop for cruisers in southern and southwestern winds. Don't even think about anchoring here if a blow from the north or the northeast is forecast. Of course, those of you who like to imitate Mexican jumping beans during the evening hours can ignore this advice.

Reasonable depths of 5½ to 6 feet hold to within .25 nautical miles of the sound's extreme southwestern shoreline. We like the waters near 25 12.134 North/080 24.490 West. Be advised that nighttime traffic running the causeway to and from Jewfish Creek Bridge can be prolific, particularly on weekends. Headlights are clearly visible from this anchorage, and some auto noise is noticeable on otherwise quiet nights.

While it's farther from the Waterway, we prefer the 5½-to 6-foot waters off (south of) charted Division Point (25 12.870 North/080 25.055 West). Good depths hold to within 250 yards of the westerly shoreline. Here, you are further removed from the automobile traffic, and the adjacent shoreline is in its natural state.

Thursday Cove Anchorage
(Standard Mile 1132)
(25 12.134 North/080 22.505 West)

Let's not make any secret about it. Our favorite Barnes Sound anchorage is located on the waters of Thursday Cove, just to the northeast of Jewfish Creek's northerly entrance. This is an absolutely perfect spot to spend a tranquil evening on the hook, unless winds over 10 knots are blowing from the north or northwest. There is superb shelter from eastern, southeastern, southern and, to a lesser extent, southwesterly breezes. The shores look as if they have never known the hand of mankind. Typical depths at low water run from 6 to 7 feet, but you can get into 5-foot soundings if you venture closer than 100 yards to the cove's shoreline. Seldom do we cruise through the northern mouth of Jewfish Creek and not find a cruising craft or two swinging idyllically on the hook in Thursday Cove. We hope you, too, will be able to join that happy throng!

Jewfish Creek and Associated Facilities
(Standard Mile 1133—Northern Entrance)
(Standard Mile 1134.5—Southern Entrance)
(Various Lat/Lons—see below)
To be such a short section of the ICW-inside

Florida Keys route, Jewfish Creek is a very important body of water. First and foremost, it serves as the connector between those cruising grounds stretching south from Miami and what many feel are the true waters of the Florida Keys to the south. For another, Jewfish Creek is the sight of the first really serious pleasure-craft-oriented marinas south of Biscayne Bay.

On a less happy note, Jewfish Creek is spanned by a bascule bridge with a closed vertical clearance of only 11 feet and, you guessed it, a restrictive opening schedule. And

Gilbert's Resort Marina (Jewfish Creek)

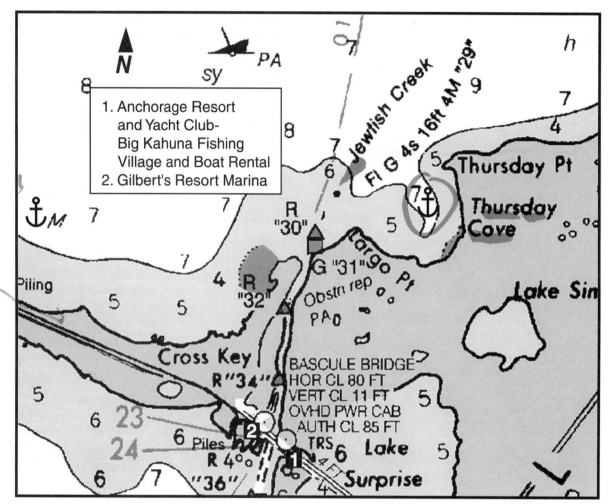

1. Anchorage Resort and Yacht Club- Big Kahuna Fishing Village and Boat Rental
2. Gilbert's Resort Marina

you thought you had left all those pesky restrictive spans behind in Miami!

By the way, just so you know, Jewfish is a Floridian name for very larger grouper. One of this guide's authors (Morgan) once caught a 450 pound Jewfish, with which he fed the entire neighborhood.

All the Jewfish Creek facilities lie south of the bridge. Gilbert's Resort Marina (25 11.072 North/080 23.437 West) overlooks the creek's westerly banks. This place was rather famous once upon a time, it being

what many considered the first stop on the way down from Miami when one gets to the "real" Keys. Landlubber tourists can turn into the resort prior to crossing the bascule bridge over Jewfish Creek.

Transient dockage is afforded at fixed wooden face piers with fresh water and 30- to 50-amp hookups. Depths alongside are a more than adequate 8 feet. Shoreside showers are old but clean, and there is an on-site Laundromat. Gasoline and diesel fuel can be purchased dockside.

This entire facility is quite old and the wear shows. Motel rooms are small and have window-type air-conditioning units. The on-site dining spot, Gilbert's Restaurant, is a sandwiches-only kind of place and has a slightly down-at-the-heels atmosphere. There is also a tiki bar on the premises, and that probably is a going concern on the weekends. On the other hand, if you are tied up along the dock and the tiki bar is roaring, you could find it hard to take a snooze. They are close.

Use the swimming pool. Swimming off your boat, even though this is the Keys and the water is clear, is probably a bad idea. There are saltwater crocodiles in these waters. No one has told the saltwater crocs that humans, and not crocs, are at the top of the food chain, and it is entirely possible that the crocs could make a nasty mistake.

There is a boat service facility and high and dry storage on site, around the western corner and up a creek. It's called The Service Center (305-451-9955). It's run by Al Papineau, a Honda outboard dealer, and his wife Claire, both transplanted from Maine. The approach to the Service Center is 6 feet, with 6 feet alongside also, and the available dockage is comprised of finger piers. Repairs can be made to diesel, gas, or outboard engines. There is also a canvas shop on the premises. The Service Center has 30-amp service and water connections and a ship's store for marine supplies. It's skimpy.

Gilbert's is 2.6 miles from the nearest real grocery store, which is a Winn-Dixie Marketplace, located in Largo, Bayside.

Gilbert's Resort Marina (305) 451-1133
http://www.gilbertsresort.com

Approach depth—8-10 feet
Dockside depth—8-10 feet

Accepts transients—yes
Type of docking—fixed wooden piers and alongside docking
Dockside power connections—up to 50 amp
Dockside water connections—yes
Showers—yes, old but clean
Laundromat—yes
Fuel available—gas and diesel
Mechanical repairs—at adjoining facility
Restaurant—on site

Anchorage Resort and Yacht Club (25 10.957 North/080 23.198 West) lies just across Jewfish Creek from Gilbert's. This facility is dominated of an ugly monolith of a building, but the dockside facilities for transients are very nice. The fixed concrete piers are in excellent repair and feature fresh water and power connections up to 50 amps. We would estimate that 10 visiting vessels of average length could be accommodated at one time. Soundings dockside vary from a minimum of 6 feet to 8 feet on the outermost pier. The rest rooms and showers for transient use are small, but they were clean. The grounds are also well maintained. There is a hard-surfaced tennis court on the property and shuffleboard, too. The swimming pool and the Jacuzzi are excellent and in perfect shape.

We didn't find a restaurant here, but it appears that the one next door accommodates all comers. The rental units in the main building look like condos.

The staff here was pleasant and courteous and helpful. You could do a lot worse.

Though some of the extras transients might want are lacking here, they are almost within spitting distance. There is gasoline at The Big Kahuna, which is within 100 yards, and repairs are available on the other side of Gilbert's.

Anchorage Resort and Yacht Club (Jewfish Creek)

Anchorage Resort and Yacht Club (305) 451-0500

Approach depth—8-12 feet
Dockside depth—6-8 feet
Accepts transients—yes
Type of docking—concrete finger piers &
   alongside docking
Dockside power connections—up to 50 amp
Dockside water connections—yes
Showers—yes
Restaurant—next door

The Big Kahuna Fishing Village and Boat Rental (also known as BK Marina, 25 11.010 North/080 23.230 West) lies just south and east of the Anchorage Resort—up the creek, actually—and this is a funky little spot that is short on fancy amenities but long on charm. The people who run it are Cuban, and you can bet your last buck that one cup of Cuban coffee will fire you up for about half of a day. If you have ever wondered why Cubans are so industrious, think about how strong (and good) their coffee is. It comes in a small cup but packs a great punch. The Cuban sandwiches are delicious, too.

The marina itself has only about 12 slips, and there are some live aboards already tied up there, so availability of slips may be questionable, particularly "in season." All berths do offer cable and phone hookups. This marina is pretty small for those kinds of amenities, but they are there nevertheless. Go figure.

Dockage consists of small, wooden finger piers, with fresh water and power connections up to 30 amps. Some slips have only 20-amp hookups. We sounded approach and dockside

Jewfish Creek Bascule Bridge

depths of around 6 feet, even though the marina advertises 7-foot depths. Gasoline can be purchased here, but you will have to look elsewhere for diesel fuel.

The rest rooms service the restaurant as well as the marina. They are clean, but they get shared with landlubber transients, so they are subject to what comes in the door. The shower for the marina—just one—is unisex, necessarily, and on the low end of the spectrum. But it's clean. When we stopped by to have a look at this place, we were struck by how truly appealing it all is. It's not elegant, but it is real and the people who wait on you are courteous and friendly. There's a Cuban flag flying out front, beside the automobile gas pumps.

Joe Diaz and Luis Guerra, the owners and operators, feature a restaurant next door called the Latin American Bayfront Grill (305-451-3311). Give this place your most serious gastronomical attention.

Big Kahuna Fishing Village and Boat Rental
   (305) 451-3094

Approach depth—6 feet
Dockside depth—6 feet
Accepts transients—yes
Type of docking—small, wooden finger piers
Dockside power connections—up to 30 amp,
   depending on slip

Dockside water connections—yes
Cable and phone hookups—yes
Shower—yes (one)

Fuel available—gas only
Variety and tackle store—yes
Restaurant—on site

CARD SOUND TO JEWFISH CREEK NAVIGATION

If you thought that aids to navigation were a bit widely spaced on Biscayne Bay, wait till you see some of the runs between markers on Card Sound, Little Card Sound, and Barnes Sound. To be succinct, there are LONG markerless stretches. Be sure to keep a good DR plot and have your GPS up, running, and locked in on these waters. Of course, as we've said repeatedly throughout this guide (and will undoubtedly say yet again), having your GPS interfaced with a laptop computer, and a digitized version of chart 11451 loaded with appropriate navigational software (such as Nobeltec's "Visual Navigational Suite" or Maptech's "Offshore Navigator"), makes a navigator's life ever so much simpler.

While most of the three sounds encompassed within this section are uniformly deep, they are separated by banks and shoals where soundings run in the inches. It is essential to correctly identify and follow the navigational aids marking Card Bank, the northern headwaters of Barnes Sound, and the northerly entrance into Jewfish Creek.

Be advised that Card Sound and Barnes Sound in particular, allow the wind plenty of fetch to foster a healthy chop during blows. Smaller cruising vessels should approach these sounds with the greatest respect.

Navigation of the various side trips outlined above and below can be a bit exacting at times. Markers are not plentiful, and it's all too easy to wander into the surrounding shallows. Take your time, and proceed with caution.

With that said, most mariners will enjoy their run from Card Sound to the southerly exodus of Jewfish Creek. Take your time, soak in the sights, and before you know it, "paradise" will be before you!

ICW and Card Sound South of unlighted daybeacon #15, where we last left the ICW, the Waterway cuts to the southwest and runs for 4.5 nautical miles across the wide open waters of Card Sound, sans aids to navigation. Eventually, skippers must identify flashing daybeacon #17 and unlighted daybeacon #16, the northeasternmost markers on the dredged cut traversing the huge Card Bank shoal. Before considering our transit of Card Bank, let's take a look at the anchorages and side trips available from Card Sound.

Angelfish Creek Tidal currents make their presence known on Angelfish Creek, often in a big way. Watch for lateral leeway as you cruise along. If you should choose to pitch out the hook on one of the creek's side waters, be very sure the anchor is well set before kicking back for the evening.

Use Inset 3, Page B of chart 11451 when navigating Angelfish Creek. It's greater detail is a must.

The outermost (westernmost) marker on the Angelfish Creek entrance is flashing daybeacon #14. Pass some 20 yards to the south of #14, and then set course to pass about the same distance south of unlighted daybeacon #12.

Stop and consider for a moment. You are now headed "toward" the open sea (in this case, Hawk Channel), so it makes sense to pass red, even-numbered aids to navigation to your port side and take green markers to starboard.

East of #12, two good anchorage opportunities open out to the north and south. First up is Little Pumpkin Creek, which cuts the southerly banks. Enter this body of water on its midwidth. For best depths, continue cruising upstream for at least 50 yards before dropping the hook. Be sure to anchor north of the stream's first lazy turn to the west. Soundings deteriorate quickly in the body of this turn.

Turning now to the north side anchorage, notice the connector stream that runs north to Middle Creek. Enter this body of water, favoring the west side banks slightly. Continue on to the north until the main body of Middle Creek opens out to the west-northwest. Cruise into the centerline of this stream and drop anchor anywhere short of (east of) the small island that bisects the creek's westerly mouth.

Do not try to cruise into the waters of Card Sound directly from Middle Creek. In spite of the tongue of 10-foot water depicted on chart 11451, very shallow depths are soon encountered.

Back on the main body of Angelfish Creek, eastbound cruisers should pass to the south of unlighted daybeacon #10. East of #10, Angelfish Creek is unmarked for the next .8 nautical miles. You will not sight another set of aids to navigation short of the seaward channel. Hold to the creek's midline and continue to watch for tidal currents. Soon, yet another potential anchorage will come abeam to the north.

Here the combined mouths of Linderman and Middle creeks meet up with their larger sister. The southerly portion of this stream exhibits soundings of 4½ feet at mean low water, but depths improve markedly northwest of the "T-shaped" intersection with Middle Creek.

If your craft can stand these thin soundings, enter the creek along its centerline and continue holding to the middle until the T-shaped juncture with Middle Creek is in your wake. Now, good depths of 7 feet or better stretch out almost from shore to shore.

One of the first anchor-down spots you might consider comes up abeam of the first small offshoot that cuts the northeasterly banks, northwest of the "T" intersection. Drop anchor in the middle of the widening waters.

The intrepid explorers among us can continue upstream to the waters abeam of the small island formed by the first two small offshoots running north to Linderman Key. Anchor south of the island on the midwidth, and settle down for a night of peace and security.

The passage from Angelfish Creek to Hawk Channel is a bit more complicated than one would expect from a quick study of chart 11451. As you exit the easterly mouth of Angelfish Creek, it is necessary to turn far more sharply to starboard than you might think to pick up the first set of markers, unlighted daybeacons #5 and #8. Point to pass between #5 and #8.

We have noted a tendency to slip a little bit too far to the south between Angelfish Creek's easterly mouth and unlighted daybeacon #5 . Such a mistake may land you in 4½- to 5-foot depths. Stick to the centerline for depths of 8 feet or better.

From this point, the channel cuts to the east-southeast and continues its merry way on to Hawk Channel. The passage twists a bit here and there, but it remains quite well marked. Just be sure to pass each aid to navigation to its appropriate side.

The outermost (easternmost) aids to navigation on the Angelfish Creek-Hawk Channel entrance cut are flashing daybeacon #2 and unlighted daybeacon #1. Cruisers will most likely encounter the shallowest depths of the entire passage between these two markers. Low-water soundings of as little as 6 feet are usually in the offing.

Pumpkin Key Anchorages The only trick to anchoring off the western or southern shores of Pumpkin Key is to correctly identify the island and to stay at least 200 yards offshore. As predicted by chart 11451, a shelf of shallows rings the island, so a closer approach is not a smart option.

Dropping the hook off the isle's northeasterly banks is complicated by the presence of the charted, but definitely unmarked, 4-foot rock. You must carefully pass between this obstruction and the shoal

water shelving out from Pumpkin Key. Once these hazards are in your wake, it's a simple matter to anchor, again some 200 yards offshore.

Don't try to cruise south, past the eastern shores of Pumpkin Key. While chart 11451 suggests a narrow channel is to be found here, pinched between a large patch of shallows making out from the easterly shoreline and a smaller shoal abutting Pumpkin Key, we found 4-foot depths along this passage, no matter where we cruised.

Captains anchoring off or exploring the waters off the southern side of Pumpkin Key will sight a series of daymarkers to the southeast. These serve some very private docks associated with the Ocean Reef Yacht Club. Visiting cruisers should keep clear.

Card Sound Anchorages Unless you already have the location of the two anchorages in southeastern Card Sound saved as way points on your GPS, they can be a bit difficult to locate. There are no aids to navigation close to either haven, and we found the shoreline is a bit short on identifiable landmarks.

We suggest that you depart the ICW some 300 yards northeast of flashing daybeacon #17. Cruise to the south-southeast, keeping at least 300 yards off the shallows of Card Bank. Use your binoculars to watch ahead for the fixed, low-rise Steamboat Creek Bridge. Ease farther from the southwesterly shoreline as you approach this span to avoid the correctly charted bubble of 2-foot waters. Anchor some 300 yards north of the entrance to ultrashallow Steamboat Creek.

Cruisers making for the more northeasterly of the two overnight havens should follow the southeasterly shores of Card Sound as they track their way to the northeast. Keep 200 yards offshore. After easing along for some 1.2 nautical miles, a cove will come abeam to the southeast. Ease into this offshoot, being sure not to approach within less than 100 yards of the banks. You're now ready to drop anchor and break out the evening libations.

On the ICW As mentioned above, Card Bank is a very shallow tongue of shoals that separates Card Sound from Little Card Sound. Fortunately, the good folks at the Army Corps of Engineers maintain a reliable, well-marked channel, which allows vessels to safely transit this hazard.

Southbound captains should bring their vessels between the northeasternmost aids to navigation on the Card Bank cut, flashing daybeacon #17 and unlighted daybeacon #16. Swing to the southwest, and point for the gap between unlighted daybeacons #18 and #19. Continue on the same heading, eventually passing between flashing daybeacon #20 and unlighted daybeacon #21. After leaving #20 and #21 behind, cruisers will pass out into the wider and far deeper waters of Little Card Sound.

Mariners must next traverse the 1.3 nautical mile section of the ICW that cuts southwest across the heart of Little Card Sound. That's right; there is only one aid to navigation whatsoever on this entire body of water. Flashing daybeacon #22 comes

up just short of the fixed, high-rise Card Sound Bridge. Before passing through this span, cruisers can break off to the east to anchor.

Little Card Sound Anchorage Depart the Waterway some 25 yards to the northeast of flashing daybeacon #22. Cruise to the east-southeast of the causeway leading to the Card Sound Bridge, keeping at least 350 yards off the southerly banks. This maneuver will serve to help you avoid the charted sunken wreck. Once you are east of this potential obstruction, consider dropping the hook a good 350 to 400 yards off the sound's southeasterly corner (near 25 17.242 North/080 21.405 West). DO NOT make a closer approach to any of the surrounding shorelines, unless you want Sea Tow's stock to take a rise.

ICW into Barnes Sound Please take your time when cruising under the Card Sound Bridge and entering the northern headwaters of Barnes Sound. This is a rather difficult stretch of the Florida Keys' ICW, and it demands careful attention to business.

Come abeam of flashing daybeacon #22 to its southeasterly side, and then set course for the central pass-through of the Card Sound Bridge. This fixed span has a vertical clearance of the usual 65 feet.

Once through the bridge, continue on more or less the same course, pointing for the gap between flashing daybeacon #24 and unlighted daybeacon #23. This is where it gets a bit tricky. The channel now turns rather quickly to the south-southeast. You must be SURE to make this swing, or you will land almost immediately in 2 feet of water. Set course to pass some 20 yards (NO more) to the west of unlighted daybeacon #25 and then continue on, passing between flashing daybeacon #26 and unlighted daybeacon #27. You made it! Now the wide waters of Barnes Sound stretch out before you to the south.

The turn in the Waterway passage at flashing daybeacon #24 and unlighted daybeacon #23, described above, is an even greater problem for northbound navigators. It's all too easy to head for the bridge's central pass-through, thinking that you are doing just what needs to be done.

WRONG! This strategy will almost certainly lead to that sad sound of your keel meeting with the bottom. Instead, you must deviate quite some distance to the east, to pick up the cut's first pair of markers, flashing daybeacon #26 and unlighted daybeacon #27. Be SURE to pass through these two aids to navigation BEFORE turning to the north-northwest and beginning your approach to the bridge. On the water, #26 and #27 will seem to be much farther to the east than chart 11451 would lead you to expect.

Continuing our help for a moment to northbound mariners, after leaving #26 and #27 behind, pass unlighted daybeacon #25 by no more than 20 yards to its westerly side, and then come between flashing daybeacon #24 and unlighted daybeacon #23. Only now does the channel cut to the north-northeast and head towards the bridge's pass-through. Who planned this channel—some Washington bureaucrat?

On the ICW Are you getting a little tired of long treks between aids to navigation on the Florida Keys ICW? Well then, sorry to say, you won't be happy with the Waterway's passage across Barnes Sound either. How does a cruise of some 4.85 nautical miles from flashing daybeacon #26 at the sound's northern entrance to the northerly entrance into Jewfish Creek grab you?

We are happy to report that Barnes Sound is generally deep, and there is virtually no danger of running aground if you stay anywhere within shouting distance of its centerline. Between the Card Sound Bridge and Jewfish Creek, there are several excursions off the Waterway for cruising skippers to consider.

Alabama Jack's Cruisers bound for Alabama Jack's should cut 90 degrees to the west-northwest, immediately south of the Card Sound Bridge. This channel is completely unmarked, and it can be quite difficult for newcomers to find the good water. All the locals are constantly telling us that, "you can't miss the channel." Translation: It can be hard to find for those who don't already know where it is.

Even under the best of circumstances, depths at low water can run to 5 feet. Eventually, a small canal will open out before you. Alabama Jack's will be sighted a bit farther upstream overlooking the northerly banks.

Glades Canal and South Dade Marina As long as 5-foot depths are not a problem for your vessel, the approach channel leading to Glades Canal and South Dade Marina is adequate. The channel markings are anything but adequate, however, and they aren't correctly depicted on the current edition of chart 11451. The outer marker is actually a small unlighted daybeacon #3, not unlighted daybeacon #2 as shown on the chart. Come abeam and pass #3 by some 25 yards to its easterly side, and set a course to the northwest across the body of Manatee Bay.

There is only one other navigational aid on this channel. Unlighted daybeacon #5 (NOT unlighted daybeacon #3 as shown on 11451) sits hard by the point where the channel passes into the southeasterly mouth of Glade Canal. Pass #5 to your port side and continue upstream holding the midline. It is a lengthy passage of almost 1.5 nautical miles between #3 and #5. Good luck!

Depths on the Glade Canal deepen to 10+ feet. Eventually, the offshoot leading to South Dade Marina will cut off to the west. Several low-key markers lead you into the dockage basin.

Manatee Bay Anchorage Cruisers making for the shallow anchorage on Manatee Bay should begin running the approach channel leading to Glades Canal, described above. Abandon this cut about halfway between unlighted daybeacons #3 and #5. Slow to idle speed and cruise carefully northeast into the main body of Manatee Bay, feeling your way along with the sounder. Be SURE to drop anchor at least 200 yards (preferably 300 yards) off any of the surrounding banks. Sea Tow would love for you to make a closer approach to shore.

Cormorant Rookeries Anchorage The outermost markers on the Manatee Creek channel (see below) are useful in helping to locate the more southerly of the two keys that chart 11451 labels as "Cormorant Rookeries." These small keys lie a short hop north-northeast of unlighted daybeacon #2. Set course to come abeam of the island by some 250 yards to its easterly side. This is the place to anchor. Please remember that landing by dinghy is not permitted on these islands.

Manatee Creek Channel To find your way to Manatee Creek, cruise towards Division Point. As you approach this promontory, use your binoculars to pick out unlighted daybeacons #1 and #2, the outermost marks on this entrance channel. Pass between #1 and #2 and set course to the north-northwest.

Now it gets more than a little tricky. You have to bypass a semisunken wreck and pick between two competing pairs of unlighted daybeacons. Once again, use your trusty binocs and look to the north-northwest for a hull sticking out of the water. Point to pass this old wreck by some 25 yards off your port side. As you pass, it becomes apparent that this derelict is the remains of a once proud sailcraft.

Not to be repetitive, but for the third time, pick up the binoculars. First, look to the northwest. You will see a pair of markers, unlighted daybeacons #1 and #2. These two aids serve a private dock and should be ignored. Instead, continue on to the north-northwest, hunting for a whole series of markers. These aids to navigation outline an eventual turn to the west and an entry into the interior section of Manatee Creek. While running this cut, you will spot a whole bevy of vessels on the surrounding waters. Some seem to be partially sunk, while others (obviously vessels with very shallow draft) are anchored. We can only tell you that we sounded a mere 3 feet of water every time we tried to check out this seeming anchorage. We suggest that you leave anchoring (or sinking) on the waters adjacent to Manatee Creek strictly to the locals.

Southwestern Barnes Sound Anchorages It doesn't require any sort of sophisticated navigation to make good your cruise to the two anchorages (at least) that occupy the waters of southwestern Barnes Sound. We suggest departing the ICW several hundred yards north of flashing daybeacon #29 (which is itself several hundred yards north of Jewfish Creek's northerly mouth).

Cruise to the west, for about 1.3 nautical miles before turning south and feel your way to within some 400 yards (no closer) of the southern banks. This cruising plan's initial track due west will help to avoid the shallows lying west and northwest of Jewfish Creek's northerly entrance.

Wise captains, bound for the more sheltered overnight stop off Division Point, should continue working their way west towards this point of land. You may spot unlighted daybeacons #1 and #2, north of the point. We met these aids in regards to the Manatee Creek entrance cut reviewed above. They can serve to identify Division Point for mariners looking to anchor on these waters.

Drop the hook some 100 yards south of Division Point and 100 yards off the westerly banks. We like the waters near 25 12.870 North/080 25.055 West.

Thursday Cove Anchorage It doesn't get much simpler than this fellow cruisers. Leave the comfortable confines of the Waterway about 200 to 300 yards north of flashing daybeacon #29. Cruise into the midwidth of the cove, which will open out to the southeast. Be sure to drop anchor before approaching to within less than 100 yards of the shoreline. Closer in, soundings rise to 5-foot levels. Captains piloting craft that are comfortable with these sorts of soundings can squeeze to the south and southeast just a bit more.

ICW into Jewfish Creek Be sure to identify flashing daybeacon #29. This is an important aid to navigation. It serves as the northernmost marker on the dredged cut leading into northerly Jewfish Creek. The waters outside of the ICW are very shallow between #29 and the creek. Slow down and be sure to pick out all the marks, and pass each one to its appropriate side.

From a position abeam of #29 (to its westerly side), point to pass between unlighted daybeacons #30 and #31. It's then only a quick hop south into the stream's northerly entrance.

Jewfish Creek is very sheltered and in all but the very strongest northerly blows, you will quickly leave any choppy water behind. Two more unlighted daybeacons, #32 and #34, will be spotted north of the Jewfish Creek Bridge. Pass both these markers to their easterly sides.

Soon the Waterway will bring cruisers within sight of the low-level Jewfish Creek bascule bridge. Slow to idle speed. The waters immediately north and south of the bridge are an official no-wake zone.

The Jewfish Creek span has a closed vertical clearance of only 11 feet and a semirestrictive opening schedule. Siggghhhh! This span opens only on the hour and half-hour Thursday through Sundays, year round, from 10:00 A.M. 'til sunset. The rest of the time, it opens on demand. Wonder who determines when sunset is going to occur on any particular day?

Immediately south of the Jewfish Creek Bridge, Gilbert's Resort Marina will be quite obvious to the west, while the high-rise condo associated with Anchorage Resort and Yacht Club towers over the easterly banks.

Cruisers bound for small but friendly Big Kahuna Fishing Village and Boat Rental should cut east of the Waterway and pass just south of the Anchorage Resort and Yacht Club's docks. Very soon, a small creek will open out to the east. Big Kahuna lines the northerly shores.

Now, it's only a proverbial hop, skip, and a jump south into Blackwater Sound. You've made it—by all accounts your hull is now slipping through the waters of the Florida Keys. Let's hurry on to the next chapter and see what lies ahead.

Hawk Channel to Largo Sound

Captains who choose to head south by way of Hawk Channel have their first opportunity to enter this passage south of Cape Florida. It's worthwhile to pause for a moment and reiterate our advice about Hawk Channel, found in this guide's introduction. If your craft exceeds 45 feet in overall length, or most importantly, if she draws 5 feet or more, then by all means, follow the "way of the Hawk" as opposed to the inside-ICW passage.

Most larger cruising craft will want to leave Biscayne Bay by way of Biscayne Channel (see below). After running this cut and turning your bow to the south on Hawk Channel, be advised that it is a run of almost 40 nautical miles before you meet up with the Largo Sound channel, home of the first cruiser-friendly marina and anchorage (also known as "mooring field") south of Key Biscayne.

There are a few other marinas along the way, most notably the elegant Ocean Reef Resort and Marina, south of Angelfish Creek. Unfortunately, this facility offers only fuel to visiting cruisers, unless you are lucky enough to own property in the complex or you are a guest of a member. Garden Cove Marina near Rattlesnake Key does not accept transients, and the entrance channel is, shall we say, challenging.

Happily, this situation changes for the better in Largo Sound. While the entrance channel sports a few 5½-foot dead-low-tide soundings, most of the route is deep. After traversing a fairly lengthy but marked passage, cruisers can find their way to the John Pennekamp Coral Reef State Park Marina. Several slips are kept open for transients, and there is an adjacent mooring field.

Anchorages along this initial portion of

Hawk Channel are minimal. You can anchor inside of Caesar Creek and Angelfish Creek, but only the latter stream boasts a truly reliable channel. Swinging room on the various Angelfish havens is not sufficient for craft larger than 38 feet. Don't even think about dropping the hook overnight in the open waters off of Hawk Channel, unless there is nary a chance of foul weather in the forecast for the next several days.

In addition to the four channels south of Cape Florida outlined immediately below, there are three other streams north of Largo Sound that connect Hawk Channel to the inland route. Of these three, only Angelfish Creek has a reliable, well-marked channel.

A run of 40 nautical miles through semi-open water is nothing to—proverbially—sneeze at. For our money, we always make sure that our craft is in top condition, and the tanks are topped off, before beginning this run. It would also be a very smart idea to check the latest NOAA weather forecast once and then twice before committing to this passage. Good luck!

Cape Florida Passages to Hawk Channel

There are actually four routes a short hop south of Cape Florida that cruisers could theoretically use to make the watery transition from Biscayne Bay to Hawk Channel. However, only the northernmost and southernmost are fit for larger pleasure craft. The two middle cuts are very treacherous, even though they boast a few low-key aids to navigation.

Moving north to south, the first channel

Stilt house on Biscayne Bay (Cape Florida Lighthouse in background)

(which we shall hereafter call the Cape Florida Channel) is the same passage we met earlier in this chapter as part of our review of the No Name Harbor anchorage. This cut has minimal markings, and the northwesterly portion of the run borders on shallow water to the south and southwest. Minimum depths seem to run 6 feet or better. The charted 5-foot sounding immediately west of Cape Florida did not show up during our repetitive soundings we took on these waters. We think it's safe to say that this obstruction has been removed.

However, as one cruises southeast from Cape Florida to eventually intersect the easterly reaches of the Biscayne Channel, it is quite possible that your sounder may only show 6 feet of water as you make your approach to flashing daybeacon #6. Be SURE to check out the navigational account of the Cape Florida Channel in the next navigational section of this chapter BEFORE attempting to run this cut.

As mentioned above, the two middle channels are doubtful at best. The northern of the two is marked on its westerly extreme by unlighted daybeacon #1 and flashing daybeacon #A. While we did eventually find these two aids to navigation, they are not easy to spot, and there are no other markers of any kind on this cut. The southern of the two middle passages sports unlighted daybeacon #3 on its westerly tip. This is the soul aid to navigation on this channel. Both passages border on very shoal waters to the north and south; need we say more? We highly suggest that you use either the Biscayne Channel (preferably—see below) or the Cape Florida route.

Unless you are on your way to or from No Name Harbor, or have a yen to see the Cape Florida Lighthouse up close and personal, your best bet for putting out into Hawk Channel from northerly Biscayne Bay is the

extremely well-marked Biscayne Channel, southernmost of the four cuts, south of Cape Florida. This fortunate passage carries minimum 8-foot depths, with typical soundings of 10 to 15 feet or better. Careful attention must be paid, however, to the copious aids to navigation. An unintended departure from the channel could easily land you in 1 foot of water.

With these standard precautions in mind, pleasure vessels of most any size that draw 6½ feet or less can make use of the Biscayne Channel with as much confidence as is ever possible on those often tenuous connections between inland and offshore waters. Take your time, sort out all the markers, and be sure to review the navigational account of this passage below.

Caesar Creek

The easterly tip of the marked channel leading to Caesar Creek comes up west of flashing daybeacon #20, at approximately 25 23.100 North/080 11.622 West. Both the creek's seaward entrance cut and its counterpart leading into Biscayne Bay are well outlined by aids to navigation. However, minimum low-water depths of 5 feet on the Hawk Channel portion of the cut, and low-tide soundings of 4 feet on the connector to Biscayne Bay render these waters unfit for vessels larger than 36 feet or (more importantly) those boats drawing 4 feet or better. Be advised, tidal currents run fiercely on Caesar Creek.

That's the bad news. On the other hand, if your boat fits the somewhat rigorous size and draft requirements outlined above, then Caesar Creek offers interesting scenery and access to the Biscayne National Park Adams Key Visitors' Center, a backwater anchorage, and to Biscayne Bay (plus the nearby ICW-inside route).

Moving east to west, first up is the Adams Key Park Service dock, which overlooks Caesar Creek's northerly shores, hard by unlighted daybeacon #22 (approximately 25 23.851 North/080 14.081 West). While no overnight stays are allowed, visitors can tie temporarily (during daylight hours) to the outer edge of the 125-foot face pier in 6-foot minimum depths. It's then an elementary matter to step ashore and make use of the visitors' center's shaded picnic ground, public bathrooms, and charcoal grills. There is also an adjacent half-mile hiking trail. The Park Service has informed us that the Adams Key facility is the least frequented of its centers. During our three visits, we have never seen another boat and only once observed anyone making use of the picnic tables.

Have your largest fenders ready when approaching the Adams Key Park dock. The strong tidal currents can sometimes make for a brusque meeting between your boat's rub rail and the pier's pilings.

Cruisers looking to anchor off on the waters of Caesar Creek can cut southwest off the main channel, some 30 yards southeast of unlighted daybeacon #23, and follow a narrow, unmarked track to the sheltered waters lying between beautifully undeveloped Reid and Rubicon Keys. Be warned that this unbuoyed track is surrounded by 1-foot shallows. On a clear, sunny day, or with a GPS interfaced with a laptop computer (plus a digitized version of chart 11451 and appropriate navigational software), you can probably follow this passage with relative ease. Caution should still be your watchword. In low light or stormy conditions, this task may be all but impossible.

If you persevere, this side channel eventually leads to a creeklike patch of good water lying between Reid and Rubicon Keys. Here, you can anchor a vessel as large as 36 feet amidst at least 8 feet of water, near 25 23.701 North/080 14.441 West. There is excellent shelter from all but strong southwesterly winds. Once the tricky entrance channel is left behind, this stream is an idyllic overnight haven. During September of 2000, we dropped the hook here and watched the sun slowly sink into the waters of Biscayne Bay to the west. We could have sworn we heard it sizzle as it disappeared into the mirror-smooth waters.

One of the best things about Caesar Creek is its connection with Biscayne Bay. As correctly forecast by chart 11451, the channel curves north around the southwestern and western shores of Adams Key, and then takes a 90-degree turn to the west-northwest near unlighted daybeacon #25. This westerly track leads, in turn, to the deeper waters of Biscayne Bay. Unfortunately, you must cruise through some 4-foot low-water soundings to get there.

There is yet another nearby anchorage possibility for shallow-draft vessels only. Notice that a second channel continues north-northeast past the main cut's westerly turn. Several markers outline this passage. After cruising between unlighted daybeacons #5 and #6, you can turn to the east-southeast and anchor at approximately 25 24.358 North/080 13.724 West. While the initial section of this cut holds at least 6 feet, depths drop to low-water soundings of about 4 feet as you cruise east into the anchorage. Obviously, this haven is ONLY meant for boats drawing 3½ feet or (preferably) less. There is good shelter to the south-southeast and east. There is no protection from northern or northwestern winds. The surrounding shores of both Adams and Elliott Keys are about as beautiful as any cruiser has a right to expect.

Be SURE to read the navigational narrative of Caesar Creek in the following section. It contains mandatory information for first-timers.

Broad Creek

The shallow entrance to Broad Creek cuts the westerly banks, west of unlighted daybeacon #24. In a word or two, this is one of those passages between Hawk Channel and Biscayne Bay that should be strictly relegated to our outboard and I/O brethren.

On a calm, sunny day in August 2000, fearless research assistant, Bob Horne, and Claiborne actually did make it through Broad Creek in a shallow draft, 25-foot, outboard-powered craft. It is not an experience that we would want to quickly repeat. The channel, such as it is, is completely unmarked, and the only possible way to proceed is by eyeball navigation. Even with these perfect conditions, we would never even consider taking a cruising-sized vessel through this cut. Depths outside of the channel run to a half-foot, and the westerly passage into Card Sound is a "take your best guess" situation. Our advice: keep on trucking!

Angelfish Creek

Angelfish Creek makes into the westerly flank of Hawk Channel, west-southwest of unlighted daybeacon #24. The easterly extreme of the creek's entrance channel can be found at (approximately) 25 19.639 North/080 15.012 West.

This fortunate body of water (at last) provides a reliable means to cruise from Hawk

Channel to the inside-ICW route and vice versa. Minimum MLW depths run about 6 feet, with the vast majority of the stream exhibiting much deeper soundings. There are also, thankfully, no bridges spanning Angelfish to worry with. If it weren't for the presence of some prodigious tidal currents, this channel would be a breeze.

Angelfish Creek boasts marked entrance channels running into its interior reaches from both Hawk Channel and Card Sound (the inside-ICW passage). The shallowest portions of the entire Angelfish Creek passage are found at the western and eastern ends of these two approach cuts. Here, captains can expect their depth sounders to show some 6-foot readings, but once into the stream's interior reaches, don't be surprised to find yourself in 7 to 15 feet of water.

A small portion of the sumptuous Ocean Reef development (see below) is visible to the south, but for the most part, the shores of Angelfish Creek are delightfully undeveloped. Quite simply, this is a beautiful stream whose passage will undoubtedly engender more than its share of eye candy for nature lovers.

Now, as if all that weren't enough, Angelfish Creek offers overnight anchorage for vessels as large as a 38-footer. All are set in completely natural surroundings, and most boast good shelter, even in really foul weather. Before reviewing these havens, however, allow us to once again call your attention to the strong tidal currents, which regularly scour these waters. Be SURE the anchor is well set before heading below to begin a memorable evening meal.

Moving east to west, study chart 11451, Page B, Inset 3 and notice the combined mouths of Middle and Linderman creeks making into the northerly flank of Angelfish Creek, east of unlighted daybeacon #10. If you can stand the initial 4½-foot depths, Linderman Creek can lead to two potential havens. Good depths of 6 feet or better are in the offing northwest of the intersection with Middle Creek.

The first anchor-down spot to consider is found on the widening body of Linderman Creek, abeam of the unnamed offshoot, which makes off from the northeasterly banks some .12 nautical miles north-northwest of the juncture with Middle Creek (near 25 20.385 North/080 16.085 West). Here, amidst 7-foot depths, cruisers will find plenty of swinging room for a 38-footer.

Those who are up for a bit more exploration can continue tracking their way upstream to the waters abeam of the first two of the three small, unnamed islands south of charted Linderman Key (near 25 20.556 North/080 16.266 West). Here minimum depths also run around 7 feet, and there should be enough room for a boat as large as 38 feet (at least). Particularly strong winds from the west blowing up the mouth of Linderman Creek could be a bit of a problem here.

The next two anchorages lie west of unlighted daybeacon #10. Here, a southerly offshoot of Middle Creek cuts into the northern shores. By holding to the centerline, it's a relatively simple proposition to cruise north into the main body of Middle Creek. Cut to the west and drop anchor near the point where chart 11451 (Page B, Inset 3) shows a 10-foot sounding (near 25 20.253 North/080 16.422 West). Minimum depths are 6 feet, and there should be enough elbowroom for a 36-footer.

Finally, captains who pilot boats 34 feet and smaller, and whose craft can cruise

through 5-foot (low-water) depths without finding the bottom, might consider charming Little Pumpkin Creek. This stream cuts the southern banks of Angelfish Creek, some .2 nautical miles west of unlighted daybeacon #10. The mouth of the stream carries only 5 feet of water, and these depths continue upstream for a short stretch. Then, depths improve to 6 and 7 feet. Drop anchor before cruising into the correctly charted, lazy turn to the west. Some light residential development associated with Ocean Reef is visible from Little Pumpkin Creek, but the presence of the palatial homes adds to, rather than detracts from, the visual appeal of this anchorage.

Ocean Reef

The two channels serving the Ocean Reef Yacht Club cut the waters of Hawk Channel a short hop south of Angelfish Creek, almost 3 nautical miles west-southwest of unlighted daybeacon #2. The more southerly passage provides access to the complex's marina, fuel dock, and repair facilities. This cut's easterly entrance lies near 25 18.505 North/080 16.050 West.

Any of you who have had the good fortune to visit the elegant Ocean Reef Club will not be surprised when we term it the "Palm Beach of the Florida Keys." The palatial homes look as if they have just been magically transported from Beverly Hills, and the accommodations are enough to make Worth Avenue proud.

If you are a member of the Ocean Reef Yacht Club (305-367-9021) or a guest of an accredited member, you will discover a fine, well-sheltered marina a short hop up the entrance canal. After passing the fuel pier to starboard, the dockage basin will open out to the north. If they are open to you (see below), slips consist of fixed concrete piers, sporting (as you might have guessed) every power, fresh water, telephone, and cable television connection imaginable. Absolute minimum depths in the entrance channel are 8 feet, with typical soundings in the 9 to 15 foot range. Impressive soundings of at least 13 feet are found dockside. Waste pump-out service is available for those staying at the marina only.

Now for the less-than-happy news: the only services open to visitors are gasoline and diesel fuel purchases from the fuel dock on the canal. Several conversations between the Ocean Reef marina personnel and both authors of this guidebook made it very, very clear that uninvited visitors are not welcome. Oh yes, if you should purchase fuel here, hold on to your wallet. In September of 2000, we pumped the most expensive gasoline of our entire cruising careers at Ocean Reef.

So, unless you are one of the select few, or you are in immediate need of fuel, keep your bow pointed south. Of course, it doesn't hurt to pick up your binoculars and scope out all the stately Ocean Reef structures visible from the water. Just try not to sigh too loudly.

The "Nevermore" Marina

Some older cruising guides list a marina located on the T-shaped harbor that indents the shores of Key Largo, northwest of unlighted daybeacon #29. One bright September day, this guide's authors went looking for this facility. While we could see what appeared to be a dockmaster's office and some piers in the distance, it proved impossible to find an entrance channel. We later learned that the one-time entry cut has now been completely walled off by rocks. The approach channel from the Gulf is now completely unmarked, and while we were able to find it by eyeball navigation this sunny day, this old passage is NOT recommended for any size vessel. All this is a long-winded way of saying, "It's not there anymore, and don't try to get to it."

Garden Cove Marina
(25 10.240 North/080 22.251 West)

A prolifically marked channel lies west of Hawk Channel's flashing daybeacon #32. This cut leads first southwest and then west to a sheltered canal that serves as the home for Garden Cove Marina (305-451-4694). Low-water depths in the entrance passage of only 4 feet (possibly 3½ feet in a few places), the nebulous presence of underwater rocks, and an old derelict barge lying near the channel, lead off a list of less-than-fortunate qualities.

The dockmaster at Garden Cove Marina told us about a big rock in the middle of the channel just shoreward of the unlighted daybeacon #1 at the cut's entrance. He said that local boats made some big course changes to avoid it, but he had never been out there to see about it personally. We sounded this portion of the channel several times, and did not find any rocks, but you may not be so fortunate.

If you do successfully make your way into the canal west of unlighted daybeacon #19, depths improve surprisingly to 12 feet or better. The marina will be spotted overlooking the stream's westerly terminus.

Garden Cove Marina doesn't accept transients, which is probably a blessing in disguise. The condition of the marina itself is rather poor. We have seen worse, but this is the low end on Key Largo proper. On top of that, the way in is something of a riddle, wrapped in a mystery and surrounded by an enigma. It seems odd that Garden Cove is the closest marina on the ocean side to the Ocean Reef Club, which is absolutely the most exclusive facility around, and private to boot; yet Garden Cove has gained nothing by its proximity. There are water connections on the docks, but no waste pump-out, no showers, and no Laundromat. They sell gas but no diesel.

There is a restaurant in the marina. While it is architecturally attractive, we were there on a Saturday night and the place was virtually vacant, which tells you something. It offers standard Keys fish and fowl and beef. We think that the marina and the restaurant are ripe for a time-share or something equally unappealing.

John Pennekamp Coral Reef State Park, Marina, and Mooring Field
(25 07.459 North/080 24.439 West—Marina Position)

The most important channel on this entire portion of Hawk Channel comes up south of Lower Sound Point, north-northwest of Mosquito Bank's flashing daybeacon #35 (approximately 25 05.773 North/080 23.839 West). This west-northwestward-running cut boasts 5½- to 6-foot minimum depths and leads to a deep, sheltered canal that, in turn, carries cruisers northeast to the headquarters of the John Pennekamp Coral Reef State Park,

John Pennekamp Coral Reef State Park Marina

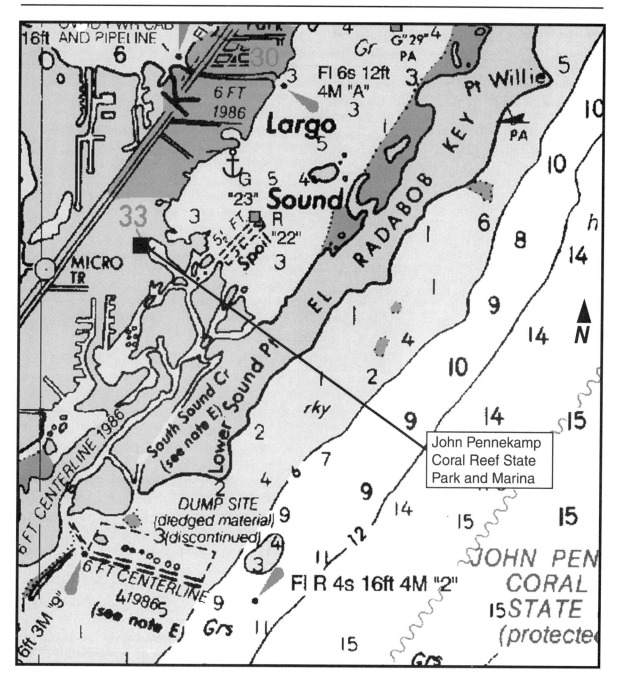

its like-named marina, and eventually, the enchanting waters of Largo Sound.

The John Pennekamp Coral Reef State Park

is a big state park with lots of people, most of whom are interested in diving. This is the first undersea park in the country. In fact, it features the only living coral reef in the United States. It encompasses a total of 63,000 acres (uplands and submerged) and has coral heads, mangrove swamps, and seagrass beds in its offshore sections. It's named after Miami newspaper editor John D. Pennekamp, who was a mover and a shaker behind the establishment of the Everglades National Park, when ecology was a word that no one knew anything of and cared less about.

There are two nature trails in the park, and two man-made beaches are also available for swimming. The visitors' center has a 30,000-gallon saltwater aquarium, as well as smaller aquariums. Also present are educational displays and a theater where videos about the park and natural resources are shown.

The park features its own marina. Captains bound for this facility should take a 90-degree turn to the to the northwest, off the main canal, at unlighted daybeacon #19. There are two sizes of slips available and a total of nine. The large, fixed wooden slips will take a vessel with a 14-foot beam and 60-foot length. The small slips (also of the fixed wooden variety) will take a vessel with a 10-foot beam and 35-foot length. Depths alongside run 6 feet or better in most berths, though some of the smaller, inner slips may only have 5 feet of water. Fresh water hookups, as well as power connections up to 30 amps and waste pump-out service, are in the offing.

There are showers ashore, but they are outside affairs. The food available is concession sandwiches. This is a state park, remember? Other things available are: glass-bottom boat tours, snorkeling tours, sailing and snorkeling tours, scuba tours, scuba instruction, scuba equipment rentals, and boat rentals.

If the sandwich fare at the park sounds a bit skimpy and you want a break from your boat, there are restaurants up on U.S. 1, but the selection within walking distance is sparse. If you are looking for a better choice, call a cab and surf U.S. 1 both ways. Something will tickle your fancy.

John Pennekamp Coral Reef State Park, Marina, and Mooring Field (305) 451-1202
http://www.pennekamppark.com

Approach depth—5½-15 feet
Dockside depth—6 feet (a few smaller slips have some 5-foot depths)
Accepts transients—yes
Type of docking—fixed wooden piers
Dockside power connections—up to 30 amp
Dockside water connections—yes
Waste pump-out—yes
Showers—yes (outside)
Restaurant—none on site and but a meager selection nearby

Cruisers who prefer to spend their evening in a bit less frequented setting can continue following the main canal out into the wide, and usually tranquil, reaches of Largo Sound. This is a beautiful body of water that is well sheltered from all but particularly strong northern and northeastern blows. The westerly shores show moderate, though not unsightly, residential development, while the ocean-side banks are entirely in their natural state. Northeast of unlighted daybeacons #22 and #23, the good people at John Pennekamp State Park have established a mooring field to the east and west of the main channel. Anchoring is NOT allowed on the sound's waters, so your only option is to pick up a buoy. In total, there are 11 mooring buoys for transients, and the average water depth is 5½ feet in the mooring buoy field. The buoys rent for $15 a day, which includes trash disposal and holding tank pump-out. The time limit in the mooring buoy field is two weeks. Check at

Public Beach (John Pennekamp Coral Reef State Park)

John Pennekamp State Park Tour Boat (Largo Sound)

the park marina or call (305) 451-1202 to make arrangements to moor in the field.

Marvin D. Adams Waterway

Small, shallow-draft boats (ONLY) can follow a narrow canal, officially known as the Marvin D. Adams Waterway, from Largo Sound to the southern foot of Blackwater Sound. A short spurt to the west on the waters of Blackwater Sound will bring you to the inside-ICW route. The canal's easterly entrance is outlined by flashing daybeacon #A, while flashing daybeacon #B denotes its westerly mouth.

This small passage would be a very useful shortcut between Hawk Channel - Largo Sound and the ICW if it were not for its 4 1/2 foot depths (at the eastern and western entrances), a 14-foot fixed bridge crossing the canal along its passage, and the strong tidal currents that regularly boil through this waterway. Are you beginning to get the idea? We once successfully piloted a 31-foot, fly bridge equipped powercraft through this stream, but it's a feat that neither of us would choose to repeat again.

If you pilot an outboard or I/O powered vessel 25 feet and smaller, don't hesitate to make cautious use of the Marvin D. Adams Waterway. Otherwise, it's certainly best to keep trucking south down Hawk Channel to either Tavernier or Snake Creek before making the transition from the outside to inside routes.

HAWK CHANNEL—KEY BISCAYNE TO LARGO SOUND NAVIGATION

The northerly extreme of Hawk Channel intersects deep Government Cut Inlet, running seaward from Miami Beach. This passage is covered in our *Cruising Guide to Eastern Florida,* so we need pause here only to say that cruisers exiting this cut can turn south-southwest from flashing buoy #1 and begin their trek down Hawk Channel.

Many other cruisers, particularly those interested in visiting the waters and facilities of northerly Biscayne Bay will choose to make use of the Biscayne Channel (south of Key Biscayne), outlined below.

There are no unusual navigational difficulties on this initial section of Hawk Channel from Key Biscayne to Largo Sound. This run is very typical of the entire route. Aids to navigation are tall, but widely spaced. We always keep a good DR track while making this run, and it's not a bad idea to have the GPS up and running as well. Oh yes, be sure to keep chart 11451 at hand to quickly resolve any questions that might arise.

At times, shallows associated with the reefs guarding the easterly flanks of Hawk Channel brush elbows with the main passage. Be mindful of these very real hazards as you are cruising gaily along.

As with all other sections of Hawk Channel, these waters can become more than slightly choppy if the wind gets its dander up. By all accounts, this is not a trip to be undertaken by pleasure craft in foul weather. It's far better to stay in port, play another hand or two of bridge or two, and wait for fair weather to once again appear over the horizon.

With these elementary precautions in mind, sit back, relax, and enjoy the clear and sparkling waters. Try not to grin too widely as you make your way south into "paradise."

Key Biscayne Passages to Hawk Channel
Study the waters south of Key Biscayne on chart 11451 and you will soon discern that there are actually four channels, all of which have at least some markings, that provide access from Biscayne Bay and the ICW passage to Hawk Channel. The southernmost, Biscayne Channel, is by far the best marked and most reliable. The northernmost, Cape Florida cut is also useable, but more caution is required. The two middle passages are best avoided.

Moving north to south, let's first turn our attention to the Cape Florida Channel. To run this cut, come abeam of flashing daybeacon #4 by at least 50 yards to its southerly side. Then point for the gap between unlighted daybeacon #2 and (currently uncharted) unlighted daybeacon #1. Daybeacons #4 and #2, mark a large patch of very shallow water making out from the westerly shores of Key Biscayne. It is fortunate that unlighted daybeacon #1 has been added since the last edition of chart 11451 went to press. This aid marks a clearly and correctly charted patch of 2- and 3-foot shoals south of the cut. Keep both these hazards very clearly in mind as you run the initial portion of the Cape Florida Channel.

After passing between #1 and #2, turn to the southeast and follow the shoreline, keeping some 200 yards off the banks. Not to be repetitive, but please let me once more warn you about the 2- and 3-foot depths flanking the channel's southwesterly limits in this section. There is also a much smaller shelf of shallows making out from the Key Biscayne shoreline east of #2.

Eventually, you will leave the just mentioned shoals behind, and No Name Harbor will come up along the northeasterly banks. This anchorage was discussed earlier in this chapter.

We did not find the charted 5-foot patch, south of No Name Harbor, in spite of repeated soundings taken on these waters. Our readings indicated that minimum 8-foot depths can be expected.

Soon Cape Florida will come abeam to the northeast. Pause for a moment to admire the tall lighthouse. It makes for quite a sight from the water.

After coming abeam of Cape Florida, point directly for flashing daybeacon #6. This aid to navigation is actually part of the Biscayne Channel. It is a far better idea to run the easterly portion of this cut rather than the completely unmarked eastern extreme of the shoal-plagued Cape Florida Channel. Just before reaching #6, alter your course slightly to the south, and come abeam of #6 to its immediate southerly side.

Between Cape Florida and flashing daybeacon #6, very shoal water flanks the channel to the south and southwest. If depths start to rise, you are probably impinging on these shallows. Alter your course a bit to the northeast, and see if soundings improve. Also, don't be surprised to find yourself cruising through some 6-foot low-water depths as you make your approach to #6.

Once abeam of #6, turn a bit farther to the southeast, and point for the gap between unlighted daybeacon #4 and flashing daybeacon #3. Now, use your binoculars to identify flashing daybeacons #1 and #2 to the southeast. These two aids to navigation are the outermost markers on the Biscayne-Cape Florida channel, and it is a healthy run of slightly better than .6 of a nautical mile from #3 and #4 to the gap between #1 and #2. This portion of the channel is often replete with choppy water, so proceed with caution.

After passing between #1 and #2, turn south, and point to pass well east of the tall, 37-foot, unnumbered daybeacon that lies a short hop south of the Biscayne-Cape Florida channel's easterly terminus. This impressive marker heralds your entrance into Hawk Channel. Next stop, Key Largo!

As mentioned repeatedly in this chapter, the two middle channels are best avoided. The northern of the pair is marked on its westerly extreme by unlighted daybeacon #1 and flashing daybeacon #A, while the southern middle cut is denoted by an unlighted daybeacon #3. In spite of the presence of these aids to navigation, we strongly suggest that you use either the Biscayne Channel (see below) or the Cape Florida cut (see above).

The westerly entrance to the deep, exceptionally well-marked Biscayne Channel lies 1.2 miles southeast of the ICW's flashing daybeacon #B, at approximately 25 39.366 North/080 11.139 West. The cut's westernmost markers are flashing daybeacons #20 and #21. Pass between #20 and #21, and then point to come abeam of unlighted daybeacon #19 to its northerly side. Now, pick out the next pair of markers, unlighted daybeacons #18 and #17. Set a course to the east-southeast designed to pass between #18 and #17. At this juncture, the Biscayne Channel turns almost due east. As you continue along, pass south of all red, even-numbered markers, and take green beacons to their northerly quarters.

After running the gap between unlighted daybeacons #7 and #8, continue on more or less the same course until you come abeam of flashing daybeacon #6 to its southerly side. At this point, the channel turns just a bit farther to the southeast. Point to pass between flashing daybeacon #3 and unlighted daybeacon #4. Now, use your binoculars to identify flashing daybeacons #1 and #2 to the southeast. These two aids to navigation are the outermost markers on the Biscayne Channel, and it is a healthy trek of slightly better than .6 of a nautical mile from #3 and #4 to the gap between #1 and #2. This run often takes you through choppy water, so proceed with caution.

After passing between #1 and #2, turn south, and point to pass well east of the tall, 37-foot, unnumbered daybeacon that lies a short hop south of the Biscayne-Cape Florida channel's easterly terminus. This impressive marker heralds your entrance into Hawk Channel.

On Hawk Channel Cruisers southbound on Hawk Channel should generally pass to the east of red, even-numbered aids to navigation and take green markers to their (the markers') westerly sides.

From the unnumbered 37-foot flashing daybeacon, set course to eventually pass between unlighted daybeacons #2 and #3. Daybeacon #3 lies just west of the Fowey Rocks's 110-foot light. Fortunately, no shallow water is found near #3. It is a run of 2.6 nautical miles between the 37-foot marker and the gap between #2 and #3.

Next up is a run of 1.6 nautical miles to a point some 50 yards east of unlighted daybeacon #4. Watch out for the charted, semisunken wreck .4 of a nautical mile east-northeast of #4. Once #4 is in your wake, you must cross a gap of some 3.3 nautical miles before coming abeam and passing unlighted daybeacon #7 to its westerly quarter. It's then only a short hop south to flashing daybeacon #8. As its color would indicate, come abeam of #8 fairly close by its easterly side.

South of flashing daybeacon #8, things become a bit more complicated. Between flashing daybeacon #11BS and unlighted daybeacon #17, Hawk Channel runs hard by the shallows of Bache Shoal and Morgot Fish Shoal, just east of the marked track. Be SURE to stay west of flashing daybeacon #11BS and unlighted daybeacons #13, #15, and #17. Also, be advised that unlighted daybeacon #14, which denotes the channel's westerly flank, marks a rock. It might really make your whole day to pass #14 by at least 25 yards to its easterly side.

From #17, set course to bring unlighted daybeacon #18 abeam by some 25 yards to its easterly side. Between #17 and #18, more shallows lie east of Hawk Channel. Watch for a side-setting wind or current pushing you to the east.

Continue cruising south from #18 for another 2 nautical miles, pointing to bring unlighted daybeacon #19 abeam to its westerly quarter. South of #19, navigators should set course to come abeam of the flashing daybeacon #20 by some 25 yards to its easterly side. West of #20, adventurous cruisers (with shallow-draft vessels) can explore Caesar Creek and its associated visitors' center and anchorage.

Caesar Creek Please remember that minimum depths on the seaward approach channel to Caesar Creek run as thin as 5 feet at mean low water. Also, if you follow the marked channel from Caesar Creek's westerly reaches to Biscayne Bay, low-tide soundings of 4 feet can be expected. This passage is NOT recommended for boats larger than 36 feet or those vessels drawing 4 feet or more.

Also, it would be advisable to remember our earlier admonition about the strong tidal currents that regularly race in and out of Caesar Creek. This is a really good spot to watch the track over your stern, as well as your course ahead, to make sure a lateral current is not easing you out of the channel.

To make good your entry into the seaward approach channel, cut 90 degrees to the west off Hawk Channel, and pass south of flashing daybeacon #20. Then, cruise between unlighted daybeacons #1 and #2, the easternmost aids to navigation on the Caesar Creek cut. The channel winds a bit as you move westward, but it is very well marked with unlighted daybeacons. Anyone who remembers their good, old, "red, right, returning rule", will know to pass all subsequent red aids to navigation to their vessel's starboard side and take green markers to port.

Note that ALL the aids to navigation on this passage are of the unlighted variety. While fair-weather, daylight entries are relatively routine, you will never catch yours truly trying to enter this channel at night or in low-light conditions. May you, too, heed this advice.

The shallowest portion of the seaward approach is found hard by the outermost aids to navigation, unlighted daybeacons #1 and #2. Here, during low tide, don't be surprised if your depth sounder reveals a mere 5 feet of water.

Immediately after passing between unlighted daybeacons #18 and #19, the channel swings to the north-northwest. It's a bit of a long run to the next set of aids to navigation, unlighted daybeacons #20 and #21. Fortunately, the channel is rather broad along this stretch. Just point to stay some 100 yards southwest of charted Christmas Point and its adjacent shoreline. Do notice the correctly charted 2-foot waters to the west and southwest. It would obviously behoove you to stay well away from these shallows.

At #20 and #21, the channel swings again, this time to the west-northwest. Point to come abeam of unlighted daybeacon #22 to its fairly immediate southern side. The Adams Key visitors' center dock lies just north of #22. If you decide to tie up here temporarily, approach with caution, pay the most respectful attention to the tidal currents, and have your largest fenders ready.

Captains making for the enchanting but navigationally challenging anchorage between Reid and Rubicon Keys should depart the main channel some 30 yards southeast of unlighted daybeacon #23. Swing sharply to the southwest, and point for the (more or less) centerline of the passage, which you will spy ahead between the two keys. It is essential to practice eyeball navigation to pick out this unmarked approach channel. Generally, a darker color means deeper water, and a lighter shade denotes a shoal. We suggest that you attempt this side cut only on a clear, sunny day, when it is relatively easy to pick out the good water from the bad.

Once between the two keys, favor the northwestern (Rubicon Keys) shores slightly. By the time you reach the second charted offshoot running to the northwest, good depths of 8 feet or better stretch out almost from shore to shore.

Mariners continuing to Biscayne Bay on the main Caesar Creek channel should pass between unlighted daybeacon #23 and #24, and then cut to the north. Slow down! The collection of markers surrounding the intersection of the channel branch that leads to Biscayne Bay, and the northward-running cut that allows access to a shallow anchorage, can be confusing.

If you are making for Biscayne Bay and the ICW, continue tracking your way north until unlighted daybeacon #25 comes abeam to its easterly side. Swing to the west-northwest and pass between #25 and unlighted junction daybeacon #A. Then, set course to cruise between unlighted daybeacons #27 and #28. This same track will lead you between unlighted daybeacons

#29 and #30. Finally, pass to the south of the unnumbered flashing daybeacon and continue west into the deeper waters of Biscayne Bay.

Be warned that low-water depths of as little as 4 feet are found in the vicinity of #29 and #30. Obviously, captains who pilot vessels that draw 4 feet or more should keep clear.

Cruisers bound for the shallow anchorage to the north should ignore unlighted daybeacon #25, and pass unlighted, junction daybeacon #A to its immediate eastern side. Soon thereafter, you should come abeam and pass unlighted daybeacon #2 fairly close to its western quarter. Look to the northeast, and pick out unlighted daybeacons #3 and #4. Point for the gap between these two markers. Be mindful of the very shallow water on both sides of the channel. Take your time and pay strict attention to business.

Next, set course for the gap between unlighted daybeacons #5 and #6, the northernmost aids to navigation on this side channel. Continue cruising north-northeast of #5 and #6 for some 25 to 40 yards, then cut to the east-southeast and feel your way carefully along for a hundred yards or so with the sounder. Low-water depths of 4 feet are VERY common in this anchorage, so don't even think about going here if these sorts of soundings are a problem for your vessel. Drop the hook before coming abeam of Adams Key's northeasterly tip. East and southeast of this point, depths deteriorate further.

A Perilous Seaward Passage Chart 11451

depicts a scantily marked passage, east-southeast of flashing daybeacon #20, which leads (at least theoretically) through the easterly reefs protecting Hawk Channel into deeper ocean waters. We specifically do not recommend this route for any, save shallow draft, vessels. The channel strays near any number of unmarked 4-foot shoals, and as we learned in this guide's introduction, running around on the coral reefs that flank Hawk Channel can be a very expensive proposition. If you choose to ignore this advice, you're on your own. Good luck—you may need it!

On Hawk Channel South of the Hawk Channel-Caesar Creek intersection, cruisers should set course to pass west of unlighted daybeacon #21. This aid marks some very shallow water just east of its position. Then, point to pass flashing daybeacon #22 to its fairly immediate easterly quarter, and continue on the same course, passing between unlighted daybeacon #23 and #24.

West of #24, it is theoretically possible to run the two Broad Creek entrance channels, but as stated earlier, this unmarked passage is best avoided by all but the smallest powercraft, and even then, local knowledge is most definitely required.

South-southwest of #23 and #24, the main track of Hawk Channel continues on the same heading. For reasons that have always escaped our understanding, there is an unlighted daybeacon #2, which lies well east of the principal passage. We suggest you completely ignore this #2. In fact, favor the westerly side of Hawk Channel a bit to avoid the charted, sunken wreck.

About the only real use we can see to unlighted daybeacon #2 is that it lies almost due east of the Angelfish Creek Channel. This useful passage will be our next focus of attention.

Angelfish Creek Tidal currents make their presence known on Angelfish Creek, often in a big way. Watch for lateral leeway as you cruise along. If you should choose to pitch out the hook on one of the creek's side waters, be very sure the anchor is well set before kicking back for the evening.

Use Inset 3, Page B of chart 11451 when navigating Angelfish Creek. It's greater detail is a must.

The outermost (easternmost) markers on the Angelfish Creek entrance channel are flashing daybeacon #2 and unlighted daybeacon #1. Cruisers will most likely encounter the shallowest depths of the entire passage between these two markers. Low-water soundings of as little as 6 feet are usually in the offing. The remainder of the channel and the interior reaches of the creek carry 7 to 15 feet of water.

Continue cruising towards the mouth of Angelfish Creek by passing all red markers to your starboard side, and take green markers to port. That's right, folks. "Red, right, returning" is still in effect.

Between unlighted daybeacons #5 and #8 and Angelfish Creek's easterly mouth, the channel twists to the west far more sharply than a study of chart 11451 would suggest. Pass flashing daybeacon #6 to its southwesterly side, and then point for the gap between #5 and #8. West of #5 and #8, the broad mouth of Angelfish Creek will open out before you. We have noted a tendency to slip a little bit too far to the south between #5 and Angelfish Creek's easterly mouth. Such a mistake may land you into 4½-to 5-foot depths. Stick to the centerline for depths of 7 feet or better.

Moving east to west, the initial reaches of Angelfish Creek are unmarked for the first .75 of a nautical mile. Simply stay within shouting distance of the midwidth, and no problems (other than strong currents) will be encountered.

The first anchorage possibility comes up along the creek's northerly shores, well east of unlighted daybeacon #10. Here the combined mouths of Linderman and Middle creeks meet up with their larger sister. The southerly portion of this stream exhibits soundings of 4½ feet at mean low water, but depths improve markedly northwest of the T-shaped intersection with Middle Creek.

If your craft can stand these depths, enter the creek along its centerline and continue holding to the middle until the T-shaped juncture with Middle Creek is in your wake. Now, good depths of 7 feet or better stretch out almost from shore to shore.

One of the first anchor-down spots you might consider comes up abeam of the first small offshoot that cuts the northeasterly banks, northwest of the "T" intersection. Drop anchor in the middle of the widening waters.

The intrepid explorers among us can continue upstream to the waters abeam of the small island formed by the first two small offshoots running north to Linderman Key. Anchor south of the island on the midwidth, and settle down for a night of peace and security.

Back on the main body of Angelfish Creek, skippers will eventually sight unlighted daybeacon #10. Pass to the south of this aid to navigation.

A short hop west of #10, two good anchorage possibilities come abeam to the north and south respectively. First, notice the connector stream that runs north to Middle Creek. Enter this body of water, favoring the west side banks slightly. Continue on to the north until the main body of Middle Creek opens out to the west-northwest. Cruise into the centerline of this stream and drop anchor anywhere short of (east of) the small island that bisects the creek's westerly mouth.

Do not try to cruise into the waters of Card Sound directly from Middle Creek. In spite of the tongue of 10-foot water depicted on chart 11451, very shallow depths are soon encountered.

Moving back to Angelfish Creek, cruisers might also choose to drop the hook on Little Pumpkin Creek to the south. Enter this body of water on its midwidth. For best depths, continue cruising upstream for at least 50 yards before dropping the hook. Be sure to anchor north of the stream's first lazy turn to the west. Soundings deteriorate quickly in the body of this turn.

Cruisers continuing west on Angelfish Creek to Card Sound should favor the northerly shores just slightly west of the intersection with Little Pumpkin Creek. A small band of shallows abuts the southerly banks along this stretch. Pass to the fairly immediate southerly sides of both

unlighted daybeacon #12 and flashing daybeacon #14. West of #14, the wide waters of Card Sound and the nearby ICW passage wait to greet you.

On Hawk Channel South of unlighted daybeacon #24, it is a run of some 3.4 nautical miles to the next aid to navigation, unlighted daybeacon #25. Come abeam of #25 well to its westerly quarter. Between #24 and #25, the two channels serving the Ocean Reef Club cut out from the westerly shores.

Ocean Reef Club Channels Study chart 11451, Inset 3, Page B, and notice that there are actually two marked channels serving the Ocean Reef complex. The northerly cut leads to a host of private piers, while the southerly passage provides access to the Ocean Reef Club Marina. Visiting cruisers should keep clear of the north-side channel.

Remember that only members or guests of members are actually accepted for dockage at the Ocean Reef marina, though the fuel pier is open to all. Just hold on to your wallet.

To make good your entry into Ocean Reef, come abeam of the outermost marker, flashing daybeacon #2 to its southerly side, and set course to pass between the next two markers, unlighted daybeacons #3 and #4. Continue on to the west, passing all subsequent red markers to your starboard side and green beacons to port.

After leaving unlighted daybeacons #19 and #20 in your wake, slow to idle speed as you cruise into a long canal. Eventually, the fuel pier and dockmaster's office will come abeam to the north, followed shortly by the dockage basin, also overlooking the northerly banks.

Route to the Briney Blue Cruisers looking to leave Hawk Channel and make their way out into the open ocean can make use of a marked channel east-northeast of unlighted daybeacon #27. Study chart 11451 closely and notice unlighted daybeacon #6, south of the oblong 2- and 3-foot shoal. Cruise carefully from Hawk Channel to #6, pointing to come abeam of this marker by some 25 yards to its southerly side. Don't slip too far to the south on this run, or you could meet up with the correctly charted 5-foot shoal almost due east of #27.

Take a lazy turn to the north-northeast around #6, and set course to come abeam of unlighted daybeacon #4 by some 25 to 50 yards to its easterly side. You will probably spy unlighted daybeacon #5 to the east while cruising through this northerly turn. Stay well west of #5. By all accounts, DON'T slip to the west between #6 and #4. The correctly charted 2- and 3-foot reef is waiting to say hello to your keel.

Continue on the same north-northeasterly heading and pass unlighted daybeacons #3 and #1 by some 25 to 50 yards to their easterly quarters. A 3-foot shoal lies south of #1, so don't slip to the east as you approach this marker.

Cruise north-northeast of #1 for at least 100 yards, and then turn to the east. Before long, you will pass flashing buoy #4 well north of your course line. Depths now deepen to 30 feet or better. Next stop, the Bahamas?

On Hawk Channel South of unlighted daybeacon #27, set course to pass unlighted daybeacon #29 to its westerly side. From a position abeam of #29, point to come abeam of Hawk Channel's next aid to navigation, flashing daybeacon #3BH, well to the western side. The charted 9½-foot patch will not be a problem for any, save exceptionally deep-draft, vessels.

Moving south-southwest of #31BH, it's a run of about 3 nautical miles to a point abeam of the next marker, flashing daybeacon #32. This marker is located fairly close to shore, and we suggest that you bring it abeam by some .8 nautical miles to its easterly quarter. You need only make a closer approach to #32 if you plan to visit Garden Cove Marina.

Garden Cove Marina The channel to this minimalist facility carries only 3½ to 4 feet at mean low water. We have also been warned of "underwater rocks" near this cut's entrance, though none of these underwater, hardware-smashing obstructions showed up during our research.

If you decide to enter anyway, turn to the west at flashing daybeacon #32, and leave this marker just to your north side. Cruise to the west, and watch for what will appear to be a barge. This semisunken derelict is correctly portrayed on chart 11451. For best depths (such as they are) pass the old barge by about 20 yards to its southerly side.

Shortly thereafter, point for the gap between the outermost channel markers, unlighted daybeacons #1 and #2. From this point, just take all red markers to your starboard side and green markers to port as the channel works its way towards the shoreline.

After passing unlighted daybeacon #19, cruise straight ahead into the canal mouth, which will open out before you. Garden Cove Marina overlooks the westerly terminus of this stream.

You may spot some additional markers making off to the south as you enter the Garden Cove canal. Avoid these like the Black Plague. How do depths of 3 feet or less grab you?

On Hawk Channel The remaining run, 6 nautical miles southwest to a juncture with the Largo Sound approach channel, is a straightforward portion of Hawk Channel that need not be further detailed here. Just be sure to say west of unlighted daybeacon #33 and all should be well.

The next southerly Hawk Channel aid to navigation is flashing daybeacon #35. This marker warns against a large patch of shallows and rocks east and northeast of its position. Quite obviously, you should keep well west of #35.

Short of (northeast of) flashing daybeacon #35, skippers may choose to visit Largo Sound, the John Pennekamp Coral Reef State Park, Marina, and Mooring Field.

Largo Sound-John Pennekamp Coral Reef State Park Channel Chart 11451 does not do justice to the channel running first west and then northeast to Largo Sound and the Pennekamp Marina. The entrance cut and

the canal it leads to are actually marked with a prolific array of daybeacons, very few of which are actually charted. Not to worry—elementary coastal navigation should see you through.

To enter, come abeam of flashing daybeacon #2 to its fairly immediate southerly side. Look to the east, and in spite of what chart 11451 would lead you to believe, you will quickly spy a whole collection of daybeacons outlining the entrance passage. I bet you guessed this one—leave all subsequent red markers to your starboard side and take green aids to navigation to port.

The shallowest portion of the entrance channel will be encountered between #2 and the first pair of unlighted daybeacons. Don't be surprised to note a 6-foot sounding on this stretch of the channel if your arrival coincides with low water.

At flashing daybeacon #9, the channel angles to the northwest and soon enters the mouth of a northeastward-running canal. Ample markings continue to line this stream.

Northeast of (uncharted) unlighted daybeacon #16, no-wake regulations are in effect. Even if it were not for this prohibition (which is, by the way, enforced), it would be a good idea to ease along slowly. Unlighted daybeacon #17 marks a sharp, blind turn in the canal. We noted several local vessels, including the Park Service tour boat, sounding their horns before they carefully eased around this turn. That's a pretty good word to the wise.

At (still uncharted) unlighted daybeacon #19, cruisers bound for the Pennekamp Marina should take a sharp turn to the

John Pennekamp Coral Reef State Park Marina

northwest and follow the canal, which will open out in front of them into the dockage basin. This stream soon leads to a large pool of water. The marina docks are located along the northwesterly shores. The pier you will sight to the north is used by the Park Service tour boats. Don't try to moor here.

To continue out into the waters of Largo Sound and the adjacent mooring field, follow the main canal out into the sound's wider waters. A marked cut will lead you into the sound. Stick to this channel until you are northeast of the gap between unlighted daybeacons #22 and #23. You can then cruise to your assigned mooring buoy.

Marvin D. Adams Waterway Please recall that this small waterway carries only 4½ feet of water at low tide. It is regularly plagued by strong tidal currents, and it is spanned by a fixed bridge with only 14 feet of vertical clearance. Anybody want to take a boat larger than 25 feet, or one drawing more than 3 feet on this run?

If your craft does fit these stringent requirements, continue cruising northeast on the midwidth of Largo Sound until you sight flashing daybeacon #A near the westerly banks. Turn to the west and pass a short distance south of #A. Cruise straight ahead into the centerline of the canal.

This entire passage is a no-wake zone. Slow down and, not to be repetitive, be on guard for STRONG currents. The U.S. 1 14-foot fixed bridge will come up a stone's throw from the canal's westerly terminus.

As you exit the canal to the west, point to pass flashing daybeacon #B by some 15 yards to its southerly side. This is the shallowest portion of the Marvin D. Adams Waterway, and low-water soundings of 4 feet are not at all uncommon. Continue cruising out into the wide waters of Blackwater Sound, and soundings will soon improve markedly. The ICW passage lies some .8 of a nautical mile to the northwest.

Marvin D. Adams Waterway (Largo Sound to Blackwater Sound)

The *African Queen* (Key Largo)

CHAPTER 2

Blackwater Sound and Largo Sound to Tavernier Creek

Whether you cruise the ICW or Hawk Channel from the southerly mouth of Jewfish Creek or Largo Sound (respectively) to Tavernier Creek, there is one community that dominates these waters. The name of this place conjures up faded black-and-white images from an old movie. Lauren Bacall stares unforgettably out of that hotel window with a poignant look of hope and love on her face, while Bogie gallantly pilots his old wooden-hulled craft back to port, bullet wound and all.

The place we are referring to, of course, is Key Largo, which actually encompasses the older communities of Rock Harbor and Tavernier. As we shall see, Hollywood had more than a little to do with Key Largo's present-day name, but more about that in a minute.

Before going any further, both this guide's writers must admit that Key Largo is one of our favorite cruising grounds in all of the Florida Keys. With Marathon quickly assuming the shape of a mini-Miami, and Key West's evermore teeming crowds, there are those who will argue that no better Florida Keys cruising can be found than the waters lapping about these storied isles. Life moves a bit more slowly on Key Largo, and there always seems to be time to check out one more anchorage or wet the line one more time. Many longtime members of the cruising community will be enchanted by this laissez-faire atmosphere and find themselves called back time and time again. We hope you will heed the siren's call of Key Largo yourself, and discover why Lauren and Bogie seemed so happy in this mythical setting.

From a mariner's point of view, Key Largo cruising is a very different experience, depending on whether you choose to transit the inside-ICW passage or the offshore Hawk Channel route. Each has advantages, disadvantages, and its own charms. Check out the descriptions below, assess your own tastes, as well as your vessel's size and draft, and make your decision accordingly.

The ICW between Jewfish and Tavernier Creeks is a visual delight. There are wide sounds, and narrow, almost secret streams to explore, and a potpourri of beautiful anchorages that will delight any true cruiser.

Another significant advantage to this passage can be found along its northwesterly flank. Here, the dredged confines of the Waterway give way to the broad but ever so shallow, gin-clear reaches of Florida Bay. All the locals refer to this region as "the back country." While it takes a very shallow-draft vessel to really take advantage of back-country cruising, and running aground has the potential to be an expensive proposition, the lure of these waters is unmistakable.

On the other hand, depths at low water, even smack in the middle of the ICW channel, can run as thin as 6 feet. Obviously, captains whose vessels draw more than 5½ feet had better skip directly to our coverage of the Key Largo portion of Hawk Channel (see below).

Another unexpected disadvantage of this route is the scarcity of marina facilities south of Jewfish Creek (to Tavernier Creek) that readily serve larger cruising craft (32 feet and more). In fact, with one exception, skippers

Key Largo shoreline

piloting vessels in this size range will almost certainly want to keep trucking to Islamorada before tucking into a snug slip for the night.

The stretch of Hawk Channel adjacent to Key Largo is pretty much like Hawk Channel everywhere else. It's broad, open, and offers only minimal shelter from foul weather. There is very little in the way of sheltered anchorages to appeal to passing skippers, but if you prefer to spend the night at a full-service marina, the situation is very different indeed.

Most of the Key Largo marinas serving larger pleasure craft are found off Hawk Channel. Usually, it is necessary to traverse an entrance channel and perhaps even an approach canal, but at the end of this trek, visiting mariners will find some quality facilities.

The only stream connecting the ICW and Hawk Channel passages within the scope of this chapter's coverage is Tavernier Creek. This stream has a relatively deep and well-marked channel, BUT it is spanned by a fixed bridge with a miserly 15 feet of vertical clearance. Only small powercraft need look to Tavernier Creek as a ready passage.

Well, without further ado, let's push on to learn something about Key Largo and its enchanting waters. Oh yes, if you happen to spot one (or both) of this guide's authors cruising about near Key Largo with a silly, satisfied smile on his face, don't be surprised.

Numbers to know in Key Largo include:

Thrifty Car Rental—305-852-6088
Enterprise Car Rental—800-736-8222
Key Largo Chamber of Commerce—800-822-1088
  (305-451-1414)
Key Largo Public Library—305-451-2396
Boater's World—305-451-0025
West Marine—305-453-9050

Charts Once again, you will need only a single chart for both the ICW and Hawk Channel passage within the scope of this chapter.
11451—wonderful cartographic aid continues to outline pretty much all the cruisable waters between Jewfish Creek, Largo Sound, and Tavernier Creek

Bridges
There is only one bridge that cruisers need concern themselves with along this stretch.
Tavernier Creek Bridge—crosses Tavernier Creek, north of unlighted daybeacons #12 and #13, not far from this stream's intersection with the open ocean and Hawk Channel—fixed—15 feet of vertical clearance

---

Key Largo History

Key Largo, the largest of the Florida Keys at more than 20,000 acres, had but three hundred people on it in 1950, a half-century ago. It seems amazing that such a beautiful part of Florida could be so sparsely populated, even then.

Key Largo began its modern life in 1855, when a Key West wrecker by the name of Capt. Benjamin Parker started raising pineapples on the island. Sixty years later, after hurricanes proved farming on the key a dicey proposition and the price of pineapples fell into the briny because of cheap imports from

Flying scots rounding the mark near the Upper Keys Sailing Club

Cuba—thanks to Henry Flagler's railway—Key Largo went through a stagnant period. But in the mid-1920s, land became the going currency.

What got it started was the construction of the old Card Sound Bridge, as the first part of the highway that would, in time, link Key West and the rest of the Keys with the mainland. It wasn't all peaches and cream on Key Largo, even then. There were saltwater crocodiles, alligators, rattlesnakes, mosquitoes, sand gnats, and large members of the cat family to deal with. While the panthers and the bobcats are gone, the other denizens remain. Crocs are a real concern in the upper keys, so one should watch where one swims, in salt and brackish water. The crocodiles are protected. You aren't. The crocs usually dine on much smaller fare than Homo sapiens, but you'd hate to become the exception to the rule; it would spoil your entire vacation and get you lots of unwanted tabloid notoriety on the shelves in supermarket checkout lines.

The Card Sound Bridge gave access to the Keys via automobile, but just as things were looking up, the Florida land boom went bust throughout the state. It was 1926. The Great Depression followed the land bust. Then the 1935 hurricane roared ashore in September of that year, trapping and killing hundreds people, just down the road. The Keys looked like a good place to stay away from.

Real, fresh water came to the Keys in abundance in the early 1940s. The navy in Key West needed it. Completed in 1942, a 130-mile pipeline went in from Florida City on the mainland to Key West. For the first time, the residents of Key Largo had a consistent water supply.

After victory in World War II, people started to come south to Key Largo. Gasoline, which had been severely rationed during the war, was available again, and cars starting coming off Detroit assembly lines in record numbers. During the war, those assembly lines built military vehicles.

In the 1950s, some forty-nine new subdivisions opened in Key Largo. In 1959, the Ocean Reef Club began construction. The development is still in existence and is still as exclusive as it ever was. Nonmembers are firmly and politely turned away at the gate. The 1950s were a good time to have real estate in Key Largo. You could dredge up bay bottom and fill in property as you wished. There was little to no government control over what happened on a person's private property. These days, you practically need a permit in Monroe County to install a new flapper valve in your toilet.

Modern Key Largo is a humming spot. General tourism and scuba diving in the waters around John Pennekamp Coral Reef State Park are big draws. Linked to the metropolitan centers of Miami and Fort Lauderdale by toll roads and super highways, Key Largo is the first, real key most people touch upon after they leave the mainland, and it also the last key as they trek back home. It's a busy little town, ready to help tourists have a good time.

Key Largo also includes Rock Harbor and Tavernier, with Rock Harbor somewhat in the middle and Tavernier at the southwest end.

Key Largo, the movie—we are told—was not filmed in Key Largo. Other than some random interior shots in a local bar, the movie was shot on a Hollywood sound stage. Joy Williams, in her delightful Keys guidebook, *The Florida Keys,* relates that when the movie *Key Largo* was released in 1948, the northernmost of the Keys carried the postal name of Rock Harbor. Real-estate developers loved the cachet associated with the movie, Humphrey Bogart, and Lauren Bacall. They circulated a petition seeking a name change from Rock Harbor to Key Largo. In 1952, according to Williams—others put the date seven years later—the post office granted the request and Rock Harbor officially became Key Largo, the island of adventure and romance. A rose by another other name?

Key Largo Ashore

Key Largo teems with shopping centers, delectable restaurants, and hostelries of all descriptions. These shoreside lodgings range from the humble likes of Stonelege to chain motels plus a few bed and breakfast inns. Of more immediate concern to mariners, there is a West Marine, a Boater's World, and quite a collection of hardware and auto parts stores. If you can obtain automobile transportation (rental cars are available—see above), then there is little you can't find in Key Largo.

It is only fitting that a community as friendly to visitors of all stripes, as Key Largo assuredly is, boasts a WIDE selection of fine (and, to be truthful, less than fine) places to slake a healthy appetite. We shall meet many of these memorable dining spots below in our verbal visits to Key Largo's marinas and waterside attractions. There is also another large group of eateries perched along both sides of Highway U.S. 1. While you will need automobile transportation to reach these eateries, there are a few we just have to mention.

Ballyhoo's Island Grille (Mile Marker 98,

Swimming pool at Casa Thorn (Plantation Key)

305-852-0822)is popular locally for its great seafood and clean Keys atmosphere. The inside of this delightful restaurant comes from designs of earlier times. The ceiling is beamed and the bar is vintage-Keys style without being hokey. This is the genuine article here, not something dreamed up by an interior decorator imported from New York.

Popular with Ballyhoo diners are Catch Meuniere—filet of dolphin pan sautéed with sherry, butter, lemon, garlic, and Worcestershire sauce. Catch Francaise is just as good. In fact, they do things to dolphin here that will make you think all the time you

spent eating beef was a waste. The variety is excellent; you'll have a tough time making up your mind. Prices are moderate and the help couldn't help you more or better. This is a must-stop for diners who take their repast seriously. It's open for lunch and dinner.

For something a little more down-home, and at reasonable prices to boot, Mrs. Mac's Kitchen (99336 Overseas Highway, 305-451-3722) offers all three meals of the day. There is nothing fancy here, but everything we've had during our multiple visits can only be described as quite good. Mrs. Mac's guards the westerly flank of Highway 1.

Finally, if you're up for what may be the best breakfast in all of the Florida Keys, don't spare any pains to find your way to Harriette's Restaurant (95710 Overseas Highway, 305-852-8689). This informal dining spot also overlooks the western side of Highway 1, hard by small but friendly Stoneledge Motel.

Key Largo's version of the ubiquitous West Marine is located on the bay side of Highway 1, in what is called Pink Plaza (Lat/Lon: 25 08.21 North/80 24.23 West, MM 102.5 Bayside, 103400 Overseas Highway, 305-453-9050). It has the full panoply of marine products and services. Though this store is not nearly as big as the Fort Lauderdale West Marine store, which is a yachtsman's kingdom come, it has most of everything that a cruiser needs . . . plus lots of things a cruiser really doesn't need but would like to have anyway, if he could get by all the rationalizing and whining involved in convincing his first mate.

Steve Duval, the store's resident electronics guru, said that he moved down to the Keys from Clearwater, Florida and loves working at the store. "What makes us special is the combined knowledge of everyone in here," Duval said. "We have a broad range of experience. Everyone is strong in all fields, and then we have people who are experts in different fields. We are one of the best stores as far as customer service and support; we go the extra mile."

The Key Largo version of Boater's World resides at 105660 Overseas Highway (MM 105.5 Bayside, Lat/Lon: 25 09.82 North/80 22.88 West, 305-451-0025). This is a big store, bigger than West Marine. The square footage is about 10,000 square feet. It is the closest major boating outlet—one of 105 stores nationwide—to the north end of Key Largo. When we were there, the store was vacant, except for the help; and the help consisted of a couple of lightweights who could have cared less that we were in the store. They were engaged in their own conversations.

Key Largo also plays host to a large K-Mart at 101499 Overseas Highway (305-451-5017). We have discovered a large selection of marine items, including some very cheap two-cycle outboard oil, at this store. They carry just about anything else you might need as well.

This guide does not presume to cover shoreside lodgings in any sort of comprehensive fashion. Key Largo contains an almost mind-boggling array of motels, hotels, condos, and just about every other form of hostelry that could be imagined. They range from the humble to large chain hotels, some of which we will meet below. Because tourism is the economic lifeblood and heartbeat of Monroe County, the county has a huge arrays of bars. It also gets its commensurate share of DUI arrests. In fact, along the main artery of the Florida Keys U.S. 1, one sees signs reminding you that if you drink and drive, you are apt to get arrested for a DUI. We have seen those signs nowhere else in Florida.

What does all that mean for a cruiser, someone not driving? Sometimes, you walk along the highway, from the marina where your boat is tied up, to get to a supermarket or drugstore or . . . well, you get the drift. You do it in the day and at night. It would make sense to take into account the possibility that the car coming down the road toward you might be driven by someone who had gotten over served at some bar up the road.

Another factor to consider is the sheer beauty of the Florida Keys. The ever-changing scene and the picture-perfect vistas are terribly distracting to drivers. They tend to wander just a bit on the highway. They can't seem to help it. Watch out. Your cruise will come to a sudden end if you get hauled off in an ambulance or worse, a coroner's station wagon.

You have, of course, heard of defensive driving. This is a place where defensive walking might save you great pain. Walk against the oncoming traffic, if you must walk along the highway. Better yet, where available, eschew the highway for the sidewalk. But be eternally vigilant.

One of the most interesting attractions in Key Largo, at least to our collective judgment, is the Florida Keys Wild Bird Rehabilitation Center (93600 Overseas Highway, 305-852-4486). The headquarters for this noteworthy organization is found adjacent to the northwestern side of U.S. Highway 1, just a few miles north of the Tavernier Bridge. It is WELL worth a visit.

These good people rescue wild birds and waterfowl that have been injured. Their goal

Key Largo sunset

is to treat their injuries and then release them back into the wild. In some cases, however, the injuries are so severe, or the treatment program so lengthy, that the birds must be kept in captivity for the sake of their survival.

And keep these birds they do, with sensitivity and a loving interest in the quality of their lives. You can walk past cage after cage, and see a magnificent red hawk or vibrant flamingos. Pelican feeding time in the afternoon is a great hit. Claiborne never thought he would have the opportunity to pat a pelican on the head, but he did just that here.

The Florida Keys Wild Bird Rehabilitation Center is kept operating strictly through voluntary contributions. After touring their facility, you might decide that extra $20 in your pocket could be put to good use. The dedicated volunteers at the center would be ever so happy for your help!

ICW from Blackwater Sound to Tavernier Creek

From the southerly mouth of Jewfish Creek, the ICW quickly passes out into the broad waters of Blackwater Sound. A host of anchorages and a few low-key marinas call Blackwater home and beckon the passing mariner to tarry for awhile.

The Waterway next transits Dusenberry Creek, darts across Tarpon Basin (site of additional anchorages), and then cuts through Grouper Creek on its way to Buttonwood Sound. Cruisers entering this body of water will get their first good view of the Florida Bay "back country," off to the west and northwest.

From Buttonwood Sound, the ICW follows a dredged route past Rock Harbor and Pigeon Key. Small, shallow-draft vessels can follow a sneaky cut and bypass the Waterway's detour around Pigeon Key.

Soon the inside route cuts to the southwest and makes its way through Ramshorn Cut. It's then only a quick hop to the northwesterly mouth of Tavernier Creek. This stream boasts a good channel and a marina, though this facility caters almost exclusively to smaller powercraft.

There is much to see and do along the way, so let's get started.

Blackwater Sound Anchorages and Facilities (Standard Mile 1134.5—northerly entrance) (Standard Mile 1137.5—southerly entrance) (Various Lat/Lons—see below)

Southbound cruisers will follow a dredged and well-marked channel running south-southwest from the southerly mouth of Jewfish Creek. Eventually, flashing daybeacon #38 heralds the Waterway's entrance into the deeper waters of Blackwater Sound. Northwest of #38, cruisers whose craft are not bothered by 5-foot soundings can anchor in the lee of Cross Key.

Notice the charted 7-foot waters northwest of flashing daybeacon #38. Looks nice, doesn't it? There's just one problem. It isn't there. We have no idea how long ago the soundings that appear on 11451 for these waters were taken, but they need to be updated. We discovered only 5 feet of water at low tide in this anchorage.

If 5 feet is okay for your boat, it is quite possible to track your way to the west-northwest of #38 and drop the anchor within 200 to 300 yards of the northerly Cross Key shoreline

Dock at Key Largo Marriott Hotel

(approximately 25 10.906 North/080 24.135 West). Don't try this if fresh (or even moderate) winds are blowing or are forecast to blow from the south, southwest, or southeast. This anchorage does have moderate protection to the north, northwest, and northeast, but even then, this is clearly not the place to ride out nasty weather.

Swinging room is unlimited. Some of the development associated with the facilities at the Jewfish Creek Bridge can be spotted to the northeast, and during weekends, automobile noise can waft its way out to this anchorage from U.S. 1, but otherwise, it's a fairly attractive spot. Another potential problem with this

haven is wake from powercraft speeding up after exiting Jewfish Creek. So while you can certainly spend the night swinging on the hook in this anchorage, there are even better overnight stops nearby.

One of these better spots is found on Sexton Cove. This body of water indents the shores of northeastern Blackwater Sound, immediately south of charted Lake Surprise. Good depths of 6 feet hold to within 200 yards of the shoreline, and 5 feet of water can be carried as close as 100 yards to shore. We like to drop the hook near 25 09.957 North/080 23.598 West. Swing room is once again without limit. Protection is quite good

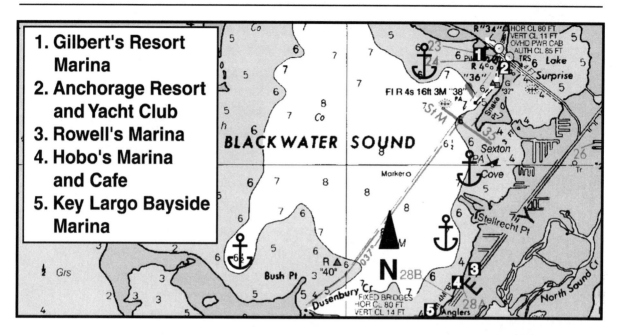

1. **Gilbert's Resort Marina**
2. **Anchorage Resort and Yacht Club**
3. **Rowell's Marina**
4. **Hobo's Marina and Cafe**
5. **Key Largo Bayside Marina**

for all but western, northwestern, and south-western breezes. The surrounding shores play host to moderate, and in a few spots, fairly heavy (mostly) residential development.

Another good anchor-down spot lies on the waters south of charted Stellrecht Point. This outcropping of land strikes out from Blackwater Sound's easterly shores, south of the just discussed Sexton Cove anchorage. Very respectable soundings of 6 feet or better extend to within 200 yards of the easterly banks. Closer in, depths rise to 4-foot levels. A good spot to drop the hook lies near 25 09.335 North/080 23.862 West. Lying between the Key Largo shoreline and the body of Stellrecht Point to the northeast, this haven would be a good spot if winds are blowing from the east, northeast, south, or southeast. There is no shelter from western and northwestern blows. Rowell's Marina (see below) is visible just to the south, and the adjoining shores are overlooked by heavy to moderate (though not unsightly) develop-

ment. With winds wafting from the appropriate direction, this is perhaps our favorite anchorage on Blackwater Sound.

Finally, as far as Blackwater Sound anchorages are concerned, the best spot to anchor when southerly winds are in the offing resides on the charted tongue of 6½-foot waters west-northwest of Bush Point. Unfortunately, while low-water depths in this haven run about 6 feet, it's a very easy proposition to wander into 5 feet of water in trying to find this haven. So, we do not suggest this anchorage for vessels drawing more than 4½ feet. If your craft fits these requirements, try dropping the old (or new) hook near 25 09.064 North/080 26.206 West. Be sure to stay a good 350 yards north of the southerly shoreline for best depths. There is ample elbowroom for any sized vessel, and the adjacent shoreline is delightfully undeveloped.

The marina facilities on Blackwater Sound all reside on the easterly banks, south of Stellrecht Point. First up is Rowell's Marina

Mariner's Hospital (Tavernier)

(305-451-1821) at 25 09.006 North/080 23.651 West. This marina is mostly a store-it-on-your-trailer facility with a launching ramp. They are also a Yamaha and Mercury dealer, and outboard repairs are available for Yamaha and Merc engines, as well as Merc Cruisers. A Winn-Dixie is about ¼ of a mile away. There's a restaurant within ⅛ of a mile.

While this may be a good place for a short stop because of its proximity to a supermarket, transients are not accepted for overnight dockage. The mostly breakwater-enclosed harbor has dockside depths of 6 feet or better, but you must cruise through some low-water soundings of 5 feet to get there. The few docks present in the harbor are of the fixed wooden variety, and do NOT boast any power or water hookups. Gasoline (no diesel fuel) can be bought at a central fuel pier, but we found the prices rather on the expensive side. It is safe to assume that Rowell's is buzzing on weekends, and tying up there, even just for a little while, would be discouraged.

Hobo's Marina and Café (25 08.850 North/080 23.790 West) lies just south of Rowell's. (The name is an amalgamation of Holly and Bob). Hobo's is mostly a dry-stack storage facility (of the semi-open-air variety), and it is not a place to stop if you are looking for luxury. Its showers and toilet facilities, which are close to the water, and the marine store/snack shop barely rate a passing grade. Hobo's does not encourage transients, as the fixed wooden docks are open to westerly/northwesterly winds. One of the ways they discourage transients, the dockmaster

Hobo's Marina (Blackwater Sound)

said, was to keep the heads and showers in barely okay shape. You know, just above the threshold where the health department might condemn them.

There's also a picture in the office that shows what Hobo's Marina's waterfront looks like when waves come rolling in from the north; it is not a sight that would please mariners. The marine store, such as it is, is sparse in supplies. There is beer, soft drinks, and water for sale, and some fishing tackle. "Don't forget the deli meat corner," said the dockmaster, "we have Slim Jims." You have to appreciate such a droll sense of humor.

Depths in the dockage basin are a meager 4 to 4 ½ feet at mean low water, and it looked to us as if the berths would not be comfortable for craft larger than 28 feet. Some fresh water and

20-amp dockside hookups are in the offing. Gasoline (high-test only) can be purchased.

The café part of the operation, Hobo's Sports Café, is about 100 yards from the water. It's is run by Holly, the distaff side of Hobo's, and it's a funky, dark place that appeals to locals. The bar top is teak and holly. Though we were unable to stop, the seafood menu looks attractive. The place must do well. Holly drives a sapphire blue Aston Martin DB-8 convertible that looks showroom new. The restaurant is open 11 A.M. to 10 P.M.

Hobo's Marina and Café Marina (305) 451-4684
  (Café phone:305-451-5888)

Approach depth—6 feet
Dockside depth—4-4¹/₂ feet
Accepts transients—very limited

Type of docking—fixed wooden piers
Dockside power connections—20 amp
Dockside water connections—yes
Showers—yes
Fuel available—gas (high test only)
Ship's & variety store—meager
Restaurant—on site

The southernmost Blackwater Sound marina is known as the Key Largo Bayside Marina (305-453-0081), formerly the Italian Fisherman. This facility resides at 25 08.589 North/080 23.995 West. Again, Bayside Marina is primarily a dry-stack facility, plus two adjacent restaurants with heavy weekend business. They do not take transients, except in an emergency. It is, however, a huge dealer in Pro-Line Boats, maybe the biggest in the world. Depths in the harbor run about 5 feet, but there is little in the way of wet slip dockage. The ship's store at the gas dock (no diesel) sells bait, ice, some charts, some tackle, beer, soft drinks, snacks, and outboard

Pelican feeding at the Florida Keys Wild Bird Rehabilitation Center

oil. It is a bare-bones operation, but it is neat and run by friendly people.

Sundowners restaurant (305-451-4502) is just next door to Key Largo Bayside. This dining spot has its own dock in the Bayside harbor, and it is a very popular local spot. Cruising craft skippers take note that depths alongside run as thin as 4 to 4½ feet at low tide. Sundowners is open 11A.M. to 11P.M., seven days a week. Prices are moderate. We had lunch there and had a grouper sandwich, which was excellent, a high compliment from a person who does not ordinarily eat such fare. The grouper had a marvelous Caribbean flavor to it and the waitress said, "We jerk it around some." We'd order the same again.

Sundowners specializes in yellowtail, grouper, and tuna. Wednesdays and Fridays are prime rib nights. Friday night is an all-you-can-eat fish fry night. The view of the bay is from either the air-conditioned dining room or the outside deck, which opens up onto Blackwater Sound. The sunsets are celebrated here with gusto. There's a tiki bar and outside tables for the those who love the sun.

Señor Frijoles (305-451-1592), also next door to the Key Largo Bayside Marina, is a Mexican restaurant with a ton of specialty rum drinks. The real specialty, as one might imagine, are the margaritas, and they sell quickly during the 4-6 P.M. happy hour. The barkeep said they have twenty-five different kinds of tequila, one of which is a tequila made in Trinidad that sells for $9 a pop. Trinidad tequila? Is there something we don't know? Nine bucks a shot? That's God's way of telling you that you are making too much money.

Fajitas are the top fare. Wednesday is all-you-can-eat taco night. Señor Frijoles is open 11 A.M. to 10 P.M., seven days a week.

Locally, we heard a woman refer to it as Senior Beans. Frijoles means "beans" in Spanish. It would be a Conch who sets the record straight, now wouldn't it?

The old (adjacent) Italian Fisherman Restaurant was closed at the time of this writing, but its huge former home is still quite visible as you approach Key Largo Bayside's harbor. You will most likely spy a fixed wooden pier just in front of this structure, with three slips. We do not suggest that you approach this structure while the restaurant is closed. If it ever reopens, cruisers planning to dine here may be able to once again berth at these slips while patronizing the restaurant. Minimum depths run 4½ feet. Be SURE to stay on the westerly side of this dock. The inner, easterly face has soundings just short of nil.

Marvin D. Adams Waterway

Small, shallow-draft boats (ONLY) can follow a narrow canal, officially known as the Marvin D. Adams Waterway, from the southeastern corner of Blackwater Sound to Largo Sound. The canal's westerly entrance is outlined by flashing daybeacon #B, while flashing daybeacon #A denotes its easterly mouth.

This small passage would be a very useful shortcut between the ICW and Largo Sound (and eventually Hawk Channel) if it were not for its 4½-foot depths (at the eastern and western entrances), a 14-foot fixed bridge crossing the canal, and the strong tidal currents that regularly boil through this waterway. Are you beginning to get the idea? We once successfully piloted a 31-foot, flybridge-equipped powercraft through this canal, but it's a feat we would not choose to repeat again.

If you cruise aboard an outboard or I/O-powered vessel, 25 feet and smaller, don't hesitate to make cautious use of the Marvin D. Adams Waterway. Otherwise, it's certainly best to keep trucking south down the Waterway to either Tavernier or (preferably) Snake Creek before making the transition from the inside to outside routes.

For continuing information on Largo Sound, check out our review of this body of water in Chapter 1, under the Hawk Channel-Key Biscayne to Largo Sound section.

Dusenbury Creek and the Strange Sailcraft (Standard Mile 1137.5—Northerly Entrance) (Standard Mile 1138—Southerly Entrance)

South of flashing daybeacon #41, the ICW follows the inner recesses of Dusenbury Creek to Tarpon Basin. As you come abeam and pass unlighted daybeacon #42, check out the eastern banks. Here you will spy a large, ferrocement-hulled sailcraft, which has several tons of junk piled haphazardly atop its cabin roof. One look will lead you to believe that this hulk is a derelict and has been abandoned for time out of mind.

Well, look again! Someone actually lives aboard this miserable excuse for a boat, and we have been told by several locals that the "vessel" in question has been perched on the shores of Dusenbury Creek for 10+ years. Go figure! We are continually amazed where some people will live.

Don't miss this one, fellow cruisers, and have the camera ready. It will make for a great story when you get back home.

Tarpon Basin Anchorages (Standard Mile 1139.5)

South-southeast of unlighted daybeacons

Derelict sailcraft on Dusenbury Creek

Fierce K-9 guardians (Tarpon Basin)

#44 and #42, the Waterway passes out into Tarpon Basin. As you come abeam of flashing daybeacon 46, you may well spy a sailcraft, or several such vessels, anchored on the seemingly open waters to the southeast. DON'T try to enter this anchorage from #46. Normally, this sort of warning would appear only in our navigational account of these waters below, but we've seen so many mariners make this mistake, it seemed a good thing to mention it here as well.

Tarpon Basin does offer at least three good spots to spend the evening swinging on the anchor. With northerly, northeasterly or northwesterly breezes blowing, the charted

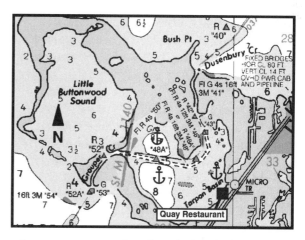

deep water north of unlighted daybeacon #48A is a good bet (25 07.858 North/080

25.955 West). Good low tide depths of 6 to 7 feet run to within 200 yards of the northerly banks. Closer in, soundings rise to 5 feet or less. The surrounding shores are beautifully undeveloped, but wake from larger power-craft passing on the Waterway could be a problem, particularly early in the morning. There is little protection to the south and southeast. If winds are blowing from either of these quarters, cruisers would do better to occupy one of the havens described below.

A bit more open, but still better sheltered for winds blowing from the south and south-west, is the charted 7- to 8-foot bubble south of unlighted daybeacon #48A (near 25 07.438 North/080 25.937 West). Entrance into this anchorage is not as easy as chart 11451 would lead you to expect. However, with the info presented in our navigational section below, most navigators can carry at least 6 feet of water into this haven. Swing room is without limit. We wouldn't want to be caught here with a strong blow wafting down from the northeast or east, but other-wise, protection is pretty good. Tarpon Basin's southeastern and southwestern shorelines (which abut each other) are divided as far as development is concerned. The banks to the southwest are untouched, while the shoreline lying to the southeast is guarded by moderate development.

The most sheltered Tarpon Basin anchor-age, but by far the most difficult to access, is found along the southeasterly banks. The waters northwest of the charted "Micro Tr" (near 25 07.439 North/080 25.180 West), east of the small charted island, offer depths of 5 to 6 feet and superb shelter from all but unusually brisk southwesterly breezes. During our last visit here, no less than four sailcraft were taking advantage of this haven.

The adjacent shoreline exhibits moderate development, and there is enough room for a 46-footer to swing to and fro on the hook comfortably. Be SURE to read the naviga-tional directions in the next section of this chapter BEFORE trying to make your way to these waters. This is NOT a straightforward passage, though it is quite doable if you know what to look for.

The Quay Restaurant flanks the easterly shores of Tarpon Basin, just south of the charted "Micro Tr," near 25 07.282 North/080 25.114 West. We skipped this restaurant because it was understaffed and the people who worked there appeared to be on the low end of the waitperson spectrum. Walking into The Quay down a covered walk, one notices the canvas cover is sun-rotted and the place is patchworked with spider webs.

Grouper Creek
(Standard Mile 1140)

Moving west from Tarpon Basin, the ICW enters the sheltered reaches of Grouper Creek and quickly turns to the south. This cut encompasses only slightly more than .5 of a nautical mile of the Waterway.

The only aid to navigation in the creek is unlighted daybeacon #52. A narrow offshoot cuts to the northwest near #52 and eventually leads into the shallows that buffer the south-ern side of Little Buttonwood Sound. Depths between the ICW channel and this little con-nector creek run as thin as 4 feet.

We mention this stream only because we have seen several groups snorkeling on these waters during our many transits of Grouper Creek. We gave in to the temptation on one occasion and checked the depths out for our-selves. The water was gin clear, and the plant life was quite colorful, though we saw little in the way of fish population during our dive. Fortunately, we didn't see any saltwater crocs either.

Buttonwood Sound Anchorages

Southwest of unlighted daybeacons #52A and #53, the Waterway exchanges greetings with Buttonwood Sound. The southeasterly corner of this body of water is known as Sunset Cove. Buttonwood boasts quite a selection of overnight anchor-down spots abutting its eastern and southeastern shoreline, particularly in Sunset Cove.

Several local Key Largo cruisers have warned us that holding ground in Sunset Cove is not the best. They have gone on to suggest that visiting captains not back down very hard on their anchors, or the hook might pull right out. After relating this advice, we have never suffered these problems while repeatedly anchored on these waters. You, however, may not be so fortunate, so be SURE the anchor is well set, particularly if foul weather is in the forecast. In really nasty conditions, an anchor watch might be a tiring, but nevertheless a smart, idea.

One real advantage to anchoring in Sunset Cove is the free dinghy dockage, afforded by the good folks at the Upper Keys Sailing Club (see below). This is particularly fortunate as there is a drugstore, a supermarket, and several restaurants within walking distance. Thank you Upper Keys Sailing Club—the cruising community is appreciative!

First up are the waters northeast of flashing daybeacon #54. To enter this 6½-foot minimum depth anchorage, you must depart the ICW southwest of #54. Then, cruisers can curl around to the north-northeast and follow the charted tongue of deep water to within 250 yards of the northerly banks (near 25 07.116

North/080 26.604 West). The undeveloped shoreline gives a good lee from northern, northeastern, and (to a somewhat lesser extent) northwestern winds. There is ample elbowroom for any sized pleasure craft, but because of the unmarked entry channel, we would be hesitant to pilot a boat larger than 46 feet to this anchorage.

A broad band of deep-water buffers both sides of the Waterway as it crosses the midsection of Buttonwood Sound. During light airs (ONLY), cruisers can anchor 100 to 200 yards east and west of the ICW. Minimum depths are 6 to 7 feet, and obviously, there is enough room for anything short of the Queen Mary. East of the channel, we like the waters southeast of the charted "Marker" (which is actually an Everglades National Park Boundary sign), near 25 06.402 North/080 27.122 West. West of the Waterway, try 25 06.540 North/080 27.708 West or anywhere thereabouts.

Far more sheltered are the waters west of the charted position of Newport (near 25 07.438 North/080 25.937 West). Minimum soundings of 5½ feet are held to within 200 yards of the easterly banks. Swinging room is unlimited and this anchorage is protected from eastern, northeastern, and southeastern winds. There is no shelter to the west, northwest, and southwest. The teeming development, which cruisers anchoring on these waters will undoubtedly spy to the northeast, is a huge trailer park.

Sunset Cove brings on another set of overnight stops. Shallow-draft vessels can anchor northwest of tiny (but charted) Pelican Key (near 25 05.645 North/080 27.385 West). Depths run to 5 feet at low water, some 200 yards from shore, but drop to 4-foot levels closer in. Pelican Key gives good shelter to the south, and the point just southwest of this haven provides a lee from southern and southwestern breezes. Don't drop the hook here if stiff winds are blowing from the north or northwest.

The most popular anchorage on Buttonwood Sound is found on the waters of Sunset Cove. Seldom have we visited these waters, even during high summer, when there were not several cruising craft anchored in this cove. The only problem is that low-water soundings can run to 5 feet, so only vessels drawing less than 5 feet need apply. These minimum depths hold to within 200 yards of the southeasterly banks. We like to drop anchor near 25 05.570 North/080 26.926 West. The adjoining shoreline is festooned with fairly heavy, but not unattractive, development.

Shelter is good for easterly, southeasterly and northeasterly winds but nil from all other quarters.

Upper Keys Sailing Club
(Standard Mile 1143)
(25 05.968 North/080 26.497 West)

The Upper Keys Sailing Club occupies the sharp point of land, west of the twin charted "Micro Trs," south of the charted position of Newport. It is depicted as facility #35 on chart 11451. This is a private sailing club, with a lovely view and spotless grounds. What is so appealing is that the club will accept transients. Depths alongside at the fixed wooden finger piers run about 5 feet at low water, with similar approach soundings. Dockside power hookups are of the 15- to

Upper Keys Sailing Club (Key Largo)

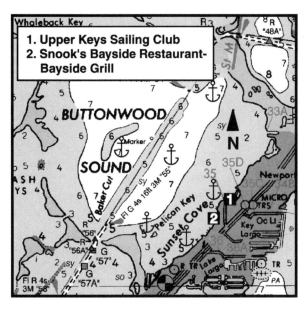

1. Upper Keys Sailing Club
2. Snook's Bayside Restaurant-
   Bayside Grill

Upper Keys Sailing Club (305) 451-9972
http://www.geocities.com/uksc_2000

Approach depth—5 feet
Dockside depth—5 feet
Accepts transients—yes
Type of docking—wooden finger piers
Dockside power connections—15 to 30 amp,
   fee based
Dockside water connections—yes, via hose
Showers—yes
Laundromat—commercial type, three blocks
   away
Restaurant—several close by

Sunset Cove Dining

A short hop southwest of the Upper Keys Sailing Club, Snook's Bayside Restaurant (25 05.741 North/080 26.578 West, MM 99.9 Bayside, 305-453-3799) likewise overlooks the southeasterly shores of Sunset Cove. Its fixed wooden face dock carries a bare 3-3½ feet at low tide, however. Many cruisers will wisely choose to visit this restaurant by dinghy (or automobile). Patrons are welcome to use the dock while partaking of the fine fare—no overnight stays allowed.

Snook's features a lovely view, with both outside and inside dining available. In the cooler months, outside has to get the nod. Also outside is Patrick's Waterfront Bar, which has all the libations necessary to enjoy the evening . . . or the entire day. The menu is enchantingly diverse. If yellowtail snapper topped with fresh crab cake and béarnaise sauce doesn't make your mouth water, you might be happier cruising the Chicago River and Sanitary Canal. Snook's is open from 11:30 A.M. to 10 P.M., seven days a week. Sunday brunch buffet is $7.95 and definitely worth the price of admission.

30-amp variety, and there is an extra charge to hook up. The club is within walking distance of a drugstore (Eckerd's) and a super market. Also a short stroll away is a Wendy's, Burger King, McDonald's and a Denny's Liquor Store, the latter having prices that are twenty percent higher than mainland prices. The UKSC clubhouse is airy and clean. While the club is closed on Tuesdays and Wednesdays, it is open the rest of the time. There's a full-service bar in the clubhouse, and club guest memberships, which allow one to sit and drink at the bar, are available for $1 per day. While there is no charge for tying up a dinghy, there are tariffs involved with other services. It's $15 per night to stay at the dock. There's a shower on the dock and another inside, but the club prefers that transients use the dock shower. Showers cost $1.50 each. Really. Save money; shower with a friend. Ten pounds of bagged ice is $1.25. Water connections are via hose, but remember that water in the Florida Keys is a valuable commodity.

Bayside Grill (305-451-3380) is just next door to Snook's. This restaurant is on the second floor with an elevator ride for those who are just too tired from yachting to climb the stairs. Like Snook's, depths at this restaurant's fixed wooden pier are only 3-4 feet. The dining room looks out over the popular Sunset Cove anchorage to the southwest. Open for both lunch and dinner, this is a popular stopping place for hungry mariners. Try the cracked conch that's marinated before being golden fried. Dinner entrées run the gamut from Cajun smothered chicken to dolphin and steak. The 16-ounce, brandy-flamed, Angus strip steak with peppercorns, demi-glacé and a touch of cream makes a meat eater's juices start to flow.

Rock Harbor Facilities (Standard Mile 1144-1145)

The Waterway bids a fond farewell to Buttonwood Sound, and the really good people at the Upper Keys Sailing Club, south of unlighted daybeacon #56. The channel quickly passes through a dredged cut running between two large mangroves and enters a rather open section of easterly Florida Bay. The shoreline to the southeast is part of the old Keys community of Rock Harbor, a name that predates "Key Largo" by more than a few years. Two pleasure-craft facilities call the shores of Rock Harbor home.

America Outdoors Camper Resort lies southeast of flashing daybeacon #58, near 25 04.510 North/080 27.920 West (Standard Mile 1144). Chart 11451 shows its location as

America Outdoors Marina (Rock Harbor)

facility designation #34A. This facility is essentially an extensive RV campground, but it has a long, fixed, wooden face dock and one slip. Try to find a berth on the dock's inner face, as protection on the outer side is nil. Transients are accepted, but approach and alongside depths of only 4 feet (at low water) will be a problem for many cruising-sized vessels. Power connections up to 30 amps and fresh water hookups are also in the offing.

There's a waterfront restaurant on site—mostly sandwiches, but with a grill—and they sell beer and tackle inside as well. The restaurant is named Fishtales (305-852-9121) and it's open 8 A.M.-6 P.M., seven days a week. You can also get a lite breakfast there. Also available at this location are propane, ice, and beer.

There are two shower/rest room facilities shoreside, both climate controlled. The one closer to the water is less attractive than the one near the highway, which is cleaner, probably because it is closer to the main office. There is an on-site Laundromat as well.

Oddly, and also conveniently, there's a phone line hookup for laptop computers with modems at a pay phone right at the dockside restaurant. You can be "in touch" while looking out over the pristine waters of Florida Bay. If you don't have an 800 number for getting in touch with your ISP, check out that possibility. It is most convenient.

Also at the resort is a sandy bayside beach that is protected and a great place for cruisers who have kids along to let the youngsters play in shallow water and shake off some of that energy they have been using to bug adults.

America Outdoors Camper Resort
   (305) 852-8054 (Marina 305-852-9121)

Approach depth—4 feet
Dockside depth—4 feet

Accepts transients—yes
Type of docking—170-foot-long wooden face dock
Dockside power connections—up to 30 amp
Dockside water connections—yes
Showers—yes
Laundromat—yes
Fuel available—gas only (Texaco)
Variety store—yes (plus fishing tackle)
Restaurant—on site

The Westin Beach Resort will be spotted southeast of unlighted daybeacon #58A, near 25 04.041 North/080 28.367 West (Standard Mile 1145). This is a Westin, so we are talking a 200-room major resort with all that entails. Right off the dock, there is a carnival of stuff—para-sailing, jet skis, tube boat rides for the kids, some sailing, beach volleyball.

The dock itself amounts to a fixed face dock made of concrete, and one comes in around the southwest end of it and docks behind it, stern to. There are some 20 slips, bracketed by wooden finger piers, most of which appear to have never been used. There are no facilities whatsoever on the dock. It is just a place to park a boat and then go up to the front desk to register. The catch would be that you'd have to stay in the hotel. It appeared to us as if this place is not really cruiser friendly, in that boating doesn't seem to be part of the mix, but the staff is nice. Max size of boats that can tie up here would be about 45 feet.

Should you obtain a berth anyway, expect to discover meager 4-foot dockside depths. Obviously, many larger cruising craft will find these soundings to be a very limiting factor.

The hotel has a couple of restaurants and bars. The prettiest thing is the huge swimming pool with a stunning waterfall. What God cannot produce on his own, irrigation engineers can manufacture. Is this a great world or what?

Westin Beach Resort (305) 852-5553
http://www.1800keylargo.com
info@1800keylargo.com

Approach depth—4-6 feet
Dockside depth—4 feet
Accepts transients—only if you stay at the hotel
Type of docking—fixed concrete with finger
    piers
Restaurant—several on site

Rock Harbor Anchorage
(Standard Mile 1145.5)
(25 03.256 North/080 29.525 West)

South of flashing daybeacon #58, the Waterway swings to the southwest and runs away from the Rock Harbor-Key Largo Shoreline. This turn is designed to bypass the shallows southeast of Pigeon Key. A whole passel of 5- to 6-foot (low-tide) waters lie southeast of the ICW along this stretch. It is quite possible for mariners to track their way to within 100 yards of the Rock Harbor-Key Largo shoreline and drop the hook. Our favorite spot is found near 25 03.256 North/080 29.525 West. There is plenty of shelter from southeasterly, easterly and southerly winds. Woe be unto you if you get caught here during a strong blow from the northwest or west. The adjoining shores are overlooked by moderate, mostly residential, development that is very easy on the eyes. Don't try to dinghy ashore here, as almost all the adjacent property is private.

Pigeon Key Anchorage
(Standard Mile 1146.5)
(25 03.465 North/080 30.475 West)

Cruisers whose craft is not bothered by some 4½-foot soundings can anchor off the easterly shores of Pigeon Key with protection to the west. This anchorage is wide open to all other wind directions. Typical soundings are 5 feet at mean low water, but the occasional 4½-foot reading does creep in from time to time. Drop the hook before approaching to within less than 100 yards of the banks.

Pigeon Key is undeveloped and looks as if it is begging for exploration by dinghy. DON'T give in to this temptation. Landing is not allowed on Pigeon Key, and this prohibition goes for pretty much all the undeveloped keys in Florida Bay, particularly those which are within the boundaries of the Everglades National Park.

Back-country Anchorages
(Standard Mile 1147.5)
(Various Lat/Lons—see below)

Okay, listen up out there all you off-the-beaten-path types. Southwest of flashing daybeacon #61 and Pigeon Key, the Waterway intersects a broad patch of 6- and 7-foot waters that run north, northeast, and northwest out into the back country. While a 5-foot draft can certainly be carried on these waters, there is the possibility of wandering into shallower depths, so we usually confine our explorations of even these deeper Florida Bay waters to times when we have a boat drawing 4½ feet or less (and 45 feet or less in length) under our feet.

Also, be advised that navigation of these waters can be, shall we say, challenging. There are NO official aids to navigation once you leave the Waterway. You may spot some stakes stuck here and there by the locals, but we have always found these informal markers to be more of a hindrance than an aid. Some denote deep water and some do not.

Yes, sports fans, once again we are going to mention how wonderful it is to have a GPS, interfaced with a laptop computer, running navigational software and loaded with a digitized version of chart 11451. This arrangement makes successful navigation of these backcountry waters ever sooooo much easier.

Well, with all that out of the way, there are at least three anchor-down spots to consider. First up are the waters well east of Bottle Key (approximately 25 04.184 North/080 32.690 West). The only unusual characteristic of this stop is that you must stand off the banks of Bottle Key at least .5 of a nautical mile to remain in at least 5 feet of water. Closer to shore, soundings rise dramatically.

In spite of its standoff requirement, this anchorage boasts some good shelter. Bottle Key and the charted shallows of Upper Cross Bank protect cruisers swinging on the anchor here from western and southwestern breezes. There is no lee at all from northern, northwestern and northeastern breezes. Bottle Key is completely in its natural state, but once again, landing is not allowed.

Next up, cruisers might consider anchoring southwest of Butternut Key near 25 04.869 North/080 31.208 West. Good depths of 5 feet or better are held to within 300 yards of the key's southwesterly banks. Winds from the northeast and east should not be too much of a problem, but choose another spot to spend the night if fresh breezes are wafting from the northwest or west.

Finally, for those cruisers who are willing to take a lengthy trek of 5.1 nautical miles off the ICW, a fair-weather anchorage east of Manatee Keys can be reached near 25 04.588 North/080 36.287 West. Chart 11451 seems to indicate that minimum 6-foot depths can be held during this entire passage, but we observed many low-water soundings in the 5-foot regions.

Drop the hook some .35 of a nautical mile

east-northeast of the larger of the two Manatee Keys for best depths. Here, mariners will discover at least 5- to 6-foot soundings at low water. Once again, closer to shore, it's almost a sure bet that your keel will say hello to the bottom (and let's once again remember that can be an expensive proposition in the Florida Keys).

The Manatee Keys provide a lee to the southwest, but this anchorage is wide open in all other directions. Don't try this spot if there is even a mention of foul weather or afternoon thunderstorms in the forecast.

Community Harbor Anchorage and Mangrove Marina (Standard Mile 1150) (Anchorage—25 00.760 North/080 31.254 West) (Mangrove Marina—25 00.760 North/080 31.075 West)

After rounding Pigeon Key and flashing daybeacon #61, the ICW takes a sharp turn to the south and heads back toward the Key Largo shoreline. Flashing daybeacon #62 marks the northerly beginnings of a lazy turn back to the southwest. After passing through this turn, cruisers can break off to the south at unlighted daybeacon #64A and visit an anchorage and a marina on the waters of Community Harbor.

The first thing to say about Community Harbor is that its entrance doesn't even bear a vague resemblance to what is pictured on chart 11451 (Page E, Inset 5). Even the charted configuration of aids to navigation is different (see navigational account below).

In actuality, the entrance, marked by unlighted daybeacons #1 and #2 (charted as #3 and #4), leads mariners between a series of mangroves and small islands. These indistinct bodies of land provide some shelter to the entire Community Harbor basin, which partially explains the popularity of this anchorage.

Mangrove Marina (Community Harbor)

The second thing to say about Community Harbor is that it is on the shallow side. Low-water soundings of 4½ feet are not at all uncommon. Dockside depths at Mangrove Marina run about 5 feet. Obviously, this entire side trip is pretty much relegated to vessels drawing less than 4½ feet.

The best spot to anchor is found where the deeper (relatively speaking) waters of Community Harbor spread out in a fairly wide pool, southwest of the mangrove. Stay as near to the middle as possible. Try 25 00.760 North/080 31.254 West.

Mangrove Marina occupies the southeasterly shoreline, northeast of the charted "Foul" bottom (25 00.760 North/080 31.075 West). This is a facility in what appears to be serious regeneration. It was once called Campbell's.

The local buzz is that when the owner of Campbell's got sick, all kinds of ugly family things happened and the marina was sort of caught in the middle. Eventually, after court battles over the estate, it went down a slippery slope and was sold to the current owners.

They have 130 slips here, overall, most of the fixed concrete variety. Dockside power connections up to 50 amps are available. Fresh water connections are metered for long-term yachts. Cable television and phone hookups are located on the docks as well. Both gasoline and diesel fuel are available for purchase. The shoreside showers (three men's and three women's—older but clean) are in a separate building that also contains three washers and three dryers, coin ops. There's also a small cruisers' library.

Mangrove Marina offers waste pump-out service. It seems that the newer marinas all have waste pump-out, and it could be a requirement for the necessary permitting, which is hard to get in the Keys.

Mechanical repairs are available for both gasoline and diesel-power plants. A 35-ton travel lift was on the way, marina officials said.

The closest restaurant is the Copper Kettle (305-852-4131). It is about three blocks away, across U.S. 1. The Copper Kettle was in the process of changing hands when we were there. It was open for only breakfast and lunch and seemed under-air-conditioned and understaffed, but the food was excellent. The existing atmosphere was not Keys kitsch, which was a bit of a relief. It was more English country. There is alfresco courtyard dining. The restaurant is separated from the inn part of the operation by the courtyard, so things are enclosed.

There is great shopping within about ⅓ mile, certainly within walking distance. It's in a new strip mall, which contains a Winn-Dixie, several restaurants, and a movie theater. Between the marina and the mall is a 42-bed hospital, Mariner's Hospital, with standard and emergency medical care.

When they get it all together, and they seem to be intent on doing so, this marina will be a great stopping-off place. It has all the necessary ingredients and location, location, location. The anchorage in front of the docks features some local boats and some vessels that have just been left to sink. It's colorful.

Mangrove Marina (305) 852-8380
http://www.mangrovemarina.com

Approach depth—4½-5 feet (low water)
Dockside depth—5 feet (low water)

Accepts transients—yes
Type of docking—concrete finger piers
Dockside power connections—up to 50 amp
Dockside water connections—yes
Cable television and phone hookups—yes
Waste pump-out—yes
Showers—yes
Laundromat—yes
Fuel available—gas and diesel
Mechanical repairs—yes (gas and diesel engines)
Below-waterline repairs—planned
Ship's and variety store—modest
Restaurant—nearby

Tavernier Creek and Tavernier Creek Marina

After passing through a dredged channel known as Ramshorn Cut, the Waterway soon approaches an intersection with the northwesterly reaches of Tavernier Creek. The juncture of these two channels can be VERY confusing for first-timers. All mariners cruising these waters should be SURE to read our navigational review below before entering this region.

If you are successful in sorting out the markers, captains can expect at least 7 feet of water between the ICW and the mouth of Tavernier Creek. Once you slip past its entrance, it will become quickly apparent just how sheltered Tavernier Creek really is. There are some tidal current and blind turns, so watch for these hazards.

Eventually, the 15-foot fixed bridge, spanning Tavernier Creek, will come within sight dead ahead. Just before reaching this span, Tavernier Creek Marina (305-852-5854, 25 00.193 North/080 31.838 West) will come abeam to the west. This facility is huge and quite attractive, but it is solely a dry-stack facility or long-term wet slip rental facility. Transients are not accepted. Period.

The only parts of Tavernier Creek Marina

Tavernier Creek Homeplace

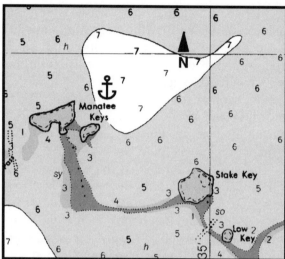

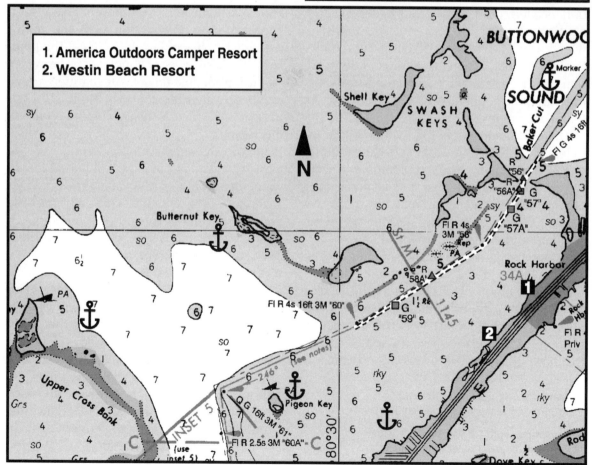

1. America Outdoors Camper Resort
2. Westin Beach Resort

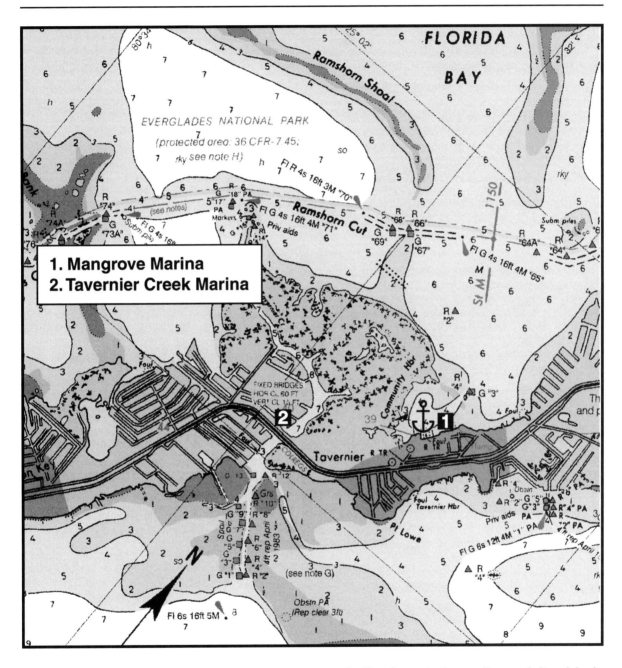

1. Mangrove Marina
2. Tavernier Creek Marina

readily accessible to visiting cruisers are Chris's Bait and Tackle (305-853-0191) and Las Brisas Café (305-853-0042). Chris's fronts the marina's entrance, on its southerly flank, and offers beer, fuel (gasoline and diesel fuel), and sandwiches. Depths at the fuel dock run as thin as 4½ to 5 feet, but soundings in the harbor are in the 8+-foot region.

Las Brisas Café is a small operation that sits immediately adjacent to Chris's. It is so new that we have not been able to review its cuisine, but we are told it is open for breakfast and lunch.

Those vessels that can clear the 15-foot fixed bridge may continue seaward on a well-marked channel leading from the southerly mouth of Tavernier Creek to Hawk Channel. This cut has shoaled a bit over the last year or two, and currently some 5-foot soundings at low tide can be expected.

ICW FROM BLACKWATER SOUND TO TAVERNIER CREEK NAVIGATION

The ICW channel from Jewfish Creek to Tavernier Creek is a thoroughly typical section of the Waterway running south and west to Marathon. The channel moves between large, open sounds and narrow, protected connector streams. No one will ever properly characterize a cruise through these waters as being dull.

While it is quite possible for captains to depart the ICW track in some of the sounds along the way, other sections require close attention to markers and a good knowledge of coastal navigation. Sailors, in particular, will be delighted to safely leave the rigid confines of the Waterway here and there, but just be sure to return to the marked cut when it's time to continue your journey south and west.

As with virtually every section of the ICW between Jewfish Creek and Marathon, it is quite possible to find yourself cruising through only 6 feet (possibly 5½ feet in a few spots) of water, even when your craft is directly between the Waterway markers. As we have said repeatedly throughout this guide, this inside, ICW route is not appropriate for boats drawing more than 5 1/2 feet.

So, with those provisos in the works, let's push off and take a look at the navigational characteristics of these waters. Next stop, Islamorada!

ICW—Jewfish Creek to Blackwater Sound

The southerly mouth of Jewfish Creek is joined to the wider waters of Blackwater Sound by a dredged cut. Southbound ICW cruisers should continue at idle speed until the facilities on Jewfish Creek are well in their wake, and then point for the gap between unlighted daybeacons #36 and #37. After passing between #36 and #37, swing a bit farther to the southwest, and point to pass flashing daybeacon #38 to its fairly immediate southeasterly quarter.

Southwest of #38, the deeper waters of Blackwater Sound open out before you. It's a long run of slightly better than 2 nautical miles across the southeasterly ⅓ of Blackwater Sound to the next ICW navigational marker, unlighted daybeacon #40. Eventually, you should come abeam of #40 by some 50 yards (or even a bit more) to its southeasterly side.

Along the way, you may spot what appears to be a navigational aid near the midpoint of your trek across Blackwater Sound. Upon closer inspection, this "Marker" is really a sign that denotes a boundary of the Everglades National Park.

Between #38 and #40, cruisers have several opportunities to anchor and three marinas to check out.

Blackwater Sound Anchorages and Facilities The first anchorage to consider lies south of Cross Key, on the charted 7-foot waters west-northwest of flashing daybeacon #38. Please remember that depths in this region are NOT as they are portrayed on chart 11451. Instead of depths ranging from 6 to 7 feet, expect low-water soundings of around 5 feet. To access this haven, continue cruising on the Waterway for some 200 yards southwest of #38. Then, take a turn to the northwest, and cruise into the bubble of charted 6-foot (in reality, 5-foot) soundings. Be mindful of the correctly charted sunken wreck to the southwest of your course line. Be sure to anchor at least 300 yards south of the northerly banks. We suggest dropping the hook near 25 10.906 North/080 24.135 West.

You might also choose to anchor on Sexton Cove (near 25 09.956 North/080 23.597 West). Depths 200 yards from shore run about 6 feet, with 5½-foot soundings carrying to within 100 yards of the banks. Stick to center of the bay's southwest to northeast axis for the best water.

There's no trick to anchoring southwest of Stellrecht Point. Just stay at least 200 yards southwest of the point, and don't approach to within less than 200 yards of the southeasterly banks. Try the waters near 25 09.334 North/080 23.862 West. It doesn't get much simpler than that.

Cruisers bound for the anchorage west of Bush Point should depart the ICW some 300 yards northeast of unlighted daybeacon #40. To maintain best depths, you must cruise through a very long, lazy turn to the south. This maneuver will hopefully help you to locate the charted tongue of 6½- to 7-foot water, west of #40. Don't be surprised if you wander into 5 feet of water along the way. Drop anchor before closing to within less than 350 yards of the southerly shoreline.

Blackwater Sound Marinas All three marinas on Blackwater Sound guard the southeasterly banks, ranging in a line that starts at the charted location of Angler's Park and runs up the banks to the northeast. The northeasternmost facility is Rowell's Marina. This marina's dockage basin is enclosed by a rock breakwater. Simply cruise straight through the cut in the rock wall. Depths improve markedly once within the dockage basin.

Hobo's lies between Rowell's and Key Largo Bayside Marina. The entrance to the dockage basin is obvious from the water.

The southwesternmost of the three is Key Largo Bayside Marina. Cruisers approaching this facility will sight a long, fixed, wooden face dock immediately northeast of the harbor entrance. This dock is associated with the, now closed, Italian Fisherman Restaurant. We do not recommend tying up at Italian Fisherman until this eatery is reactivated. Depths on the inside face of this restaurant dock are practically nil.

To enter the Key Largo Bayside Marina dockage basin, cruise straight in through the harbor entrance. The dockmaster's office and fuel dock will quickly come up to starboard.

Marvin D. Adams Waterway The westerly entrance into the treacherous Marvin D. Adams Waterway makes into the extreme southeastern corner of Blackwater Sound. Please recall that this small waterway carries only 4½ feet of water at low tide. It is regularly plagued by strong tidal currents, and it is spanned by a fixed bridge with only 14 feet of vertical clearance. Anybody want to take a boat larger than 25 feet, or one drawing more than 3 feet, on this run?

If your craft does fit these stringent requirements, point to pass flashing daybeacon #B by some 15 yards to its southerly side. This is the shallowest portion of the Marvin D. Adams Waterway, and low-water soundings of 4 feet are not at all uncommon. Cruise straight ahead into the centerline of the canal.

This entire passage is a no-wake zone. Slow down and, not to be repetitive, be on guard for STRONG currents. The U.S. 1 14-foot, fixed bridge will come up a stone's throw from the canal's westerly genesis.

Continue cruising on the canal's centerline until you near its easterly terminus. Pick out flashing daybeacon #A quickly, as you pass out into the wider waters of Largo Sound. Pass a short distance south of #A.

You can now turn safely south-southwest into the heart of Largo Sound. Check out our navigational account of this sound in Chapter 1 for further details.

ICW Through Dusenbury Creek From a position abeam of unlighted daybeacon #40, to its southeasterly side, look to the south-southwest. Use your binoculars to pick out flashing daybeacon #41. This aid to navigation marks the northerly entrance to Dusenbury Creek. Set course to come abeam of #41 to its immediate northwesterly side. Don't slip too far to the northwest between #40 and #41. The correctly charted 4- and 5-foot waters in this quarter are waiting to greet you.

Once on the interior reaches of Dusenbury Creek, consider slowing down a bit. This stream is not an official no-wake zone, but it does contain some blind turns. Wise captains will take a bit of extra time in order to avoid any abrupt and unplanned meetings with fellow vessels.

Look to the east as you pass unlighted daybeacon #42 for a good view of the decrepit sailcraft (topped with several tons of junk) described earlier. Go figure!

As you exit the southerly mouth of Dusenbury Creek, point to pass between unlighted daybeacons #44 and #43. The waters of Tarpon Basin now lie before you.

On the ICW The Waterway follows a slow turn to the west as it traverses Tarpon Basin. Come abeam of flashing daybeacon #46 to its southeasterly side. Curve around to the southwest, and point to pass unlighted daybeacon #46A to its southeasterly side.

Between #46A and the next aid to navigation, flashing daybeacon #48, the Waterway completes its turn to the west. Come abeam of #48 to its southerly side.

If you happen to spot any anchored craft east of #46 or #46A, DON'T try to leave the ICW and access this anchorage. Safe passage to the anchorages on the inner portion of Tarpon Bay can only be gained by a very different route (see below).

From #48, southbound vessels should pass to the south of unlighted daybeacon #48A, and continue on more or less the same course to a position just south of flashing daybeacon #50. This marker denotes the ICW's entrance into the northeasterly mouth of Grouper Creek. We shall consider this stream after taking a look at the anchorages of Tarpon Basin.

Tarpon Basin Anchorages Two of the three Tarpon Basin anchorages are about as simple to enter as running aground on Florida Bay—just kidding. Skippers bound for the northside haven can depart the ICW at unlighted daybeacon #48A, and cut 90 degrees to the north. Just be sure to stop your forward progress before approaching to within less than 200 yards of the northerly banks.

To make good your entry into the anchorage south of #48A, look towards the southeasterly banks. You will notice that the starboard side of the cove is undeveloped, while the more easterly banks contain moderate residential development. For best depths, point for the initial portion (the southwesterly portion) of the developed banks. Drop anchor after cruising some .2 nautical miles from the ICW.

The most sheltered anchor-down spot on Tarpon Basin calls for a longer cruise and far more attention to navigational detail. This anchorage is discovered along the basin's southeasterly banks, opposite the charted "Micro Tr". Navigators bound for

this haven should use their binoculars to pick out two small uncharted and unlighted daybeacons that lie just east of the anchorage discussed above. Cruise between these markers, and head straight on into the banks ahead. Some 75 yards before reaching the southeasterly shoreline, swing to port, and keeping about the same distance from the banks, follow the shoreline around as it curves to the northeast. Soon, you will be passing shallows to your port side. Keep within 50 to 75 yards of the shoreline for good depths.

We suggest dropping anchor just west-northwest of the "Micro Tr". During our several visits to these waters, we noticed that some local craft continued cruising farther to the north before anchoring. This maneuver is NOT recommended, even if you see some boats swinging on the hook farther to the north. We found that the channel you must negotiate to successfully reach these more northerly waters (and we are being charitable to call it that) to be quite winding and difficult, north of the "Micro Tr". Wise cruisers will spend the night only a short hop north of a position abeam of the "Micro Tr".

ICW and Grouper Creek West of flashing daybeacon #50, the ICW ducks into sheltered Grouper Creek. This stream slowly curves to the south on its way to Buttonwood Sound.

Immediately northeast of unlighted daybeacon #52, passing cruisers will encounter the small offshoot we described earlier, which seems so popular with snorkelers. Watch for "diver down" flags, and slow to idle speed when passing if you spot any of these warning decals.

Cruising-sized craft should not attempt to enter the "snorkel stream." Depths soon rise to 4 feet or less.

The Waterway leaves the southerly mouth of Grouper Creek, and as almost always seems to be the case in this region, passes through a dredged channel, on its way to the far deeper waters of Buttonwood Sound.

To run the dredged channel, pass between unlighted daybeacons #52A and #53, and then come abeam of flashing daybeacon #54 to its easterly quarter. South of this point, depths improved greatly.

On the ICW and Buttonwood Sound

Buttonwood Sound must be another one of those stretches of the Florida Keys ICW where the Army Corps of Engineers was running short on their aids to navigation budget. It is a run of 1.7 nautical miles across the sound from flashing daybeacon #54 to the next southerly marker, flashing daybeacon #55. Fortunately, the ICW channel does not border on any shallows. In fact, for the vast majority of this run, the Waterway is flanked by a wide buffer of 6- to 7-foot waters. We shall explore some anchorage possibilities here just below.

Cruisers continuing southbound should come abeam of flashing daybeacon #55 to its fairly immediate westerly side, and then point to pass unlighted daybeacon #56 by some 15 yards to its easterly quarter.

A dredged cut begins south of #55 and carries the Waterway into the waters adjacent to Rock Harbor. Here, let's pause for a few moments in our sojourn south down the ICW to review the various anchorages and facilities on Buttonwood Sound.

Buttonwood Sound Anchorages and Marinas

If your goal is the overnight stop east-northeast of flashing daybeacon #54, leave the familiar confines of the Waterway some 50 yards southwest of #54. Curl slowly back around to the north, dropping the hook before cruising to within less than 250 yards of the north side shoreline.

Don't slip too far to the east while entering this anchorage. As chart 11451 correctly forecasts, depths of 4½ to 5 feet lie in this direction.

The two fair-weather overnight havens on the midsection of Buttonwood Sound, east and west of the Waterway respectively, call for simply leaving the ICW and cruising about 200 yards off the channel. If you need more directions for these anchorages, better invest in the latest edition of *Chapman's*.

The anchor-down spot north of Upper Keys Sailing Club, west of the charted position of Newport, is also easily entered. Just cruise from the Waterway, pointing for the waters anywhere near 25 06.237 North/080 26.422 West. Good soundings hold to within 200 yards of the easterly shoreline.

Let's turn our attention now to the two excellent overnight stops on Sunset Cove. Allow us to remind you, once again, that locals have warned us of poor holding ground on these waters, though we have not been so unfortunate during our stays.

Cruisers who decide to anchor off Pelican Key's northwesterly banks should remember that depths run as thin as 5 feet within 200 yards of the key's shoreline. Closer in, soundings rise to 4-foot levels.

The favorite anchorage on Sunset Cove is found near the centerpoint of the cove's northeast to southwest axis, about 200 yards offshore. No tricks to be concerned with here, except to remember that low-water depths do run to 5 feet.

The Upper Keys Sailing Club makes its home on the sharp point of land that comprises the northeastern corner of Sunset Cove. For best depths, approach the docks from their northwesterly quarter.

If you choose to visit Snook's Bayside Restaurant, southwest of the Upper Keys Sailing Club, be sure to dock on the outer face of the fixed wooden pier. Even here, soundings are a mere 3 to 3½ feet at low water.

On the ICW After slicing between two islands, the ICW follows a dredged cut through the waters adjacent to Rock Harbor. Some of the cruising grounds outside of the Waterway in this region are shallow, and some are not. Take care when leaving the comfortable confines of the ICW behind.

Unlighted daybeacon #56 marks the Waterway's passage between two small islands. Immediately thereafter, cruisers should continue on course, pointing to pass between unlighted daybeacons #56A and #57, and then come abeam of unlighted daybeacon #57A to its northwesterly side. Continue on the same track, pointing to come abeam of flashing daybeacon #58 to its southeasterly quarter.

The ICW channel swings farther to the southwest at #58. The remainder of the track across Rock Harbor to Pigeon Key is well marked and presents no unusual navigational difficulty. Southwest of unlighted daybeacon #59, good depths of 5 to 6 feet open out, southeast of the Waterway. Let's pause here for a moment to consider the various Rock Harbor facilities and anchorages.

Rock Harbor Marinas The northeasternmost marina on the Rock Harbor shoreline is America Outdoors Camper Resort. There are two routes you might choose to access this small facility, but both lead through low-water soundings of 4 feet. You can cruise directly from flashing daybeacon #58 to the dockage basin. Another approach, particularly useful for captains approaching from points south, is to leave the Waterway between flashing daybeacon #60 and unlighted daybeacon #59. Cruise to within several hundred yards of the southeasterly banks, and then turn northeast. Parallel the shore, staying at least 200 yards off the banks, and you will eventually sight America Outdoors off your starboard side.

Don't try departing the ICW between flashing daybeacon #58 and unlighted daybeacon #59. A 3-foot shoal flanks the ICW to the southeast along this stretch.

The Westin Beach Resort marina occupies the sharp point of land .6 nautical miles southwest of America Outdoors. Again, the best access to this facility is gained by leaving the ICW between flashing daybeacon #60 and unlighted daybeacon #59. For maximum depths, don't cruise directly from #59 for the position of Westin Beach Resort. This track would take you perilously near the 3-foot waters to the northeast. Instead, take a more southerly passage towards the southeasterly shoreline, and then turn northeast to head for the Westin marina when you are about 200 yards from shore.

It is very important to approach the single concrete pier that serves Westin Beach Resort from its southwesterly quarter ONLY. The slips front the inner, or southeasterly face of the pier. Cruise past the docks southwesterly tip, then cut in behind, and track your way forward as close to the end of the slips as is practical. Don't try to access the slips from the northeasterly side of the pier. Very shallow water lies in this quarter.

Rock Harbor and Pigeon Key Anchorages Southwest of flashing daybeacon #60, the ICW continues tracking its way to the southwest in order to round the shallows shelving out from the Key Largo shoreline, southeast of Pigeon Key. A large bubble of 5- and 6-foot waters occupies a position south of #60. You can anchor most anywhere on these waters, but we suggest a spot near 25 03.256 North/080 29.525 West. Good depths are maintained by tracking your way directly from #60 to this position.

Captains who choose to anchor east of Pigeon Key, can leave the ICW at flashing daybeacon #60 and cruise carefully towards the key's easterly shores. Drop the hook before approaching to within less than 100 yards of Pigeon Key's eastern

banks. Remember, some 4½-foot soundings will be encountered on these waters.

On the ICW From flashing daybeacon #60, the ICW passes Pigeon Key to the south. Be SURE to pick up flashing daybeacon #61, to the west of Pigeon Key. It is important to pass #61 by at least 50 yards to its northwesterly side.

From #61, southbound ICW mariners must follow a sharp turn to the south. Before reviewing this stretch, however, let's take a look at both the back-country anchorages that will be discovered to the northwest and an interesting shortcut for smaller craft.

Back-country Anchorages The first step in making your way to all three of the back-country anchorages described earlier is to cut northwest off the ICW at flashing daybeacon #61. From this point, however, navigation becomes, shall we say, challenging. There are virtually no aids to navigation in the back country, and navigators learn pretty quickly that one key looks pretty much like the next. Your only recourse is to keep a good DR track, or better yet, employ that wonderful combination of a GPS, interfaced with a laptop computer.

If you anchor east of Bottle Key, be sure to set the hook at least .5 of a nautical mile off the key's easterly banks. Take note of the correctly charted tongue of Upper Cross Bank to the southwest. Depths across this bank are nil. If you wander into these shallows, trust us, you will be giving Sea Tow some business.

The only trick to anchoring off Butternut

Key is to correctly identify the isle, and anchor at least 300 yards offshore. Consider breaking out the dinghy and cruising around the northwesterly tip of Butternut Key. During fair weather this is a great gunkhole. Just don't try going ashore. Landing is prohibited.

The adventurous anchorage off the Manatee Keys calls for a far longer cruise from the Waterway. Having made this trip ourselves on several occasions, we can tell you with certainty that it's easy to lose track of just where you are. Pay attention to business.

Pass at least 400 yards north of Bottle Key, and set your course almost due west. When the Manatee Keys come into sight, deviate your track to the southwest a bit,

and anchor .35 nautical miles east-north-east of the larger of the two Manatee Keys.

Sneaky Shortcut Captains who pilot vessels drawing 3 feet or less can follow a sneaky shortcut that, heretofore, only the locals have known about. This informal pass cuts through the tongue of very shallow water south-southeast of Pigeon Key.

The channel runs almost immediately adjacent to the shoreline, near 25 02.512 North/080 30.122 West. It is marked by stakes, a few of which are decorated with toilet seats. This is NOT the famed Toilet Seat Cut," however. We shall meet that off-beat channel in the next chapter.

This particular sneaky channel carries

Toilet Seat Cut

about 3 feet at low tide, and some navigation by eye is necessary. However, for smaller powercraft with outboards, or I/Os, or sailing vessels with a fully retractable keel, this nifty little passage avoids the loooong swing in the Waterway as it rounds Pigeon Key.

The locals use this shortcut on a daily basis, and you will appear to be in the know if you take advantage of it also. Just don't try it with a boat drawing more than 3 feet, okay?

On the ICW As mentioned above, the ICW takes a sharp cut to the south at flashing daybeacon #61 and heads back for the Key Largo Shoreline. For best definition, switch to Inset 5, Page E of chart 11451 while navigating the Waterway between Pigeon Key and the Cowpens Cut.

South of flashing daybeacon #62, the channel begins a slow turn to the west-southwest. This portion of the Waterway is well marked. That's a really good thing, as there is a large patch of shallows just north and northwest of the channel. Be sure to stay east of unlighted daybeacon #62A and southeast of unlighted daybeacon #64.

After making its turn to the west-southwest, the ICW's next aid to navigation is unlighted daybeacon #64A. As you would expect, pass this marker to its southeasterly side. South of #64A, cruisers can choose to visit the anchorage or an up-and-coming marina on Community Harbor.

Community Harbor and Mangrove Marina Okay, listen up out there all you coastal navigators. NOAA really dropped the ball on this one. The entrance to Community Harbor has very little resemblance to what is pictured on chart 11451, Page E, Inset 5. First of all, the aid to navigation shown on the chart south-southeast of flashing daybeacon #65, unlighted daybeacon #2, has apparently been removed entirely. Secondly, chart 11451 depicts the two markers denoting the entrance into Community Harbor as unlighted daybeacons #3 and #4. Wrong! These aids are now unlighted daybeacons #1 and #2.

But wait, that's not all. Do you see any islands or mangroves pictured on chart 11451, forming the northerly boundary of Community Harbor? We don't either, but trust us, they are there. In fact, captains running this passage will find themselves cruising between quite a collection of small islets to reach the inner harbor.

So, with all that out of the way, here's how to get to Community Harbor. Cut south from unlighted daybeacon #64A, and set a careful compass course toward unlighted daybeacons #1 and #2 (pictured on chart 11451 as #3 and #4). Use your binoculars to help pick out these aids to navigation.

Pass directly between #1 and #2, and continue tracking your way to the south-southwest into the midwidth of Community Harbor. If your intention is to anchor, continue cruising into the heart of the harbor, until the somewhat deeper waters spread out in a larger bubble. This is the one aspect of Community Harbor that is correctly shown on 11451. Anchor somewhere near the bay's center. Don't approach any of the shorelines or mangroves closely. The already meager 4-foot depths shelve up even more dramatically nearer shore.

Mangrove Marina occupies the harbor's southeasterly shoreline. Continue following the channel to the south from #1 and #2, and don't turn into the docks until they are directly abeam to port. Only then should you turn into the marina. Don't set a direct course from #1 and #2 towards the piers. Such a plan would land you in the 1-foot depths, south of #1 and #2.

On the ICW Southwest of flashing daybeacon #65, the ICW passes through a dredged passage known as Ramshorn Cut. This man-made channel subdivides, appropriately enough, Ramshorn Shoal. Two sets of closely spaced daybeacons lead navigators though this passage. Simply pass between unlighted daybeacons #66 and #67, and between #69 and #68.

Then, set course to come abeam of flashing daybeacon #70 to its southerly side. There are no further markers for the next .7 nautical miles. At this point, the ICW intersects the channel leading to Tavernier Creek.

Confusion Corner Slow down, have your binoculars on your lap, and chart 11451 in hand as you approach the junctures with the Tavernier Creek channel. It's VERY easy to become confused by the various markers. Let's sort through them below.

All southbound craft should come abeam and pass flashing daybeacon #71 to its northwesterly side. Use your binocs to correctly identify #71. Don't mistake the markers to the south and southeast as #71. These smaller aids to navigation are part of

the Tavernier Creek entrance channel and will be covered below.

From #71, the Waterway turns a bit farther to the southwest. Even if you are planning to enter Tavernier Creek, you must continue tracking your way down the ICW from #71. Eventually, the gap between unlighted daybeacons #17 and #18 will come abeam to the east. These are the outermost markers on the Tavernier Creek channel. If you are bypassing Tavernier Creek and continuing south on the Waterway, ignore #17 and #18 completely. Keep on trucking to the next Waterway marker, flashing daybeacon #73, which lies some .65 nautical miles to the southwest.

Tavernier Creek Cruisers intent on visiting Tavernier Creek must continue cruising southwest on the Waterway until the gap between unlighted daybeacons #17 and #18 is directly abeam to the east. Don't try to run directly from the ICW's flashing daybeacon #71 into the creek's mouth. This is a sure and certain recipe for a grounding.

Cut to the east and pass between #17 and #18. Then, point for the gap between unlighted daybeacons #15 and #16. The channel now takes a hard turn to starboard and soon enters the creek. Pass unlighted daybeacon #14 hard by its westerly quarter, as you pass into the stream's interior reaches.

Note that vessels entering Tavernier Creek from the ICW will be passing red, even-numbered aids to navigation to their (the cruisers') port side and taking green markers to starboard. This is just as it should be. You are now headed "toward" the open sea, so "red, right, returning" is properly reversed.

Let's insert a quick word of caution here for captains and crews northbound on Tavernier Creek, headed towards a juncture with the ICW. We have noted on more than one occasion, the tendency of captains exiting the northerly mouth of Tavernier Creek to pass between #15 and #16, and then head directly for the ICW's flashing daybeacon #71. Don't do that, unless you are a fan of Sea Tow. Be sure to pick up #17 and #18 immediately after passing #15 and #16. Turn to the west and run the gap between #17 and #18. Then, you can track your way safely a bit farther to the west to an intersection with the Waterway.

Returning our attention to cruisers seaward bound on Tavernier Creek, the interior reaches of this stream are deep almost from bank to bank, and are easy to run. Or rather, they would be easy to run if it weren't for some very sharp, blind turns along the way. It would be just like some hot dog in a Cigarette boat to come flying around one of these turns and plough right into your vessel, which, trust us, can ruin your entire day on the water. So, we suggest taking it slowly on Tavernier Creek, even in the unrestricted portion of the creek.

An official no-wake zone begins on Tavernier Creek, east and south of 25 00.542 North/080 32.225 West. This prohibition is actually welcomed on the twisty, turny track of Tavernier Creek. The slow speed zone continues to be in effect all the way to unlighted daybeacons #12 and #13, south of the fixed Tavernier Creek Bridge.

Eventually, you will begin to pick up some residential development along the southern and western shorelines. Some of these houses are quite elegant, and many have private docks decorated with a very impressive array of huge powercraft.

Eventually, Tavernier Creek turns to the south, and the 15-foot fixed Tavernier Creek Bridge will be sighted dead ahead. Just before reaching this span, Tavernier Creek Marina will come abeam to the west. The fuel dock fronts directly onto the creek.

Once the fixed bridge is in your wake, Hawk Channel-bound mariners should hold to the middle of the passage, and point to pass between unlighted daybeacons #12 and #13. The remaining portion of the channel connecting the creek to the ocean and Hawk Channel is very well marked by unlighted daybeacons. Just remember that depths at low water can rise to 5-foot levels, particularly near unlighted daybeacons #1 and #2.

The outermost marker on the Tavernier Creek approach channel is an unnumbered flashing daybeacon. You can actually pass to either side of this aid to navigation, but for best depths, come abeam to its northeasterly quarter.

Hawk Channel—Largo Sound to Tavernier Creek

The Key Largo portion of Hawk Channel is a 180-degree contrast from the ICW passage reviewed above. Protected anchorages are scarce, but there are a fine group of marina facilities that stand ready to serve cruising craft. Depths are also not a problem in the deep Hawk Channel, but some of the marina approach channels can be a little thin.

Most larger cruising craft choose to run this stretch of Hawk Channel, rather than plow through the ICW. Of course, this same principle pretty much goes for the entire ICW versus Hawk Channel routes from Miami to Marathon, so there is nothing unique about the waters lapping along the shores of Key Largo.

Key Largo Canal
(Various Lat/Lons—see below)

A 1.9 nautical mile, westward trek from Mosquito Bank and Hawk Channel's flashing daybeacon #35 will bring cruisers face to face with the outermost marker (flashing daybeacon #2) of an entrance channel that, in turn, leads to a heavily developed body of water that we call Key Largo Canal. A host of marina and repair facilities, plus several large hotels, make their home along the banks of this stream. Flashing daybeacon #2 is located near 25 04.606 North/080 25.631 West.

From #2, the channel runs to the north and soon passes into the initial reaches of the canal. Minimum soundings on the approach cut run as shallow as 5 feet, but 6-foot low-water soundings are typical. Once inside the canal, depths deepen to an amazing 15+ feet.

Eventually the canal takes a 90-degree turn to the west. This turn is known as "crash corner." Local boats of any size use VHF Channel 16 to warn that they are approaching this turn. It might be wise to monitor Channel 16 yourself when coming in here, just to be on the safe side. Watch out for water lice, also known as personal watercraft. They have no radios, of course.

As you would expect, all the marina facilities on Largo Canal are well sheltered from bad weather. This would be a great spot to ride out anything short of a hurricane.

First up is Key Largo Harbour (25 05.824 North/080 25.866 West), which overlooks the northerly banks at "crash corner." The manager of this facility is David Lavish, who also is affable, courteous and—maybe most important—knowledgeable and precise.

Transients are accepted for overnight dockage at the marina's fixed wooden finger piers and concrete face dock. Large party boats, which take tourists offshore for gambling, use this marina as a point of departure. Pleasure craft as large as 65 to 70 feet can be accommodated. Full dockside fresh water and power hookups (up to 50 amps) are in the offing, and both gas and diesel can be purchased dockside. Waste pump-out is also available.

Key Largo Harbour has a deal with the Ramada Inn up the street for use of the Ramada's facilities, which include showers, pool, Jacuzzi, and Laundromat. The boatyard has its own shower facilities, too.

There's a restaurant on the property, an inside/outside affair called Captain's Cabin Too (305-453-7930)! Bigger outside than inside, it is a tiki-type arrangement outside with picnic tables. It sits right on "crash corner," so diners may get to see a boating accident in the making or maybe just a near miss. It's better than television. The fare is mostly Keys sandwich stuff and the prices are reasonable. They have nine different beers on draft. This is a local's kind of place.

Key Largo Harbour features a full-service repair yard with a 60-ton travel lift and mechanical servicing for both gasoline and diesel-power plants. If you need to get out of the water in Key Largo, this would be the place.

Key Largo Canal

Key Largo Harbour (305) 451-0045

Approach depth—5-6 feet (low water)
Dockside depth—15+ feet
Accepts transients—yes
Type of docking—fixed wooden piers and concrete dock
Dockside power connections—up to 50 amp
Dockside water connections—yes
Waste pump-out—yes
Showers—yes
Laundromat—yes
Fuel available—gas and diesel
Mechanical repairs—yes, extensive
Below-waterline repairs—yes, extensive
Ship's store—yes, (minimal, but practical selection)
Restaurant—on site, more close by

The Marina del Mar Resort and Marina (25 05.700 North/080 26.180 West) lies along the south side of the Key Largo Canal, a bit farther upstream. This is a lovely place, which, if you can afford it, readily accepts overnight transients.

The minimum overnight fee is $65, but there are weekly and monthly rates . . . and also a holiday rate, which is appreciably higher. There is a separate charge for water and electric, with a minimum of $5 per day for each. Showers and a Laundromat are found on the bottom story of the four-story building, which overlooks the docks, just about in the middle of the facility. The Laundromat has two washers and two dryers, both coin ops. The showers/heads are clean.

Dockage is afforded at fixed wooden piers and wooden face docks. Power connections (30 amp) and fresh water hookups are found at all berths.

The operation has a wonderful swimming pool area that we found inviting. There's shade around, too, which is blissful on a hot day when the sun makes a little bit of hell on earth out of Key Largo. For tennis fans, there are also a couple of tennis courts, hard-surfaced. Hotel guests get a twenty-five percent discount off the marina rates.

Next door is a restaurant/bar/night club called Coconuts (305-453-9794). The place has an outside bar and restaurant overlooking the canal. The food is typical Keys. Prices are moderate. But one must remember that this is a bar first and foremost, so the food is an add on. There's dancing at night. And entertainment is varied, from blues to karaoke to a pajama party. (Yawn.)

Marina del Mar Resort and Marina (305) 451-4107
http://www.marinadelmarkeylargo.com

Approach depth—5-6 feet (low water)
Dockside depth—15+ feet
Accepts transients—yes
Type of docking—fixed wooden piers
Dockside power connections—30 amp
Dockside water connections—yes
Showers—yes
Laundromat—yes
Fuel available—nearby
Mechanical repairs—nearby
Below-waterline repairs—nearby
Restaurant—on site

Farther up the channel is the hurly-burly commercial area of a Best Western (305-451-5081), a Ramada Inn (305-451-3939), and a Holiday Inn (305-451-2121). At the Holiday is the original *African Queen,* a small steamboat which was in the movie by the same name.

This film movie featured Humphrey Bogart and Katherine Hepburn. If you feel so compelled, and for a price, you can go for a ride in the boat, to touch cinematic immortality. The *African Queen* and other commercial attractions are available at the end of the canal, hard by the Overseas Highway (U.S. 1).

Lake Largo Facilities
(25 05.279 North/080 26.422 West)

The same channel that provides access to Largo Canal also allows cruisers to visit well-protected Lake Largo and its adjoining canal. Instead of continuing on to the north, captains bent on a visit to Lake Largo and its marinas should turn to the west at unlighted daybeacon #6. Again, low-water entrance depths can run to as little as 5 feet, but we didn't find many soundings of less than 5½ or 6 feet.

Eventually, the canal will approach Lake Largo. The fuel dock associated with Pilot House Marina will be spotted to the north, just before entering the lake. This marina's dockage basin will be spotted just beyond, on the lake's northerly banks.

Pilot House Marina (25 05.250 North/080 26.470 West) is well kept and a great place to be in bad weather. They accept transients, in fact, they cater to transients at Pilot House Marina. There are 10 transient slips, more or less, depending on circumstances. In addition to the standard connections (water and electricity up to 50 amps) there are also cable television and telephone hookups available. Waste pump-out is coming in a few months.

Depths alongside vary widely from 15 to as little as 4½ feet, depending on slip location. Captains of deep-draft vessels should be sure to make the dockmaster aware of their needs when slip selection is in progress.

On Golden Pond's Chris Craft

The marina showers are in several places and they are locked. They are also as clean as you will find, even if they are not this year's model. There are few marinas that take such good care of transients as Pilot House Marina does, and it shows.

The Laundromat has four machines, coin ops. There's a library in the clubhouse out on the pier, and here, visitors will also find a most welcome phone hookup to the Internet.

Mechanical repairs are on an "on call" basis. (A serious crisis on a boat would best be handled at Key Largo Harbour.)

Pilot House Marina also features a restaurant called Tiki Bar and Grill (305-451-3142), with typical Keys fare. Come to think of it, there are probably more tikis in the Florida Keys than there are in all of the Pacific Ocean.

Pilot House Marina (305) 451-3452
http://www.pilothousemarina.com

Approach depth—5-6 feet
Dockside depth—4$^1/_2$ feet to 15 feet, depending on slip locatio

Accepts transients—yes
Type of docking—fixed wooden finger piers in excellent condition
Dockside power connections—up to 50 amp
Dockside water connections—yes
Waste pump-out—on the way
Showers—yes
Laundromat—yes
Fuel available—gasoline and diesel fuel
Mechanical repairs—independent technicians on call
Restaurant—on site

Ocean Bay Marina also overlooks the northern shores of Lake Largo, just to the west of Pilot House Marina. We found this marina in a state of flux during our visit. Fuel was no longer for sale, and the ship's store was barely stocked. We'll give it a look for the next edition of this guide, but for now,

The *African Queen* (Key Largo)

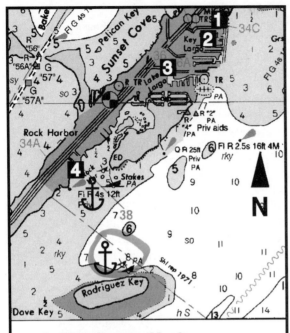

1. Key Largo Harbour
**2. Marina del Mar Resort
   and Marina**
3. Pilot House Marina
4. Mandalay Marina

visiting cruisers should probably not count on finding too much in the way of marine services here.

Mandalay Marina
(25 04.368 North/080 27.590 West)

Study chart 11451 for a moment and notice the position of "Rock Hbr," well southwest of Lake Largo. Mandalay Marina and Tiki Bar (305-852-5450) guards the northwesterly banks, a short hop southwest of these waters. Unfortunately, the unmarked entry channel carries a minimal 3 feet of depth at low water, though soundings alongside deepen to 4- and

5-foot levels. Obviously this is a shallow-draft-vessel-only stop.

Mandalay Marina is a friendly place with a decidedly local flavor to it. The people in here are real, though the boats look a little worn, and the food in the restaurant is great. Transients are accepted for overnight dockage, but berth availability is on a first-come, first-served basis. So if you plan to stop here, it would be wise to call ahead. Showers are available, and there is a Laundromat close by. Fuel is not currently on site. However there is a big condo development going in immediately to the southwest, which will reportedly have fuel.

This isn't a big marina, and there's a small fleet of sailboats anchored about 200 yards off the dockage basin, behind Rodriguez Key. According to marina management, there is a waste pump-out on the way, but it needs to be seen to be believed. Things in the Keys have a way of slowing down.

Mandalay Marina (305) 853-0296

Approach depth—3 feet
Dockside depth—4-5 feet
Accepts transients—yes
Type of docking—fixed wooden piers
Dockside power connections—30 amp
Dockside water connections—yes
Showers—yes
Laundromat—close by
Ship's and variety store—beach, bait, and tackle
Restaurant—on site

Rock Harbor Anchorage
(25 04.048 North/080 27.454 West)

During our perusal of the Hawk Channel waters, we were surprised to see quite a host of local sailcraft anchored on the waters of "Rock Hbr," just a short hop southeast of Mandalay Marina, reviewed above. Many of these vessels were swinging on mooring buoys, but it is certainly possible to anchor here as well. Low-water soundings seem to run about 5 feet, and there is unlimited swinging room, as long as you don't get too close to a neighboring craft. There is shelter to the west and northwest, and to a lesser extent, the north. Don't even think about stopping here with blows coming in from the south, east, or southeast.

Rodriguez Key Anchorage
(25 03.373 North/080 27.285 West)
Some cruising craft occasionally drop the

Aid to navigation on Hawk Channel

hook to the north of Rodriguez Key, northwest of Hawk Channel's unlighted daybeacon #37. There are a lot of down sides to this anchorage. First, to maintain 6- to 7-foot depths, you must anchor at least .2 nautical miles north of the isle's northern banks. While this might be okay in light to moderate southerly and southwesterly winds, woe be unto the mariner who is caught swinging on the hook here if strong winds happen upon them from any other quarter. Not only would it make for a miserable evening, but it is quite possible to drag anchor into the band of shallows that shelve out from Rodriguez Key. To the west and southwest, there are even broader patches of shallows.

So, anchor here if you choose in fair weather and light airs (particularly if they are blowing from the south), but you'd better be ready to move at a moment's notice if bad weather comes calling. For our money, we would far rather choose to stop at one of the nearby marinas. But, hey, that's just us.

Snapper's Restaurant
(25 02.532 North/080 29.352 West)
Snapper's Restaurant (305-852-5956) is one of Claiborne's favorite watering holes in all of the Florida Keys. There are two outdoor bars, both of which have a good view of Hawk Channel. There is also quite a collection of tables set up for outside dining. The food is simply wonderful, even if you have to hang onto your wallet a bit, come time to pay the check.

Snapper's is located on the Key Largo shoreline, west-southwest of Rodriguez Key and northeast of charted Long Point. There is a scantily marked entrance channel and some small craft wet slip dockage, but don't get your hopes up.

That's the good news. The bad is that

entrance depths run from 2½ to 3 feet at low tide. Dockside soundings improve to between 6 and 8 feet, but you have to traverse the thin approach cut to get here. It's quite possible to wander into even less water. Clearly, this is only a stop for small powercraft with outboard or I/O power. Should you make it to the slips through these shallow soundings, water-borne visitors are permitted to moor while dining, but no overnight stays are allowed.

Snapper's is so good that you might consider visiting here by automobile, if motorized transportation is available to you. Unfortunately, with its scanty soundings, very few cruising craft will be able to take advantage of Snapper's from the water.

Curtis Marine and Blue Waters Marina (25 01.163 North/080 30.475 West)

West-southwest of Hawk Channel's unlighted daybeacon #39 (itself located adjacent to the "Triangles"), cruising craft can follow a long and involved channel that curves around the large shoal north of Tavernier Key. Then, a well-marked cut leads you into a canal that sports some of the heaviest residential development that you will ever see. At this point, you will probably wonder, Why have Morgan and Claiborne sent us here?

Keep the faith. Eventually a larger, pool-like body of water will open out to the west. Both Curtis Marine and Blue Waters Marina guard the small bay's northerly banks of this body of water. Depths in the canal and harbor run up to 30 feet (see below) and you will find at least 9 feet of water dockside. Unfortunately, the innermost portion of the marked approach channel drops to 4½ feet at low water, but deeper-draft vessels can always time their entry and egress for high tide. That will add another 2½ feet or so to

these soundings (giving about 7 feet of water at high tide).

Don't try to anchor on the wide pool, south of the marinas described below. According to J. D. Howard at Blue Water Marina (and we believe him), the bottom of the basin off his docks is rocky and terrible holding ground, in addition to being some 35 feet deep.

First up is Curtis Marine, Inc. While transient space is slim here, because there are live aboards and people who rent slips year round, this is one of those marinas that you dream about stopping in. For one thing, depths in the marina are very impressive; it was a burrow pit for fill for the Overseas Railroad before it became a marine cul de sac. The rest rooms look as if they have just been cleaned, and it appears that's the way they always look. If you could get your own kids to leave bathrooms and showers this neat at home, you would be able to feel that your parenting role was complete. The entire grounds are like this, spotless, and the on-site marine store is as neat as a pin. What is more, Curtis Marine sells useful merchandise that mariners can appreciate. The "trash" factor is nil. There is a shop on the premises where boat owners can work on projects, too. Cruisers will also discover a large, semi-open-air Laundromat, which is under a roof but open on three sides.

We suggest that you call ahead to check on slip availability. If you are lucky enough to secure a berth (and we do mean lucky), expect to tie up to fixed concrete finger piers, with fresh water connections. Some spaces have 30-amp power and others 50 amp.

When it comes time to satisfy the old appetite, cruisers will find a nearby Papa John's Pizza (305-853-0999). There is a better selection of dining spots within walking

Snapper's Restaurant (Key Largo)

distance in Tavernier. Ask any of the friendly marina staff for recommendations.

The same shopping center that plays host to Papa John's Pizza also sports a Winn-Dixie supermarket, a McDonald's, a movie theater, a Chinese restaurant, and a video rental store.

If you want peace and quiet, you'll love Curtis Marine, if they can find a place for you. If you want bright lights and lots of action, this is not for you.

Curtis Marine (305) 852-5218

Approach depth—4½ feet (low water)
Dockside depth—9-30 feet
Accepts transients—yes, but best to call ahead
Type of docking—fixed concrete finger piers
Dockside power connections—30 to 50 amp, depending on the slip
Dockside water connections—yes

Showers—yes
Laundromat—yes, large and outside, under roof
Ship's store—clean and well stocked
Restaurant—nearby

Blue Waters Marina (305-853-5604-days, 305-852-1810-evenings) occupies the little charted northward offshoot, just past Curtis Marine. This marina is as clean, neat, secluded, and quiet as Curtis Marine (above) is, but the difference is that Blue Waters is full most of the time and takes no transients. Run by J. D. and Yvonne Howard, who live on the property, it is a pleasant place with many beautifully maintained yachts in evidence.

Tavernier Creek and Marina

Cruisers following the main path of Hawk Channel can cut to the west-northwest and

Dive boat on Hawk Channel

visit Tavernier Creek, some 2.9 nautical miles southwest of unlighted daybeacon #39. All mariners cruising these waters should be SURE to read our navigational review below before entering this region.

The well-marked Tavernier Creek approach channel comes up southwest of charted Tavernier Key. Some shoaling has occurred in this cut over the past several years, and low-water soundings of as little as 5 feet are now in the offing. There is also PLENTY of tidal current boiling through this stream.

Tavernier Creek's usefulness to cruising-sized craft is severely limited by the 15-foot fixed bridge that crosses the stream a short hop north of its Hawk Channel approach cut. Immediately north of the bridge, Tavernier Creek Marina (305-852-5854, 25 00.193 North/080 31.837 West) will come abeam to the west. This facility is huge and quite attractive, but it is solely a dry-stack facility or long-term wet slip rental facility. Transients are not accepted. Period.

The only parts of Tavernier Creek Marina readily accessible to visiting cruisers are Chris's Bait and Tackle (305-853-0191) and Las Brisas Café (305-853-0042). Chris's fronts the marina's entrance, on its southerly flank, and offers beer, fuel (gasoline and diesel fuel), and sandwiches. Depths at the fuel dock run as thin as 4½ to 5 feet, but soundings in the harbor are in the 8+-foot region.

Las Brisas Café is a small operation that sits immediately adjacent to Chris's. It is so new that we have not been able to review its cuisine, but we are told it is open for breakfast and lunch.

Moving up Tavernier Creek toward the ICW and Florida Bay, it will become quickly apparent just how sheltered this creek really is. There are blind turns and tidal currents to worry with, so watch for these hazards.

The juncture between Tavernier Creek and the ICW holds at least 7 feet of water, but captains must get past some confusing markers. Be SURE to read the navigational account below BEFORE running this passage for the first time.

HAWK CHANNEL—LARGO SOUND TO TAVERNIER CREEK NAVIGATION

We pick up our navigational account of Hawk Channel where last we left it at flashing daybeacon #35, west of Mosquito Bank. Two hazards distinguish the passage down to Tavernier Creek from other portions of the Hawk cut. The islands of Rodriguez Key and Tavernier Key indent the channel's northwesterly flank. Navigators should make use of all of their available prowess to stay away from both isles. They are surrounded by shoal water.

Otherwise, it's just the usual long runs between aids to navigation, so typical of Hawk Channel. Side passages can be a bit more challenging, but we'll guide you through all these smaller cuts below.

Key Largo Canal and Associated Facilities Cruisers bound for the marinas and facilities on Key Largo Canal should probably continue cruising southwest on Hawk Channel for about .5 nautical miles past flashing daybeacon #35 (off Mosquito Bank). You can then turn to the west-northwest and track your way 1.15 nautical miles to flashing daybeacon #2. This aids to navigation is the outermost marker on the canal's approach channel.

Come abeam of #2 to its southerly side and swing to the north. Point to pass unlighted daybeacons #4 and #6 to their fairly immediate westerly quarters. Then, continue straight ahead for the gap between

Sea gulls on Hawk Channel

flashing daybeacon #7 and unlighted daybeacon #8. From this point, the entrance to the canal is obvious to the north.

Slow to idle speed. The initial stretch of the Key Largo Canal is lined by an incredibly dense collection of residences, many with their own private docks. Any wake at all could get you in a world of trouble on these waters.

Eventually, it will appear as if the canal dead-ends. Actually it hangs a 90-degree turn to the west. These waters are known as "crash corner." Proceed at maximum alert, and be sure to have your VHF on and tuned to Channel 16. Many of the local captains make a safety call on 16 as they are approaching this turn from the inner reaches of the canal.

After proceeding through "crash corner," Key Largo Harbour will come up along the northerly banks, followed by Marina del Mar Resort and Marina a bit farther upstream, overlooking the southerly shores.

Lake Largo Facilities If you are making for Lake Largo and/or Pilot House Marina, follow the tracks outlined above as far as a position abeam of unlighted daybeacon #6. Turn to the west-northwest at #6, and watch for a small lighthouse-shaped structure that marks the easterly entrance of the canal leading to Lake Largo. Simply stay within shouting distance of this stream's midwidth as you work you way up to the lake. Pilot House Marina will eventually be spied to starboard.

Rock Harbor Anchorage and Mandalay Marina Both these stopovers lie 1.3 nautical miles southwest of the Key Largo Canal, discussed above. Try departing Hawk Channel about 1.6 nautical miles southwest of flashing daybeacon #35. Turn to the

Westin Resort Dock

west, and set course for the waters south-west of the charted half-foot soundings on the inner portion of Rock Harbor. The trick is to stay well north of the shallows sur-rounding Rodriguez Key to your south, and well southwest of the very shoally depths in inner Rock Harbor.

As you approach the northwesterly banks, the anchorage will become quite apparent, courtesy of the many local sail-craft moored on these waters. Be sure to leave plenty of swing room between your craft and any neighbors.

The entrance to Mandalay Marina will be spotted immediately west-northwest of the anchorage basin and local mooring field. Just cruise straight in between the breakwater entrance.

Rodriguez Key Anchorage Cruisers bound for this fair-weather (at best) anchorage can follow pretty much the same route as one would take to the Rock Harbor Anchorage. After passing Rodriguez Key by AT LEAST .55 nautical miles to its easterly side, you can begin a lazy turn around to the north side of the key. Do not approach to within less than .2 nautical miles of the this shore-line. Rodriguez Key is surrounded by a broad shelf of shallows along its entire shoreline.

On Hawk Channel Moving southwest on Hawk Channel from flashing daybeacon #35, it is a run of almost 2.8 nautical miles to a position abeam of unlighted daybea-con #37. Be sure to come abeam of #37 by at least 200 yards to its westerly side. This plan of action will help to avoid the

correctly charted 5-foot reef, northeast of #37.

As you come abeam and pass #37, Rodriguez Key will be to the west of your course line. Be sure to stay well off the shores of this key. It is surrounded by a broad band of shoal water.

From #37, it is a shorter trek of 2.35 nau-tical miles to the next Hawk Channel aid to navigation, unlighted daybeacon #39. Again, come abeam of #39 by at least 200 yards to its westerly side. This daybeacon marks another 5-foot reef.

Between #37 and #39, vessels with a draft of LESS THAN 3 feet can cut off to the west and find their way to Snapper's Restaurant, northeast of Long Point.

Snapper's Restaurant Please remember that depths coming into the docks at Snapper's Restaurant rise to 2½-foot levels at low or even mid-tide. Only shallow-draft, outboard, and I/O-powered craft need apply.

If you do make the attempt, look for one floating green marker. This is the outermost aid to navigation on the approach passage. The remainder of this minimal channel is outlined by white PVC pipes.

Eventually, you must hug the starboard side, mangrove shore, then round a half-pipe, and pass close aboard a launching ramp. You then round a point of land and swing to starboard into the restaurant dock-age basin.

Sounds fun doesn't it? (Grin!) Good luck—you may need it!

On Hawk Channel Even for Hawk

Snappers Restaurant—Key Largo

Fishing craft at Molasses Reef—Hawk Channel

Channel, it is a very long passage indeed moving southwest from unlighted daybeacon #39 to the next marker on this major offshore cut. You will have to cross 6.8 nautical miles of water to make your way to the 35-foot flashing daybeacon #40, lying south and east of the Hen and Chickens Reef. Be SURE to come abeam of #40 by several hundred yards to its EASTERLY quarter. Passing to the west of #40 is a sure recipe for disaster.

After leaving unlighted daybeacon #39 in your wake for some 1.4 nautical miles, Tavernier Key will begin to come abeam, well northwest of your course line. Stay way away from this key. It is flanked by a huge body of shoal water on all sides.

There are two side trips for cruisers to consider between #39 and #40. Only .8 nautical miles southwest of #39, captains can follow a somewhat intricate, but reasonably well-marked, passage to Curtis Marine and Blue Water Marina.

Farther along, a turn to the north-northwest will lead cruisers to the Tavernier Creek approach channel.

Curtis Marine and Blue Water Marina Take your time on this one, and be sure to pick out the next marker before proceeding. The first aid to navigation you will meet up with is flashing daybeacon #2. Come abeam of #2 to its southwesterly side, and set course to the west.

Use your binoculars to pick out the next aid to navigation, unlighted daybeacon #3. Be sure to stay several hundred yards (at least) north of #3. This aid marks the huge shelf of shallows surrounding Tavernier Key.

It doesn't take too much in the way of smarts to figure out you that you should not get anywhere near #3.

Next up is unlighted daybeacon #4. A little better than .9 nautical miles separates #3 and #4, so again, you may want to use your binoculars to pick out this marker. Come abeam of #4 to its immediate southerly side.

At this point, the channel passes through a long turn to the northeast. For maximum depths, point to come abeam of the southeasternmost markers on the canal approach channel, flashing daybeacon #1 and unlighted daybeacon #2, by about 100 yards to their southerly side. Only when the gap between #1 and #2 is directly abeam to the north-northwest, should you turn to pass between these two markers.

The remainder of the canal approach channel is well marked. Continue straight ahead into the stream's mouth, and immediately slow to idle speed. In a situation very similar to what we encountered in the Key Largo Canal, this creek is lined by a multitude of sumptuous homes with private docks.

Soon the canal slants to the north. Keep trucking upstream, until the westerly shores open out into a wide, square-shaped cove. Curtis Marina guards the cove's northern banks. Blue Water Marina lies just to the west of Curtis, on the charted northerly offshoot.

Tavernier Creek and Tavernier Marina The well-marked entrance channel leading from the open waters adjacent to Hawk Channel to Tavernier Creek, is found approximately 1 nautical mile west-southwest of Tavernier

Tavernier Creek Marina

Key. Remember that low-water depths in this cut have shoaled to 5 feet, and that the creek is crossed by a 15-foot fixed bridge.

The interior reaches of this stream are deep almost from bank to bank, and are easy to run. Or rather, they would be easy to run if it weren't for some very sharp, blind turns along the way. It would be just like some hot dog in a Cigarette boat to come flying around one of these turns and plough right into your vessel, which, trust me, can ruin your entire day on the water. So, we suggest taking it slowly on Tavernier Creek, even in the unrestricted portion of the creek.

The outermost set of markers on the Tavernier Creek approach cut are unlighted daybeacons #1 and #2. The remainder of this cut is very well outlined by pairs of unlighted daybeacons. The innermost set is numbered #12 and #13. After passing between #12 and #13, enter the southerly mouth of Tavernier Creek along its center-line.

Slow to idle speed at unlighted daybeacons #12 and #13.7 An official no-wake zone begins on Tavernier Creek at this point and continues upstream to 25 00.542 North/080 32.225 West. This prohibition is actually welcomed on the twisty, turny track of Tavernier Creek.

Immediately after passing under the 15-foot Tavernier Creek Bridge, Tavernier

Creek Marina will come abeam to the west. The fuel dock fronts directly onto the creek.

Farther upstream, residential development picks up along the southern and westerly shorelines. Some of these houses are quite elegant, and many have private docks decorated with a very impressive array of huge powercraft.

Eventually, and rather suddenly, all the homeplaces come to an end, and you will find yourself cruising on an undeveloped tract. From this point to the creek's northwesterly mouth, you will find the sharpest bends and blind turns. Take your time and watch out for the other guy.

As you approach the creek's northwesterly mouth, it's time for even more caution. We have noted on more than one occasion, the tendency of captains exiting the northerly mouth of Tavernier Creek to pass between unlighted daybeacons #15 and #16, and then head directly for the ICW's flashing daybeacon #71. Don't do that, unless you are a fan of Sea Tow. Be sure to turn to the west immediately after passing between #15 and #16, and then pick up unlighted daybeacons #17 and #18. Only after passing between #17 and #18 can you safely turn southwest into the ICW channel. Even here, we suggest you track your way 100 yards to the west of #17 and #18 before making the turn into the ICW passage.

If all this sounds a little challenging, that's because it is. Of course, local Key Largo cruisers will probably read this and wonder what all the fuss it about. First-timers, however, will want to know about all this and proceed with extra care.

Tavernier Creek Marina

Estes Fishing Camp

CHAPTER 3

Tavernier Creek to Channel Five

Just as the waters we met in the last chapter were dominated by the loosely jointed community of Key Largo, the cruising grounds between Tavernier Creek and Channel Five are part and parcel of the place known as Islamorada. Islamorada is actually a collection of keys—a Village of Islands—starting with Plantation Key, which begins on the west side of Tavernier Creek and ends with Lower Matecumbe Key.

From a cruiser's point of view, there are some differences between these waters and the ones reviewed in the last chapter. Most importantly, there are at least two marinas accessible from the inside-ICW route that cater to larger cruising craft. Only one will win a depth award, but nevertheless, this happy situation does make for a welcome change.

Anchorages continue to pepper the waters adjacent to the ICW, like grains of sand on a beach. Several are well sheltered, while others lie within sight of historic keys, which look pretty much the same as they have for the last several hundred years.

By contrast, there are actually fewer marina facilities on the Hawk Channel side, though passing cruisers need not be concerned about finding a secure place to coil the lines. At least two first-rate marinas are ready, willing, and able to serve transient craft, but there is one other that we always think of as the black hole of Calcutta.

As you would probably have guessed without the benefit of us telling you, there is very little in the way of sheltered places to drop the hook along this portion of Hawk Channel. Of course, you can always enter one of the inlets-connector streams (see below) and find your way to any number of good overnight havens without leaving Hawk Channel too far behind.

And as you've probably guessed by now as well, another noteworthy difference in this region of the Florida Keys is the many streams that provide ready access between the inside and outside passages. Snake Creek features a bascule bridge, while Channel Five is crossed by a fixed, high-rise span with a blessed 65 feet of vertical clearance. There are many other inlets to check out as well, but all of these are crossed by fixed bridges ranging in vertical clearance from as little as 6 to as much as 27 feet. Powercraft, in particular, will easily be able to use any number of these streams to make the transition from inland to offshore waters (or vice versa).

By the time you make it to Islamorada, the Keys begin to run on a more or less east to west trajectory, rather than a north to south axis. In recognition of this geographical truth, we will now begin to refer to those cruising craft headed to Key West and Marathon as "westward bound" while vessels on their way to Miami will earn the moniker of "eastward bound."

The cruising potential of the waters lapping about the various Islamorada shorelines is almost without limit. We strongly suggest that you build sufficient time in your itinerary to fully enjoy this region. Your cruising experience will be ever so much richer for the effort.

Phone numbers to remember in Islamorada include:

Thrifty Car Rental—305-852-6088

Enterprise Car rental—305-451-3998
Islamorada Chamber of Commerce—1-800-FAB-KEYS/305-664-9767
Islamorada Public Library—305-664-4645

Charts 11451—continues to provide complete coverage of both the Hawk Channel and ICW routes, plus the various connector streams that allow access from one to the other
Bridges
Snake Creek Bridge—crosses Snake Creek, north of unlighted daybeacon #9—bascule—27 feet (closed) vertical clearance—opens on demand
Whale Harbor Bridge—crosses Whale Harbor Channel, northwest of unlighted daybeacon #9—fixed—12 feet of vertical clearance
Upper Matecumbe-Lower Matecumbe Bridge—crosses a whole series of different channels between the southwestern tip of Upper Matecumbe Key and the northeasterly genesis of Lower Matecumbe Key—fixed—7 feet of vertical clearance crossing the unnamed, northeasternmost channel—10 feet of vertical clearance crossing Teatable Key Channel—27 feet of vertical clearance crossing Indian Key Channel—10 feet of vertical clearance crossing Lignumvitae Channel
Channel Two Bridge—crosses Channel Two, north of unlighted daybeacon #2—fixed—10 feet of vertical clearance
Channel Five Bridge—crosses Channel Five, north of flashing daybeacon #2—fixed—65 feet of vertical clearance

Islamorada Geography and History

Islamorada is a collection of townlets on a number of separate islands that have banded together to call themselves, collectively, the Village of Islands . . . Islamorada. The origin of the Islamorada name is so fraught with conflicting and unreasonable stories, that to come up with one over others is like spitting into the wind; nothing good will come of it.

Though it can get confusing, Islamorada incorporates Plantation Key, Windley Key, Teatable Key (also spelled Tea Table Key), Indian Key, Lignumvitae Key, Upper Matecumbe Key, and Lower Matecumbe Key.

Teatable Key is privately owned, and both Indian Key and Lignumvitae Key are state properties, so you need not concern yourself with them except in a historical or a botanical sense.

Plantation Key is quiet and peaceful. There is some serious money here, but it does not show. Plantation Key, too, was planted with pineapples, like Key Largo. And the pineapple business went down for all the same reasons that it failed on Key Largo—less expensive "pine" from Cuba and the vagaries of the weather. Pineapples and hurricanes were not compatible.

Windley Key is next in line. It is on this key that the quarrying of Key Largo limestone was still a going business in the 1960s. The Windley Key Fossil Site is run by the state here and is worth a visit, if you have an interest in the geological background of this unique part of Florida.

Flats fishing (Islamorada)

When you leave Windley Key, the next island is Upper Matecumbe Key. Lots of things of local import and impact have happened on Upper Matecumbe. In the very old days, both Matecumbe keys had supplies of fresh water, and sailing ships used to send men ashore to stock up. Some of those ships never got off the reefs, and their bones still litter the ocean bottom offshore.

On September 2, 1935, a hurricane of devastating intensity smashed ashore in the entire Islamorada chain of islands. The storm surge was 25 feet high and the winds reached 200 miles an hour. The Matecumbes were leveled. Five hundred people died. Many of them, more than half, were men working on the highway, which was being built alongside the Florida East Coast Railway's roadbed.

The workers came close to being saved, but fate conspired against them and dealt them a dead man's hand. When the upcoming weather looked bad down in Upper Matecumbe, and with the barometer heading for the lowest reading ever recorded in this hemisphere, a crew foreman from the workers' camp called Miami for a rescue train. The distance was 90 miles.

And then events started to move in malignant slow motion. It took a couple of hours to get a train crew together, get steam up on a locomotive, and assemble six coaches, two baggage cars, and several boxcars. Repairs needed to be made to one of the cars before it was ready to move on the rescue run. The train was delayed again as a drawbridge over the Miami River opened for boat traffic.

In Homestead, the train's engineer switched the engine, a 4-8-2 locomotive, "Old 447," from the front of the train to the back, so he would be able to pull forward on the return trip, even if it required him to back the train all the way to Upper Matecumbe Key. That ate up more time.

An hour and a half later, about 6:45 P.M., the train stopped at Snake Creek to pick up refugees, but here, a loose cable snagged the engine, and it took eighty more minutes to cut the engine free. The rescue train reached its destination at 8:20 P.M., about six hours after the call for help was issued.

Taking into account all the delays, the train had sped south on its rescue mission at a dawdling 15 miles an hour, which is 25 percent slower than cars are allowed to travel in a school crossing zone today.

The train arrived just in time to meet the storm surge, and all the train's cars, save the 106-ton locomotive, were swept off the tracks.

The storm struck in failing light. The next day's sunrise illuminated the ruinous horror that the maelstrom had brought. Parts of the land where people lived and laughed and worked were devoid of life and structure. The landscape was carpeted with bodies. Funeral pyres burned sporadically into November.

Today, just south of the Matecumbe United Methodist Church, on the ocean side of the highway, a monument stands honoring the memories of those people who died in that storm. Many are buried there, in a mass grave, unidentified. As late as 1965, construction workers dredged up a car that had 1935 license plates on it. Inside the car were five skeletons.

Meridith Jones survived the storm. She wrote a poem about what her life was like in the wake of tragedy. It was published in the *Miami Herald* a year later.

The poem went . . .

> I don't believe that I could bear
> The sight of a gleaming Christmas tree
> Shining through the silent night
> On the waste of Matecumbe Key.
>
> A year ago my life was good

> With the limes we raised and the fish we caught
> The house was full of mystery
> As we guarded the secrets of the gifts we'd bought.
>
> A bright red wagon for Billy Boy
> A doll with curls for little Sue
> Christmas berries, a Christmas tree
> With lights of green and red and blue.
>
> We did not know that a hurricane
> Could tear our little world apart
> Splinter all that made our home
> And leave me here with my aching heart.
>
> There is no one to buy a wagon for
> Billy was lost in the raging sea
> They found him later where he had caught
> In the twisted roots of a mangrove tree.
>
> And Sue was torn from my clinging arms
> By a great black thing that came in the dark
> I looked for days in the pounding sea
> But all I saw was a great black shark.
>
> My husband died in a hospital
> Pneumonia and an injured head
> But I believe he would be here now
> If they hadn't told him the kids were dead.
>
> My house has been rebuilt for me
> By a crew of sympathetic men
> I look at the dark blue sky and know
> That Christmas time has come again.
>
> But I don't believe that I could bear
> The sight of a gleaming Christmas tree
> Shining through the silent night
> On the waste of Matecumbe Key

Kind of takes your breath away, doesn't it?

On a less solemn note, Upper Matecumbe Key has some sensational restaurants. They are covered elsewhere in this tome, but a stop in an Upper Matecumbe Key upscale restaurant will surely tickle your taste buds, while it will also most likely lighten your wallet just a bit. Sometimes, however, a sybaritic lifestyle is just plain necessary. Rationalize it.

The fishing around this part of the Keys is

Hurricane Victims' Monument (Islamorada)

reputed to be world class. Guides who know the waters and what to fish for, and with what kind of gear are a luxury you cannot afford to do without. On top of that, there are retail outlets in Islamorada that have exactly the piece of gear an avid fisherman might want. If you can pay $1,500 for a fly-fishing reel (rod extra), you are in high cotton in Islamorada, and the cotton doesn't get any higher than at The World Wide Sportsman. It is a must-stop just to see the place and what they sell; if you are keen about fishing, this is like F. A. O. Schwartz when you were 12 years old and had just been given an American Express Gold Card, no strings attached.

Islamorada Lodging

Like Key Largo, Islamorada has a long, long list of shoreside lodgings. We will leave the details of these to our fellow author Joy

Williams' wonderful book, *The Florida Keys: A History & Guide*. There is one exception, however.

A bed and breakfast in a nautical cruising guide? Yes, but only the best. We stumbled upon Casa Thorn Inn (MM 87.5 Bayside, 114 Palm Lane, Plantation Key, FL 33036, 305-852-3996, Thorn Trainer, proprietress) by pure good luck, and by having looked at other places to stay for several nights, and after finding the selection bad, awful, or prohibitively expensive. Ever stopped at a motel where the feel of the bath towels reminds one of 40-grit sandpaper?

This charming and secluded B&B is like walking into a bit of heaven after experiencing some of the tackiness that is evident in the Florida Keys. For cruisers who want a few days off the boat, this is, without a doubt, one of the nicest places to stay you ever will experience in the Keys. It's about four blocks from the wonderful Marker 88 Restaurant (see below).

We know a diamond when we see one. This one has many facets. The lady who runs the place, and lives there, is a former New York model who also dabbled in show biz. She has the most exquisite taste in decorating of anyone we have ever met. Her house is a B&B, to be sure, but it is also a museum to the art of good taste. You find something new and intriguing with every glance. Each bedroom—there are five—is decorated differently and to perfection. One of them has antiques—including a carved four-poster bed of immense proportions—that reminds one of the time when the British Empire included India, and the raj was close by. There's a secluded patio and pool area off the living room. The pool is personal sized and not very deep, but it is spotless and feels like a little bit of heaven on a hot afternoon. Personal checks or cash. No credit cards.

Islamorada Dining

As alluded to above, there are some simply wonderful places in Islamorada to satisfy an appetite whetted by the brisk salt breezes. Many of these will be covered in the accounts below, but there are two off-the-water dining spots that we believe deserve special mention.

The Green Turtle Inn (MM 81.5 Oceanside, 305-664-9031) is a truly famous Keys restaurant, which has been open since 1947. Today, it is owned by Henry Rosenthal, a mentalist and magician whose show biz name is Bastille. The interior of the Green Turtle is dark and cozy, decorated with broadsides, posters, and photos that Rosenthal has collected of others in his line of work.

The big menu hit is dolphin, Green Turtle style: broiled dolphin complimented by a spinach soufflé, and crabmeat topped with hollandaise sauce. We didn't have it because of the time of day we stopped by, but had it been later, it would have been worth a shot. Hollandaise sauce makes everything better.

The Green Turtle Inn is something of a Keys landmark. The operation started out as a roadside café, which also rented a few rooms on the Overseas Railroad. The name of the place came from the number of local sea turtles that ended up on people's plates as steaks or soup or chowder. These days, that kind of fare would get the owners thrown in a federal jail for a couple of decades. Turtle soup is actually something else.

Alligator and conch steaks are on the menu here, and we think they are tasty and good, even if they require a little more chewing than other seafood.

Rosenthal does shows on cruise ships and also does them in his own restaurant, when he is in town. You can call ahead to see when he will be performing. The restaurant is open from noon to 10 P.M., Tuesdays through Sunday, but it is closed on Monday.

Bentley's Rawbar and More (MM 82.8, 305-664-9094) has a super local reputation with people who have been around enough to know the difference between average food and excellent food. On top of that, the restaurant has won all kinds of "people's choice" awards from local media polls. So, it is consistently good, not a flash in the pan.

If you go to Bentley's, which sits hard by Bayside Marina at World Wide Sportsman (see below), pay attention to the specials board on the wall. The afternoon we were there, it had about 20 specials on it, so missing this might mean settling for something that might not be as exciting or adventurous.

Bentley's is open from 4 P.M. to 10 P.M., seven days a week, but a reservation is a good idea. If the locals like something well enough to keep voting it into first place, it is likely that Bentley's has turned away its fair share of people just because there is not enough capacity.

If you are driving to Bentley's, it's right on the ocean side of the Overseas Highway, but it is easy to miss. The sign isn't very big and the restaurant sits back just a bit from the highway. It's in a two-story building with blue trim, just west of the Islamorada Post Office.

The seafood is the big draw. The raw bar has clams, oysters, and peel and eat shrimp. Then there are steamed clams or oysters, oysters Muscovite, oysters Rockefeller, and crazy, upside-down oysters. All are pleasingly prepared and we watched one aficionado go through two dozen raw oysters without batting an eye.

All the entrées on the menu made us glad that we had not arrived in a state of starvation, where replenishment would require some hard choices; everything looked scrumptious.

The prices at Bentley's are moderate, with the high-end entrées listed at market price.

ICW—Tavernier Creek to Little Basin

Just to make life a little easier, we are going to subdivide the ICW stretch from Tavernier Creek to Channel Five into two sections. There are sooo many marinas and anchorages to deal with, that it would be confusing to address the entire run to Channel Five at one fell swoop.

There is little we need add here concerning these waters, except to note once more that they are marina and anchorage-rich. If you can't find a stop here to your liking, it's time to try another vocation.

Cowpens Anchorage
(Standard Mile 1154.5)
(Various Lat/Lons—see below)

The ICW leaves the northwesterly entrance to Tavernier Creek in its wake and cuts southwest through a dredged passage known as Cowpens Cut, between the arms of Cross Bank and an adjoining bank of shallows. This passage leads, in turn, to a wide, open body of water called Cotton Key Basin. Charted Cowpens Anchorage comprises the southeasterly section of this basin and borders on Plantation Key.

Historic Tavernier hotel

The Cowpens Anchorage cove is a popular overnight haven with many choices as to where you might drop the hook. Minimum depths run around 5 feet in all these anchor-down spots, but first-timers should be sure to read the navigational account of these waters in the next section of this chapter before attempting entry.

The anchorage easiest to access, though the least sheltered, resides on the waters some 250 yards west of the point that is itself northeast of Plantation Yacht Harbor Marina (see below). Good low-water soundings of 5 to 6 feet can be found near 24 58.228 North/080 33.941 West. Swinging room is completely unlimited, and the nearby shore is flanked by heavy residential development. These waters afford pretty good protection

from southeastern and eastern winds, but there is little shelter in any other direction.

Probably our favorite stop on Cowpens Anchorage is located west-northwest of the charted "R Tr," near 24 58.911 North/080 33.300 West. More than adequate soundings of 5 to 6 feet are carried to within 150 yards of the easterly banks. The correctly charted point to the south gives a good lee when breezes are blowing from the south, and there is also some protection to the north, courtesy of the correctly charted shallows, which act as the northeasterly boundary to Cowpens Anchorage. Of course, the body of Plantation Key is a good buffer for eastern and south-eastern winds. Strong blows from the west and southwest call for another strategy.

Finally, with winds wafting out of the south

or southwest, cruisers can anchor some 400 yards northwest of Plantation Yacht Harbor Marina (see below) and the charted "Tr," near 24 58.029 North/080 34.371 West. Don't try this during times of fresh northern, northeastern, or northwestern breezes.

Please understand that the three choices outlined above are only a few of the many spots you might choose to spend the night on Cowpens Anchorage. Veteran Keys cruisers will undoubtedly already have their own favorites picked out. However, we thought these three anchorages were good places to start for first-timers.

Marker 88 Restaurant
(Standard Mile 1154.5)
(24 58.312 North/080 33.506 West)

The single, fixed wooden pier of Marker 88 gourmet restaurant (MM 88 Bayside, 88000 Overseas Highway, 305-852-9315) guards the southeasterly banks of Cowpens Anchorage about halfway between the charted "R TR" and "Tr." This structure is easily spotted from the water, courtesy of the many colorful flags that seem to be always flying from its dock.

There is probably room for two cruising-sized craft to dock on the outer face of the restaurant pier, and perhaps another could fit on the inner side. However, low-water soundings on the outer face run only 3½ to 4 feet, with about 3 to 3½ feet of water on the inner berth. Obviously, many cruisers will need to visit this wonderful dining attraction by dinghy or motorized land transportation. It's well worth the effort.

Marker 88 Restaurant (closed Mondays and for the entire month of September) is our kind of place. It is not overly large inside, and rather dark, but we like it that way. The restaurant is

pricey, but the menu is varied and all the selections are delicious. The restaurant sits on 1½ acres of land on Florida Bay. There is an outside facility for either waiting or eating, with bar service. The owner, Andre Mueller, is a friend of President (George Prescott) Bush's. Bush is featured in a number of photos in the restaurant, and there are a number of shots of Mueller and Bush together.

An appetizer that caught our eye was Gulf Shrimp Aztec. That's sautéed shrimp flambéed in sherry wine and cooked with chopped garlic, shallots, and tarragon in sauce demi-glacé. Then it is sprinkled with a medley of cheeses and baked. Sounds great!

Most of the entrées are in the mid-twenties in price. Some are in the mid-thirties. The menu is a la carte.

Marker 88 has been written up in *Florida Trend, Miami Magazine, Gourmet Magazine,* and the *New York Times,* among others. The reviews have all been good.

Plantation Yacht Harbor Marina
(Standard Mile 1155)
(24 57.896 North/080 34.165 West)

Would you believe that we aren't finished with Cowpens Anchorage yet? In fact, one of the few marinas that caters to larger cruising craft on the entire ICW run from Miami to Marathon guards the southeasterly banks of Cowpens Anchorage, immediately west of the charted "Tr." Plantation Yacht Harbor Marina features a fully breakwater-enclosed harbor. The entrance resides on the northeastern end of the basin, and it can be readily identified, courtesy of a small, red-and-white, candy-cane-striped, lighthouse-shaped structure.

Though this facility is on Plantation Key, it belongs to the municipality of Islamorada. Just a few short years ago, the city bought out

Plantation Yacht Harbor Marina

the previous owners, and took over the marina lock, stock, and barrel. There are mixed feelings among locals and marina residents about city government getting into the marina business. So the jury is out on this experiment. However, the city of St. Petersburg, farther north, has run a first-class marina for years, so it is possible.

What makes this marina unique is the riprap breakwater, which protects the dockage basin. It would take a good storm to breach the breakwater, so this is a secure location in all but a hurricane. A few of the 92 slips are in need of repair. The rebar inside the existing concrete has rusted and some mortar has fallen away. There are slips for transients, about 12. This marina will tend toward permanent and long-term slip rentals as time goes on.

Depths in the harbor run about 5½ to 6½ feet at low water, with one or two 5½ foot soundings at the harbor entrance. All berths feature fixed, concrete piers plus fresh water and power connections up to 50 amps. Gasoline and diesel fuel can be purchased at the inner fuel dock. Some light mechanical repairs can be accomplished by local, independent technicians, whom the dockmaster can call for you.

The showers—two stalls and sinks per gender—are old, but they are clean. There are four pairs of coin-op washers and dryers in a large Laundromat on premises.

There was no ship's store, but there is a library in the dockmaster's office. The dockmaster monitors Channel 16 and can talk people who feel a little timid right into the

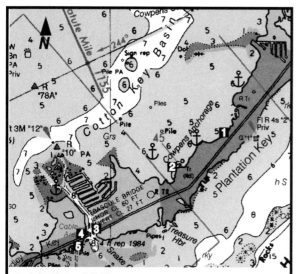

1. Marker 88 Restaurant
2. Plantation Yacht Harbor Marina
3. Cobra Marine
4. Smuggler's Cove Marina
5. Big Conch Oceanside Bar and Grill

to the west of the entrance, but on the other side of the road, are a couple of places to dine. Treasure Village Courtyard Café (305-852-1911) is located in the Treasure Village Shopping Center. It serves a great breakfast and offers a first-class deli, to boot. Next to Treasure Village is a little shopping center with a restaurant/sports bar called Jammer's Grill and Pub (305-852-8786). The back of the menu is a funny read. Don't miss it. The food won't set the world on fire in creativity, but we had no complaints.

Plantation Yacht Harbor Marina (305) 852-5424
http://www.plantationboat.com

Approach depth—5 ½ feet (minimum)
Dockside depth—5½-6½ feet (low water)
Accepts transients—yes
Type of docking—fixed concrete finger piers and
    alongside docking
Dockside power connections—up to 50 amp
Dockside water connections—yes
Waste pump-out—approved but not installed
Showers—yes
Laundromat—yes
Fuel available—gas and diesel
Mechanical repairs—mechanic on call
Restaurant—nearby

marina. Soft drinks are available via machines. Other amenities include a bayside beach, two hard-surfaced tennis courts, a basketball court, and an on-site swimming pool.

There is some real skepticism as to whether the city of Islamorada, which owns this marina, can pull this off. Municipal governments often move slowly and sometime erratically. There were a lot of "in the future" references in dockmaster Parker's discussion with us of the marina's future. If the city backs its play with money and innovation, this facility can be a winner. If it doesn't—and one experienced live-aboard we spoke with was intelligently caustic about the possibilities—it will be just another marina whose potential was never realized because people got tired of making the effort, fighting the good fight.

Out on Highway 1, the main drag, and just

Snake Creek and Associated Anchorages and Facilities (Standard Mile 1155.5) (Various Lat/Lons—see below)

The outer marker on the Snake Creek approach channel (flashing daybeacon #12) lies some .7 nautical miles south-southeast of the ICW's unlighted daybeacon #78A. This is an important connector stream spanning the gap between the Waterway passage and the offshore, Hawk Channel route. It provides the first opportunity for larger cruising craft to make the transition between these two alternate routes, south of Angelfish Creek.

Typical low-water depths are in the 7- to

Cobra Marine (Snake Creek)

10-foot region, though some 5½-to 6-foot soundings are sometimes encountered between flashing daybeacon #12 and the charted Y-shaped split in the stream.

Snake Creek is crossed by a bascule bridge with 27 feet of closed vertical clearance. Fortunately, this span opens on demand. It is the presence of this "opening" bridge that makes Snake Creek so attractive to larger vessels and sailcraft in particular—no having to mess with lower-level, fixed spans. Thank you, Florida DOT!

On the down side, Snake Creek is a member in good standing of the strong tidal current club. We sat in awe one warm September afternoon, while we watched the tide boil under this stream's bascule bridge. Cruisers should be on the lookout for these swiftly moving waters, and be ready to take instant corrective action.

Snake Creek's channel, out into the briny blue, is very well marked, but it twists this way and that. All but one of the aids to navigation on this cut are unlighted daybeacons. Nighttime and foul-weather passage of this channel are not recommended.

Snake Creek also features its own anchorage. Note the Y-shaped split in the stream south of unlighted daybeacon #10. With care, cruisers can depart the main Snake Creek channel and cut back to the west-northwest on the stream's errant northwesterly arm. Here, boats as large as 36 feet will find room to anchor amidst 6- to 7-foot minimum depths. The best place to drop the hook is found on the initial 150 yards of this offshoot's

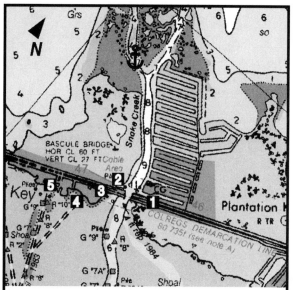

1. Cobra Marine
2. Smuggler's Cove Marina
3. Big Conch Oceanside Bar and Grill
4. Hog Heavan Bar and Restaurant
5. Tropical Reef Resort

passage to the west-northwest and northwest (near 24 57.684 North/080 35.721 West). Farther upstream, the channel narrows, and it's an all too simple process to find your way into 4 feet of water.

We don't mean to sound like we are working for the Snake Creek Chamber of Commerce, but wait, there's more. This fortunate stream boasts several facilities that line the creek's shores immediately north of the bascule bridge. Unfortunately, only one of these marinas offer anything in the way of minimal transient dockage.

First up is Smuggler's Cove Marina (305-664-5564, 1-800-864-4363) (24 57.145 North/080 35.337 West). This facility guards the westerly-Windley Key shores of Snake

Creek, immediately north of the bascule bridge. The entrance is a little tricky, courtesy of both a shoal that fronts the fuel dock and the usual, swift tidal currents. Check out our navigational account of this marina below for some hints as to how to make good your entry.

Once past its tricky entrance, cruisers will discover good low-water depths of about 6 feet or so. The fuel dock and ship's store will come up quickly to starboard. Here, all craft can purchase gasoline, diesel fuel, and basic ship's store, variety store, and bait-and-tackle items.

The marina's well-sheltered dockage basin, backed by a motel and adjacent café lies farther to the west. Unfortunately, no transient space is available here, and consequently, we will not further detail these facilities.

A whole series of canals pierce Snake Creek's easterly banks between the "Y" split and the bascule bridge. The southernmost of these cuts (immediately north of the Snake Creek Bridge) provides access to Cobra Marine. Note that as you enter this canal, the Islamorada Coast Guard Station will be quite visible to port. Cobra Marine will soon come up along the southerly banks, in the body of the correctly charted crook in the canal.

Cobra Marine (24 57.202 North/080 35.136 West) is primarily a motorboat place, and the maximum size craft they could take alongside would be 40 feet. Some transients are occasionally accepted at Cobra's fixed wooden pier on a space-available basis. We found dockside soundings to be about 6 to 6½ feet at low water, with some 6-foot soundings in the approach canal. Some berths have 30-amp power hookups, others 50 amp, while all have fresh water connections. The on-site ship's store is excellent, with a good cross section of things that cruisers need, plus food,

Smuggler's Cove Marina (Snake Creek)

snacks, beer, ice, and soft drinks. The closest restaurant is Big Conch Oceanside Bar and Grill (see below), across the bridge, on Windley Key. Hog Heaven Bar and Restaurant (305-664-9669) is just a few steps farther. Both are fine, but Big Conch will give you a touch of refinement that Hog Heaven will not. It's not like comparing, say, the Plaza Hotel in New York with McDonald's, but there's a difference.

Cobra Marine (305) 664-3636
http://www.cobramarineinc.com

Approach depth—6 feet (minimum)
Dockside depth—6-6½ feet
Accepts transients—yes, on a space-available basis
Type of docking—some fixed wooden finger piers, some alongside

Dockside power connections—mostly 30 amp, some 50 amp
Dockside water connections—yes
Fuel available—gasoline only
Mechanical repairs—mostly outboard engine variety
Ship's and variety store—yes
Restaurant—nearby

Just south of the Snake Creek bascule bridge, a small, poorly outlined channel cuts back to the west and leads to Big Conch Oceanside Bar and Grill (305-664-0020). The channel, such as it is, is outlined by two scanty, white PVC pipes and carries bare 3-foot soundings at low water. Craft that can make it through these skinny depths will quickly come abeam of the restaurant along the northerly banks (near 24 57.082

Big Conch Oceanside Bar and Grill (Snake Creek)

North/080 35.371 West). Two boats might be able to tie up to the wooden piers immediately adjacent to the Big Conch. Additional dockage of the floating, wooden-decked variety is found a bit farther upstream, also abutting the northerly shores.

The Big Conch Oceanside Bar and Grill is a pretty standard Keys restaurant that does enjoy a good local reputation. The commanding officer of the nearby Coast Guard station recommended it. It is casual and light inside. You can see Snake Creek or the Atlantic from your table, inside or outside. Cracked conch, cooked up with an airy batter, is great. We had it with "island sauce." Then we partook of a Cajun wrap, which is either blackened chicken breast or the catch of the day. The catch of the day was dolphin, our favorite. We went for it,

rolled in a garlic-herb tortilla, and had Caesar salad included in the wrap. The entrée came with channel fries, which were crunchy. We hate soggy fries. All was topnotch.

Whale Harbor Channel
(Standard Mile 1156.5)
(Various Lat/Lons—see below)

East of Cotton Key, a marked, but incorrectly charted, channel cuts south to another inlet that connects the ICW and Hawk Channel. This complicated stream is known as the Whale Harbor Channel. Unlike Snake Creek, it is spanned by a fixed bridge with a mere 12 feet of vertical clearance.

Whale Harbor Channel would probably rate only a very small mention in this guidebook, were it not for the presence of some

Whale Harbor Channel anchorage

minimal marina facilities, and more importantly, two very funky anchorages. One of these overnight havens is a study in Florida Keys alternate lifestyles.

We guess that the U.S. Coast Guard and NOAA must feel that our life on the water needs a bit more spice. So, being the considerate folks that they are, the current configuration of aids to navigation on Whale Harbor has only a passing resemblance to what is pictured on chart 11451 (Page E, Inset 6). The various daybeacons are numbered pretty much as they appear on the chart, but they are not anywhere near the shown locations. Go figure. Don't worry, we'll straighten all this out in the navigational section below.

First, notice the charted offshoot cutting to the south-southeast, north of Wilson Key. Chart 11451 depicts this cutoff as being north of unlighted daybeacon #13. In actuality, the entrance lies abeam of #13.

These waters serve as a semipermanent anchorage for several craft that looked to us as if they have not moved in years and were not about to anytime soon. There is room for visiting cruisers to anchor, and we noticed a hearty bonhomie while talking with some of these waterborne residents. To be sure, this is the opportunity to get a quick look at what one authority has described as that "maverick" lifestyle, for which the Keys are so famous (rightly or wrongly).

While 6-foot minimum depths are maintained in the unmarked channel, it is a tricky proposition at best to keep to the good water. We found it a very easy thing indeed to wander into 4 feet of water, even when we were trying to be careful. Check out our navigational account of this anchorage in the next section below for some tips on how to maintain the best possible depths.

Even with the difficult entrance in their

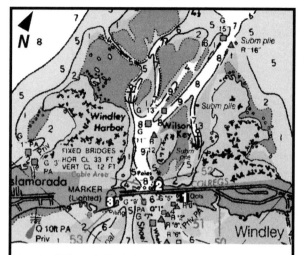

1. Holiday Isle Marina
2. Estes Fishing Camp and Marina
3. Whale Harbor Inn and Marina

wake, skippers must drop the hook before proceeding too far upstream. The rear (southerly) half of this side water is quite shallow, with depths of 4 feet very much in evidence. Swing room is only ample enough for a 34-footer, and we do not suggest that captains piloting craft larger than 36 feet attempt to access these waters at all. We suggest anchoring near 24 56.734 North/080 36.568 West. Again, we strongly recommend that you read our navigation info below before trying to drop the hook.

To its credit, this anchorage is well sheltered from all but strong northwesterlies. The rear of the cove is landlocked, and this contributes to a welcome absence of strong tidal currents. Of course, if you are so inclined, you might also find some cruising comradery with the live-aboards who call this pocket home, but not everyone will be comfortable with this arrangement. There also seems to be some sort of dinghy dock bordering the cove's

shallow southerly tip. We could not determine what the access rules might be, if any, for using this small pier, but we did observe several of the semipermanent residents landing here. Check carefully for any "no trespassing" signs before using this dock. We didn't see any, but things might have changed by the time of your arrival.

Leaving the "alternate lifestyle anchorage" behind and continuing south toward the Whale Harbor Bridge, the next possible stop comes up abeam of the charted position of unlighted daybeacon #11. Notice that we said "charted" position. Once again, this marker is actually located farther to the north than the position indicated on 11451, but at least for this discussion, its charted location helps to identify the side water in question.

Wow, was that a mouthful—all a complicated way of saying notice the branch of the Whale Harbor Channel that cuts first west and then north, west of #11's charted position. This side cut carries 7 feet at low water along its centerline, though both shorelines are shoal. A series of small, uncharted, floating markers outline the good water along this stream, and they are ever so helpful.

Craft as large as 40 feet can anchor on the midwidth of this cut, within 200 yards of its southeasterly mouth. We suggest 24 56.679 North/080 37.058 West. Be sure to set the hook so as not to swing near either of the shorelines, unless you relish the idea of waking up aground.

Farther upstream, the informal aids to navigation continue, and it's actually possible for small craft to continue tracking their way to the north and rejoin the deeper waters southeast of Cotton Key. This portion of the passage, however, exhibits low-water soundings of only 4 to 4½ feet, and it is quite narrow and twisting in places. This may be fine for smaller outboard and I/O-powered craft, but it is not acceptable for larger cruising vessels.

Returning our attention to the main body of Whale Harbor Channel, a wide swath of deep water continues south-southeast towards the 12-foot, fixed bridge. Just before reaching this span, Estes Fishing Camp and Marina (24 56.444 North/080 36.596 West) will be spotted overlooking the northeasterly point.

This marina/fish camp is virtually indescribable. Let's see now, for starters, it looks as if they are saving their scrap in case the Conch Republic rises against the Union. There are boats and parts of boats here that have not been wet since Richard Nixon was in office.

The fish camp's entrance channel is outlined by two pilings, one white PVC pipe and the other wooden. Perched atop the woodpile is an arrow that indicates on which side it should be passed.

However you enter this facility, depths quickly fall to 4 and 4½ feet at low water. The older, fixed, wooden finger piers are not in the best of condition either. Transients are occasionally accepted, but this is far more the exception than the rule. No dockside power or water connections are to be had. Clearly, this is a minimal stop for cruising craft. Many captains will wisely choose to berth elsewhere. But that's not all.

The gas pump appears not to have been used in years, but that is the one that is broken. The one that works dispenses 93 octane. The docks are not exactly in prime condition. And the people who frequent this place cannot seem to find a trash barrel to get rid of their refuse. It's all over the ground.

There is a bait-and-tackle shop on the premises, and that is the high point. You can get live shrimp and crab and beer and soft drinks. Prices are far lower here than they are in other, more upscale haunts. Jay, the owner, said that they take care of outboard repairs, too. There is an array of what appear to be reconditioned outboard propellers for sale here.

If it's raining and you need to get out of the rain, then the bait-and-tackle shop probably has a roof that doesn't leak. No guarantees, though.

This is the way the fish camps in the Keys used to look, kind of weary. But if you don't mind a loss of luster, this is quaint (or just plain run-down) in a way that many of the things in the Keys no longer are.

It should also be noted that Holiday Isle Marina is located just across U.S. 1 from Estes Fishing Camp. You can often hear the "music."

Estes Fishing Camp and Marina (305) 664-9059
http://www.esteswatersportsandmarina.com

Approach depth—6-8 feet
Dockside depth—4-4½ feet
Accepts transients—limited, space-available basis
Type of docking—old, fixed wooden finger piers
Fuel available—gasoline (93 octane only)
Mechanical repairs—outboards
Ship's and variety store—BB&T, with some
    modest additional supplies
Restaurant—across the highway

Both Holiday Isle Marina and Whale Harbor Inn and Marina flank Whale Harbor Channel (to the northeast and southwest respectively), southeast of the 12-foot, fixed bridge (on the Hawk Channel side). Very few cruising craft will be able to clear this 12-foot span, so we shall cover these facilities, as well as the seaward approach cut connecting the Whale Harbor Channel to Hawk Channel, as part of our review of the offshore route, later in this chapter.

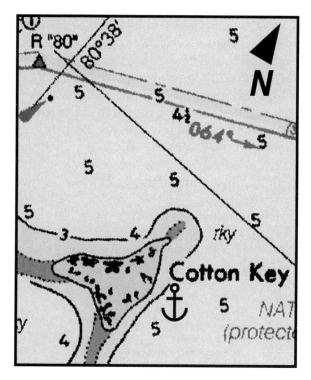

Cotton Key Anchorage
(Standard Mile 1157)
(24 57.674 North/080 37.313 West)

A good anchorage in western, southwestern, and to a lesser extent, southern winds will be discovered off the eastern banks of Cotton Key. This small, completely natural, low-lying body of land lies southeast of the ICW's flashing daybeacon #81. Depths of 5 feet or better extend to within 200 yards of the isle's easterly shoreline. Closer in, depths shelve up to 4 feet or less. There is absolutely no shelter to the north and precious little to the east. Don't even think about dropping the hook here if winds above 7 knots are forecast from these quadrants. By all accounts, this is not a foul-weather anchorage in any case.

Islamorada Anchorage
(Standard Mile 1160)
(24 55.534 North/080 38.227 West)

One of the most popular anchorages along this stretch of the Florida Keys' ICW is found on the correctly charted deep waters northeast of Little Basin, and within 500 yards of the Upper Matecumbe Key shoreline. It's a good trek of some 1.6 nautical miles from the Waterway's unlighted daybeacon #86 to this haven, but scores of cruisers make this journey year after year.

Keeping to the good water can be a bit tricky, particularly for newcomers. Be sure to leave the ICW at #86, even though this plan will seem to take you a bit out of your way to the west. Trust us. We also, once again, suggest that you check out our navigational review of these waters in the next section below, unless these cruising grounds are already familiar to you.

As you cruise into the heart of the Islamorada Anchorage, it will become quite clear that these waters are regularly shared by a host of moored and anchored vessels. Some have obviously been here a long time and probably won't be going anywhere else soon, while others are just in for a short visit.

Low-water depths are a very respectable 6 to 7 feet, though you must stay at least 100 yards off both the southeastern and southwestern shorelines to maintain these soundings. Be advised that a few of the anchored craft you will spot in the extreme southwesterly corner of this anchorage are sitting in 4 feet of water or less. You might just be a bit happier dropping anchor a wee bit farther to the north and northeast, rather than joining these sad vessels in the Islamorada mud.

As long as you don't anchor too close to any of your neighbors, there is ample elbowroom for most any sized pleasure craft. The shores of Upper Matecumbe Key give an excellent lee to the south and southeast, as do the indistinctly charted mangroves flanking Little Basin to the southwest. Even though many local live-aboards seem to ride out blows from the north, northeast, and northwest on these waters, we don't think it's a good idea for you to join them. As you've undoubtedly surmised by now, there is very little available in the way of shelter from these directions.

Lorelei Restaurant, Cabana Bar, and Marina (Standard Mile 1160)
(24 55.316 North/080 38.000 West)

This is one of those sorts of marinas that you ONLY find in the Florida Keys. Lorelei sits perched on the northwesterly shores of Upper Matecumbe Key, hard by the southeastern corner of the popular anchorage reviewed above. It's entrance is very hard to spot from the water. We must admit to searching for it in vain on two widely separated occasions and having to ask a local for directions both times. Fortunately, the NOAA folks have seen fit to locate Lorelei Marina via facility designation #54. Wish we'd know that in times past!

If you keep working your way to the southeast, pointing for the waters just northeast of facility #54, the entrance will finally open out to the southwest. This is a case of "keep the faith," and all will eventually be clear.

There are one or two transient slips at Lorelei Marina, depending upon circumstances. Dockage is afforded at fixed wooden face piers with fresh water and 30 to 50-amp power connections. Depths in the harbor run 4½ to 5 feet at low tide.

Dockside guardian (Lorelei Marina)

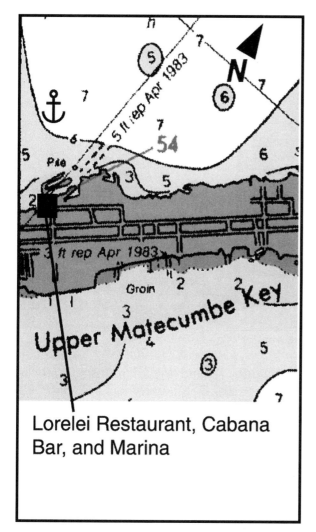

Lorelei Restaurant, Cabana Bar, and Marina

There is also a popular on-site restaurant that also goes under the name Lorelei (305-664-4656) and an equally favored outside operation, the Cabana Bar (305-664-4338), where people enjoy the sunsets. Watching the sunsets in the Keys has the same cachet as a Playboy calendar in a boy's reformatory. There is entertainment seven days a week here, and the marina is in the heart of Islamorada, so everything downtown is within walking distance. Judging by the number of cars here in

November, this is a popular place with the locals. If you were in Keokuk, Iowa, for example, and asked where the locals hung out, you couldn't put much faith in what you'd find. We think that in the Keys, however, you can count on local taste to find you good food and a fair value.

The marina—which is perfectly protected—has alongside docking and showers, but it isn't large and many of the slips are already used by live-aboards. The Laundromat, should you want to use one, is across the street and owned by others, but it's close by.

Lorelei Restaurant, Cabana Bar, and Marina (305) 664-2692
http://www.florida-key.fl.us./lorelei.htm

Approach depth—4^1/$_2$-6 feet (low tide)
Dockside depth—4^1/$_2$-5 feet (low tide)
Accepts transients—yes, space-available basis
Type of docking—alongside docking, fixed wooden piers
Dockside power connections—30 to 50 amp
Dockside water connections—yes
Showers—yes
Laundromat—nearby
Restaurant—yes, on site and popular

Little Basin and World Wide Sportsman

Two sets of markers (actually correctly charted for a change) cut off from the southwestern corner of the Islamorada Anchorage (reviewed above) and lead into a small pocket of water known as Little Basin. The northeasterly entrance to this cut lies near 24 55.354 North/080 38.566 West. Skippers cruising from the ICW channel for Little Basin should abandon the Waterway at unlighted daybeacon #86.

Little Basin is well protected from all wind directions by its flanking mangroves. While we would not want to ride out a hurricane

Lorelei Marina

here, this is a great foul-weather hidey-hole for anything up to a full gale.

The waters of Little Basin comprise a popular anchorage. Just be sure your craft can stand some 4-foot (possibly a 3½ feet here and there) soundings before deciding to drop the old hook. Simply select a spot anywhere within shouting distance of the basin's midline and settle down for a night of security.

Little Basin is home to the fabulous World Wide Sportsman's Bayside Marina and several unforgettable restaurants. These facilities guard the small bay's southeasterly flanks, immediately northeast of the charted "Wks" designation. Before considering these wonderful possibilities, however, let's have a word about water depths. During two visits in September of 2000, we sounded typical depths of 4½ to 5 feet at low water. However, local captains, including the completely trustworthy World Wide Sportsman dockmaster, Capt. Don Sorenson, have informed us that low-water, 4-foot soundings in Little Basin are not an unusual occurrence. Fortunately, soundings alongside at WWS Bayside Marina improve to 5- and 6-foot levels.

So, with that out of the way, let's feast our eyes on the World Wide Sportsman (near 24 54.923 North/080 38.407 West). This is far more than a marina. It is a complex and an experience all rolled into one sensory sandwich. Behind the marina and fronting on U.S. 1 is a two-story retail store that contains, it is our guess, the most exotic collection of fishing equipment and clothing under one roof in this country. There are two restaurants on the premises, Zane Grey's, upstairs in the main building, and the Islamorada Fish Company, next door.

World Wide Sportsman (Bayside Marina)

Even if you don't fish, the World Wide Sportsman is worth a serious look. In the middle of the store, and available for boarding and inspection, is a sister ship to Ernest Hemingway's beloved *Pilar*. This boat is a Weeks, built in Brooklyn in 1933. Hemingway had a Wheeler, New York built—down the street and around the corner. The boat at World Wide Sportsman has been rechristened *Pilar*. It had an interesting life before being purchased by Johnny Morris of Bass Pro Shops, which owns this property. Morris had the boat transported to Springfield, Missouri and completely refurbished before being returned to Islamorada. Even if you don't care for power craft, look this one over. It's a worthy experience.

There's a ship's store on site. Also on the docks is the most expensive live bait setup, the dockmaster said, in the world. The water is treated, oxygenated, and cooled to make the environment for the crabs, shrimp, and bait fish most friendly. If it strikes you that this is like putting gladiators up at the Roman equivalent of the Ritz Carlton—"We who are about to die salute you"—then you get the idea. On the other hand, it says something about how thorough people can be when they set their minds to it.

This marina is clean, beautifully maintained, and protected from virtually all directions by a buffer of mangrove islands between the marina and the ICW. Transients are accepted for overnight berths at the marina's fixed wooden piers. All berths feature fresh water connections and power hookups up to 50 amps. Gasoline and diesel fuel are readily available, and there is a waste pump-out on site as well.

The showers and bathroom at the World Wide Sportsman are located about 100 feet to the west of the docks, hard by the Islamorada Fish Company restaurant (see below). A rarity in the Keys, they are blessedly air-conditioned. They are also spotless. There is a men's rooms and a ladies' room, one each, both with shower stalls. There is also an additional toilet for each sex, sans showers.

To the immediate southwest is the Islamorada Fish Company (305-664-9271),

which is part of this complex. The food here is seafood for the most part. It is good. Our fried clams, chased down with a cold beer, were tasty and filling. On another occasion, we discovered that the broiled grouper sandwich was also quite noteworthy. Much of the dining is outside on the docks, so one would want to consider that when figuring out what to wear. Islamorada Fish Company features its own fixed wooden pier, which is just about big enough for two 20-footers or one 36-footer to squeeze in. Depths run about 4 feet at low water. Dining patrons are free to moor here, but overnight stays are not in the offing.

Next door, to the northeast and under different ownership, are two lovely restaurants,

World Wide Sportsman (Interior)

Morada Bay and Pierre's. Morada Bay (305-664-0604) has a typical Keys motif, but it's certainly upscale. It's a beach café. The building has a metal roof, inside and outside dining, and a sandy beach area—the sand was trucked in, so it is not natural, but it is very nice—with wooden, slatted Adirondack chairs to relax in while sipping something cool.

A hundred feet further northeast is the building that houses Pierre's Restaurant (305-664-3225), one of the Keys' premiere dining spots. It could just as well house the owner of a plantation; it has that look to it . . . wide verandas, beautiful view, lovely architecture, clean as a whistle. Pierre's was closed when we passed by in the morning, but we were able to get a look at the menu. If you care about fine dining, albeit at a price, then Pierre's is absolutely worth a visit. Someone in the know about the service and the food and the wine selections put it into one word, "perfect." Our guess is that if Pierre's doesn't offer it on the menu, then you wouldn't enjoy it anyway. A dress code requires slacks for gentlemen and a nice frock for miladies, because who would want a slice of perfection marred by having to sit next to some yahoo

World Wide Sportsman (Bayside Marina)

with a tank top and shorts on . . . unless that yahoo was an actress from *Baywatch*? Then she wouldn't be a yahoo, would she?

And just in case that's not enough to slake your appetite, both the Green Turtle and Bentley's restaurants, reviewed earlier in this chapter, are both within easy walking distance. Boy, talk about an embarrassment of riches!

World Wide Sportsman's Bayside Marina
  (305) 664-4615
http://www.worldwidesportsman.com

Approach depth—3½-4½ feet (low water)
Dockside depth—5-6 feet
Accepts transients—yes
Type of docking—fixed wooden finger piers
Dockside power connections—up to 50 amp
Dockside water connections—yes
Waste pump-out—yes
Showers—yes
Fuel available—gas and diesel
Ship's and variety store—yes
Restaurant—two on site and many other close
    by—all topnotch

Other Little Basin Facilities

Though you would never guess it from chart 11451, a canal cuts off from the extreme northeasterly corner of Little Basin and leads to two additional facilities. Depths in this stream are actually better than those in the basin. We sounded typical 5-foot, low-water depths.

First up is Caribee Boat Sales, just southwest of Coral Marine (see below). This is primarily a dry-stack operation that uses a large forklift to transport their customer's vessels in and out. They sell Yamaha engines and Grady White and Pursuit boats, and offer some mechanical repairs for Yamaha engines. No other transient services are in the offing.

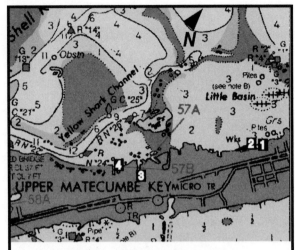

1. World Wide Sportsman's Bayside Marina
2. Islamorada Fish Company
3. Max's Marine and Boatyard
4. Matecumbe Marina

Coral Bay Marina overlooks the canal's southeasterly banks, just a bit farther upstream (24 55.179 North/080 38.180 West). This is a serious boatyard that also, surprisingly, offers some transient dockage for cruisers. Clearly the forte here, however, is service work. Mechanical repairs are available for both gasoline and diesel-power plants. These folks will even install new engines and far lesser items. Haul-outs are accomplished by a 60-ton Travelift, and all the usual below-waterline repairs are readily available.

No frills here, but it appears that no job is too complicated for them to handle. This would certainly be *the* place to come in Islamorada if you need serious work done to your vessel.

It is pretty rare for a repair yard to provide

Pierre's Restaurant (Islamorada)

transient dockage, but Coral Bay is the exception to this rule. They have about 15 slips set aside for visitors. All are on a first-come, first served basis. Power connections of the 15- or 30-amp variety are to be had, as are fresh water hookups. Depths alongside run at least 5½ feet. There is even a waste pump-out on site. The bathrooms/showers are clean, but no frills, and there is also a Laundromat located on the premises. Gasoline and diesel fuel can be purchased dockside. All the restaurants reviewed above in our account of World Wide Sportsman are within walking distance.

Coral Bay Marina (305) 664-3111

Approach depth—5 feet (approach from Little Basin)
4½ feet (minimum—northeasterly canal entrance)

Dockside depth—5½-6 feet
Accepts transients—yes
Type of piers—fixed wooden finger piers
Dockside power connections—15 to 30 amp
Dockside water connections—yes
Waste pump-out—yes
Showers—clean, but no frills, one stall per sex
Laundromat—yes, in the building housing the showers/heads
Fuel—gas and diesel
Mechanical repairs—yes
Below-waterline repairs—yes
Travelift—60-ton
Restaurant—six within walking distance in Islamorada

Finally, the canal exits into the wider waters of the Islamorada Anchorage, just southwest of Lorelei Marina. This portion of the cut is outlined by white PVC pipes. We sounded nothing less than 4½ feet at low tide along this passage.

Vessels making directly for Coral Bay or Caribee Boat Sales can certainly make use of this northeasterly entrance to the canal, rather than wander all the way into Little Basin, and then cruise back up the canal. Just take your time and keep an eagle eye on the sounder if you choose to make this approach.

TAVERNIER CREEK TO LITTLE BASIN NAVIGATION

The ICW channel between Tavernier Creek and the waters abeam of Little Basin is a typical stretch of the Florida Keys Waterway. The route remains reasonably well outlined by aids to navigation, but depths right smack in the middle of the ICW sometimes reach 5½-foot levels at low water. Typically, you can count on finding at least 6 feet of water.

None of the side waters we will address individually below present any unusual difficulty, outside of the all-too-usual swift tidal currents. The interior reaches of the Whale Harbor Channel are somewhat more challenging, courtesy of some out-of-date charting by NOAA. Be sure to the read this section BEFORE wandering into these waters for the first time.

The ICW flows through several dredged cuts that lead between shoals and mangroves along its run from Tavernier Creek to Little Basin. It almost goes without saying, but let's say it anyway, be sure to identify all Waterway aids to navigation and pass them to the appropriate side.

On the ICW After leaving the confusing juncture with Tavernier Creek behind, the ICW cuts southwest on its way to Cowpens Cut, a dredged passage through Cross Bank. This "bank" is actually a far more substantial mangrove than chart 11451 indicates. Don't get confused (like we first did), expecting to find a low shoal.

Eastbound (northbound) navigators should be aware that it's an all too simple proposition to confuse the markers leading to Tavernier Creek with the ICW daybeacons. Use your binoculars to help pick out flashing daybeacon #71 and be SURE to pass northwest of this aid to navigation.

Returning now to our westward (southward) trek, come abeam of flashing daybeacon #73 to its northwesterly side and bend your course a bit farther to the south. Point for the gap between unlighted daybeacons #73A and #74. Immediately after passing between these markers, cruisers will enter Cowpens Cut.

We have often found a host of local fishing craft trying their luck on the clear, clear waters of Cowpens Cut. It's a very good idea for larger powercraft to slow to idle speed on the cut if any fishing craft happen to be present.

Eventually, you will exit the Cowpens Cut after passing between unlighted daybeacons #74A and #75. Point to come abeam of the next southwesterly aid to navigation, unlighted daybeacon #76, to its fairly immediate southeasterly side. Then, continue on, pointing to come abeam and pass unlighted daybeacon #76A, also to its southeasterly side. The Waterway now takes a sharp cut farther to the southwest. Set course to pass flashing daybeacon #78 to its southeasterly quarter.

Toilet Seat Cut There is another, very interesting way for shallow-draft, outboard, and I/O-powered vessels to transit Cross Bank. Some 450 yards west-northwest of the bank's junctures with the Plantation Key shoreline, local boating folk have marked a passage that is known far and wide as toilet seat cut. The reason for this unusual moniker is that the piles that mark both sides of this passage are adorned by a rather incredible collection of toilet seats. It makes for a colorful passage, whose tale will be retold for many years to come.

The northerly entrance to toilet seat cut lies near 24 59.964 North/080 33.087 West. We do not suggest attempting this channel with anything larger than a 36-foot craft. More importantly, your vessel should draw 3 feet or less. Low-water soundings are in the 3-foot range.

Notice that there is another unnamed bank, south of Cross Bank, that also makes out from the shores of Plantation Key. We discovered that it was also possible to find fairly decent water across this shoal by staying some 25 yards off the easterly shoreline. Be advised, however, that this route is COMPLETELY unmarked, and it's quite possible to wander into very shallow water. Again, we strongly recommend that this adventurous route be the sole province of smaller, shallow-draft powercraft.

If you do make it through both Toilet Seat

Cut and the unnamed Plantation Key bank, these twin passages will land you in the deeper waters of Cowpens Anchorage to the southwest. All the shoreside marina facilities and these water's impressive collection of anchorages will then be easily accessible.

On the ICW After passing flashing daybeacon #78, the ICW continues on to the southwest for some 2.1 nautical miles before meeting up with its next aid to navigation, unlighted daybeacon #78A. It's a good idea to have your binoculars handy to help pick out #78A.

Along the way, you may notice two unadorned wooden pilings southeast of your course line. These unofficial aids to navigation mark the westerly extreme of the unnamed bank, south of Cross Bank, discussed above. You don't want to get anywhere near these piles. Be sure to pass them by several hundred yards to their northerly and westerly sides.

Between #78 and #78A, cruisers can break off to the southeast and take advantage of the many cruising possibilities of Cowpens Anchorage. Also of great interest, the entrance to the Snake Creek approach channel lies south-southeast of #78A. Let's pause to consider both of these interesting bodies of water.

Cowpens Anchorage and Facilities There are only three (rather obvious) tricks to successful navigation of Cowpens Anchorage. Avoid the extreme southwesterly corner, where chart 11451 correctly indicates 4-foot depths, stay well south of the unnamed bank that comprises the anchorage's northern limits, and don't approach the southeasterly banks to within less than 200 yards. That's really all there is to it.

As will be apparent to any cruiser entering this large cove, there are myriad anchorage choices. As outlined earlier, there are three spots that particularly caught our attention. The first is found on the waters west, northwest of the charted "R Tr." Not to be repetitive, but stay 200 yards off the easterly shoreline and well south of the unnamed bank to the north, and you're in fat city.

The (what we shall term) middle anchorage lies 400 yards off the southeasterly banks, northeast of the charted "Tr" and Plantation Yacht Harbor Marina (see below). No problems here.

The southernmost haven will be discovered just west-northwest of the very visible Plantation Yacht Harbor Marina dockage basin. Captains need to exercise a bit more caution here. Shallower waters are waiting to greet your keel to the west and southwest. Feel your way along with the sounder, and if the bottom starts to shelve up, retreat a bit to the northeast before dropping the hook.

Marker 88 Restaurant guards the Plantation Key shoreline about halfway between the "R Tr" and "Tr." This dining spot's pier is usually quite visible, courtesy of a host of colorful flags that are usually gaily flying in the wind. If your vessel can stand the thin 3½- to 4-foot dockside depths, cruise straight into the outer face of the fixed wooden pier. Don't try to moor to this dock's inner face or to the shoreside connector. Depths here are all but nil.

Plantation Yacht Harbor Marina sits in its enclosed basin, just west of the charted "Tr." Approach this facility from its northeasterly side. Watch for a red-and-white, candy-cane "lighthouse." This colorful structure marks the marina's only entrance. Leave the lighthouse to your starboard side and cruise straight into the harbor. Call the dockmaster ahead of time to get a slip assignment, as there are many, many slips to choose from. See if you can get her or him to meet you on the docks and direct your vessel to its proper slip.

Snake Creek and Associated Anchorages and Facilities
Be sure to use Inset 6, Page E (of chart 11451) when navigating Snake Creek. This inset's greater detail is ever so helpful.

From the ICW's unlighted daybeacon #78A, cruise south-southeast towards flashing daybeacon #12. This is the northernmost marker on the Snake Creek approach cut. Note that #12 can be hard to spot from the water. Use the good old binocs to help with this process.

Come abeam and pass #12 to its fairly immediate westerly side. Notice that you are now headed "toward" the open sea, so all subsequent red, even-numbered aids to navigation should be passed to your port side, and green marks should be taken to starboard.

Continue on, passing unlighted daybeacon #10 to its fairly immediate westerly side. The entrance to Snake Creek will then lie dead ahead. Stick to the centerline.

Eventually, Snake Creek curves just a touch farther to the south and hurries on towards the charted "Y" split in the stream. Favor the easterly banks as you approach the split. Chart 11451 correctly forecasts a ribbon of shallows shelving out from the westerly shoreline, beginning some 350 yards north of the split.

If you choose to anchor on the north-westerly arm of the "Y" split, be sure to enter on the stream's midline. Drop anchor before proceeding more than 150 yards upstream. Past this point, depths begin to shelve upward. Carefully set the hook so as not to swing into any of the shallows flanking all the surrounding shorelines. Also, be SURE the anchor is well set before heading below to begin the evening libations. As we have mentioned repeatedly throughout this account, tidal currents are fierce on Snake Creek.

Continuing seaward on the principal branch of Snake Creek, no-wake regulations are in effect, south of the "Y" split. Slow to idle speed. I mean, after all, the Islamorada U.S. Coast Guard Station is located a bit farther downstream on Snake Creek, so if there ever was good place to obey speed regulations, this is it!

Cruising south on Snake Creek towards the bascule bridge, you will notice that the eastern banks are penetrated by a whole series of canals. These small streams are overlooked by an incredibly dense collection of private residences. None of the canals has room enough for overnight anchorage, so we suggest that visitors keep clear of these waters.

The Islamorada U.S. Coast Guard Station occupies the point of land between the two southernmost canals making into the easterly shoreline, immediately north of the bascule bridge. Its position is quite apparent from the water.

The southernmost of the east-side canals plays host to Cobra Marine. Simply enter this stream along its centerline and forge on to the east at idle speed. Cobra's docks will soon be spotted dead ahead, in the charted crook of the canal.

Smuggler's Cove Marina guards the westerly banks, just north of the Snake Creek bascule bridge. You can't cut directly in toward the fuel dock or the dockage basin. As indicated by a whole collection of small floats and white PVC pipes, this marina is fronted by a shoal. To enter without finding these shallows, you must ease your way in from the north. This process is often complicated by the swiftly moving waters running under the Snake Creek Bridge. All captains should be ready for this current and take immediate remedial action if their vessel is knocked off course by the tide. This is a maximum-alert entry-way, and you'd better be ready for it.

These same strong currents plague the Snake Creek bascule bridge. Seldom have we seen more swiftly moving waters racing under a coastal bridge than the tidal flow we observed at the Snake Creek span. Thank goodness this bridge has a closed vertical clearance of 27 feet and opens on demand for vessels that require more clearance.

If you must wait for a bridge opening, stop well back from the span's fenders and wait for the bridge to fully open before proceeding along. These currents can push you into the bridge before you even know what's happening.

Immediately south of the bascule, two white PVC pipes mark a small, westward-running channel, which leads to the Big Conch Oceanside Bar and Grill. Remember that low-water depths in this cut run as thin as 3 feet. If you decide to enter anyway, keep strictly to the midwidth. Eventually, the restaurant and one face dock will come up to starboard, followed by additional dockage a bit farther upstream, also to starboard.

The seaward approach cut serving Snake Creek is very well marked, but it has a bad case of the "snakes." It coils first one way and then the other. Perhaps, this is where Snake Creek derives its name.

It would serve no purpose here to try and verbally catalog all the many unlighted daybeacons that outline this channel. Suffice it to say that it is critically important to correctly identify the next marker, or set of markers, before proceeding onward from a position abeam of a preceding aid to navigation. Keep chart 11451 at hand and detail a member of the crew to tick off your progress by daybeacon numbers as you go along.

Keep a sharp watch for any temporary, floating markers that may have been recently placed to warn of new encroachments by the surrounding shoals. We spotted several of these temporary beacons during our last visit, and it was to our good fortune that we let them guide us to the good water. May you, too, be so fortunate.

The outermost (southernmost) markers on the Snake Creek seaward channel are flashing daybeacon #2 and unlighted daybeacon #1. Once the gap between these two markers is in your wake, it's a run of almost 1.5 nautical miles southeast into the main path of Hawk Channel.

On the ICW Slightly better than 2 nautical miles of water separates the Waterway's unlighted daybeacon #78A and the next pair of markers, flashing daybeacon #81 and unlighted daybeacon #80. Before reaching #80 and #81, cruisers can split off to the south and visit Whale Harbor Channel and its anchorage (plus one low-key facility), or find their way to the anchorage abeam of Cotton Key.

Whale Harbor Channel As mentioned repeatedly earlier in this chapter, some of the markers on the Whale Harbor Channel are no longer located where chart 11451 would indicate them to be. Unlighted daybeacons #13, #12, and #11 have all been moved farther to the north. That's not all bad news. Daybeacon #13 now sits squarely opposite the "alternate lifestyle anchorage" and provides an easy means of identifying this offshoot.

Again, be sure to use Inset 6, Page E when navigating the Whale Harbor Channel. It gives far more navigational detail than the general chart.

To enter the northerly reaches of the Whale Harbor Channel, track your way from the ICW to a position between unlighted daybeacons #15 and #16. These aids to navigation ARE properly pictured on 11451. Continue on to the south, using your binoculars to pick out the next southerly aid to navigation, unlighted daybeacon #13.

If you arrive during a clear, sunny day, it will be quite obviously that a huge shelf of shoal water flanks this portion of the Whale Harbor Channel to the west. Favor the easterly side of the passage slightly and be sure to come abeam of #13 by some 25 yards to its easterly quarter. Do not approach #13 closely. The shallows to the west seem to be building around this marker.

Once abeam of #13, skippers may choose to enter the anchorage on the offshoot cutting to the southeast. Be advised that this is NOT a simple entrance. It is quite possible to wander into 3½ to 4 feet of water, even when you are trying to be careful.

For best depths, abandon the main Whale Harbor Channel a short hop north of #13. Cruise into the anchorage, favoring the port-side mangroves. Once past the entrance, begin slowly working your way back towards the starboard banks. Favor this side of the channel slightly as you work your way upstream. We suggest dropping the hook shortly after the sandy shores of Wilson Key come abeam to the southwest. Farther into the cove, depths begin to shelve up sharply.

Back on the principal Whale Harbor Channel, point for the gap between unlighted daybeacons #11 and #12, after coming abeam of #13. Like #13, #11 and #12 are located farther to the north than indicated on chart 11451. Pass between #11 and #12.

Between #13 and this pair of markers (#11 and #12), continue to be mindful of the shallows to the west. They are still waiting to trap the unwary.

Cruisers intent on anchoring along the waters of Whale Harbor Channel's northwesterly offshoot, opposite the charted position of unlighted daybeacon #11, should enter this stream on the midwidth. Drop anchor before proceeding through the stream's charted turn to the north. Shortly thereafter, soundings begin to rise.

After leaving the gap between #11 and #12 behind, begin a slow turn to the southsoutheast. The Whale Harbor Channel now begins to widen and becomes a substantial passage by the time it makes its approach to the 12-foot fixed bridge. Just before reaching this span, Estes Fishing Camp will come abeam to the northeast.

As most cruising-sized craft will not be able to clear the 12-foot fixed bridge, we will not further review the seaward passage of Whale Harbor Channel here. Just be advised that there is a reliable channel running southeast from the bridge to Hawk Channel, and two facilities are to be found near the seaward side of the bridge. We shall meet up with this passage and these two marinas later in this chapter as part of our perusal of this portion of Hawk Channel.

Cotton Key Anchorage Cruisers who plan to anchor east of Cotton Key should depart the ICW some .8 nautical miles northeast of flashing daybeacon #81. Cruise to the south, making sure to stay well east of the shallows running off from the northern side of Cotton Key. Anchor at least 200 yards east of the Key's easterly shores. Closer in, depths deteriorate rapidly.

On the ICW From #80 and #81, cruisers

must cross a gap of some .9 nautical miles before encountering the Waterway's next aid to navigation, unlighted daybeacon #82. Be SURE to come abeam of #82 by 25 yards (no more) to its southeasterly side. Shallows lie north and south of #82.

Even by following this outlined maneuver, don't be surprised if your sounder shows only 5 feet of water at low tide along this stretch of the Waterway. Let's hope the Army Corps of Engineers gets busy on these waters in the near future.

Next up is unlighted daybeacon #84. Come abeam of this marker by about 20 yards to its southeasterly side. Again, a shoal flanks the channel, immediately north of #84. Obviously, it would behoove one to stay south of this marker.

It's then only a short hop to flashing daybeacon #86. For the same reasons, be sure to come abeam of #86 to its southerly side.

From unlighted daybeacon #86, mariners may choose to break off to the south and visit the popular Islamorada Anchorage, Lorelei Marina, Little Basin, World Wide Sportsman, and a smattering of other facilities.

Islamorada Anchorage Cut to the southeast at #86 and track your way along for about 1.6 nautical miles. Soon, you will catch sight of the armada of vessels almost always anchored on these waters. Avoid the southwesterly side of the cove, even if you see some other craft moored there. Depths on this pocket of the bay rise to 4- and 5-foot levels. We suggest dropping anchor near 24 55.534 North/080 38.227 West. This will get you close enough to shore to provide

some protection, and you will still be northeast of the shallower southwesterly corner of the bay.

Lorelei Marina To find your way to Lorelei Marina, locate facility designation #54 on chart 11451 (Inset 6, Page E). Set course so as to approach this harbor from its northeasterly side. As the chart indicates, it is from this quarter that cruisers can take advantage of an improved channel leading to the dockage basin's entrance.

On the water, it is never easy to identify the entrance to Lorelei, even when you've been there before. Usually, your only clue will be some sailcraft masts sticking above the trees. If you are navigating electronically, it is helpful to know that the entrance lies near 24 55.425 North/080 37.962 West.

Swing to the southwest and cruise through the entrance. The first slips will come up to starboard. The restaurant, tiki bar, and some small craft slips guard the harbor's southwesterly tip.

Little Basin and World Wide Sportsman and other Nearby Facilities NOAA has really knocked themselves out this time. The Islamorada Anchorage, discussed above, is covered on Inset 6, Page E of chart 11451, while most of the immediately adjacent Little Basin, is detailed on Inset 7, Page F. In between, there is a little sliver, which is not covered on either inset. It just so happens that Caribee Boat Sales and Coral Bay Marina are found here. Be ready for some serious chart manipulation.

From the ICW's unlighted daybeacon #86, cut southeast as if you were going to visit the Islamorada Anchorage. Watch to the southwest for two sets of unlighted daybeacons that lead between two mangroves. Don't mistake the northernmost aids to navigation, unlighted daybeacons #21 and #22, on the Shell Key Channel, for the Little Basin entrance marks. We shall meet the Shell Key passage in the next section of this chapter. For now, we need only note that the Little Basin entrance is located a good .9 nautical miles southeast of the Shell Key Channel.

As noted above, use Inset 6, Page E for your approach, then switch to Inset 7, Page F to actually navigate the entrance to Little Basin. Cruise directly between both sets of daybeacons. Stick strictly to the midline—both mangrove shores are quite shoaly.

Once into Little Basin, avoid all the shorelines like the Black Plague, except for the World Wide Sportsman Bayside Marina dockage basin (and the adjacent Islamorada Fish Company dock). This complex will be spotted on the basin's southeasterly shoreline.

If you choose to anchor on Little Basin, drop the hook as near the middle to the northern half of the bay as possible. Be sure to set your hook so as not to swing near any of the shorelines. They are all quite shallow.

Captains cruising from Little Basin to the small canal that provides access to Caribee Boat Sales and Coral Bay Marina will discover the entrance to this stream on Little Basin's northeasterly corner. Cruise into the canal's centerline at minimum speed. These waters can get shallow, so take your time. You must immediately switch to Page E of chart 11451 (no inset) to navigate the canal. Both Caribee and Coral Bay will eventually come up on the southeasterly shoreline.

It is also possible to enter this canal from the wider waters just southwest of Lorelei Marina. Two white PVC stakes outline this passage. Cruise directly between these crude markers. Expect some 4½-foot soundings at low tide when following this route.

ICW—Shell Key to Channel Five

Are you ready for a little confusion? Well, just get out your handy-dandy copy of chart 11451 and peruse the waters that separate Upper Matecumbe and Lower Matecumbe Keys. This wide swath of water is traversed by as complicated a series of channels as you will ever find in the Florida Keys. Some lead to a few facilities, others to anchorages, and all, one way or another, to the long highway bridge that provides the link between the two Matecumbe keys. For discussion purposes, we will call this collection of cuts and small passages, the Matecumbe channels.

Be advised that the bridge spanning the Matecumbe channels is a fixed structure. Only one of the passages crossing under this span, the Indian Key Channel, offers anything in the way of vertical clearance, 27 feet as a matter of fact. All the other channels leading under the bridge have a mere 10 feet of vertical clearance, except for the northeasternmost, unnamed channel that has 7 feet of clearance.

Sailcraft skippers should take careful note of the fact that a long, high-tension power line parallels the northern face of the bridge spanning the Matecumbe channels. While, quite surprisingly, the shocking obstruction's vertical clearance is not noted on chart 11451, the lines looked to be about 50 feet off the water. The electrical wires are, to say the least, daunting. It would be a terrible place to make a mistake in a sailboat. Anchoring in a channel where a dragging anchor could take you into some power lines AND into a bridge would get you the lead story on local television and front-page coverage in the newspaper. You probably could do without that.

All the Matecumbe channels will come abeam south of the ICW passage, between unlighted daybeacon #86 and the Peterson Key Bank. We heartily suggest that you keep chart 11451 close at hand as we detail these many, convoluted channels. This is about the only way that you have a chance to keep all of this straight.

Within the body of this cruising ground, captains and crews will find Lignumvitae Key and Indian Key. Both isles are Florida state parks and enjoy a rich natural and man-made history. There are provisions for pleasure craft to visit both parks, so be sure to check out our account of these storied keys below.

Southwest of Peterson Key Bank, which the ICW traverses by way of a dredged channel, cruisers can choose to continue following the Waterway or cut south-southwest to Channel Five. This inlet allows ready passage by most any sized pleasure craft to and from the ICW and the offshore, Hawk Channel route. Channel Five is spanned by a fixed bridge with a wonderful 65 feet of vertical clearance. Several nearby anchorages and a few facilities

add to the appeal of the waters lapping about Channel Five.

So put on your strongest reading glasses, take a deep breath, and here goes!

Shell Key Channel
(Standard Mile 1160)

The easternmost of the Matecumbe channels is the Shell Key Channel. The entrance to this cut is located some .8 nautical miles south-southeast of the ICW's unlighted daybeacon #86. The northernmost markers are unlighted daybeacons #21 and #22. The markers on the Shell Key Channel do not show up on earlier editions of chart 11451 (Inset 7, Page F), but thankfully, they are correctly depicted on the current version. This renders the channel relatively easy to run for careful navigators. However, there are, as the late Howard Cosell would have said, a "plethora" of markers on these waters, courtesy of the all the intersecting channels. Take your time and have your binoculars at hand to help sort out all the confusing aids to navigation.

The Shell Key Channel maintains minimum depths of 6 feet. This track allows access to the southeasterly foot of Race Channel (southwest of unlighted daybeacons #11 and #12), and more importantly, the westerly genesis of the Yellow Shark Channel, which is the next track we will detail below.

Southwest of unlighted daybeacons #11 and #12, the Shell Key Channel turns to the south and eventually heads toward the 50-foot (estimated) power lines and a pass-through under the long bridge and causeway that stretches between Upper and Lower Matecumbe Keys. Unfortunately, this portion of the fixed bridge has only 10 feet of vertical clearance. All but small craft will have to take an alternate track north of the span.

Fortunately, it's possible to turn west-south-west or east-northeast and run the Power Line Channel (see below).

For those low-lying vessels that can make it under the 10-foot span, a reasonably well-marked track known as the Teatable Key Channel continues seaward towards Hawk Channel. This passage maintains minimum 10-foot depths, but, as usual, there is plenty of tidal current in evidence. In spite of this, the Teatable Key Channel is a good route for smaller powercraft who are set on a visit to the briny blue.

Yellow Shark Channel and Associated Facilities (Various Lat/Lons—see below)

Yellow Shark Channel actually begins just north of the easternmost pass-through of the Upper Matecumbe-Lower Matecumbe Bridge. This very low-level portion of the span has a mere 7 feet of vertical clearance.

The Yellow Shark is outlined by small nun and can buoys. It runs first north, past one marina, then takes a sharp turn to the east, and wanders on toward an intersection with Little Basin. Minimum depths are 6 feet, with typical low-water soundings of 8 feet or better.

This is not a simple cut to run successfully. It wanders first one way, then another. The small aids to navigation are not always easy to spot, so again, take your time and be sure to correctly identify all markers before proceeding forward.

It is also quite possible to access the Yellow Shark Channel from the Shell Key Channel. Cruisers on the Shell Key passage

Entrance to Matecumbe Marina (Yellow Shark Channel)

can abandon this cut at either unlighted day-beacon #10 or just south of unlighted day-beacon #8 and cut east into the Yellow Shark. Minimum soundings on this transition are about 5 feet.

Immediately north of the Yellow Shark's meeting with the eastern limits of the Upper Matecumbe-Lower Matecumbe Bridge, Papa Joe's Marina, Restaurant (305-664-8109), and Tiki Bar (24 53.896 North/080 39.582 West) guards the eastern banks. This is not the place where you might want to spend a long time, as this marine facility is short on amenities. On the other hand, the restaurant appears popular and the fact that it's upstairs and has an open-to-breezes bar makes it fun. It attracts more people off the highway than it does off the water, but back-country fishing expeditions are staged from these docks in some quantity, and apparently, with rather consistent success.

This operation is more restaurant than anything else and it has some tenure in the Keys. The fixed wooden finger pier slips are small and would probably work best for outboard boats. Transients are accepted, however, and dockside fresh water and 15-amp (only) power connections are available. Depths alongside run around 5½ to 6 feet at low water. There are no on-site showers, but marina customers can use the rest rooms associated with Papa Joe's Restaurant. A beach-bait-and-tackle store just behind the docks add to the marina's offerings.

**Papa Joe's Marina, Restaurant, and Tiki Bar
    (305) 664-5005**
http://www.papajoesmarina.com

**Approach depth—6-8 feet
Dockside depth—5½-6 feet
Accepts transients—yes
Type of piers—fixed wooden and alongside
    docking
Dockside power connections—15 amp only
Dockside water connections—yes
Showers—no, but there are rest rooms that
    serve the restaurant
Ship's store—BB&T
Restaurant—Papa Joe's Landmark Restaurant on
    site, full menu, moderate pricing**

Papa Joe's Marina (Yellow Shark Channel)

There is a seaward branch of the Yellow Shark Channel that provides access to popular Bud N' Mary's Marina. Since no vessel of any size can clear the 7-foot portion of the bridge to reach these waters from the inside portion of Yellow Shark, we will cover Bud N' Mary's as part of our Hawk Channel section later in this chapter.

At unlighted nun buoy #22 and unlighted can buoy #21, the Yellow Shark Channel takes a sharp turn to the east and begins to parallel the northerly shoreline of Upper Matecumbe Key. As mentioned earlier, this portion of the Yellow Shark is very twisty and turny. At unlighted nun buoy #24, the channel turns to the northeast and eventually wanders on to a shallow meeting with the northwesterly extreme of Little Basin. The juncture between the Yellow Shark and Little Basin is not for the faint of heart and is definitely off-limits to vessels drawing 4 feet or more. Check out our navigational review of Yellow Shark Channel below for some hints on how to keep to the best water when entering Little Basin via this route. Even with the best case in the offing, don't expect more than 4 feet of depth.

This easterly section of the Yellow Shark Channel plays host to two smaller marina facilities. First up is Matecumbe Marina (24 54.487 North/080 39.004 West). The white, PVC-pipe-lined entrance channel breaks off to the east, near unlighted nun buoy #24. This entrance cut eventually wanders through a mangrove to the dockage basin. Low-water depths are only 3½ feet or so.

Matecumbe Marina is the home to a bunch of laid-back people, some of whom live on houseboats or houses built on small barges. It is also the home of Nautilimo, which has to be seen to be believed. This strange machine is a Lincoln Continental that has been converted into a boat, tires and all. Obviously, all the heavy stuff has been taken out. The trunk sports a hidden outboard motor, which powers this unusual mode of transportation. The driver sits in the usual place and steers with a conventional steering wheel, which is attached to the outboard engine. Paying customers sit in the back as they are chauffeured to and fro. Pub crawling in the Nautilimo is probably an option, but do it on calm seas. You don't what to hit potholes.

A local character by the name of Joe Fox launches the Nautilimo for special occasions. It has been featured in television shows. Rent it for a tour if you want. Joe is affable and clever and funny. It will be a trip.

Transients are accepted at Matecumbe Marina, but berth space at the fixed wooden pier is limited. Fresh water and 30-amp power connections are the in the offing. Surprisingly, dockside cable television and telephone connections are also available. Typical low-tide soundings in the harbor are about 5 feet, so the 3½-foot entrance depths will be the limiting factor. Speaking just for us, we would not want to try and jockey a vessel larger than 36 feet into this harbor.

Waste pump-out service is available on call. The on-site showers are large and clean, but it's a pretty good walk from the docks to get there. A small Laundromat is located alongside the showers.

When it comes time to satisfy an appetite gleaned from a long day on the water, there are several nearby choices. Dino's of Islamorada Ristorante (305-664-0727) is the closest, open for lunch and dinner. This dining spot is located about a half-mile to the east. Put your hiking shoes on. There are also four other restaurants nearby. A cab might be a good call here. Outback Steak House (305-664-3344) is a

Nautilimo (Matecumbe Marina)

half-mile west, along U.S. 1. And a little further down the road is Papa Joe's (see above). No breakfasts are to be had at any of these eateries.

Matecumbe Marina (305) 664-2402

Approach depth—3 1/2 feet (minimum, low water)
Dockside depth—5 feet (low water)
Accepts transients—yes
Type of docking—fixed wooden piers with alongside docking
Dockside power connections—30 amp
Dockside water connections—yes
Cable televsion hookup—yes
Phone hookup—yes
Waste pump-out—yes, waste pump-out service truck on call
Showers—yes
Laundromat—yes
Restaurant—walk a half-mile or call a cab

The second facility off the Yellow Shark Channel is Max's Marine and Boatyard (24 54.523 North/080 38.881 West, 305-664-8884). This facility's entrance passage cuts southeast off the Yellow Shark, immediately northeast of unlighted can buoy #25. It is outlined by a combination of white PVC pipes and unadorned wooden pilings. Low-water depths run around 4 feet, with at least 4½ feet of water in the dockage basin.

Max's Marine is a marina and boatyard that has enough local business; transient services are not part of what it offers. However, Max's Marine is a Mercury outboard and Merc cruiser dealer, so they would be able to repair something in that product line. In addition, they have a 35-ton Travelift, so below-waterline repairs are available here also. They sell gasoline but no diesel.

Max's Marine and Boatyard

Don't look for them on weekends. They are open 7:30 A.M. to 5:00 P.M., Mondays through Fridays.

To summarize, this is a good, clean, professional marina, which has repair services as outlined above, but does not offer transient service whatsoever. Because it is off the beaten path, you should have something very specific in mind in the way of repairs when and if you come in here. A phone call or radio call ahead to let them know that you are on the way would be a good idea, too.

Shell Key Anchorage and Mooring Field (Standard Mile 1161)
(24 55.548 North/080 40.264 West)
Shell Key is a large, all natural body of land that is found south of the ICW's unlighted daybeacon #91. It also lies near the northerly head of the various passages that we have designated as the Matecumbe channels.

Shell Key is owned by the state of Florida and is fully protected. Landings are not allowed.

On the plus side, the state maintains a series of 5 mooring buoys off the key's northwesterly shoreline. There is also PLENTY of room to anchor. Good depths of 6 feet or better are maintained to within 100 yards of the isle's northwesterly banks.

This anchorage/mooring field affords good shelter to the east, southeast, and south. The charted shoal and mangrove southwest of Shell Key contributes to this protection greatly. On the other hand, don't get caught beside Shell Key in strong northerlies, or even worse, blows coming from the northwest.

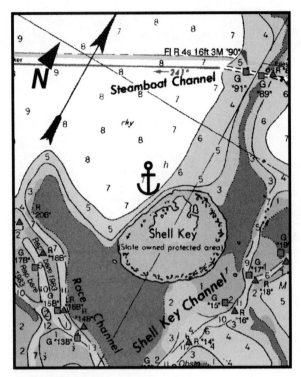

Race Channel
(Standard Mile 1162)

The Race Channel cuts to the southeast, well southeast of the ICW's unlighted daybeacon #91A. Westbound (southbound) mariners need not actually go all the way to #91A. You can abandon the Waterway a good .5 nautical miles farther to the northeast.

The Race Channel runs along its amply-marked way, well southwest of Shell Key. It is separated from the key by a wide band of shallows and mangroves. Surprisingly, cruisers will find at least 6 feet of water in the Race Channel at low tide, with typical soundings in the 7- and 8-foot region. Outside of the marked cut, however, soundings run to 1 foot or less. Need we remind you? It would be a very good idea, indeed, to stay within the bounds marked by the various aids to navigation.

Southeast of unlighted daybeacon #12B, the Race Channel meets up with the Shell Key Channel that we reviewed earlier. A turn to the south on this latter cut will lead to Papa Joe's, and a meeting with the Yellow Shark Channel.

Indian Key Channel
(Standard Mile 1162.5)
(Various Lat/Lons—see below)

South-southeast of unlighted daybeacon #91A, the Indian Key Channel provides the best means along this stretch of the Waterway for mariners to cruise outside to Hawk Channel, or alternately, leave Hawk Channel behind and cruise inland to the ICW.

Even so, this passage is fit only for power-craft, courtesy of the 50-foot power lines and the 27-foot, fixed bridge that crosses the passage, south-southeast of unlighted daybeacons #7 and #8. This clearance is plenty for most vessels who travel without the need of wind power.

Indian Key Channel provides access to two very interesting historic sites: Lignumvitae Key and Indian Key. The visitor and tour-boat dock for the Florida state park on Lignumvitae Key sits almost due west of the Indian Key Channel's unlighted daybeacon #15 (24 54.191 North/080 41.667 West), close by the "Dol" notation on chart 11451 (Inset 7, Page F). It is a fixed concrete structure with some outlying wooden piles and finger piers. Depths alongside run 4 to 4½ feet at low water. Deeper-draft vessels can always anchor on the correctly charted 7-foot waters farther to the east and dinghy in.

Indian Key is found on the seaward - Hawk Channel side of the Lower Matecumbe-Upper Matecumbe Bridge, west of the Indian Key Channel's southerly terminus. This isle is also a state park. There is one park pier on the southeasterly tip of the isle and a series of mooring buoys off the key's southeasterly shores. Depths at the small, fixed wooden pier run only 4 feet or so, and most of the space here is set aside for a tour boat that brings visitors out from the mainland. Depths in the mooring field run from 5 to 7 feet at low water.

We shall consider both the parks on Lignumvitae Key and Indian Key separately below. For now, we only wanted to note the position and mariner-friendly amenities.

Returning our attention to Indian Key Channel, navigators should be ready for trouble as their craft approaches the northern face of the 27-foot, fixed bridge. At this point, the main cut intersects what we call the Power Line Channel (see below). It's very, very easy to confuse the markers on this latter passage with aids to navigation on the Indian Key cut. Such a mistake will most likely result in a grounding. PLEASE read our navigational reviews of both the Indian Key Channel and the Power Line Channel below before entering these waters for the first (or even the second) time.

Lignumvitae Key State Park
(Standard Mile 1162.5)
(24 54.191 North/080 41.667 West—location of visitors' dock)

Lignumvitae Key is a state botanical park, and you get to it by boat from Robbie's Marina (see below). The fare for the trip out and back is $15 per person, plus tax. The tour boats depart a half-hour before the park tour starts. Park tours are offered twice a day, at 10 A.M. and at 2 P.M. The park is closed on Tuesdays and Wednesdays, a fact that you might well keep in mind. You cannot go ashore on your own.

If you'd like to avoid the boat ride tariff, you can tie up to a mooring buoy off the park (there are five off the northwest side of Lignumvitae Key, near 24 54.410 North/080 42.246 West) and dinghy in. Or, if your craft doesn't draw more than 4 feet, you may tie right up to the park dock. There is a small admission charge to the park, but it's insignificant, about $1 per person, and children under six get in for free. A third plan of action for deeper-draft vessels would be to anchor on the correctly charted 7-foot waters just east of the park pier and break out the dinghy.

Probably one of the reasons that people like to visit the Keys is that they remind us of simpler times. There are a number of uninhabited islands in the Keys, small ones that only support wildlife and vegetation that arrived on the wind or waves. Lignumvitae is such a Key—it's just larger than most—and when you visit here you step back into history . . . geological, human, and verdure. Some of the trees that grow on Lignumvitae Key grow in no other place in the Keys. Elsewhere, they have been sacrificed to make way for modern needs, modern accommodations, and modern comforts.

Trees here have names like gumbo-limbo, poisonwood, strangler fig, pigeon plum, mastic, and not surprisingly, of course, lignumvitae, from which the key draws its name. Lignumvitae is an incredibly dense, hard wood, harder than oak, that was once used to make billy clubs for police. It dulled saw blades quickly. It also dented heads beautifully.

Lignumvitae Key began its existence as a living coral reef. During one of the ice ages, as water began to freeze at the poles, the level of the water around the world dropped, and what was under water emerged and became islands. Over time—lots of time—bits of seaweed and other detritus washed up on the rock, decayed, and became soil when it was deposited in depressions in the rock. Then, most likely, some migrating birds shed some seeds in their droppings and the seeds took hold and grew. How many years did it take? Thousands, probably. But now Lignumvitae Key represents how the Keys might have looked if mankind had not found the waters so rich with sea life and the islands so beautifully attractive. The contrast between what might have been and what is, is breathtaking.

The mosquitoes on Lignumvitae Key look forward to your visit, especially on Thursdays, after two days of near famine. Take precautions.

Indian Key State Park

Indian Key should be approached from its southern, Hawk Channel side. Shoals envelop the island to the north, and a bank of shallows shelves out from both the eastern and western banks as well. The visitors' dock is perched off the southeasterly tip of Indian Key. It is rather small, and most of the space here is given over to a tour boat, which brings visitors to this park from Lower Matecumbe Key. It would be far better for captain and crew of most cruising-sized craft to dinghy in to the dock.

There is a mooring field off Indian Key's southeasterly shores. If any are available, you can pick up a buoy in 5 to 7 feet of water, or alternately, drop anchor. This anchorage/mooring field is well sheltered from northwesterly breezes, and there is also some protection to the north. Forget it if a hard wind is blowing from the south, southwest, or the southeast. However you get ashore, Indian Key is well worth a visit. Few other Florida Keys can

claim such a historically colorful past.

Indian Key encompasses some 11 acres and once had a town on it, albeit not a very big one. The key was colonized in the 1830s by a wrecker—a man who salvaged shipwrecks—whose name was Jacob Housman. He came from Key West, where there was more competition and where some of the judges had the inside track, for they, too, were wreckers. Housman bought Indian Key in 1831. There was nearby fresh water on the Matecumbe Keys, but most of the houses on Indian Key had cisterns, too. At one time, Indian Key had its own post office, several streets, wharves, warehouses, some 20 residences, and a hotel that was called the Tropical. The Tropical even had a bowling alley. Automatic pinsetters and televised bowling contests had not been invented yet, so the bowling alley never made the big time.

Jacob Housman grew rich on Indian Key. The reefs on which ships foundered were not far off. The ships' bad fortune and his good luck and near monopoly on the wrecking business brought him lots of money. Though historical accounts of Housman's tenure on Indian Key attribute some of his success to his business acumen, they also infer that he may have been involved in some shady dealings. He was, however, successful in getting the Florida Legislature to establish a separate Dade County, independent from Key West, and make Indian Key the county seat.

According to one source, Housman's political successes paralleled his financial decline. He was in court a great deal, presumably in a turf battle with Key West wreckers, and he lost far more than he won. He was found guilty of embezzlement of goods from a vessel he was salvaging in 1836. He lost his

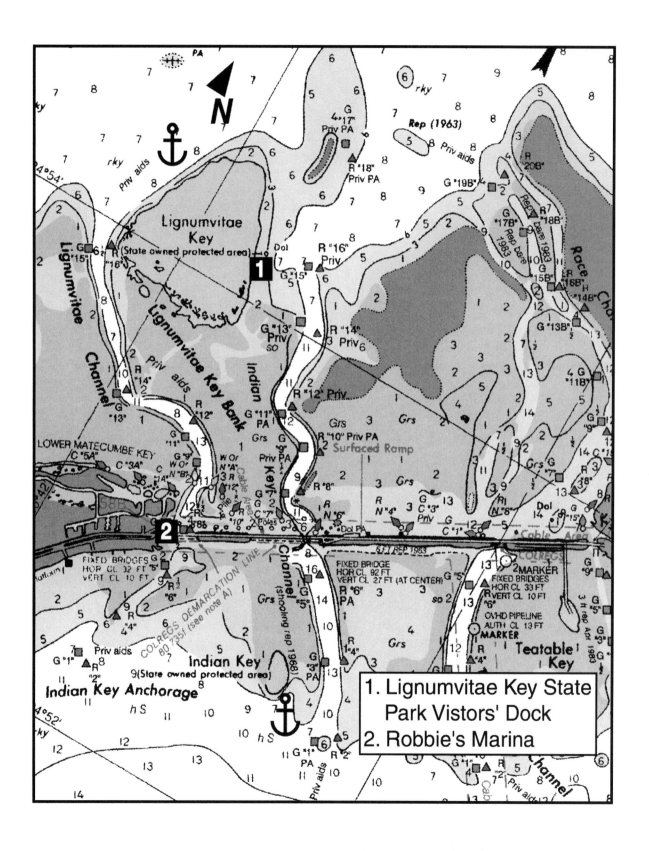

1. Lignumvitae Key State Park Vistors' Dock
2. Robbie's Marina

wrecker's license in 1838. And when the Second Seminole War began in late in December of 1835, he also lost the trade of the Indians who used to come to the key and buy goods at the key's general store.

His former customers became his adversaries and his worst nightmare. By 1840, there were about 55 people living on Indian Key. Housman, ever the opportunist, was negotiating with the United States government around that time for permission to hunt down Seminoles at the going rate of $200 a head. It is assumed that $200 a head was a literal interpretation. Housman also had enough sway with the government that he succeeded in having the United States Navy's Florida Squadron stationed at Teatable Key, just to the east of Indian Key.

Housman's luck ran out on August 7, 1840. The Florida Squadron was away chasing savages around Cape Sable or possibly restocking its medicinal rum supply, which was known to evaporate extremely quickly in the Florida heat, summer or winter, when Seminoles arrived on Indian Key, uninvited. The Indians burned down every house but one, killed some sixteen people, and then left. Housman and his family lived through it all and escaped injury, but the good old days, wherein Jacob Housman was a law unto himself, were gone forever. He moved shortly thereafter to Key West and continued to work as a wrecker for another man, but his days were short. He died within six months in an accident, crushed between two vessels while plying his trade.

Jacob Housman's body was brought back to Indian Key and buried. But someone stole his skeletonized remains and his tombstone. There is a replica of the original in place today.

In the 1930s and 1940s, treasure hunters, who used explosives in the search for treasure, scoured the island to little avail. Today, you may visit Indian Key from 8 A.M. to sunset. You are on your own, however. There are no facilities on the island. On the other hand, you may find a mosquito or two. Some things never change.

Lignumvitae Key Channel (Standard Mile 1163.5)

The entrance to the 6-foot minimum depth Lignumvitae Channel lies just west of the like named key. Cruisers headed for this cut from the ICW can leave the Waterway's track .6 nautical miles southwest of unlighted daybeacon #91A.

Between the Waterway and the northern entrance to this channel, the mooring field off the northwestern shores of Lignumvitae Key will be passed to the east. As observed above, this is a great spot, with eastery winds in the offing, to spend a few hours or even an evening.

The northernmost aids to navigation on the Lignumvitae Channel are unlighted daybeacons #15 and #16. From this point, the passage weaves its way generally south to a juncture with the 10-foot (fixed) westernmost pass-through of the Upper Matecumbe-Lower Matecumbe Key Bridge. Not only are some the channel's twists and turns a bit navigationally challenging, but just north of its meeting with the 10-foot fixed span, this cut intersects the Power Line Channel (see below). The various markers at the juncture can be monumentally confusing. We will carefully detail this stretch in our navigational section below. All cruisers are strongly advised to review this upcoming account in detail.

Powercraft aground at edge of Lignumvitae Channel

During our last visit to this passage, we noted a large powercraft aground north of unlighted daybeacon #8. I'm sure the captain of this vessels was northbound, and after passing under the bridge, mistakenly headed for a nun and can buoy that he thought marked the Indian Key Channel. Not so, and the result was an afternoon of sitting on the hard, contemplating the value of good coastal navigation.

Just north of the 10-foot span, Robbie's Marina (24 52.976 North/080 41.415 West) overlooks the western flank of the Lignumvitae Channel. A large shoal separates this facility's docks from the channel. This hazard is indicated by a series of floats on a rope. To safely access the marina, you must cruise either south or north of this shoal. Take your time—this is not an easy entry.

Assuming you bypass the shoal described above successfully, captains can expect 5-foot entrance depths at low water. Soundings alongside run at least 6½ to 7½ feet.

Robbie's Marina also sits perilously close to the 50-foot power lines mentioned at the beginning of this section. The electrical wires are, to say the least, daunting. It would be a terrible place to make a mistake in a sailboat, trying to get into the marina. Dinghying in would make far more sense, but remember that the current in these channels can get very, very strong, so you need to pick your times carefully and make no errors. Anchoring in a channel where a dragging anchor could take you into some power lines AND into a bridge would get you the lead story on local television and front-page coverage in the newspaper. You probably could do without that.

Robbie's Marina is smallish, with an Old Florida look, ripe with fishing boats of some years. The dockage consists of mostly fixed wooden finger piers, but their state of repair is a bit depleted. While the people at Robbie's couldn't be nicer or more accommodating, there is, unless you are into some serious

Tarpon feeding at Robbie's Marina

funk, not a lot here to look forward to. It sometimes seems not fair to define a marina by what it is not, but this one has no showers or other amenities that most cruisers deem necessary.

Nevertheless, transients are accepted, though many of the slips are occupied by local craft. Fresh water hookups are available, and there are also some dockside 15-amp (only) power connections. Gasoline (no diesel) can be purchased. There is an on-site bait-and-tackle shop.

Robbie's has its own restaurant known as the Hungry Tarpon (305-664-0535). It's sort of funky Keys style with funky Keys food. No gourmet dining here. However, they do serve all three meals of the day.

The big attraction at Robbie's is the presence of free-swimming tarpon (and jacks) that have become accustomed to people feeding them by hand. It's quite thrilling, really, to see the legendary, silver-sided game fish up close and personal as they wait for a handout. You can buy baitfish by the bucketful, just yards away from where you feed the fish. A tarpon is a big fish and moves with great speed, so you want to make sure you get all your fingers back when you present one with an offering.

Tour boats leave from Robbie's Marina to ferry tourists to the state park on Lignumvitae Key. Inquire about times of departure in the bait store.

Robbie's Marina (305) 664-9814
http://www.robbies.com

Approach depth—5 feet (low water)

Dockside depth—6½ -7½ feet
Accepts transients—yes
Type of piers—fixed wooden with some
  alongside docking and some finger piers
Dockside power connections—15 amp only
Dockside water connections—yes
Fuel—gas only
Ship's store—BB&T
Restaurant—on-site

Power Line Channel

While there is nothing navigationally easy about it, a marked channel parallels the entire northern face of the Upper Matecumbe-Lower Matecumbe Bridge. We have dubbed this east-west-running cut the Power Line Channel, and it has been referred to as such several times above. Along its easterly section, this passage runs between the 50-foot power lines and the bridge (plus causeway), but just west-southwest of its intersection with the Indian Key Channel, it darts under the lines and remains north of these shocking obstructions for the remainder of its length.

Minimum depths are 5½ feet, with most of the channel showing soundings of 6 to 8 feet at low water. These depths presuppose that you will be able to stay in the marked cut. That's not always easy, particularly when the Power Line Channel crosses the Teatable Key, Indian Key, and Lignumvitae Channels at right angles. It's very easy to confuse the floating markers on the Power line cut with the day-beacons marking these three major channels. Again, we exhort you, gentle reader, to check out our navigational section below pertaining to these waters.

As it approaches its intersection with the Lignumvitae Channel, the Power Line passage begins to bend to the northwest and then cuts west. While it would be almost impossible to discern it from chart 11451 (Inset 7, Page F), this cut actually leads across Lignumvitae Channel, and then into a narrow, canal-like passage, which connects with the fine anchorage on Matecumbe Bight (see below). Only small craft are eligible to even contemplate running this secret, almost mysterious, stream but it is surprisingly well marked and holds minimum 5-foot depths with most soundings in the 6- to 8-foot region. Much of the connecting canal is completely overhung with leafy branches, and at times, it appears as if you are cruising into a tunnel.

The first time we found it, we came upon this passage by accident and were utterly enthralled with this unusual canal. We heartily suggest that all small craft give this westernmost section of the Power Line Channel a try. We don't think you will be disappointed!

Heading Toward Channel Five

After passing Lignumvitae Key well south of its track, the ICW follows the dredged Bowlegs Cut through Peterson Key Bank. Soon, cruisers can break off to the south-southwest and visit two different anchorages hard by Lower Matecumbe Key, plus Channel Two and the very important passage known as Channel Five.

Matecumbe Bight Anchorage (Standard Mile 1166) (24 52.255 North/080 42.856 West)

The large bubble of deep water known as Matecumbe Bight lies south-southeast of the ICW's unlighted daybeacon #97. To avoid the 1-foot shallows of Peterson Key Bank, west-bound (southbound) cruisers must follow the Waterway's track for another .6 miles or so southwest of #97 before turning to southeast and heading for the bight.

Hidden channel to Matecumbe Bight

Good soundings of minimum 6½- to 7-foot depths run to within 100 yards, or even slightly closer, of the bight's southeasterly shoreline. These banks alternate between residential development and some all-natural stretches, some with palm trees, while the point to the southwest is overlooked by a stand of Australian Pines. Highway U.S. 1 sits just behind this shoreline, and nighttime traffic might be a bit of an annoyance from time to time.

Avoid Matecumbe Bight's southwesternmost corner. The charted 4-foot depths are for real. Take our bent prop's word for it.

As we learned above, Matecumbe Bight can also be accessed via the southwesternmost section of the so-called Power Line Channel, through a tree-enshrouded canal.

Check out our account above for additional details.

Matecumbe Harbor Anchorage (Standard Mile 1168) (24 51.057 North/080 44.520 West)

The marked entryway into Matecumbe Harbor lies some 1.9 nautical miles southwest of the anchorage in Matecumbe Bight. This latter haven boasts one flashing daybeacon, with the remainder of the channel outlined by white PVC pipes. Minimum depths run around 5 feet, with typical 6- to 7-foot soundings.

The Matecumbe Harbor channel dead-ends against the same high-tension power lines we met in our discussion of the Matecumbe channels above. The shoreline of Lower Matecumbe Key sits just behind the power poles.

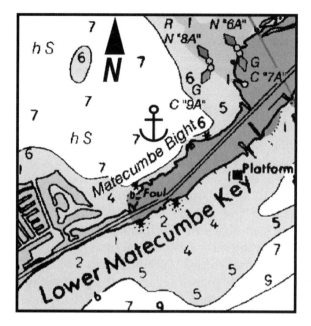

If it weren't for the power lines, the southerly portion of the Matecumbe Harbor channel would make for a superb anchorage for all vessels. With these shocking obstructions in mind, however, we would be loath to recommend this haven to sailcraft in any but fair weather. After all, a dragging anchor on these waters could make for a real problem of the many-kilowatt variety.

For best depths, anchor some 75 to 100 yards short of (north of) the power poles. Closer to the lines, soundings rise to 4-foot levels.

It is possible to ease just a bit to the west, but don't go beyond a point where you come abeam of the eastern tip of the small island that lies just west of the anchorage. Depths shelve up to nil as this island comes abeam.

The southeasterly corner of Matecumbe Harbor plays host to an Explore (Boy Scout) Sea Scout headquarters. This is a wonderful youth facility, with a good harbor, featuring 5-foot minimum depths. Unfortunately, there are no facilities for visiting cruisers.

The Matecumbe Harbor anchorage is well sheltered from all but strong northerly and northwesterly winds. In fact, this is one of the most protected anchorages in this region of the Florida Keys. Swing room is sufficient for a 38-footer. Just please don't forget those power lines if you pilot a ship with masts.

Channel Two
(Standard Mile 1169)

The long, long combination fixed bridge and causeway that spans the gap between Lower Matecumbe Key and Long Key actually crosses two channels. The easternmost is known as Channel Two. The inside or ICW-side portion of this cut is actually of little use to cruising-sized craft. It is crossed by a portion of the bridge with only 10 feet of vertical clearance. To make matters a little more interesting, the northerly section of Channel Two borders on some rather strange-looking concrete structures. These were actually lower sections of piers that were to be part of the Overseas Highway, built by WPA workers in

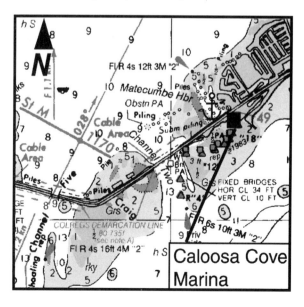

the 1930s. They were left uncompleted after the Labor Day Hurricane of 1935.

Channel Two is decidedly not a good place to anchor, and there are no marinas north of the 10-foot, fixed bridge. Skippers of all but small, shallow-draft, outboard and I/O vessels are advised to keep clear.

The seaward side of Channel Two is a rather different story. It provides access to Caloosa Cove Marina, on the Hawk Channel (ocean) side of Lower Matecumbe Key. However, since only very small craft will be able to clear the 10-foot Channel Two Bridge, we shall review this facility as part of our Hawk Channel coverage later in this chapter.

Channel Five
(Standard]Mile 1169)

Channel Five is the second of the two marked passages that are spanned by the Lower Matecumbe Key-Long Key Bridge. It is an important passage, not the least reason for which is the full 65 feet of vertical clearance afforded by the fixed bridge that spans its width. This is the first ICW to Hawk Channel route south of Miami that enjoys such a high-rise clearance, with nary the necessity of a bridge opening.

NOAA places such importance on Channel Five, that chart 11451 indicates an approach to the cut, south-southwest of flashing day-beacon #98 and unlighted daybeacon #97, as an alternate passage of the ICW. This is really not the case. The ICW continues wending its way to the southwest, on the inner (northern) side of the Florida Keys to Marathon (but that's another story for the next chapter).

Channel Five enjoys minimum depths of 7 feet. Most cruisers will not find much of anything less than 8-foot readings on their sounders. This does not mean that Channel Five is not without problems, however.

What has always surprised us about Channel Five is that for a channel of its obvious importance, there are very, very few aids to navigation outlining its track. And it's not like there aren't any surrounding shallows to worry with. North of the bridge, shoals flank

Channel Five Bridge

Channel Five to the east and west. South of the fixed span, shallow water is even more of a problem, with depths of 1 to a half-foot lying to the west and 2-foot shoals to the east.

Yet, in spite of all these problem stretches, there are NO aids to navigation outlining Channel Five north of the bridge, and only two markers (only one of which is lighted) south of the high-rise. We think that the U.S. Coast Guard should expend a bit more of its budget for aids to navigation on these waters. Another half-dozen lighted daybeacons would be ever soooo welcome.

The upstart of this dearth of markers is a hazardous entry during nighttime or low-light conditions. If you have a GPS, interfaced with a laptop computer (with navigational software and the latest digitized version of chart 11451), running Channel Five is child's play. Otherwise, you may rest assured that this important passage is, shall we say, more than slightly challenging from the navigational point of view.

Long Key Bight Anchorage

After leaving the fixed 65-foot bridge in its wake, Channel Five continues south toward a meeting with Hawk Channel. Some .3 nautical miles south of the span, cruisers can turn west and visit a somewhat open, and rather shallow, anchorage on Long Key Bight.

Captains making for this haven must stick strictly to the midline. Don't even think about approaching any of the bight's shorelines. They are uniformly shoal. Even by following this plan, an occasional 4½-foot sounding might be noted, though most low-water readings fall in the 5- to 5½-foot range. Clearly, this is not an anchorage for deep-draft vessels, and we suggest that captains jockeying pleasure

craft with more than 4 feet of draft look elsewhere.

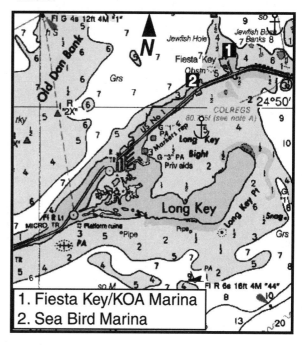

1. Fiesta Key/KOA Marina
2. Sea Bird Marina

If these soundings are not a problem for your boat, Long Key Bight is not a bad place to spend an evening with light to moderate winds blowing from the south, southwest, west, northwest, or north. Any breeze over 10 knots from the east or northeast would make for a decidedly uncomfortable evening. Swinging room is unlimited, and it is also only fair to note that Long Key Bight is a pretty body of water.

Navigators perusing chart 11451 will note that there are a few charted unlighted daybeacons near Long Key Bight's northwesterly corner. Actually, our on-the-water research revealed even more markers. Unfortunately, these lead only to some private docks, and you must cruise through 4-foot depths to get there. Visiting craft should keep clear of this uncertain passage.

ICW—SHELL KEY TO CHANNEL FIVE NAVIGATION

If you read the introduction to the descriptive section above, you probably noticed that the word "confusing" made a prominent appearance. Well, just wait until you get into our navigational review of these waters, which is below.

Allow us to impart the same advice here—have a copy of chart 11451 by your elbow as you read through this section. Otherwise, you will almost certainly become lost in mind and soul amid the many twists, turns, and intersections along the way. Get out a fresh bottle of Murine and let's get going.

Shell Key Channel Be sure to use Inset 7, Page F when navigating the Shell Key Channel. This same inset provides excellent detail of all the Matecumbe channels reviewed below.

The northeasterly entrance to Shell Key Channel is found .8 nautical miles south-southeast of the ICW's unlighted daybeacon #86. The first two markers are unlighted daybeacons #21 and #22. Pass between #21 and #22 and set course to the south-southwest, pointing to pass between the next set of markers unlighted daybeacons #19 and #20. During this run, you will pass a landmass to the west that is far more substantial than chart 11451 would seem to indicate. Be sure to stay well off the shores of the indistinct isle. A definite shelf of shallows abuts its easterly banks.

From #19 and #20, you will next pass through another pair of unlighted daybeacons, #17 and #18. Immediately after running the gap between #17 and #18,

swing farther to the south and pick up unlighted daybeacons #15 and #16. Set course to pass between these markers.

You will notice that in all the maneuvers outlined above, we have been passing red markers to their westerly side and taking green aids to navigation on their easterly quarter. As the Shell Key Channel is heading "toward" the open sea, this is just as it should be.

After #15 and #16 are in your wake, use your binoculars to help pick out the next marker, unlighted daybeacon #14. Be SURE to come abeam and pass #14 on its fairly immediate westerly side. Shallow water lies south and southeast of #14, waiting to greet your keel.

From this point, the Shell Key Channel continues on its merry way until passing between unlighted daybeacons #11 and #12. This is a stretch that demands caution. Just west of #11 and #12, the markers associated with Race Channel (detailed below) make in from the northwest. All navigators, but particularly those northbound on the Shell Key Channel, must be sure to sort out the various aids to navigation correctly.

So, after passing between #11 and #12, ignore unlighted daybeacons #11B and #12B to the west. These are the Race Channel markers. Turn south and point for the gap between unlighted daybeacons #9 and #10.

Captains and crews bound for the Yellow Shark Channel can abandon the Shell Key Channel just south of unlighted daybeacon #10 and cut east-northeast, eventually passing between the Yellow Shark's unlighted can buoy #21 and unlighted nun buoy #22.

South of #9 and #10, the combined paths of Shell Key Channel and Race Channel continue relatively easy to follow all the way to the fixed 10-foot pass-through of the Upper Matecumbe-Lower Matecumbe Bridge. Watch out for the correctly charted, 3-foot shoal north of unlighted daybeacon #8. Be sure to pass between #7 and #8, favoring the western side of the channel slightly as you make your approach to this pair.

South of #8, skippers have another opportunity to cut east and intersect the Yellow Shark Channel. Stay some 25 yards south of #8 and head directly for unlighted nun buoy #16. You can then cut south to Papa Joe's Marina, or north and eventually east to the remainder of this passage.

Back on the Shell Key Channel, mariners will sight the easternmost markers on the Power Line Channel (unlighted can buoy #1 and unlighted nun buoy #2) just west-southwest of the 10-foot fixed pass-through. This cut will be outlined later in this section.

With but a 10-foot clearance, only very small craft will be able to transit the bridge passing over the southerly foot of the Shell Key Channel. If you can make it, the ocean-side passage changes its name to the Teatable Key Channel. This cut is reasonably well marked, but a few additional aids to navigation would not be amiss.

Immediately after passing under the 10-foot bridge, swing a bit to starboard and point to pass between the northernmost marks on the Teatable Key Channel, unlighted daybeacons #5 and #6. From this point, the Teatable passage follows a long, slow arc to the southeast. Take your time and be sure to pick out the various charted markers.

After passing between unlighted daybeacons #1 and #2, swing to the southeast. A shoal is building into the southerly foot of the Teatable Key Channel, south of #1.

Yellow Shark Channel and Associated Facilities The southern genesis of the Yellow Shark Channel lies just north of the easternmost, fixed, 7-foot span of the Upper Matecumbe-Lower Matecumbe Bridge. Incidentally, the easterly tip of the Power Line Channel, which we will consider below, lies just to the west-southwest.

Papa Joe's Marina, Restaurant, and Tiki Bar will be sighted just to the east, immediately north of the 7-foot fixed span. The entrance to this facility is obvious.

Cruisers continuing north on the Yellow Shark Channel should pass all subsequent red markers to their (the cruisers') starboard side and take green markers to port. You are "returning" from sea now, so anyone who remembers the good, old, "red, right, returning" rule will not be surprised by this scheme of aids to navigation.

Favor the easterly side of the channel, slightly between unlighted nun buoy #16 and the pair of unlighted nun buoy #18 and unlighted can buoy #19. Be mindful of the correctly charted 3-foot waters north of the Shell Key Channel's unlighted daybeacon #8, lying to the west of this portion of Yellow Shark Channel.

At unlighted nun buoy #22 and unlighted can buoy #21, the Yellow Shark

Channel takes a 90-degree turn to the east. Pass between #21 and #22, then continue on ahead, pointing to eventually come abeam of unlighted nun buoy #24 to its northwesterly side.

Soon, you will find yourself cruising between a whole collection of mangroves off your port side, with the mainland to starboard. Chart 11451 fails to take note of many of these isles.

At #24, the channel swings sharply to the northeast. Cruisers bound for Matecumbe Marina should depart the Yellow Shark immediately northeast of #24 and follow the white PVC-pipe-lined channel. Remember, depths at low water in this cut run as shallow as 3½ feet.

The Matecumbe Marina approach channel will eventually bring you close aboard a mangrove to your starboard side. The cut then takes a turn to starboard and leads you through an almost tunnel-like opening in the mangrove. The dockage basin will then lie dead ahead.

Returning now to the Yellow Shark Channel, the next aid to navigation that marks the way is unlighted can buoy #25. Pass #25 to its fairly immediate southeasterly side.

A short hop northeast of #25, the marked channel to Max's Marine cuts off to the southeast. This cut is marked by a combination of unadorned wooden piles and white PVC pipes. It is straightforward and leads directly into the U-shaped dockage basin.

Back on the Yellow Shark, this cut continues on to the northeast and passes unlighted nun buoy #26 to its northwesterly side. From this point, the channel cuts to the north and eventually wanders through a split in the flanking mangroves to Little Basin. This portion of the Yellow Shark is narrow, winding, and not really fit for vessels larger than 28 feet. On the plus side, however, uncharted and unlighted can buoy #27 and nun buoy #28 help mariners keep to the good water.

If you do make it as far as the juncture with Little Basin, slow immediately to idle speed. The waters before you are quite shallow and plagued with a variety of shoals. For best depths (and even so, they are none too good), favor the northerly side of Little Basin as you cruise out into its interior reaches. Only after coming abeam of its north to south mid-axis should you turn south and find an anchorage, or make your way to World Wide Sportsman.

On the ICW West-southwest of unlighted daybeacon #86, the Waterway soon approaches a dredged cut known as the Steamboat Channel, which passes through Shell Key Bank. This little passage is well outlined by aids to navigation, and successful daylight passage should not be a problem.

The westernmost pair of aids on the Steamboat Channel is comprised of flashing daybeacon #90 and unlighted daybeacon #91. Cruise directly between #90 and #91 and remain on the same course for about 100 yards. You should then turn a touch farther to the southwest and continue to follow the ICW's track.

It is a long run of slightly better than 1.9 nautical miles between #91 and the next southwestward, Waterway marker, unlighted daybeacon #91A. To the south, cruisers might choose to visit the mooring field northwest of Shell Key or run the Race Channel. Again, switch to Inset 7, Page F for the best cartographic detail.

Shell Key Mooring Field/Anchorage Captains bound for the mooring field/anchorage northwest of Shell Key should leave the Waterway behind some .6 nautical miles southwest of unlighted daybeacon #91. It's then only a .65 nautical mile run through open, deep water to the mooring field. Be sure to pick up a buoy or drop the hook at least 100 yards offshore.

Race Channel To access the Race Channel from the ICW, cut to the south-southeast .5 nautical miles northeast of unlighted daybeacon #91A. You must then cross .9 nautical miles of deep water to discover the northwesternmost markers on the Race Channel, unlighted daybeacons #19B and #20B.

Quite obviously, you should set course to pass between #19B and #20B. From this point, moving generally southeast on the Race Channel, pass all subsequent red, even-numbered aids to navigation to your port side and take green markers to starboard.

The third pair of daybeacons are numbered #15B and #16B, respectively. From our on-the-water observations, it appears that shallow water is impinging on #16B from the northeast. Favor #15B when passing between these two markers.

Soon you will run the gap between unlighted daybeacons #13B and #14B. Moving farther to the southeast, it is essential to correctly identify the southeasternmost marks on the Race Channel, unlighted daybeacons #11B and #12B. Confusing these aids with the various markers on the Shell Key Channel is an all too frequent occurrence.

Cruise between #11B and #12 B, favoring #12B slightly. Once #12B is in your wake, you have found the southeasterly terminus of the Race Channel. Assuming you can correctly sort out all of the confusing markers, it is relatively simple to turn either north or south and follow the Shell Key Channel.

On the ICW A run of 1.95 nautical miles separates the Wateway's unlighted daybeacon #91A from the next set of southwesterly aids to navigation. Flashing daybeacon #93 and unlighted daybeacon #92 signal the ICW's northeasterly entrance to Bowlegs Cut. This dredged section of the Waterway leads cruisers safely through the shallows of Peterson Key Bank.

South-southeast of #91A, cruising mariners might choose to explore the important Indian Key Channel. The anchorage described earlier, off the northwestern shores of Lignumvitae Key and the marked Lignumvitae Channel, can be accessed southwest of #91A.

Indian Key Channel Indian Key Channel is an important passage that provides power-craft (that can clear the overhead 50-foot power lines, and a 27-foot fixed pass-through of the Upper Matecumbe-Lower

Matecumbe Bridge) fairly reliable access from the ICW, inside passage to the off-shore, Hawk Channel route, or the other way around. It's also allows access for pleasure craft to the visitors' docks associated with both Lignumvitae Key State Park and Indian Key State Park. Finally, power vessels can cruise from the Indian Key Channel into the Power Line Channel (see below) but not without some navigational contretemps.

Unfortunately, after saying that, it's only fair to note that this passage could be renamed, the "Indian Snake Channel." When we say that it winds one way, then another, that is simply doing the convoluted turns along the way an injustice. As if all that weren't enough to give you on-the-water eyestrain, there is the confusing situation with aids to navigation where the Power Line Channel meets up with the Indian Key Cut. What's a navigator to do?

To make good your entry into the northern mouth of the Indian Key Channel, cut south off the path of the ICW some .35 nautical miles northeast of unlighted daybeacon #91A. It's then a southward run of .8 nautical miles to find the channel's northernmost marks, unlighted daybeacons #17 and #18.

As you might have already guessed, #17 and #18 can be hard to spot on the water, And it's essential to pick out these daybeacons, as shallow water lies west and southwest of #17. If you pilot an especially deep-draft vessel, the correctly charted 5-foot patch, northeast of #18, might also be a cause for concern. Pass between #17 and #18, then swing immediately to port and

make use of your binocs to pick out the next southward-running aids to navigation, unlighted daybeacons #15 and #16.

The Lignumvitae Key State Park visitors' pier will be spotted west of unlighted daybeacon #15. Please don't forget that dockside depths at this structure run only about 4½ feet at low tide. Anchoring off and then dinghying ashore is complicated by the swift tidal currents that plague this entire region. It would really ruin your whole afternoon to be strolling through the Lignumvitae Key nature trails, only to spot your boat gaily drifting onto a nearby shoal. Our advice is to be SURE the anchor is well set before breaking out the dinghy.

Now, the channel swings just a bit to the south-southeast. Set course to pass between unlighted daybeacons #13 and #14. Next up is the gap between unlighted daybeacons #11 and #12. Here, the channel shifts again, this time to the southeast. Pick out unlighted daybeacons #9 and #10 and point for the gap between the two. Are you tired of turning? Well hold on, because here's another swerve. Immediately after leaving #9 and #10 in your wake, cut back to the south, and point to pass between unlighted daybeacons #7 and #8.

At this point, all cruisers should slow to idle speed and proceed with the greatest caution. The reason for this "alert" status is the intersection of the Power Line Channel and the Indian Key Channel, immediately north of the 27-foot fixed bridge and the 50-foot power lines. Many, many visiting mariners have come to grief by confusing the markers.

There is actually a simple way to avoid

all these problems, though Sea Tow will probably never forgive us for telling you so. After passing between #7 and #8, point for the 27-foot bridge pass-through, which you will spot almost dead ahead. For the first 50 yards of your passage between #7 and #8 and the bridge, favor the western side of the channel slightly. This maneuver will serve to help avoid the shallows and charted rock south of #8.

Then, point for the bridge, IGNORING all floating markers you might see. These floaters are part of the Power Line Channel, NOT the Indian Key cut.

Skippers northbound on Indian Key Channel should follow the reverse of this advice after crossing under the 27-foot bridge. Again, IGNORE all the floating markers you will see north of the span and head for the gap between unlighted daybeacons #7 and #8, favoring the westerly side of the channel as you approach to within 50 yards of the markers.

Returning to our review of Indian Key Channel's southbound trek, cross under the 50-foot power lines (this doesn't apply to sailors of course) and then through the 27-foot fixed bridge. Once the span is in your wake, set course to pass between unlighted daybeacons #5 and #6.

The remainder of Indian Key Channel's seaward passage is outlined by two additional pairs of unlighted daybeacons. Stick to the marked track! Very shallow water (1-foot depths) flanks the channel to the east and west.

The Indian Key Channel ends after passing between unlighted daybeacons #1 and #2. Cruisers bound for Hawk Channel can intersect this route some 1.2 nautical miles south-southeast of #1 and #2.

Cruisers intent on a visit to Indian Key should take a lazy turn around unlighted daybeacon #1. Approach the key in line with its southerly tip. Don't ease too far to the east. The charted shallows in this quarter are for real. The visitors' dock will be spotted on the southeastern corner of Indian Key, with the mooring field just off the southeasterly shores. We strongly recommend that you pick up a mooring buoy, or anchor and dinghy in to the visitors' pier.

Lignumvitae Key Channel and Mooring Field/Anchorage It's easy to reach the mooring field off the northwestern shores of Lignumvitae Key. Simply leave the Waterway behind .5 of a nautical mile southwest of unlighted daybeacon #91A. Cruise south-southeast for about .8 nautical miles until you are some 200 yards off Lignumvitae Key's northwesterly shoreline. Here you will find the mooring field. If there are no available buoys, you can also anchor, but the Florida Park Service would prefer that you pick up a mooring buoy if at all possible.

The northern entrance to Lignumvitae Channel cuts through the shallows west of the like-named key. The northernmost marks are unlighted daybeacons #15 and #16. Let' see now, what should we do with these two aids to navigation? How about passing between them? Sounds like a good idea to us!

The Lignumvitae Channel runs to the southeast from #15 and #16 and next encounters unlighted daybeacons #13 and

#14. Pass between these markers as well. You must now cut to the east-southeast and be sure to pick out the gap between the next pair of aids, unlighted daybeacons #11 and #12.

The passage now turns again, this time to the south. Use binoculars if necessary to find the next channel marker, unlighted daybeacon #9. Make sure to come abeam of #9 by some 15 yards to its EASTERLY side. Very shoal water lies west and northwest of #9.

Let's pause in our southbound journey for a moment to note that on two different occasions, we have found ourselves cruising north on the Lignumvitae Channel from a position abeam of unlighted daybeacon #9. Both times, we mistakenly headed for the gap between unlighted daybeacons #13 and #14, rather than, as we should have done, tracking our way to a position between unlighted daybeacons #11 and #12. It was simply thrilling, and of course, not at all embarrassing to have to get out and push our research vessel off the bottom both times. May you not make the same error.

So you successfully left #13 and #14, passed between #11 and #12, and are now abeam of #9. Your troubles must be over—right! Wrong! Now, you must face the confusing intersection of the Lignumvitae and Power Line Channels. Once again, the conflicting aids to navigation make on-the-water passage a bit of a nightmare.

On several occasions, we have noted powercraft aground just north of the 10-foot fixed bridge. What seems to have happened in all of these instances is that the vessels in question came under the bridge, passed between unlighted daybeacons #7 and #8, and then spotted the nun and can buoys associated with the Power Line Channel off to the north-northeast. While cruising towards these floating aids to navigation, it soon came to be bottom crunch time.

Both southbound and northbound vessels plying the Lignumvitae Channel should completely IGNORE all the floating markers they might see along this stretch (unless, of course, you plan to run the Power Line Channel). From a position abeam of unlighted daybeacon #9, captains piloting their craft toward the 50-foot power lines and the 10-foot bridge should point to pass between unlighted daybeacons #7 and #8. Vessels headed for points north should set course from a position between #7 and #8 to come abeam of unlighted daybeacon #9 by some 15 to 25 yards to its easterly side. Not to be repetitive, but it is important to say once again, IGNORE any floating markers you may spy along the way.

Those small craft that can clear the 10-foot fixed bridge crossing the southerly foot of the Lignumvitae Channel will find an indistinct seaward track south of the span. This is not a terribly reliable route, and we do not suggest it for vessels larger than 25 feet.

If you do run this seaward cut, from the bridge, curve around to the southwest and pass between unlighted daybeacons #5 and #6. Continue on pretty much the same track, coming abeam and passing unlighted daybeacon #4 to its fairly immediate northwesterly side. Then, you need only pass between the outermost pair, unlighted day-beacons #1 and #2, to find the open off-shore waters.

Robbie's Marina Cruisers running the Lignumvitae Channel will spot Robbie's Marina to the west-southwest, just north of the 10-foot fixed bridge and unlighted day-beacons #7 and #8. Don't attempt to enter the docks from a position directly abeam of the marina. A huge shoal, partially outlined by small white floats strung on ropes, fronts Robbie's.

To safely reach the marina, you must pass to the north or south of the shoal and its attendant floats. While accomplishing this maneuver, you will find yourself in close proximity to the poles that support the 50-foot, high-tension power line. There are NO aids to navigation marking either the northerly or southerly entrance, and the lack of any markers makes entry into this marina ever so much more difficult.

Our best advice is to stay well south or north of the little white floats and feel your way along with the sounder. If you're enter-ing from the southern side, leave the big power pole to port. Good luck, you may need it!

Power Line Channel Those of you who have been reading through this chapter sec-tion-by-section have already heard a lot about the Power Line Channel and the nav-igational difficulties it causes where it inter-sects other channels. Actually, though, this passage provides a ready means of access along the entire northern face of the long bridge/causeway that spans the gap between Upper Matecumbe Key and Lower Matecumbe Key.

Along its eastern section, the Power Line Channel passes between the bridge/cause-way and the 50-foot power lines. West-southwest of its intersection with Indian Key Channel, this route ducks under the power lines and remains north of these shocking obstructions for the remainder of its length. As the passage approaches the Lignumvitae Channel, it darts northwest and then west into a tree-shrouded canal.

Our review of this channel will run east to west, beginning at its easterly genesis, just west-southwest of Papa Joe's Marina and the southern foot of the Yellow Shark Channel. The easternmost section of the Power Line Channel is not marked, and it's easy to come to grief.

To avoid a most unpleasant grounding, you MUST cruise west-southwest from Papa Joe's BETWEEN THE BRIDGE/CAUSE-WAY AND THE FIRST POWER POLE! On the water, this will look all wrong. It would appear as if the best water is to be found north of the easternmost power pole. WRONG! You can take our word for it. I'm sure a video shot of our crack research team pushing our research vessel off the shoal north of the power pole would have a real shot at making *America's Funniest Home Videos*.

Got the idea. Cruise between the bridge and the power pole, and hold to the cen-terline of the waters between this fixed span and all subsequent power poles, as your cruise across the Shell Key-Teatable Key Channel.

Immediately after leaving this latter cut

in your wake, the first floating buoys marking the course of the Power Line Channel will be spotted. Cruise between unlighted can buoy #1 and unlighted nun buoy #2. From this point on, all craft westbound on the Power Line Channel should pass all subsequent red, even-numbered aids to navigation to their (the markers') southerly sides and green, odd-numbered markers to their northerly quarters.

The Power Line Channel remains relatively easy to follow until it intersects the Indian Key Channel, immediately west-southwest of unlighted nun buoy #6. Cruisers running the Power Line cut should scrupulously ignore the daybeacons associated with Indian Key Channel.

Just a short hop west-southwest of its passage across Indian Key Channel, the Power Line Channel cuts to the northwest and passes under the 50-foot power lines. Need we say it? Please don't try this if you pilot a sailcraft.

Point to pass between unlighted can buoy #7 and unlighted nun buoy #8. DON'T confuse these floating markers, numbered #7 and #8, with unlighted daybeacons #7 and #8, which lie just to the north and are part of the Indian Key Channel. From buoys #7 and #8, cut back to the west-southwest, pointing to pass between unlighted can buoy #9 and unlighted nun buoy #10.

Now things get really, really confusing. This next section of the Power Line Channel calls for the greatest caution, some serious navigational prowess, and probably a bit of luck as well.

West of #9 and #10, the Power Line Channel turns sharply to starboard (to the northwest) and runs between unlighted can buoy #11 and unlighted nun buoy #12. It's not always easy to find #11 and #12 on the water. Use your binoculars to help with identification.

At this point, the Power Line Channel swings to the west-southwest, crosses the Lignumvitae Channel, and heads between unlighted can buoy #1A and unlighted nun buoy #2A. Again, be sure to ignore the daybeacons on the Lignumvitae passage, unless, of course, your plans are to turn north or south into this major channel.

A series of floating markers leads cruisers westbound on this extreme western portion of the Power Line Channel to the westerly mouth of a narrow canal. Look down this tunnel-like passage, and it will quickly be quite obvious that you should stick to the midline.

The overgrown canal exits into the waters of Matecumbe Bight. Two additional pairs of markers show the way out into the bight's deeper waters. Simply pass between unlighted nun buoy #6A and unlighted can buoy #7A, then between unlighted nun buoy #8A and unlighted can buoy #9A. Maintain the same course line for some 200 yards to the east of #8A and #9A. You can then cut southwest to the anchorage on the inner part of Matecumbe Bight or east to the ICW.

On the ICW The ICW transit through the shallows of Peterson Key Bank is, fortunately, very well outlined by three pairs of aids to navigation. That is very good thing indeed, as depths on Peterson Key Bank outside of the Waterway channel can be measured in 1- and 2-foot levels.

Pass between the three sets of markers, and soon the southwesternmost pair, flashing daybeacon #98 and unlighted daybeacon #97, will be in your wake. Continue on the same course for about 200 yards. Cruisers continuing westbound (southbound) on the Waterway should then cut a bit farther to the west and set a careful compass course for flashing daybeacon #1, north of Old Dan Bank. Even for the Florida ICW, this is a long run indeed, with some 6.2 nautical miles of deep water separating #97 and #98 from #1. Cruisers lacking the electronic marvels of GPS should practice their best DR navigation on this lengthy trek. Fortunately, there is no shallow water to worry with, until #1 is in sight.

Chart 11451 (Page E) would seem to indicate that an alternate branch of the ICW breaks off to the south-southwest from #97 and #98 and heads for Channel Five. This is misleading. The actual ICW passage is the one outlined above, which eventually passes flashing daybeacon #1 at Old Dan Bank. Be sure to come abeam of #1 by at least 50 yards to its northerly side. Shallower depths lie south and southeast of #1. From this point, as we shall learn in the next chapter, the Waterway hurries on towards Marathon.

NOAA's choice of showing the cutoff to Channel Five as an alternate ICW passage reflects the importance of this latter channel. Before considering this passage, however, let's take a look at the anchorage on Matecumbe Bight, a similar haven on Matecumbe Harbor, and then give brief consideration to Channel Two.

Matecumbe Bight Anchorage Joy of joys, the entrance to Matecumbe Bight boasts a wide swath of deep water. Simply avoid the broad band of shoals to the northeast, and you're home free. To facilitate this avoidance, continue tracking your way southwest on the ICW for .6 of a nautical mile past flashing daybeacon #98 and unlighted daybeacon #97. Then, you can swing to the southeast and enter Matecumbe Bight along the centerline of its deep-water section. If the sounder should start to show the bottom shelving up, retreat a bit to the southwest and see if the depths improve.

Drop anchor after cruising to within 100 yards of the southeastern banks. Then, it's time to head below and begin the evening festivities.

Matecumbe Harbor Anchorage To access this smaller anchorage, cut south-southwest from the foot of Bowlegs cut as if you were headed for Channel Five. After cruising for slightly better than 2.7 nautical miles, pick out flashing daybeacon #2 to the east-southeast of your track. This is the northernmost aid to navigation, and the only official marker, on the Matecumbe Harbor entrance channel.

Pass #2 to your starboard side, and watch sharply for a series of white PVC pipes that outline both sides of the channel as you move to the south-southeast. These informal markers give out sooner than you might think, but just stick to the centerline thereafter. For best depths, anchor 75 to 100 yards north of the power lines. Sailcraft skippers, make SURE you're not dragging anchor.

It is possible to ease off just a bit to the west, but DON'T go any further than a point abeam of the small, charted island's easterly tip. In fact, for our money, we suggest you stop at least 50 yards east of this small isle.

The Explorer Sea Scouts Harbor, which occupies lower Matecumbe Harbor's northeasterly tip is best avoided by visitors, as is the extreme southerly section of the harbor. The Sea Scouts have no facilities for visiting craft, and the southern tip of Matecumbe Harbor is plagued by 4-foot shallows.

Channel Two We might easily sum up our navigational account of Channel Two by saying, "Don't go here." In the first place, the northerly section of the channel, southwest of Matecumbe Harbor and flashing daybeacon #2, is plagued by a whole series of concrete obstructions. In the second, the channel is spanned by a 10-foot fixed bridge.

The seaward side of Channel Two is far more hospitable with a well-marked channel and a nice marina. We shall consider this section of Channel Two in our coverage of Hawk Channel between Tavernier Creek and Channel Five, below.

Channel Five Okay, come on you guys in the USCG. Why are there NO markers outlining the passage from the ICW's track through Peterson Key Bank to the Channel Five, 65-foot fixed bridge? I mean, this is a rather important route! Go figure!

Sorry to say, you will have to traverse some 4.4 nautical miles without aids to navigation between flashing daybeacon #98 and unlighted daybeacon #97 and the northerly face to the Channel Five Bridge. Thankfully, there are no shallows impinging directly on this route.

Along the way, you will most likely sight the concrete obstructions north of the Channel Two Bridge, southeast of your course. Ignore these rather strange-looking structures and continue on toward the bridge.

As you make your approach to the 65-foot high-rise, be mindful of the correctly charted shallows to the east and west. Fortunately, there is wide buffer of good water between the channel and these shoals. Of course, a few aids to navigation showing where these potentially grounding spots are located are apparently just too much for the USCG to trouble with!

Cruise under the 65-foot high-rise and pause for just a second to admire this structure. It is only one of two fixed bridges in all of the Florida Keys that enjoys this vertical clearance.

Point to pass 35 yards west of flashing daybeacon #2 and then about the same distance east of unlighted daybeacon #1. I know this is getting repetitive, but let's just note once again that there *should* be several additional markers south of the 65-foot span as well.

Continue on course south of #1 for 1 nautical mile on the same track before cutting to the northeast or southwest. This maneuver will serve to help you avoid the ring of shallows abutting the southeasterly tip of Long Key, and the 5-foot depths east and northeast of #1.

Hawk Channel will be intersected 1.3 miles south of #1. Next stop, Marathon?

Long Key Bight Anchorage The trick to anchoring in Long Key Bight is to stay way away from all the various shorelines and anchor in the middle of the bight. Shallows abut all the surrounding banks and shelve out into the bight for an amazing distance.

Abandon Channel Five .25 miles north of flashing daybeacon #2. Turn west and cruise carefully into the central waters of Long Key Bight. You can follow the mid-width for a short distance farther to the west-southwest, as the bight turns slightly in this direction, but again, STAY AT LEAST SEVERAL HUNDRED YARDS OFF ALL THE VARIOUS SHORELINES.

If you happen to spot some unlighted daybeacons on Long Key Bight's northwesterly corner, we suggest ignoring these markers. In fact, don't go anywhere near them. The daybeacons eventually lead to a shallow, narrow canal that serves a series of private docks. There is no room to anchor, and no facilities are available for visitors.

Hawk Channel—Tavernier Creek to Channel Five

The Hawk Channel section between Tavernier Creek and Channel Five continues this passage's tradition of good marina facilities but minimal anchorages. Additionally, this stretch offers several good opportunities to make the transition between the outside and inside route. Snake Creek and Channel Five are fit for any sort of pleasure craft, while Indian Key Channel is a good choice for powered vessels.

Indian Key itself hosts a state park that we met above. It is accessible from Hawk Channel and makes for one of the most historic stops along this entire portion of the Florida Keys. Even if you have to anchor off and dinghy ashore (which is the correct strategy for larger cruising vessels), this site is well worth your time.

A few reefs abut the northerly portion of Hawk Channel run from Tavernier Creek to Channel Five. These potentially deadly obstructions require extra navigational caution and your most serious respect. One of these rocky shallows even complicates a marina entrance along the way.

Treasure Harbor Marina
(24 57.402 North/080 34.358 West)

This little mom-and-pop operation occupies the northerly tip of the charted "Treasure Harbor," well northwest of Hawk Channel's flashing daybeacon #40 and the Hen and Chickens Reef. Another reef, known and charted as "The Rocks," lies between Hawk Channel and Treasure Harbor.

Treasure Harbor Marina can be accessed by continuing southwest on Hawk Channel until you are past the southwestern tip of "The Rocks" and the Hen and Chickens Reef. You can then cut to the north, round the southwesterly tip of "The Rocks," and make a slow turn to the northeast. It is then necessary to follow the charted ribbon of deeper water between the reef and the shallows cutting out from the northwesterly banks.

Treasure Harbor Marina

and #2. The remainder of the cut is outlined by white PVC pipes, whose tops have been painted red and green to designate which side of the channel they mark.

While the run from #A to #1 and #2 has depths of 6 to 8 feet, the inner part of the approach channel, between the PVC pipes, carries only 3½ to 4 feet of water at low tide. Once into the harbor, however, soundings improve to 9 feet or better. A call on VHF Channel 16 may yield some helpful navigational advice.

Treasure Harbor Marina is a low-key sort of mom-and-pop operation, run by Pam and Pete Anderson. It is closed Wednesdays and ALWAYS on May 8. The basin in which this marina resides was dredged out for the Overseas Railroad and the spoil was used for fill. Art McKee, a famous Keys hard-hat salvage/treasure diver, bought the land surrounding the basin and started Treasure Harbor Salvage. He had a glass-bottomed boat and he used to take people out to show them the wrecks of ships on the bottom. All the treasures and artifacts that McKee recovered were brought out over the existing docks.

Treasure Harbor Marina rents out its slips on a first-come, first-served basis. If the marina should happen to be full, the best time to find that out is before you make the long and exacting journey up the entrance channel. A VFH radio call is a very good idea with this facility. The docks are wooden finger piers, clean, and in good repair. Electricity available is 15- and 30-amp service, and there is also water dockside. The showers are clean, close by, and about standard for the Keys. There is also an on-site Laundromat.

The Andersons have owned Treasure Harbor Marina since 1990. The nearby

Eventually, if you're lucky, you will sight a large, yellow, drum-shaped marker with the designation, #A. The marina entrance channel runs north-northwest from #A. From #A, you have to locate two small floating buoys, #1 restaurant is Jammer's (305-852-8786), open 11 A.M. to midnight, and it's only three blocks away. There is a small shopping center called Treasure House, the site, we believe, of Art McKee's original museum, within about three blocks, too. Here you will find the Treasure Village Courtyard Café (305-852-1911), a very nice deli, which also serves an excellent breakfast. More restaurants are available along Snake Creek, which is about a 10-minute walk away.

Treasure Harbor Marina (305) 852-2458
(800) 352-2628
http://www.treasureharbor.com

Approach depth—3½-4 feet low water (call on VHF 16 for navigational assistance)
Dockside depth—6 feet minimum
Accepts transients—yes, but it is best to call ahead
Type of docking—fixed wooden finger piers
Dockside power connections—15- and 30-amp service
Dockside water connections—yes
Showers—yes
Laundromat—yes
Ship's and variety store—small, sells ice
Restaurant—nearby

Snake Creek
(Various Lat/Lons—see below)

Cruisers westbound (southbound) on Hawk Channel can make a turn toward the Snake Creek approach channel 1.1 nautical miles southwest of flashing daybeacon #40. This aid to navigation marks the Hen and Chickens Reef. It's then another trek of 1.5 nautical miles from Hawk Channel to Snake Creek's outermost markers, unlighted daybeacon #1 and flashing daybeacon #2.

Snake Creek's channel, from the briny blue to its bascule bridge, is very well marked, but it twists this way and that. All but one of the

aids to navigation on this cut are unlighted daybeacons. Nighttime and foul-weather passage of this channel are not recommended.

Snake Creek is an important connector stream, spanning the gap between Hawk Channel and the inside-ICW passage. It provides the first opportunity for larger craft to make the transition between these two alternate routes, south of Angelfish Creek.

Typical low-water depths are in the 7- to 10-foot region, though some 5½- to 6-foot soundings are sometimes encountered on the northernmost portion of the creek, between the charted Y-shaped split in the stream and flashing daybeacon #12.

Snake Creek is crossed by a bascule bridge with 27 feet of closed vertical clearance. Fortunately, this span opens on demand. It is the presence of this "opening" bridge that makes Snake Creek so attractive to larger vessels and sailcraft in particular—no having to mess with lower-level fixed spans. Thank you, Florida DOT!

On the down side, Snake Creek is a member in good standing of the strong tidal current club. We sat in awe one warm September afternoon, while watching the tide boil under this stream's bascule bridge. Cruisers should be on the lookout for these swiftly moving waters, and be ready to take instant corrective action.

Snake Creek boasts several facilities, which line the creek's shores immediately north of the bascule bridge. There is also one restaurant with dockage and a rather shallow channel just south of the span. Unfortunately, only one of these marinas offers minimal transient dockage.

First up is Big Conch Oceanside Bar and Grill (305-664-0020, 24 57.082 North/080 35.371 West). Just south of the Snake Creek bascule bridge, a small, poorly outlined channel cuts back to the west and leads to this dining attraction plus its two dockage piers. The channel, such as it is, is outlined by two scanty, white PVC pipes and carries a bare 3 feet of depth at low water. Craft that can make it through this skinny water will quickly come abeam of the restaurant, along the northerly banks. Two boats might be able to tie up to the wooden piers immediately adjacent to the restaurant. Additional dockage of the floating, wooden-decked variety is found a bit farther upstream, also abutting the northerly shores.

The Big Conch is a pretty standard Keys restaurant that does enjoy a good local reputation. The commanding officer of the nearby Coast Guard station recommended it. It is casual and light inside. You can see Snake Creek or the Atlantic from your table, inside or outside. Cracked conch, cooked up with an airy batter, is great. I had it with "island sauce." Then we partook of a Cajun wrap, which is either blackened chicken breast or the catch of the day. The catch of the day was dolphin, our favorite. We went for it, rolled in a garlic-herb tortilla, and had Caesar salad included in the wrap. The entrée came with channel fries, which were crunchy. All was topnotch.

North of the 27-foot bascule bridge, Smuggler's Cove Marina (24 57.145 North/080 35.337 West) guards the westerly-Windley Key shores. The entrance is a little tricky, courtesy of both a shoal that fronts the fuel dock and the usual, swift tidal currents. Check out our navigational account of this marina below for some hints as to how to make good your entry.

Once past its tricky entrance, cruisers will discover good low-water depths of about 6 feet or so. The fuel dock and ship's store will come up quickly to starboard. Here, all craft can purchase gasoline, diesel fuel, and basic ship's store, variety store, and bait-and-tackle items.

The marina's well-sheltered dockage basin, backed by a motel and adjacent café, lies farther to the west. Unfortunately, no transient space is available here, and consequently, we will not further detail these facilities.

A whole series of canals pierce Snake Creek's easterly banks between the "Y" split and the bascule bridge. The southernmost of these cuts (immediately north of the Snake Creek Bridge) provides access to Cobra Marine. Note that as you enter this canal, the Islamorada Coast Guard Station will be quite visible to port. Cobra Marine will soon come up along the southerly banks, in the body of the corrected charted crook in the canal.

Cobra Marine (24 57.202 North/080 35.136 West) is primarily a motorboat place, and the maximum size craft they could take alongside would be 40 feet. Some transients are occasionally accepted at Cobra's fixed wooden pier on a space-available basis. We found dockside soundings to be about 6 to 6½ feet at low water, with some 6-foot soundings in the approach canal. Some berths have 30-amp power hookups, others 50 amp, while all have fresh water connections. The on-site ship's store is excellent, with a good cross section of things that cruisers need, plus food, snacks, beer, ice, and soft drinks. The closest restaurant is Big Conch Oceanside Bar and Grill (see above), across the bridge on Windley Key. Hog Heaven is just a few steps farther. Both are fine, but Big Conch Oceanside Bar and Grill will give you a touch of refinement that Hog Heaven will not. It's not like comparing, say, the Plaza Hotel in New York with McDonald's, but there's a difference.

Cobra Marine (305) 664-3636

Approach depth—6 feet (minimum)
Dockside depth—6-6$\frac{1}{2}$ feet
Accepts transients—yes, on a space-available basis
Type of docking—some fixed wooden finger piers, some alongside
Dockside power connections—mostly 30 amp, some 50 amp
Dockside water connections—yes
Fuel available—gasoline only
Mechanical repairs—mostly outboard engine variety
Ship's and variety store—yes
Restaurant—nearby

Snake Creek also features its own anchorage (24 57.684 North/080 35.722 West) just off its northerly reaches. Note the Y-shaped split in the stream, south of unlighted daybeacon #10. With care, cruisers can depart the main Snake Creek Channel and cut back to the west-north-west on the stream's errant northwesterly arm. Here, boats as large as 36 feet will find room to anchor amidst 6- to 7-foot minimum depths. The best place to anchor is found on the initial 150 yards of this offshoot's passage to the west and northwest. Farther upstream, the channel narrows, and it's an all too simple process to find your way into 4 feet of water.

The main branch of Snake Creek continues on to the north and follows a marked passage out into the waters of Cotton Key Basin. Another .7 nautical miles will bring you face-to-face with the ICW's unlighted daybeacon #78A and the inside passage.

Tropical Reef Resort

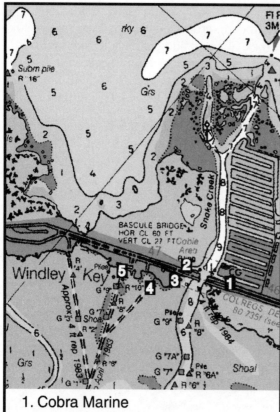

1. Cobra Marine
2. Smuggler's Cove Marina
3. Big Conch Oceanside Bar and Grill
4. Hog Heaven Bar and Restaurant
5. Tropical Reef Resort

Tropical Reef Resort (24 56.908 North/080 35.637 West) and Hog Heaven (24 56.972 North/080 35.453 West)

Take a gander at chart 11451 and notice the three-pronged channel making in from the offshore waters to the southerly shores of Windley Key. These cuts will be spotted just a short hop west of Snake Creek's seaward approach channel.

The westernmost of the three cuts leads only to some private piers, while the center channel provides access to Tropical Reef

Resort, and the easternmost brings cruisers to the infamous Hog Heaven Bar and Restaurant.

The channel to Tropical Reef is by far the most reliable of the three. It maintains minimum 5-foot depths at low water, and the track is well delineated by unlighted daybeacons. Eventually, this cut leads cruisers into a partially breakwater-protected harbor, with 4½-foot minimum soundings.

Tropical Reef (305-664-8881) is a resort on the Atlantic side of Windley Key. Inside the protection of a rock and mangrove breakwater lies the marina, sitting in its own little lagoon with good protection from southerlies . . . or just about anything. There is a collection of about 10 finger piers, which are available for guests of the resort only—no staying overnight on board. There are a couple of dive operations on site. It appears that people who stay here trailer their boats in and tie them up for weekend use. Customary transient services for cruisers are not available. But customary motel services and amenities are. We received a definite "get lost" attitude from the front desk.

The Hog Heaven channel breaks off from the Tropical Reef approach a short hop south of the latter cut's unlighted daybeacon #7. The initial marker on the Hog Heaven passage is some sort of piling with a funky orange rectangle perched atop it. The remainder of this cut is haphazardly outlined by a few white PVC pipes. Depths are a mere 3 to 3½ feet at low water.

This thin channel soon leads to a small dockage basin flanked by fixed wooden piers to the east and west. Depths in the harbor improve to 4 feet or better.

Hog Heaven (305-664-9669) isn't a marina; it's an oceanfront bar with a reputation for

Hog Heaven Bar and Restaurant

excellent cheeseburgers, "real cold beer," and rowdy entertainment, mostly from fellow customers. Hog Heaven opens in the morning and does not close until 4 A.M., so it gets the late, late night crowd, which has really already had enough . . . and maybe doesn't recognize it. There is a live pig of considerable size in a pen on the dock. It is named Oink. It can be petted when it feels like it. The rest of the time it snoozes in its house. The outside bar has a collection of about 40 women's bras hanging from overhead pipes. Women who feel compelled to take off restrictive undergarments and place them in the permanent collection are roundly cheered by male customers present, it is assumed. While waterborne patrons can tie up while eating or drinking, there are no marina facilities at Hog Heaven.

People rarely spend the night here by choice, anyway. Trying to get some shuteye in a cove hard by a bar that stays open until nearly first light and with a pig as a mascot is an exercise in futility.

We have eaten in Hog Heaven a couple of times. On both occasions we saw the same two guys in there; they looked like raisins because they had been out in the sun far too long. They were in their fifties, but they dressed like they were in their twenties. One had his obligatory baseball cap on backwards. The other had wavy, stiff, long blonde hair that appeared to have been dyed. They stood at the bar, their eyes watery enough to enliven an oasis, and looked like a couple of sure fire stand-ins for actors Jim Carrey and Jeff Daniels in the movie *Dumb and Dumber*.

Look for them when you go here; they are probably still around.

Whale Harbor Channel and Associated Facilities (Various Lat/Lons—see below)

The seaward approach passage serving the Whale Harbor Channel cuts through the banks of Windley Key north-northeast of Hawk Channel's unlighted daybeacon #41. Cruisers heading west (south) on Hawk Channel should split off some 2.2 nautical miles southwest of the Hen and Chickens marker, flashing daybeacon #40.

Whale Harbor Channel is a complicated stream that is spanned by a fixed bridge with a mere 12 feet of vertical clearance. Whale Harbor would probably rate only a very small mention in this guidebook, were it not for the presence of some marina facilities.

The upstream portion of the Whale Harbor Channel, north of the 12-foot fixed bridge, was covered in the last section of this chapter. With a vertical clearance of only 12 feet, virtually no cruising-sized craft will be cruising under this span. We will, therefore, in this Hawk Channel section, confine our scrutiny of the Whale Harbor Channel to the waters southeast of the fixed span.

The Whale Harbor seaward branch is well marked and carries at least 5 feet of water at low tide. Typical soundings are in the 6- to 8-foot range.

A separate channel breaks off from Whale Harbor's unlighted daybeacon #7 and cuts north to Holiday Isle Marina. Minimum depths run about 5½ to 6 feet, with at least 5 feet of water in the semiprotected dockage basin.

Holiday Isle Marina

Holiday Isle Marina (24 56.488 North/080 36.429 West) is actually a collection of bars and restaurants with a full panoply of fishing-guide services and marina services. The charter fleet available here is enormous. There are many restaurants on the grounds and a collection of bars that will boggle the mind for weeks at a time if you visit them all. By staying in the marina, you get the full run of the resort, its swimming pools, bars, and food offerings. Holiday Isle has been put together a piece at a time; as a result, it has sort of a rumble/jumble air of confusion about it. For example, on a hot day, the roar of air-conditioning units and fans—one of these things lurks around every corner like a troll—gives the place a unique buzz, sometimes muffling normal conversation. Every open door seems to sell something: never have you seen so many T-shirts for sale at one place at one time. The sound of a distant jukebox booms across the landscape, lyrics unintelligible, but the pulsing bass notes sufficiently strong enough to stir your bowels.

The marina itself is close by all the action, so if you stay here, you will not miss a thing (even if you want to). Low-water approach depths run 5½ to 6 feet with at least 5 to 6 feet of water dockside. Transients are welcome here, of course, and you can tie up to fixed wooden piers. Some of the slips closest to where the charter boats are tied up are of the covered variety, a real blessing in the Florida summer sunshine, where shade is a commodity to be coveted like two tickets on the 50-yard line at the Super Bowl. We cannot guarantee the covered slips are available for transients, but it never hurts to ask when you talk to the dockmaster. Note that there are also some outer slips, which are not nearly as well sheltered as the berths in the inner harbor.

Dockside electricity is available with up to 50-amp service, and there are water connections on the docks. On shore, you'll find a Laundromat, showers that are not air-conditioned, a ship's store that is more convenience type than truly shippy, and all the action that you might want. Holiday Isle serves up both gas and diesel, and there's waste pump-out available, too, always a blessing. Some light mechanical repairs can be obtained by way of independent mechanics, which the dockmaster will call for you.

Holiday Isle Marina (305) 664-2321
http://www.holidayisle.com

Approach depth—5½-6 feet
Dockside depth—5-6 feet (minimum)
Accepts transients—yes
Type of docking—fixed wooden piers
Dockside power connections—up to 50 amp
Dockside water connections—yes
Waste pump-out—yes
Showers—yes, but not climate controlled
Laundromat—yes
Fuel available—gas and diesel
Mechanical repairs—mechanic on call
Ship's store—convenience type
Restaurant—eight on site

Whale Harbor Inn and Marina (24 56.213 North/080 36.766 West) (305-664-4959-inn and restaurant, 305-664-4511-dockmaster) guards the southwestern flank of Whale Harbor Channel, immediately southeast of the 12-foot fixed bridge. This is a facility that most visiting cruisers will wisely choose to avoid. Successfully reaching Whale Harbor Inn by water is an interesting proposition. One strategy is to parallel the southeastern face of the fixed span and work your way slowly around to the marina's inner dockage basin. Unfortunately, this plan may well land you in only 4 to 4½ feet of water at low tide.

There is also a second route, running in from the deeper offshore waters. This channel is actually charted, just southwest of the marked Whale Harbor passage. It is barely outlined by several hard-to-see, white PVC pipes. The local captains obviously know where these informal aids to navigation are located, but visiting cruisers may not be so lucky. If you can stay in the channel (problematic at best), minimum depths in this approach channel run around 5 feet.

Whale Harbor Inn and Restaurant has but one slip available for restaurant patrons, and that's it in the way of services for visitors. The marina does boast a big and busy charter-fishing fleet operation and the dockage basin is almost always full of these craft. There is no overnight transient dockage. In fact, transients are discouraged. However, there is an all-you-can-eat seafood restaurant and lodging on site. The prices are moderate.

Matecumbe Channels

Northwest of Hawk Channel's unlighted daybeacon #43, the long combination fixed bridge and causeway connecting Upper Matecumbe Key and Lower Matecumbe Key spans a whole collection of channels along its 1.9-nautical-mile length. All but one of these cuts lead to low-level fixed bridges with 7- to 12-foot vertical clearances. As virtually no cruising-sized vessel will be able to clear such low spans, we will not repeat our coverage of the various cuts north of the long bridge and causeway (with one exception). Small-craft skippers that can make it under the low-level bridges should consult the last section of this chapter for a full review of this complicated set of passages.

Bud N' Mary's Marina
(24 53.843 North/080 39.504 West)

There are two cruising destinations (one

Bud N' Mary's Marina

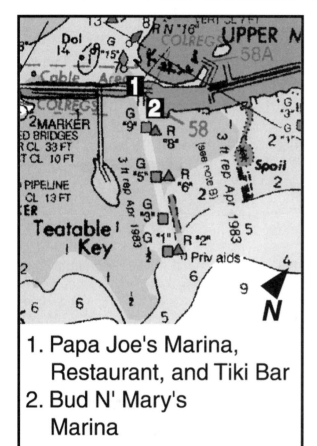

1. Papa Joe's Marina,
   Restaurant, and Tiki Bar
2. Bud N' Mary's
   Marina

marina and one channel) near the Upper Matecumbe-Lower Matecumbe Bridge/causeway that are worthy of attention. First up is the marked, but unnamed, easternmost passage, which lies 1.9 nautical miles north-northwest of #43. This cut also leads to a low bridge, in this instance with a mere 7 feet of vertical clearance. So, why are we bringing this little cut to your attention? Well, just south-southeast of the 7-foot span, cruisers can break off to the east and visit Bud N' Mary's Marina. Chart 11451 (Inset 7, Page F) notes the location of this marina by way of facility designation #58.

Bud N' Mary's marked approach parallels a

stone breakwater to the east for the initial portion if its run. Navigation on these waters is a little tricky. Check out our navigation sketch below BEFORE attempting first-time entry.

Minimum depths in the approach cut run around 5 feet, complimented by dockside soundings of 6 to 7½ feet. Do NOT attempt to run this approach passage at night, unless you are intimately familiar with the channel.

Bud N' Mary's is all fishing, fishing, and more fishing. If you don't enjoy fishing and all that goes with it, including a charter fleet, then this is not the place for you. There are, however, off-the-boat accommodations here, including a penthouse suite and motel rooms. The view of the channel and the Atlantic is gorgeous.

Transients are welcome at either fixed wooden slips or alongside docking. The outer slips, within sight of the bridge, have very little in the way of protection from foul weather. Berths on the inner harbor are far better sheltered. Power connections of 30 and 50 amps are available, and there are dockside water hookups. There is no waste pump-out here, and the showers are unisex but nice. Nice means clean and neat, not glorious. Glorious is in rather short supply in the Keys. The Laundromat is a bit worn, but serviceable. As you might expect, the ship's store is on the beer-bait-tackle side of the pendulum swing, with very heavy emphasis on things that will help you catch fish.

Papa Joe's Restaurant (305-664-8109—see above) is across the street and an Outback Steak House (305-664-3344) is within walking distance (several blocks) to the north.

Bud N' Mary's Marina (305) 664-2461
(800) 742-7945
http://www.budnmarys.com

Approach depth—5 feet (low water)
Dockside depth—6-7½ feet
Accepts transients—yes
Type of piers—fixed wooden, alongside docking
Dockside power connections—30 and 50
Dockside water connections—yes
Showers—yes, unisex but nice
Laundromat—yes, but a little run-down
Fuel—gas and diesel
Ship's store—BB&T and convenience type with heavy emphasis on fishing gear
Restaurant—two nearby

Teatable Key Channel

The Teatable Key Channel is the next passage cutting under the Upper Matecumbe-Lower Matecumbe Bridge/causeway, moving east to west. This is a reasonably well-marked passage featuring 10-foot depths. However, it leads to a fixed pass-through with only 10 feet of vertical clearance. Keep on trucking!

Indian Key Channel
(Various Lat/Lons—see below)

The most important of the routes passing under the Upper Matecumbe-Lower Matecumbe Bridge is Indian Key Channel. Mariners whose craft can clear a 27-foot fixed bridge can cruise from Hawk Channel to the inside ICW route in relative security. Minimum low-water soundings run about 6 feet with average depths of 8 to 15 feet. While the entire channel is well marked, there are some navigational concerns to be addressed.

Obviously, with the fixed bridge and some adjacent 50-foot power lines, the Indian Key Channel is strictly relegated to powercraft. Sailors should use Snake Creek (see above) or continue down Hawk Channel to Channel Five (see below).

Indian Key Channel provides access to two very interesting historic sites: Lignumvitae Key and Indian Key. Indian Key is found short

hop west of Indian Key Channel's southerly genesis. There is one park pier on the southeasterly tip of the isle and a series of mooring buoys off the key's southeasterly shores. Depths at the small, fixed wooden pier run only 4 feet or so, and most of the space here is set aside for a tour boat that brings visitors out from the mainland. Depths in the mooring field run from 5 to 7 feet at low water. Most cruisers will wisely choose to pick up a mooring buoy, or anchor and then dinghy in to the visitors' pier.

Well north of the 27-foot bridge, Lignumvitae Key flanks the western side of Indian Key Channel. The visitor and tour boat dock for the Florida state park on Lignumvitae Key sits almost due west of unlighted daybeacon #15 (24 54.191 North/080 41.667 West), close by the "Dol" notation on chart 11451 (Inset 7, Page F). It is a fixed concrete structure with some outlying wooden piles and finger piers. Depths alongside run 4 to 4½ feet at low water. Deeper-draft vessels can always anchor on the correctly charted 7-foot waters farther to the east, and dinghy in.

We shall consider both the parks on Lignumvitae Key and Indian Key separately below. For now, we only wanted to note the position and mariner-friendly amenities.

Returning our attention to Indian Key Channel, navigators should be ready for trouble as soon as they pass under the 27-foot, fixed bridge. At this point, the main cut intersects what we call the Power Line Channel (see above). It's very, very easy to confuse the markers on this latter passage with aids to navigation on the Indian Key cut. Such a mistake will most likely result in a grounding. PLEASE read our navigational reviews of both the Indian Key Channel below, and our coverage of the Power Line Channel in the section presented earlier in this chapter before entering these waters for the first (or even the second) time.

Indian Key State Park

Indian Key and its associated Florida state park should be approached from its southern, Hawk Channel side. Shoals envelop the island to the north, and banks of shallows shelve out from both the eastern and western banks. The visitors' dock is perched off the southeasterly tip of Indian Key. It is rather small, and most of the space here is given over to a tour boat, which brings visitors to this park from Lower Matecumbe Key. It would be far better for captain and crew of most cruising-sized craft to dinghy in to the dock.

There is a mooring field off Indian Key's southeasterly shores. If any are available, you can pick up a buoy in 5 to 7 feet of water, or alternately, drop anchor. This anchorage/mooring field is well sheltered from north-westerly breezes, and there is also some pro-tection to the north. Forget it if a hard wind is blowing from the south-southwest or the southeast. However you get ashore, Indian Key is well worth a visit. Few other Florida Keys can claim such a historically colorful past.

Indian Key encompasses some 11 acres in size and once had a town on it, albeit not a very big one. The key was colonized in the 1830s by a wrecker—a man who salvaged shipwrecks—whose name was Jacob Housman. He came from Key West, where there was more competition and where some of the judges had the inside track, for they, too, were wreckers. Housman bought Indian Key in 1831. There was nearby fresh water on the Matecumbe Keys, but most of the houses

on Indian Key had cisterns, too. At one time, Indian Key had its own post office, several streets, wharves, warehouses, some twenty residences, and a hotel that was called the Tropical. The Tropical even had a bowling alley. Automatic pin setters and televised bowling contests had not been invented yet, so the bowling alley never made the big time.

Jacob Housman grew rich on Indian Key. The reefs on which ships foundered were not far off. The ships' bad fortune and his good luck and near monopoly on the wrecking business brought him lots of money. Though historical accounts of Housman's tenure on Indian Key attribute some of his success to his business acumen, they also infer that he may have been involved in some shady dealings. He was, however, successful in getting the Florida Legislature to establish a separate Dade County, independent from Key West, and make Indian Key the county seat.

According to one source, Housman's polit-ical successes paralleled his financial decline. He was in court a great deal, presumably in a turf battle with Key West wreckers, and he lost far more than he won. He was found guilty of embezzlement of goods from a ves-sel he was salvaging in 1836. He lost his wrecker's license in 1838. And when the Second Seminole War began in late in December of 1835, he also lost the trade of the Indians who used to come to the key and buy goods at the key's general store.

His former customers became his adver-saries and his worst nightmare. By 1840, there were about 55 people living on Indian Key. Housman, ever the opportunist, was negotiat-ing with the United States government around that time for permission to hunt down Seminoles at the going rate of $200 a head. It is assumed that $200 a head was a literal interpretation. Housman also had enough sway with the government that he succeeded in having the United States Navy's Florida Squadron stationed at Teatable Key, just to the east of Indian Key.

Housman's luck ran out on August 7, 1840. The Florida Squadron was away chasing savages around Cape Sable or possibly restocking its medicinal rum supply, which was known to evaporate extremely quickly in the Florida heat, summer or winter, when Seminoles arrived on Indian Key, uninvited. The Indians burned down every house but one, killed some sixteen people, and then left. Housman and his family lived through it all and escaped injury, but the good old days, wherein Jacob Housman was a law unto himself, were gone forever. He moved shortly thereafter to Key West and continued to work as a wrecker for another man, but his days were short. He died within six months in an accident, crushed between two vessels while plying his trade.

Jacob Housman's body was brought back to Indian Key and buried. But someone stole his skeletonized remains and his tombstone. There is a replica of the original in place today.

In the 1930s and 1940s, treasure hunters, who used explosives in the search for treasure, scoured the island to little avail. Today, you may visit Indian Key from 8 A.M. to sunset. You are on your own, however. There are no facilities on the island. On the other hand, you may find a mosquito or two. Some things never change.

Lignumvitae Key historic homeplace

Lignumvitae Key State Park
(Standard Mile 1162.5)
(24 54.191 North/080 41.667 West—location of visitors' dock)

Lignumvitae Key is a state botanical park, and you get to it by boat from Robbie's Marina (see above). The fare for the trip out and back is $15 per person, plus tax. The tour boats depart a half-hour before the park tour starts. Park tours are offered twice a day, at 10 A.M. and at 2 P.M. The park is closed on Tuesdays and Wednesdays, a fact that you might well keep in mind. You cannot go ashore on your own.

If you'd like to avoid the boat ride tariff, you can tie up to a mooring buoy off the park (there are five off the northwest side of Lignumvitae Key, near 24 54.410 North/080 42.246 West) and dinghy in. Or, if your craft doesn't draw more than 4 feet, you may tie right up to the park dock. There is a small admission charge to the park, but it's insignificant, about $1 per person, and children under six get in for free. A third plan of action for deeper-draft vessels would be to anchor on the correctly charted 7-foot waters just east of the park pier and break out the dinghy.

Probably one of the reasons that people like to visit the Keys is that they remind us of simpler times. There are a number of uninhabited islands in the Keys, small ones that only support wildlife and vegetation that arrived on the wind or waves. Lignumvitae is such a Key—it's just larger than most—and when you visit here you step back into history . . . geological, human and verdure. Some of the trees that grow on Lignumvitae Key grow in no other place in the Keys. Elsewhere, they have been sacrificed to make way for modern needs, modern accommodations, and modern comforts.

Trees here have names like gumbo-limbo, poisonwood, strangler fig, pigeon plum, mastic, and not surprisingly, of course, lignumvitae, from which the key draws its name. Lignumvitae is an incredibly dense, hard wood, harder than oak, that was once used to make billy clubs for police. It dulled saw blades quickly. It also dented heads beautifully.

Lignumvitae Key began its existence as a living coral reef. During one of the ice ages, as water began to freeze at the poles, the level of the water around the world dropped, and what was under water emerged and became islands. Over time—lots of time—bits of seaweed and other detritus washed up on the rack, decayed, and became soil when it was deposited in depressions in the rock. Then, most likely, some migrating birds shed some seeds in their droppings and the seeds took hold and grew. How many years did it take? Thousands, probably. But now Lignumvitae Key represents how the Keys might have looked if mankind had not found the waters so rich with sea life and the islands so beautifully attractive. The contrast between what might have been and what is, is breathtaking.

The mosquitoes on Lignumvitae Key look forward to your visit, especially on Thursdays, after two days of near famine. Take precautions.

Lignumvitae Channel

The westernmost of the channels that cross under the Upper Matecumbe-Lower Matecumbe Key Bridge/causeway is known as the Lignumvitae Channel. The passage from the deeper offshore waters to the bridge is rather scantily marked, and this channel's pass-through is of the fixed, 10-foot variety. Not to be even more repetitive, but with all these negative qualities, cruising-sized vessels should probably avoid the seaward portion of the Lignumvitae Channel.

Lignumvitae Key State Park dock

Caloosa Cove Marina

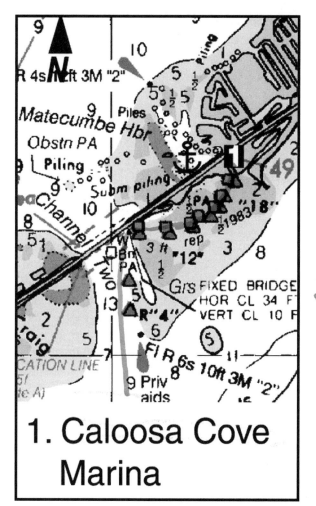

1. Caloosa Cove Marina

Caloosa Cove Marina and Channel Two
(24 51.004 North/080 44.296 West)

The marked passage known as Channel Two cuts the causeway/bridge spanning the gap between Lower Matecumbe Key and Long Key 6. 5 nautical miles southwest of Hawk Channel's unlighted daybeacon #43. This cut has impressive depths of 7 to 13 feet, with an occasional 6-foot sounding thrown in. Unfortunately, it leads north to yet another 10-foot fixed bridge.

Happily, a second marked channel cuts sharply east and then northeast, just south of the 10-foot span, and leads to Caloosa Cove Marina. This well-outlined approach passage carries at least 5½ feet of water, with good alongside depths of 6 to 8½ feet in the marina harbor.

Caloosa Cove is home to an impressive charter-fishing-boat fleet, but there is also room and a warm welcome for visiting cruisers. The basin is protected and well operated, though a few of the outer slips do not offer nearly so much shelter. Dockage is found at fixed wooden finger piers featuring 30- and 50-amp electrical service on the east side of the dockage basin and 30 on the west. If you need 50 amps of shore power, you will want to request an east-side slip when you contact the dockmaster. There are also dockside water hookups but no waste pump-out. Showers are in a separate building, close by the ship's store, and there is an on-site Laundromat.

Gasoline and diesel fuel can be purchased at Caloosa Cove, and mechanical repairs are also available. The ship's store is a good one. It is well stocked and begs for more than a few minutes of exploration.

Those who have seen one-too-many waves lately will be glad to learn that Caloosa Cove offers attractive shoreside lodging. This service consists of condo units, which may be rented. They are very nice, and all have a magnificent ocean view, in case you have not seen enough magnificent ocean views from your boat. There are also other non-condo rooms, nice ones, on the premises. This is a place where you will want for little.

Raylyn's Breakfast and Lunch (305-664-0607), the restaurant which fronts on the marina basin, is operated by a married couple who moved down to the Keys from North

Carolina. It is open from 7 A.M. until 2 P.M., seven days a week. Maybe Yankees won't appreciate their fresh homemade sausage, gravy, and biscuits, but those of us who grew up south of the Mason/Dixon Line surely will. The breakfasts they prepare are made-to-order and will give people who cherish their first meal of the day a marvelous start.

Caloosa Cove Marina (305) 664-4455

Approach depth—5½ feet (minimum)
Dockside depth—6-8½ feet
Accepts transients—yes
Type of piers—fixed wooden finger piers
Dockside power connections—30 and 50 on east side, 30 on west
Dockside water connections—yes
Showers—yes, in separate building next to ship's store
Laundromat—yes
Fuel—gas and diesel
Mechanical repairs—yes
Ship's store—complete and thorough and large
Restaurant—on site. It is called Raylyn's, and it is open from 7 A.M. until 2 P.M.

Channel Five

Channel Five is the second of the two marked passages that are spanned by the Lower Matecumbe Key-Long Key Bridge. It is an important channel, not the least reason for which is the full 65 feet of vertical clearance afforded by the fixed bridge that spans its width. This is the first Hawk Channel to ICW route south of Miami that enjoys such a high-rise clearance, with nary the necessity of a bridge opening.

Channel Five features minimum depths of 7 feet. Most cruisers will not see much of anything less than 8-foot readings on their sounders. This does not mean that Channel Five is not without problems, however.

What has always surprised us about Channel Five is that for a channel of its obvious importance, there are very, very few aids to navigation outlining its track. And it's not like there aren't any surrounding shallows to worry with. North of the bridge, shallow water flanks Channel Five to the east and west. South of the fixed span, shoals are even more of a problem, with depths of 1 to half-foot lying to the west and 2-foot shoals to the east.

Yet, in spite of all these problem stretches, there are only two markers outlining Channel Five (only one of which is lighted) south of the high-rise, and NO aids to navigation north of the bridge. We think that the U.S. Coast Guard should expend a bit more of its budget for aids to navigation on these waters. Another half-dozen lighted daybeacons would be ever soooo welcome.

The upstart of this dearth of markers is a hazardous entry during nighttime or low-light conditions. If you have a GPS interfaced with a laptop computer (with navigational software and the latest digitized version of chart 11451), running Channel Five is child's play. Otherwise, you may rest assured that this important passage is, shall we say, more than slightly challenging from the navigational point of view.

Long Key Bight Anchorage

Some .3 nautical miles south of Channel Five's 65-foot fixed bridge, cruisers can turn west and visit a somewhat open, and rather shallow, anchorage on Long Key Bight. Captains making for this haven must stick strictly to the midline. Don't even think about approaching any of the bight's shorelines. They are uniformly shoal. Even by following this plan, an occasional 4½-foot sounding might be noted, though most low-water readings fall in the 5- to 5½-foot range. Clearly, this is not an anchorage for deep-draft vessels, and we suggest that captains jockeying pleasure craft with more than 4 feet of draft look elsewhere.

If these soundings are not a problem for your boat, Long Key Bight is not a bad place to spend an evening with light to moderate winds blowing from the south, southwest, west, northwest, or north. Any breeze over 10 knots from the east or northeast would make for a decidedly uncomfortable evening. Swinging room is unlimited, and it is also only fair to note that Long Key Bight is a pretty body of water.

Navigators perusing chart 11451 will note that there are a few charted unlighted daybeacons near Long Key Bight's northwesterly corner. Actually, our on-the-water research revealed even more markers. Unfortunately, these lead only to some private docks, and you must cruise through 4-foot depths to get there. Visiting craft should keep clear of this uncertain passage.

HAWK CHANNEL—TAVERNIER CREEK TO CHANNEL FIVE NAVIGATION

This is going to come as a big surprise, but the Hawk Channel section between Tavernier Creek and Channel Five carries on the tradition of REALLY LOOOONG runs between aids to navigation. And markers are very important along this stretch. There are a whole host of flanking reefs, which, while a boon to scuba divers, can really ruin your whole day on the water. Remember, running aground in the Florida Keys, particularly on a coral reef, can be far more expensive than just the cost of having your craft pulled off and repairing any damaged underwater hardware. Courtesy of our good friend Larry Dennis, cruising writer extraordinaire for the *Florida Times Union* (in Jacksonville, Florida), we learned there was one instance recently when a professional captain was delivering a new Hatteras motor yacht and ran aground on three occasions. The total fine amounted to MORE than $100,000. Need we say more? It would be a really, really good idea to stay off the reefs!

On Hawk Channel Picking up our travelogue of Hawk Channel at unlighted daybeacon #39, where we left in earlier in the last chapter, it is a somewhat daunting run of slightly better than 6.7 nautical miles southwest to the next marker, 40-foot flashing daybeacon #40. Be SURE to bring #40 abeam by about 100 yards to its southeasterly side.

North and northwest of flashing daybeacon #40, the Hen and Chickens Reef sits waiting with 3-foot depths and a shallow, sunken wreck. Once again, it's a paradise for divers, but a place that cruisers want to avoid at all costs.

Approaching #40, you may spy a series of two yellow, warning nun buoys, which mark the northeastern extreme of the Hen and Chickens Reef. Another team of two such aids denotes the reef's southwesterly boundary. Stay well east and southeast of all these warning markers.

Continuing southwest of #40, it is a shorter cruise of 4 nautical miles before coming abeam of Hawk Channel's next marker, unlighted daybeacon #41. Come abeam of #41 by about 100 to 200 yards to its northwesterly side. Don't get too far from #41, however, as the opposite side of the channel is bounded by the Cheeca Rocks Reef. Two more floating, yellow, warning nun buoys give some indication of where these shallows are located. We know this is a "duh," but we have to say it anyway, be SURE to stay well southeast of the Cheeca Rocks.

Between #40 and #41, mariners can cut northwest and visit a variety of cruising destinations, all of which are outlined below.

Treasure Harbor Marina Successful entry into Treasure Harbor Marina is complicated by the presence of a large, large reef charted as "The Rocks," immediately southeast of its entrance channel. To access the marina, you must work your way carefully around the unmarked southwesterly tip of "The Rocks" and then cut northeast, behind the reef. After making this turn to the northeast, navigators have the unenviable task of threading a path between "The Rocks" and the extensive shelf of shallows striking well out from the northwesterly, Plantation Key shoreline.

Watch to the southeast for the 40-foot flashing daybeacon #40, signaling the Hen and Chickens Reef marker. When this aid to navigation comes abeam well to your starboard side, watch for a large, drum-shaped sea buoy designated as #A (near 24 56.880 North/080 33.906 West). Turn to the north-northwest once abeam of #A and use your binoculars to pick out the outermost aids to navigation on the marina approach channel, two small floating markers designated as #1 and #2. The remainder of the entrance cut is outlined by white PVC pipes.

Be careful to completely ignore any orange and white "No Wake" buoys you might see. These errant markers almost led us onto the shallows southwest of the entry cut. Eventually, you will pass into a sheltered harbor. The marina will be spotted on the northerly tip of this small bay.

Trust us when we tell you, don't do this at night. Even the management at Treasure Harbor Marina thinks nighttime passage is a decidedly bad idea.

Snake Creek Be sure to use Inset 6, Page E (of chart 11451) when navigating Snake Creek. This inset's greater detail is ever so helpful.

The seaward approach cut serving Snake Creek is very well marked, but it has a bad case of the "snakes." It coils first one way, and then the other. Perhaps this is where Snake Creek derives its name.

It would serve no purpose here to try and verbally catalog all the many unlighted daybeacons that outline this channel. Suffice it to say that it is critically important to correctly identify the next marker, or set of markers, before proceeding onward from a position abeam of a preceding aid to navigation. Keep chart 11451 at hand and detail a member of the crew to tick off your progress by daybeacon numbers as you go along.

Keep a sharp watch for any temporary, floating markers that may have been recently placed to warn of new encroachments by the surrounding shoals. We spotted several of these temporary beacons during our last visit, and it was to our good fortune that we let them guide us to the good water. May you, too, be so fortunate.

North of unlighted daybeacons #8 and #9, the Snake Creek cut begins its approach to the 27-foot, bascule bridge, which spans its width. Strong currents run under this structure with surprising rapidity. Seldom have we seen more swiftly moving waters racing under a coastal bridge. Thank goodness this span has a closed vertical clearance of 27 feet and opens on demand for vessels that require more clearance.

If you must wait for a bridge opening, stop well back from the span's fenders and wait for the bridge to fully open before proceeding along. Trust me, these currents can push you into the bridge before you even know what's happening.

Just short (south) of the bascule bridge, two white PVC pipes mark a small, westward-running channel, which leads to the Big Conch Oceanside Bar and Grill. Remember that low-water depths in this cut run as thin as 3 feet. If you decide to enter anyway, keep strictly to the midwidth. Eventually, the restaurant and one face dock will come up to starboard, followed by additional dockage a bit farther upstream, also to starboard.

No-wake regulations are in effect, north of the Snake Creek bascule bridge to the "Y" split in the stream, well south of unlighted daybeacon #10. Slow to idle speed. I mean, after all, the Islamorada U.S. Coast Guard Station is located on Snake Creek, so if there ever was good place to obey speed regulations, this is it!

Speaking of which, the Islamorada U.S. Coast Guard Station occupies the point of land between the two southernmost canals making into the easterly shoreline, immediately north of the bascule bridge. Its position is quite apparent from the water.

The southernmost of the east-side canals plays host to Cobra Marine. Simply enter this stream along its centerline and forge on to the east at idle speed. Cobra's docks will soon be spotted dead ahead, in the charted crook of the canal.

Smuggler's Cove Marina guards the westerly banks, just north of the Snake Creek bascule bridge. You can't cut directly in towards the fuel dock or the dockage basin. As indicated by a whole collection of small floats and white PVC pipes, this marina is fronted by a shoal. To enter without finding these shallows, you must ease your way in from the north. This process is often complicated by the swiftly moving waters running under the Snake Creek Bridge. All captains should be ready for this current and take immediate remedial action if their vessel is knocked off course by the tide. This is a maximum-alert entryway, and you better be ready for it.

Moving generally north on the interior reaches of Snake Creek, cruisers will notice that the eastern banks are penetrated by a whole series of canals. These small streams are overlooked by an incredibly dense collection of private residences. None of the canals has room enough for overnight anchorage, so we suggest that visitors keep clear of these waters.

After running through a long markerless stretch, Snake Creek splits. The main channel continues up the northerly arm, but the northwesterly branch offers good anchorage. If you choose to anchor on the northwesterly waters, be sure to enter on the stream's midline. Drop anchor before proceeding more than 150 yards upstream. Past this point, depths begin to shelve upward. Carefully set the hook so as not to swing into any of the shallows flanking all the surrounding shorelines. Also, be SURE the anchor is well set before heading below to begin the evening libations. As we have mentioned repeatedly throughout this account, tidal currents are fierce on Snake Creek.

Returning our attention to the main Snake Creek passage, captains should favor the eastern banks for 350 to 400 yards north of the charted "Y" split in the stream. Chart 11451 correctly forecasts a ribbon of shallows shelving out from the westerly shoreline along this stretch.

Swing back to midchannel after proceeding for 400 yards or so past the "Y" split. Then, point to pass unlighted daybeacon #10 to its fairly immediate westerly side.

The outermost (northernmost) marker on the Snake Creek channel is flashing daybeacon #12. Note that #12 can be hard to spot from the water. Use the good old binocs to help with this process. Come abeam and pass #12 to its fairly immediate westerly side.

Cruisers looking to enter the path of the ICW from #12 should set course for the Waterway's unlighted daybeacon #78A. This marker lies about .7 nautical miles to the north-northwest. For a continuing account of the ICW passage, check out our ICW—Tavernier Creek to Channel Five section earlier in this chapter.

Tropical Reef Resort and Hog Heaven Bar and Restaurant The three-fingered set of channels that provides access to Tropical Resort and Hog Heaven bar resides a short hop west of the Snake Creek seaward channel. The center cut leads to Tropical Reef. It is fairly well marked by unlighted daybeacons and relatively easy to run in daylight conditions. The resort harbor's entrance will be spotted north of the innermost set of markers, unlighted daybeacons #9 and #10. Cruise straight into the basin through the entrance in the partial breakwater.

The northwesterly channel provides access to some private docks. It is outlined solely by white PVC pipes, contrary to what chart 11451 indicates. We suggest that you bypass this cut entirely.

The easternmost channel runs north to Hog Heaven Bar. Please remember that this is a shallow passage, with scanty markings. If you choose to enter, depart the center, Tropical Reef channel 150 yards south of unlighted daybeacon #7. The outermost marker (which is charitably called an aid to navigation) is a wooden piling topped by some sort of funky orange rectangle. Leave this informal mark to your port side. The remainder of the cut is outlined by haphazardedly placed white PVC pipes. They are not terribly easy to find. Don't even think about trying this in darkness or bad weather.

If you make it that far, the channel eventually leads you past a stone breakwater to starboard, followed closely by the dockage basin. Fixed wooden piers will be spotted to both port and starboard.

Whale Harbor Channel and Associated Facilities About the only reason that skippers of cruising craft might choose to enter the seaward side of Whale Harbor Channel is that they are bent on a visit to Holiday Isle Marina. Otherwise, cruisers will come face-to-face with a 12-foot fixed bridge, which will mean it's time to turn around for all but small craft.

Captains and crew bound for Holiday Isle should come abeam of Whale Harbor Channel's outermost marker, flashing daybeacon #1 to its northeasterly side. From #1, the channel runs to the northwest. Pass all subsequent red, even-numbered aids to navigation to your starboard side and take green markers to port. Did you remember "red, right, returning"?

Take care to stay in the marked channel by carefully identifying all aids to navigation. Soundings outside of the Whale Harbor cut run from one half to 1 foot. "Ouch," says your underwater hardware!

The plentifully marked cut leading to Holiday Isle Marina cuts off to the north, immediately northwest of the Whale Harbor Channel's unlighted daybeacon #8. The first markers are #1 and #2. Pass between #1 and #2, and continue on, still taking red markers to starboard and green to port.

Soon the dockage basin will come up dead ahead. Cruise straight into the harbor.

Those few mariners who choose to visit the scant marine facilities (at least for visitors) at Whale Harbor Inn must follow one of two rather perilous routes. Shallow-draft vessels (drawing LESS THAN 4 feet), might try cutting to the southwest, immediately southeast of the 12-foot fixed bridge. Parallel the bridge, keeping fairly close to this structure. You might then be able to carefully curl around to the south and enter the harbor at Whale Harbor Inn. No guarantees though!

The other entrance to Whale Harbor is gained via the charted channel a short hop southwest of the Whale Harbor Channel. This cut is barely outlined by a few white PVC pipes. Even under ideal conditions, running this passage can be a white-knuckle experience for first timers. If you make the attempt, proceed at super slow speed and keep an eagle eye on the sounder. Good luck!

On Hawk Channel For Hawk Channel, the run from unlighted daybeacon #41 to the next southwesterly lying marker, unlighted daybeacon #43, is relatively short, only a measley 2.5 nautical miles. As you begin your approach to #43, don't mistake the huge, 136-foot Alligator Reef light for #43. This mammoth aid to navigation lies well southeast of Hawk Channel. Unless you are bound to Alligator Reef for the great scuba diving, you should stay well north and northwest of the 136-foot marker.

Northwest of unlighted daybeacon #43, the long causeway/bridge connecting Upper Matecumbe Key with Lower Matecumbe Key spans a whole collection of channels. All but one of these passages are spanned by fixed, low-level sections of the bridge. Indian Key Channel is the exception. It is crossed by a 27-foot portion of the bridge and a 50-foot power line. Cruisers will also be interested in the easternmost cut, which provides access to Bud N' Mary's Marina.

Bud N' Mary's Marina From unlighted daybeacon #43, it is cruise of about 1.9 nautical miles north-northwest to the outermost marker on the small channel that leads to Bud N' Mary's Marina. Pass between the first two markers, unlighted daybeacons #1 and #2, and then point to pass unlighted daybeacon #3 to its fairly immediate easterly side.

The initial portion of this channel is flanked by a rock breakwater to the east. Craft running the cut must pass between #3 and this rocky barrier. On the water, it can look as if you should go west of #3, in spite of its color. In three words, don't do that. Stay east of #3 but also west of the breakwater.

Eventually, you will pass between unlighted daybeacons #5 and #6, then between unlighted daybeacons #8 and #9. The marina entrance will come up to the east shortly thereafter.

Teatable Key Channel The next route (moving east to west) to pass under the Upper Matecumbe-Lower Matecumbe Bridge/causeway is the Teatable Key Channel. While this cut is well marked and has good depths, it eventually leads to a 10-foot fixed portion of the bridge. With this limitation in mind, most cruising-craft skippers and crew should look elsewhere.

Indian Key Channel and Indian Key State Park Indian Key Channel is an important passage that provides powercraft (that can clear the overhead 50-foot power lines and a 27-foot fixed pass-through of the Upper Matecumbe-Lower Matecumbe Bridge) fairly reliable access from Hawk Channel to the ICW-inside route, or the other way around. It's also allows access for pleasure craft to the visitors' docks associated with both Lignumvitae Key State Park and Indian Key State Park.

Unfortunately, after saying that, it's only fair to note that this passage could be renamed, the "Indian Snake Channel." When we say that it winds one way then another, that is simply doing the convoluted turns along the way an injustice. As if all that weren't enough to give you on-the-water eyestrain, there is the confusing situation with aids to navigation where the Power Line Channel meets up with the Indian Key Cut. What's a navigator to do?

Also, note that ALL the aids to navigation

on Indian Key Channel are unlighted. That would make a nighttime entry perilous at best.

The seaward portion of the Indian Key Channel is outlined by three pairs of unlighted daybeacons. Stick to the marked track! Very shallow water (1-foot depths) flanks the channel to the east and west.

The southernmost (outermost) markers on Indian Key Channel are unlighted daybeacons #1 and #2. Obviously, it would behoove you to pass between these markers. However, captains intent on a visit to the Florida state park on Indian Key should break off their approach to Indian Key Channel some 100 yards south of #1 and #2.

Those bound for Indian Key should take a lazy turn around unlighted daybeacon #1. Approach the key in line with its southerly tip. Don't ease too far to the east. The charted shallows in this quarter are for real. The visitors' dock will be spotted on the southeastern corner of Indian Key, with the mooring field just off the southeasterly shores. We strongly recommend that you pick up a mooring buoy, or anchor and dinghy in to the visitors' pier.

Returning now to the main track of Indian Key Channel, north-northwest of the gap between unlighted daybeacons #5 and #6, the passage quickly approaches the 27-foot fixed bridge, followed closely by the 50-foot power line. Immediately after passing under the fixed span and the power lines, slow to idle speed, and proceed with the GREATEST caution.

The reason for this "alert" status is the intersection of the Power Line Channel with the Indian Key Channel, immediately north of the 27-foot fixed bridge and the 50-foot power lines. Many, many visiting mariners have come to grief by confusing the markers.

There is actually a simple way to avoid all these problems, though Sea Tow will probably never forgive us for telling you so. After passing under the fixed bridge, point for the gap between unlighted daybeacons #7 and #8. As you approach this pair of markers, begin favoring the western side of the channel slightly. This maneuver will serve to help avoid the shallows and charted rock south of #8. IGNORE all floating markers you might see. These floaters are part of the Power Line Channel, NOT the Indian Key cut.

Head for the gap between unlighted daybeacons #7 and #8, favoring the westerly side of the channel as your approach to within 50 yards of the markers. Again, and we think it important enough to be repetitive at this point, IGNORE any floating markers between the bridge and the pair of daybeacons (#7 and #8).

Immediately after leaving the gap between #7 and #8 in your wake, cut to the north and point to pass between unlighted daybeacons #9 and #10.

Now, the channel swings to the northwest. Set course to pass between unlighted daybeacons #11 and #12. Here, the channel shifts again, this time to the north. Point to pass between unlighted daybeacons #13 and #14.

Are you tired of turns? Well there are

several more yet to come. From #13 and #14, turn to the north-northwest and set course for the midwidth between the next two aids to navigation, unlighted daybeacons #15 and #16.

The Lignumvitae Key State Park visitors' pier will be spotted west of unlighted daybeacon #15. Please don't forget that dockside depths at this structure run only about 4½ feet at low tide. Anchoring off and then dinghying ashore is complicated by the swift tidal currents that plague this entire region. It would really ruin your whole afternoon to be strolling through the Lignumvitae Key nature trails, only to spot your boat gaily drifting onto a nearby shoal. Our advice is to be SURE the anchor is well set before breaking out the dinghy.

Next up is unlighted daybeacons #17 and #18. It's essential to pick out these daybeacons, as shallow water lies west and southwest of #17. Pass between #17 and #18, favoring #18. Then, turn to the northeast and cruise out into the charted, wide patch of deep water.

The ICW lies some .8 nautical miles to the north. If you pilot an especially deep, draft vessel, the correctly charted 5-foot patch northeast of #18 might also be a cause for concern.

Lignumvitae Channel The westernmost of the Matecumbe channels is known as the Lignumvitae Channel. Sparse markings on the seaside portion of this cut and a 10-foot fixed bridge lead off a list of less-than-sterling qualities. Again, cruising-sized vessels are advised to ignore this passage and continue southwest on Hawk Channel to Channel Five.

On Hawk Channel Well, you probably guessed that after a brief respite, it's back to a lot of water between markers on Hawk Channel. In fact, you must cruise across 8.8 nautical miles of open water between unlighted daybeacon #43 and the next aid to navigation, flashing daybeacon #44. Come abeam of #44 by at least 100 yards to its southerly side. Shallows are found north and northwest of #44.

Short of #44, cruisers can run the southerly stretch of Channel Two to visit Caloosa Cove Marina, or cruise through Channel Five and pass under its wonderful 65-foot fixed bridge on the way to a meeting with the ICW-inside route.

Caloosa Cove Marina and Channel Two Captains making for Caloosa Cove Marina can turn north after cruising 6.25 miles southwest of Hawk Channel's unlighted daybeacon #43, and track their way through the southerly portion of Channel Two. This cut soon leads to a 10-foot fixed bridge, but fortunately, a profusely marked channel cuts off to the east and northeast, just short of the fixed span, and leads to Caloosa Cove Marina.

Enter Channel Two by passing some 25 to 50 yards to the west of the first marker, flashing daybeacon #2. Be sure to stay west of #2 and the subsequent two red daybeacons. Truly shoal water of 1/2 foot is

Caloosa Cove Marina

encroaching on these aids to navigation from the east.

Continue on, passing unlighted daybeacons #4 and #6 by about the same distance to their westerly sides. Then, point for the bridge, as if you were going to pass under its 10-foot pass-through. Immediately before reaching the span, the Caloosa Cove channel cuts off to the east. Be SURE to pick up the first two markers, unlighted daybeacons #8 and #9, and pass directly between them.

The remainder of the marina cut is prolifically marked. Just pass all red markers to your starboard side and take green markers to port (as if you were expecting something else). Eventually, the channel curls around to the northeast. You will first pass some rather open slips to port, backed by a huge, metal dry-stack storage building, followed by the far-better-sheltered harbor farther to the north.

Channel Five Okay, come on you guys in the USCG. Why are there only two markers outlining the seaward portion of Channel Five and NO aids to navigation between the 65-foot fixed bridge and the ICW? I mean, this is a rather important route! Go figure!

Point to pass 35 yards east of unlighted daybeacon #1 and then about the same distance west of flashing daybeacon #2. Be very mindful of the 1- to half-foot shoals to the west, southwest, and northwest of #1 and the 2-foot depths east and southeast of #2.

West of flashing daybeacon #2, captains piloting non-deep-draft vessels might choose to anchor in Long Key Bight. This haven will be considered separately below.

From #2, swing just a bit to the north-northeast and head toward the central pass-through of the 65-foot fixed bridge. Pause for just a second to admire this structure. It is only one of two fixed bridges in all of the Florida Keys that enjoys this vertical clearance.

North of the fixed span, continue on to the north-northeast, being careful to avoid the two patches of 1-foot shallows to the west and the equally unhappy 2-foot depths just southwest of the Channel Two Bridge. Eventually, you may sight the concrete obstructions north of the Channel Two

Bridge, southeast of your course. Ignore these rather strange-looking structures and continue north-northeast on the same course line.

Cruisers northbound (eastbound) on the ICW should continue cruising on this same track for approximately 4.4 nautical miles to unlighted daybeacon #97 and flashing daybeacon #98. These Waterway markers denote the southwestern tip of the Bowlegs Cut channel.

Mariners who intend to turn west, toward Marathon and Key West on the ICW, can save a chunk of distance by cutting northwest, once abeam of the Channel Two concrete obstructions. Unfortunately, there are no Waterway markers to aim for, but you will intersect the ICW passage after cruising just over 1.8 nautical miles. While it would take a gross navigational error for this to be a problem, do be very sure to pass well north of the charted bubble of 1-foot shallows northwest of the 65-foot bridge's pass-through.

Once you've found your way to the ICW, cut southwest and point to come abeam of flashing daybeacon #1, north of Old Dan Bank, by at least 50 yards (no closer) to its northerly side. Shallower water lies south and southeast of #1.

Long Key Bight Anchorage The trick to anchoring in Long Key Bight is to stay way away from all the various shorelines and anchor in the middle of the bight. Shallows abut all the surrounding banks and shelve out into the bight for an amazing distance.

Abandon Channel Five .25 miles north

of flashing daybeacon #2. Turn west and cruise carefully into the central waters of Long Key Bight. You can follow the mid-width for a short distance farther to the west-southwest, as the bight turns slightly in this direction, but again, STAY AT LEAST SEVERAL HUNDRED YARDS OFF ALL THE VARIOUS SHORELINES.

If you happen to spot some unlighted daybeacons on Long Key Bight's northwest-erly corner, we suggest ignoring these markers. In fact, don't go anywhere near them. The daybeacons eventually lead to a shallow, narrow canal that serves a series of private docks. There is no room to anchor, and no facilities are available for visitors.

Bud N' Mary's Marina (Islamorada)

Mangrove Walk—Long Key Recreation Area

CHAPTER 4

Long Key to Moser Channel

Whether you find yourself tracking to the west on the Florida Keys ICW or along Hawk Channel, Long Key is the next body of land you will spot west of Channel Five. This island offers some low-key marina facilities on the ICW side.

Then, cruisers can stare in wonder at the Long Key Viaduct, which connects Highway U.S. 1 to Duck Key. This isle plays host to a fine marina and a shallow-draft dry-storage facility, both of which can only be accessed from the Hawk Channel side.

Another bridge (or you might just think of it as an extension of the Long Key Viaduct) leads west to Grassy Key and the westerly genesis of the long, sprawling, and often confusing community known as Marathon. If someone ever was to take a small piece of Miami and deposit it in the Florida Keys, it would resemble nothing so much as Marathon.

Marathon encompasses Grassy Key, Crawl Key, Little Crawl Key, Long Point Key, Fat Deer Key, Key Colony Beach, Vaca Key, Boot Key, Hog Key, Knight Key, and Pigeon Key. You can find just about anything here a cruiser might ever need and some things that most who go on the water would rather avoid.

Marathon is peppered with marina and repair facilities. Anchorages are also numerous, including the very popular and well-protected haven on Boot Key Harbor. We will take an extensive look at both the charms and the controversies surrounding Boot Key within the body of this chapter.

West of Marathon, Moser Channel boasts the second of only two fixed, high-rise bridges (63 feet) in the Florida Keys. In spite of its less-than-sterling scheme of aids to navigation, mariners can make use of this passage to cut inside or outside.

The bridge spanning Moser Channel is a story in itself. It is aptly named "the Seven Mile Bridge." You may take our word for it, after missing Seven Mile Grill via automobile and accidentally getting onto this span, it IS 7 miles across and seven miles back. The new bridge sits cheek by jowl with the older span, which was a true engineering marvel in its day.

There are three different take-off points along this stretch of the ICW that lead cruisers north to an intersection with Cape Sable, and thence to the many charms of cruising the western (mainland) coast of the Sunshine State. These popular passages are particularly important routes for sailcraft, and even tall-powered vessels that can not clear the old, decrepit, lift railway-bridge at Port Mayacca on the Okeechobee Waterway. The only method by which these sorts of vessels can readily cruise between the east and west coasts of Florida is by way of Marathon.

There is much to see, much to do, and a whole passel of attractions to explore in Marathon. Let's roll up our collective sleeves and take a look.

Charts11451—our old friend continues to provide the best cartographic coverage of both the ICW-Florida Bay route and Hawk Channel, as far west as the Moser Channel—also details the Florida Bay Yacht Channel from Old Dan Bank to just short of Cape Sable **11442**—general Gulf of Mexico chart that covers a portion of the Moser Channel to Cape Sable (western mainland Florida) passage **11431**—another offshore Gulf of Mexico chart that details another portion of the Moser Channel to Cape Sable passage **11433**—provides excellent navigational coverage of the Cape Sable region, including the route to the marina at Flamingo and points north, including Little Shark River

Bridges
Vaca Cut Bridge—crosses Vaca Cut, north of unlighted daybeacon #6 and southwest of unlighted daybeacon #1—fixed—13-feet vertical clearance

Seven Mile Bridge—crosses both Knight Key Channel and Moser Channel between Marathon (Vaca Key) and Little Duck Key—fixed—19 feet of vertical clearance across Knight Channel—63 feet (minimum) vertical clearance across Moser Channel

Boot Key Bridge—spans the western entrance to Boot Key Harbor, east of unlighted daybeacon #14—bascule—24 feet closed vertical clearance—opens on demand, except between the hours of 10:00 P.M. and 6:00 A.M.—openings during this nighttime period require a 2-hour notice (call 305-289-2430)—24 feet of (closed) vertical clearance

Sea birds (Marathon)

Marathon

The Middle Keys are dominated by Marathon, a city of many diversions. When one cruises in the Keys, the blandishments of modern society are often left far behind, out of sight and out of mind. But if you thought you escaped all that, when you get to Marathon, you will feel as if much of it followed you here. Marathon has modern everything. There's a Home Depot and a Super K-Market. Supermarket chains are represented by Publix and Winn-Dixie. There are fast-food restaurants galore for burgers, tacos, fish, or whatever. If you have been loafing along at a snail's pace, Marathon could shock you like a cattle prod.

It can be a bit of a problem, surprisingly enough, to restock your galley in Marathon. Only three marinas (all of which are located on the waters of Boot Key Harbor) are within easy walking distance of the local Publix and Winn-Dixie supermarkets. Unless you happen to obtain a slip at these facilities, a cab ride will most likely be necessary to and from your harborside berth.

On the other hand, Marathon could be just the stopover point you need to restock, resupply, and regenerate your vessel. West Marine (2055 Overseas Highway, 350-289-1009) and Boater's World (5001 Overseas Highway, 350-743-7707) both have ample marine stores in Marathon. For people with more exotic diversions in mind, there is Lion's Den, an adult toystore which advertises on big billboards along the highway. You will have missed those, of course, because you will have been cruising along by watercraft ,such a nasty break.

All the various isles of Marathon teem with marina and repair facilities. While a few of these operations are best forgotten, others are absolutely first rate. The local service yards can cover everything from a bent prop to a major engine rebuild. If you need repairs, particularly extensive repairs, this is *the* place to stop in the Florida Keys, even more so (surprisingly) than Key West.

As you would expect of a budding metropolis like Marathon, there is a huge collection of shoreside lodging ranging from the less-than-memorable to chain motels. A few of these have some small docks adjacent to their property, but these are all pretty much geared to small, fishing-sized craft, not cruising-sized vessels.

You will have to decide for yourself how the hustle and bustle of Marathon compares to a quiet anchorage off Whale Harbor or even the artistic confines of Key West. As life usually is, Marathon is clearly a trade-off between its many welcome and varied services, and a faster-paced lifestyle that is so counter intuitive in the Florida Keys.

Marathon Restaurants

While Islamorada is justly famous for its restaurants, we must say in all sorrow that, by and large, the same can not be said of Marathon. While there are some dining attractions worth noting, particularly Seven Mile Grill, there are also many best forgotten. The level of gastro-culinary delights in Marathon is just "fair," based on our own collective enjoyment meter. Maybe your own experience will prove us wrong, and we hope that is so. But it is our duty to call them as we see them . . . or taste them.

We will cover several dining establishments in our various marina accounts below, but there are three other spots, without direct water access, that we think deserve a mention. For the best breakfast in town, do what the locals do: beat a path to the Wooden Spoon (7007 Overseas Highway, 305-743-7469). Trip after trip, even in the foulest of weather, we always found a broad selection of those who live in Marathon year round breaking their morning fast here. Located on the southern side of U.S. 1, The Wooden Spoon is only a quick taxi ride from all the area marinas.

Herbie's Restaurant (6350 Overseas Highway, 305-743-6373) is a perennial Marathon favorite. We found the food here, particularly in the evenings, to be excellent. All our seafood entrees and appetizers were as fresh as they could be and prepared with excellent seasonings. The atmosphere was pure bonhomie, with some semi-open-air dining for those who prefer such a venue.

And, of course, as mentioned above, don't dare miss the Seven Mile Grill (305-743-4481), located on the northern side of U.S. 1, immediately east of the Seven Mile Bridge (as its name so aptly implies). We will present a full review of this, our favorite restaurant in Marathon, later in this chapter, but for now, let's just note that the food is great, the service is superb, and the atmosphere is pure Florida Keys.

Numbers to know in Marathon include:

Avis—305-743-5428
Budget—305-743-3998
Enterprise—305-289-7630
Island Auto Rental—305-289-3200
Customs (clearance)—800-458-4239, 800-451-0393
Action Taxi—305-743-6800
Fisherman's Hospital—305-743-5533
Greyhound—800-410-5397
Marathon Airport—350-743-2155
West Marine—350-289-1009
Boater's World—350-743-7707
Chamber of Commerce—350-743-5417

Marathon Waters

Like everything else in this little piece of Miami that has found its way to the Florida Keys, the waters in and around Marathon are more than a little complicated. West of Vaca Cut, mariners can think of the local cruising grounds as being divided into three sections. First, there is the inside-Florida Bay route, which flanks the northerly Marathon shoreline, and through which the ICW runs west on its way to a meeting with the Moser Channel. There's a good smattering of marinas here and even a few fair-weather anchorages.

Then, there are the ocean-side, Hawk Channel waters, which feature a wealth of facilities around Key Colony Beach and Coco Plum Beach. There is even one intriguing anchorage near Crawl Key that will speak to the heart of any true cruiser.

Arguably the most intriguing cruising region in Marathon are its "middle waters." This cruising ground is dominated by Boot Key Harbor and its two connecting streams. There is also a whole collection of marinas and repair yards set about Boot Key Harbor, particularly its west side approach stream. Boot Key Harbor is, without a doubt, the most popular anchorage in the Florida Keys, but this reputation does not come without some controversy.

We will consider these three cruising regions in three distinct sections (and several subsections) below. You can show yourself to be a very wise mariner by keeping charts 11451, 11442, 11431, and 11433 close at hand while we wander through these complicated waters.

Marathon History

Marathon is really a collection of several keys, but for the purposes of this guide, we will lump them under just one name.

The main island here is called Vaca Key. If the name sounds Spanish, it is because that's its derivation. "Vaca" is the Spanish word for cow. Some suggest that Vaca Key was named thusly because there were a lot of manatees—sea cows—in the area. Manatees were prized by Indians for their meat. There were no singers of songs in the Keys back then to make the Indians more aware of the consequences of dining on manatees, so the plunder continued unabated and probably without much impact. There were a lot more manatees back then than there were Indians.

About 1822, a year after Florida was ceded to the United States by Spain, a couple of wreckers, Joshua Appleby and John Fiveash, established a small settlement on the western end of Vaca Key, possibly not far from where the Seven Mile Grill is now. They called their settlement Port Monroe.

It didn't amount to much. But then Captain Appleby—all wreckers back then also claimed the title of "Captain"; it is similar to the meaningless "Esquire" that gets appended to the rear end of lawyers' names—came up with a great plan.

Privateers—civilians commissioned to operate armed vessels against the shipping of an enemy, in this case Spain—from South America were required to take their seizures back to their home ports so that the legality of what they had done could be sanctioned, and they could get paid. That requirement meant that privateers had to spend a lot of time in transit, back and forth, to and from home, time that could have been put to better and more profitable use in looting, pillaging, and plundering.

Appleby made a deal with a Colombian privateer. The Colombian would intentionally wreck the ships he had captured on reefs near Vaca Key, thus relieving himself of the obligation of taking the ships back to Columbia, and Appleby would buy the cargo at a caved-in price. He later was able to sell the bargain-basement merchandise at a great profit up North, and he made lots of money. Appleby's success and Port Monroe, both operating on the razor's edge of legality and lawlessness, soon attracted men of like minds and a similarly refined sense of business ethics. Vaca Key blossomed.

At the time, there was an anti-piracy squadron of warships down the islands, in Key West, under the command of Commodore David Porter. Between 1823 and 1825, Porter's job was to stop pirates from preying on shipping in the Caribbean. Porter heard of the shenanigans at Port Monroe, but it took a murder on Vaca Key to gird him into action. He sent a squad of marines to put the lid on the nefarious goings-on at Port Monroe; they arrested Appleby, too. Appleby was released in time, but he had lost his edge and Port Monroe faded into historical obscurity.

From time to time, Indian attacks elsewhere emptied Vaca Key of residents as they sought refuge in Key West. When the danger—real or imagined—passed, they returned. On January 4, 1836, a Seminole Indian raid on a New River plantation in what is now Fort Lauderdale set Vaca Key residents to flight. Seminoles had killed the plantation owner's wife, their three children, and the children's tutor.

When the Vaca Key settlers decided that it was safe to come home, they returned to find out that, in their absence, their island had become part of the newly-minted Dade County. The county seat for Dade County was Indian Key, a small island between Upper Matecumbe Key and Lower Matecumbe Key.

The original Dade County was huge. Today it would encompass half of Monroe County, all of Dade County, all of Broward County, and a part of what is now Palm Beach County. It's hard to imagine that the first county seat of sprawling Dade County was an island so small that four years after it became the county seat, it was overrun—on August 7, 1840—by Indians during the Second Seminole War, and by the end of the war, it was deserted.

Vaca Key itself suffered the same sort of depopulation. By 1860, the key only had twenty-six residents. Ten years later it had none.

The construction of the Overseas Railroad put Marathon on the map to stay, literally and figuratively. As the railway made its way down the Keys, reaching the island in 1908, Vaca Key became a supply depot for the construction work. The next jump of the railroad required a bridge of seven miles in length to be built. Vaca Key filled up with railroad workers. The town was named during this railroad period. However, as with many of the names in the Florida Keys, the origin of the Marathon name is disputed. Some say a railroad worker, stating that the building of the railroad had become a marathon, named the town. Others maintain that the name came from a passage written by the Right Honourable George Gordon (Noel) Byron, Lord Byron, VI Baron Byron of Rochdale. Conundrums abound everywhere, even in the Keys.

Though the advent of the railroad may have given Marathon its name, the railroad didn't make much of an impact on the hamlet. In 1930, there were only about thirty people in Marathon. The opening of the Overseas Highway in 1938 brought more people. Some came to fish. Some came to retire. More stayed than left.

By the early part of the 1950s, Marathon was comprised of a western part that had grown out of what Henry Flagler had left behind when his railroad operation moved on. Commercial fishing interests moved into the west end, and some are still there. Much, but not all, of the east end of Vaca Key was dredged-up land. Developers like Phil Sadowski, who built Key Colony Beach, pumped up sand from the ocean and put it in behind seawalls to make real estate. The lots were sold, but the building of houses on them went on over a long period of time, making for architectural disparity within neighborhoods.

In the 1960s, the Keys, and Marathon, became a more expensive location in which to live. The escalation of real-estate values also took place in other parts of the country too, like Aspen. Paradise, wherever people discovered it, came with an ever-steeper price tag attached. The people who work in service industries, many in low-paying jobs, have been squeezed into low-rent neighborhoods. And some have chosen to live aboard, many of them in boats anchored in Boot Key Harbor.

Today, Marathon is the third-most-populous city in the Keys, the other two being Key West and Key Largo.

ICW—Long Key to Vaca Cut

Some of the most beautiful anchorages that this guide's writers have ever witnessed lie just south of the ICW's run from Long Key and Channel Five to a position abeam of Vaca Cut.

None are appropriate for truly heavy weather (particularly with strong winds blowing out of the north), but with fair breezes or even moderate blows from the south, you can while away an evening or two here and be readily excused for deciding that this is really what cruising is really all about.

Only a few small marinas offer anything in the way of services for pleasure craft east of Vaca Cut. As usual, this is in marked contrast to the offshore Hawk Channel passage. Be aware, however, that this dearth of marinas adjacent to the ICW changes somewhat dramatically on the waters west of Vaca Cut, in the heart of what we shall term downtown Marathon. That, of course, is a story we shall peruse in the next full section of this chapter.

**Jewfish Bush Banks Anchorage
(Standard Mile 1169.5)
(24 50.918 North/080 46.952 West)**

Take a perusal of chart 11451, and check out the waters west and north of the Channel Five Bridge. Note the small islet and 1-foot shoal that bears the name of Jewfish Bush Banks. Cruising craft of most any size can anchor 300 yards west of the correctly charted 1-foot shelf of shallows in minimum 7-foot depths. The very shallow water running north from Fiesta Key to the west affords good shelter when winds are blowing from this quarter, while the shoal and small island of Jewfish Bush Banks gives a lee to the east, and the causeway leading to the Channel Five Bridge provides shelter to the south. You will notice that nowhere in this lengthy discourse has there been any mention of protection to the north, northwest, or northeast. Don't even think about anchoring here if the wind is forecast to blow from any of these quarters at a speed greater than 7 knots.

We have never found this to be much of a problem, but some fellow cruisers have informed us that headlights and auto noise from the nearby bridge and causeway have disturbed their rest. Perhaps we have always been so ready to hit the proverbial hay that it would have required a small nuclear device to keep us from a good night's sleep.

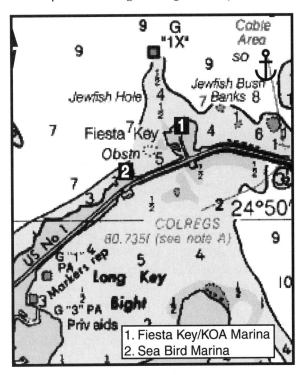

1. Fiesta Key/KOA Marina
2. Sea Bird Marina

**Fiesta Key/KOA Marina
(Standard Mile 1170)
(24 50.594 North/080 47.569 West)**

Fiesta Key/KOA Marina is a campground with a marina in the backyard. This facility lies south of the ICW, south-southeast of Jewfish Hole's unlighted daybeacon #1X. Note that marker #1X is NOT part of the Waterway.

Entrance depths run as thin as 4 feet, with only 3½ to 5 feet of water dockside, depending on the slip location. The approach channel is very scantily marked and can be a real bear for first-timers. Check out our navigational review of this facility in the next section of this chapter for some hints.

Fiesta Key Marina operates on a strict time clock, 8 A.M. to 4 P.M., and if you arrive later than that, you can expect the door to be closed. Come back tomorrow.

The dockage basin is enclosed by a breakwater and during the summer and early fall months, there is plenty of space available. In peak season, the vacancy ratio might be much, much smaller, so it would make sense to call ahead. Transients are accepted, but most of the people who use this marina facility are residents of the campground and their boats are of the kind one might tow behind a recreation vehicle. This facility is clearly geared toward this type of small craft. The docks are fixed wooden finger piers but nothing fancy.

All berths feature 30- and 50-amp dockside power service and fresh water connections, no waste pump-out, though. The showers here are big and clean and neat. They are not air-conditioned, but that's the norm in the Keys, not the exception. The Laundromat at Fiesta Key is open-air, large, and has a number of big machines. This is the Cadillac of Laundromats . . . or maybe we should say the Trumpy or Hinckley. Having said that, we can also write that the ship's store is kind of puny, a beer-bait-and-tackle type. There is no diesel here, only gas, and mechanical repairs are nil. The campground has an above-ground swimming pool, at which transient cruisers are welcome. That appeared to be quite nice.

Cruisers who anchor-off nearby in the deeper waters near Jewfish Bush Banks (see above) should be advised that dinghies ARE NOT welcome at Fiesta Key Marina. The campground authorities are vigilant about interlopers. Don't do it.

Fiesta Key has an on-site restaurant that goes by the moniker of Beach House Grill. Small and more of a lunch counter than a full-fledged restaurant, it is adjacent to a game room. You won't need to wear your tux or best party dress. In season, Beach House Grill (305-664-5252) is open from 8 A.M. until 9:30 P.M. However, the hours of operation depend upon the season and the capacity of the campground.

Fiesta Key/KOA Marina (305) 664-4922
http://www.koa.com

Approach depth—4 feet
Dockside depth—3$\frac{1}{2}$-5 feet, depending on the slip
Accepts transients—yes
Type of piers—fixed wooden slips
Dockside power connections: 30 and 50 amp
Dockside water connections—yes
Showers—yes, not climate controlled, but clean and neat
Laundromat—yes
Fuel—gas only
Ship's store—convenience type with BB&T
Restaurant—on site

Sea Bird Marina
(Standard Mile 1171)
(24 50.307 North/080 47.954 West)

Sea Bird Marina is found just a short hop west of Fiesta Key Marina, on the northern shores of Long Key. There is nothing standard about this marina. Everything is an exception to the rule. For example, they have two basins and two approaches. The southwesterly basin, in which shallower draft vessels are placed, has a 3$\frac{1}{2}$-foot approach and 3 to 3$\frac{1}{2}$ feet of water alongside. The more northeasterly dockage complex, where sailcraft and larger powercraft are lodged, has a 6$\frac{1}{2}$- to 7-foot approach depth and a 10- to 15-foot dockside depth. There are both fixed wooden and fixed concrete piers and alongside docking and finger-pier docking.

Sea Bird Marina is peopled by some nice folks. This is kind of a homey place that accepts transients willingly. If you are looking for bright city lights, though, go elsewhere. This is laid back.

There are showers available but nothing fancy. Dockside water is standard, and there is 30- and 50-amp electrical service dockside, too. For a funky place such as this, there is also cable hookup and phone service at the slips, which may surprise some.

Gasoline can be purchased dockside at Sea Bird, and the owners will arrange for diesel to be delivered by truck. We would assume that if you need only a couple of gallons, they could be the most expensive two gallons of diesel you have ever purchased.

No waste pump-out here and the ship's store is kind of a minimalist's dream. This is no West Marine, but a look around could be rewarding. You might find a part or item that hasn't been produced for twenty years.

There's a restaurant by the name of Little Italy (68500 Overseas Highway, 305-664-4472) one mile to the south. The restaurant was rated "excellent" with moderate prices by the marina staff, and they will provide shuttle service for you, both to and from. There are other services that the folks who run this marina are willing to provide, and it seems that you just have to ask in order for your wishes to be satisfied. They will help you get a rental car and pick you up at the airport . . . in Marathon. Miami, Newark, and Atlanta are just not in the cards.

The one inviolate caveat at this marina is: NO PETS. Not maybe. Not now. Not ever.

Sea Bird Marina (305) 664-2871 (800) 640-3303
www.seabirdmarina.com

Approach depth—6¹/₂-7 feet (northeasterly basin)
3¹/₂ feet (southwesterly basin)
Dockside depth—10-15 feet (northeasterly basin)
3-3¹/₂ feet (southwesterly basin)
Accepts transients—yes
Type of docking—fixed wooden piers
Dockside power connections—30 and 50 amp
Dockside water connections—yes
Cable television hookup—yes
Phone hookup—yes
Showers—yes
Fuel—gas at the marina; diesel delivered by truck
Ship's store—minimally and eclectically stocked past the usual fishing gear
Restaurant—transportation provided

Route to Western Florida

Flashing daybeacon #1 marks the ICW's passage past the northern tip of a huge bank of shallow water known and charted as Old Dan Bank. This marker also serves as the southeasternmost point of an alternate passage that cuts northwest and north to an eventual intersection with the western mainland Florida coastline. This is the easternmost (northernmost) of three possible routes to reach this destination from the Florida Keys, and Marathon in particular. We shall take a careful look at all three of these routes in a separate section at the end of this chapter.

Long Key Viaduct

After skirting past the northern tip of Old Dan Bank, the ICW continues on to the southwest for an eventual meeting with the Channel Key Banks and Channel Key Pass. This is a long run of almost 5 nautical miles. For much of this distance, the Long Key Viaduct will be visible south of your course

Long Key Viaduct

line. This is one of the most amazing man-made structures in the Florida Keys, particularly amazing when you consider that it was constructed in 1905.

Anyone who even knows a smattering of Florida history will recognize the name of Henry Flagler. This giant of a man almost single-handedly brought development to the eastern coastline of Florida, eventually pushing "his railroad" all the way south to Key West. Out of all the many bridges that were constructed as part of this remarkable railway system, Mr. Flager was proudest of the Long Key Viaduct. In fact, he used it in publicity photo after publicity photo.

Long Key Viaduct spans a width of 2¾ miles, and is composed of 180 concrete, semicircular arches, each some 50 feet wide. There was no other bridge in the USA of this type in those days, and it was considered a marvel.

Today, a new bridge has replaced Mr. Flagler's remarkable achievement, but the old Viaduct is still quite visible, just south of the new bridge. Pause for a few minutes in your waterborne trip to admire this monument from an earlier age that will not come again.

For those who are interested in learning more about the Long Key Viaduct and Mr. Flager's amazing railroad, we highly recommend the Web site, "Mike's Railway History" at http://mikes.railhistory.railfan.net/r053.html

Grassy Key Bank Anchorage (Standard Mile 1181) (24 46.483 North/080 56.506 West)

After cutting through Channel Key Pass, the

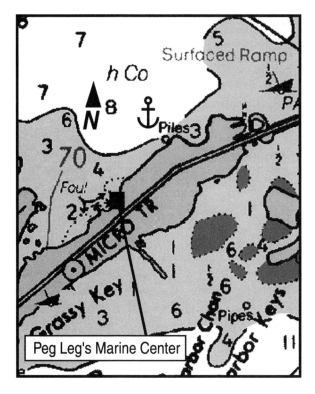

Peg Leg's Marine Center

Waterway skirts well north of the long shoal that flanks the western side of Tom's Harbor Channel, and then north also of another lengthy shoal known as Grassy Key Bank. East of this latter patch of shallows, cruisers can find good anchorage off the shores of Grassy Key to the south, near the charted notation, "Piles." Excellent soundings of at least 6½ to 7 hold to within 150 to 200 yards of the shoreline. As you might imagine, there is superb shelter to the south, southeast, and southwest, with some protection to the east and west as well. Strong blows from the north or northeast call for another strategy.

The adjacent Grassy Key shoreline is overlooked by a trailer park fronted by a cordoned-off swimming area. Just east of the park, cruisers will spy a private residence with its own dock. We usually try to drop the hook 150 yards north of this private pier.

In all save fresh northerly winds, this is a superior anchorage with pleasant surroundings. However, before committing once and for all to the idea of spending the evening here, may we suggest that you read on. There are some even more attractive havens just a bit farther along.

Peg Leg's Marine Center (Standard Mile 1181) (24 46.094 North/080 56.694 West)

Peg Leg's Marine Center overlooks the northerly banks of Grassy Key, northeast of the charted "Micro Tr" and southwest of the anchorage reviewed above. The approach channel is leanly outlined by a few white floats and one white-and-orange "No Wake" buoy. Low-water approach depths run to only 4½ feet, with similar soundings dockside. Only vessels drawing 4 feet or less need apply here for dockage.

Peg Leg's boasts six transient slips and a huge dry-stack storage building. There's not much in the way of razzle-dazzle here, and it would be bumpy in a fresh north wind. Nevertheless, this is a clean marina. Should you decide to stay, you'll find fixed wooden piers, 30- and 50-amp electrical service, waste pump-out, dockside water connections, plus (surprisingly enough) cable television hookups. There are no showers, but they do have an on-site Laundromat, plus propane fill-ups and gasoline. No diesel fuel is available. Mechanical repairs are offered for both gasoline and diesel-power plants. The adjacent ship's store is one of the better non-chain operations of its type that we reviewed in and near Marathon.

Peg Leg's is located right next to the

Peg Leg's Marine Center (Grassy Key)

Dolphin Research Center (see below) on Grassy Key, a definite plus if you have a shred of interest in marine mammals. Check with the marina staff for more information.

The food facilities are a bit on the thin side when it comes to selection, pizza and deli items being the principal offerings. Hours of operation are 3 P.M. to 9 P.M. There is also a Tiki Hut with beer and wine sales on site. If want to hang out where you're going to be offered a sit-down dinner, then you might opt to keep going.

Peg Leg's Marine Center (305) 289-9320

Approach depth—4 1/2 feet (minimum)
Dockside depth—4$\frac{1}{2}$ feet (minimum)
Accepts transients—yes
Type of piers—fixed wooden

Dockside power connections—30 and 50 amp
Dockside water connections—eyes
Waste pump-out—yes
Cable hookup—yes
Laundromat—yes
Fuel—gasoline only
Mechanical repairs—yes, both gas and diesel
Ship's store—yes (complete)
Restaurant—pizza parlor and deli on site

Grassy Key Anchorage (Standard Mile 1183.5) (24 45.832 North/080 57.913 West)

After clearing Grassy Key Bank, cruisers can take a lazy turn to the south (being SURE to stay well west of the bank) and anchor northeast of the "Obstn" notation, off the northwesterly shores of Grassy Key. Minimum 6-foot depths hold to within 100 yards of the

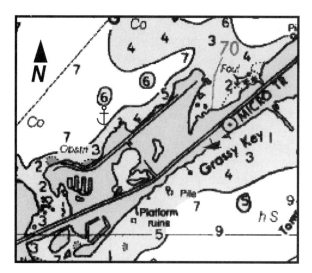

shores, though you must take care to avoid the correctly charted 3-foot cove just to the southwest.

Cruisers approaching this anchorage will sight an artificial breakwater that resembles a point of land just to the east. You can come close to slipping behind the lee of this point, but depths start to rise if you actually come abeam of its northerly tip. We suggest that you feel your way along with the sounder and drop anchor about 100 yards west of the artificial point, just before coming abeam of its northerly tip.

The adjacent shoreline is overlooked by some fine homeplaces, which make for interesting viewing from the water. There is good protection to the south, southeast, and southwest, but this anchorage is wide open to winds blowing from any other direction. Check out the latest NOAA weather forecast (hoping that it might be correct this time) and make a decision about whether to stop here accordingly.

Grassy Key Dolphin Research Center

The Grassy Key Dolphin Center will be discovered just southwest of Peg Leg's Marine Center, reviewed above. For those of you who can remember back far enough to the days of black-and-white television, anyway, you can connect to Flipper, the television star, here. This is where Flipper is buried. And you thought that he—it was really a she—was buried in Hollywood.

The facility is open, for a price, to the public. You can have a dolphin "encounter" here, which is what the Dolphin Research Center calls swimming with the dolphins. This exercise is so popular that you will need a reservation and something around $100 to have your encounter. Call (305) 289-0002. Of course, you will have to know something about swimming to do this; otherwise, your experience would be called "drowning with the dolphins." If you'd like to leave some more of your money behind, you can adopt a dolphin and become "parents" to the critter for $200 a year. There is no word on whether you'll have to fight for parental rights when your year runs out.

When not encountering with humans in an up-close-and-personal style, the dolphins put on shows, which are pretty much like dolphin shows everywhere else in the country. Dolphins are usually a big draw wherever they are; even sailors who have sailed across oceans can't resist pointing out a pod of the things in local waters. They are intelligent and they appear to be friendly because of that smile they always have on their faces. It is not always the case.

A free-swimming dolphin that hangs out in the Intracoastal Waterway, north of Venice, Florida, has gotten so many free handouts that the people up that way call him (her?) Beggar. It's against the law for humans to feed wild dolphins. It is, however, not against the law for wild dolphins to bite the hand that feeds them, which Beggar has managed to do upon occasion, engendering a special marine warning from the Florida Fish and Wildlife Commission.

"My, Beggar, what big TEETH you have!"

Long Point Key Anchorage
(Standard Mile 1185)
(24 45.182 North/080 59.481 West)

Now, we know it's not the deepest anchorage to be found in this part of the Florida Keys, and you must avoid an unmarked shoal to get there, but for our money, the waters northwest of Long Point Key (southwest of charted Burnt Point) make for one of the most beautiful places that you will ever find anywhere to spend an evening, or even several evenings. During our last visit, we spotted a

Catboat in Long Point Key Anchorage

classic wooden-hulled, catboat swinging languidly on the hook in this anchorage. Set against the backdrop of swaying palms and attractive homes, our picture of this craft will always remind us of what it's really like to go a-cruising in the Florida Keys.

Well, with all that out of the way, let's get down to the nuts and bolts of this anchorage. Low-water depths of 5 feet can be maintained as long as you stay at least 300 yards off Burnt Point's shallow easterly shoreline and 400 yards short of the rear (southern) tip of the cove.

If winds are wafting from the south, southeast, southwest, or even the east and northeast, no problem, you are in fat city. On the other hand, strong blows from the north and northwest call for, sadly, continuing your cruise in search for another overnight haven.

Bamboo Key Anchorage
(Standard Mile 1185.5)
(24 45.335 North/081 00.412 West)

Bamboo Key is found just to the west of the anchorage reviewed above, north of Fat Deer Key. It is a small landmass, which is delightfully in its natural state. Minimum depths of 5 feet can be held to within 300 yards of its northwesterly shoreline. In fair weather and light airs or with moderate winds blowing from the southeast, this is yet another delightful spot to while away an evening. Don't do this if bad weather appears to be in the offing. Even if you are careful, one of those unforecast nighttime thunderstorms could come along, as they often do, and help you practice your imitation of a Mexican jumping bean.

Russel Key Anchorage
(Standard Mile 1187.5)
(24 44.435 North/081 01.990 West)

South of the ICW's flashing daybeacon

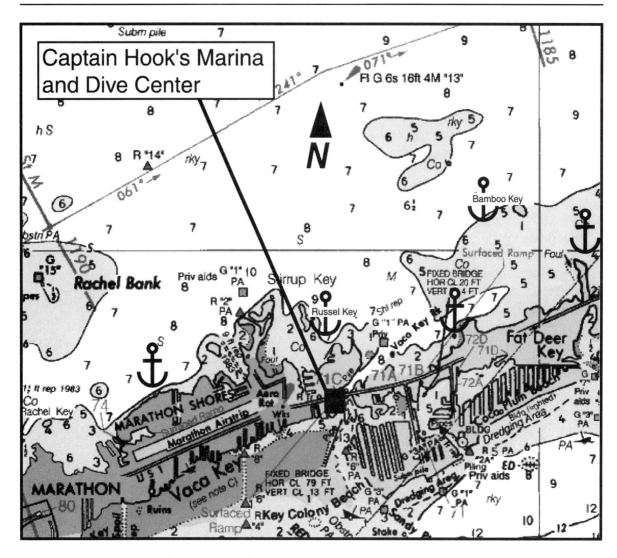

#13, cruisers can cut to the south and begin an approach to treacherous Vaca Cut. Between the Waterway and this channel's northerly entrance, there are two additional anchorage opportunities to the east and west, respectively.

First up are the waters east of charted Russel Key, west of the Vaca Cut approach passage. This key is privately owned, and cruisers visiting these waters will gaze longingly at the elegant home, private beach, and dock, not to mention the lush vegetation. Don't even think about dinghying ashore. This is very private property. Nothing can prevent us cruisers from enjoying the crystal-clear water and the island's eye candy, however.

Another unsuspected aspect of Russel Key is that, contrary to what chart 11451 would lead you to believe, on the water, this island actually appears to be two keys. The southerly isle is the site of the private residence.

Try anchoring about 75 yards east of the private pier. Minimum depths run about 6 feet, but don't be surprised by soundings of 8 to 8½ feet. The key and the adjacent mainland provide a good lee to the west, southwest, and (to a lesser extent) the southeast. This anchorage is wide open to the north, northeast, and the east. This would be a decidedly bad spot to spend the night if the wind exceeds 8 knots from any of these quarters.

We did notice that the bottom east of Russel Key is a little on the rocky side. We were able to get our Danforth anchor to catch on the first try, but be aware that you might have to take a little extra time to find just the right spot to secure the hook.

This is another of our favorite overnight anchorages on these waters. If nothing else, be sure to give Russel Key a look. It is well worth the extra effort.

Fat Deer Key Anchorage
(Standard Mile 1187.5)
(24 44.547 North/081 00.657 West)

Check out the approach passage to Vaca Cut on chart 11451. Locate unlighted daybeacon #1, the northeasternmost marker on the channel, and trace your way to the east-northeast. Notice the tongue of deeper water that lies north of the blunt point of land on the northwestern shores of Fat Deer Key. This spot can make for a good overnight anchorage with southerly winds in the offing, but depths are not as good as those promised by 11451.

In reality, we discovered that low-water 5-foot soundings continued only to a position abeam of the westerly extreme of the blunt point lying to the south. Farther to the east, depths rise to 4-foot levels at low water. We suggest dropping anchor off the northwesterly tip of the blunt point.

Clearly this anchorage is only good for vessels drawing 4½ feet or (preferably) a bit less. Swing room is virtually unlimited, as has been true for all the anchorages reviewed so far in this chapter. Currents can run swiftly on these waters, courtesy of nearby Vaca Cut, so be SURE the anchor is well set.

The adjacent shoreline supports moderate residential development, as well as some all-natural stretches. There's nothing visually unpleasing about this haven; it's just not quite as pretty as some of the anchorages described above.

Vaca Cut
(Standard Mile 1187.5)

Are you getting tired of hearing the words, "strong tidal currents"? Well, sorry to say you are going to have to hear them one more time. Vaca Cut, south of the Waterway's flashing day-beacon #13, has the dubious distinction of having some of the swiftest Florida Keys currents yet. One warm, humid, September afternoon, we sat in awe as we watched the current race under the Vaca Cut Bridge. This is NOT the spot where one would want the motor to conk out.

In our next breath, we should quickly note that Vaca Cut is crossed by a fixed bridge with a measly 13 feet of vertical clearance. There are some low-key marina facilities and one possible anchorage south of the bridge, but all but small craft will need to approach these cruising finds from the Hawk Channel side. As such, we will detail the seaward side of Vaca Cut as part of our Hawk Channel coverage later in this chapter and will not further review these waters here.

ICW—LONG KEY TO VACA CUT NAVIGATION

The ICW section between Long Key and Vaca Cut is, in some ways, a very typical stretch of the Florida Keys Waterway. There is one cut between a shallow bank and some seriously long distances between aids to navigation. If you don't have a GPS interfaced with a laptop aboard, be ready to practice your best DR navigation, and be sure to have compass courses computed ahead of time.

What is atypical about this section of the ICW, however, is that many of the various markers actually sit a surprisingly long distance south or north of the Waterway's ideal track. Don't worry, we'll outline all these anomalies below in detail.

The various side waters and anchorages along the way, all of which lie south of the ICW, present no unusual navigational difficulty, but you must still pay attention to business. Shallow water is not uncommon in this region, and a navigational mistake could make Sea Tow's whole day.

On the ICW We have already met some really long runs between aids to navigation on the Florida Keys ICW, but the trek from the southwesterly terminus of the Bowlegs Cut (unlighted daybeacon #97 and flashing daybeacon #98) to flashing daybeacon #1, north of Old Dan Bank, may be the grand-daddy of them all. Would you believe the distance is slightly better than 6.2 nautical miles?

Be SURE to come abeam of #1 by at least 200 yards to its northwesterly side. South of this aid to navigation, the half-foot depths of Old Dan Bank are a real hazard.

Between Bowlegs Cut and flashing day-beacon #1, skippers can break off to the south and visit two marinas plus one anchorage.

Jewfish Bush Banks Anchorage Unlighted daybeacon #1X, north of Fiesta Key, is a great help in finding your way to the otherwise unmarked anchorage west of Jewfish Bush Banks. Set course from the ICW to come abeam of #1X by about .6 nautical miles to its easterly side. Then, ease your way a bit farther to the east-southeast, dropping the hook before approaching to within less than 300 yards of the 1-foot bank shallows. You should also be on guard against drifting too far to the south. This unhappy maneuver would land you in the large shelf of shallows that shelve out from the westerly end of the Channel Five cause-way.

Fiesta Key/KOA Marina Approach this facility strictly by way of the deeper waters east of unlighted daybeacon #1X. We made the mistake of trying to following a white PVC-pipe-outlined channel across the long tongue of shoal that extends north from Fiesta Key. It was a really hot day to have to push the boat off the bottom, but we had that privilege.

Unless you cherish thoughts of having

the same experience, stay a good 200 yards east of #1X. Cruise to the south, watching for a single white PVC pipe with an orange warning cone perched atop it. Leave this unusual aid to navigation off your port side, and cruise straight into the enclosed dockage basin.

Be it known that this procedure can be a little tricky. There is PLENTY of shallow water all around this approach. We suggest that you take your time and keep an eagle eye on the sounder.

Sea Bird Marina Successful entry into this marina is pretty much just the opposite of the strategy outlined above. In this case, you want to be SURE to stay 300 yards (or more) WEST of unlighted daybeacon #1X and the shallows striking north from Fiesta Key. If depths start to rise, retreat a bit to the west, and see if soundings improve.

Cruise south, keeping well west of Fiesta Key, and watch for the twin dockage basins associated with Sea Bird Marina. The northeasterly basin is the deeper of the two, and most cruising-sized craft will want to cruise directly into this harbor. Call the dockmaster ahead of time on the VHF or cellular phone for instructions as to slip assignment.

Alternate Old Dan Bank Channel As noted above, the ICW skirts just north of the shoal known as Old Dan Bank. There is also a scantily marked passage nearer to shore, which begins with unlighted daybeacon #1X, north of Fiesta Key. We discovered some definite 4-foot low-water depths on this passage, possibly even an occasional 3½-foot sounding or two. If this relatively thin water is not a problem for your vessel, and for some reason, you want to pass closer to shore, this alternate route is a possibility.

To run the cut from east to west, come abeam of #1X by about 100 yards to its northerly side. Turn to the southwest and cruise along for some 2 nautical miles. Use your binoculars to carefully pick out unlighted daybeacon #2X. Pass about 50 yards southeast of #2X. Continue on the same heading, pointing to pass unlighted daybeacon #4X by about the same distance to its southeasterly quarter. After leaving #4X behind by some .6 nautical miles, your track will lead to a wide swath of deeper water.

On the ICW From a position northwest of flashing daybeacon #1, at Old Dan Bank, continue on a southwesterly heading. After about 1.7 nautical miles, unlighted daybeacon #2 will come abeam well north of your course line. Don't approach #2 closely. It is located hard by a patch of rocky shallows.

Another 2.1 nautical miles will see you abeam of unlighted daybeacon #4. Be SURE to pass at least 100 yards southeast of #4. Shoal water is encroaching on this aid to navigation from the north.

Between #1 and #4, the ICW parallels the fabulous Long Key Viaduct, some 2 nautical miles south of the Waterway's track. Be sure to use your binocs for a better view of this engineering marvel.

Next up is an important series of three markers outlining Channel Key Pass. Very shallow water (would you believe a half-foot or less) lies immediately to the north and south of this cut. Navigators with enough sense to get out of the rain will want to pay very close attention to this passage. Come abeam and pass flashing daybeacon #5 to its fairly immediate northerly side, and then pass between unlighted daybeacons #7 and #8.

The next ICW marker is flashing daybeacon #9. This aid to navigation actually sits almost .6 nautical miles south of the Waterway's nominal track. We suggest that you stay .6 nautical miles north of #9, as this aid marks very shoal water to the south that seems to be slowly spreading around the daybeacon itself.

From #9, you should next set course to pass at least 300 yards north of flashing daybeacon #11. This marker denotes the northerly tip of Grassy Key Bank. This shoal's half-foot depths demand the greatest respect. Stay well north of #11 and all will be well. Between #9 and #11, mariners can cut south and visit the anchorage east of Grassy Key Bank and nearby Peg Leg Marina.

Grassy Key Bank Anchorage Leave the Waterway about halfway between flashing daybeacons #9 and #11. Cut south and set course for the point of land immediately west of the small, charted, 3-foot cove. As you approach shoreline, watch for a trailer park with a swimming area, outlined by small white floats. Just to the east of the park, you will spy a private home with its own pier. Drop anchor some 150 yards north of this dock.

Peg Leg's Marine Center This entrance channel to Peg Leg's Marine Center is

located southwest of the anchorage described above, and northeast of the charted "Micro Tr." Use your binoculars to pick out the few white floats and one orange-and-white "No Wake" buoy that outline the marina approach cut. Cruise between these informal aids to navigation and enter the partially enclosed harbor. Remember that low-water depths are only about 4½ feet on this entrance channel.

On the ICW From a position well north of flashing daybeacon #11, it's a much shorter run of only 2.3 nautical miles to the next Waterway aid to navigation, unlighted daybeacon #12. Point to come abeam of #12 by some 200 yards to its southern side. After cruising 1.4 miles from #11, captains might choose to cut south-southeast and visit the anchorage off Grassy Key.

Grassy Key Anchorage The real trick to accessing this anchorage, without meeting up with the bottom, is to stay well west of the shallows associated with Grassy Key Bank. Don't cut farther to the southeast until your craft is within .7 nautical miles of the Grassy Key banks. Watch for a large private home with its own pier, with an artificial breakwater/point just to the east. Drop anchor just as the northerly tip of this point comes abeam. Do NOT make a closer approach to shore as depths quickly begin to shelve up!

Long Point Key Anchorage South of unlighted daybeacon #12, skippers can track their way 2.1 nautical miles south-southeast to the delightful anchorage behind Burnt Point and Long Point Key. Don't go anywhere near Burnt Point, and stay at least .2 nautical miles west of the Long Point Key Shoreline. A very broad band of 4-foot waters extends well out from these east-side banks. Drop the hook near the charted "Co" notation on 11451. Settle back for an evening of relaxation, and enjoy the eye candy.

Bamboo Key Anchorage Also accessible south-southwest of unlighted daybeacon #12 is the anchorage northwest of Bamboo Key. Set course so as to pass east of the slightly shallower, rocky patch of charted waters southeast of flashing daybeacon #13. Once this hazard is in your wake, cut just a tiny bit farther to the west, and point to come abeam of Bamboo Key by some 300 yards off its northwesterly shoreline.

When leaving this anchorage, cruisers headed for points west (south) can cut west, bypass the rocky shallows mentioned above, and rejoin the ICW at unlighted daybeacon #14. This will cut a nice corner off the Waterway and not bring you near to any shoals. What a treat!

On the ICW From unlighted daybeacon #12, continue on the same track, pointing to come abeam of flashing daybeacon #13 by about 100 yards to its northerly side. At this point, the channel swings a bit farther to the southwest. Your next mark will be unlighted daybeacon #14, which should be passed to its southeasterly side. A short stretch southwest of #13, captains might choose to break off to the south and visit the two anchorages near Vaca Cut or even risk this current strewn channel.

Russel Key Anchorage Steer south from the Waterway's flashing daybeacon #13 for 1.9 nautical miles, and point to come abeam of Russel Key by some 100 yards to its easterly side. Do NOT attempt to approach from the isle's westerly quarter, and cruise around its southerly tip. Depths rise to 2-foot levels at lightning speed.

On the water, Russel Key will actually appear to be two different islands. Watch for a private pier stretching out from the easterly shores of the more southerly of the two. Try anchoring about 75 yards east of this structure. Remember, DON'T try to dinghy ashore. Russel Key is VERY private!

Fat Deer Key Anchorage Entry into this anchorage is complicated by the fact that chart 11451 no longer accurately represents bottom contours on these waters. According to the chart, a wide tongue of deep water extends well east of the blunt point of land, east of Vaca Cut's unlighted daybeacon #1. We discovered during our on-the-water research that 5-foot minimum depths can only be carried to a point where the northwesterly tip of the blunt point comes abeam to the south. Even a stone's throw farther to the east will land you in 4 feet of water.

Come abeam of #1 by some 50 yards to its easterly side. Turn to the east-northeast. Note that a turn due east from #1 would encroach on the tongue of correctly charted, 2-foot shallows striking north from the southerly banks. Ease your way to a position off the blunt point's northwesterly corner. Drop anchor here amidst 5 feet of water at low tide (NOT the 7-foot depths shown on chart 11451). Don't attempt to cruise any farther to the east unless your vessel is very comfortable with 4-foot depths.

Vaca Cut Chart 11451 depicts a single aid to navigation, unlighted daybeacon #1, outlining the approach to Vaca Cut. Actually, there are now two markers, the second being an unlighted daybeacon #2.

As you would have probably surmised without our telling you, pass between #1 and #2.

To continue on to the 13-foot fixed bridge, hold to the passage's midwidth and be ready for some serious tidal currents. As most cruising-sized vessels will not be able to clear this fixed span, we will cover the marinas and anchorage possibilities along the southerly half of Vaca Cut in our Hawk Channel section later in this chapter.

ICW—Vaca Cut to Moser Channel

West of Vaca Cut (and particularly west of Marathon Shores), the ICW begins to parallel the heart of the Marathon community. Marinas and other pleasure-craft facilities begin to pepper the shoreline south of the Waterway. There are also a few anchorages near the easterly portion of the waters covered in this section, principally off Marathon Shores and Rachel Key.

Of course, this section of the ICW eventually leads to important Moser Channel. While it's really NOT the end of the ICW, many cruisers, even veteran captains, tend to the think of the Moser Channel as the westerly (southerly) terminus of the Florida Keys inland Waterway. We will see that this is not the case, but there is no denying that the Moser cut is one of the principal routes by which cruising captains can cut inside from Hawk Channel or leave the ICW and head for the briny blue.

Marathon Shores Anchorage
(Standard Mile 1189)
(24 43.937 North/081 03.608 West)
South of the Waterway's unlighted daybeacon #14, mariners can cruise 1.7 nautical miles

to within 100 yards of the Marathon Shores banks. We suggest anchoring south of the capital "R" in the charted notation "Surfaced Ramp." This spot features minimum depths of 6 feet and tons of elbowroom, plus excellent shelter to the south, southeast, and southwest. There is even a little shelter to the east, courtesy of the oblong landmass known (and charted) as Stirrup Key. Strong or even moderate winds blowing out of the north, northeast, or northwest call for getting back out the chart and this guidebook and selecting an alternate spot.

The Marathon Airport and some very dense residential development sit just south of these waters. While anchored tranquilly in this haven, we have watched many small planes winging their way in and out of this small airstrip. If you happen to see what appears to be a Communist jet fighter, emblazoned by a red star, taking off or landing, don't worry. You're not about to be strafed, but you will have just observed one of Marathon's most unique shoreside attractions. Morgan got to go up in this plane and wrote the following first-person account.

Czech Fighter Plane (Marathon)

Tropical Fighters of Florida

The green-and-brown camouflage paint job and the prominent red star of Communism on the jet fighter airplane are what first catch your attention at Paradise Aviation, a fixed base operator at the Marathon Airport in the Florida Keys.

What is a Communist aircraft doing here, parked right by U.S. Highway 1? Cuban defector?

Not quite. The jet fighter is Czech, a 1978 Aero Vodochody L-39, an aircraft identical to the one that James Bond "appropriated" to escape certain death in the movie *Never Say Die*. The aircraft is a tactical fighter with all its systems operating. If it had rockets or bombs

attached, they'd work. It is owned and flown by Ed Steigerwald of Marathon. He'll let you fly it. And I did.

It is, as they used to say at Walt Disney World, a definite E-Ticket Ride.

If you have never flown a jet fighter before, and I had not, you sit in the rear-tandem seat, behind Steigerwald. If you've put a few hours (and many dollars) into the aircraft, you get to fly up front.

Steigerwald operates Tropical Fighters of Florida, which flies out of Marathon. His brochure offers the thrill of a lifetime. It all starts with a preflight indoctrination, where Steigerwald describes what the plane is all about and what you can expect when you get into the air. He is thorough, low-key, and direct. You've heard that voice of quiet competency before, from the public address system emanating from the cockpit of commercial airliners.

Next comes a walk-around, out on the hard. Up close and personal, you get to look at the wings, the landing gear (three-finger clearance on the struts), the wheels, the flaps, ailerons, the engine intakes, and exhaust. Then you get into the plane by climbing up the side, putting your feet onto a retractable step, and then into slots on the side of the aircraft. Steigerwald climbs up behind you and helps you into your parachute harness and then the seat and shoulder belts.

You don't get that kind of service on Delta. And neither does Delta explain to you that in case there is a problem with the aircraft, the pilot will flip it upside-down and you can undo your seatbelt, fall free, and trip your own parachute. If you've flown much, you've probably ignored the safety briefing on a commercial airliner. On the ground in Marathon, Ed Steigerwald had one hundred percent of my attention.

There are some caveats associated with the experience of flying in a jet fighter. A couple of red handles in the back are "no touch." One will jettison the canopy and the other will take control of the landing gear. You learn the location of controls for the flaps, what the green and red warning lights associated with the landing gear mean, where the brakes are, and what the stick in front of you will do. You put on the headset with the voice-actuated microphone. You feel ready. Steigerwald's filtered voice comes into your head. *Are you ready?* "Roger that."

The payoff is when the fighter is lined up on the runway, with the white centerline stripe on the concrete bisecting the aircraft. Steigerwald pushes the throttle forward and the aircraft surges ahead, gathering speed, creating lift over the wings. The sound is behind you, and the headset insulates you from cockpit noise. But nothing takes away from the 270-degree view you have as Marathon drops away and you climb out. The ocean and Florida Bay are visible all around you.

Low clouds pop up ahead and Steigerwald turns the controls over to me. I execute a 180 turn in a 30-degree bank back to the west, losing altitude in the process and then gaining too much back. Things happen very, very quickly at 250 miles an hour.

Steigerwald takes the controls, and we execute a 3-G turn and climb. I start to sweat just a little bit. And I grunt with the strain of flexing my stomach muscles to keep my blood from leaving my head and pooling in my lower extremities. Then we pull some negative Gs, where you become weightless. The straps hold you in your seat.

And would I like an aileron roll? (That's a 360-degree roll around the aircraft's horizontal axis.) Sure. Steigerwald did it slow. Your world turns and your perspective goes right out the window. It's part of the experience.

Down below I see a sailboat, small as a tiny, floating toy in a bathtub, etching a feather of a wake onto the green water behind it, as it moves east to west on Hawk Channel. Speedboats leave long white trails behind them. The channels around Vaca Key, upon which Marathon sits, show up in graphic relief. This kind of perspective is what mariners pray for and will never get.

We cross the active runway at Marathon at several thousand feet, turn left to enter the traffic pattern, and execute a downwind leg that nearly takes us to the Seven Mile Bridge.

Then it's left again into a descending turn that keeps us over U.S. Highway 1. The runway appears ahead and we touch down at 130 knots with nary a bump. Steigerwald kisses the fighter onto the concrete.

It's over. I have flown a tactical jet fighter, albeit not with the precision I'd like to remember. It is an experience to put away, to cherish from the comfort of an easy chair. And point of fact, it only took my body about three hours to adjust to being back in a 1-G environment, something I am very comfortable with. My body loves 1-G.

For more information on Tropical Fighters of Florida, you can call (305) 289-0007. Toll-free, the number is 1-877-JET-8234. If you talk personally with Ed Steigerwald, tell him that "Ace" suggested you call.

Rachel Key Anchorage
(Standard Mile 1189.5)
(24 43.693 North/081 04.549 West)

Rachel Key is a tiny, all-natural island that sits between the shallower waters of Rachel Key Bank and the sharp point of land west of Marathon Shores and the Marathon Airport. It lies almost due south of unlighted daybeacon #15.

It is best to depart the Waterway well northeast of #15 and then work your way slowly south and then west (more on these maneuvers in the next section below). You can then come abeam of Rachel Key by some 50 yards to its northerly side and anchor. Cautious navigators might also choose to drop the hook 75 yards or so off the isle's westerly shoreline. The first of these havens offers shelter from southerly breezes, while the second gives a lee to the east. By all accounts this is NOT a foul-weather stop, however. Winds from any other direction would almost certainly make for a

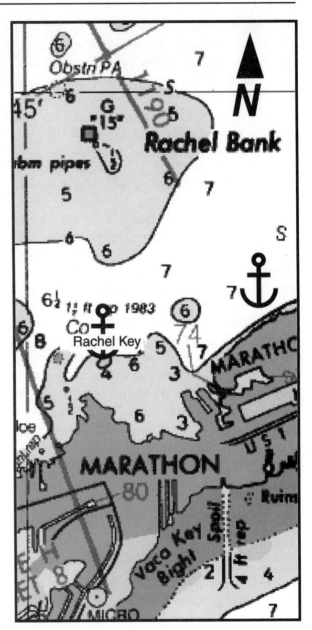

rather bumpy evening, possibly with your hard-won dinner ending up in your lap.

Marathon Northern Shore and Associated Marina Facilities

After skirting just north of Rachel Bank, the

ICW channel continues on to the southwest and passes between unlighted daybeacon #18 and flashing daybeacon #17. Once these aids to navigation are in your wake, there's nothing but deep water to the south, between the Waterway and Marathon's northerly banks. An extensive collection of marinas, yacht clubs, and repair yards guards this shoreline. Below, we will review these various facilities moving east to west.

Blackfin Resort and Marina
(Standard Mile 1191.5)
(24 43.026 North/081 04.972 West)

Blackfin Resort and Marina is the easternmost of the two marinas, east of charted Pretty Joe Rock. Impressive approach soundings of 8 feet (more typically 9 to 12 feet), with at least 10 feet of water dockside, are a distinctive characteristic of this marina. You won't find many deeper dockage basins anywhere in the Florida Keys.

Captains must take GREAT care, however, to stay well east of charted Pretty Joe Rock. A portion of the "Rock" is actually a small island with its own little house precariously perched on its shores. Shallows stretch out for surprising distances from the small isle. The easterly portion of this shoal is marked with a piece of PVC pipe. Careless mariners still manage to find the bottom here.

Blackfin Resort is transient friendly. Dockage is found at fixed wooden finger piers. They aren't new but are carefully maintained and in first-class shape. Dockside power connections are of the 30- to 50-amp variety and the obligatory fresh water hookups are there for taking, too. Some light mechanical repairs can be arranged through local, independent contractors.

The showers here are vintage Florida Keys—clean, not new. Just two but they get the job done. There's also a Laundromat on premises.

Blackfin has the obligatory swimming pool, a saltwater swimming area, and man-made sandy beach on the bay side, and kayak and boat rentals. If you need something (anything), Home Depot is across the street and Boater's World (5001 Overseas Highway, 305-743-7707) is only a block away. Both are located on the opposite side of U.S. Highway 1.

The on-site Hurricane Raw Bar and Restaurant (305-743-2220) is open seven days a week, with blues and jazz in the lounge for the late-night crowd.

Wanda Brock, who runs Blackfin, hails from Montana and has the air about of her of a woman who does not suffer fools gladly. You can imagine her running a cattle spread back home, had she not moved to the Florida Keys.

Blackfin Resort and Marina (305) 743-2393
(800) 548-5397
www.blackfinresort.com

Approach depth—8-12 feet (low tide)
Dockside depth—10 feet (minimum)
Accepts transients—yes
Type of piers—finger piers, wooden
Dockside power connections—30 to 50 amp
Dockside water connections—yes
Showers—yes
Laundromat—yes
Mechanical repairs—mechanic on call
Restaurant—on-site

Banana Bay Resort and Marina
(Standard Mile 1191.5)
(24 43.036 North/081 05.050 West)

Banana Bay Resort and Marina sits hard by Blackfin Resort (reviewed above), just to the west. Banana Bay is a small marina that has about 40 slips. Entrance depths are considerably shallower here than at nearby Blackfin, with some low-water soundings in the approach channel of only 4½ feet. Happily, in the dockage basin, cruisers will discover at least 10 feet of water.

As we warned above for Blackfin Marina, visiting navigators must watch out for Pretty Joe Rock just to the west. It's on the charts, but careless mariners still manage to find it.

Banana Bay accepts transients and even live-aboards. Boats are tied up at fixed wooden finger piers, which are in good repair. Many of the vessels we observed at this marina were tied up stern to, in the Mediterranean manner. Dockside power connections run 30 to 50 amps, and there is a fresh water hookup at every slip. Cable television and telephone connections are in the offing as well. For the sportsminded, there are also two tennis courts and a swimming pool.

The showers at Banana Bay total four. They are unisex, clean, but not fancy. The rest room and shower are together, Old Florida-style, and in a separate building on the eastern side of the marina. The rest room/showers have hair dryers as standard. All these facilities are a bit small, but they smelled great. That is either a sign of cleanliness or a jaded nose on the part of your friendly reviewer.

The on-site Laundromat is by the swimming pool. Go for a swim and do your laundry at the same time. "Lemme see now, do I need another beer, and did I put the laundry in the dryer yet?"

The on-premises, full-service restaurant is known as the Banana Cabana Restaurant (305-289-1232). The Sunset Tiki Bar, adjacent to the marina, opens at 5 P.M. This is a great spot to watch the sunset, and you'll not suffer from dehydration while you're waiting for the sun to sink below the horizon.

People in the Keys take sunsets seriously.

Maybe that is because there is usually something cold and tasty to drink, readily available each and every sunset. It is easy to become a "traditional" in the Keys. If you become too much of a traditional, however, you will probably end up riding a bicycle, eschewing shaving and bathing, and carrying all your possessions in a plastic grocery sack.

Banana Bay is located in the heart of downtown Marathon. It is close to everything, though you must walk through the property—and its full array of banana trees—to get to U.S. 1. West Marine (2055 Overseas Highway, 305-289-1009) is 1½ miles west. Boater's World (5001 Overseas Highway, 305-743-7707) is two blocks to the east.

Banana Bay Resort and Marina (305) 743-3500
http://www.bananabay.com

Approach depth—4½ feet (minimum)
Dockside depth—10 feet
Accepts transients—yes
Type of piers—fixed wooden finger piers
Dockside power connections—30-50 amp
Dockside water connections—yes
Cable hookup—yes
Phone hookup—yes
Showers—yes
Laundromat—yes, located by the swimming pool
Restaurant—on-site

Keys Boat Works (Standard Mile 1191.5) (24 42.975 North/081 05.389 West)

The largest pleasure-craft repair facility on the ICW side of Marathon lies some 1.5 nautical miles southeast of the Waterway's flashing daybeacon #17. Keys Boat Works overlooks Marathon's northerly shores, between Pretty Joe Rock and the unlighted daybeacon #1 associated with the Marathon Yacht Club (see below).

Keys Boat Works is a commercial, full-service boatyard and dockage basin. With storage for 185 boats, it's huge, but one must not mistake this for a marina or resort. While overnight transients are accepted, there are no frills here. On the other hand, they can get done what you need to have done and big jobs, heaven forbid that you should need one while cruising, are right up their alley.

There are fixed wooden piers in the well-sheltered dockage basin and some alongside docking as well. Minimum entrance depths run around 7 feet, and there is amazing 10+ feet of water in the yard's harbor. You can get 30- to 50-amp electrical service, dockside water, and a well-stocked on-site ship's store, but for the most part that's it. In no way do we mean for this review to denigrate this facility, but if you don't have a significant repair problem that needs immediate attention, there are other, fancier places to dock, which you would probably enjoy more.

Extensive mechanical repairs are offered for both gasoline and diesel-power plants. Haul-outs are accomplished by way of either a 15- ton or a 50-ton Travelift. If you can't get it fixed here, better check on how the new boat market has been doing lately.

The showers and bathrooms, one per gender, are in a separate temporary building in the marina. They are adequate, but you'll never feel that you are at the Ritz. The ladies facility carries this notice on the door: "WARNING TO ALL MEN. Do Not Use This Restroom. Lorena Bobbitt is watching!"

Nearby restaurants include the Stuffed Pig (3520 U.S. Highway 1, 305-743-4059) on the corner at U.S. 1, a few blocks away. For those with more refined tastes, Barracuda Grill (305-743-3314), also nearby, offers fine dining.

A word of caution: this boatyard is adjacent to a neighborhood that is at the bottom of the housing scale. It would be a bad place to "flash" a lot of money, unless you had Clint Eastwood along as a bodyguard. It is an area that gets constant police attention, however.

Keys Boat Works (305) 743-5583

Approach depth—7 feet
Dockside depth—10+ feet
Accepts transients—yes
Type of piers—fixed wooden, some alongside docking
Dockside power connections—30-50 amp
Dockside water connections—yes
Waste pump-out—honey wagon only
Showers—yes
Mechanical repairs—extensive
Ship's store—yes, no frills but all you will ever need
Restaurant—several nearby

Marathon Yacht Club
(Standard Mile 1191.5)
(24 42.813 North/081 05.759 West)

The impressive headquarters and dockage basin of the Marathon Yacht Club lie some 1.5 nautical miles south-southeast of the ICW's flashing daybeacon #17. Cruisers can cut a bit of distance off this run by leaving the Waterway .3 nautical miles northeast of #17.

There is one charted marker (unlighted daybeacon #1) and one uncharted one (unlighted daybeacon #2) that sit just north of the yacht club's dockage basin. A stone breakwater lies just to the east and serves to protect the entrance channel.

Minimum entrance depths are 8+ feet, and these impressive soundings are complimented by better than 10 feet of water alongside. If you have an especially deep-draft vessel in Marathon, then let's hope you can meet this club's dockage requirements, because you won't find a deeper slip any-where in the region.

Marathon Yacht Club accepts transients who are members of other yacht clubs with appropriate reciprocal privileges. The MYC is a member of the Florida Council of Yacht Clubs (FCYC), and those who belong to another club in this distinguished group are given full privileges. Members of non-FCYC yacht clubs may also stay here, but you will pay cash for the services that you require.

The Marathon Yacht Club does not employ a regular dockmaster. It is best to make certain you know the rules and slip availability before you arrive, so an advance call to the club is definitely in order.

The Marathon Yacht Club dockage basin is well sheltered from all but fresh northerly breezes. Slips will be discovered at fixed wooden piers (in good condition), featuring 30- to 50-amp power hookups, plus fresh water, cable television, and telephone con-nections. Waste pump-out is also available.

The club has two spotless, unisex showers. Surprising for a yacht club, MYC also features its own Laundromat with one washer and one dryer. And of course, there is a restaurant and bar on site.

The MYC dining room is open Tuesday through Saturday. Lunch is served from 11:30 A.M. to 1:30 P.M., while dinner is offered between the hours of 6:00 P.M. to 8:30 P.M. (except on Sundays when serving stops at 8:00 P.M.). There is also a Sunday brunch from 11:00 A.M. to 1:30 P.M.

Marathon Yacht Club (305) 743-6739

Approach depth—8+ feet
Dockside depth—10+ feet
Accepts transients—yes
Type of piers—fixed wooden

Dockside power connections—30-50 amp
Dockside water connections—yes
Waste pump-out—yes
Showers—yes, two unisex and very clean
Cable hookup—yes
Phone hookup—yes
Laundromat—one dryer and one washer
Restaurant—on site

Faro Blanco Marine Resort, Florida Bay Side (Standard Mile 1192) (24 42.652 North/081 06.234 West)

For many years now, captains have made a 90-degree turn to the south, some 300 yards southwest of the ICW's flashing daybeacon #17, and crossed the intervening 1.6 nautical miles of water to one of the most recognized marinas in the Florida Keys. Faro Blanco Marine Resort, Bayside is located hard by the charted "Tower Q Lt," east of the Fanny Keys.

This facility is famous, among other attrib-utes, for its easy access from the ICW and its signature lighthouse, which is lighted and even has a couple of apartments in it for those who have never stayed in a lighthouse before, which is most of us.

The entire Faro Blanco operation has recently changed hands, and the new owners are now operating the venerable, popular facility. Expect an infusion of cash and some updating of the physical plant and services.

Marina hours are 7 A.M. to 6 P.M. in the winter (the peak season) and 8 A.M. to 5 P.M. in the summer. The marina monitors VHF Channel 16 and the staff is very helpful in guiding people in. Transients are accepted, of course, because transient business is the backbone of what Faro Blanco is all about.

Faro Blanco, Bayside features two dockage basins, each with its own entrance. The har-bor to starboard (west side) seems destined for larger craft, while the one to port (east

Faro Blanco Marine Resort, Florida Bay Side

side) accommodates smaller vessels. Both basins are well sheltered by a concrete sea wall.

Minimum approach depths run 7 feet or better, with at least 6½ feet of water in the eastern harbor and 7 to 13 feet of depth in the west-side basin.

The marina's piers are of the fixed-wooden variety, and all are in good repair. All berths boast 30- to 50-amp electrical service, phone connections, cable television hookups, and dockside water. Waste pump-out is via a "honey wagon," and there is a $15 charge for this service.

Gasoline and diesel fuel are available at the fuel dock, adjacent to the lighthouse. There is access from both basins. In case of engine trouble, there is a mechanic on call.

The marina showers, while squeaky clean, are a bit of a hike from the marina, and they are rather old. The showers are located down low, in a tunnel behind the swimming pool and underneath the pool deck. In one, the black porcelain sink and commode remind us of what one might see in a house of someone "lost in the 1970s." The Laundromat is adequate, but it is found next to the showers, which puts it a far piece from the marina.

Just as you would expect of a full-service facility such as this, there is an on-site ship's and variety store, located just behind the gas dock. The offerings consist of a few basic ship items, plus beach-bait-and-tackle inventory.

We were reminded by the Faro Blanco personnel that the marina is "pet friendly." However, as the grassy pet-walking area is

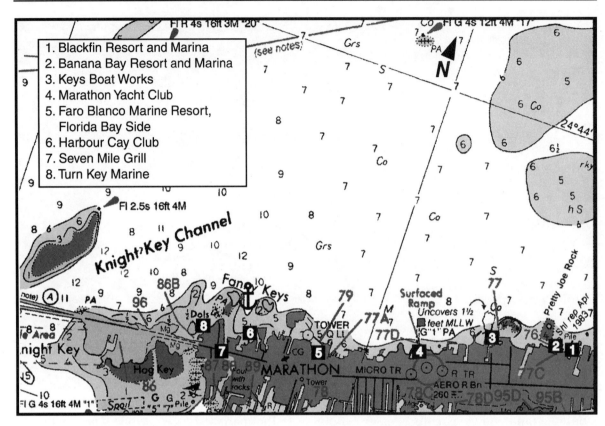

1. Blackfin Resort and Marina
2. Banana Bay Resort and Marina
3. Keys Boat Works
4. Marathon Yacht Club
5. Faro Blanco Marine Resort,
   Florida Bay Side
6. Harbour Cay Club
7. Seven Mile Grill
8. Turn Key Marine

also a shortcut to the showers, we were exceedingly careful where we stepped.

Faro Blanco, Bayside also features what it calls "garden cottages," which this writer stayed in a number of years ago. They were quiet, air-conditioned, and comfortable.

The upscale eatery at Faro Blanco, once known as Chelsea's, has closed. However, the Angler's Lounge is still serving. You can get lunch and dinner here. The fare varies from full meals to snacks and sandwiches. Prices are "moderate." Off premises and nearby is Pancho's (305-289-1629), which is a Marathon version of Tex-Mex.

Those up for a bit longer hike can cut west down U.S. Highway 1 and visit Seven Mile Grill (reviewed later in this chapter). It is also possible to visit this dining spot by water,

which we will detail shortly. To be brief here, the food is marvelous, and the atmosphere is pure Florida Keys.

Both the Marathon versions of West Marine (2055 Overseas Highway, 305-289-1009) and Boater's World (5001 Overseas Highway, 305-743-7707) are within walking distance (about ¼ of a mile), but it is a 2½-mile hike to the nearest grocery store, which happens to be a Publix Supermarket. That's a cab ride in anyone's vernacular.

We found it interesting that the people who worked "Bayside" were not really familiar with what was going on in the "Oceanside" portion of this operation (see below). One would think that when people work for one owner, they would have an idea of what the entire entity was about.

Faro Blanco Marine Resort, Bayside (305) 743-9018
http://www.spottswood.com

Approach depth—7 feet
Dockside depth—6$\frac{1}{2}$ feet (minimum—east side harbor)
7-13 feet (western dockage basin)
Accepts transients—yes
Type of piers—fixed wooden, all in excellent shape
Dockside power connections—30-50 amp
Dockside water connections—yes
Waste pump-out—yes (via a honey wagon at the gas dock)
Showers—yes, at the nearby swimming pool
Cable hookup—yes
Phone hookup—yes
Laundromat—yes, in shower area
Fuel—gas and diesel
Mechanical repairs—independent technicians
Ship's store—yes, and West Marine is across U.S. 1, about a $\frac{1}{4}$-mile walk
Restaurant—several on site and more within walking distance

Fanny Keys Anchorage
(Standard Mile 1192.5)
(24 42.736 North/081 06.656 West)

Cruisers can turn south .7 nautical miles northeast of the ICW's unlighted daybeacon #19 and cross 1.3 nautical miles of open water to the tongue of good depths between the two charted Fanny Keys. This same route provides access to the two shoreside facilities, which we will review below.

If you are careful to anchor just as soon as the midwidth of the two keys' north-to-south axis comes abeam, minimum depths in this anchorage run to 6 feet. Farther to the south, the bottom shelves up to 5-foot levels at low water. There is enough room for a 40-footer, but be mindful of the fact that there might be some boat traffic to and from the nearby Harbour Cay Club (see below).

There is plenty of shelter to the east, west, southwest, southeast, and some to the south. Don't try spending the night here if fresh northerlies are in the offing.

The two Fanny Keys are undeveloped, but the adjacent Marathon shoreline is overlooked by dense residential and commercial development. This is not what one would call a quiet, isolated Florida Keys haven.

One of this anchorage's great advantages is the easy dinghy access to nearby Seven Mile Grill. This wonderful dining attraction is reviewed below.

Harbour Cay Club
(Standard Mile 1192.5)
(24 42.608 North/081 06.598 West)

Cruisers whose craft can stand 5-foot soundings without a meeting of keel and bottom can track their way to the Fanny Keys Anchorage described above and then continue to the south-southeast. Here, they will discover the (mostly) private Harbour Cay Club, perched on the Marathon shores, almost due south of the easternmost (of two) Fanny Keys.

Harbour Cay Club is a private, 24-member marina. How does one get into a private marina? When a slip space is available, then other boats may use the vacant berth for a fee. Be SURE to call first to check availability. Ask for either Harvey Roitman or the current fleet captain. This is not a "drop in" marina. Advance arrangements must be made. A marina informational package is available. Just call and ask for one.

The marina sports fixed wooden piers, with a full array of dockside connections, including 30- to 50-amp power service, fresh water hookups, cable television, and telephone jacks. Minimum approach depths run to 5 feet, with at least 6 feet of water dockside. Some slips feature soundings of 9 feet or better.

The dockage basin is not at all well-sheltered, except to the south.

Harbour Cay Club sports small, unisex showers and toilet facilities. They are the usual vintage Florida style, but they are also immaculate. We think now, by just looking at showers and rest rooms—which we have seen by the hundreds—that you can gauge a facility by its "facilities." Generally, the ones in the Florida Keys are a bit dated, rarely air-conditioned, and usually very clean. In the Florida Panhandle, we ran into a few that we turned around and ran right out of. You get the picture.

There's a lovely clubhouse here that makes for a great a place to spend a few idle hours. Don't miss the veranda that overlooks the marina. The clubhouse also boasts a large cruising library. The people who own slips here are nice, friendly, and they know their stuff.

Harbour Cay Club (305) 743-5390
http://www.home.earthlink.net/~harbourcayclub

Approach depth—5 feet (minimum)
Dockside depth—6-10 feet, depending on slip
Accepts transients—limited
Type of piers—fixed wooden piers
Dockside power connections—30 to 50 amp
Dockside water connections—yes
Cable television hookup—yes
Phone hookup—yes
Showers—yes
Laundromat—yes
Restaurant—several blocks away, along U.S.
   Highway 1

Seven Mile Grill
(Standard Mile 1192.5)
(24 42.549 North/081 06.717 West)

Yet another destination that can be reached by cruising between the two Fanny Keys is the small, fixed, wooden dock associated with Seven Mile Grill (305-743-4481), named, as you might have surmised, for the adjacent Seven Mile Bridge. The cove that plays host to this facility lies due south of the westernmost of the two Fanny Keys. The restaurant pier guards this cove's westerly banks.

The approach is tricky, but minimum 5-foot depths can be carried to the dock, with 7-foot soundings alongside. Owner Pat Farrell suggested hugging the west-side sea wall on the way in (and out). A navigational mistake could land you in about 6 inches of depth.

There is just about enough room at the Seven Mile Grill dock for one or two thirty-footers. Visiting mariners are free to tie up while dining, but no overnight stays are allowed, and there are no other marine facilities.

Some cruisers who pilot larger cruising craft may choose to anchor in the deeper water between the two Fanny Keys and then dinghy in to Seven Mile Grill. That's not a bad plan of action. Be SURE to check out our navigational write-up of this channel below BEFORE attempting to access this dining attraction by water.

Seven Mile Grill has been operating since 1954 and calls itself "a last little touch of the old Keys." The appellation is accurate. One of the pictures on the wall inside is a collection of faded color photos of the men of Meisner Marine, who were part of the construction crew of the Seven Mile Bridge (see below). There are other photos of men with huge, dead sharks. Open for breakfast, lunch, and dinner, the Seven Mile Grill is a great stop. "There are no dress codes here," Farrell said, so you can dine in your swimsuit. A birthday suit might cause a raised eyebrow or two. The menu looks inviting and the prices are moderate. If entering a genuine time warp is for you, then so is the Seven Mile Grill.

Turn Key Marine
(Standard Mile 1192.5)
(24 42.577 North/081 06.841 West)

The small facility known as Turn Key Marine (305-743-2502) lies south of the charted finger of 9-foot waters, west of the westernmost (of two) Fanny Keys. Approach depths are an impressive 6 to 9 feet at low tide.

Turn Key is a dry-stack storage facility that does not accept transients and offers little else in the way of marine services for visitors. On the other hand, they are a Yamaha and Mercury dealer, so people having mechanical problems with these sorts of engines might find this facility of use.

Knight Key Channel
(Standard Mile 1193.5)

Cruisers can think of Knight Key Channel as the extreme eastern end of the wide swath of water, west of Marathon, known as the Moser Channel. The Knight Key passage will be discovered south of the ICW's unlighted daybeacon #19. Unlike the Moser cut, however, the Knight Key Channel is crossed by a fixed portion of the Seven Mile Bridge with only 19 feet of vertical clearance. Couple this meager, vertical, height limit with some flanking shoals, and you can readily understand why we recommend this passage only for powercraft up to 36 feet in length.

Of course, local power captains use the Knight Key Channel as a shortcut on a daily basis. It's a good, quick way to access the westerly approach to Boot Key Harbor (see below). If your craft can clear the bridge and if you know how to avoid the flanking, unmarked shoals, then it makes sense to use this channel, rather than wander considerably farther to the west in search of the Moser Channel. Otherwise, this latter route will serve you far better.

Seven Mile Bridge (storm in the distance)

Moser Channel
(Standard Mile 1196.5)

Many captains who are not dyed-in-the-wool, Florida Keys veterans think that the ICW ends just west of Marathon at the Moser Channel. Cruisers of this ilk almost inevitably head out to sea via the Moser passage thence west by way of Hawk Channel to Key West. As we shall discover in the next chapter, this is not really true. In fact, the ICW passage, which cuts northwest through Big Spanish Channel and then skirts the northern flank of the Keys all the way to Key West, can be one of the greatest backwater cruising finds in this entire region.

With that said, let's do be sure to note that the Moser Channel is a very important passage that connects the inside-ICW-Florida Bay waters with the offshore Hawk Channel route. Like Channel Five, the Moser Channel is spanned by a portion of the fixed, Seven Mile Bridge that features an official vertical clearance of 65 feet. However, we have noted a clearance as low as 63 feet during an unusually high tide. Skippers of tall sailcraft take note!

Unlike Channel Five, the Moser cut is reasonably well marked. It is also deep, and in fair weather, easily run during daylight. Nighttime passage is quite difficult, due to the almost total lack of lighted aids to navigation. Come on USCG, if you are going to put up markers, why not have a few flashers among the group. Go figure!

The 63-foot pass-through section of the bridge is located south of the Waterway's track, between unlighted daybeacons #22 and #24 (at bit closer to the #24 or westerly side of this run). Another series of markers leads off to the north, and these are important to navigators making for the mainland coastline of Western Florida. The three alternative routes to this destination will be carefully considered in

a separate section at the end of this chapter.

There are some flanking shoals to be concerned with, though none of these shallows directly impinge on the Moser Channel. The largest batch of shallow water runs out for a considerable distance from historic Pigeon Key (see below), east of Moser Channel. There are also some shallows to be concerned with that are associated with Molasses Keys, west of the Moser cut.

While we have never experienced this phenomenon, veteran cruisers and even the NOAA charting folks have warned that Moser Channel can become very rough indeed when strong winds and tide oppose one another. A warning note appears on some NOAA charts to the effect that "overwash" can occur when these conditions are present. Overwash means that the waves become so tall, that they wash right over the decks of a craft, possibly causing it to capsize. From all indications, conditions this extreme are fairly rare, but it does call to mind the notion that the Moser Channel might best be avoided in really heavy weather.

South of unlighted daybeacon #2, it's only a short hop out into Hawk Channel. We will pick up coverage of this offshore route just a little bit later in this chapter.

Pigeon Key, the Seven Mile Bridge, and the Amazing Mr. Flagler

Pigeon Key, the small island west of Marathon and east of the Moser Channel, upon which the original Seven Mile Bridge rests for support, is a trip back in history that is worth your time and money.

When Henry Morrison Flagler built his railroad over the Florida Keys, he altered this string of islands for eternity. One of the things left behind after the railroad was finished was

Pigeon Key passenger train

the construction camp, on Pigeon Key, for the original Seven Mile Bridge. Pigeon Key is less than 5 acres in size, yet during the construction period (1908-1912) it housed some 400 construction workers in barracks-type housing and in tents.

In modern times, a new bridge has replaced the amazing span built by Mr. Flagler's faithful construction workers. The old bridge now lies just north of the newer span and is by far the more visual of the two. The centermost section of the Flagler bridge has been removed to allow for easy passage by both pleasure and commercial craft. The easterly section of the old bridge is used as both a fishing pier and a foot (and tram) path to the attractions on Pigeon Key.

What one sees of Pigeon Key today doesn't reflect the earlier times, when outhouses were built out on long piers over the water and the tide carried human waste, and the rest of the garbage and trash they generated, away. What one sees today is what came after the construction period, when a village was begun to house the bridge tenders, supervisors, and bridge maintenance workers who kept the railroad going.

Little has changed on Pigeon Key since 1912. The houses have the same pine floorboards that went down almost 100 years ago. The architecture is attractive and practical and has been duplicated many, many times in other parts of Florida. The main building on the property, now a meeting room with modern rest rooms, was once the old section-gang quarters and mess hall.

The assistant bridge tender's house (Pigeon Key)

Behind the old section-gang quarters is what is called Negro Quarters. It housed the blacks who lived on the island. They were, for the most part, cooks. But they were not allowed to live with the people who ate the food they cooked. This was America, land of the free, if you were the right color.

A small house, called the Honeymoon Cottage, sits just beyond the Negro Quarters. Today it houses a deputy sheriff, who provides security for the island. Though some will say differently, it was built in the 1950s to house the maid of the man who was responsible for the Overseas Road and Toll District.

The old Seven Mile Bridge became an overseas highway bridge in 1938. The 1935 Labor Day Hurricane destroyed the railroad in the Islamorada area, shutting it down. The right of way was sold to the State of Florida, which subsequently built a highway all the way to Key West.

There is one two-story house on the island; it is the bridge tender's house. And this homeplace is supposed to have its own ghost. Back when bridge tenders actually worked on the original Seven Mile Bridge—it had a railroad turnstile on it which would swing open to allow sailing ships in Moser Channel to pass through—history has it that the wife of the bridge tender got involved with the assistant bridge tender. Because the bridge tenders went to and from work on gasoline-powered handcars, the sound of their return preceded them by several minutes. Though never actually caught in a compromising situation, the woman is said to have been riddled with guilt and committed suicide in this house. You be the judge.

The most attractive house on the island, for our money, is the Assistant Bridge Tender's House, which doubles as the Pigeon Key Museum. It is lovely both inside and out. When we were there, the morning sunlight shone through a south-facing window and silhouetted a model of a working schooner, *Louisa,* against the backdrop of the section-gang quarters seen through the crisscross of window grates. The moment was magic.

The Pigeon Key Historic District (305-289-0025) is open 9 A.M. to 5 P.M., seven days a week. You can get out to Pigeon Key by walking down the old Seven Mile Bridge or by taking the tram from the Pigeon Key Visitors'

Center (305-743-5999) on Knight Key. There is NO water access, due to the surrounding shallows. A $7.50 admission fee for adults is charged, with a $5 fee for children under twelve. Preschool kiddies get in free.

Even though it's a long way out there, this is one of those Florida Keys attractions that you simply can't miss. Tell them we sent you.

Western Entrance to Boot Key Harbor

South of the Moser Channel's unlighted daybeacon #2, captains can hang a turn to the east and track their way to the westerly approach channel, which serves Boot Key Harbor. These "middle waters" of Marathon are so important that they demand their own subsection presented later in this chapter.

ICW—VACA CUT TO MOSER CHANNEL NAVIGATION

Navigation of the ICW between Vaca Cut and the Moser Channel is a surprisingly simply proposition, at least during daylight and fair weather. Runs between daybeacons are not too lengthy, and there is not much in the way of surrounding shallows to worry with. The Knight Key Channel is an exception to this rule. It demands very strict attention to business.

Even the various shoreside marinas and nearby anchorages are relatively easy to access. Of course, sometimes you must favor one side of the channel or bank over the other, but armed with the data presented below, most cruisers will probably come through with nary a scratch.

In all but heavy weather, Moser Channel is also generally a joy to navigate, at least when the sun is in the sky. At night, a navigator's

task is a far chancier proposition with an almost total lack of lighted aids to navigation.

On the ICW It's a nice, simple run of only 1.7 nautical miles from flashing daybeacon #13 to unlighted daybeacon #14, the next southwesterly marker on the Waterway. At #14, captains may choose to leave the ICW in their wake and cut south to the anchorage north of Marathon Shores.

Marathon Shores Anchorage This overnight haven lies almost due south of unlighted daybeacon #14. Depart the Waterway once abeam of #14 and cruise south for some 1.7 nautical miles. Drop the hook before approaching to within less than 100 yards of the Marathon Shores banks to the south.

Between #14 and this anchorage, you

may well spot several small, unlighted daybeacons stretching out from Stirrup Key, east of your course line. These informal aids to navigation mark a channel that serves a small canal and several private docks. They are of no interest to visiting cruisers.

On the ICW It is only a quick hop of 1.1 nautical miles from unlighted daybeacon #14 to a point abeam of the next Waterway marker, unlighted daybeacon #15. Take out your old, tattered copy of chart 11451 (at least ours was after only one trip) and notice that #15 sits smack in the middle of Rachel Bank. The "magenta line" suggests that you should pass .3 nautical miles northwest of #15, right over a charted "Obstn" (obstruction). We always make it a practice to come abeam and pass #15 by some 200 to 300 yards northwest of its position, then adjust course slightly farther to the west in order to pass between the next pair of Waterway aids to navigation, flashing daybeacon #17 and unlighted daybeacon #18.

Before pushing on too much farther to the west on the ICW, let's take a look at the anchorage north of Rachel Key, south of unlighted daybeacon #15.

Rachel Key Anchorage For best possible depths, cruise south from the ICW some .6 nautical miles northeast of unlighted daybeacon #15. This maneuver will serve to keep you on the eastern extreme of Rachel Bank and nowhere near the half-foot shoal immediately south of #15.

As you cruise to within .6 nautical miles of the southerly banks, cut sharply to the southwest, and use your binoculars to pick out the small, natural mass of Rachel Key. Come abeam of this isle by some 50 yards off its northerly tip. This is the best place to anchor.

Captains piloting smaller, shallower-draft cruising vessels might also try CAREFULLY easing their way some 75 yards off Rachel Key's westerly shoreline. There are some shallows shelving out from this portion of the key, so take the greatest care, and keep an eagle eye on the sounder.

Blackfin Resort and Banana Bay Resort and Marina Both these facilities lie just east of charted Pretty Joe Rock. We advise mariners making for either of these two marinas to take a wide berth around the shallows on the interior reaches of Rachel Bank. Even though this maneuver will add a bit of extra distance to your cruise, it is the safer plan of action.

With this in mind, we suggest turning south off the Waterway, some .5 nautical miles northeast of flashing daybeacon #17. Cruise to the south-southeast for 1.45 nautical miles, keeping a sharp watch for Pretty Joe Rock. Though you would barely guess it from the chart, this "rock" is actually a tiny isle with a small but most interesting little house perched atop its shores. Of far more concern is the long, sinister patch of shallows that stretch out on all quarters from this "rock."

We need not say it, but let's say it anyway. Don't get anywhere near Pretty Joe Rock. Pass at least 200 yards north of the small isle, and stay at least this far to the east of its position as well.

If you are successful in avoiding Pretty

Joe Rock, the entrances to both Banana Bay and Blackfin Resort will be spotted hugging the southerly shoreline. Blackfin is the easternmost of the two, with Banana Bay lying closer to Pretty Joe Rock.

Keys Boat Works Keys Boat Works will be discovered 1.4 nautical miles southeast of flashing daybeacon #17. The first ninety percent of the approach is a breeze, with little in the way of nearby shallows to worry with. Just be sure to stay west of the somewhat shallower water associated with Rachel Bank.

Things change as you approach the entrance to Keys Boat Works. You will sight a harbor with a semiround, breakwater enclosure just to the west of the repair yard's entrance. You must HUG the eastern (outer) face of this breakwater as you track your way south into the yard's harbor. Even a small deviation to the east can land you in a whole passel of shallows.

The entrance to Keys Boat Works is rather tiny, but you can usually identify it, courtesy of the tall Travelift in the background, not to mention any number of tall masts and flybridges from the boats that are docked and being repaired there.

Marathon Yacht Club The Marathon Yacht Club (MYC) can be accessed by leaving the Waterway's track about 300 yards northeast of flashing daybeacon #17. By cutting to the south, northeast of #17, you will avoid the sunken wreck marked by #17. Then, it's a run of 1.6 nautical miles across open water to the yacht club.

As you near the MYC, you will spot unlighted daybeacon #1 and (uncharted) unlighted daybeacon #2. Slow down! The entrance to the yacht club's dockage basin passes a public launching ramp, immediately north of the clubhouse. Any wake at all could seriously hamper operations at this ramp. Believe me, we have had the unfortunate experience of discovering this fact for ourselves.

Pass directly between #1 and #2, and continue south into the yacht club harbor. The slips and the clubhouse will quickly come abeam to port.

Faro Blanco Marine Resort A very exciting cruising destination lies almost due south of flashing daybeacon #17. Faro Blanco Marine Resort, Bayside is a great pleasure-craft facility.

To avoid the sunken wreck marked by flashing daybeacon #17, we suggest that you cut to the south some 200 to 300 yards southwest of #17. It's then a run across open water to this large marina.

Faro Blanco, Bayside is not hard to spot. Long before you reach its actual location, the marina's famous lighthouse will be quite visible. It is even lighted to facilitate nighttime approaches.

As you may recall from our earlier descriptive account of this marina, it has two very distinct dockage basins, each with its own entrance. It would be a good idea, indeed, to call ahead and discover which harbor holds your slip for the night.

If the easterly basin turns out to be your home away from home, cruise directly in toward the lighthouse. You will soon be paralleling an extensive rock breakwater off your starboard side. Continue on toward the lighthouse, and soon the east-side harbor will open out (you guessed it) to the east.

The western basin can be reached by skirting across the northern face of the rock breakwater. The entrance will come up between the western tip of this protecting structure and a concrete sea wall, which is overlooked by a host of palm trees.

On the ICW Once between flashing daybeacon #17 and unlighted daybeacon #18, continue along on the same course, pointing for the gap between unlighted daybeacon #19 and flashing daybeacon #20. Once again, there are no shallows to contend with on this passage. Just be sure to say south of #20. The same cannot be said for the waters northwest of this aid to navigation.

Between #17 and #19, cruisers can strike off to the south yet again, and access three cruising destinations.

Fanny Keys Anchorage, Harbour Cay Club, and Seven Mile Grill Whether you plan to anchor between the two charted Fanny Keys, visit semiprivate Harbour Cay Club, or slake your appetite at wonderful Seven Mile Grill, continue tracking your way southwest on the ICW for about .45 nautical miles from flashing daybeacon #17.

Then, turn south, and cruise along for 1.3 nautical miles. As you near the southerly extreme of this run, the two, undeveloped Fanny Keys will be quite visible. Cruise between the two isles, and drop the hook as soon as the midwidth of their north-to-south axis comes abeam.

Skippers continuing on to Harbour Cay Club should hoist their binoculars and look to the south-southeast. The good folks at Harbour Cay have been kind enough to erect a range that will keep you to the good water as you cruise into their harbor. Remember, dockage is only available at this mostly private facility by way of advance arrangements.

The third destination on these waters, the dock at Seven Mile Grill, is a bit more difficult to enter safely. The Seven Mile pier flanks the westerly banks of the second cove, west of Harbour Cay Club. The midwidth of this cove is shoal. You must heavily favor the western banks as you enter this cove or risk a grounding just where you would least expect to find the bottom.

Stick close to the starboard-side sea wall, and soon the Seven Mill Grill dock will be spotted dead ahead. Be sure to favor the cove's westerly shores as you exit this facility.

On the ICW Flashing daybeacon #20 and unlighted daybeacon #19 mark an important juncture in the Florida Keys ICW. Chart 11451 notes a split in the magenta line at this point.

The more northerly passage is the true Florida Keys Waterway. This route skirts across the northerly half of Moser Channel and then enters the southeastern mouth of Big Spanish Channel. This passage, as we shall see in detail in the next chapter, provides a reliable means to cross to the key's northerly flank and thence west to Key West.

The southerly of the two routes provides access to both the Moser Channel and the

20-foot fixed bridge crossing Bahia Honda Channel. We shall deal with this latter cruising location in our next chapter. For now, we will concentrate on the track to Moser Channel, after taking a quick look at the adjacent Knight Key Channel.

Knight Key Channel Small, mostly local craft use the Knight Key Channel on a daily basis to quickly skirt between the ICW (and all the Florida Bay waters), the offshore Hawk Channel passage, and the westerly entrance to Boot Key Harbor. Please remember, however, that this cut is spanned by a fixed 19-foot portion of the Seven Mile Bridge. There are also some surroundings shallows to worry with.

Cruisers making for Knight Key Channel should cut south at unlighted daybeacon #19. Set a careful compass and/or GPS course designed to stay well east of the huge patch of shallows flanking the westerly side of Knight Key Channel. This extensive hazard is marked by one flashing but unnumbered daybeacon. Again, not to be repetitive, but keep at least 300 to 400 yards east of this marker.

Eventually, the older of the two Seven Mile bridges spanning the great width of the Knight Key-Moser Channel will be spied dead ahead. Cruise straight through the older span, while taking a few moments to admire the incredible engineering of a far earlier day. This bridge will be immediately followed by the new span. Cross under it as well.

Once both bridges are behind your stern, cut to the southwest. This course change will help to avoid the long tongue

of 2- to 5-foot waters striking west from Knight Key. On the water, this won't look right, particularly if you are making for the westerly approach to Boot Key Harbor. It will appear as if you are headed almost directly away from the place you are trying to reach. Trust us, this IS the way to do it. Wait until Boot Key's westerly entrance is abeam, well east of your course line, before turning east and running this marked cut.

On to Moser Channel Set course from the gap between flashing daybeacon #20 and unlighted daybeacon #19 to come abeam of flashing daybeacon #21 by some 50 yards to its northerly side. Don't slip south of #21. The mammoth shoal flats surrounding Pigeon Key reach almost to the southern flank of #21.

Stay on the same course line for another 1.2 nautical miles. At this point, the removed center span of the old bridge and the central pass-through of the newer Seven Mile Bridge will come abeam to the south.

Turn south and track your way toward the bridges. There are no aids to navigation between your turn off the ICW and the northern face of the two spans. You may spy some aids to navigation to the north. These help to outline the passage from Moser Channel to Cape Sable (the southwestern tip of mainland Florida). As we have noted several times already in this section, this valuable route will be reviewed in its own subsection at the end of this chapter.

The center span of Mr. Flager's remarkable version of the Seven Mile Bridge has been completely removed, negating any height restrictions. However, the newer span is another matter entirely.

Chart 11451 lists the official vertical clearance of the new Seven Mile Bridge at 65 feet. Our on-site observations, however, show that at spring tides, this height can shrink to 63 feet. We observed just such a reduced clearance, courtesy of an on-the-water tidal gauge in September of 2001. Skippers of tall sailcraft who need a full 65 feet should time their passage under this bridge to coincide with low water!

After passing under the new, high-rise, Seven Mile Bridge, cruisers should immediately pick up a series of unlighted daybeacons to help them along the way. BE VERY SURE to stay WEST of all three unlighted daybeacons (#6, #4, and #2). East of #6, those same pesky shallows surrounding Pigeon Key are waiting to say hello to your bottom (of your boat that is). There is also an unlighted daybeacon #5, which, as you probably surmised, should be passed by some 20 yards to its easterly side.

South of the southernmost Moser Channel marker, unlighted daybeacon #2, it's a quick hop south of 1.28 nautical miles to the midwidth of Hawk Channel. A turn to the west points your bow toward (guess where) Key West.

Hawk Channel—Channel Five to Moser Channel

The Hawk Channel section southwest of Channel Five's seaward exodus (and flashing daybeacon #44) to the Moser Channel is a mixed bag of opportunities for visiting skippers. From Duck Key to Vaca Cut, these waters might well be accurately described as a marina-rich environment. Then, quite suddenly, cruisers will find themselves without facilities west of Vaca Cut. Of course, small cruising craft could always run Sister Creek to Boot Key Harbor, but these various marinas and repair yards there are part of Marathon's "middle waters," not Hawk Channel.

There is but one good anchorage to consider along this entire stretch, but it's (as we said in the 1950s) a doozy. And it doesn't hurt anything that this overnight haven sits hard by a shoreside motel (rental cottages actually) and a small marina.

Our jaunt on this portion of Hawk Channel comes to an end at important Moser Channel. The Moser cut is one of the principal routes by which cruising captains can cut inside from Hawk Channel or leave the ICW and head for the briny blue. It's fixed, 63-foot (officially 65 feet of vertical clearance) bridge is a joy after all the low-level spans we have encountered north of this point.

Long Key Recreation Area

Well west-northwest of Hawk Channel's flashing daybeacon #44, the state of Florida's Long Key Recreation Area occupies the southerly shores of Long Key, just east of the fabulous Long Key Viaduct. We had heard that there was some dockage and/or water access associated with this facility, but alas, an extensive on-the-water check up and down the beach that fronts the park revealed no piers or even a good spot to anchor. There is also a huge band of shallows running south and southwest from the park's shoreline. All in all, while it's a good spot for landlubber tourists to visit and even camp, Long Key Recreation Area is not a valid cruising destination.

Long Key Viaduct

Between flashing daybeacons #44 and #45, the Long Key Viaduct Bridge will be visible north of your course line, east of Duck Key. This is one of the most amazing man-made structures in the Florida Keys, particularly amazing when you consider that it was constructed in 1905.

Anyone who even knows a smattering of Florida history will recognize the name of Henry Flagler. This giant of a man almost single-handedly brought development to the eastern coastline of Florida, eventually pushing "his railroad" all the way south to Key West. Out of all the many bridges that were constructed as part of this remarkable railway system, Mr. Flager was proudest of the Long Key Viaduct. In fact, he used it in publicity photo after publicity photo.

Long Key Viaduct spans a width of 2¾ miles and is composed of 180 concrete, semicircular arches, each some 50 feet wide. There was no other bridge in the USA of this type in those days, and it was considered a marvel.

Today, a new bridge has replaced Mr. Flagler's remarkable achievement, but the old Viaduct is still quite visible, just south of the new bridge. Pause for a few minutes in your waterborne trip to admire this monument from an earlier age that will not come again.

For those who are interested in learning more about the Long Key Viaduct and Mr. Flager's amazing railroad, we highly recommend the Web site, "Mike's Railway History" at http://mikes.railhistory.railfan.net/r053.html

Duck Key Canal

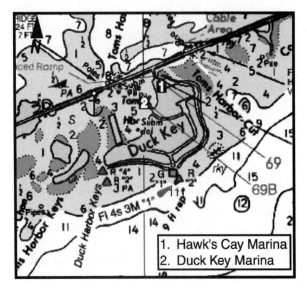

1. Hawk's Cay Marina
2. Duck Key Marina

Duck Key—Hawk's Cay Marina
(24 46.633 North/080 54.815 West)

Duck Key thrusts its bulk well out into the offshore water, immediately west of the Long Key Viaduct. The entrance to its canal system lies off its southerly banks, some 2.7 nautical miles north-northeast of Hawk Channel's flashing daybeacon #45.

Don't even think about trying to access Duck Key and its marinas from the ICW-inside route. One local magnanimously set the bridge clearance at 6 feet, but we barely made it under in a 22-foot powercraft.

For reasons known only to the island's developers, Duck Key is the home of Hawk's Cay Marina. By following a series of markers (some uncharted) through an entrance cutting the isle's southerly banks, cruisers can turn to the east and follow this outermost canal around to the marina. Most approach depths run 8 feet or better but there is one spot that shelves up to 5½ feet at dead low-water as you enter the dockage basin. The marina piers will eventually be sighted to the west as you near the canal's northerly tip. Soundings alongside seem to run at least 5½ to 6 feet. First-timers should be sure to check out our navigational account of Hawk's Cay in the next section below.

Hawk's Cay Marina is a first-class destination resort, and you can have just about anything money can buy here. The service is perfect most of the time, though one of the marina crew we encountered was a lot happier saying "No" than "How can I help you?" On the whole, however, you couldn't want for anything here. There is tennis, swimming, sport fishing, a nearby dolphin habitat, and lovely architecture. Plus plenty of other amenities that you need to check up on personally.

When they were filming the movie *True Lies* in the Florida Keys, Arnold Schwarzenegger and his wife Maria Shriver stayed at Hawk's Cay, as did Jamie Lee Curtis, who, when she was but six years old, sat on Morgan's lap at a radio station in Aspen, Colorado, while her mother was being interviewed in the next studio. Little girls sometimes grow into very foxy ladies, but you can't always call it ahead of time. Darn.

Transients are welcome at Hawk's Cay, and the fixed wooden piers and concrete piers are all very nice. Out on the docks you will find 30- and 50-amp electrical service and water connections, plus telephone and cable television hookups. There is waste pump-out here, too.

Cruisers will want to spend some time in the very well-stocked ship's and variety store, located in the building just behind the docks. Some basic, convenience-store-type food items can be purchased here as well. This is also the location for the marina's squeaky-clean, air-conditioned showers. An on-site Laundromat adds to the marina's offerings.

There are five (count them, five) restaurants within walking distance in Hawk's Cay. We particularly like the Palm Terrace with its 80-item breakfast buffet and made-to-order omelets. The Water's Edge Café features outdoor dining, the freshest of seafood, and it overlooks the marina dockage basin. The Cantina offers inspired Mexican dishes for the midday meal. Hope you weren't planning to diet while you're here.

The fuel dock sells both gas and diesel, and there is a mechanic on call for repairs.

Hawk's Cay has it all. It is the kind of place that one might like to stay for several days while cruising, just to get the salt off. Bring cash or credit cards. You will be using them.

Hawk's Cay Marina (305) 743-7000
www.hawkscay.com

Approach depth—5^1/$_2$-8 feet
Dockside depth—5^1/$_2$-6 feet

Accepts transients—yes
Type of piers—fixed wooden and concrete finger piers
Dockside power connections—30 to 50 amp
Dockside water connections—yes
Cable television hookup—yes
Telephone hookup—yes
Waste pump-out—yes
Showers—yes, first-rate
Laundromat—yes
Fuel—gas and diesel
Mechanical repairs—mechanic on call
Ship's and variety store—complete with both food and hardware, excellent
Restaurant—five on site

Duck Key Marina and Tom's Harbor Anchorage
(Marina—24 46.505 North/080 54.992 West)
(Anchorage—24 46.531 North/080 55.398 West)

Mariners who jockey small, shallow-draft

Hawk's Cay Marina

vessels (that can stand 3-foot depths) might possibly choose to follow the scantily marked channel immediately west of Duck Key. This cut has only two aids to navigation, not nearly enough to insure that you keep to the channel. Even if you are able to find the best water, expect some 3-foot soundings at low tide.

Cruisers who are willing to risk all of this can eventually round the northwesterly tip of Duck Key and cruise into Tom's Harbor, where you will find Duck Key Marina. Before going on to review this facility, we should also note that there is an alternate route to the waters of Tom's Harbor by way of the Duck Key canal system. You must negotiate a winding passage and pass under several 10-foot fixed bridges to use this route. Obviously, this is a trip appropriate for small powercraft only.

Those cruisers who do make it to Duck Key Marina (305-289-0161) will find a dry-stack storage facility, with a resident MercCruiser and OMC dealer. Duck Key does not take transients and they have no amenities that visitors would need. They do, however, sell gas and make mechanical repairs. There's a small marine store connected to the office.

Captains who manage to run the partially marked channel west of Duck Key have a surprising anchorage opportunity. Notice the charted bubble of 6-foot water, just west of Tom's Harbor's northwesterly entrance. These soundings are for real. Swinging room is restricted, and we don't suggest that you try anchoring any vessel larger than 30 feet here. The bridge provides some protection to the north, while the body of Duck Key gives a good lee to the south-southeast and east. This is not the spot to anchor during strong westerly blows.

Don't even think about cruising farther to

Picnicking on Crawl Key

the west. Even though the waters look deep and inviting, depths quickly rise to 2-foot levels.

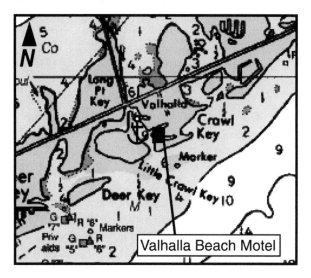

Valhalla Beach Motel

Valhalla Beach Motel and Little Crawl Key Anchorage
(Marina—24 44.586 North/080 58.804 West)
(Anchorage—24 44.643 North/080 58.882 West)

Using chart 11451, locate Crawl Key and Little Crawl Key 2.7 nautical miles west-northwest of Hawk Channel's flashing daybeacon #45 (or 2.5 nautical miles north-northwest of unlighted daybeacon #47). The cove that separates these two islands plays host to a small marina (plus rental cottages) and one of the best anchorages available off Hawk Channel. For our purposes here, we will name this body of water "Crawl Cove."

Some small, uncharted daybeacons outline the entrance channel coming in from the deeper offshore waters. There are a few tricks to this process, and visitors will occasionally note a 4½-foot low-water sounding. Typical depths run 6 to 8 feet. Check out our navigational account below BEFORE attempting to visit the adjacent marina or anchorage for the first time.

Entering Crawl Cove, the cottages associated with Valhalla Beach Motel will be spotted along the eastern banks. DON'T attempt to turn east into the first canal that fronts the cottages. On the water, this seems the obvious choice, but such a maneuver will land you in less than 3 feet of water. The marina is actually located on a second canal that cuts east from the easterly shoreline BEHIND the cottages. You have to look hard to find this second canal for the first time, but it is there, and so is the marina.

Valhalla Beach Motel is actually a little resort motel that is off the beaten track, with water on two sides of the property. They have rooms to rent, and if you are renting a room, which is air-conditioned, you get everything else for free. The rooms are simple, clean, and neat—sort of vintage 1960-1970. And there is a private, sandy beach right on the premises. The dockage is protected, big-time, and there is both alongside docking and slips outfitted with fixed, wooden, finger piers. The owner is a former Stiletto sailor and catamaran racer.

Valhalla is happy to accommodate transient craft that are the property of motel patrons (only). These slips are probably not appropriate for vessels larger than 28 feet. Depths alongside run 5½ to 7 feet. While there is not a great deal of room here, it is safe to say that there are probably not a great many boats that come here; it is off the beaten track. For some, that is a handicap; for others, it is a blessing.

While there are no dockside electrical connections, there is dockside water. The showers are in the individual motel units. The only fuel available is from a truck, which will deliver diesel, and there's a mechanic on call.

If you don't want to be a big spender ($65-$140 a night) you can anchor in the nearby lagoon for free (see below). But then you won't be sleeping in an air-conditioned room either. Valhalla is simple, but it is clean, and you couldn't find a better place to have your boat tied up when the weather is nasty than outback at this motel. It would truly be a Valhalla for you—no Valkyries, though, and no credit cards either.

If you stop here, you will be "off soundings," so to speak. There are no restaurants nearby. Plan accordingly.

Valhalla Beach Motel (305) 289-0616

Approach depth—4¹/₂ feet (minimum)
Dockside depth—5-7 feet
Accepts transients—yes (motel guests only)
Type of piers—fixed wooden piers
Dockside water connections—yes
Fuel—none on site, but a truck delivers diesel
Mechanical repairs—local, independent
  technician

Another very viable alternative is to continue past the Valhalla complex and drop anchor in the midwidth of the cove, just north of the marina canal. Minimum depths of 6 feet can be maintained if you stop well short of Crawl Cove's northerly shoreline. As these banks are approached, soundings deteriorate to 5 feet or maybe even slightly less.

The Valhalla cottages overlook the easterly shores, and there is a small park along the westerly banks. Otherwise, this anchorage is in its natural state and offers a backwater, almost secret, feeling that makes it a real cruising find.

The same caveat to the approach channel applies here, in regards to approaching the Valhalla marina. There are a few tricks, so check out our navigational write-up of Crawl Cove in the next section.

Coco Plum Beach Facilities
(Coco Plum Beach Yacht Club)
(24 43.988 North/081 00.293 West)

One of the most surprising channels anywhere near Marathon cuts between Deer Key, Fat Deer Key, and Coco Plum Beach, 1.8 nautical miles north-northwest of Hawk Channel's unlighted daybeacon #47. This cut carries 5-foot minimum depths with far more typical soundings of 6 feet or better.

After passing between the innermost set of markers, an undeveloped island will be sighted almost dead ahead, while a private home and dock will lie to the west, flanked by a west-running canal. Turn WEST on the canal. Do NOT try and enter the large body of water to the north. Depths here are measured in inches.

After turning into the canal, your first thought will be, "What are Morgan and Claiborne trying to pull on us?" This seemingly isolated stream seems to run by a few private homes and then disappear into the mangroves. Keep the faith.

After rounding a small turn, some .6 nautical miles west of the canal's mouth, you will, just where you would least expect it, come upon a marina that features a rather incredible collection of large cruising craft of both the sail and power variety. The wonderfully well-sheltered Coco Plum Beach Yacht Club's dockage basin will open out to the south, and if you're like this writer, you'll wonder how all those really big boats got up the canal you have just traversed.

First and foremost, Coco Plum Beach Yacht Club is a condominium association for live-aboard sailors. That means that it is a tight-knit community of people who already know each other. It's not fancy, and the no-see-ums that come out in weak light are savage. Large pets and small children are discouraged, but they are not prohibited.

That said, transients are accepted. Dockage is found at fixed, wooden, finger piers with widely varying soundings, from as little as 4½ feet up to 10 feet. Typical depths are 6 feet or better. There is 30- to 50-amp electrical service, dockside water, and dockside waste pump-out. Telephone and cable television hookups are in the offing as well. Adequate showers and the Laundromat are found just down the street. You'll have to get fuel, food, and supplies elsewhere.

The problem with being a transient at Coco Plum is the lack of any office telephone, and thereby, the lack of any way to make advance arrangements. Your only option is to just show up, and since there is, at least to our knowledge, no regular dockmaster, it could be a real challenge trying to find a slip, pay for it, and discover the lay of the land. Good luck, you may need it!

Coco Plum's most endearing quality is its more-than-adequate distance from the "action" in nearby Marathon. Cruisers who prefer the quiet of an isolated anchorage off a Florida Bay key might find much to admire in this facility, particularly when contrasted with other Marathon facilities located in the heart of this community's hustle and bustle. Coco Plum would also be a great place to stay if you had a boy-crazy teenage daughter on board. She'd be bored to tears, of course, but you'd be able to sleep rather well.

Coco Plum Beach Yacht Club (NO phone)

Approach depth—5 feet (minimum)
Dockside depth—4½-10, depending on slip
Accepts transients—yes
Type of piers—fixed wooden finger piers
Dockside power connections—30-50 amp
Dockside water connections—yes

Waste pump-out—yes, on the dock
Cable television hookup—yes
Telephone hookup—yes
Showers—yes
Laundromat—yes

The vast majority of cruising-sized craft will wisely choose to cease their explorations at Coco Plum Beach Yacht Club. Small craft skippers in search of storage can follow a complicated channel farther to the west, and then cut north to Driftwood Marina and Storage (305-289-0432) (24 44.039 North/081 00.757 West). This is a dry-stack storage facility with no transient services.

Key Colony Beach Facilities (Various Lat/Lons—see below)

West of Coco Plum Beach, a marked channel cuts north-northwest and leads from the offshore waters to two marinas in the Key Colony Beach community, plus a dry-stack storage facility. The entrance cut carries at least 7 feet of water, and there are actually far more markers (which is a good thing) than chart 11451 indicates.

Cruisers running this cut for the first time should be advised that there are significant shoals flanking the channel here and there. Be sure to read our navigation info later in this chapter to avoid any close encounters of the grounding variety.

Just north-northwest of unlighted daybeacon #2, the region's first facility will come up along the easterly banks. Bonefish Marina C. A. (24 43.493 North/081 00.722 West) is a condominium association, which is what the C. A. stands for above. However, transients are accepted, but all arrangements MUST be made prior to arrival. There's a $50 application fee and the fee for dockage is established with the individual dock owner.

The applications are channeled through Harry Nettles, who is the dockmaster and also a source for information concerning what is available.

The marina itself is impeccably maintained and, because of its location, has nearly bulletproof protection from the elements. Depths in the basin run 9 feet or better. Anyone got a keel deeper than that?

Bonefish's fixed wooden piers are perfect.

There is dockside power up to 50 amps, dockside water, and dockside cable television connections. The showers are a quarter-century old, but they are neat and clean. You'll also find a Laundromat on the premises.

As nice as this marina is, it is also only fair to note that it is a fair piece from shopping, repairs, and shoreside dining. One would be wise to take all that into account before reserving a berth here.

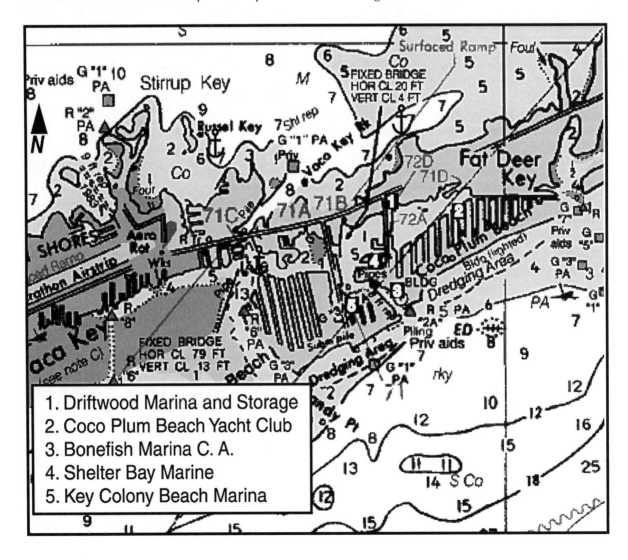

1. Driftwood Marina and Storage
2. Coco Plum Beach Yacht Club
3. Bonefish Marina C. A.
4. Shelter Bay Marine
5. Key Colony Beach Marina

Bonefish Marina C. A. (305) 743-7015

Approach depth—7 feet (minimum)
Dockside depth—9+ feet
Accepts transients—yes (but ONLY with
   advance arrangements)
Type of piers—fixed wooden, excellent
   condition
Dockside power connections—up to 50 amp
Dockside water connections—yes
Cable television hookup—yes
Showers—yes
Laundromat—yes

Alternately, cruisers can continue following the marked channel north-northwest to yet another good, transient-friendly facility. Northwest of unlighted daybeacons #8 and #10, the waters open out into a wider pool. This is deceptive, as much of this breadth is shallow, more about that in a minute.

For now, let's note that a canal cuts back to the south on the southwestern corner of this small bay. Key Colony Beach Marina occupies both the western shores of the canal's northerly mouth and the extreme southerly banks of the small bay. In other words, this facility runs around the corner in both directions.

Key Colony Beach Marina is a very nice pleasure-craft facility. When cruisers spend an evening here, they receive a complimentary social membership at the Cabana Club (½ of a mile away). Visitors at the club are treated to a swimming pool and bar, plus showers and bathrooms. These are the only showers available to transients at Key Colony Beach Marina, and while clean, with an "old Florida" look, one could not exactly call them convenient, courtesy of the half-mile walk necessary to reach them. The Laundromat is also located at the club. In the busy season, December through April, there may be no room at the inn.

The only bathrooms available, sans the half-mile walk, are located in the on-site restaurant, Smuggler's Landing. Marina patrons may use these facilities, but the restaurant may not always be open when the urge hits you. Sometimes a boat's holding tank is a precious commodity.

Transients are welcome at Key Colony Beach Marina, but it might be nice to have an advance reservation. The fixed concrete finger piers are in good repair and feature 30- to 50-amp power service, cable television jacks, fresh water connections, and adjacent waste pump-out. Gasoline and diesel fuel can be purchased at a fuel dock that fronts the canal's western banks. With an approach depth of 8 feet or better, and 10-foot soundings at the docks, this marina can be used by even deep-draft vessels.

Key Colony's Smuggler's Landing Restaurant (305-289-0141) features a nice view of the marina and seems to be well operated. Good food. Good service. Good attitude. Our waitress, Lisa, was from Long Island and as sunny as a Florida spring afternoon. We wanted for nothing. Were they all as good as she.

Key Colony Beach Marina (305) 289-1310

Approach depth—8 feet (minimum)
Dockside depth—10 feet
Accepts transients—yes
Type of piers—fixed concrete
Dockside power connections—30-50 amp
Dockside water connections—yes
Cable television hookup—yes
Waste pump-out—yes
Rest rooms—in the on-site restaurant or a ½-
   mile walk away
Showers½-mile away
Laundromat—also ½-mile away
Fuel—gas and diesel
Mechanical repairs—mechanic on call
Restaurant—on site

It is possible, though not necessarily a good idea, to continue following the Key Colony Beach Channel as it cuts northeast and hugs the small bay's southeasterly banks. There is a whole passel of flanking shallows to worry with, and the channel can be a bit confusing in places. This route does eventually lead to a charter diving agency, a couple of private marinas, and a dry-stack storage facility that goes by the moniker of Shelter Bay Marine (305-743-7008) (24 43.641 North/081 00.842 West).

Shelter Bay is accessed by way of a 7-foot, eastward-running canal that cuts the southeasterly banks between unlighted daybeacons #11 and #13. This is a dry-stack storage facility that sells gas and diesel and offers mechanical repairs. There are no other transient facilities here except for a very complete ship's store.

Vaca Cut and Associated Facilities and Anchorages
(Various Lat/Lons—see below)

The small inlet known as Vaca Cut divides Fat Deer Key (Key Colony Beach) and Vaca Key, north of Hawk Channel's unlighted daybeacon #48. Don't even consider turning north from #48 to run this cut, however. The approach channel is FAR more complicated and demands a careful and meticulous review in our navigational section below. For now, suffice it to say that Vaca Cut's seaside approach channel, if you can find it, maintains minimum 6-foot depths. Soundings as deep as 15 feet will be noted at places along the way.

North of unlighted daybeacon #6, a side water opens out in the easterly banks. At first glance, this would seem to be a fairly wide bay, but be advised that the northerly shoreline is shoal. Nevertheless, this is an acceptable anchorage (24 43.635 North/081 01.647 West)

during fair weather or when moderate winds are blowing from the east-northeast or southeast. Low-water depths run 5 to 6 feet. The north-side shoals vastly reduce the swinging room, and we do not suggest trying to anchor vessels larger than 36 feet here. There is the usual tidal current sweeping through these waters, so be sure your anchor is well set.

Captains of the devil-may-care variety can continue upstream on this offshoot by following a marked, but completely uncharted, channel that hugs the southerly banks. Immediately after passing unlighted daybeacon #5 (uncharted), you can turn to the north and track your way to Boat House Marina.

Ask three different people about the best track between #5 and this marina, and you will probably get six different opinions. To be on the safe side, we suggest that you count on no more than 4½ feet of depth as you approach Boat House.

Boat House Marina (305-289-1323) (24 43.776 North/081 01.446 West) is yet another in the long string of Marathon dry-stack storage marinas. The semienclosed dockage basin has around 6 feet of water and features a few fixed wooden piers. The wet-slip space is obviously geared mostly to vessels smaller than 30 feet. The marina's huge dry-stack storage building dominates the skyline. Gasoline can be purchased, but there are no other transient services available.

Moving back to the main Vaca Cut channel, cruisers can continue north to the 13-foot fixed bridge spanning the inlet. Just south of this span, Captain Hook's Marina and Dive Center (305-743-2444) (24 43.770 North/081 01.828 West) overlooks the westerly banks. Getting into Captain Hook's can be a bit tricky, courtesy of the viscous tidal currents that regularly run under the adjacent bridge.

This passage is not for the fainthearted or those who are low on skill. In fact, do it the easy way. Try another place.

Even if you can survive the swiftly moving water, Captain Hook's is just not set up to handle transients. Gasoline can be purchased in the dockage basin (5½-foot approach depths, 7 to 8 feet in the partially enclosed harbor), and there is an on-site store, which is pointed mostly toward scuba diving customers. Otherwise, cruisers would do well to look elsewhere.

Sister Creek

The marked entry channel into Sister Creek is located 1.4 nautical miles north-northwest of Hawk Channel's flashing daybeacon #49 (marking East Washerwoman Shoal). This stream is the southerly access channel leading to Boot Key Harbor. It will be considered in the separate section dealing with this popular cruising destination later in this chapter. For now, we need only note that larger, deep-draft vessels may want to pass up Sister Creek in deference to Boot Key Harbor's deeper (and wider) westerly entrance, making off from Moser Channel.

Knight Key Channel

From a position abeam of flashing daybeacon #49, it is a westward run of some 2.8 nautical miles on Hawk Channel to a point abeam of the Knight Key Channel, lying slightly better than 2.2 miles to the north. The actual channel is spanned by a 19-foot fixed portion of the Seven Mile Bridge, and there are some adjoining shoals that navigators need to be concerned about. Nevertheless, many local captains, particularly those who pilot smaller powercraft, use Knight Key Channel on a regular basis as a shortcut

between the inside-ICW route and the offshore-Hawk Channel waters.

Cruisers plying their way west (south) on Hawk Channel have far more reason to appreciate the Knight Key cut than their brethren wending their way down the ICW. That's because the well-marked, deep, westerly entrance to Boot Key Harbor makes off from the southerly reaches of this inlet channel, well south of the worrisome fixed bridge. Thus, captains cruising Hawk Channel can use the southerly portion of the Knight Key passage as the most direct means to enter Boot Key Harbor via its westerly approach. There is little in the way of adjacent shallows to worry with, and your only problem on this stretch will most likely be the scarcity of aids to navigation.

On the other hand, skippers bypassing Boot Key Harbor and heading north to the ICW and the waters of Florida Bay will have to pass under the 19-foot fixed bridge and avoid several nearby shoals. Larger cruising craft, particularly of the deep-draft and sailcraft persuasion, would find Moser Channel far better suited to their purposes.

Moser Channel

A little better than 5 nautical miles west of a position abeam of flashing daybeacon #49, Hawk Channel cruisers will come abeam of the Moser Channel to the north. It's another run of 1.3 nautical miles from the Hawk to the southernmost aid to navigation on the Moser cut, unlighted daybeacon #2.

The Moser Channel is a very important passage that connects the the offshore Hawk Channel route with the inside-ICW—Florida Bay waters. Like Channel Five, the Moser Channel is spanned by a portion of the fixed, Seven Mile Bridge, which features an official

Seven Mile Bridge (new and old), as seen from Pigeon Key

vertical clearance of 65 feet. However, we have noted a clearance as low as 63 feet during an unusually high tide. Skippers of tall sailcraft take note!

Unlike Channel Five, the Moser cut is reasonably well marked. It is also deep, and in fair weather, easily run during daylight. Nighttime passage is quite difficult, due to the almost total lack of lighted aids to navigation. Come on USCG, if you are going to put up markers, why not have a few flashers among the group? Go figure!

The 63-foot pass-through section of the bridge is located north of unlighted daybeacons #5 and #6. North of the bridge, another series of markers leads off to the north, and these are important to navigators making for

the mainland coastline of Western Florida. The three alternative routes to this destination will be carefully considered in a separate section at the end of this chapter.

There are some flanking shoals to be concerned with, though none of these shallows directly impinge on the Moser Channel. The largest batch of shoal water runs out for a considerable distance from historic Pigeon Key (see below), east of Moser Channel. There are also some shallows to be concerned with, which are associated with Molasses Keys, west of the Moser cut.

While we have never experienced this phenomenon, veteran cruisers and even the NOAA charting folks have warned that Moser Channel can become very rough indeed when strong winds and tide oppose one another. A warning note appears on some NOAA charts to the effect that "overwash" can occur when these conditions are present. Overwash means that the waves become so tall, that they wash right over the decks of a craft, possibly causing it to capsize. From all indications, conditions this extreme are fairly rare, but it does call to mind the notion that the Moser Channel might best be avoided in really heavy weather.

North of the Moser Channel-Seven Mile Bridge, it is only a short hop to the main ICW channel and an even quicker run to the alternate channel cutting west-southwest to Bahia Honda. Both of these routes will be reviewed in the next chapter.

Pigeon Key, the Seven Mile Bridge, and the Amazing Mr. Flagler

Pigeon Key, the small island west of Marathon and east of the Moser Channel, upon which the original Seven Mile Bridge rests for support, is a trip back in history that is worth your time and money.

When Henry Morrison Flagler built his railroad over the Florida Keys, he altered this string of islands for eternity. One of the things left behind after the railroad was finished was the construction camp, on Pigeon Key, for the original Seven Mile Bridge. Pigeon Key is less than 5 acres in size, yet during the construction period (1908-1912), it housed some 400 construction workers in barracks-type housing and in tents.

In modern times, a new bridge has replaced the amazing span built by Mr. Flagler's faithful construction workers. The old bridge now lies just north of the newer span and is by far the more visual of the two. The centermost section of the Flagler bridge has

been removed to allow for easy passage by both pleasure and commercial craft. The easterly section of the old bridge is used as both a fishing pier and a foot (and tram) path to the attractions on Pigeon Key.

What one sees of Pigeon Key today doesn't reflect the earlier times, when outhouses were built out on long piers over the water and the tide carried human waste, and the rest of the garbage and trash they generated, away. What one sees today is what came after the construction period, when a village was begun to house the bridge tenders, supervisors, and bridge maintenance workers who kept the railroad going.

Little has changed on Pigeon Key since 1912. The houses have the same pine floorboards that went down almost 100 years ago. The architecture is attractive and practical and has been duplicated many, many times in other parts of Florida. The main building on the property, now a meeting room with modern rest rooms, was once the old section-gang quarters and mess hall.

Behind the old section-gang quarters is what is called Negro Quarters. It housed the blacks who lived on the island. They were, for the most part, cooks. But they were not allowed to live with the people who ate the food they cooked. This was America, land of the free, if you were the right color.

A small cottage, called the Honeymoon Cottage, sits just beyond the Negro Quarters. Today it houses a deputy sheriff, who provides security for the island. Though some will say differently, it was built in the 1950s to house the maid of the man who was responsible for the Overseas Road and Toll District.

The old Seven Mile Bridge became an overseas highway bridge in 1938. The 1935 Labor Day Hurricane destroyed the railroad in the Islamorada area, shutting it down. The right of way was sold to the State of Florida, which subsequently built a highway all the way to Key West.

There is one two-story house on the island; it is the bridge tender's house. And this homeplace is supposed to have its own ghost. Back when bridge tenders actually worked out on the original Seven Mile Bridge—it had a railroad turnstile on it which would swing open to allow sailing ships in Moser Channel to pass through—history has it that the wife of the bridge tender got involved with the assistant bridge tender. Because the bridge tenders went to and from work on gasoline-powered handcars, the sound of their return preceded them by several minutes. Though never actually caught in a compromising situation, the woman is said to have been riddled with guilt and committed suicide in this house. You be the judge.

The most attractive house on the island, for our money, is the Assistant Bridge Tender's House, which doubles as the Pigeon Key Museum. It is lovely both inside and out. When we were there, the morning sunlight shone through a south-facing window and silhouetted a model of a working schooner, *Louisa,* against the backdrop of the section-gang quarters seen through the crisscross of window grates. The moment was magic.

The Pigeon Key National Historical is open 9 A.M. to 5 P.M., seven days a week. You can get out to Pigeon Key by walking down the old Seven Mile Bridge or by taking the tram from the Pigeon Key Visitors' Center on Knight Key.

Model of the schooner *Louisa* (Pigeon Key)

There is NO water access, due to the surrounding shallows. A $7.50 admission fee for adults is charged, with a $5 fee for children under twelve. Preschool kiddies get in free.

Even though it's a long way out there, this is one of those Florida Keys attractions that you simply can't miss. Tell them we sent you.

HAWK CHANNEL—CHANNEL FIVE TO MOSER CHANNEL NAVIGATION

This portion of Hawk Channel contains the longest run between markers that we have yet encountered. How does 9.1 nautical miles grab you? If you don't have the miracle of GPS aboard, better preplot your compass courses, and be ready to practice your best DR navigational skills.

Much of Hawk Channel between Channel Five and the Moser Channel passes well north or south of what aids to navigation you will find. Some of these beacons mark shallow reefs, and it's a really good idea to give them a wide berth.

The various side waters along this stretch all have marked entry channels, but some (Vaca Cut comes immediately to mind) can be tricky propositions. We strongly suggest that you read the navigational info below with care and keep a copy of chart 11451 at hand to help interpret this data.

On Hawk Channel We last left Hawk Channel at flashing daybeacon #44, just southwest of Channel Five's southerly terminus. Well, there's nothing like starting off a section with a bang. If you noticed the comment about a looong stretch between markers above, this is it! It is a run of slightly better than 9.1 nautical miles between #44 and the next Hawk Channel aid to navigation, flashing daybeacon #45.

Flashing daybeacon #45 marks the shallower water of East Turtle Shoal, south of its position. To maintain the best soundings, come abeam of #45 by some 200 yards to its northwesterly side.

Cruisers can cut to the north off Hawk Channel, 1.4 nautical miles east-northeast of flashing daybeacon #45, and make their way to Duck Key and Hawk's Cay Marina.

Long Key Viaduct As you are cruising between flashing daybeacons #44 and #45, use your binoculars to look north for a view of the old Long Key Viaduct. Even from this distance, it's an impressive sight.

Duck Key and Hawk's Cay Marina The approach channel cutting into the southern banks of Duck Key actually boasts far more markers than what is shown on chart 11451. Many of these informal aids to navigation are nothing more than unadorned pilings, but at least during daylight, they do a pretty good job of outlining both sides of the channel.

This short passage will soon lead you through a rock breakwater and bring you face-to-face with a three-way split. Take the starboard (eastern) canal and immediately slow to idle speed. It's a long, long cruise at idle speed up this channel to the marina. Use the extra time to admire the many sumptuous homes guarding the port-side banks.

Eventually the approach canal will turn to the north, and you will approach a second fork. Take the starboard branch, which has a sign to clue you into the fact that this is the way to the marina.

The portion of the channel between this second fork and the marina dockage basin is the shallowest part of this passage. Expect some extreme low-water depths of 5½ feet.

Soon you will pass an enclosed swimming area to port. Be sure to continue cruising along strictly at idle speed.

Watch to port as you approach the marina for a good view of the dolphin habitat. During our last visit, feeding was in progress. You should have seen all those eager, smiling faces waiting to receive their daily ration of baitfish. It made for a truly memorable sight from the water.

Hawk's Cay dockage basin will soon open out along the port (western) shore. For best depths, stick fairly close to the docks as you cruise to your assigned slip.

Duck Key Marina and Tom's Harbor Anchorage Let's be real clear about this. There is nothing easy or simple about the channel running north, just west, of Duck Key to Tom's Harbor, Duck Key Marina, and the nearby anchorage. We suggest that all but very shallow-raft vessels leave this possibility to our outboard and I/O brethren.

If you decide to make the attempt anyway, pass unlighted daybeacons #2 and #4

to their fairly immediate westerly side and continue ahead, favoring the easterly banks. Expect some soundings as shallow as 3 feet, between the southwesterly point of Duck Key and the channel's easterly swing into Tom's Harbor.

Eventually, you will round Duck Key's northwesterly point. Here, you can squeeze to the north just a bit and anchor in the correctly charted 6-foot bubble of water.

Don't be tempted by the seemingly open waters farther to the west. Even though they look inviting, depths quickly rise to 2- and 3-foot levels.

Captains continuing on to Duck Key Marina should take a somewhat lazy turn to the southeast and cruise straight for the marina. Its position will be more than obvious, courtesy of its huge dry-stack storage building.

On Hawk Channel After the mammoth run between flashing daybeacons #44 and #45, cruisers will be happy to learn that it's a mere 2.4 nautical miles to the next marker, unlighted daybeacon #47. This aid to navigation sits hard by the northwesterly corner of a fish haven. Be sure to pass at least 300 yards northwest of #47.

Some .4 nautical miles northeast of #47, cruisers can turn to the north and visit Valhalla Beach Motel and the excellent anchorage between Little Crawl Key and Crawl Key.

Valhalla Beach Motel and Little Crawl Key Anchorage It would be ever soo much easier to navigate the channel leading to

Valhalla Beach Motel and the Crawl Key anchorage if NOAA had seen fit to chart the channel markers outlining the approach cut. Oh well, at least the channel is marked, so we shouldn't ask for everything.

Use your compass or GPS to help set a course for the gap between Crawl Key and Little Crawl Key. Along the way, you may spot the markers serving the Coco Plum Beach channel, west of your course line. Ignore these markers, at least until we turn our attention to them below, and continue on to the north. Use your binoculars to help pick out the Crawl Key markers, which will be spotted considerably closer to shore.

These uncharted aids to navigation consist of small, unlighted daybeacons. Cruise between the various markers, passing red beacons to your starboard side and taking green markers to port. You were expecting something else?

This channel leads into a surprisingly broad basin. Favor the easterly shores slightly as you cruise into this baylike body of water. Shallower depths are found near to the westerly banks.

The cottages associated with Valhalla Beach Resort will be spotted along the easterly banks. DO NOT turn into the first eastward running canal, which fronts these structures. These waters are shoal.

Similarly, do NOT approach a small, fixed wooden pier that you will spot on the point of land between the first and second east-side canals. Depths beside this old structure are nil.

Instead, mariners bound for the Valhalla marina should continue north on the midwidth of the bay, until the second (moving south to north) eastward canal comes abeam to starboard. Cut into the centerline of this stream. The marina docks will quickly come up along the southerly banks.

Captains who choose to anchor on the bay between Crawl Key and Little Crawl Key should drop anchor shortly after coming abeam of the second east-side canal, described just above. Farther to the north, depths shelve upward to 4-foot levels.

Coco Plum Beach Channel and Facilities
Cruisers will discover the outermost markers of the Coco Plum Beach channel, unlighted daybeacons # 1 and #2, 1.8 nautical miles north-northwest of Hawk Channel's unlighted daybeacon #47. The initial portion of this cut is well marked by pairs of unlighted daybeacons. Simply cruise between the various markers.

After passing between the innermost set of aids to navigation, unlighted daybeacons #7 and #8, it will appear that the channel continues straight ahead, beside a small, undeveloped island. WRONG! Watch to port, and you will sight a private home with its own pier. Favor the westerly shores slightly, bordering on this house and its dock, until a canal opens out to the west. Turn into the midwidth of this stream, and cruise west along its length. Some small canals will soon begin to open out along the southerly shoreline. Some of these display light development, while others display all-natural banks.

Ignore all these side waters, until the canal takes a small jog to port. At this point, the slips associated with Coco Plum Beach

Yacht Club will open out on a southward-running canal, along its easterly banks. If this facility is your destination, turn to the south and parallel the slips as you work your way to a berth.

Those few cruisers (and we mean VERY few) who continue on to Driftwood Marina and Storage should favor the southerly banks heavily as they cruise on to the southwest. Soon the waters open out into a much wider, baylike region. Continue favoring the southerly banks heavily, even though you may spy several boats north of your course. Don't imitate these guys; they are stuck in the mud.

Eventually, you will sight a very low-level bridge ahead, abutting the bay's westerly limits. Just before reaching this little span, cut 90 degrees to the north. Stay just off the commercial fishing piers, which will come abeam to your port side. Continue favoring this western shoreline as you work your way north to a small canal that will open out on the northerly banks. Driftwood is found on the upstream tip of this tiny stream.

Key Colony Beach Channel and Facilities
The marked cut leading to Key Colony Beach lies between the Coco Plum Beach passage, reviewed above, and Vaca Cut. Successful navigation of this cut is facilitated by the presence of far more aids to navigation than what is pictured on chart 11451.

Come abeam of the outermost marker, unlighted daybeacon #2, to its westerly side. As if you expected something else, just pass all subsequent red marks to your starboard side and take green beacons to port.

Just upstream from #2, the entrance to Bonefish Marina C. A. opens out along the easterly banks. Cruise into the harbor along the entrance's centerline if this facility is your destination.

After passing unlighted daybeacons #5 and #7, be SURE to pick up unlighted daybeacons #8 and #10. These aids to navigation direct you to a course hard by the westerly banks. A large shoal lies just east of the channel along this stretch. It is marked by a sign.

Upstream of #10, the waters widen considerably, and the channel takes a rather bizarre turn to the northeast. Before following this twist, however, let's note that cruisers can cut back to the south and visit Key Colony Beach Marina. The fuel dock fronts the eastern banks of the adjacent, south-running canal.

Most visiting captains will want to halt their explorations of these waters at Key Colony Beach Marina. Those few who continue on to Shelter Bay Marine, or one of the private marinas farther to the northeast, will have to negotiate a tricky transition in the Key Colony Beach channel.

After passing unlighted daybeacon #10, the channel takes a hard turn to starboard and then runs hard by the southeasterly banks. Be SURE to pass unlighted daybeacons #11 and #13 to your port side.

Soon thereafter, the markers peter out, but reasonable depths can be maintained by continuing to favor the southeasterly banks heavily. The canal providing access to Shelter Bay will open out to the east.

Vaca Cut Any captain who tries to head

directly from Hawk Channel to Vaca Cut is in for a big surprise of the grounding variety. This small inlet is abutted by a huge shoal that lies south of its interior reaches. To avoid this considerable hazard, you must follow a very circuitous route.

To begin, set course from Hawk Channel as if you planned to run the route to Key Colony Beach, reviewed above. Some 100 to 150 yards south of this cut's outermost marker, unlighted daybeacon #2, swing to the west-southwest and point to pass unlighted daybeacon #1 by about 50 yards to its northerly side.

On the water, this will look all wrong. It would seem that you should be south of #1, but you MUST be north of this marker. Very rough and shoal water lies to the south and southwest.

Next up, use your binoculars to pick out some small, orange-and-white floating buoys. Well, these informal aids to navigation were present during our last visit in early 2001, but who knows if they are permanent features. If you do see these floaters, be sure to pass some 25 yards south of them.

Now, pick out unlighted daybeacon #3. Again, be SURE to pass at least 25 yards north of #3. Once abeam of #3, begin to bend your course to the north. Favor the easterly shoreline. On a clear, sunny day, the huge shoal to the west is quite obvious.

After a long markerless stretch, point to pass unlighted daybeacon #6 to its immediate westerly quarter. Shortly after #6 is in your wake, the baylike side water described earlier will open out to the east.

To anchor on this body of water, enter the small bay, favoring the southerly shoreline. An uncharted channel runs hard by these banks. Remember, the northerly portion of this bay is shoal, so ease just a bit off the south-side channel before dropping the hook.

Cruising craft continuing upstream to Boat House Marina can benefit from an uncharted aid to navigation, unlighted daybeacon #5. Continue to favor the southerly banks heavily as you approach and pass #5 to its southern side. Immediately after passing #5, cut sharply to the north and point for the marina basin, which you will sight on the bay's northwesterly corner.

The approach from #5 to Boat House Marina is a very problematic passage. Sometimes we seem to maintain best depths by favoring the westerly shoreline, while at others, a straight-in approach seems best. After several conversations with local captains, we've decided there is no one right way to do this, just be ready for some low-water 4½-foot soundings between #5 and the marina basin, no matter how you structure your approach.

Back on the main body of Vaca Cut, stick to the channel's centerline as you approach the southern face of the 13-foot fixed bridge. Be ready for VICIOUS tidal currents, and believe, the word *vicious* is not used here just to show we know how to read a dictionary.

Just south of the bridge, captains can cut west to Captain Hook's Marina and Dive Center. Again, watch out for those strong currents as you approach the harbor. Fortunately, a breakwater blocks the current within the harbor itself.

Pass under the fixed bridge (if you can) and don't scrimp on the RPM's. I know it's becoming repetitive, but when you see the speed with which the water races under this span, you will want to have plenty of engine power working for you.

North of the 13-foot span, the Vaca Cut channel angles to the northeast. Stick to the centerline, and use your binoculars to pick up unlighted daybeacons #1 and #2. These aids to navigation mark the channel's northeasterly terminus. Unlighted daybeacon #2 is uncharted, but just pass between #1 and 2. Continue on the same course for 50 yards or so, and then swing northwest into naturally deep water.

On Hawk Channel From a position abeam of Hawk Channel's unlighted daybeacon #47, cruisers must ply their way across approximately 3.1 nautical miles of water to the next marker, unlighted daybeacon #48. Come abeam of #48 by some 100 yards (or more) to its southeasterly quarter.

To help avoid the charted rocks (though none are shallower than 8 feet), continue on the same course, past #48 for about 1 nautical mile, then swing a bit farther to the west, and point to come abeam of flashing daybeacon #49 by .5 of a nautical mile to its northerly side. This 36-foot aid to navigation sits hard by East Washerwoman Shoal. With depths of 2 feet or less, no one (except scuba divers) will want to get anywhere near #49.

Northwest of #49, the marked Sister Creek channel cuts north to an eventual intersection with Boot Key Harbor. We will take a detailed look at this passage in the next section of this chapter.

Maintain the same course for another 2.8 nautical miles west of flashing daybeacon #49. Begin watching to the south for a glimpse of the tall (142 feet, no less) Sombrero Key light. It is an impressive sight from the water, but cruisers running the midsection of Hawk Channel or making for Boot Key Harbor, Knight Key Channel, or Moser Channel will pass a good 2.6 nautical miles north of this beacon.

Knight Key Channel and Boot Key Harbor
After cruising 2.8 nautical miles west of #49, captains making for Boot Key Harbor can turn north at 24 40.100 North/081 07.614 West and run the deep southerly portion of Knight Key Channel. The marked westerly approach channel serving Boot Key Harbor will come up to the east, about .6 of a nautical mile south of the 19-foot fixed bridge. This passage will be detailed below.

Captains continuing north on Knight Key Channel must swing their vessels out to the west in order to avoid the correctly charted tongue of shallow water striking west from Knight Key. Soon thereafter, cross under the 19-foot bridge, and immediately bend your course to the northeast.

Study chart 11451 and notice the large shoal marked by one unnumbered flashing daybeacon, on its northern tip. Need we say it? Stay well southeast of this considerable obstruction.

After passing the unnumbered, flashing daybeacon mentioned above, the ICW track lies just to the north, while a turn to the east will lead you to the Marathon facilities located along the inside route.

Moser Channel Cruisers bound north on the Moser Channel should cut north off Hawk Channel and set course to come abeam of the Moser's southernmost marker, unlighted daybeacon #2, by some 25 yards to its westerly side. Continue cruising north, being sure to stay west of unlighted daybeacons #4 and #6. Very shallow water associated with Pigeon Key Banks is found east of #6. Also, pass unlighted daybeacon #5 by about 25 yards to its easterly quarter.

As you come abeam of #6, look to the northeast for a glimpse of historic Pigeon Key. Unfortunately, there is no water access, and the outlying shallows are extensive. Visit Pigeon with the aid of land-side transportation only.

North of #6, the southern face of the new, fixed, high-rise Seven Mile Bridge will be quite apparent. Remember that during unusually high tides, this span's official 65-foot clearance can shrink to 63 feet. Sailcraft skippers take note.

Immediately after passing under the new span, cruisers will pass between the two sections of the old Seven Mile Bridge. The intervening span between the two halves has been permanently removed.

Continue cruising north-northwest for at least .6 nautical miles before making any turns. This strategy will help your vessel clear the Pigeon Key shallows to the east and the sunken (and charted) "Boiler" to the west.

A most useful series of Moser Channel markers continues on to the north, after crossing the path of the east-west-running ICW. This route is one of the passages that cruisers can use to reach mainland Florida's western coastline. As we have noted repeatedly above, these waters will be considered separately at the end of this chapter.

Moonrise over Boot Key Harbor

Boot Key Harbor

Marathon's "middle waters" consist of a western approach via a deep, well-marked channel from Knight Key Channel, a southerly inlet known as Sister Creek, and most importantly, Boot Key Harbor. You can think of this body of water as an oblong bay, lying between Marathon to the north and Boot Key to the south. Its east-to-west axis covers better than 1.6 nautical miles from the bridge spanning its westerly entrance to Boot Key's extreme easterly reaches.

Much of Boot Key Harbor is deep and easily adapts itself to anchored vessels. However, there is a surprising amount of shallow water as well. Don't assume just because you see boats in a particular part of the harbor that depths are adequate for cruising craft. Some of those boats are sitting square on the muddy bottom, while others are in a semisunken state (see below).

The majority of Boot Key's marinas and repair yards overlook the northern banks of the western approach channel. Almost all of these operations are of the first-class variety. There are also three major marinas and some smaller facilities along the shores of upper (easterly) Boot Key Harbor. Two of these are very important for their dinghy dockage service.

Boot Key Harbor is, without a doubt, the

Boot Key Harbor (Marathon)

most popular and populous anchorage in all of the Florida Keys. To put a Marathon twist on a phrase, "Nothing exceeds like success." Dozens and dozens of boats can be found swinging idly on Boot Key Harbor's waters, even during high summer. Couple this profuse anchorage with a host of good marinas and repair yards and almost total protection from foul weather, and you can readily understand why this natural harbor draws cruisers like a giant magnet. Some move on. Others never do. And it is the popularity of Boot Key Harbor that has put it on the cusp of controversy.

"Boot Key Harbor is the last stop of safety for an east-coast cruiser," said a local resident. "When east coast people have some romantic ideas about cruising and sailing and heading for the Caribbean, then Boot Key Harbor is where they stop. Some never leave. It is as far as they will ever get."

Boot Key harbor is polluted. Where you expect to find the water in the Keys gin-clear, Boot Key Harbor has a milky-greenish color to it. No one with any brains swims in it. One person, referring to the sad situation of the live-aboards, estimated that few of the boats anchored either had or used a holding tank. "If there are 100 boats like that out there," he said, "and they each flush nine times a day, that's an amazing amount of pollution which they generate."

Is this unfortunate situation a Monroe County problem, a state dilemma, or a federal conundrum? No one seems to know. It is definitely Monroe County's problem right now. But Florida's Fish and Wildlife Commission, which is charged with keeping Florida's waters clean, has not, according to one source, done anything about checking up on boats that might be polluting. The Coast Guard, which can do something about boats that don't meet the code, has apparently sort of closed its eyes to its "potty patrol" responsibilities. There's a Coast Guard station in Marathon.

If you think back to earlier times in the American West, the people who live aboard and anchor in Boot Key Harbor are latecomers; they are the "sod busters" and the "sheep farmers" whose arrival in the West made the previous denizens, cattle men who believed in free-range rights, apoplectic. The cattle men, of course, had their own earlier tiff with the Indians, who didn't understand white men's occupation with property claims and who lived, in some cases, to regret it. The story is an old one, with conclusions hard to draw. If you liken the Marathon marine establishment to the cattle barons, then the live-aboards will suffer some before the two sides come to some kind of accommodation.

Help, local help, is apparently on the way. The Florida Keys Marina, Marathon will, many pray, be the answer to the predicament. Operated by a group of private citizens with a mandate from Monroe County, the marina has a pump-out station. Dinghy space is also available here. Currently, there are toilet facilities and showers and a book exchange, all the things that either appeal or should appeal to cruising sailors and/or live-aboards.

Future plans call for a paid harbor master, and all the boats that tie up in the mooring field will be required to have holding tanks. "I see good things happening out in that harbor," said Sharon Bossert of Keys Boat Works. "There is a good plan in place, and it is a matter of getting the right things started."

The long-term goal is to get the harbor cleaned up and phase in a mooring field, where live-aboards and cruisers can hook up.

Then all the harbor activity will flow through the Florida Keys Marina, Marathon. There will be no other option and for good reason. In the 30 days following the opening of the pump-out station, we were told, only one boat in the anchorage bothered to use it.

An additional challenge is cleaning up the harbor bottom. We were informed that the bottom is littered with sunken boats. This sunken nautical junkyard, locals said, comes from people who buy boats and then live on them until they sink. The sunken wrecks are visible throughout the harbor. The level of yachtsman who does this, my source speculated, was about one step up from "homeless." As a result, it will take many, many tax dollars and a lot of time to clear it up.

Don't let all these problems blind you to Boot Key Harbor's good points. It's shelter from really foul weather, the bonhomie that runs rampant among many in this waterborne community, and the nearby facilities demand that you at least give the harbor a look-see.

Western Approach Channel

Boot Key Harbor's western approach channel cuts east from the Knight Key Channel, just south of Knight Key and Hog Key. This cut is well marked and carries minimum, low-water soundings of 7 feet, with typical soundings in the 9- to 11-foot region. This should be enough for all but the very deepest-draft pleasure craft (we saw one sailor recently who piloted a vessel with a 7½-foot draft) and even this esoteric variety of vessel can certainly enter and leave at high water.

The westernmost pair of markers on this channel are unlighted daybeacon #2 and

Dinghy dock at the Florida Keys Marina, Marathon

flashing daybeacon #1. Daybeacon #1 is the ONLY lighted aid in this whole grouping. Consequently, nighttime entry for strangers could be a bit, shall we say, challenging.

An impressive collection of marinas lines this approach channel's northerly banks, west of the 24-foot bascule bridge. Let's take a good look at these below.

Marathon Marina
(24 42.272 North/081 06.679 West)

First up, in more ways than one, is Marathon Marina. Its well-protected harbor will just about smack you in the eyeballs, north of unlighted daybeacon #9.

This is a big, classy, well-managed operation. Looking west, one sees the arch of Seven Mile Bridge. Marathon Marina is big enough to accommodate 130 vessels, short-term or long-term. If it doesn't exist at Marathon Marina, it is because it hasn't been invented yet.

Transients are welcome here, and the marina and its staff are set up perfectly to handle any and all comers. Docking is found at fixed concrete piers (face docks) and slips, but finger piers dominate. Soundings alongside are an impressive 8 to 14 feet, depending on slip location. That should keep even the 7½-foot draft sailcraft that we met in our discussion above off the bottom. Dockside power connections run up to 100-amp service with complimenting fresh water and cable television and telephone hookups. Boy, talk about having ALL the slip-side amenities.

Gasoline and diesel fuel are ready for pumping. Waste pump-out service is also in the offing. This service is currently offered by

Marathon Marina

way of a "honey wagon," but the marina management hopes to have pump-out connections available at every slip by 2002. Repairs are readily available on site. There is also a complete ship's store.

There are four men and four women on-site showers that are as clean as any we saw in the Florida Keys. Then, there is the Laundromat, which is simply the very best. Read that as total approval and even a bit of awe. We don't know what make the machines are, but they are made of stainless steel and they fairly glisten. Men generally don't get too excited about washing machines and things like that, but these have such an industrial air about them that they got our total attention. Dirty laundry inserted into these metal giants just HAS to come clean. It would not dare do otherwise.

Pets are allowed here, but dogs must be leashed and their roaming is restricted to a dog-walk area. In some marinas they are thought of as bad news and unwanted, so it is always a good idea to check ahead if traveling with a pet.

Interestingly, the handout presented to every guest at Marathon Marina is cleverly designed along the lines of an airline ticket jacket. There are places for the marina staff to write in the boat's name, captain's name, slip assignment, and the code numbers for the lock on the showers. It is the best design we have ever seen. Everything you need to know about the marina and surrounding environs is contained in this handout.

There is a fully stocked, on-site ship's store, with what appears to be a very large parts inventory. Many cruisers will find what they need here, without having to resort to a visit to the local West Marine or Boater's World.

The on-site restaurant at Marathon Marina is closed as of this writing, and it has been shut down for some time. Several other dining choices are within easy walking distance, including the Seven Mile Grill, Pancho's (305-289-1629—a Marathon version of Tex-Mex), and Angler's Lounge (305-743-9018). If you have not read our review of Seven Mile Grill earlier in this chapter, check it out immediately. We think your hungry feet will head on over to Seven Mile Grill pretty much by themselves after reading this account. Angler's is reviewed above.

Unfortunately, as with most marinas in Marathon, there is nary a supermarket within walking distance. Thankfully, it's only a quick cab ride to either Publix or Winn-Dixie.

The staff we met at Marathon Marina has also called our attention to the fact that eighty percent of the marina's long-term guests started out as overnight drop-ins. That says something about how far the staff will go to please you.

Now, as if that isn't enough in and of itself, would you believe that Marathon Marina features its own full-service repair yard? Yes, that's right. Extensive mechanical repairs are readily available for both gasoline and diesel engines. Haul-outs are accomplished by way of a 50-ton Travelift, and the popularity of this service is also very much in evidence by way of the many hauled craft that we have always observed during our visits here.

To paraphrase a very old television commercial, "If you can find a better marina, stay there." We don't think you will, and we give Marathon Marina our most hearty recommendation.

Marathon Marina (305) 743-6575

Approach depth—7-9 feet
Dockside depth—8-14 feet, depending on the
   slip location

Accepts transients—yes
Type of piers—fixed concrete piers
Dockside power connections—30-50-100 amp
Dockside water connections—yes
Cable television hookup—yes
Telephone hookup—yes
Waste pump-out—yes
Showers—yes
Laundromat—gorgeous
Fuel—gas and diesel
Mechanical repairs—extensive (gasoline and
   diesel engines)
Ship's store—yes, complete
Restaurant—on site with 10 others within
   walking distance, ¹/₂ mile

Pancho's Fuel Dock and Marina (24 42.197 North/081 06.580 West)

Pancho's is a marina and fuel dock oriented toward commercial fishing craft that also accepts transient pleasure craft. It's long, fixed, wooden, face dock and fuel pier fronts the northern side of the western Boot Key Harbor approach cut, a short hop east of Marathon Marina. Additional slip space is located on a canal-like body of water around the corner to the west.

Pancho's is long on practicality and short on amenities. An educated guess is that you could get some great prices here on stone crab claws and lobster if your timing was right and you had cash money.

From what we could see, the gasoline and diesel fuel prices at Pancho's are some of the best in Marathon. It's an almost sure bet that you will see any number of fellow craft fueling up at the face dock fronting onto the main channel.

Pancho's Fuel Dock and Marina (Boot Key Harbor)

Somewhat surprisingly, Pancho's does take transients. The docking here is via concrete finger piers and alongside docking. A third of the slips have 30-amp electrical service. There is dockside water and some minimal shore-side showers. On the other hand, given the commercial nature of this establishment, many services that cruising people want—cable, phone, restaurant, mechinical repairs, and a ship's store—are lacking.

Pancho's Fuel Dock (305) 743-2281

Approach depth—7-9 feet
Dockside depth—12-14 feet
Accepts transients—yes
Type of piers—fixed concrete w/ alongside
    docking and finger piers
Dockside power connections—about 1/3 of the
    slips have 30-amp
Dockside water connections—yes
Showers—yes
Fuel—gas and diesel
Restaurant—many nearby

Burdine's Waterfront Marina (24 42.207 North/081 06.531 West)

This facility also guards the westerly approach channel's northerly banks, just a quick hop east from Pancho's Fuel Dock. Burdine's is a nice marina. It seems busy and clean and in the process of getting better. When the conditions are right, the setting sun sinks into the sea right at the end of the channel that leads into Burdine's, doubtless to cheers and huzzahs from Conchs who take the setting of the sun with the seriousness approaching a religious quest. Or maybe it is just an excuse to get together for a drink.

Burdine's Waterfront Marina (Boot Key Harbor)

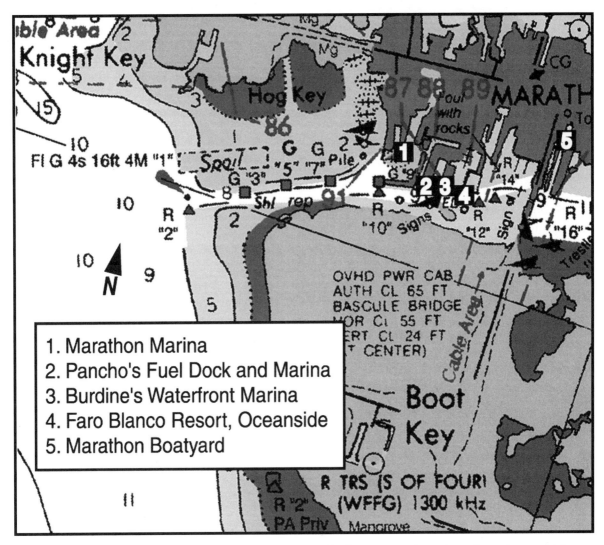

1. Marathon Marina
2. Pancho's Fuel Dock and Marina
3. Burdine's Waterfront Marina
4. Faro Blanco Resort, Oceanside
5. Marathon Boatyard

Burdine's has an outside patio, the Chiki Tiki Bar and Grill (305-743-9204), upstairs over the dockmaster's office. There's a nice breeze blowing through here most of the time. Large shutters cover the windows, in case there is more wind than is comfortable. Upstairs, when conditions are right, dining and sunset can coordinate in a lovely tableau. The menu is Keys cuisine, nothing fancy. The blackened fish sandwich is delicious; order it with fries,

which are terrific. The place has ambiance and charm and is worth a shot. There's entertainment some nights, Fridays especially.

Approach depths are the usual 7-foot minimums, with typical 8 to 9 feet of water in the channel. Dockside at Burdine's, expect good soundings of 8 feet or better.

Transient yachtsmen are welcome here. The piers are of the fixed wooden, finger type with 30- and 50-amp electrical service, cable television hookups, telephone jacks, and dockside water connections. Waste pump service is available at the fuel dock, where gas, diesel, and dive tank fills are also in the offing. There is also an on-site ship's store that seems very well stocked.

The showers and Laundromat at Burdine's were in the process of being replaced when we were there. They will be housed in separate buildings. They will be new, but it's a good bet they will not be air-conditioned.

The only downside to both Burdine's and Faro Blanco Oceanside (next door) appears to be several blocks of low-income housing that create a barrier—real or psychological— between the marinas and U.S. 1, which is where the action is in Marathon. If you are nervous about this, call a cab. With this motorized transportation, it's a very quick ride to all the restaurants reviewed both above and below, plus you can also head for the local supermarket.

Burdine's Waterfront Marina (305) 743-5317

Approach depth—7-9 feet
Dockside depth—8+ feet
Accepts transients—yes
Type of piers—wooden finger piers
Dockside power connections—30-50 amp
Dockside water connections—yes
Cable television hookup—yes
Telephone hookup—yes
Waste pump-out—yes, on the fuel dock
Showers—yes, but in the process of being replaced with updated units
Laundromat—yes, but in the process of being updated, same as the showers
Fuel—gas and diesel
Mechanical repairs—mechanic on call
Ship's store—yes, rather thorough
Restaurant—yes

Faro Blanco Resort, Oceanside

Faro Blanco Resort, Oceanside
(24 42.209 North/081 06.468 West)

Would you believe there is yet one more facility guarding the northern banks, northwest of unlighted daybeacon #12 and west of the Boot Key Bridge? Well, we hope you believe it, as this is the location of the marina known as Faro Blanco Resort, Oceanside.

Hurricane Georges hit Marathon in November of 1998 and whacked the south side of Marathon hard. At the time, there were about 20 houseboats moored at Faro Blanco Resort, Oceanside. These were what amounted to two-story rectangular buildings that were built on floating barges and permanently attached to the dock. Make that semipermanently. According to a Faro Blanco employee on the Bayside, "Half of them sank. They were later taken out. The adjacent docks were all torn up." Not all of the houseboats were taken out. Eleven remain at the back of the marina, and they are actually quite attractive.

The marina still has not completely recovered to its pre-Georges level. During our on-site visit, Faro Blanco Resort, Oceanside was about seventy-five percent restored and getting better. There were some destroyed finger piers still in evidence, but the main dock is concrete and virtually new. More houseboats are not in the future.

Transients are welcome here. The dockage consists of fixed concrete and some fixed wooden piers. Low-water depths vary from a typical sounding of 8 feet to a minimum of 6 feet. Both slip space and alongside docking are used. Dockside power of 30 to 50 amps is present, along with fresh water connections. Cable television and telephone hookups are also provided. There is waste pump-out on dock B only, as of this writing, but it will be universal in time.

There is a mechanic on call but no fuel here. It is readily available from the other nearby facilities reviewed above.

We found a cruising library in the dockmaster's office, which also has a simple array of commercial items, but nothing serious in the line of boating gear. Variety items consisted of mostly soft drinks and beer. The average showers and Laundromat are a fair piece from the end of the dock, but cruisers berthing at an inner slip will like the convenience.

The former on-site restaurant is closed, and the same caveat about the neighborhood north of the dockage basin, which was discussed in connection with Burdine's Waterfront Marina above, applies here. Many cruisers will probably want to take a taxi to visit the local restaurants or grocery stores.

The co-dockmasters, Bill Shook and Hank Osgyn, are easy-going and affable. Were but everybody in Marathon so nice.

Faro Blanco Resort, Oceanside (305) 743-9018
http://www.spottswood.com

Approach depth—7-9 feet
Dockside depth—6 to 8 feet, varies with slip location
Accepts transients—yes
Type of piers—fixed concrete and fixed wooden piers
Dockside power connections—30-50 amp
Dockside water connections—yes
Waste pump-out—available on B dock only
Showers—yes, only average
Cable hookup—yes
Phone hookup—yes
Laundromat—yes, three washers and two dryers
Mechanical repairs—mechanic on call
Ship's store—limited
Restaurant—not open now

Marathon Boatyard

Marathon Boatyard
(24 42.413 North/081 06.238 West)

After passing through a motley collection of sunken and semisunken vessels and then under (or through) the 24-foot bascule bridge spanning the westerly entrance to Boot Key Harbor, cruisers can turn north up a narrow canal and visit one of Marathon's largest repair facilities.

Marathon Boatyard is not a place that one might choose for its cachet and tourism appeal. Read on, though. This is a full-service boatyard with a 60-ton Travelift. "Anything that has gone wrong with a boat we can fix," said owner Bruce Popham. They are Detroit Diesel, Volvo, and Lugger diesel dealers. They also sell Northern Light gen sets. This is a very big boatyard; they have room for 110 boats on the dry at the same time. The service is focused on the customer, and they seem ready to go the extra mile at every opportunity.

If something on your boat went bump in the night, you'd count yourself lucky to be here. This is a serious boatyard in every sense of the word, a place to cherish when things go ping or thump or ta-pocketta-pocketta-pocketta. It's in downtown Marathon, and everything you might need to keep you occupied while your boat is being worked on is within walking distance. Watch out for the Marathon vehicular traffic; it's fierce.

Transients are welcome here, but this operation's focus is clearly on service, not overnight dockage. The usual visiting cruiser amenities—pool, restaurant(s), guest services, and the like—are absent. Minimum approach depths run 7 feet with at least 10 feet or more dockside and on the entrance canal.

Berths are found alongside at fixed wooden piers. There are fresh water and 30- to 50-amp connections dockside. The one shower on the premises is unisex and rather old, but it is clean. Waste pump-out, cable hookups, a Laundromat, and phone hookups are not found here.

In a rather unusual arrangement, the local West Marine store sits just behind the dockage basin, apparently, on property leased from Marathon Boatyard, and so is a dinghy dock, which allows transients who are anchored out to come ashore and visit West Marine store. You had best stick to your knitting when you use this pier, however. The sign on the dinghy dock reads:

PLEASE FOLLOW THESE RULES
THIS IS PRIVATE PROPERTY
NOT OWNED BY WEST MARINE
1. ONE HOUR LIMIT WHILE SHOPPING AT WEST MARINE. PLEASE DO NOT USE THIS DOCK FOR TRIPS TO THE LAUNDROMAT, RESTAURANT OR OTHER BUSINESSES.
NO EXCEPTIONS
2. NO BIKES, FUEL JUGS OR PETS AT ANY TIME.
3. NO DOCKING SUNDAYS OR BEFORE 8 A.M. or AFTER 5:30 P.M.
4. NO DUMPING OF OIL OR BATTERIES
ANYONE FAILING TO HONOR THESE RULES WILL HAVE THEIR DINGHY IMPOUNDED AND CHAINED.
YOU WILL BE CHARGED $50 A DAY STORAGE FEE.

West Marine Sign (Marathon Boatyard)

We found the people who run this marine facility to be forthright and as competent as one could want. There is, however, a kind of outlaw mentality among some of the live-aboards who are anchored out in Boot Key Harbor. It seems that this sign is aimed their way. While it does not convey a laissez-faire attitude on the part of the marina and could strike some as harsh, it is meant to get a message across in terms that are implicit. We think that you would be wise not to test the resolve of the boatyard management on this matter. There are other places, other dinghy docks (see below), for those with business in establishments other than West Marine. None are quite so convenient, though. All the good things in life are a trade-off, eh?

Across the street is a Mexican restaurant by the name of Pancho's (2010 Overseas Highway, 305-289-1629). We ate there and the food was average, but the service was excellent. This dining establishment offers a full bar as well. There are many other places to dine close by.

Marathon Boatyard (305) 743-6341
http://www.yardofficeatmarathonboatyard.com

Approach depth—7-9 feet
Dockside depth—10+ feet
Accepts transients—yes
Type of piers—fixed wooden piers (all alongside docking)
Dockside power connections—30-50 amp
Dockside water connections—yes
Showers—yes (one that is old and unisex, but clean)
Mechanical repairs—extensive (gasoline and diesel engines)
Ship's store—West Marine, next door.
Restaurant—many nearby

Seven Mile Grill, Marathon

Lower Boot Key Anchorage
(24 42.233 North/081 06.168 West)

Some captains choose to anchor their vessels on the waters of western Boot Key Harbor, east of the 24-foot bascule bridge. These boats are less numerous, and some seemed to be in poorer state of repair than those anchored on upper portion of the harbor. Nevertheless, depths here run from 6 to 11 feet, as long as you avoid the shallow southerly shoreline. Watch out for a few sunken and semisunken boats in this anchorage. Fouling your anchor on one of these derelicts would almost certainly result in losing your hook.

Upper Boot Key Harbor Anchorage
(24 42.362 North/081 05.432 West)

Many a Boot Key Harbor newbie has sailed under the Boot Key Bridge, taken one look at the huge collection of pleasure craft anchored on the waters to the east, and set course straight for this popular anchorage. After passing unlighted daybeacon #18 and #19, the next sound they hear is their keel meeting up with the muddy, slimy bottom.

While on the water it looks as if you can just cruise straight into the upper (easterly) reaches of Boot Key Harbor, there is actually a very large shoal that cuts across the bay's breadth, east of unlighted daybeacon #19 and north of unlighted daybeacon #21.

To avoid this considerable hazard, navigators must pick their way through the initial section of the Sister Creek approach channel. Then, south of unlighted daybeacon #21, you can cut to the east and bypass the shoal. We will give a far more detailed account of this

Sombrero Marina and Dockside Lounge

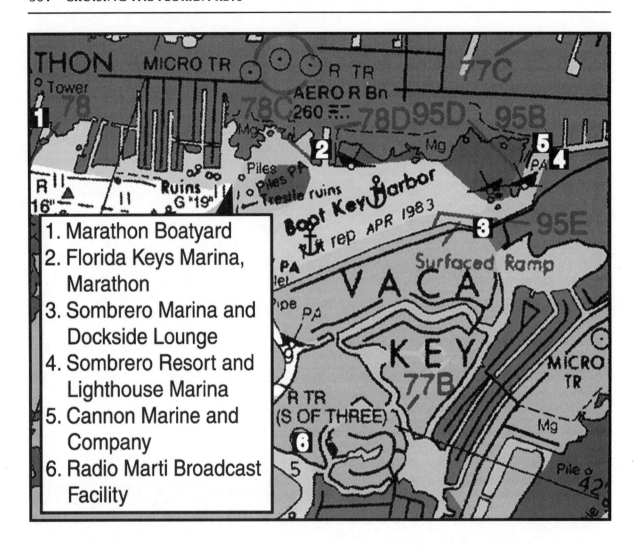

1. Marathon Boatyard
2. Florida Keys Marina, Marathon
3. Sombrero Marina and Dockside Lounge
4. Sombrero Resort and Lighthouse Marina
5. Cannon Marine and Company
6. Radio Marti Broadcast Facility

scheme in our navigational account of Boot Key Harbor below.

By the time you have made your way to unlighted daybeacon #A, captains can cut to the north and try to pick out a place to anchor amidst the crowd, and we do mean crowd, of vessels. Depths vary from 8 to as much as 12 feet, even at low tide. Just stay away from that shoal mentioned above.

If it weren't for your neighbors, there would be enough swing room for the *Queen Mary* in this anchorage. On-the-water reality demands that you pick a spot that will allow plenty of elbowroom between your craft and any adjacent vessels. Be warned, this can require a bit of hunting, particularly during the winter cruising season.

As noted in our introduction to Boot Key Harbor above, it doesn't get much more sheltered than this. Nothing short of a full gale should give much in the way of problems when snugly ensconced within this haven.

Florida Keys Marina, Marathon

Turd Tug (Boot Key Harbor)

One live-aboard, who seemed to know his stuff and was large enough to get your attention just by his sheer size, told us that a Bahamian Moor is the accepted way of anchoring at Boot Key Harbor. The holding ground is good, he said, but swinging on a Bahamian Moor gives others a little more (pun intended) room in an anchorage that gets very, very crowded at times.

Florida Keys Marina, Marathon (24 42.562 North/081 05.483 West)

An increasingly important facility known as the Florida Keys Marina, Marathon overlooks the northern shores of Boot Key Harbor, north of unlighted daybeacon #2B. A few low-key navigational markers outline the route to this marina. These aids serve mostly to keep cruisers clear of the large shoal mentioned above, which lies just to the west.

Florida Keys Marina is operated by the Marathon Community Council, a nonprofit organization of private individual Marathon citizens who have chosen to trod the road-little-taken. While the frills are few here—the building which houses the offices is an old, concrete fish-processing warehouse and looks it—the concept of having local people running a municipal marina business was born, apparently, out of frustration with the way things were going with live-aboards in Boot Key Harbor. The marina offers a supremely useful dinghy dock, and the rate for its use is $10 less per month than its competition (see below).

For live-aboards, the warehouse offers locked storage in plywood houses. The interior space in the warehouse is plentiful, and the inside temperature is cool and shaded all the time.

Maybe most importantly, the Florida Keys Marina, Marathon is an enlightened step in the right direction, socially and environmentally. It is close to everything in Marathon.

This is also the berthing place for the Turd Tug, an outboard-powered pump-out vessel that will service boats anchored out on the waters of Boot Key anchorage for a fee. The Tug's slogan is: "We're Number 1 with Your Number 2!"

Transients are welcome here. This is not the plushest facility in Marathon, but it undoubtedly has the best purchase on the future. You can probably pay more and probably pay less than what it will cost you to spend some time here, but no where else will you support an idea whose time has come as much as you will when you tie up here.

Currently dockage is afforded alongside a concrete sea wall, with wooden pilings in close attendance. Depths alongside are a very impressive 12 feet or more of water at low tide, with minimum 8-foot approach soundings. Power connections are of the 30- to 50-amp variety, and fresh water hookups are available at all berths. There are even telephone connections to be had. Waste pump-out service is also in the offing. Showers, clean but without much in the way of frills, are only a few steps away, as is an excellent Laundromat. All in all, we can attest to the fact that this entire facility is well maintained and will get better with time and the availability of money.

Several local restaurants, including the Stuffed Pig (3520 U.S. Highway 1, 305-743-4059), are within easy walking distance. There is also a convenience store close by, but it is a bit of a hike to make your way to the nearest supermarket.

The future Boot Key Harbor plan calls for a

mooring field, fees for using the moorings, an enforceable plan for making certain that live-aboards do not continue to pollute Boot Key Harbor, and the right amount and type of people on staff who will make sure that all those regulations are carried out.

Florida Keys Marina, Marathon (305) 289-8877
flkeysmarina@marathonkey.com

Approach depth—8-10 feet
Dockside depth—12+ feet
Accepts transients—yes
**Type of piers—alongside docking at a concrete
   sea wall**
Dockside power connections—30-50 amp
Dockside water connections—yes
Telephone hookup—yes
Waste pump-out—at the dock
Showers—yes
Laundromat—yes, excellent
Restaurant—many nearby

Sombrero Marina and Dockside Lounge (24 42.511 North/081 05.017 West)

Sombrero Marina and Dockside Lounge resides on Boot Key Harbor's southerly banks, near the bay's easterly limits, just east of unlighted daybeacon #5A. East of this point, the harbor narrows to a canal-like body of water.

If Florida Keys Marina, Marathon (above) is an attempt to bring order out of chaos in Boot Key Harbor, then Sombrero Marina and Dockside Lounge, and the people who enliven this place, are its reason d'être.

Sombrero Marina is the other side of the coin, and it is famous. This is where the salty, gnarly cruisers hang out. This is where the live-aboards dinghy ashore. This is where tales are told, interviews are given, and marine writers come to get a story or two. Sombrero Marina, with its open-16-hours-a-day bar—which is as

integral to its survival as your heart and brain are to yours—has been around so long and has become such a revered location in the cruising world that it is, truly, a legend in its own time.

Cruisers—whether they do it by sail or power—are an independent lot of people. This is where the most independent of the independent hang out. Some might go so far as to call them feisty.

"We don't go by last names down here," said a barkeep by the name of Rosie, who refused to give her last name. "It is not like working in the real world."

Doubtless.

Rosie was dead set against having a mooring field in Boot Key Harbor. "We are fighting to keep some of the more desirable anchoring spots in the anchorage," she said. However, live-aboards, who pay no property taxes, have little say in local governmental decisions. The handwriting is on the wall. There are those who say, "It's about time." There are those who say, "You are trampling on my rights." Time will tell.

People in positions of responsibility in Marathon all agree that Boot Key Harbor is polluted. Even Rosie said it was. But she contended that the pollution did not come from live-aboards pumping effluent into the water; rather, she said, it came from the fertilizer runoff from a nearby golf course.

Political issues aside, Sombrero Marina has a dinghy dock where for a fee—$3 a day, $15 a week, or $55 a month—you can dinghy in and tie up. Dinghies that are left unattended at the dock with tools and other valuables in them are virtually guaranteed to be left alone. There's a policy of unassailable honesty here, we were told, and no one dares breach it.

The bar at Sombrero Marina is a joyous and jumping place on Friday, Saturday, and Sunday nights, and one power cruiser, who had either the good fortune or misfortune to be tied up near where all the action was, said that it got a mite noisy on those evenings. Breakfast is served on weekends. Lunch is available from 11:30 A.M.-3 P.M., seven days a week; and a fast-food dinner is available at a separate facility within a few feet of the bar and lunch counter. The bar opens at 8 A.M. and serves until midnight.

On the definite plus side is the location of a Publix and K-Mart within walking distance of this marina. If you pushed it, you could even carry ice cream back without it melting, provided you had a freezer on board.

Now that you know all you need to know— or never wanted to know in the first place—let us press on to the facilities. Transients are welcome here. There are about 30 slips, which cruisers may rent when available. All berths feature 30- to 50-amp electrical service, cable television hookup, and dockside water. The showers are in the same building as the bar, so they will be easy to find. The Laundromat is right there, too. No fuel and no mechanical repairs available, but these are close by. Nothing in Marathon comes with as much gnarly color as the Sombrero Marina and Dockside Lounge. You need to sample this, even if you don't stay here.

Sombrero Marina and Dockside Lounge
  (305) 743-0000

Approach depth—7-9 feet
Dockside depth—6 feet
Accepts transients—yes
Type of piers—30 slips, fixed wooden docks,
  some alongside, some finger piers
Dockside power connections: 30-50 amp
Dockside water connections—yes
Waste pump out—no, but the Turd Tug is close by

Showers—yes, two unisex
Cable hookup—yes
Phone hookup—available
Laundromat—yes
Restaurant—on site.

Sombrero Resort and Lighthouse Marina (24 42.735 North/081 04.885 West)

Whoever came up with the idea of naming two virtually adjacent facilities both "Sombrero?" Let's be clear on this. There is no connection other than a naming similarity between Sombrero Marina and Dockside Lounge and Sombrero Resort and Lighthouse Marina. Period!

Sombrero Resort and Lighthouse Marina lies along the southerly banks, northeast of Sombrero Marina and Dockside Lounge, just as Boot Key Harbor narrows to a canal and turns sharply back to the east-northeast (almost opposite Cannon Marine—see below). The marina itself is huge, 72 slips total. In season most of them are filled up, but there may be room at the end of the line. The adjacent resort features all the amenities—pool, beach, hotel rooms, tennis courts, fitness workout room, and a sauna.

Lighthouse Marina is glad to accept transients. Overnight and more permanent dockage is found at both fixed wooden finger piers and alongside larger fixed wooden piers, depending on the location. Visiting mariners will discover a full array of dockside connections, including 30- to 50-amp power service, fresh water, telephone, and cable television hookups.

The harbor is very well protected. The only thing that might dislodge a cruiser is the possibility of a hurricane.

The on-site Laundromat is open-air but covered. It is clean, with six washers and eight dryers. And it has a cruisers' library. The showers and bathrooms are vintage Keys, not

Sombrero Marina dinghy dock (Boot Key Harbor)

quite good enough to delight and not quite bad enough to cause despair. That is not to say that they are not clean. They are, however, a bit dated as to fixtures and amenities.

A one-mile walk to the east along U.S. 1 will lead visiting cruisers to a Publix supermarket and all kinds of other stores. This may be a bit far for most, particularly when carrying groceries back to the galley. A quick taxi ride is a pleasant alternative.

This facility, as a whole, seems to be in a state of flux, with better things in the offing. Oddly, some of the answers that one might expect to be on the tips of employees' tongues were not there. They were, however, willing to find out.

There's a poolside tiki bar. The on-site restaurant is in the process of being renamed to Lighthouse of Blues (305-743-4108). We are always put a little on edge by changes of restaurant names and fare. If it wouldn't work with Plan A, how can we be assured that Plan B will be any better? That's a rhetorical question, of course, but one that is fair to ask when one is putting up the bucks for dinner. In any case, the restaurant sits at the end of the swimming pool.

One of the real assets here is Bob Robinson, the dockmaster, who is jovial and knowledgeable and doesn't seem to be able to do enough to make your stay enjoyable.

Sombrero Resort and Lighthouse Marina (305) 743-2250
http://www.FL-WEB.com/sombrero

Approach depth—8+ feet
Dockside depth—12+ feet
Accepts transients—yes
Type of piers—fixed wooden
Dockside power connections—30-50 amp
Dockside water connections—yes
Cable television hookup—yes
Telephone hookup—yes
Showers—eight showers, four for each sex, no connecting doors.
Laundromat—yes
Restaurant—on site

Cannon Marine and Company
(24 42.751 North/081 04.916 West)

Northeast of Sombrero Marina and Dockside Lounge, Boot Key Harbor narrows to an almost canal-like body of water. It cuts first north and then strikes east-northeast to an eventual dead end. Cannon Marine and Company (305-289-0505) guards the northerly banks, just as the canal makes its swing to the east.

This facility is primarily a dry-stack storage facility that neither wants nor accepts transients. They do feature some seriously good Mercury mechanics, and we owe Cannon a vote of thanks for getting one of our research vessels up and running again in jig time.

Sister Creek

A marked channel leaves the southerly reaches of Boot Key Harbor and flows into the mouth of Sister Creek. This stream provides a second inlet and egress between the harbor and the offshore-Hawk Channel route. It is reasonably easy to run, but it is not as deep as the westerly approach, and there are several shoals that impinge on the channel's flanks here and there. Minimum dead low-water depths are 5 feet, though we have seldom sounded less than 6 feet.

Sister Creek demands navigational caution, particularly as you approach its seaward entrance. Vessels drawing less than 5 feet should not meet with any undue difficulty, unless the usual, swift tidal currents facilitate a meeting between your keel and an adjoining sand bar.

South of unlighted daybeacon #21, Sister Creek flows first to the southeast and then back to the south. While cruising this southern-running stretch, look to the east, and you will spy four radio towers and a legion of "U.S. Government Property—No Trespassing" signs. This semisecret federal facility provided a unique happening for one of this guide's authors.

Marathon Radio Curiosity

One of the interesting things that you can find in Marathon is an official United States government installation, surrounded by a high chain-link fence topped with two rows of barbed wire. Two rows. It is an island flanking the easterly shores of Sister Creek and can be identified, day or night, by four radio towers.

Land access is gained via a locked gate port with a television camera on the outside that shows your image to the armed guard, who resides in a guardhouse inside two gates.

If admitted, you pass through an outer gate, which closes behind you before the inner gate opens up. Then the inner gate opens and then closes behind you. You're in. If you have ever been in a prison, just as a visitor of course, you know the feeling of finality when those two gates shut behind you.

This facility, though it doesn't say so anywhere, is Radio Marti, the 24-hour-a-day radio station that has for years beamed Spanish-language radio broadcasts to Cuba. The aim of the station is to get the United States point of view across to Cubans, and possibly, influence Cuban policy.

Radio Marti Broadcast Facility (Sister Creek)

This writer got into Radio Marti just by a fluke. I was wearing, by chance, a baseball cap with a Central Intelligence Agency emblem on it. I had gotten it as a birthday present from some Washington, D. C. friends a couple of years previous to this occasion. The guard must have thought I was the genuine article because he let me in, and we chatted about Viet Nam, where he had served and where I have never been. Driving to where I had a good view, I took my picture of the building that houses the Radio Marti transmitter, turned around, and left. Right through those double chain-link gates, which were so nicely opened for me, both ways.

Devoid of any landscaping and designed by government architects, the broadcast facil-ity is as hard-featured as you'll see anywhere and only rivals the closed Russian embassy in Havana and the Southern Bell concrete-microwave monolith on Key Largo in its general unsightliness. The only saving grace it has is that it is smaller and less conspicuous than either the Russian Embassy or Southern Bell's cement blunder.

Interestingly, most of the people in Marathon are unaware of its existence, and if they are aware, they still don't know what it does. The only person who knew exactly what was out there was a postal delivery lady driving a mail truck.

The United States has broadcast to Cuba ever since the 1959 Cuban Revolution. It started with Radio Swan, a pure propaganda station. Over time that operation eventually became Radio Marti, but it went through many permutations as a CIA-sponsored station with CIA-originated programming.

Jose Marti—the Cuban patriot and influential Hispanic writer for whom the station is named—was born in Havana in 1853, but for much of his life he lived outside his own country. He had been "political" in Cuba and was jailed for his ideals. When he was seventeen years old, and after he had spent some time in Cuban prisons, he was exiled to Spain. After graduating from college in Spain, he moved to Mexico and then Guatemala. It seemed to be his destiny to land in countries whose politics he disagreed with. A military coup forced him out of Guatemala, and in 1878 he went back to Cuba under a general amnesty. After again conspiring against Spanish colonial authorities in Cuba, he was banished anew. He went to Spain and then to the United States. He stayed a year, went to Venezuela, and then came back to New York City, where he lived from 1881 to 1895. In 1895 he left New York to go back to Cuba to join the war for independence. He died in Cuba in one of the first skirmishes of the war he so vehemently advocated.

When Ronald Reagan was president in 1981, he made a speech in which he announced that it was his administration's intent to establish what he called Radio Free Cuba. The United States Senate voted down the money for this entity in 1982. However, in 1983, legislation allocating the money for the radio station passed through Congress, and in October of that year, Ronald Reagan signed the Radio Broadcasting to Cuba Act. Radio Marti was then placed under the authority of the Voice of America.

Radio Marti signed on for the first time in May of 1985 from its transmitter in Marathon, and it got Fidel Castro's attention right away. He threatened to have Cuban stations transmit on some of the same frequencies used by commercial stations in the United States, but he never carried through on his threat.

Radio Marti started with 14½ hours of programming a day. Now it runs 24 hours a day, seven days a week. But it is not a propaganda outlet, in the conventional sense of the word. It broadcasts soap operas, news, entertainment shows, music, and even messages "back home" for relatives of Cuban Americans who are now living in the United States. Eschewing a heavy-handed approach, the station has found a responsive audience in Cuba, and some say that it is the most listened-to station in that island-nation.

The Cuban government slanders the station in its own broadcasts, which shows that both the guys in the white hats and the guys in the black hats are all tuning in. In Cuba, that fact may make Radio Marti what every radio station in the United States says it is after the latest ratings period is over—Number One!

One question remains. How can you ever be Caller Number Nine and win all the prizes when you live across the Straits of Florida?

BOOT KEY HARBOR NAVIGATION

Both approach channels serving Boot Key Harbor are very well marked and reasonably deep. The primary, western cut has minimum 7-foot depths and easy access to many of the harbor's marina and repair yard facilities. Sister Creek, the southerly entrance, runs north from the offshore, Hawk Channel waters to the southerly flank of central Boot Key Harbor. This entrance is very convenient to the major harbor anchorage, but dead low-tide soundings can run as thin as 5 feet. There are also a host of shoals adjoining the channel that are waiting to trap the unwary.

Boot Key Harbor itself is a bit more navigationally complex than it first appears on the water. It looks as if all you need to do is cruise east on the centerline. Wrong! A huge shoal north of the Sister Creek inlet can be a major problem for first-timers.

Western Approach Channel Pass between the outermost markers, flashing daybeacon #1 and unlighted daybeacon #2, and continue to the east by passing to the fairly immediate southerly sides of unlighted daybeacons #3, #5, and #7. From #7, point to pass between the next pair of markers, unlighted daybeacons 9 and #10.

Cruisers making for the first-class facilities at Marathon Marina should cut north just short of unlighted daybeacon #9 and cruise into the dockage basin. The entrance is obvious.

East of #9 and #10, there are two additional markers west of the bascule bridge, unlighted daybeacons #12 and #14. Pass to the north of both #12 and #14, and in general, favor the northerly banks along this stretch. The southerly shoreline is shoal.

East of #9, Pancho's Fuel Dock, Burdine's Waterfront Marina, and Faro Blanco Resort, Oceanside will all come abeam along the northerly banks, in the order listed here. A short hop east of Faro Blanco, cruisers will say hello to the 24-foot (closed vertical clearance) bascule bridge that spans the gap between Marathon and virtually undeveloped Boot Key.

The Boot Key Harbor Bascule Bridge opens on demand (surprisingly enough), except between the hours of 10:00 P.M. and 6:00 A.M. Openings during this nighttime period require a 2-hour notice (call 305-289-2430), but we suggest not holding your breath unless you have a very good reason to request that the bridge open during this time period.

Once through the bridge, the lower Boot Key Harbor anchorage will lie before you.

Lower Boot Key Harbor Anchorage Cruisers who arrive on the eastern face of the Boot Key Harbor Bascule Bridge will undoubtedly find a host of anchored vessels in front of them. Good depths stretch out in a broad band along the midwidth.

Just don't be lured towards the southerly banks by any vessels that might seem to be anchored on these waters. These boats are sitting in the mud. Stay at least 150 yards off the southerly shoreline to avoid this hazard.

Marathon Boatyard Captains bound for this truly world-class repair yard should cut north immediately after passing under the Boot Key Bascule Bridge. Look towards the shoreline, and pick out the easternmost of the two small canals, which will open out before you. A sign at the canal's southerly tip helps in the identification process.

Cruise into the centerline of this small stream. Skippers of larger cruising craft may be taken aback by the narrow nature of this approach stream, but keep the faith. It is deep and wide enough for anything short of the former *Trump Princess*.

The repair yard will appear dead ahead and along the easterly shores. The West Marine dinghy dock will also come up to the east, about ⅔ of the way between the canal's southerly entrance and its northerly terminus.

East on Boot Key Harbor Cruisers continuing east on the broad waters of Boot Key Harbor should pass unlighted daybeacon #16 fairly close to its northerly side. Look to the east, and you will see what will appear to be a forest of masts. These vessels are all moored on the popular Upper Boot Key Harbor Anchorage. First-timers could be readily excused for thinking all they need do is forge straight ahead and join this happy throng. Such a course of action would not, however, take into account the large shoal, already mentioned several times in this chapter, which lies just north of Sister Creek. Many a bent prop or mud-covered keel can attest to the fact that all cruisers must follow a very different course of action.

To make good your entry into upper (easterly) Boot Key Harbor, pick out unlighted daybeacons #18 and #19. Come abeam of these markers by some 35 yards to their northerly side, then turn to the southeast, and cruise between #18 and #19. Continue on the same course, pointing to pass between the next set of markers unlighted daybeacons #20 and #21.

What you are actually doing by running the gap between the pairs of #18 and #19 and #20 and #21 is following the northwesterly approach to Sister Creek, Boot Key Harbor's southerly entrance. This is the only way to bypass the large patch of shallows to the north and east.

After passing between #20 and #21, look to port for a small island. Cruisers bound for the upper reaches of Boot Key Harbor should cut to the east-northeast and hold to the centerline between this small islet and the southerly shoreline.

Pick out unlighted daybeacon #1A ahead, and be SURE to pass south of this marker. This course will lead you hard by the southerly banks, which is exactly where you need to be to avoid the northern shallows. Just past #1A, captains might choose to swing north and visit Florida Keys Marina, Marathon.

Florida Keys Marina, Marathon From unlighted daybeacon #1A, three daybeacons outline a northerly track to Florida Keys Marina, Marathon. Pass just to the west of unlighted daybeacons #2B and #4B and east of unlighted daybeacon #5B. North of #5B, the long, thin harbor of Florida Keys Marina will open out before you. The dinghy dock will be discovered at the basin's northerly limits.

Upper Boot Key Harbor Anchorage East of #1A, cruisers can cut north and drop anchor amidst a whole host of their fellow pleasure craft. The harbor remains deep as it moves to the northeast. This will not come as a surprise to those on the water. The masts and flybridges stretch away seemingly to infinity.

Your only real challenge in this anchorage is to find a place that allows sufficient elbowroom between your vessels and the neighbors. This can be quite a challenge during the winter cruising season.

Upper Boot Key Harbor Facilities Captains and crews continuing on to Sombrero Marina and Dockside Lounge, Sombrero Resort and Lighthouse Marina, or Cannon Marine and Company should continue following the channel paralleling Boot Key Harbor's southerly banks by passing south of unlighted daybeacons #3A and #5A. Of course, you don't really have to follow the marked channel, as the waters to the north of #3A and #5A are deep as well, but hey, we've always thought following buoyed cuts where they are available is a good cruising notion. Hope you agree.

East of Sombrero Marina and Dockside Lounge, Boot Key Harbor's waters narrow substantially and cut to the northeast and then east. At the easterly turn, Cannon Marina will come abeam to the north.

This canal-like section of Boot Key Harbor finally dead-ends at some unused fixed wooden piers. Your only course of action is to turn around and retrace your steps.

Sister Creek Cruisers cutting south on Sister Creek should not turn to the east after passing between unlighted daybeacons #20 and #21, as we described in our navigational section concerning upper Boot Key Harbor above. Instead, continue cruising to the southeast into the mouth of Sister Creek.

As you work your way downstream on Sister Creek, hold scrupulously to the centerline. Shoaling flanks the channel all along this route.

Eventually, as you approach the seaward Sister Creek Channel, you will sight unlighted daybeacon #8. It is VERY important to observe #8 and all its sister markers as you cruise south into Hawk Channel and the offshore waters. Shoals flank the southerly mouth of Sister Creek to the east and west.

As you are now headed TOWARD the open sea, pass all subsequent red, even-numbered aids to navigation to your port side and take green markers to starboard. Of course, if you are headed north on Sister Creek from Hawk Channel to Boot Key Harbor, do just the opposite.

Be especially careful to pass some 20 yards west of unlighted daybeacons #6 and #4. Very shallow water is found east of #6 and #4.

Pass Sister Creek's outermost marker, flashing daybeacon #2, by some 20 yards to its westerly side, and cruise south-southeast out into the deeper offshore waters. Be careful not to slip to the west. As chart 11451 correctly predicts, there is a finger of 4-foot waters south and southwest of #2 waiting to exchange greeting with any vessel that makes this error.

Routes to Western Florida

Navigators not familiar with Floridian waters will probably be asking themselves at this point, Why anyone would journey all the way south and west to Marathon to make a jump across to the western mainland coastline of the Sunshine State? There are actually two answers to this question.

First, north (and east) of Marathon, the very shallow depths of Florida Bay simply do not allow any but very shallow-draft vessels to cruise across its breadth and then turn north to Cape Sable, the southwesternmost tip of mainland Florida.

An even more significant reason lies in the form of an old, decrepit, lift-type railway bridge that spans the Okeechobee Waterway just east of Lake Okeechobee itself, near the tiny community of Port Mayaca. The problem with this span is that even when completely open, it only allows 49 feet of vertical clearance from the water's surface.

For those of you not familiar with the Okeechobee Waterway, this wonderful route normally provides reliable access between the city of Stuart, on the eastern Florida coastline, and Fort Myers, on the state's western shores. During 2000-2001, this passage met with its share of troubles due to some incredibly short-sighted drainage by the Florida Water Management Board, but now, thankfully, depths have returned to normal levels. Complete coverage of the Okeechobee Waterway is to be found in our *Cruising Guide to Eastern Florida*.

The rub is that to cruise the Okeechobee ICW, vessels must be able to clear the 49-foot Port Mayaca Bridge. As can be quickly appreciated, this is not a viable option for most larger sailcraft. Many a sailor has exhausted their entire vocabulary of four- and five-letter words when contemplating this unfortunate span.

Thus, the only alternative is to cruise south to (or almost to) Marathon, where three alternate routes offer safe passage to Cape Sable and Flamingo. However you choose to reach Cape Sable, all three possible routes lead to East Cape and the old village of Flamingo, the first port of call moving south to north on Florida's western (mainland) coastline. We will consider this stopover below. For continued coverage of the Western Florida coastline, please check out our *Cruising Guide to Western Florida*.

Florida Bay Yacht Channel

The first of these three passages cuts northwest from flashing daybeacon #1 (Standard Mile 1173.5), just north of Old Dan Bank. This route is known (and charted) as the Florida Bay Yacht Channel. It is the best choice for cruisers coming south and west from the upper keys. For one thing, it's the first of the three you will reach; and for another, it is the best marked. For our purposes, we will refer to this passage as "route #1."

The Florida Bay Yacht Channel (or route #1) features the shortest runs between the various aids to navigation. It does border on any number of shoals, and navigators must take great care to identify each marker and pass to its appropriate side. Minimum depths are 6 feet along route #1 between Old Dan Bank and Cape Sable, but a navigational mistake could land you in depths as shallow as 1 foot.

Route #2

The second alternative is to cut northwest from flashing daybeacon #13, north of Vaca Cut, and pass just north of Bullard Bank. Once you reach this point, "route #2" follows the same path as "route #3," described below.

Moser Channel and Route #3

And speaking of route #3, this cut jumps north from the northerly reaches of Moser Channel and then weaves its way past several banks and shallows. All these trouble spots are marked, but again, cruisers must take care to pick up each daybeacon and pass them correctly.

Another problem with route #3 is the markerless, 16-nautical-mile run to flashing daybeacon #2, west of First National Bank (no, we didn't make up that name). This loooong passage is ever so much easier to run with a GPS aboard, or better, a GPS interfaced with a laptop computer.

Flamingo

Flamingo was once one of the wildest frontier towns in all of Florida. Sadly, nothing is now left of the Flamingo of yesteryear. Today,

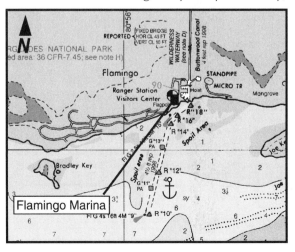

visiting cruisers will find only a lodge, marina, and restaurant, operated by a U.S. Park Service concessionaire.

It is a run of better than 12 nautical miles from the waters off the "East Cape" section of Cape Sable through the northerly waters of Florida Bay to the southerly dockage basin of Flamingo Lodge and Marina. Minimum depths on the entrance channel are about 4½ to 5 feet (found near unlighted daybeacon #16). Typically, soundings range from 5 to 9 feet. Boats drawing less than 4 feet should not have any problems. If you need more water, wait for a higher tide before attempting the passage.

Flamingo Marina has a rather unique situation. There are two dockage basins at this facility that are separated by a concrete floodgate. The harbor north of the gate is used by small craft engaged in cruising the so-called Wilderness Waterway through Everglades National Park. This shallow passage leads adventurous, small-craft skippers through the heart of the great sea of trees and grass north of Flamingo to Everglades City. The waterway is only appropriate for very small (18 feet or less), outboard-powered craft and thus will not be further discussed in this guide. The marina at Flamingo maintains a hoist that can actually lift smaller powercraft over the concrete barrier and deposit them safely in the waters to the north or south. This lift is not heavy enough for larger vessels, but as mentioned, that point is mostly moot anyway.

Of more interest to cruising-sized craft is the sheltered dockage basin on the bay side of the marina, just north of unlighted daybeacon #18. Here you will find fixed wooden piers where transients may dock in 4½- to 6-foot dockside depths. Water and 30-amp power connections are available. Gasoline and diesel can be purchased at a fuel dock just south of the concrete floodgate, where you will also discover a waste pump-out service. Shoreside showers and a Laundromat are at hand beside the full-line variety-and-ship's store. For those wanting to take a break from the live-aboard routine, the adjacent lodge is quite convenient. The restaurant in the complex is not open during the summer months, but you can still get pizza and sandwiches at the bar, which is in operation year round.

Flamingo Marina (941) 695-3101
http://www.flamingolodge.com

Approach depth—$4^{1}/_{2}$-9 feet
Dockside depth—$4^{1}/_{2}$-6 feet
Accepts transients—yes
Fixed wooden piers—yes
Dockside power connections—up to 30 amp
Dockside water connections—yes
Waste pump-out—yes
Showers—yes
Laundromat—yes
Gasoline—yes
Diesel fuel—yes
Ship's and variety store—yes
Restaurant—on site

Flamingo makes an ideal base of operations for those wanting to explore Everglades National Park. Check at the lodge office concerning information about tram tours for those who arrive by water and lack landside automobile transportation. These sorts of excursions are usually offered, except during certain times of the summer. Call ahead of time to see if the park trams are operating.

We cannot leave Flamingo without a word about the mosquitoes. Never have this guide's authors seen such bloodthirsty mosquitoes as those in the Florida Everglades. At times they swarm so thickly that it seems as if everything (and everyone) will be completely covered within a few minutes by frenzied, buzzing, biting insects the size of condors. They practically carried us off during the night and early morning while we were docked at Flamingo. According to Park Service employees, the mosquitoes are at their worst between May and November. They really seem to come out after a rain—the more rain, the more mosquitoes. It should also be noted that calm conditions seem to encourage the little beasts. On a calm summer night or early in the morning after a heavy rainfall, it could be a battle for your life.

To save yourself from these pests, the locals swear by a body lotion produced by the Avon cosmetic company called Skin-So-Soft. While it is most certainly not an insect repellent, apparently mosquitoes hate the taste of this fragrant, perfumy liquid and will not bite if you have slopped the oily concoction on your skin. By all accounts, I would have a large bottle of Skin-So-Soft on board before anchoring or tying up to the docks anywhere between Cape Sable and Marco Island.

Flamingo History

In his fascinating book, *True Tales of the Everglades,* Stuart McIver comments about Flamingo's roots:

"When the settlers at the tip of Cape Sable established a post office in 1893, they were told they had to give their settlement a name. . . . They considered 'End of the World.' Instead they picked a romantic, exotic name for their own personal hell-hole. They called it Flamingo. . . . In the 1890's flocks of the spectacular tropical birds were commonly seen in the Cape Sable area . . . so the name made sense. So did 'End of the World,' since the Cape at that time was an isolated society populated mostly by people who were running away from something—the law, civilization, or maybe their wives."

This short, quaint description tells all, and the term "hell-hole" seems particularly appropriate in view of the climate and the mosquitoes. In those early days, the few residents of Flamingo made a living fishing, cultivating sugarcane, and distilling more than a few quarts of moonshine.

Apparently, mosquitoes were at least as big a problem then as they are now. Each house was equipped with a room fronting the outdoors that was called a "loser." Before anyone entered a house, they were supposed to beat away or "lose" their mosquitoes with a palmetto branch in the little room.

In 1901, Flamingo received one of its most prominent early citizens, Steve Roberts. Uncle Steve, as he came to be called, migrated south from Gainesville, Florida with "cattle rustling" rumors snapping at his heels. He raised a big family which eventually became the most prominent in the tiny settlement.

In 1908 the village's sugarcane was beset by a horde of hungry rats. Desperate to save their one, cash crop, Uncle Steve's son Gene took a boat to Key West, where he advertised, "Will pay 10 cents Apiece for Every Cat." It wasn't long before he had a boat full of snarling, fighting felines. It must have been a long, trying trip back to Flamingo, but the effort was worth it. In no time at all, the new swamp cats had routed out almost every rat within miles.

However, the real fame of Flamingo lies not in fishing, sugarcane, or even rats, but in the wholesale slaughter of the exotic birds that lived in the Everglades and high-ground "hammocks" near the village. At the turn of the century, a truly unfortunate trend in fashion resulted in the stylish practice of decorat-

ing women's hats with colorful bird feathers or plumes. The demand rose so quickly that hunters in the Everglades soon could make more money than they had ever dreamed of before. At one point, egret feathers were selling for $32 an ounce, more than the price of gold at the time. The mass killings drove many of the Everglades' winged species to the brink of extinction after only a few years.

Finally, the state of Florida came to the rescue and outlawed the killing of birds for their plumage in 1901. For several years thereafter, it was a battle between the local game wardens and the plume hunters, but finally this sad trend in fashions crept into the pages of history.

In 1922, a road was pushed through the Everglades from Miami to Flamingo. Surprisingly enough, this artery of commerce was the death knell of the tiny community. As Stuart McIver comments in his other, equally fascinating book, *Glimpses of South Florida History,* "People had found a way to get out." Many of the original homes were destroyed in the great hurricane of 1926 and the rest rotted away, with not a trace remaining today.

Flamingo Legend

It was during that tense period when plume hunting had been outlawed but before the fashion went out of style, that the National Association of Audubon Societies hired a group of wardens to enforce the new state law. Several of these heroic individuals operated out of Flamingo, and one of the most famous was Guy Bradley.

On July 8, 1905, the sounds of distant gunfire were heard over Florida Bay. Guy walked out of his front door and sighted a schooner in the distance, which he recognized as the boat of Capt. Walter Smith. He had already arrested Smith twice before for plume hunting, and the gunfire left little doubt about the captain's present activities.

The intrepid warden got his gun and began rowing his small dinghy across Florida Bay. It was a trip from which he would never return. His body was found soon afterward. Guy Bradley had become the first warden to die in the defense of Florida's native bird population.

Captain Smith fled to Miami, where he managed to successfully avoid indictment through political connections. Nevertheless, the warden's sacrifice was not to be in vain. As a direct result of the anger engendered by Guy Bradley's death, new legislation was passed in both Tallahassee and Washington to end the plume trade within a few years, once and for all.

Guy Bradley was buried on the tip of Cape Sable, and a deeply grateful Audubon Society erected a plaque over his grave. In 1960, Hurricane Donna washed the grave away, but the brave warden and his untimely but honorable death have not been forgotten. Today a notable monument has been erected to Guy Bradley's memory at the Flamingo Visitors' Center.

Flamingo and Cape Sable Anchorages

A few boats occasionally anchor in the waters off Cape Sable during fair weather. None of these havens are particularly sheltered, and they should not be employed if there is a hint of foul weather in the forecast.

Captains wanting to anchor off Flamingo, rather than tie up at the marina docks, might consider doing so in the 4- and 5-foot waters east of unlighted daybeacon #11. Don't stray too far from the marked channel, or depths may deteriorate further.

In light winds, cruisers may consider anchoring in the charted 7- and 8-foot waters northwest and southeast of Middle Cape. Anchor abeam of the cape's westerly tip, either to the north or south. Do not attempt to make a closer approach to the beach except by dinghy, as depths rise quickly.

Middle Cape is surrounded by a beautiful white-sand beach backed by tall trees that look as if they have not known the hand of man since time immemorial. You explorer types might try dinghying ashore through the surf for an unforgettable visit. Just don't forget about the mosquitoes if the winds are calm.

North along the Western Florida Coastline

Cruisers continuing north from Flamingo and Cape Sable (and that will be most everyone who journeys from Marathon to this region) have an incredible host of cruising opportunities before them, including the fascinating backwater anchorages not far to the north on Little Shark River. May we be so bold as to recommend our *Cruising Guide to Western Florida* for those continuing their northward trek. This volume can be had at a mere fraction of its real value at all West Marine, Boat/U.S., and many private marine stores, or by ordering on-line from our Web site at http://www.CruisingGuide.com. Happy cruising!

ROUTES TO WESTERN FLORIDA NAVIGATION

The only other general tip we have to give you, besides the old saw of being sure to "take care of business," is to yet again recommend that you cruise with a GPS interfaced with a laptop computer, onto which is loaded digitized versions of ALL the NOAA charts along the way, plus appropriate navigational software (such as Nobeltec's "Visual Navigational Suite" or Maptech's "Offshore Navigator"). You simply will not believe what a difference it will make in your passage making.

Florida Bay Yacht Channel, alias Route #1
From flashing daybeacon #1, north of Old Dan Bank, set course to the northwest, pointing to come abeam of yet another flashing daybeacon #1, southwest of Arsenic Bank. After crossing the intervening 3 nautical miles between the two #1s, navigators are right away presented with one of the most difficult sections of the Florida Bay Yacht Channel.

Check out chart 11451, and notice the tongue of 1- and 2-foot waters south of #1 and yet another patch of equally shallow water north of its sister marker, flashing daybeacon #2. These shoals are for real, and cruisers must take the greatest care to bypass these hazards, or you could well be aground just where it seems least likely to occur.

To avoid the twin shoal, come abeam of flashing daybeacon #1 by about 20 yards to its northerly side. Immediately, alter course to the southwest and point to pass between #1 and flashing daybeacon #2. Take a very lazy turn around #2, eventually coming back to a northwesterly heading. Be SURE to stay at least 50 yards south and southwest of #2.

Wasn't that fun. Well, the worst is behind you. The next marker is unlighted daybeacon #3, which should be passed by at least 200 yards to its northeasterly quarter. The same heading will bring you abeam of flashing daybeacon #5, north of Sprigger Bank. Don't get anywhere near #5. There is NO water south of this marker. We suggest coming abeam and passing #5 by 300 to 400 yards to its northeasterly side. If depths start to rise, give way to the northeast to find better soundings.

From #5, it is a run of slightly better than 3.6 nautical miles to the next Florida Bay Yacht Channel aid to navigation, flashing daybeacon #6. This beacons sits hard by the westerly reaches of another large shoal known as Schooner Bank. Come abeam and pass #6 by at least 300 yards to its southwesterly side.

For reasons which will remain forever known only to those who placed the markers, a very strange unlighted daybeacon #7 is located on the interior reaches of Schooner Bank. Another set of marks, beginning with unlighted daybeacons #9X and #10X and ending with unlighted daybeacons #11 and #12, have been placed east and north of Oxfoot Bank. We STRONGLY suggest that you ignore all these highly questionable markers. Instead, continue on to the northwest, pointing to come abeam of flashing daybeacon #10, marking the southwestern foot of Oxfoot Bank by at least 300 yards to its southwesterly side. Along the way, you will pass well southwest of unlighted daybeacon #8.

Cruisers will now face the longest run between aids to navigation on this passage. It is a run of slightly better than 7.1 nautical miles from #10 to flashing daybeacon #2, well west of First National Bank. Wonder what joker came up with the name for this shoal?

For best depths, run a compass and/or GPS course designed to come abeam of #2 by some .6 nautical miles to its westerly side. This plan will keep your craft well west of the shallows associated with First National Bank.

From #2, cruisers can continue north to Cape Sable or take a lazy turn to the east and head for Flamingo. For the moment, let's turn our attention to route #2 and route #3. We will review the track to Flamingo at the very end of this chapter.

Route #2 Route #2 is really just a shortcut for westbound (southbound) craft that want to make the run from Marathon to Cape Sable. After coming between the first set of marks, it follows the same path as route #3.

From the ICW's flashing daybeacon #13, cut to the northwest and set course to come abeam of unlighted daybeacon #16, southeast of Bullard Bank by some 200 yards to its northeasterly side. Once abeam of #16, continue on the same course for another 200 yards or so, and then swing to the north, pointing to pass well east of flashing daybeacon #17, which marks Bullard Bank. Don't approach #17 closely. It sits in the heart of the Bullard Bank shallows and is surrounded by 2- to 3-foot waters.

At this point, you will have joined route #3, and it is now a long run north to flashing daybeacon #2, west of First National Bank. This portion of the passage is described below in our account of route #3.

Route #3—Moser Channel to Cape Sable
We will follow this route from the northerly face of the old Seven Mile Bridge, but the same directions apply to those cruisers turning north off the ICW and heading for Cape Sable via Moser Channel.

After passing through the old Seven Mile Bridge (the center span has been permanently removed), set your course to the north, pointing to come abeam of flashing daybeacon #8 to its westerly side. Along the way, sharp-eyed navigators will probably spot unlighted daybeacon #24, west of their course lines. This marker is part of the ICW and does not enter into this account.

From #8, it is a short hop for the gap between flashing daybeacon #10 and unlighted daybeacon #9. Once between #9 and #10, set a careful course to come abeam and pass flashing daybeacon #12, west of Red Bay Bank, by some 250 yards to its westerly side. Be sure to stay well west of #12. The half-foot waters of Red Bay Bank lie east of this beacon, and the shoal has begun to impinge on the marker itself.

Next up is flashing daybeacon #13. This aid to navigation denotes 1-foot waters west and northwest of its position. Guess what? You should pass at least 100 yards east of #13.

After coming abeam of #13, turn a tiny bit farther to the north-northeast and set course to come abeam and pass unlighted daybeacon #15 by some 300 to 400 yards to its easterly quarter. This marker sits hard

Sunset over Boot Key Harbor's western entrance

by a patch of 2-foot waters, and you don't want to be anywhere near it.

It's another 1.3 nautical miles to a position between flashing daybeacon #17 and unlighted daybeacon #16. Favor #16, the southeasterly side of the channel. Daybeacon #17 sits in the heart of the 3-foot waters of Bullard Bank. Don't make a close approach to #17.

Now comes the really loooonng leg of this route. It is a run of slightly more than 16.5 nautical miles from a position abeam of #17, to a position abeam of flashing daybeacon #2, west of First National Bank.

This is clearly a good spot to have a GPS aboard (preferably interfaced with a laptop computer). If you are not so fortunate, run a careful compass course and practice your best DR navigation.

Point to eventually come abeam of flashing daybeacon #2 by some .6 nautical miles to its westerly side. From #2, cruisers can continue north to Cape Sable or take a lazy turn to the east and head for Flamingo.

Entrance into Flamingo Take a long, very lazy turn to the east, around flashing daybeacon #2, and cruise through the wide

Seven Mile Bridges (old and new)

gap between #2 and unlighted daybeacon #1A to the north. Deep-draft vessels should probably cruise north from #2 for .9 nautical miles before turning east. This maneuver will avoid the charted patch of 5- and 6-foot depths, north of #2.

From flashing daybeacon #2, the channel is reasonably straightforward, though there are wide gaps between the various aids to navigation along the way. Be sure to have compass courses preplotted and faithfully follow them as you work your way along.

Come abeam and pass unlighted daybeacon #4 by 300 yards or so to its northerly side. Also, stay well south of flashing daybeacon #5. Shoal water lies west and northwest of #5.

Pass unlighted daybeacons #6 and #8 to their northerly sides (as you would expect from the good old "red, right, returning" rule). Shallow water lies south of these markers. From #8, point to come abeam of flashing daybeacon #9 and unlighted daybeacon #10 to their immediate southerly sides.

At #9 and #10, the channel turns sharply north-northeast and cuts through a dredged passage into Flamingo Marina's southerly dockage basin. This is the shallowest portion of the passage to Flamingo. Expect some 5-foot (possibly 4½ at extreme low water) depths abeam of unlighted daybeacon #16.

If you should decide to anchor east of unlighted daybeacon #11, ease your way about 50 yards due east from #11. Drop the hook before proceeding any farther. To the east, soundings rise to 4-foot levels or less.

At unlighted daybeacon #16, the channel swings a bit to starboard then cuts back north at unlighted daybeacon #18. The harbor's entrance will then be obvious dead ahead. As you cruise into the creek, the marina docks will come abeam to port.

Anchored between the Bahia Honda bridges

CHAPTER 5

Little Duck Key to Stock Island

If you are one of those cruisers who cherishes the feeling that every turn of the screw, or every puff of air, carries your craft a bit farther from the maddening crowd, then the waters between Moser Channel and Stock Island will be a genuine treat. Perhaps, nowhere else in all of the Florida Keys is there such an incredible selection of isolated, sometimes well-sheltered, overnight anchorages. Some of these havens will be remembered for a lifetime.

On the other hand, marina facilities are definitely fewer and farther between. The ICW route features a grand total of one marina along its entire run, short of Key West. Even Hawk Channel boasts only a few marinas until Stock Island is sighted in the distance.

West of the Moser Channel, captains must make a very basic choice that they will have to live with all the way to Key West. A majority of cruisers seem to choose the Hawk Channel route. There is little we need add to an overview of this passage here. It is pretty much the same as the upper portion of this channel, which we have been following since Miami, except to note that there are far more anchorages available here than on the waters to the east and north.

The Intracoastal Waterway route is, at least to our collective mind, the more interesting of the two, even though it sees far less pleasure craft traffic. The selection of overnight anchorages is, quite simply, mind boggling. And cruisers traveling this portion of the ICW get to see a portion of the Keys that is still pretty much in its virgin state. That is a rare treat in our modern, well-planned world.

So, whether you choose the well traveled Hawk Channel or the far more remote recesses of the ICW, there is much to recommend to the explorers and adventurers among us on this stretch of the Florida Keys. If you are one of those cruisers who likes to spend every evening at a full-service marina, then you might want to crank out the jib or lay on the throttle a bit more so as to arrive at Key West a bit sooner. Captains and crews of most any other ilk will relish in this opportunity to explore a portion of the keys that often looks as if it has seldom been touched.

Charts For the first time, well-prepared navigators will need a full array of charts to cover all the waters and side passages for both the ICW and Hawk Channel routes.
11451—our old friend has one last, brief fling as it details the waters of Hawk Channel from Moser Channel to Money Key and outlines the ICW, also from Moser Channel to Money Key

11445—an important chart—covers the ICW approach to Big Spanish Channel, including the various alternate channels and anchorages north and east of the ICW track—also details Big Spanish Channel, north to Crawl Key, and the northern keys, just east of Northwest Channel - also depicts Hawk Channel and its many adjoining alternate cuts all the way to Key West

11448—covers the ICW and the northernmost Keys, including the wide assortment of anchorages along this section, as far west as Johnson Key Channel

11442—a very useful chart for those plying the ICW passage from Big Spanish Key to Key West's Northwest Channel—it provides a clearer view of this route through the offshore waters than does 11445—however, it does not give nearly as much detail on the northerly keys themselves—wise navigators running the ICW to Key West will have 11445, 11448, and 11442 aboard

11441—an excellent chart for cruisers planning to run either the Boca Chica Channel or the Stock Island Channel—gives the clearest picture of these waters, though they are also pictured on 11445—also useful when approaching Key West from Hawk Channel and more offshore waters

Bridges

Ohio Key-Bahia Honda Key Bridge—crosses the gap between Ohio Key and Bahia Honda Key south of unlighted daybeacon #3—fixed—14 feet of vertical clearance

Bahia Honda Bridge—crosses the gap between Bahia Honda Key and Spanish Harbor Keys—fixed—20 feet of vertical clearance

Old Bahia Honda Bridge—crosses the gap between Bahia Honda Key and Spanish Harbor Keys, south of the newer bridge detailed above—easternmost portion of this old span has been permanently removed to allow for ready passage by all vessels, particularly sailcraft

No Name Key Bridge—crosses the northerly reaches of the Bogie Channel between Big Pine Key and No Name Key—fixed—15 feet of vertical clearance

Big Pine Key Bridge—spans the gap between Spanish Harbor Keys and Big Pine Key, along the southerly reaches of Spanish Harbor—fixed—11 feet of vertical clearance

Newfound Harbor Channel Bridge—runs the wide gap between Big Pine Key and Little Torch Key, north of unlighted daybeacon #8—fixed—eastern pass-through has 9 feet of vertical clearance, while the larger, western pass-through has 15 feet of vertical clearance

Niles Channel Bridge—crosses Niles Channel between Ramrod Key and Summerland Key—fixed—40 feet of vertical clearance

Kemp Channel Bridge—spans Kemp Channel between Summerland Key and Cudjoe Key, north of unlighted daybeacon #25—fixed—8 feet of vertical clearance

Bow Channel Bridge—runs the breadth of Bow Channel between Cudjoe Key and Sugarloaf Key—fixed—8 feet of vertical clearance

Cow Channel Twin Bridges—runs the gap between Stock Island and Key West—fixed—9 feet of vertical clearance

ICW—Moser Channel to Northwest Channel

As mentioned in the last chapter, many cruisers new to the Florida Keys, or even those who have just followed the crowd year after year, believe the ICW ends at Moser Channel. This bunch thinks their only option is to cruise under the Seven Mile Bridge, meet up with Hawk Channel, and turn west for, where else, Key West.

Well, let us be the first to inform these cruisers that the ICW does not end at Moser Channel. In fact, not only does it not end, but the Waterway route to Key West provides some of the finest wilderness anchorages we have ever reviewed.

Chart 11451 shows a split in the magenta line northeast of the Moser Channel. This is a bit of a misnomer. The northerly track is actually the Waterway, while the indicated southerly passage leads to the only real cruising-craft-oriented marina anywhere near the inside-ICW route and to an inlet known as the Bahia Honda Channel. This cut boasts a wide path to the open sea, but it is bridged by a fixed span with only 20 feet of vertical clearance.

The primary ICW skirts well north of Little Duck Key, Missouri Key, Ohio Key, and Bahia Honda Key then turns northwest on broad, Big Spanish Channel. It then skirts through one tricky section abeam of Big Spanish Key and finally flows out into the waters of the open Gulf of Mexico, north of Harbor Key Bank. The Waterway then turns to the southwest and skirts along the northerly banks of the Keys as it works its way along. Some 28 nautical miles later, cruisers can turn to the southeast on Northwest Channel, which leads, in turn, to Key West.

With winds out of the south, southeast, or southwest, waters along this stretch of the ICW are usually considerably calmer than their Hawk Channel counterparts. However, with strong blows coming from the north, northeast, northwest, or west, the Waterway north and west of Big Spanish Channel can be a real bear. We specifically do not suggest running the ICW if winds are forecast to blow 20 knots or above from any of these quarters.

It should also be noted that the ICW channel is probably most appropriate for cruising craft 45 feet and smaller. While larger vessels could probably run this passage safely, at least by way of cautious navigation, most of the interesting side anchorages would not be easily accessible. Keep this in mind when choosing between the Waterway and Hawk Channel.

The anchorages along this stretch of the ICW can be divided into three definite groups. The first set is found along the alternate passage running to Bahia Channel. The second collection lies abeam of the many small, uniformly undeveloped keys east and west of Big Spanish Channel. Some of these are directly adjacent to the Waterway, while others demand that cruisers follow side channels to reach their location. The third set lies either just off the northerly keys or along the various deep-water streams and channels that run the gaps between these small islets. These latter havens boast by far the best shelter, but they are also more of a navigational challenge.

One word of warning, very few of this myriad collection of overnight havens qualify as foul-weather hidey-holes. If bad weather is in the offing and you want to follow the ICW, better wait for fair weather while securely tucked in Boot Key Harbor or one of Marathon's many marinas.

As mentioned earlier in the introduction, there is but a single cruising-craft-oriented marina along the entire ICW passage between Moser Channel and Key West. Even this facility calls for a fairly long detour off the Waterway's direct path.

To make life easier for you, gentle reader, we will divide our account of the ICW from Little Duck Key to Key West into three sections, dealing first with the alternate route to Bahia Honda Channel, secondly Big Spanish

Channel and its nearby anchorages, and finally, the passage running along the northern edge of the keys to Key West.

Over and above all these dry statistics, this guide's authors would like to note, with a certain amount of glee, that the ICW passage between Moser Channel and Key West is just a whole bunch of fun, at least when the weather cooperates. Who would not be tempted by the "Fat Albert" anchorage off Cudjoe Channel or the secret recesses of Jewfish Basin? These waters will, without question, speak to the heart of any true cruisers who is always wondering just what is really around the next bend.

Alternate Bahia Honda Channel

As noted in the last chapter, the magenta line splits on chart 11451 at unlighted daybeacon #19 and flashing daybeacon #20, north of Knight Key Channel. While the northerly leg is the real ICW passage, the marked southerly route works its way west, across Moser Channel, and then passes north of a series of small keys, including Little Duck Key, Missouri Key, and Ohio Key.

Next up is Bahia Honda Key. The unnamed channel that separates Ohio Key and Bahia Honda Key plays host to Sunshine Key Resort and Marina (reviewed below), which is the one and only cruising-craft-oriented marina anywhere near the ICW between Moser Channel and Key West.

The marked cut eventually turns to the southwest and joins up with the Bahia Honda Channel. After passing a potential anchorage, the combined routes flow under a 20-foot fixed bridge. South of this span, the older Bahia Honda Bridge has been left in place, with a portion of its east side removed to allow for ready access to the open sea. This unhindered passage through the old span renders the anchorage between the bridges and the adjoining state park marina (also reviewed below) an excellent stopover for vessels plying Hawk Channel. Cruisers from the ICW side have to pass under the 20-foot fixed bridge AND deal with some really wicked tidal currents.

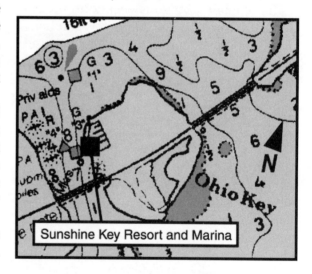

Sunshine Key Resort and Marina

Sunshine Key Resort and Marina
(24 40.360 North/081 14.908 West)

Note the marked channel pictured on chart 11445 between Ohio Key and Bahia Honda Key. This cut leads south and then east into the sheltered harbor serving Sunshine Key Resort and Marina. Minimum approach channel depths run 5½ feet (with typical soundings of 6 to 7 feet), with at least 5½ feet of water in the

Old Bahia Honda Bridge

Sunshine Key Resort and Marina

dockage basin. Don't be surprised to find a few places in the harbor where incredible 35-foot soundings appear on your depth finder. South of the marina entrance, this passage is blocked by a fixed bridge with 14 feet of vertical clearance.

Sunshine Key is a 172-slip, transient-friendly marina that is protected from foul weather blowing in from any quarter. That's the neat part. On the downside, if you have been staying in first-class-resort-type marinas east and north of here, you're in for a little letdown. That is not to say that there aren't some nice features here—there are. On the other hand, this is a travel-trailer resort with a marina added, and you need to keep that in mind. If you are looking for space and real privacy, forget it.

Dockage is provided at wooden-decked floating docks. The available slips are obviously designed for runabout-sized vessels. Bigger boats will want to tie up alongside. Power connections in this marina are skimpy, only four slips feature 30-amp service. All berths feature fresh water hookups, and waste pump-out is available as well, which we think is a definite plus. The marina sells only gas, no diesel. There is also a small, beach, bait, tackle, and variety store on site. Light mechanical repairs can be addressed by local, independent technicians, which the marina staff will be glad to contact for you.

There's supposed to be a Laundromat in the RV park, but we couldn't find it. Out by the highway, which is rather close, is a gas station and convenience store.

On the plus side, Sunshine Key boasts a swimming pool, a couple of tennis courts, and a 12-seat modest restaurant—call it the Sunshine Grill (305-872-2217)—on the premises. The Grill is closed on Mondays and Tuesdays. There are terrific bathroom and shower facilities here. They are not just for marina people, though; they are for everyone, but the ones we saw were modern, clean as a whistle, and well lit. You get to be a bit of a bathroom guru when you look at as many of them as this cruising guide requires, and these were up there with some of the best.

Sunshine Key Resort & Marina (305) 872-2217 (800) 852-0348
http://www.rvonthego.com

Approach depth—5½ feet (minimum at mean low water)
Dockside depth—5½+ feet
Accepts transients—yes
Type of docking—floating wooden piers
Dockside power connections—four slips with 30-amp service
Dockside water connections—yes
Waste pump-out—yes
Showers—yes
Laundromat—yes
Fuel available—gas only
Mechanical repairs—mechanic on call
Ship's and variety store—BB&T
Restaurant—on site

Bahia Honda Key Anchorage (24 39.937 North/081 16.267 West)

A little better than halfway between the Bahia Honda alternate channel's turn to the southwest and the 20-foot fixed bridge, a bubble of deep water cuts in toward the southeasterly banks. Depths of 5 to 7 feet turn to within 200 yards of the southerly banks. However, the charted cove lying to the southeast has only 2 feet of water, so don't try to cruise into this recess. Protection is fair from southern and southeastern winds, and there is a bit of shelter to the southwest as well. This is not an appropriate anchorage in northern, northwestern, or northeastern winds above 10 knots. The adjoining shores are entirely

Anchored between the Bahia Honda bridges

undeveloped, though you can catch sight of headlights during darkness from the nearby track of U.S. 1.

Bahia Honda Channel Anchorage (24 39.442 North/081 16.819 West)

Craft that can clear the 20-foot fixed, Bahia Honda Bridge will find a good anchorage between this span and the old bridge, just off the westerly shores of Bahia Honda Key. Impressive depths of 9 feet extend to within 300 yards of the easterly banks, with at least 5 feet of water 200 yards from shore. The body of Bahia Honda Key shelters this anchorage beautifully from southern, southeastern, and eastern winds. The new bridge provides a bit of shelter to the north, and the point of land to the south gives some lee from this quarter as well. Strong southwesterly winds call for another strategy. Swinging room is unlimited.

The entrance to the Bahia Honda State Park dockage basin (see below) is visible to the

east from this anchorage, as are some of the cabins and the nearby beach. We have found these sights add to, rather than detract from, this haven's charms.

We have never had trouble with the holding ground in this anchorage, and indeed, seldom have we been here when several other cruising-sized vessels were not comfortably ensconced on these waters. Nevertheless, one of the park rangers at nearby Bahia Honda State Park characterized the bottom strata here as "poor holding ground." As we say, you can't tell it by our experience, but based on this advice, you might do well to look elsewhere in really heavy weather.

The Bahia Honda Channel anchorage is actually even more important to cruisers following Hawk Channel, as their craft can make their way to these waters without having to cross under any bridges. ICW captains must contend with the 20-foot span of the Bahia Honda Bridge.

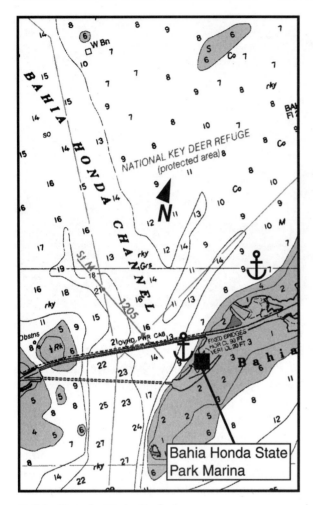

Bahia Honda State
Park Marina

Bahia Honda State Park

Bahia Honda State Park occupies the southwesterly tip of Bahia Honda Key. A dockage basin and small marina are a part of this park, and the harbor's unmarked entrance can be run from the deeper waters of the anchorage described above. Just remember, all you Waterway cruisers, that you have to get under the 20-foot Bahia Honda Bridge to get here.

Unfortunately, entrance depths into the Bahia Honda State Park basin are a mere $3\frac{1}{2}$

feet at mean low water. The dockage harbor boasts much better depths of 5 to 9 feet.

Bahia Honda State Park marina offers 19 slips for transients in a very well-protected harbor. All dockage is found alongside a concrete sea wall, with attached wooden pilings. Spaces are assigned on a first-come, first-served basis. Dockside electrical service of the 30-amp variety is offered, as are fresh water hookups and waste pump-out.

Keeping in mind that this is a state facility, you might not be distraught to find out that the only shower available is an outside type. Mostly, it is for washing off salt water from swimmers.

The marina is clean and has ready access to the marina office and concession building, where the state sells items that appeal mostly to tourists who arrive by automobile. Don't depend on its having anything that mariners might need for boats. Also in the building is a snack-bar type of fast-food service. It is open 8 A.M. to 5 P.M.

The nearby Bahia Honda beaches are some of the best that the Florida Keys have to offer. Inside or outside, they are beautiful.

Bahia Honda State Park Marina (305) 872-2353
http://www.myflorida.com

Approach depth—$3\frac{1}{2}$ at low tide
Dockside depth—5 to 9 feet, depending on location
Accepts transients—yes
Type of docking—alongside concrete sea wall with wooden pilings only
Dockside power connections—30 amp
Dockside water connections—yes
Waste pump-out—yes
Showers—yes, outside only and at a nearby bathhouse
Ship's and variety store—minimal
Restaurant—fast-food concession service

Pelicans at Bahia Honda State Park Marina

Bahia Honda Key History

Bahia Honda Key is the geological transition point where the Key Largo limestone subducts and the overlaid Miami Oolite begins. Bahia Honda means "deep bay" in Spanish. This key has a part of the original Florida East Coast Railway Extension steel bridge attached to it. The bridge—with a section missing so that sailboats may access Hawk Channel at Bahia Honda State Park on its eastern side, or if you like, with a section missing to keep adventurers from transiting the span in pickup trucks or motorcycles as they utter their famous last words, "Hey, guys, watch **this!**"—is a piece of engineering history. Because of the deep water, this bridge was far more difficult for Henry Flagler's engineers to build than the Seven Mile Bridge, which they had just completed. How discouraging it must have been to have just finished a bridge seven miles long, a wonder of construction skill the world over, and then have to face the seemingly bottomless depths of the waters around Bahia Honda. With the waters as deep as they were (about 25 feet), they are subject to higher surges in storms, so the Bahia Honda Bridge was built higher than the others. It was (and still is) 5,356 feet long and has a clearance above the water of 20 feet. At its maximum, the height of the bridge is 65 feet. The clearance is still 20 feet, though, and you need to know the difference.

Entrance to Bahia Honda State Park Marina

When the bridge was used for the Overseas Highway, the descendant of the railway, the road builders discovered that the part of the bridge where the tracks were laid was not wide enough for a two-lane road, so they built the roadway on *top* of the bridge structure. It is still there today, looking rather silly so far up in the air. Some think it resembles a carnival ride more than a highway. The new bridge connecting Bahia Honda with Spanish Harbor Keys is a modern, four-lane affair and offers an excellent view of the old span.

The currents that surge through the channels here are the fastest moving in the entire Florida Keys. Read that again so you have it firmly in mind.

Spanish Harbor Keys-West Summerland Key

The almost indistinguishable twin islands of Spanish Harbor Keys and West Summerland Key form the western tip of both the new and old Bahia Honda Channel bridges. Spanish Harbor Keys get their name from Spanish Harbor to their north, but there is no way for larger craft to access this natural harbor (see below).

Also found in this menage of coral and rock is West Summerland Key, which is 10 miles to the *east* of Summerland Key. In her simply wonderful book, *The Florida Keys,* Joy Williams relates that a number of years ago, people found some coral rock storage houses on West Summerland that had been used to store dynamite used in construction. The underbrush claimed the structures again over time. It makes one wonder what would happen if someone found the houses again and

they still had seventy-year-old, crystallized dynamite in them. Ka-boom!

ALTERNATE BAHIA HONDA CHANNEL NAVIGATION

The alternate ICW passage to Bahia Honda Channel and inlet features some lengthy runs between aids to navigation, but as you've probably figured out by now, that is the rule in the Florida Keys rather than the exception. Have your compass and/or GPS courses preplotted, keep charts 11451 and 11445 handy, and before you know it, the fixed Bahia Honda Bridge will appear over the bow.

Past Moser Channel From a position between the Waterway's flashing daybeacon #20 and unlighted daybeacon #19, turn to the west-southwest and set course to come abeam of flashing daybeacon #21 by some 150 yards to its northerly side. Approaching #21, sharp-eyed navigators will spy unlighted daybeacon #22 north of their track. This aid to navigation is part of the principal ICW passage, which eventually leads to Big Spanish Channel. Ignore #22 if your destination is the Bahia Honda Channel or one of its associated anchorages or marinas.

Continue on the same course for about 3.3 nautical miles. As you cruise along on this run, you will pass at a right angle across the breadth of the Moser Channel. To the south, the removed section of the old Seven Mile Bridge and the raised section of the newer span will be quite obvious.

Carefully point to come abeam of flashing

daybeacon #25 by at least 200 yards to its northerly side. Don't miss this marker! Rocky shallows lie south of #25 and seem to be building toward the marker itself. Need any more reason to give #25 a wide berth?

Well, would you believe the same course will lead you along for another 3.0 nautical miles? This run will take you past a series of small islands south of your course line, including Little Duck Key, Missouri Key, and Ohio Key. North of Missouri Key, pass some 200 yards north of the charted warning beacon ("W Bn").

Use your binoculars to pick out the unnumbered, 16-foot flashing daybeacon, located well north of Bahia Honda Key's northernmost point of land. For best depths, come abeam of this marker by some .15 nautical miles to its southerly side. This maneuver will help to avoid the 5-foot waters northeast of the unnumbered flashing daybeacon.

Of course, if Sunshine Key Resort and Marina is your goal, you need not cruise all the way to a position abeam of the unnumbered daybeacon.

Sunshine Key Resort and Marina Abandon the alternate channel about .5 nautical miles east of the unnumbered, 16-foot flashing daybeacon, located well north of Bahia Honda Key's northernmost point of land. Turn south and pick up the northernmost of the two sets of daybeacons outlining the channel between Ohio Key and Bahia Honda Key. Pass between these markers, unlighted daybeacons #1 and #2, and continue almost straight ahead, pointing to pass between unlighted daybeacons #3 and #4.

After leaving the gap between #3 and #4 in your wake, continue on toward the low-level fixed bridge. Watch to the east, and the marina's entrance will open out to port. Wait until you are directly abeam of this stream, and then turn 90 degrees to port, and enter on the centerline. The entrance cut is protected by two small, stone breakwaters lying along its southern and northern flanks. By waiting until the entrance is directly abeam to turn into it, you can easily avoid these twin hazards.

South of the marina entrance, this passage is crossed by a fixed, 14-foot bridge. Even if you could clear this span, the channel south of the bridge is unmarked and treacherous. Leave these waters to those with very specific local knowledge.

On to the Bahia Honda Bridge Once abeam of the unnumbered 16-foot flashing daybeacon, located well north of Bahia Honda Key's northernmost point of land, turn sharply to the southwest, and set course for the center section of the 20-foot, fixed Bahia Honda Bridge. It is a run of some 2 nautical miles to this span. Don't allow leeway to ease you off to the east or southeast. While there is a broad band of deep water to keep you out of trouble, shoals do shelve out from the northwesterly shores of Bahia Honda Key for quite some distance.

Short of the bridge, cruisers may choose to turn southeast and check out the anchorage off Bahia Honda Key.

Bahia Honda Key Anchorage Abandon the approach to Bahia Honda Bridge 1.13 miles southwest of the unnumbered daybeacon. Turn sharply to the southeast, and feel your way along with the sounder for about .3 nautical miles. Closer in, depths rise sharply; the seemingly inviting cove farther to the southeast exhibits 2-foot depths. Your best bet is to stay at least 200 yards north of the blunt point of land, southwest of the shallow cove.

On Bahia Honda Channel Cruisers southbound on the Bahia Honda Channel must contend with the 20-foot, fixed Bahia Honda Bridge. We suspect it won't come as a complete shock to learn that some wicked tidal currents regularly make themselves felt under this span. Take your time, and be SURE your vessel can clear the bridge before making a close approach.

Once through the fixed bridge, cut to the southeast. Cruisers continuing on to Hawk Channel should pass through the removed span of the old bridge. This section is located hard by the easterly end of this most impressive structure.

Bahia Honda Channel Anchorage and Bahia Honda State Park Marina Good depths are held to within 200 yards of the easterly banks between the new and old Bahia Honda bridges. Simply select a spot to your liking and drop the hook. Closer to shore, depths run markedly.

Skippers bound for the marina at Bahia

Honda State Park might want to make use of their binoculars to help pick out the small entrance cut, piercing the easterly shoreline. The approach canal is unmarked.

Cruise straight into the marina entrance canal on its centerline. Soon, the dockage harbor will open out to the north.

The ICW, Big Spanish Channel, and Nearby Anchorages

The main ICW channel runs north of the Moser Channel and then south of a series of broad but unmarked side channels cutting to the north. Eventually, the Waterway cuts to the northwest on wide Big Spanish Channel. Except for one narrow stretch south of Big Spanish Key, this section is easy to run all the way to the open waters of the Gulf of Mexico, north of Harbor Key Bank.

In looking at the huge collection of available anchorages in this region, these havens fall into two groups. First, there are those that must be accessed by one of the channels east of Little Pine Key and Big Spanish Channel. These are some great fair-weather overnight stops, but keep in mind that none of these broad channels has any sort of navigational markers. That's not too big a problem if you

Waterfowl on channel marker (Big Pine Key)

are proceeding along with computerized navigation aboard, but if you're navigating by compass and eye, it soon becomes apparent that one undeveloped key in this region looks pretty much like the next. All of which is to say, it can be a bit of a challenge to find your way safely to this set of anchorages.

The second group lies adjacent to the ICW's track through Big Spanish Channel. Some of these overnight stops are located just off the marked cut, while others, particularly the havens just off Big Pine Key and No Name Key, demand a short trip off the ICW.

Be advised that almost all (though not quite all) these anchorages, both directly off Big Spanish Channel and those accessed by the alternate passages, lie abeam of small keys (or islands if you will) that are completely in their natural state. This condition is so uniform that unless we tell you differently in our specific accounts of these various anchorages below, you can assume correctly that the adjacent body of land looks pretty much as it has for the last several hundred years.

Please also remember our admonition at the beginning of the ICW to Key West section that almost all the various overnight anchorages along this stretch are not fit for really heavy weather. In fact, most are comfortable only with light airs in the offing, or at worst, a moderate breeze blowing across an adjacent key.

Marinas along Big Spanish Channel are confined to two fish camps. You must be able to cruise safely under some very low, fixed bridges (15 feet and 11 feet respectively) to access either facility. For cruising-sized craft, this is essentially a marinaless region.

Again, please allow us to note that the Big Spanish Channel and its adjacent waters simply make for good cruising. The anchorages are wonderful (as long as the weather chooses to cooperate), and the virgin shores are a genuine visual treat. If you don't enjoy Big Spanish Channel and its close-by environs, better think about taking up offshore powerboat racing.

East Bahia Honda Key Anchorage (Standard Mile 1198) (24 46.414 North/081 13.966 West)

Northwest of unlighted daybeacon #24, cruisers can follow an unnamed channel that runs between East Bahia Honda Key and Hardup Key (plus Cocoanut Key). Minimum depths are 6 feet in the channel, but it's quite possible to wander into a half-foot of water via a navigational error.

Minimum 6-foot depths can be maintained to within 400 yards of East Bahia Honda Key's southwesterly banks. Closer in, soundings quickly rise to 3- and 4-foot levels.

This anchorage gives some lee to the north and the northeast. All other wind directions will be straight in your face.

To be honest, probably only the intrepid explorers among us will choose to make use of this anchorage. Couple the lengthy cruise off the Waterway necessary to reach its location with the lack of any other good nearby havens and it's easy to see why there are better choices not far away. For those who just have to see it all, however, we will present a navigational sketch of this overnight stop in the next section of this chapter.

Cocoanut Key and Hardup Key Anchorages (Standard Mile 1201) (24 44.480 North/081 14.293 West - Cocoanut key Anchorage) (24 45.342 North/081 14.969 West - Hardup Key Anchorage)

North of the Waterway's flashing daybeacon #27, captains might choose to navigate yet another monikerless channel. This cut runs the gap between Cocoanut Key and Hardup Key to the east, and Teakettle Key and Sandfly Key to the west. It's a cruise of 2.5 nautical miles to the first potential overnight haven off Cocoanut Key, with another .9 nautical miles of water to cross before arriving at a better anchorage off Hardup Key.

The first anchorage lies about 425 yards off the southwesterly shores of Cocoanut Key. A closer approach is not possible, courtesy of the huge patch of 1- to 3-foot waters that surrounds this key on all sides.

Minimum depths run about 7 feet, and there is some protection to the northeast (ONLY). This is clearly a fair-weather, light-air anchorage. If there is even a hint of unhappy weather, or just for winds over 10 knots, we suggest you look elsewhere.

Better sheltered from northerly and northeasterly winds are the minimum 6½-foot waters 300 yards off the southwesterly shores of small Hardup Key. You still cannot make a close approach to the key's shoreline, thanks to the all-too-usual shelf of shallows making out from all of the key's banks.

Again, this is not a spot to consider in heavy weather, but if light winds are in the offing or lower moderate breezes are wafting from the northeast, this is a pretty spot to spend an evening, in about as far removed a place as you are likely to find anytime soon.

Harbor Key light at northern head of Big Spanish Channel

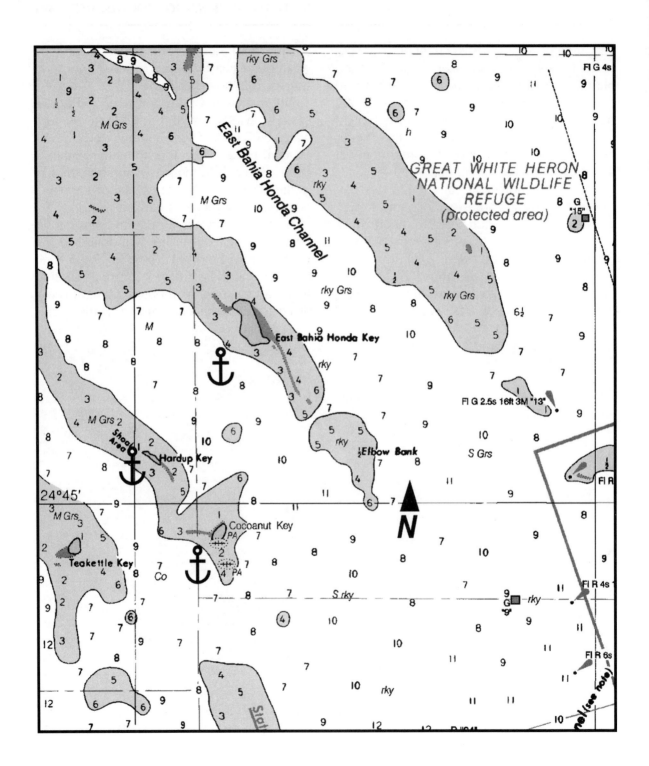

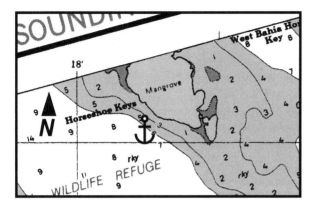

Horseshoe Keys Anchorage
(Standard Mile 1202)
(24 46.120 North/081 17.546 West)

A far broader channel pierces the gap between Teakettle Key, Sandfly Key, and Horseshoe Keys to the east and the two Johnson Keys to the west, north of the gap between flashing daybeacon #27 and unlighted daybeacon #30. A rather lengthy cruise of 4.5 nautical miles will carry vessels to an anchorage off the southwesterly shores of Horseshoe Keys.

The Horseshoe Keys are far larger bodies of low-lying land and mangrove than we have met above in our reviews of the other anchorages off the passages east of Big Spanish Channel. This isle provides a pretty good lee from northern, northeastern, and eastern winds. There is no shelter to the northwest and the south, with precious little to the southwest and west.

Good depths of 6½ feet extend to within 300 yards of the isle's southwesterly banks. Consider breaking out the dinghy and exploring the 1- and 2-foot waters all around Horseshoe Keys. While landing is not permitted, the clear waters make for fascinating exploration.

Johnson Keys Anchorages
(Standard Mile 1204)
(24 44.180 North/081 17.707 West—off southern Johnson Key)
(24 44.765 North/081 18.403 West—off northern Johnson Key)

Yet another unmarked channel strikes north between unlighted daybeacon #30 and flashing daybeacon #32. A trek of some 2.5 nautical miles north and northwest along this narrower channel will bring you to an anchorage west of the southernmost of the two charted Johnson Keys, while another .8 nautical miles affords an even better overnight stop off the southwesterly shores of the (larger) northern Johnson Key.

Minimum 5-foot depths can be held to within 200 yards west of the southern (of the two) Johnson Key's northwesterly point. There is good shelter to the east and southeast, but that's all.

The northerly anchorage lies 200 yards off the northern Johnson Key's southwesterly shoreline. This is a much larger island and affords excellent shelter to the northeast and north. The body of Little Pine Key, to the southwest, gives some shelter with winds blowing out of the west, southwest, or (to a lesser degree) the south. Minimum depths seem to be about 5½ to 6 feet.

Little Pine Key Anchorage
(Standard Mile 1204)
(24 44.086 North/081 18.197 West)

With strong breezes blowing from the southwest or west, cruisers can use the same channel that leads to the two Johnson Keys anchorages, described above, to find their way to an overnight stop off the northeasterly shores of Little Pine Key. Minimum

Big Spanish Channel (from No Name Key)

6-foot depths are found as close as 300 yards off this isle's banks. You can squeeze a little closer to shore in 5 feet of water, but then the bottom suddenly rises to 2-foot levels.

The best spot to anchor lies just slightly south of a point abeam of the northerly tip of the southern Johnson Keys (well to the east). Note that chart 11445 correctly predicts that the deeper water makes its closest approach to the northeasterly shores of Little Pine Key at this point.

Little Pine Key may not be as big as Big Pine Key (see below), but it's still a substantial island. It would take a really fresh breeze from the southwest or west, blowing across this large landmass, to be a problem in this anchorage. However, strong winds from most any other quarter will call for a different selection of an overnight stop.

**Big Spanish Channel
(Standard Mile 1205)**

At flashing daybeacon #32, the ICW follows a turn to the northwest and flows into the southerly reaches of Big Spanish Channel. Contrary to what you may have heard, this passage is broad, mostly deep, and well marked. If it were not for but one constricted section (between Big Spanish Key and Cutoe Key), running the entire channel would be a breeze. Even so, armed with the navigational account of Big Spanish Channel in the next section of this chapter, captains piloting pleasure craft up to 46 feet in length, drawing less than 6 feet, need not fear this passage.

Anchorages line the whole length of Big Spanish Channel. Some are immediately adjacent to the Waterway's track, while another set adjacent to No Name Key and Big Pine Key require a quick jaunt off the ICW by way of a

Cruising on Big Spanish Channel

marked, side channel. No one will ever want for anchorage selection on these waters.

No Name Key Anchorage
(Standard Mile 1206.5)
(24 42.350 North/081 19.816 West)

Southwest of unlighted daybeacon #34, cruisers can anchor off the northern shores of No Name Key in at least 5½ feet of water. Try dropping anchor northeast of the "5 ft rep 1983" channel notation. Keep at least 200 yards north of the banks. Closer in, 2-foot depths are quickly encountered.

This spot is very convenient to the Waterway, and it affords superb protection from southern, southeastern, and southwestern winds. There is also a bit of shelter to the west, courtesy of No Name Key's extended northwesterly point. Don't even think about trying to pass the evening here if boisterous winds are blowing from the north, northeast, or northwest.

Unlike every other anchorage that we have met thus far in our review of overnight stops both on and just off Big Spanish Channel, there is some light residential development visible to the south on No Name Key. Nothing to worry about, however. This anchorage still has a happy backwater feeling.

No Name Key History

Everything in the Florida Keys has a name, even the key without a name, No Name Key. It's adjacent to Big Pine Key, across a concrete bridge that was once a rickety wooden bridge. When the Overseas Highway went into business in 1938, No Name Key, which had been the western terminus of a ferry connection between Marathon and the Lower Keys, kind of lost its *raison d'être*.

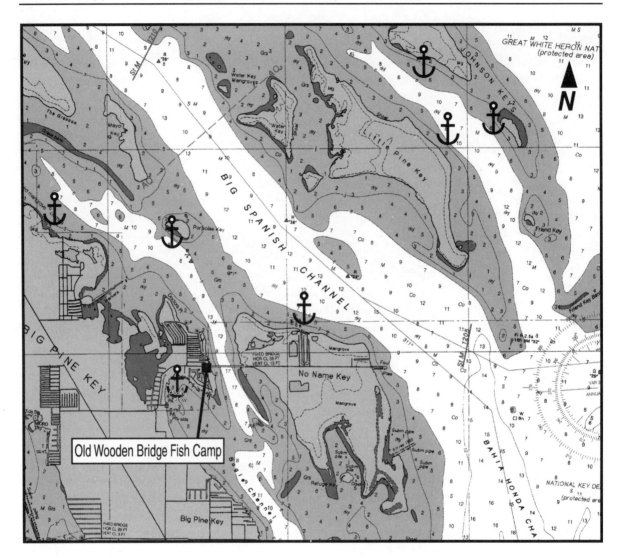

The question of how this particular key was named often comes up. We couldn't find out. We estimate that someone once asked what the name of the key was and someone else responded, "Oh, that key? It doesn't have a name."

Aha!

The ferry ride was 14 miles long, and that translated to a couple of hours time when tourists could watch life in the very slow lane before getting back on the road again. No Name Key has some people living on it now, but it has no electricity and no fresh water of its own. Ironically, the largest supply of natural, fresh water in the entire Keys is close by, at Blue Hole on Big Pine Key. Blue Hole was once a rock quarry. Now it is home to some alligators, Key deer, water birds, and raccoons. It's an interesting place to visit if you are lucky enough to have motorized land transportation available to you.

There was once a small town and a real U.S. Post Office on No Name Key, but they disappeared when the auto traffic started going to Key West via Seven Mile Bridge and Bahia Honda Bridge.

The road that connects Big Pine Key with No Name Key ends at some big rocks, right by the water's edge on No Name Key. That's the old ferryboat landing. People often come to No Name Key to see the Key deer, which are nearly habituated to human presence. The best time to see them is near dusk. Do not feed the deer.

Porpoise Key Anchorage and Big Pine Key Anchorage
(Standard Mile 1208)
(24 43.115 North/081 21.282 West—Porpoise Key Anchorage)
(24 43.333 North/081 22.584 West—Big Pine Key Anchorage)
Peruse chart 11445 for a moment, and notice the two unlighted daybeacons (#1 and #2) well west of unlighted daybeacon #36. The aids to navigation mark a westward-running channnel that leads to the long, charted tongue of deep water east of Big Pine Key. Minimum low-water depths on this connecting cut run from 6 to 6½ feet.

At unlighted daybeacon #2, mariners can turn northwest and easily find their way to two pretty good overnight anchorages. Alternately, a cut to the south will eventually bring captain and crew face-to-face with a 15-foot fixed bridge. If you can clear this span, there are additional anchorage opportunities, a friendly fish camp, and even the opportunity to experience one of the most unique dining spots in the Lower Keys, but more on that in a moment.

For now, let's focus our attention on Porpoise Key, north of unlighted daybeacon #2. Soundings of 5½ to 6 feet can be expected 200 yards off this islet's southwesterly shoreline. A rim of 1-foot shoals rings the key closer in.

Classic sailcraft (Big Pine Key)

Porpoise Key offers a good lee to the northeast, north, and east. There is little shelter in any other direction. While the key is, as usual, entirely in its natural state, the Big Pine Key shoreline to the west and southwest does exhibit some light development.

Cruisers whose crafts are not bothered by 5-foot soundings can anchor on the cove northwest of the blunt point of land on Big Pine Key, west of Porpoise Key. Minimum 5-foot soundings are held to within 200 yards of the southwesterly shores. Try anchoring on the waters northeast of the charted "3-foot" sounding.

The Big Pine Key shoreline to the southwest is in its natural state and boasts superb shelter from southwestern, southern, and northwestern winds. The blunt point also gives a lee to the south. Fresh winds from the east and southeast are an entirely different story.

Bogie Channel, Doctor's Arm, and Spanish Harbor
(Standard Mile1208)
(Various Lat/Lons—see below)

After running the same westward channel described above in regards to the anchorages off Porpoise Key and Big Pine Key, cruisers can alternately choose to turn south and follow a broad, deep but unmarked channel to the charted 15-foot fixed bridge. If your craft is small enough to clear this span, Old Wooden Bridge Fish Camp will immediately

Between the old and new Spanish Harbor bridges (Big Pine Key)

come abeam along the westerly banks, south of the bridge, and a protected anchorage is available on Doctor's Arm, a bit farther along. Old Wooden Bridge is within easy walking distance of No Name Pub, one of the best places to slake a healthy appetite (or thirst) between Key Largo and Key West. Even if you can't clear the bridge, consider anchoring north of the span. After being SURE your hook is not dragging in the prodigious tidal current that sweeps under the bridge, you can blow up the old dinghy and visit the fish camp by way of this more modest mode of waterborne transportation.

The entrance to Old Wooden Bridge Fish Camp (24 41.855 North/081 20.898 West) will be sighted to the west, immediately south of the 15-foot fixed bridge. Low-water entrance depths run only 3½ to 4 feet, but there is 5 to 6 feet of water in the reasonably well-sheltered dockage basin.

Old Wooden Bridge Fish Camp is "the way Florida used to be." Really. And it is a fishing camp first and foremost. Anything else would be an overstatement. That is not to say that the Old Wooden Bridge Fish Camp is not charming. It is. But part of that charm is all the things that seem to have been left over from a time warp.

Transients are welcome. The docking is a mix between tying up to larger, fixed wooden pier and a few fixed wooden finger piers. There is a hose bib outside so you can lead a hose to your boat, but there is no electric service available dockside. A small, on-site store sells mostly beer, bait, and tackle in a building that has been around since the 1950s. Gas can also be purchased, but that's it.

During our last Sunday afternoon visit, the woman we bumped into was as local as an oyster bed and as nice as Key lime pie. She had the time to talk and exuded the pleasantness of a favorite aunt. It was like the hustle and bustle of the modern world had never touched her. And maybe it never had.

Even if you cannot or do not want to stay at the Old Wooden Bridge Fish Camp, it might be worth your while to stop here because of the No Name Pub.

Old Wooden Bridge Fish Camp (305) 872-2241

Approach depth—3¹/₂-4 feet
Dockside depth—5-6 feet
Accepts transients—yes
Type of docking—alongside and wooden finger piers
Dockside water connections—hose bib
Fuel available—yes, gasoline
Ship's and variety store—yes, mostly beer, bait, and tackle in a building that has been around since the 1950s
Restaurant—nearby

The No Name Pub (305-872-9115) is less than ¼ of a mile away from the Old Wooden Bridge Fish Camp. Walk west down the hard-surfaced road. The restaurant will soon be spied on the northern side of the road.

No Name Pub is a great dining attraction with scads of local color. Built in 1936, this place was once a local general store, with a brothel operating upstairs. "I'll have two quarts of milk, a half-dozen hotdogs, three Hershey's candy bars, some soda pop, and a quickie." When the upstairs enticements closed down, the owners added a bait-and-tackle shop. The restaurant went in during the 1950s. The inside is decorated with dollar bills signed by the people who put them on the walls and on the ceiling. It occurred to us that allowing people to use their own money is a great idea in interior decorating. You get sound damping, decoration, color, and an annuity out of it, with no work on the part of the owner.

Old Wooden Bridge Fish Camp (Big Pine Key)

Because this is an eclectic place, it draws an eclectic crowd. Bikers come here. We sat next to a paleontologist at the bar. There could have been movie stars in here, too. There is an air or irreverence about this place, typified by the old mayonnaise jar that is full of free condoms, courtesy of the Monroe County Health Department.

One of the truly big draws here is the pizza. It's gourmet, to be tasted to be believed. People talk about it long after the food has been digested, so it must be good.

The waters running off south from the fixed bridge and the Old Wooden Bridge Fish Camp are known as the Bogie Channel. Some .9 nautical miles south of the span, shallow-draft vessels (ONLY) can turn back to the northwest and enter an arm of Bogie Channel known and charted as Doctor's Arm. Low-water entrance depths can run as thin as 3½ feet, though 4- to 5-foot soundings are typical. If your vessel is not put off by this thin water, you can anchor on the correctly charted 4-foot tongue of water, off Doctor's Arm's northerly banks (near 24 41.644 North/081 21.152 West). This haven is very protected from all but southeasterly winds. The adjoining Big Pine Key Shoreline alternates between an undeveloped patch at the very back of this cove, to moderate residential development overlooking the other banks.

Brave captains who continue following the unmarked, shoal-ringed Bogie Channel south will run into the wider waters of Spanish Harbor, south of Big Mangrove Key. There are plenty of 4-foot waters in Spanish Harbor, and the southern end of this bay is spanned by twin fixed bridges with only 11 feet of vertical clearance. Obviously, only small craft will be able to fit under this restricted height.

Big Pine Key Fishing Lodge guards the western banks, south of the 11-foot bridges.

Big Pine Key Fishing Lodge

The ultratricky entrance to this facility calls for cutting under and between the two 11-foot bridges. Few captains of cruising-sized craft will even begin to contemplate such a passage. However, just so you know we are on the job, a quick sketch of this facility will be presented here.

Big Pine Key Fishing Lodge (305-872-2351) takes no transients vessels unless one is a guest of the lodge, which has both lodging and camping sites. It seems possible, however, that when the season is low, one might be able to stop here if your boat is 25 feet or shorter. The fixed wooden slips cannot handle larger vessels. No dockside connections nor any other marine services are available.

Big Pine Key History and the Key Deer

Of the numerous lower keys, Big Pine Key has the best natural resources. Fresh water was available on the key when the first settlers arrived, and with its 5,816 acres, it was (and is) the second largest of all the Florida Keys. Physically, it's ten miles long and about three miles wide. As early as 1843, two families lived on the island, most likely farming. Indians inhabited the island back in the 1500s.

The first settlers on Big Pine Key came from Key West. They farmed the land and got a good deal of food from the sea, too. The deer that lived on Big Pine Key were also a source of food. The deer, now called Key deer, are smaller than a conventional white-tailed deer. The Key deer is only a couple of feet tall at the shoulder. Mature males may weight as much as eighty pounds and the females about sixty-five pounds. Key Deer are an endangered and protected species. Did hunters cull the herd? No. Destruction of habitat? No. Disease? Not that either. The biggest threat to the Key deer is Automobilus detroiti, which comes in many sizes, shapes, and colors. All have the capacity to turn the protected Key deer into endangered road kill. If solid lines of traffic discourage motorists in the Keys, imagine how confusing they must be to the deer.

In the 1940s, laws were established to save the deer when their number dropped to about 50. Now, there's a herd of several hundred on Big Pine Key and the adjacent No Name Key. The best place to view these deer, which have become habituated to human presence, is on No Name Key.

Out on the Overseas Highway, because of the deer, the speed limit is reduced on Big Pine Key to 45 miles an hour during the day and 35 miles per hour at night. The lower speed at night is because deer tend to freeze up when illuminated by car headlights.

In 1870, Big Pine Key had about 130 inhabitants. About half were engaged in farming. The remainder made their living from the sea. People also made charcoal here. When the Overseas Highway went into service in 1938, the gap between Knight Key at Marathon and Big Pine Key was closed by ferryboats that brought cars and their passengers to No Name Key, which had a ferry dock. The 14-mile trip was a welcome respite for tourists, because it put them to sea on the dazzling azure waters of the Keys.

A shark fishery and processing plant opened on Big Pine Key in the 1920s, sharks being valuable for their hides and their livers. Shark liver is full of vitamins. The hide was

Key deer (Big Pine Key)

made into an abrasive called shagreen, which was used to put smooth finishes on fine furniture. The company bagged about one hundred sharks a day, often in ways that would make people squeamish today. Sharks' bellies were cut open to see what they had been eating. According to June Keith's book, *Key West and the Florida Keys,* everyone's twisted fantasies were realized one day when the belly of one shark coughed up a human arm clothed in part of a blue serge suit. It had belonged to a Cuban pilot who had gone down in the Atlantic a few days prior. It may have been the very first instance on record of recycling in the Florida Keys, though no one knew it at the time.

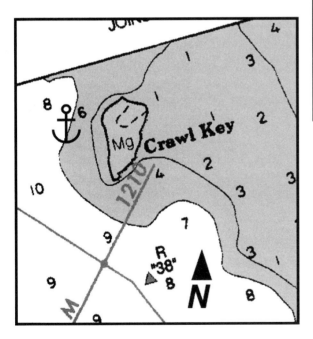

**Crawl Key Anchorage
(Standard Mile 1210.5)
(24 45.334 North/081 21.716 West)**

Returning our attention to anchorages directly off the ICW and Big Spanish Channel,

yet another haven comes up northwest of unlighted daybeacon #38. Excellent depths of 6 to 7 feet hold to within 250 yards of Crawl Key's westerly banks. This undeveloped isle provides a solid lee to the east and southeast. There is also a bit of protection to the northeast, but none for any other wind directions.

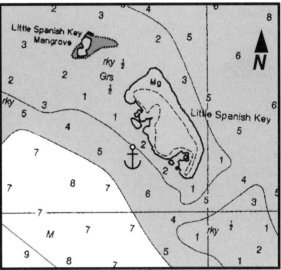

**Little Spanish Key Anchorage
(Standard Mile 1211.5)
(24 46.261 North/081 22.468 West)**

Little Spanish Key flanks the ICW-Big Spanish Channel to the northeast, well east of unlighted daybeacon #42. Cruisers northbound (eastbound) on the Waterway can actually cut northeast to the key's shoreline, well southeast of #42.

For once, depths are not as deep as the soundings predicted on chart 11448. Mariners can expect some 4½-foot soundings at dead, low water during their approach to Little Spanish Key. If these soundings do not pose a problem for your vessel, consider anchoring some 300 yards off the island's southwesterly shoreline.

While, again, landing is NOT permitted, this is a great spot to launch the dinghy and check out the surrounding, crystal-clear waters. Just be advised that depths between Little Spanish Key and Little Spanish Key Mangrove run to a half-foot at low tide. Even dinghies might stir a bit of mud between these isles.

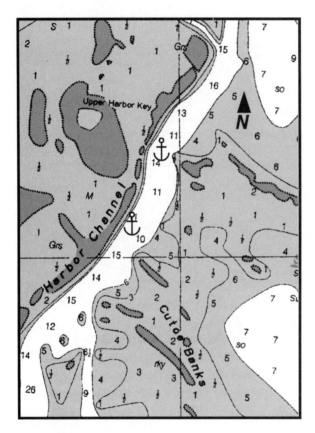

Harbor Channel Anchorages
(Standard Mile 1217)
(24 48.547 North/081 26.129 West—northern anchorage)
(24 48.149 North/081 26.288 West—southern anchorage)

After pushing northwest and then north through its only constricted section, the ICW and Big Spanish Channel rush past unlighted daybeacon #53 to its easterly side. It's then a run of slightly better than 2 nautical miles to the next marker, unlighted daybeacon #55, west of Turtlecrawl Bank. Some .6 nautical miles short of (south of) a position abeam of #55, cruisers with a bit of wanderlust in their hearts can break off to the south-southwest and run the northerly portion of the charted Harbor Channel. This cut leads to many—at least two—good anchorages (depending from which direction the wind chooses to blow).

Harbor Channel lacks any aids to navigation, and there are PLENTY of surrounding shallows to be concerned with. Some run to a half-foot or less. On a clear, sunny day, this is really not too big a problem. Cautious captains who proceed warily can spot the shoals pretty much by eye. Most stand out quite readily in bright sunshine. Trying this at night or in foul-weather, low-light conditions is an excellent exercise for the foolhardy.

Skippers who successfully navigate Harbor Channel can anchor in 10 to 14 feet of water in the portion of this cut abeam of Upper Harbor Key. The shoals, shallows, and Upper Harbor Key afford good protection to the west, southwest, and northwest, while the shallows west of unlighted daybeacon #53 give some lee to the east and southeast.

Another good spot will be discovered on the stretch of Harbor Channel northwest of Cutoe Banks. Depths run 9 feet or better, and this spot is even more protected. Only strong northeasterly and southwesterly breezes should make for an uncomfortable evening.

Be advised that some of the surrounding flats uncover completely at low tide, leaving a lot of sea weed and various other saltwater flora and fauna exposed. If the wind is blowing across these sand bars, the smell could not be accurately described as "sweet."

THE ICW, BIG SPANISH CHANNEL, AND NEARBY ANCHORAGES NAVIGATION

Successful navigation of the ICW and most of the anchorages just off the Waterway is a snap. The only real section of concern along the main track is the stretch west of Big Spanish Key. Even here, copious markers allow for most attentive navigators to follow the channel successfully, at least during daylight.

The anchorages found east of Big Spanish Channel, uniformly accessed by way of several wholly unmarked north-to-south-running channels, are another matter entirely. The lack of any navigational aids to use as references, plus the great similarity in the on-the-water appearance of the various keys, makes for more than a little navigational challenge. GPS or GPS plus laptop computer is a real, definite advantage when trying to find these overnight stops. Otherwise, have your compass courses pre-plotted and maintain a careful DR track.

On the ICW From a position between flashing daybeacon #20 and unlighted daybeacon #19, set course to pass just south of unlighted daybeacon #22. Continue on the same track, pointing to come abeam and pass the next ICW marker, unlighted daybeacon #24, to its fairly immediate southerly side.

Between #22 and #24, several markers associated with the northern leg of the Moser Channel will be passed north of your course line, while the old Seven Mile Bridge (center span removed) and the 63-foot central pass-through of the new Seven Mile span will lie to the south. Ignore all these distractions (unless your intended

destination is the Moser Channel) and continue on to #24.

Once abeam of #24, captains might choose to turn north-northwest and make use of the anchorage off East Bahia Honda Key.

East Bahia Honda Key Anchorage It is a cruise of about 4.5 nautical miles from unlighted daybeacon #24 to the anchorage off the southwestern shores of East Bahia Honda Key. Once again, there are no markers to help you along the way. The main navigational concern are the rocky shallows of Elbow Bank, southeast of Bahia Honda Key. With no markers denoting this hazard, cruisers must be very careful to pass well west of this potential trouble spot.

Also, notice the correctly charted finger of shoals running well northeast of Cocoanut Key. The best plan of action here is to stay well away from this island.

Drop anchor some 400 yards off the southwesterly banks of East Bahia Honda Key. Don't try a closer approach unless your vessel is not bothered by 3- and 4-foot soundings.

On the ICW Abeam of unlighted daybeacon #24, set course to come abeam and pass unlighted daybeacon #26 by at least 100 yards to its southern side. A large patch of shallows lies north of #26, and you don't want to make the acquaintance of this shoal. Then, it's only a quick hop to flashing daybeacon #27. Come abeam of #27 to its northerly quarter.

At #27, cruisers might decide that a wild

hair is really the order of the day and turn north to the anchorages off Cocoanut and Hardup Keys.

Cocoanut and Hardup Keys Anchorages The big problem about successfully navigating your way to the two anchorages off the southwestern shores of Cocoanut and Hardup Keys is the lack of any markers defining the western edge of the large shoal north of unlighted daybeacon #26 and a smaller patch of shallower water west of your course line.

For best depths, we suggest departing the ICW at flashing daybeacon #27 and cruising to the north-northwest for some 1.65 nautical miles. Be on guard against the 3-foot shoal, east of your track, and the smaller 5- to 6-foot waters to the west.

Cruisers bound for the haven off southwestern Cocoanut Key can cut to the north-northeast at this point and track their way through another .98 nautical miles to their goal. Be sure to drop the hook at least 425 yards southwest of Cocoanut Key's southwesterly point. A huge shelf of shallows strikes south, west, and (to a lesser extent) southwest from this small island.

To reach the Hardup Key anchorage, cruise through the broad swath of deep water between Cocoanut and Teakettle Key. Don't make a close approach to either of these islands. Eventually, if you're lucky, small Hardup Key will come abeam to the northeast. Anchor 300 yards off the key's southwesterly shoreline. Again, a closer approach will land you in very shallow water.

On the ICW From a position abeam of flashing daybeacon #27, to its northerly side, it's a cruise of slightly better than 2.0 nautical miles to the next set of markers, unlighted daybeacons #29 and #30. Pass directly between these two markers.

Horseshoe Keys Anchorage Captains making for the distant anchorage abeam of the larger (of two) Horseshoe Keys face a long, markerless run of some 4.45 nautical miles from the Waterway to this haven. We suggest leaving the ICW in your wake about .7 nautical miles east of #30. Turn to the north-northwest and begin tracking your way along the very broad channel.

Be especially careful to pass well east of Friend Key. This small island is surrounded by a very rocky, shallow shoal, which would bring any craft to grief. Similarly, stay well west of both Teakettle and Sandfly Keys. Anyone who studies chart 11445 will quickly see the whole array of shallows associated with these two keys. In fact, the best plan of action is simply to stay well off all the islands you will pass until reaching the southern, and far larger of the two, Horseshoe Keys.

Anchor 300 yards off the key's southwesterly banks. Now, its time to settle down to an evening of peace and security, at least as along as the prevailing winds are blowing across Horseshoe Keys.

On the Waterway Wow, one could almost get spoiled on these short runs between aids to navigation. Just wait, things will change in a big way once you make your turn to the west at the northwestern end of Big Spanish Channel.

From unlighted daybeacons #29 and #30, it's a relatively short hop of 1 nautical mile to a position abeam of flashing daybeacon #32. Come abeam of #32 by 300 to 500 yards off its southerly quarter. A huge shoal, with some 2-foot depths, lies north of #32 and seems to be building south toward this marker. Wise navigators will give #32 a very wide berth.

The anchorages off the Johnson Key, and the haven northeast of Little Pine Key can be accessed by leaving the Waterway .4 of a nautical mile east of #32.

Johnson Keys Anchorages—Little Pine Key Anchorage The channel running between Little Pine Key to the west and the Johnson Keys (plus Friend Key and Friend Key Bank) to the east, is narrower than the other side cuts reviewed above. You must pay strict attention to your navigation of these waters, or the afternoon might be spent perched atop a sand bar contemplating the value of good coastal piloting.

Cut north off the ICW .4 nautical miles east of flashing daybeacon #32. Thread your way carefully between the long, long shoal, running south and east from Little Pine Key, and the equally unwelcoming shallows off Friend Key Bank, to the east. Don't cut too far to the west, or you could meet up with the shoal striking out from the southeastern banks of Little Pine Key.

The next cause for concern is the rocky shoal surrounding Friend Key on all its sides. This underwater hazard could be a real boat killer. Need we say it? Stay AWAY from Friend Key.

Soon the southern (and smaller) of the two Johnson Keys will come abeam to the northeast. Drop anchor about 200 yards west of this isles northwestern tip.

Just across the channel, cruisers might also choose to drop the hook 300 yards off Little Pine Key's northeasterly shoreline. This is a great spot for southwesterly breezes.

Finally, cruisers bound for the anchorage abeam of the northern Johnson Key should anchor off this isle's southwesterly shoreline. Stay a good 200 yards offshore for best depths.

The ICW and Big Spanish Channel At flashing daybeacon #32, the ICW joins up with Big Spanish Channel and turns to the northwest. Runs between markers become lengthy once again, and it's not always possible to spot the next aid to navigation along the way, even with the use of binoculars. GPS-less captains should keep an accurate DR track, while those with electronic navigation should use these wonderful devices to stay on course.

Another problem with navigating the Big Spanish Channel portion of the ICW is the presence of a whole host of crab pots and fish traps, some right smack in the middle of the marked channel. During daylight, these obstructions can be avoided by observant helmsmen, but at night or in low-light conditions, they could foul a prop as easily as Tom Hanks seems to collect Oscar nominations. Keep these traps in mind at all times while running Big Spanish Channel, and be ready to change course at a moment's notice. This vigilance is ever so much easier than diving over the side, knife in hand, to cut away a line wrapped (and wrapped and wrapped and wrapped) around a propeller shaft.

From flashing daybeacon #32, it is a run of approximately 1.9 nautical miles to the next marker, unlighted daybeacon #34. Come abeam of #34 by at least 200 yards to its southwesterly side. Shallower (4 and 5 feet) water is found north of #34. Between #32 and #34, check out the banks of No Name Key to the southwest. The only development visible from the water on this island can be seen along this stretch.

Southwest of #34, cruisers might opt to anchor off the northerly shores of No Name Key.

No Name Key Anchorage Study chart 11445 and notice the "5 ft rep 1983" notation off the northern banks of No Name Key. Don't actually try to run this channel. It is relatively shallow and leads only to some private piers. Instead, anchor just northeast of the channel marked by this notation, some 200 yards north of the isle's northerly shoreline.

On Big Spanish Channel and the ICW Can we stand it? A mere .85 nautical miles separates unlighted daybeacon #34 and unlighted daybeacon # 36. For best depths, stay well southwest of both #34 and #36. West of #36, cruisers can leave the Waterway and explore the anchorages (and fish camps) off Porpoise Key, Big Pine Key, Doctor's Arm, and the Bogie Channel.

Porpoise Key and Big Pine Key Anchorages Once abeam of unlighted daybeacon #36,

turn to the west-southwest and use your binoculars to pick out unlighted daybeacons #1 and #2, south of Porpoise Key. Be advised that #2 is located considerably farther to the west than #1. Come abeam and pass #1 about 75 to 100 yards north of its position, and then come abeam of #2 about the same distance to its southerly side.

Continue past (west of) #2 for another 25 yards or so, and then turn sharply to the north-northwest. Work your way along until your craft is about 200 yards off Porpoise Key's southwesterly shoreline. Drop anchor here.

Captains who prefer the anchorage northwest of the blunt point of land adjoining Big Pine Key's easterly shoreline should continue past Porpoise Key, keeping at least 200 yards southwest of the island.

Use your binoculars to look toward the southwest. You may spot a whole series of small markers paralleling a thin point of land, northwest of Doctor's Point. Quite frankly, we couldn't make heads nor tails out of these informal aids to navigation, and we strongly suggest that visiting cruisers keep well clear of these waters.

Pass the blunt point of land, southwest of your course line, by staying at least 400 yards off its banks. Continue on the centerline of the main channel for another .6 nautical miles. You can then cut to the southwest and anchor northeast of the charted "3-foot" sounding. Stay a good 200 yards off the Big Pine Key shoreline to the southwest.

Bogie Channel, Old Wooden Bridge Fish Camp, and Doctor's Arm Let's continue our look at the waters adjacent to Big Pine Key's easterly shoreline, off the ICW. Instead of turning north at unlighted daybeacon #2, and thereby visiting Porpoise Key, cruisers with low-lying craft might also decide to alter course to the south and cruise to the charted 15-foot fixed bridge. There's really no reason to make this trip unless you can fit under this span, so make your decision accordingly.

Between #2 and the fixed bridge, stick strictly to the midwidth. A large pool of 1- to 3-foot shallows thrusts north from No Name Key's northwesterly point, while a smaller band of shallows strikes out from the banks of Big Pine Key to the west.

Assuming your craft can squeak under the 15-foot bridge, cruisers can turn to the west immediately south of this span and visit Old Wooden Bridge Fish Camp. The 3½-foot (minimum) channel serving this small facility is outlined by a few pairs of small floating markers. Cruise between these informal markers straight into the dockage basin. The office and store will come up to starboard.

Brave captains continuing south to Doctor's Arm will find no further navigational aids to help them along the way. You're on your own.

Watch out for the unusually loooonnng finger of 2-foot waters extending south from the easterly point of Doctor's Arm. Be SURE you are south of these shallows before turning back to the northwest into the body of this long cove.

To enter Doctor's Arm, favor the northeasterly shoreline somewhat, but don't approach to within less than 200 yards of these banks either. This plan will help to avoid the correctly charted finger of 3-foot waters, east of the charted unlighted daybeacons #1 and #2. By the way, we heartily suggest that you ignore these two small aids to navigation. They outline a shallow, local channel and lead to neither dockage nor sufficient room to anchor. Even by avoiding these shoals, don't be surprised to see only 3½ feet of water registering on your sounder.

Continue to favor Doctor's Arm's northeasterly banks until you are about 350 to 400 yards short (southeast of) the rear of the cove. Drop anchor here before proceeding any further. Shortly thereafter, soundings rise quickly to grounding levels.

South on Bogie Channel to Spanish Harbor

It's an even trickier cruise south on Bogie Channel, past Doctor's Arm to the charted 11-foot bridge. There's nothing simple about this, so don't blame us if your keel says hello to the bottom.

Should you make the attempt anyway, stay about 300 to 400 yards off the western, Big Pine Key shoreline. The east side of this cut borders on vast quantities of shoal water, striking out from No Name Key and Big Mangrove Key.

If you're very lucky, eventually the 11-foot fixed bridge will be sighted ahead. An overhead power line with an undetermined height lies just south of this span.

Small powercraft that can make it under this span might choose to visit Big Pine Key Fishing Lodge. The very tricky entrance cuts into the western, Big Pine Key banks, immediately south of the fixed bridge. We suggest that you call ahead by telephone for advice on how to enter this facility with the best depths. During our visit, we watched three locals do it three different ways. Our sounder showed minimal depths on all three access routes.

Back on the ICW and Big Spanish Channel Things begin to spread out on Big Spanish Channel, northwest of unlighted daybeacon #36. Runs between markers become much longer, and it's a very good idea to keep your binoculars close at hand to help pick out the next daybeacon.

From #36, cruisers must cross 2 nautical miles of water before coming abeam of unlighted daybeacon #38. Stay 200 yards west of #38.

Then, the ICW channel turns farther to the northwest, and another good run of better than 2.7 nautical miles must be traversed before meeting up with the next marker, unlighted daybeacon #42. Come abeam of #42 fairly close by its southwesterly side.

Notice that all the markers, from #34 all the way to #42, have been "unlighted." Care to try this portion of the channel at night? We didn't think so!

Another anchorage, off the westerly shores of Crawl Key, comes up .6 nautical miles northwest of unlighted daybeacon #38.

Crawl Key Anchorage Curl in towards the westerly shores of Crawl Key from the ICW channel. Aim for the center of the island's north-to-south axis. Drop the hook once you are within 250 yards of the westerly banks.

Little Spanish Key Anchorage Another anchorage comes up along the Waterway's northeasterly flank, 1.0 nautical miles southeast of unlighted daybeacon #42. Mariners can track their way some .65 nautical miles to the northeast and anchor 300 yards short of Little Spanish Key's southwesterly shoreline. Captains whose vessels can stand some 4½- to 5-foot soundings can carefully feel their way along with the sounder for another 100 yards. Closer to shore, depths rise to 2 feet or less.

Difficult Section A short cruise of .8 nautical miles past unlighted daybeacon #42 will bring you abeam of unlighted daybeacon #43. Be sure to come abeam of #43 fairly close to its northeasterly side. This aid to navigation introduces cruisers to the one and only difficult portion of the Big Spanish-ICW Channel. The cut narrows to a tight track between #43 and unlighted daybeacon #52, and it twists first one way and then another. Slow down, take your time, and be SURE to identify each marker and pass it to its correct side as you proceed along. Failure to follow this common-sense advice will most likely result in a grounding, far from the nearest Sea Tow or Tow Boat/US headquarters.

From #43, continue on pretty much the same course, and come abeam of unlighted daybeacon #46 by some 20 yards to its southwesterly side. At this point, the channel turns farther to the north. Swing to the north-northwest and pass unlighted daybeacon #48 fairly close to its westerly side. Continue on course, pointing to come abeam of unlighted daybeacon #49 by about 20 yards to its easterly quarter.

Now the passage swings back to the northwest. Set course to come abeam of unlighted daybeacon #52 by about the same distance to its southwesterly side.

We're not done with turns yet. The channel now cuts sharply north (actually, just a few degrees east of north). It is very important that you follow this northerly bend. Otherwise, you may just say hello to the correctly charted shoal northwest of #52. There's not enough water across these shallows to keep a sea gull afloat.

The next marker is unlighted daybeacon #53, located some .75 nautical miles to the north. You must take great care between #52 and #53, not to drift west on the charted shoals and sandbanks or cut too far to the east and encounter the long bubble of 2- to 4-foot depths. Set course to come abeam of #53 by about 150 yards to its easterly side.

Happily, north of #53, the channel soon broadens out again, though there are still unmarked shallows to the east and northeast to worry with. Proceed on the same course past #53 for about 200 yards. Then cut to the north-northwest, and point to eventually come abeam of unlighted daybeacon #55, by a good 350 yards to its easterly side.

Bringing #55 abeam by such a healthy distance to its easterly quarter will help to avoid the huge bubble of ½- to 1-foot depths south of #55. It's amazing to us that such a severe shoal, and one located so hard by the ICW channel, remains otherwise unmarked. Come on. Wake up you guys in the Army Corps of Engineers' Aids to Navigation Department.

Just to make things a little more interesting, you must also take care not to stray too far east of #55. This would take a pretty gross navigational error, but those who find themselves .37 nautical miles east of #55 will also find the half-foot shallows of charted Turtlecrawl Bank.

Before pushing out into the open waters of the Gulf of Mexico, north of Harbor Key Bank, let's take a quick look at one final set of anchorages off Big Spanish Channel.

Harbor Channel Anchorages Just one navigational marker would be ever so helpful in finding your way safely to the two, otherwise, good anchorages on Harbor Channel. "It's not to be, cherie." Navigators are on their own with this one.

On the other hand, cruisers can pretty much navigate by eye with a bright sun in the sky. The sunlight pretty much shows where the shoals are and where the deep water is located. Of course, this is not a one-hundred-reliable method of staying off the bottom, but hey, it's how most of the Florida Keys locals navigate. Couple this eyeball navigation with a GPS, and chances are you'll make it, but not without an anxious moment or two.

Don't even think about trying to find your way to this anchorage at night or in low-light, stormy conditions. You are almost certain to be practicing your best kedging-off techniques following such a foolhardy enterprise.

Try departing the Waterway about .5 nautical miles south-southeast of unlighted daybeacon #55. Ease off to the south-southwest, watching carefully for the shallows to the west. Cut south about 200 yards east of these shoals, and begin following the centerline of Harbor Channel first to the south, and then to the south-southwest.

Eventually, the channel will lead between another batch of shoals to the east, while the western shallows continue striking to the south-southwest. At this point, cruisers will spy Upper Harbor Key well west of their course line. Consider dropping the hook here, particularly if the wind is blowing across Upper Harbor Key.

Alternately, you might continue working your way south-southwest on Harbor Channel and anchoring on the portion of this cut that lies northwest of Cutoe Banks.

On to the Gulf From your position well east of unlighted daybeacon #55, it's only a short hop to flashing daybeacon #57. Pass this marker by some 400 yards (or more) to its easterly side, and continue on course for another 300 yards or so. Then, you can swing to the west-southwest and prepare for the looong but totally fascinating cruise to Key West.

ICW—Harbor Key Bank to Northwest Channel

Picture your craft floating along on glistening waters with an untouched verdant green shore just off your port side. Now throw in a whole host of anchorages and small keys to the south that almost seem to ooze a secret and mysterious character, which must be experienced to be understood.

Well, my friends, we have just described the ICW route from Harbor Key Bank to the Northwest Channel. At least we've given you some idea of what it's like during a sunny day with light airs.

Now for the bad news. There is not a single aid to navigation to help captains find their way along anywhere on the 28+-nautical-mile ICW passage from Harbor Key Bank (flashing daybeacon #57) to flashing buoy #1, the northwesternmost mark on appropriately named Northwest Channel. This latter cut provides reliable access to Key West Harbor, with all its delights and diversions.

With light winds or even moderate breezes blowing from the south, southeast, or to a much lesser extent, the southwest, this portion of the ICW makes for an idyllic crossing. Sharp blows from the north, northeast, or northwest make for a very, very different story. Mariners will find themselves at the wrong end of miles and miles and miles of wind fetch, trying to claw off a lee shore, during the entire passage to the Northwest Channel. We pointedly do not recommend this otherwise wonderful route if winds are forecast to exceed 20 knots out of the northerly (N, NE, and NW) quarters.

There is also a complete dearth of marina facilities along this entire run. Not a single marina, gas stop, or Sea Tow service center is in the offing. You are really on your own here, and if you do have trouble, it could be a very expensive proposition to get help to your craft, if you can convince anyone to come at all. Be

Back-route fishing

SURE your tanks are topped off and your craft is in first-rate condition before undertaking this journey.

We have always found the anchorages between Harbor Key Bank and Northwest Channel to be nothing short of enchanting. In fair weather, there is little better to do in this world than to anchor a few hundred yards north of the adjoining keys and shallows, don flippers, mask, and snorkel (or scuba gear if you are certified), and check out the flora and fauna below.

Even better, at least to our way of thinking, are the anchorages off the channels that regularly pierce the gap between the various keys. None of these potential overnight havens could be described as navigationally simply, and there is always the potential of finding the bottom. But if you can get past the shoals and drop your hook near the likes of Tarpon Belly Keys or (even better) Jewfish Basin, you will

have a story that can be retold among any gathering of cruisers for the rest of your life.

So, to summarize, yes, there is a navigational risk and challenge on these waters, and no, there is nothing in the way of marina or repair services, but oh, how the waters and utterly untouched keys can dance before your eyes. If by now you have sensed a certain enthusiasm for these waters on the part of this guide's authors, you are on the right track. Just be sure to take the appropriate precautions, and hopefully, your sojourn of these waters will yield nothing but happy memories.

Content Keys Anchorage #1 (Standard Mile 1221.5) (24 48.470 North/081 28.415 West)

Notice the several "Content Keys" pictured on chart 11448, southeast of the Waterway and well northwest of Harbor Channel. One of the first anchorages to consider along the

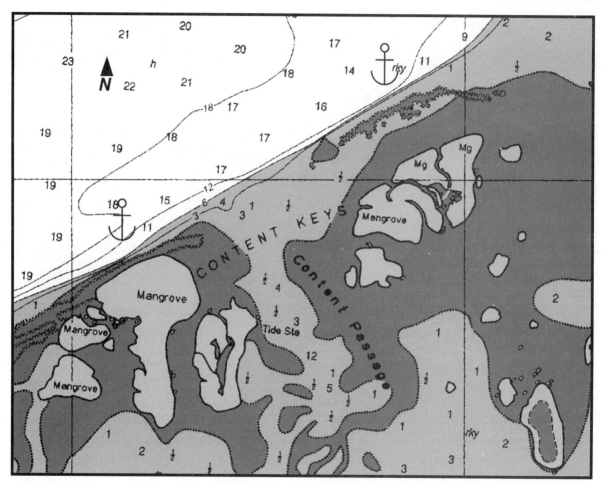

run between Harbor Key Bank and Northwest Channel comes up off the northwesterly shores of the northeasternmost Content Key, some .85 nautical miles south-southeast of the ICW channel. You must stay at least 200 yards northwest of the correctly charted shallows (.4 nautical miles off the key's northwesterly banks). The shoals can be easily spotted on a calm, sunny day, but otherwise, be sure to feel your way carefully in with the sounder, and stop well before you even begin to encroach on the shoals. These shallows have a very rocky bottom, and you don't want to be anywhere near them.

Anyway, by staying well northwest of these hazards, minimum depths of 12+ feet can be expected. As usual for the outer anchorages along this portion of the Waterway, there is good shelter to the south and southeast, as well as some lee to the east and southwest.

One of this guide's authors (Claiborne) can well recall one sunny December 11, when my ace research assistant Bob Horne and I anchored on these waters for a well-deserved lunch. We donned snorkeling gear afterwards and were amazed by the huge variety of fish

Back-route cruising

life we found languidly swimming just off the adjoining reefs and shoals. May you, too, be so fortunate.

Content Keys Anchorage #2
(Standard Mile 1222.5)
(24 47.764 North/081 29.732 West)

The second Content Key, moving northeast to southwest, is yet another good place to anchor during times of southerly winds. Keep a good 300 yards offshore, or you might meet up with the shallow reef that runs north from the isle's shoreline. By staying well off these shallows, you can expect soundings of 12 feet or better.

This anchorage is even better protected from southern and southeastern breezes than the haven mentioned above. The body of the key, and its attached mangroves, give a good lee from this quarter. Again, don't even think about trying this during strong northerly blows.

Cudjoe Key Channel Anchorages
(Standard Mile 1227)
(Various Lat/Lons—see below)

Cudjoe Channel runs the gap between Crane Key Mangrove to the east and Riding Key-Sawyer Key to the west. It's northerly mouth yawns out into the Gulf, some 1.3

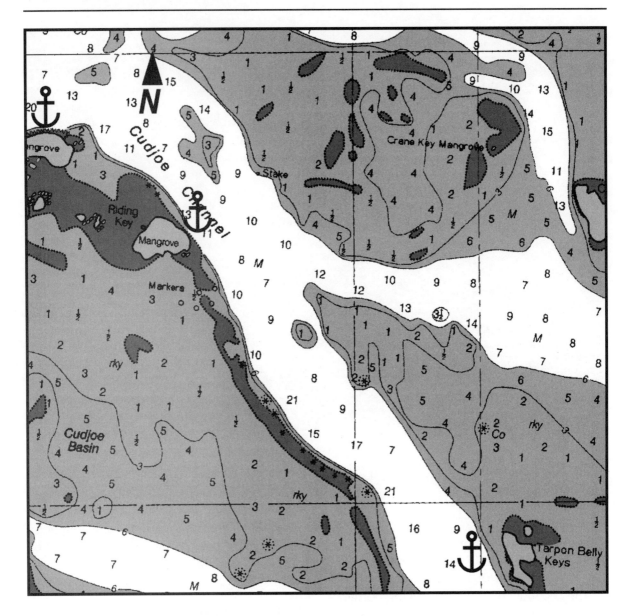

nautical miles south-southeast of the ICW's nominal track.

Cudjoe Channel is a wide, deep passage that nevertheless borders on a whole host of unmarked shoals. Most of these shallows can be spotted by eye on a sunny day, but for our money, this is yet another great spot to exercise your GPS combined with a laptop computer.

These waters feature a whole array of anchorages. Some are sheltered from one wind direction, some another, so you can pick and choose your overnight stop based on the latest forecast.

Those captains and crews up for a lengthy

5-nautical-mile trip southeast down Cudjoe Channel can track their way to what is undoubtedly the most unique overnight haven in this entire section of the Florida Keys. We call these waters the "Fat Albert Anchorage." The reason for this strange moniker will be explained below.

Moving north to south, cruisers might anchor north of the charted "Mangrove," itself northeast of Sawyer Key. Try dropping the hook near 24 45.754 North/081 33.531 West, about 200 yards north of the mangrove shoreline. Depths are an impressive 15+ feet, and there is good protection to the south and southwest.

For excellent shelter from western and southwestern breezes, continue southeast down Cudjoe Channel and drop anchor off the northeasterly banks of the charted mangrove, southeast of Riding Key. Try 24 45.292 North/081 32.756 West or about 250 yards off the mangrove shoreline. Minimum depths run to 14 feet. Note that there is little lee from a strong southern or southeastern wind in this haven.

Another 2-nautical-mile trek farther to the south-southeast on Cudjoe Channel will bring skippers and their craft abeam of an oblong island known (and charted) as Tarpon Belly Keys. This haven (24 43.777 North/081 31.374 West) boasts good shelter from eastern and southeastern breezes. For best depths, try anchoring some 250 yards west of the key's western shoreline. As usual, the Tarpon Belly Keys are completely undeveloped, and feature a pretty stand of Australian pines along its southerly banks. This is a pretty anchorage, but it is not recommended in even moderate winds blowing from any direction other than the east or southeast.

Well, by now perhaps, you think you have seen it all in the Florida Keys. A further trek of 2.1 nautical miles southeast down Cudjoe Channel will bring you abeam of the charted "Tide Sta" (Tide Station). Be advised that low-water depths can run as shallow as 4½ feet as you approach this anchorage. If you craft draws more than 4 feet, this passage is NOT recommended.

However, if you can stand this somewhat thin water, try anchoring near 24 42.048 North/081 30.118 West, about 275 yards east of the charted Tide Station. As already stated, low-water depths are in the 4½- to 5-foot region. There is superior protection to the west and southwest and also some shelter to the south, the east, and the northeast. Heavy blows whistling out of the northwest, the north, or the southeast call for another strategy.

Long before you get the anchor down, it will become quite apparent that there is far more to Cudjoe Key than just a tide station. Please don't be alarmed. Those huge, filmy, bomb-shaped spectacles that may well appear just onshore are not really UFOs. They just look that way. My friend, what you are actually seeing are the famous (or is it infamous?) "Fat Alberts" of Cudjoe Key.

Cudjoe Key History and the "Fat Alberts"

Cudjoe Key's most famous early settler was Lily Lawrence Bow, a lady from Chicago who came to settle on the key with her husband and their two boys about 1904.

She loved it. He hated it.

It could have been the Chicago winters he missed, when the wind blows so hard that it whisks the snow right off the ice on Lake Michigan. At any rate, he went back to Chicago, abandoning his brood and leaving his wife and two kids on Cudjoe Key, the only

Fat Albert blimp (Cudjoe Key)

whites there. Lily dug in, literally and figuratively. She raised chickens and grew vegetables. Her boys fished. They had food on the table. Then Lily became a teacher, allowing her to stay on Cudjoe Key for a couple of years before moving up to Homestead, which back then wasn't much more urbane than Cudjoe Key.

Bow Channel between Cudjoe Key and Sugarloaf Key is named after Lily Bow. So is the public library in Homestead. Some people leave an indelible mark on the world through their grit and courage. There isn't even a trash-strewn alley in the entire city of Chicago named after her husband.

Currently, the very northern end of Cudjoe Key is used by the United States government for a somewhat-secret facility that does not admit unauthorized personnel, which is most of us.

The United States government has two blimps tied to the north end of Cudjoe, which it flies as high as 10,000 feet. Usually one blimp flies at a time, but there are occasions when two are up at the same time.

The blimps are made of a rubberized plastic, and because of their ungainly appearance, they have been dubbed "Fat Alberts." A Fat Albert is a little larger than the Goodyear blimp. Deflated of the helium used to make the blimp weightless, the thing weighs in at about 6,500 pounds.

They are used for a couple of different missions. One Fat Albert—the Air Force prefers that they be called by a more sophisticated name, Tethered Aerostat Radar System—is used to beam TV Marti signals to Cuba, where they are routinely jammed by the Cuban government. The other Fat Albert is used to send out over-the-horizon radar signals to detect ships and planes about 150 miles out. This is for drug interdiction and monitoring the boats of Cuban refugees, which daily attempt to get people ashore in the United States.

The Air Force has tried to get people to stop calling the balloons by their nicknames, which emanated from a character in a Bill Cosby skit. One official Air Force spokesperson put it this way: "How would you like to have a nickname like Fat Albert?", as if balloons have feelings.

Tied to the ground via a ¾-inch polyethylene rope, the balloons are up because the United States felt that it needed a better radar eye on the Florida Straits. In 1969, while Air Force One was on a runway at Homestead Air Force Base in South Florida, a defecting Cuban pilot brought a MiG into Homestead, undetected.

Ooops.

In 1991 it happened all over again; this time a MiG from Cuba came into the naval flight facility on Boca Chica Key at Key West and landed there.

Fat Alberts cost the government about $4 million each. That, in and of itself, is all well and good. There is, after all, a need to protect the Leader of the Free World from the embarrassment of being run down by a Cuban MiG operated by Cuban defector. However, Fat Alberts have a habit of escaping from the 42-person group of Lockheed Martin civilians who run the secure base at the north end of Cudjoe Key for the Air Force. The compound is at the end of a long road called Blimp Road.

In 1981 a Fat Albert broke loose from its mooring and floated west to the Dry Tortugas before the Air Force scrambled some jets and shot it and its expensive radar gear down with a couple of missiles. In 1982 a Fat Albert crashed in the water as it was being reeled back in and was destroyed. In 1989 a Fat Albert deflated at about 2500 feet as it was being reeled back in. It plunged into the Gulf of Mexico. The Air Force raised it, but it was a total loss, and the radar equipment in it was pretty much history after being immersed in salt water. All these balloons are radar balloons.

Broadcasting the television signal to Cuba via the balloons began in 1990. A year later in 1991, the TV Marti Fat Albert broke loose and crashed in the Everglades after technicians managed to get it to deflate by signaling it to do so while it was in its escape mode. In March of 1993, both blimps were destroyed in the same month. High winds ripped apart the radar blimp, and the TV Marti blimp crashed as it was being lowered. At a later unspecified date, according to an article in *The Key West Citizen,* the Navy shot down a blimp that had broken loose and was drifting toward Cuba, with all its secret radar equipment aboard. In late April of 1997, another Fat Albert bit the dust; it was destroyed during a thunderstorm.

According to an official at the site, locals tired of trying to bring down the balloons with gunfire some time ago. "That hasn't happened in years," he assured. It is simply amazing what passes for sport in the Florida Keys.

If you've done the math, the government has lost $32 million worth of Fat Alberts. Your tax dollars at work.

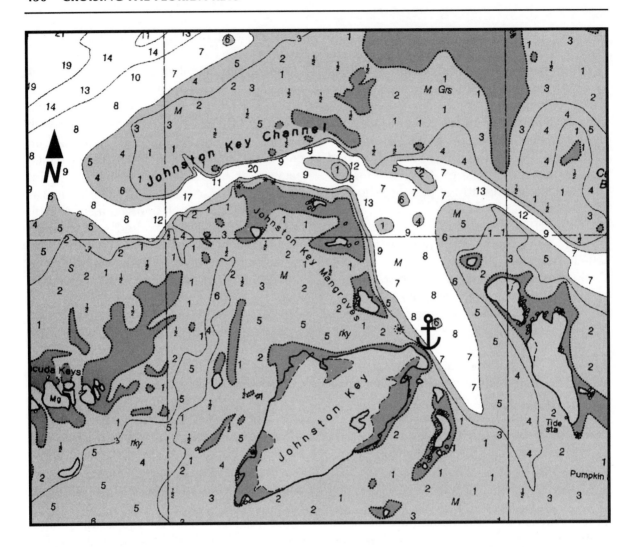

Johnston Key Channel Anchorage
(Standard Mile 1230.5)
(24 43.492 North/081 34.456 West)

Okay, let's be clear about this one. Only captains with wanderlust in their hearts, who are willing to risk finding the bottom pretty much in the middle of nowhere, should attempt to access the anchorage off the north-eastern tip of Johnston Key.

The navigational problems with this channel are many. First, it is, as usual for these waters, surrounded by unmarked shoals. The even knottier problem, however, is a large (also unmarked) shoal that bisects the channel north of Johnston Key Mangroves.

The only way that you will ever catch the writers of this cruising guide trying to access this overnight stop is either aboard a vessel equipped with a first-quality GPS interfaced with a laptop computer (loaded with appropriate navigational software and the LATEST version of chart 11448) or piloting a shallow-draft vessel 32 feet or smaller, with a calm, sunny day in the offing. By all accounts, this side channel - anchorage is strictly not recommended for vessels larger than 36 feet, or those drawing more than 4 feet.

So, with all that being said, let's take a look at the anchorage itself, assuming (and

you know what they say about those who assume) you can get there. The haven in question lies off the northeasterly tip of large Johnston Key. Minimum depths run around 6 feet, if ,and only if, you do not close to less than 225 yards of the banks.

The good news concerning this haven comes in the form of protection from foul weather. It is well buffered from southwesterly winds by the bulk of Johnston Key, and the shallows north and south of this island

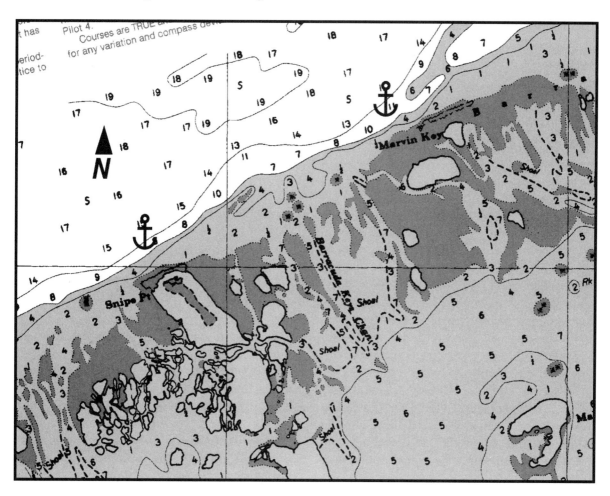

provide a lee from northwestern and southern blows. The unnamed key that flanks the eastern side of the channel, opposite Johnston Key, provides a wind break from eastern breezes. There is essentially nothing in the way of protection from fresh southeastern and northern blows.

Marvin Key Anchorage
(Standard Mile 1233.5)
(24 42.754 North/081 39.048 West)

With southern, southeastern, or southwestern breezes in the forecast, cruisers can anchor .3 miles west-northwest of Marvin Key. You must stay this far off the key, as it is buffered by a huge sand-and-oyster bar for a considerable distance off its northern banks. Minimum depths run to 9 feet, north of the just-described shallows. Farther to the south, soundings are measured in inches.

Snipe Point Anchorage
(Standard Mile 1235)
(24 42.094 North/081 40.471 West)

Check out chart 11445 and note Snipe Point, well west of charted Barracuda Keys Channel (which is, by the way, not really a channel at all!). This potential anchor-down spot is very similar to the haven we reviewed just above off Marvin Key. It also offers a good lee in southern, southeastern, and southwestern winds, but is wide open to blows from any northerly quarter.

Drop the hook at least 350 yards northwest of blunt-shaped Snipe Point. By doing this, you will always be in at least 10 feet of water. Closer to the adjoining land, even a little closer, can run you into 4 feet (or less) of water.

Snipe Point is particularly attractive, with a rind of white-sand beach flanking its

northerly extreme. Too bad landing is not allowed on any of these keys, or this would be a great spot to break out the dinghy and explore. Sigghhhh—well, maybe one day the Park System will decide that we have some rights to the land as well.

Jewfish Basin Anchorages
(Standard Mile 1238)
(Various Lat/Lons—see below)

One of our very favorite collections of anchorages will be discovered on (or near) the waters of Jewfish Basin. The basin and its entrance channel cut the banks northeast of charted West Harbor Key and Lower Harbor Keys (west of charted Mud Keys).

Wonder of wonders, there are actually some informal, uncharted, low-lying markers that denote the approach cut's westerly edge. These markers, if they are still present by the time of your arrival (no one will ever mistake these aids to navigation for USCG- or Army-Corps-of-Engineers-maintained markers), greatly facilitate a successful passage from the deeper Gulf waters to the inner reaches of Jewfish Basin. With care, minimum 5-foot soundings can be maintained, with many depths in the 6- to 8-foot region. Please don't misunderstand us. There is still plenty of shoal water to concern oneself with, but at least visiting cruisers have some indication of where these hazards are to be found.

Once the approach channel is behind you, the waters spread out into a wide, baylike body of water. This is Jewfish Basin, and waterborne visitors who are looking around for the first time can be excused for thinking they have died and gone to cruising heaven. Don't worry, it just feels that way!

There are at least three possible anchorages to consider. The first is found on the waters

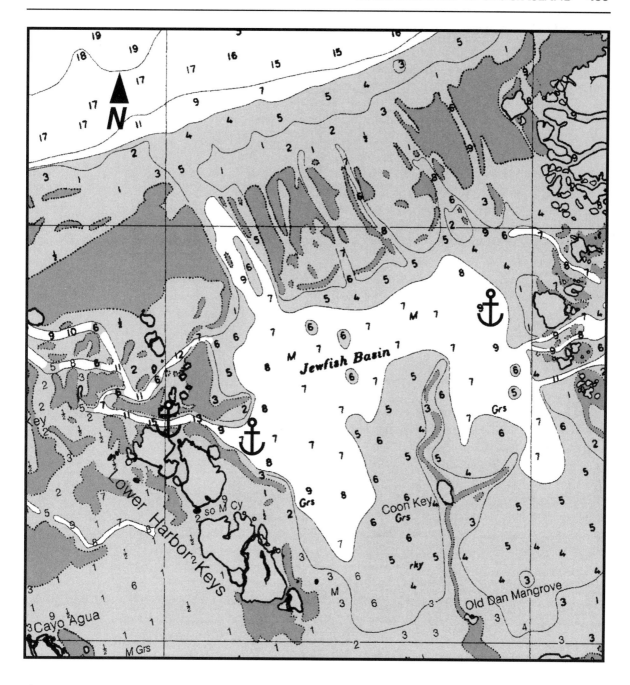

denoted on chart 11445 by an "8-foot" sounding, northeast of the shallow channel running between the second (moving northwest to southeast) and third Lower Harbor Keys. Try dropping the hook near 24 38.845 North/081 43.453 West, for minimum 7-foot soundings.

Excellent shelter is afforded from southern, southwestern, and western breezes. This anchorage is wide open on all other quarters.

Next up is a personal favorite, but only for skippers who pilot boats 30 feet and (preferably) smaller. Study chart 11445, and notice the deep but narrow channel darting just north of the Lower Harbor Keys, northwest of the just-reviewed anchorage. There are whole rafts of surrounding shallows, but if (and only if) you can navigate by eye on a sunny day, it's quite possible to keep in at least 7 feet of water as you curl between beautiful mangroves and some more solid bodies of land. We suggest anchoring south of the small island, north of the northwesternmost Lower Harbor Keys, near 24 39.055 North/081 43.962 West. Swinging room is very restricted, and you must take care to set the hook so as not to swing into any of the adjoining banks or shoals. This effort will be rewarded by protection from really foul weather and virtually all wind directions.

There is no denying that this is a navigationally challenging side trip and anchorage, but if you do make it and can get the hook down in just the right place, your craft will be in a place about as far removed from our modern, well-planned world as you are likely to get in this day and time.

Finally, with eastern, northeastern, or southeastern breezes blowing across the keys, try dropping anchor on the easterly reaches of Jewfish Basin, near 24 39.590 North/081 42.155 West. The trick is to stay 350 yards west of the large, unnamed island, itself southwest of charted Mud Keys. Here you will find 7 feet of water and unlimited swinging room. Strong westerlies will bring a sharp chop skipping across the breadth of Jewfish Basin. You will want to be elsewhere when such weather conditions are present.

We do not suggest that you attempt to explore the narrow, charted channel south of

Jewfish Basin Anchorage

the just-discussed anchorage, which connects to Waltz Key Basin, in anything larger than a dinghy. We tried to enter these cuts from several angles and hit 3-foot soundings every time.

Calda Channel
(Standard Mile 1243.5)

The northwesterly entrance to the profusely marked Calda Channel strikes into the waters of the Gulf of Mexico between charted Bluefish Channel and Calda Bank. In spite of its numerous aids to navigation, this is a shallow, small-craft channel. As such, we will not cover it in any depth here. Cruisers wanting to learn more about this wayward passage should check out our Calda Channel sections in the next chapter.

Northwest Channel to Key West
(Standard Mild 1247.5)

Northwest Channel is one of Key West's primary approach cuts. It is deep and boasts an adequate set of markings, but that is not to say there aren't loooonnng runs between markers. Its northwesternmost section is protected by a series of underwater jetties to the northeast and southwest. It's a really good idea to avoid these protective structures, unless you feel the real need for a complete new set of underwater hardware.

Eventually Northwest Channel skirts southwest of "Middle Ground" and soon makes its approach to the western face of Key West. The next chapter in this guide will be devoted exclusively to this ever-so-varied community.

ICW—HARBOR KEY BANK TO NORTHWEST CHANNEL NAVIGATION

As you round flashing daybeacon #57 at Harbor Key Bank, take a good, long look at this marker. It's the last one you will see for the entire 28+-nautical-mile run to flashing buoy #1, at the head of Key West's Northwest Channel.

That's the bad news. The good news is that all you need do for a successful passage is to stay some 1.5 to 2 nautical miles north and northwest off the various keys and shallows south and southeast of your course line. Just keep these landmasses in sight, and you can parallel the undulating shoreline until you are within striking distance of Northwest Channel.

With the exception of a few, low-key private markers on the Jewfish Basin approach channel, cruisers must negotiate the various side waters along the way by eyeball navigation. This is not what one would term sure-and-certain navigation, but except for electronic aids (GPS plus computer), this is the only game in town on these waters.

Route to Northwest Channel If your goal is simply to find your way to the head of Northwest Channel and bypass the many anchorage opportunities along the way, then all you need do is set a careful compass course (of approximately 245 degrees magnetic) from a position northwest of flashing daybeacon #57 and hold to this track for a little better than 28 nautical miles.

As you cruise along, you will pass from chart 11448 to 11445 and finally 11441. It's not a bad idea to keep 11442 at hand as well.

That's really all we need say about this

long leg of the ICW here. Just stay well offshore, and no unusual problems should be encountered, always assuming that the changeable winds choose to cooperate.

The remainder of our ICW to Key West navigational coverage will take a detailed look at the various anchorages and navigable side waters along the way. Then, at the very end of this section, we will review Northwest Channel.

Content Key Anchorage #1 The only trick to this anchorage is to correctly note the broad reef of shallows running well north and northwest of the northeasternmost Content Key. For this reason, you must stay .4 nautical miles northwest of the island and at least 200 yards north and northwest of the shallows. Drop anchor well short of the reef, and then it's time to break out the snorkel gear.

Content Key Anchorage #2 The adjoining shallows do not run out nearly as far from this Content Key as the one reviewed above. Just drop the hook 300 yards or so offshore, and you will find yourself in at least 12 feet of water.

Cudjoe Channel Anchorages While making your way into the northwesterly reaches of Cudjoe Channel, be on guard against the two, charted, 4-foot patches to the east, and particularly, the 2- and 3-foot shoals to the west.

Skippers bound for the northernmost Cudjoe Channel anchorage should point for the eastern half of the oblong "Mangrove," on which chart 11448 notes

the presence of a "Tide Sta." Drop anchor before approaching to within less than 200 yards of this isle's northerly banks.

To continue south on the Cudjoe Channel, your next challenge will be to safely pass the amoeba-shaped 3- to 5-foot shoal that bisects the channel, northeast of Riding Key. We suggest that you pass to the southwest of these shallows and hold to the centerline of the channel between the shoal and the mangroves to the southwest.

The next anchorage comes up off the northeasterly banks of the charted "Mangrove," southeast of Riding Key. Consider easing the anchor over the side about 250 yards off this isle's shores.

Southeast of the anchorage reviewed just above, Cudjoe Channel splits. We do not recommend the easterly leg without very specific local knowledge, which is another way of saying that if you don't already know these waters, don't go there.

Instead, continue south-southeast down the wide, main fork of Cudjoe Channel. Note the correctly charted 1-foot bubble just south of the split. Stay well west of this bottom killer.

Eventually, if you're lucky, the largest of the Tarpon Belly Keys will come up along the channel's easterly flank. While this island makes a great anchor-down spot during times of easterly breezes, be advised that a wide buffer of shallows rings all of this series of island's collective shorelines. Anchor 250 yards off the largest Tarpon Belly key's westerly shoreline.

Only vessels drawing 4 feet, or preferably a bit less, should consider continuing southeast down Cudjoe Channel to the Fat

Albert anchorage off the "Tide Sta." Right smack in the middle of the channel, low-water soundings can rise to 4½ feet.

If you do make the attempt, watch out for the two sand bars lining the cut's westerly banks, southwest of Tarpon Belly Keys. Also, stay a good 300 yards northeast of Little Swash Keys as your work your way along.

Soon you will sight the "Fat Albert" station on the northerly tip of Cudjoe Key to the south. Work your way into the waters 250 to 300 yards east of the charted "Tide Sta" and anchor here. If you're lucky enough to make it this far, you won't soon forget a night spent abeam of this government facility.

Johnston Key Channel Anchorage Okay gang, now listen up. There is nothing, absolutely nothing, that could accurately be described as easy when it comes to navigating Johnston Key Channel. It is flanked by very shallow water along both its flanks, and just to make things really exciting, the channel is bisected by a foot-shaped 1-foot shoal, which lacks any sort of marking. You must successfully bypass all these many and varied hazards to reach the anchorage we recommend off the northeasterly point of Johnston Key. Once you get there, it's a great spot, but don't ever say we didn't warn you if your keel finds the bottom while trying to navigate this channel.

Johnston Key Channel can only be approached from the west. The cut runs just a tiny bit north of due east as it works its way past Johnston Key Mangroves to the south. Use eyeball navigation to try and keep off the shoals to the north and south.

Soon, the foot-shaped shoal mentioned above, which bisects the channel, will be approached. Pass to the north of this considerable hazard and carefully follow the channel at is cuts to the south. Don't attempt to bypass this shoal via its southerly flank. As narrow as the northerly passage is, it's a superhighway compared to the southerly cut.

Once past the 1-foot shoal, the primary channel cuts to the south. Favor the easterly flank of this portion of the cut to avoid the correctly charted bubble of 1-foot waters northeast of Johnston Key Mangroves.

Cruisers who have more than their share of the "luck of the Irish" will eventually sight the blunt northeasterly point of Johnston Key to the southwest. Anchor at least 225 yards offshore.

If you are brave (or is it foolhardy?) enough to make it to this anchorage without finding the bottom, you will be where very, very few cruising vessels have been before you.

Marvin Key Anchorage A huge reef of shoals strikes out from the northern banks of Marvin Key and the larger but unnamed key to the southwest. Try dropping the hook a good .3 nautical miles west-northwest of Marvin Key. Don't even think about a closer approach.

Snipe Point Anchorage This one's a bit trickier. It's not just the reef-type shallows that run north and northwest of Snipe Point. There is also a buffer of 4-foot waters that lie even farther offshore, waiting to trap those cruisers who are just a little bit too adventurous. So, take a word to the wise, and drop the hook at least 350 yards northwest of Snipe Point.

Jewfish Basin Anchorages Successful navigation of the Jewfish Creek approach channel is greatly facilitated, at least during our last visit in January of 2001, by a series of stakes that outline the eastern edge of the shoals, flanking the initial portion of the channel to the west. We stayed about 50 yards east of these informal markers and were able to make it into the wider and far deeper waters of Jewfish Basin to the south without problems.

Of course, there's no absolute guarantee that these piles will still be in evidence by the time of your arrival, but hey, let's hope for the best. By the way, whoever erected these informal markers has done a great service to the cruising community.

Once into Jewfish Basin, captains must decided which of the three anchorages described above (or one of their own choosing) they will visit. To access the southernmost stop, cruise south on Jewfish Basin, favoring the westerly shores slightly. Don't ease too far to the west, or you might meet up with the charted 2- and 3-foot waters (plus a bit of a mangrove) that thrust to the east-northeast of Lower Harbor Keys.

Try to find your way to the waters shown on chart 11445 that are designated with an "8-foot" sounding. Just a bit farther to the south and southwest, the bottom rises to 3-foot levels. Be sure to set your anchor so as to swing well clear of these shallows.

The enchanting but treacherous anchorage north of Lower Harbor Keys must be accessed by the deep but unmarked channel running first west-northwest and then west from Jewfish Basin. This is eyeball navigation, country fellow cruisers, and all we can add is to take your time and detail a crew member whose sole responsibility is to watch the sounder. Eventually, you will pass through a series of mangroves. Just north of the northwestern-most Lower Harbor Key, an unnamed key will come abeam to the north. Anchor here for maximum shelter from foul weather, but remember that swinging room is limited.

The only real problem cruisers will encounter on their way to the anchorage on easterly Jewfish Basin is the long but unmarked finger of shoals and sand bars making in from the south. You must be very sure to pass well north of this obstruction. Anchor 350 yards west of the large island, north of the three small channels cutting east to Waltz Key Basin.

We pointedly recommend that cruising craft NOT attempt to run any of the three petite channels striking east from Jewfish Basin to Waltz Key Basin. We found these three small passages treacherous and hard to follow, even with careful eyeball navigation. However, exploration by dinghy can be more than rewarding. The waters associated with the Waltz Key area are wide, and the adjoining keys are just as beautiful.

Northwest Channel Break out your binoculars, and use your GPS if you have one, to locate flashing buoy #1 and the northwestern head of (guess what) Northwest Channel. It is important for you to come abeam of #1 to its NORTHERN side. Cruisers who arrive south of #1 might meet up with the "East Jetty," described below.

Be careful not to mistake the very prominent flashing daybeacon #A, which marks the northwestern end of the "East Jetty," as flashing buoy #1. For one thing, #1 is a buoy, and for another, it has a bell.

Round #1 and turn to the south. Set course to pass some 25 yards east of unlighted nun buoy #2, and then between unlighted nun buoy #4 and flashing buoy #3. From this point, vessels proceeding south to Key West should pass all subsequent red, even-numbered aids to navigation to their (the cruisers') starboard side and take green markers to port.

South and southeast of #2, a portion of Northwest Channel is protected by twin underwater jetties to the northeast and southwest, respectively. Chart 11445 would lead you to believe that a portion of "East Jetty" is "Awash at MHW" (mean high water). Maybe so, but we couldn't see it during our last traversal of this channel. In any case, don't go anywhere near either jetty.

Northwest channel is reasonably easy to follow, as far as the gap between flashing daybeacon #10 and unlighted daybeacon #11. As always, keep your old, reliable binoculars close at hand to help identify the various markers along the way.

Southeast of #10 and #11, the markers spread out, and it's a much longer run between these aids to navigation. You must pass through a little better than 1 nautical mile of open waters before sighting flashing daybeacon #12. Stay a couple hundred yards northeast of #12.

Then, another nautical mile will bring you abeam of unlighted daybeacon #14 to its northeasterly side, followed closely by unlighted daybeacon #15. There is a wide gap between #14 and #15. Wise mariners will run the centerline between these two markers.

The channel now shifts farther south. Point to come abeam of flashing daybeacon #15A by several hundred yards to its westerly quarter. Now, things get a little more interesting. An oblong shoal, charted as "Middle Ground," flanks Northwest Channel to the east and northeast south of #15A. Come abeam and pass unlighted daybeacon #16 by 500 yards or so to its easterly side. Daybeacon #16 sits hard by the shallows abutting the westerly side of Northwest Channel, and obviously, cruisers need to give this marker a wide berth. On the other hand, don't pass so far to the east of #16 that you begin to encroach on the "Middle Ground" shoal. Your eventual goal is to come abeam of the next Northwest Channel marker, flashing daybeacon #17, by about .25 nautical miles to its southwesterly quarter. This will put you smack in the middle of Northwest Channel and well away from any shallow-water problems.

Study chart 11447 for a moment, and notice unlighted daybeacons #1 and #2, south of unlighted daybeacon #16. These apparently mark some sort of local channel and are best avoided entirely.

Once abeam of #17, its only a short hop to the wide gap between flashing daybeacons #18 and #19. Now, Key West, with all its many anchorages and marinas, lies within sight. Get ready for some good times!

Hawk Channel—Moser Channel to Key West

The westernmost stretch of Hawk Channel from Channel Five to Key West is both typical and atypical of this passage's sister sections to the east (and north). It's similar in that the channel continues to follow the offshore waters between the various keys and the outlying reefs, with long runs between tall aids to navigation. It's dissimilar in that there are fewer marina facilities (short of Stock Island) but far more anchorages. These overnight havens are found along a whole series of side channels that cut north between the various keys. All these cuts are marked, but some are deeper than others.

This is clearly a portion of Hawk Channel that cruisers who are not in too big a hurry will want to take the time to explore. Some of the anchorages off the various side channels are really quite nice, and there is also the opportunity to find a marina here and there.

The shortage of pleasure-craft facilities comes to a grinding, spark-throwing halt as Hawk Channel finds its way west to Stock Island. Here, there are any number of marinas and repair yards that cater to cruising craft.

Hawk Channel finally comes to an end as it rounds Whitehead Spit, in sight of historical Fort Taylor. Soon, cruisers can cut north on the Main Ship Channel. Now, Key West is just a short hop away. All this community's many facilities, services, and attractions will be considered in the next chapter of this guide.

Bahia Honda Channel Anchorage and Bahia Honda State Park Marina
(24 39.442 North/081 16.819 West—Anchorage)
(24 39.390 North/081 16.706 West—Marina)
West of the Moser Channel, there is a very, very long portion of Hawk Channel that lacks any markers along its direct track. The nearest aid to navigation along this stretch initially is flashing daybeacon #49A. A little more than 3 nautical miles west of a position abeam of #49A, cruisers can turn north and visit the anchorage and marina bordering the westerly banks of Bahia Honda Key and the southerly foot of Bahia Honda Channel.

Check out chart 11445's depiction of the southerly foot of Bahia Honda Channel. Notice that there are two bridges pictured crossing these waters. The northerly span is a modern, fixed, 20-foot structure. The far more interesting southerly bridge is the original span, and it makes for a most fascinating sight from the water. As you pass, note the narrowness of this bridge. Two-way car traffic use to drive over that?!

The extreme easterly end of the old bridge has been permanently removed, allowing for unfettered access to the waters between the two spans. Thus, any-sized pleasure craft can take advantage of the good anchorage (described below) between the spans, and smaller vessels may visit the adjacent marina associated with Bahia Honda State Park.

Captains will find a good anchorage just off the westerly shores of Bahia Honda Key, between the two bridges. Impressive depths of 9 feet extend to within 300 yards of the easterly banks, with at least 5 feet of water 200 yards from shore. The body of Bahia Honda Key shelters this anchorage beautifully from southern, southeastern, and eastern winds. The new bridge provides a bit of shelter to the north, and the point of land to the south gives some lee from this quarter as well. Strong southwesterly winds call for another strategy. Swinging room is unlimited.

The entrance to the Bahia Honda State Park dockage basin (see below) is visible to the east from this anchorage, as are some of the cabins and the nearby beach. We have found these sights add to, rather than detract from, this haven's charms.

We have never had trouble with the holding ground in this anchorage, and indeed, seldom have we been here when several other cruising-sized vessels were not comfortably ensconced on these waters. Nevertheless, one of the park rangers at nearby Bahia Honda State Park characterized the bottom strata here as "poor holding ground." As we say, you can't tell it from our experience, but based on this advice, you might do well to look elsewhere in really heavy weather.

Bahia Honda State Park occupies the southwesterly tip of Bahia Honda Key. A dockage basin and small marina are a part of this park, and the harbor's unmarked entrance can be accessed from the deeper waters of the anchorage described above.

Unfortunately, low-water entrance depths into the Bahia Honda State Park basin are a mere $3\frac{1}{2}$ feet at mean low water. The dockage harbor boasts much better soundings of 5 to 9 feet.

Bahia Honda State Park Marina offers 19 slips for transients in a very well-protected harbor. All dockage is found alongside a concrete sea wall, with attached wooden pilings. Spaces are assigned on a first-come, first-served basis. Dockside electrical service of the 30-amp variety is offered, as are fresh water hookups and waste pump-out.

Keeping in mind that this is a state facility, you might not be distraught to find out that

the only shower available is an outside type. Mostly, it is for washing off salt water from swimmers.

The marina is clean and has ready access to the marina office and concession building, where the state sells items that appeal mostly to tourists who arrive by automobile. Don't depend on its having anything that mariners might need for boats. Also in the building is a snack-bar-type fast-food service. It is open 8 A.M. to 5 P.M.

The nearby Bahia Honda beaches are some of the best that the Florida Keys have to offer. Inside or outside, they are beautiful.

Bahia Honda State Park Marina (305) 872-2353
http://www.myflorida.com

Approach depth—$3\frac{1}{2}$ at low tide
Dockside depth—5 to 9 feet, depending on
    location
Accepts transients—yes
Type of docking—alongside concrete sea wall
    with wooden pilings only
Dockside power connections—30 amp
Dockside water connections—yes
Waste pump-out—yes
Showers—yes, outside only and at a nearby
    bathhouse
Ship's and variety store—minimal
Restaurant—fast-food concession service

Bahia Honda Key History

Bahia Honda Key is the geological transition point where the Key Largo limestone subducts and the overlaid Miami Oolite begins. Bahia Honda means "deep bay" in Spanish. This key has a part of the original Florida East Coast Railway Extension steel bridge attached to it. The bridge—with a section missing so that sailboats may access Hawk Channel at Bahia Honda State Park on its western side, or if you like, with a section missing to keep adventurers from transiting the span in pickup trucks or motorcycles as they utter their famous last words, "Hey, guys, watch *this!*"—is a piece of engineering history. Because of the deep water, this bridge was far more difficult for Henry Flagler's engineers to build than the Seven Mile Bridge, which they had just completed. How discouraging it must have been to have just finished a bridge seven miles long, a wonder of construction skill the world over, and then have to face the seemingly bottomless depths of the waters around Bahia Honda. With the waters as deep as they were (about 25 feet), they are subject to higher surges in storms, so the Bahia Honda Bridge was built higher than the others. It was (and still is) 5,356 feet long and has a clearance above the water of 20 feet. At its maximum, the height of the bridge is 65 feet. The clearance is still 20 feet, though, and you need to know the difference.

When the bridge was used for the Overseas Highway, the descendant of the railway, the road builders discovered that the part of the bridge where the tracks were laid was not wide enough for a two-lane road, so they built the roadway on *top* of the bridge structure. It is still there today, looking rather silly so far up in the air. Some think it resembles a carnival ride more than a highway. The new bridge connecting Bahia Honda with Spanish Harbor Keys is a modern, four-lane affair and offers an excellent view of the old span.

The currents that surge through the channels here are the fastest moving in the entire Florida Keys. Read that again so you have it firmly in mind.

Little Palm Island Resort

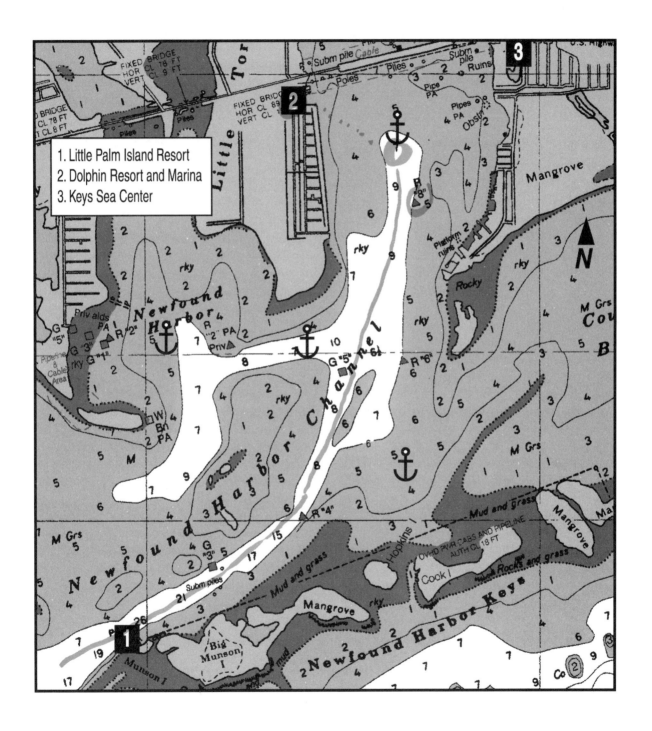

Newfound Harbor Channel—Anchorages and Facilities
(Various Lat/Lons—see below)

The next aid to navigation that comes anywhere near Hawk Channel is flashing daybeacon #50. This marker actually sits better than .5 nautical miles to the north and marks some shallows south of Big Munson Island. Another (1.0) nautical mile to the west-southwest on the Hawk will bring cruisers abeam of the entrance to Newfound Harbor Channel. This deep, reasonably well-marked track leads to a host of excellent anchorages and some smaller marina facilities.

After rounding flashing daybeacon #2, which marks the westerly tip of a long, long shoal striking west from Munson Island, Newfound Harbor Channel cuts to the east-northeast and hurries by the northerly banks of Munson Island and Big Munson Island. Mariners passing through this cut for the first time might well be surprised to gaze south and spot any number of huge yachts and a collection of elegant buildings on Munson Island. All this is part of ultraexclusive Little Palm Island Resort (24 37.468 North/081 24.136 West). Incidentally, Little Palm Island is what the locals call the body of land that chart 11445 names Munson Island.

Little Palm Island is sooo exclusive that we were denied permission to land and look for ourselves. We can tell you that soundings at the marina's two ranks of piers are 10+ feet, even at low water. The western pier (both are of the fixed, wooden variety) is wide open to foul weather.

Be advised that lodgings at Little Palm Island Resort run in the $575+ per night region. It's possible to just visit the resort for a meal, but the prices are enough to give most any cruiser a quick case of the gasps. If Little Palm Island tempts you, be prepared to say goodbye to dead presidents . . . many, many of them. It's hard, however, to put a price on perfection. If you're feeling particularly affluent, call (305) 827-2524 for more information.

The Newfound Harbor Channel works its way through a long, lazy turn to the north as it skirts past unlighted daybeacons #3 and #4. Between #4 and the next upstream markers, unlighted daybeacons #5 and #6, captains can break off to the east and anchor on the charted bubble of 5- to 6-foot waters (near 24 38.286 North/081 22.686 West). We found minimum 5½-foot depths here, with fair protection from southern, southeastern, and eastern breezes. This is not a good spot during strong northerlies or fresh southwesterly breezes. Swing room is unlimited.

North of unlighted daybeacon #5, a side channel cuts back sharply to the west and eventually leads to Newfound Harbor. There are two anchorages (at least) to consider on these waters. First up, during our last visit, we spotted a large, handsome sailcraft tucked snugly on the midwidth of the side channel near 24 38.768 North/081 23.206 West, just east of the charted "7-foot" sounding. You will discover minimum 6½-foot depths on these waters and excellent shelter from northerly winds. Strong blows from the south call for another selection of overnight stops.

Captains whose craft are not hampered by 5-foot soundings can continue west into Newfound Harbor (west of unlighted daybeacon #2) and anchor .25 nautical miles east of the charted unlighted daybeacons to the west, near 24 38.780 North/081 23.906 West. This spot offers some lee from southern, western, northwestern, northeastern, and southwestern winds, but it is wide open to the southeast and east. Incidentally, don't even think about seeing where the series of daybeacons referred to above lead. They serve some private docks on an adjacent canal, and depths are more than suspect.

Returning now to the main Newfound Harbor Channel, the cut continues north, running between Little Torch Key to the west and Big Pine Key to the east. Perhaps, the most sheltered anchorage in this region will be discovered north of unlighted daybeacon #8, near the tip of the charted tongue of deep water (near 24 39.711 North/081 22.721 West). Contrary to what chart 11445 predicts, we found 6-foot low-water depths here. This is a popular anchorage, and you will most likely find yourself amidst any number of other pleasure craft. During our last visit, we observed quite a collection of our fellow craft

anchored in the shallower waters to the northeast and northwest. Obviously, these craft must have been of the shallow-draft variety, as depths run between 3 and 4 feet as you leave the charted deep water behind and begin an approach to the 15-foot fixed bridge.

Dolphin Resort and Marina guards the easterly banks of Little Torch Key, just south of the 15-foot fixed bridge. At low water, cruisers must plow through some 3½- to 4-foot depths to get here, but once inside the basin, soundings improve greatly to 8 feet or better.

This facility has a can-do attitude, which pretty much comes from dockmaster Mike Morris, an affable guy who has been around some and probably is privy to some things "he cannot talk about."

The marina takes transients, and docking is

Dolphin Marina (Little Torch Key)

found alongside at fixed wooden piers. Electrical service is 30-amp and 50-amp, and you can expect dockside water. Gas and diesel are also available.

The bathrooms were sparkling clean and they are even air-conditioned, a rarity in the Keys. There is but one shower and that is in the men's bath. Women are invited to use the same, and there is a lock on the door that allows milady to wet up and soap down without having to worry about being surprised, midbath.

Rental cottages are available at Dolphin Marina for those who have seen one too many waves. There is also a small, on-site variety store where you will find mostly beach, bait, and tackle items. The Sandbar restaurant on Little Torch Key (183 Barry Avenue, 305-872-9989) is about ¼ of a mile away. Along the way, you will also find a roadside convenience store.

Pay particular attention to the beautiful, antique launches, which deliver high-end guests to nearby Little Palm Island. These classic craft come and go from Dolphin Marina, and they are a dream floating.

All in all, Dolphin Marina is a very clean and well-run operation, which we recommend highly. Just be sure your craft can get through those skinny entrance depths safely.

Dolphin Resort and Marina (305) 872-2685
(800) 553-0308
http://www.dolphinresort.com

Approach depth—3½-4 feet at mean low water
Dockside depth—8+ feet
Accepts transients—yes
Type of docking—fixed wooden piers
Dockside power connections—30- and 50-amp
 service
Dockside water connections—yes
Showers—yes, just one, but very clean
Fuel available—gas and diesel
Ship's and variety store—yes, mostly BB&T
Restaurant—nearby

The charted canal northeast of unlighted daybeacon #8 and south of the fixed 9-foot bridge leads east to a minimal marina facility. After traversing the 3½-foot approach canal, cruisers will suddenly find themselves in 15+ feet of water. Then, a northward turn on the first canal cutting off to port will eventually lead to the Keys Sea Center (305-872-2243, 24 40.140 North/081 22.065 West, http://www.keysseacenter.com), hard by this stream's northerly tip.

Newfound Harbor Channel anchorage

No services are available for transients at the Keys Sea Center. Though this is a clean and apparently well-run operation, this facility will be of little interest to visiting cruisers.

Smaller-cruising powercraft that can clear the 15-foot bridge north of Dolphin Marina and are not hampered by 4-foot low-water soundings, will find an additional anchorage opportunity north of the span on the charted Pine Channel. Note the lobe of deeper water cutting in toward the westerly, Middle Torch Key banks, well north-northwest of the charted "Micro Tr." You can anchor near 24 41.611 North/081 24.084 West in 4 feet of water, with a good lee to the south, southwest, and west. Strong winds from the southeast or north could make you imitate a Mexican jumping bean in this anchorage.

Torch Keys History

The Torch Keys (Little Torch Key, Middle Torch Key, and Big Torch Key) line the westerly reaches of Pine Channel and make up most of the easterly flank of Niles Channel. According to one source, they got their names from torchwood, which burns when green. These islands have never figured much in the history of the Keys. When a road went in, people followed, but few stayed very long.

Little Torch Key is the point of departure for well-heeled patrons of Little Palm Island, where a five-star resort now coddles people for big bucks. Little Palm Island was once called (and is still charted as) Munson Island. It was here that moviemakers from Hollywood came to film the movie *PT-109*, which starred Cliff Robertson, who was portraying the real-life exploits John F. Kennedy. After the movie company left, several old PT boats remained behind, beached and rusted. They are long-gone today. "Beached and rusted" is not part of the *lingua franca* at Little Palm Island these days.

Niles Channel and Associated Anchorages (Various Lat/Lons— see below)

The southern entrance to the Niles Channel lies just opposite the entrance to Newfound Harbor Channel. Instead of cutting to the east-northeast once abeam of flashing daybeacon #2 and the western tip of Munson Island, cruisers bound for the Niles cut should swing northwest and pass west of unlighted daybeacon #4.

The Niles Channel maintains minimum 6-foot depths north to the 40-foot fixed bridge. However, there are several unmarked twists and turns in this passage, where it's all too simple to find yourself in 4 feet of water. Northwest of unlighted daybeacon #6, visiting navigators must proceed with extra caution.

While Niles Channel lacks any marinas or repair-yard facilities, there are at least three anchorages that might be considered. One is an open, fair-weather-only haven, while the other two offer more shelter, at least from certain wind directions.

South of unlighted daybeacon #6, with light airs (ONLY) in the forecast, captains might choose to drop the hook just northeast of the shoal charted as "M Grs," near 24 37.779 North/081 25.537 West. This spot offers shelter only for southwesterly breezes, and even when winds are wafting from this direction, you won't catch these writers in this spot if wind speeds are forecast to exceed 10 knots.

Better sheltered are the waters northeast of Pye Key. Low-water soundings of 5 feet or more hold to within 450 yards of the Key's easterly banks. Closer to shore, depths are

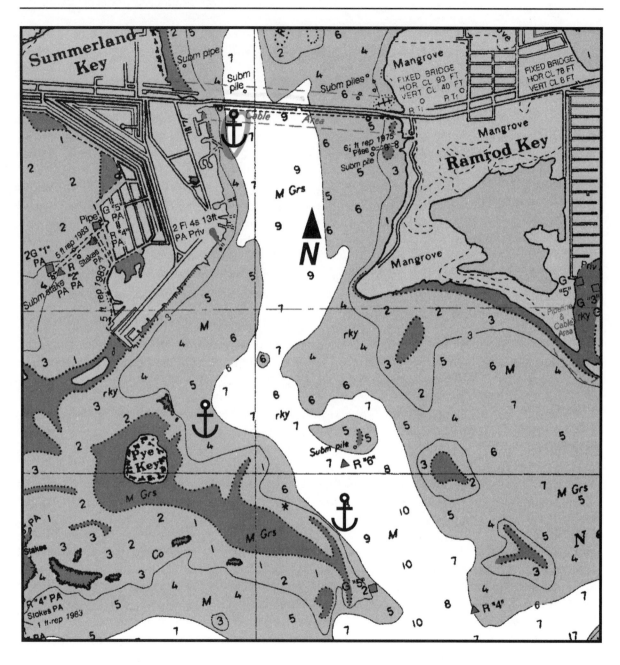

measured in inches. Try anchoring near 24 38.235 North/081 26.263 West. This is a reasonably secure spot if winds are blowing from the west or southwest, but it is pretty wide open in all other directions. These waters are particularly susceptible to a heavy chop with fresh northeasterly breezes in the offing.

For our money, the best anchorage on Niles

Channel lies 200 yards off the westerly banks and 250 yards south of the fixed bridge (near 24 39.506 North/081 26.113 West). Here, you will find at least 6 feet of water and plenty of shelter from western, northwestern, and southwestern winds. There is also a bit of protection to the east, courtesy of Ramrod Key. Don't even think about spending the night here if moderate to strong winds are forecast to blow from the north or south.

There is one SERIOUS caveat to this overnight haven. To the north, a seemingly low-lying power line crosses Niles Channel just south of the fixed bridge. We have been unable to find any published overhead clearance for these high-tension lines, but it's a safe bet that the mast of even a medium-sized sailcraft would encounter these shocking obstructions should such a vessel drag anchor to the north. For this reason, we do not recommend this anchorage for any sailcraft if there is even a hint of foul weather in the forecast. Even during fair weather, sailors should be VERY SURE their anchor is well set before heading below to the galley!

Kemp Channel

The Kemp Channels strikes north, well north of Hawk Channel's flashing daybeacon #50A. This prolifically marked channel twists and turns a tortured path north to an 8-foot fixed bridge. Low-water depths are only 3½ to 4 feet, and there are no marinas or anchorages readily accessible from this cut's track. While shallow-draft powercraft could and do run the channel almost every day, one must ask, Why would you want to? This is one passage where we suggest that even the explorers among us keep on trucking west on Hawk Channel.

Key Lois

We had heard that Key Lois, northwest of Hawk Channel's flashing daybeacon #50A, was home to a whole herd of experimental monkeys. Well, either everyone got smart and the monkey project was abandoned years ago, or the little buggers are very good at hiding. We cruised as close to this isle's southwesterly shores as possible and spent quite some time observing the key through binoculars. Nary a monkey did we spot.

Bow Channel and Associated Anchorages and Facilities
(Various Lat/Lons—see below)

Between Hawk Channel's flashing daybeacon #50A and the unnumbered Nine-foot Shoal flashing daybeacon, Bow Channel cuts off to the north between Sugarloaf Key to the west and Cudjoe Key to the east. This cut boasts a profuse set of markers, but be advised that low-water soundings of 4½ feet (possibly 4 feet in a few spots) are not uncommon. On the other hand, those cruisers who successfully run Bow Channel can find their way to a small but interesting marina and a fairly good anchorage. Clearly, this cut is pretty much consigned to shallow-draft vessels that draw less than 4 feet. If your vessel can fit these requirements, then this is not a channel you should bypass automatically.

West of Bow Channel's unlighted daybeacon #10, a marked cut runs off to the west and eventually intersects the wide but ultrashallow inner reaches of Sugarloaf Sound. Don't even look in the direction of this side cut. We found the bottom in a 22-foot outboard-powered craft, directly between the outermost markers. It can only be surmised that this so-called channel has been marked for the exclusive use of fishing skiffs and airboats.

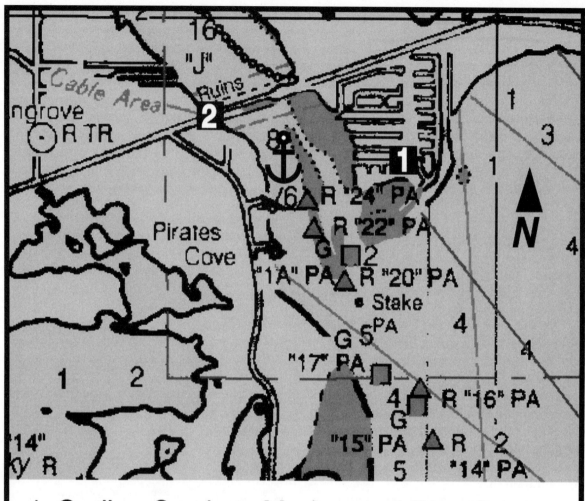

1. Cudjoe Gardens Marina and Dive Center
2. Sugarloaf Key KOA Resort Marina

At unlighted daybeacon #20, a marked side channel cuts first north and then east into a sheltered canal. This approach passage maintains minimum 4½-foot depths, with typical soundings in the 5- to 9-foot range. The deeper soundings will be encountered once your craft finds its way to the inner section of the canal.

After entering the eastward-running canal, the first side stream that cuts back to the northwest provides access to Cudjoe Gardens Marina and Dive Center (24 39.474 North/081 30.321 West). This facility resides on an ultrasheltered dockage basin at the northwesterly tip of this canal.

If you ever need a good place to ride out a heavy blow, this marina is a virtual hurricane hole. It isn't very big, and the alongside docking arrangements mean that only a few boats can be accommodated at any one time, but the protection is excellent. In this case, the smallish basin—about 100 feet across—is an advantage.

Transients are accepted, but it might be a good idea to call ahead and make sure space is available. All berths are found along a concrete sea wall, buffered with wooden pilings. Soundings alongside run 6 to 7 feet at low water. Power connections are limited in number and also limited to 30-amp. Dockside water is in the offing. There's gasoline available here but no diesel fuel.

Cudjoe Gardens also has a boat ramp for launching small boats and it is a PADI dive facility, meaning that you can buy dive gear here and get tanks filled up.

The ship's store is mostly beer, bait, and tackle with a smattering of things that cruisers might need, but don't count on the store having any esoteric parts. You'll have to get to Marathon or Key West for that kind of diversity.

The nearby Cudjoe Landing restaurant (305-745-9999) is open for the evening meal at 6 P.M. and closed on Mondays. It's Italian and right next door to the marina. The interior is set up with, say, 15 tables and was, when we stopped by, virtually devoid of ambiance.

Like some of the other marinas between Marathon and Key West, Cudjoe Gardens seems a bit short on the things that many cruisers might consider standard equipment. But the lady we spoke with was nice, courteous, and candid. You'll see friendly faces here, which is always a blessing.

Cudjoe Gardens Marina and Dive Center (305) 745-2357
http://www.cudjoegardensmarina.com

Approach depth—4 1/29 feet
Dockside depth—6-7 feet
Accepts transients—yes
Type of docking—alongside concrete sea wall
Dockside power connections—30 amp, but very limited
Dockside water connections—yes
Fuel available—gasoline only
Ship's and variety store—yes, but mostly BB&T
Restaurant—next door

Unlighted daybeacon #24 is now the northernmost marker on Bow Channel. The two charted aids to navigation, unlighted daybeacons #2B and #4B, which marked a long shoal flanking the channel to the east, were absent during our last visit.

Nevertheless, by sticking to the midline of Bow Channel, cautious mariners can continue north past #24 and anchor 350 yards south-southeast of the 8-foot fixed bridge (near 24 39.525 North/081 30.887 West). Minimum depths run around 6 feet, but captains must take care to set their anchor so as not to swing into the shallows once marked by charted #4B. The west-side Sugarloaf Key banks are essentially undeveloped, while the Cudjoe Key shoreline to the east supports moderate, but not unsightly, development. This anchorage boasts superb protection from all except strong northern and southern winds. During the nighttime hours, automobile traffic noise and headlights, courtesy of the nearby bridge, could be a bit of a problem, though they didn't disturb us during our last visit. Maybe that's because we had been performing on-the-water research since 5:00 A.M. the preceding morning.

Lastly, the Sugarloaf Key KOA Resort Marina guards the westerly shores, immediately south of the 8-foot fixed bridge, near 24 39.648 North/081 31.112 West. No transient services are available for visiting cruisers. The marina is for the exclusive use of KOA Campground-registered guests only.

Sugarloaf Key History and Bat Tower

North of Hawk Channel's unnumbered Nine-foot Shoal flashing daybeacon, the sprawling mass of Sugarloaf Key comprises the northerly shoreline. Sugarloaf Key was on its way to becoming the sponge capitol of the world, back in 1910. A couple of brothers from Chicago by the name of Chase thought that they could grow sponges in the shallow bays around Sugarloaf Key, and they paid $45,000 to buy almost the entire island. They brought in workers and equipment, and pretty soon they had a town, which was called Chase. The brothers estimated, based on some previous government research, that they could produce a viable crop of sponges in four years. They were wrong, as was the government research. While sponges did grow on the cement disks, which were placed in the water with a piece of sponge already attached, it took sponges six years—not four—to mature to where they were ready for market. The Florida Keys Sponge and Fruit Company went under; workers moved elsewhere; the town of Chase was abandoned. The Chase brothers eventually sold their real-estate holdings for $200,000 to one Richter C. Perky of Miami.

Perky had plans. He wanted to develop Sugarloaf Key into a resort and fishing camp. The mosquitoes, however, were so thick that no one in their right mind would come there to be beset by bloodsucking insects and driven half-nuts. Perky then came up with the idea that, if he built a habitat for bats, bats would come and rid him of the mosquitoes.

Bats, he had heard, can eat their own weight in insects each day. It was sort of a *Field of Dreams* concept; if you build it, they will come. So Perky built a bat tower. Not one to let an ancillary opportunity pass by untapped, Perky also planned to sell the bats' droppings for fertilizer. It was a perfect scheme, similar to the infamous but specious cat pelt plan: fatten up the cats on rats, harvest the cat skins, and then use the leftover cat carcasses to feed the rats—an ecologically closed-end operation. Anyway, at this point, historical opinion divides. Some say the bats never came. Others declare that Perky brought in a swoop of bats, put them up in his bat-o-minium, and then the bats promptly took off.

Whatever the truth, Perky was batting zero.

The bat tower is still there. There are no bats in residence. However, tourists often stop to look at it. The mosquitoes are there, too, which makes one wonder if the entire bat tower debacle was not actually orchestrated by the mosquitoes themselves to lure prey to their dinner table. Strange things happen in the Florida Keys.

Between Sugarloaf Key and Key West, there is little history, though there are plenty of islands—Saddlebunch Keys, Big Coppitt Key, Boca Chica Key, Stock Island, and finally Key West. Though it is only a guess, Key West was such a magnet for people because of its maritime tradition, that the outlying islands simply couldn't stand up to the allure of Key West. It would be like trying to set up a fundamentalist Christian community—no dancing, no movies, no music—right next door to Las Vegas. No contest.

Saddlebunch Harbor Anchorages
(24 34.923 North/081 37.613 West)

A cruise of approximately 1.3 nautical

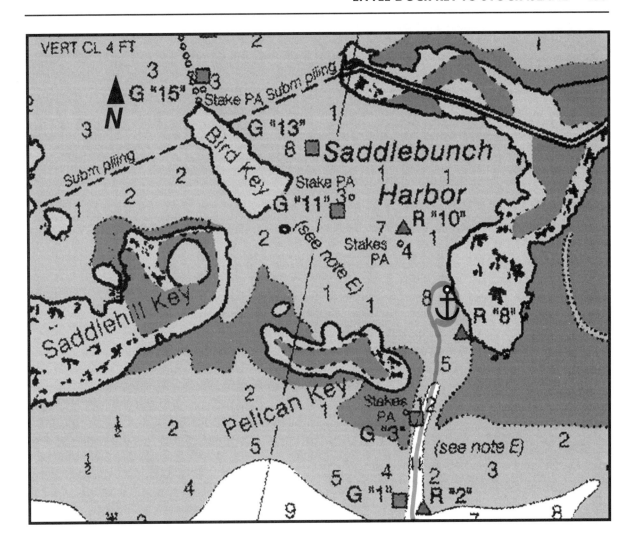

miles north from Hawk Channel's unlighted daybeacon #55 will lead captains and crews to a marked channel that serves Saddlebunch Harbor along its lower reaches and Similar Sound farther upstream. Minimum 5½- to 6-foot depths are enjoyed between this cut's southerly entrance and the anchorage detailed below, near unlighted daybeacon #8. Farther upstream, some 4½- to 5-foot soundings can be expected at low water.

Saddlebunch Harbor features a super anchorage just north-northwest of unlighted daybeacon #8. Here, cruisers can squeeze in surprisingly close to the easterly shoreline and stay in 8 to 13 feet of water. The adjacent banks are undeveloped and absolutely lovely. Shelter to the east and northeast is as good as it gets, and there is also some protection to the southwest, north, and southeast. Strong blows from the northwest would probably be the only wind direction that could really

Bat Tower (Sugarloaf Key)

chase you out of this otherwise wonderful overnight stop.

The marked passage continues upstream into the waters of Similar Sound. We sounded some low-tide depths of 4½ to 5 feet near unlighted daybeacon #18. North-northwest of unlighted daybeacon #18, brave cruisers can continue tracking their way between the two charted lines of submerged pilings. This unmarked passage eventually ends at a tiny public launching ramp. We observed some local vessels anchored just south of the ramp near 24 35.999 North/081 38.747 West, in about 7 to 8 feet of water.

We eased our vessel carefully over the charted line of underwater piles twice and could not find these potential obstructions. You may not be so lucky, and if these hazards really are there and not just some figment of NOAA's imagination, then it would render successful navigation of this unmarked upper portion of the channel tricky at best. Most cruisers would be far better served by the anchorage near unlighted daybeacon #8 in Saddlebunch Harbor.

Geiger Key Marina
(24 34.889 North/081 38.901 West)

Anyone who has read this far along with us knows that the authors of this guidebook are not shy about recommending, or at least reviewing, channels where few have gone before. So, when we tell you that visiting and resident craft would be better served to forget about trying to make their way to Geiger Key Marina, we mean it.

We thought that surely this facility was accessed by way of the marked and charted channel west of Saddlehill Key (2.2 nautical miles northwest of Hawk Channel's unlighted daybeacon #55). However, after spending an hour exploring all the adjoining canals, we learned that this channel serves a whole host of private homes with private docks but nary a marina.

After asking a local, we finally discovered two pitifully small, easy-to-miss, white PVC pipes near 24 34.504 North/081 38.897 West. We tried to follow the few additional pipes into the marina and twice wandered into only 3 feet of water. When we finally got to the "marina," we found a few docks, left over mostly to local fishing craft, and a large, semi-open-air bar. Keys gnarliness was very much in evidence.

We strongly suggest that you leave this "facility" and its forgettable channel to the locals. Your keel and underwater hardware will have a much longer life for the omission.

Boca Chica Channel and Associated Facilities and Anchorages
(Various Lat/Lons—see below)

Okay fellow cruisers, it's time to listen up. The various channels running north, between, and adjacent to Boca Chica Key and Stock Island offer a wealth of both facilities and anchorages. They are, however, confusing, to say the very, very least. PLEASE get out a copy of chart 11441 to follow along visually as you peruse the verbal account below. All will be so much clearer with this cartographic aid close at hand.

The long, very well-outlined Boca Chica Key Channel cuts to the north-northeast between Hawk Channel's flashing daybeacons #56 and #57. The southern tip of this cut and its first aid to navigation, flashing daybeacon #1, will be found near 24 32.775 North/081 43.556 West. Navigators approaching #1 must be careful to differentiate this cut from the Stock Island Channel (whose outermost marker is flashing daybeacon #2), which will be reviewed next in this section.

Boca Chica Key itself, which lies just east of its like-named channel, is U.S. military property and off-limits to civilians. In fact, the channel eventually leads to a mooring field and a marina, near unlighted daybeacon #17, which are for the exclusive use of service personnel. On the other hand, several side channels coming off the main Boca Chica cut provide reliable access to a host of anchorages and two repair yards.

Some 150 yards south-southwest of the

Anchored off the Boca Chica Channel

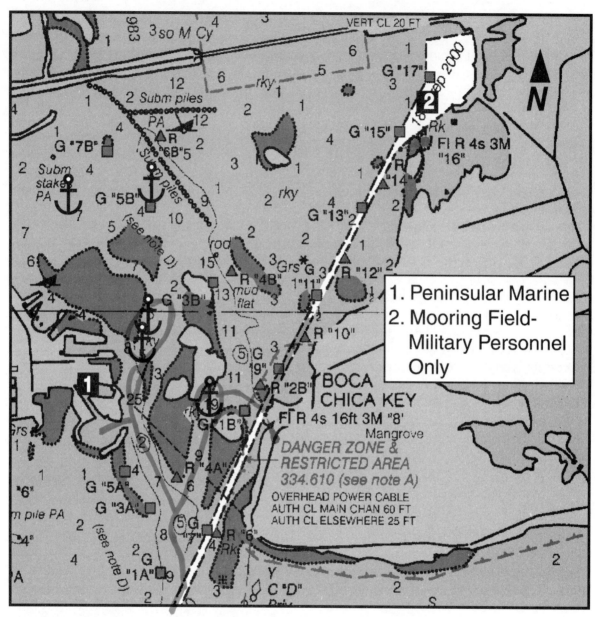

1. Peninsular Marine
2. Mooring Field-
   Military Personnel
   Only

Boca Chica Channel's unlighted daybeacon #7, cruisers can break off to the north (and eventually the north-northwest) and follow a marked but unnamed side channel to several anchorages and the two repair yards mentioned earlier.

Shortly after entering this alternate passage, the channel forks. Captains can choose to cut to the north, east of unlighted daybeacon #4A. This deep, little stream runs between a whole host of small islands and mangroves. These waters are a very popular anchorage (near 24 33.759 North/081 43.216 West), and we found a host of fellow cruising craft comfortably swinging on their hooks here during our last visit in 2001. Some were new, sleek modern yachts and sailcraft, while others would clearly never move again.

This anchorage also features good depths, running from 6 to as much as 18 feet, and if you can find elbowroom between your craft and its neighbors, there is ample swing room for a 45-footer. Cruisers will discover superior protection from all but gale-force southerly blows. The ultraprotected nature of this anchorage undoubtedly contributes greatly to popularity. The adjoining shores are completely undeveloped, and this natural character further adds to this haven's appeal.

It is possible to continue following this alternate portion of the side channel and curve around the northerly tip of the small island to the east. Then, by passing between unlighted daybeacons #1B and #2B, you can rejoin the main Boca Chica Key Channel at flashing daybeacon #8.

Now, wasn't that fun? Well, now it's back to what we might term the "main side channel," north-northwest of unlighted daybeacons #4A and #3A. In spite of the 2-foot bubble pictures on chart 11441, we sounded nothing less than 5 feet while passing right over this spot. Shortly thereafter, cruisers can turn 90 degrees to the west and discover an extensive repair yard on the easterly shores of Stock Island.

Peninsular Marine (24 33.808 North/081

Peninsular Marine (Stock Island)

43.565 West) is located at the northwesterly tip of the check-mark-shaped side water that runs northwest from the circular pool-shaped body of water, north of unlighted daybeacon #5A.

Peninsular Marine (305-296-8110) is a commercial boatyard as opposed to a marina. In fact, with just two exceptions, all of Stock Island is heavily industrialized. The amenities on Stock Island are few, but they are interesting, a point we will touch on later.

Overnight transients are not accepted here, but with an approach depth of 6½ feet and dockside depths varying from 6 to 25 feet, Peninsular Marine can service about anything you can dish up. If you want to work on your boat yourself, you can do it here. Though fuel is not available, haul-outs, mechanical repairs, and below-waterline repairs are. The 15½-acre yard has a 75-ton Travelift.

Also on site is a complete marine store. This is serious stuff here, so they don't skim the surface. If you need it, chances are that Peninsular Marine has it or can get it for you quickly.

Returning now to the alternate side channel, it is quite possible to continue following this cut to the north and then a bit to the north-northeast. This portion of the channel is unmarked, and you have to pay attention to business, or your keel may well say hello to a mud bank flanking the easterly side of the channel. Otherwise, minimum 5-foot depths with typical soundings of 6 to as much as 11 feet can be expected.

Just past the small bend to the north-northeast, this side channel slips between several small islands and mangroves. These waters are another very popular anchorage. We particularly recommend two spots, 24 33.893 North/081 43.402 West and 24 33.965 North/081 43.386 West. Both havens offer 6

to 11 feet of water, with excellent shelter from all but fresh northerly winds. While there is plenty of swing room, particularly by way of the more northern anchorage, you will assuredly find your craft amidst many neighboring vessels. It may be a bit of challenge for captains of larger cruising vessels to find sufficient elbowroom.

Don't continue cruising north past the charted 6-foot sounding. A whole raft of unmarked shallows begin to impinge on the channel opposite unlighted daybeacon #3B. We have been told that the locals know a way through these underwater hazards, but newbies had best leave this challenging passage to the veterans.

Okay, phew, there's still more to go. Let's return now to the main Boca Chica Key channel, at flashing daybeacon #8. We took a brief look at this section of the passage above, in describing how cruisers can regain the main Boca Chica cut by passing east between unlighted daybeacons #1B and #2B. Now, let's look to the north.

All of this is a complicated way of saying that captains following the main Boca Chita Key Channel, can cut to the north once abeam of flashing daybeacon #8, pass between unlighted daybeacons #1B and #2B, and thereby enter yet another side channel. Quite frankly, this cut is a bit less interesting and lacks the excellent shelter from foul weather boasted by the other alternate passages already reviewed above. However, it does lead to some anchorage opportunities, so let's take a quick look.

We found a collection of local vessels anchored north of unlighted daybeacon #5B, near 24 34.285 North/081 43.378 West, in surprising depths of 10+ feet. This spot is protected from southwesterly winds, and there is also a bit of shelter to the northeast, but it's otherwise rather open.

Lastly, vessels that are not put off by 3½- to 4-foot low-water depths can depart this side channel between unlighted daybeacons #5B and #7B and cruise west into the charted, broad basin of water. We found several craft anchored near 24 34.260 North/081 43.601 West. These were obviously shallow-draft vessels, and some appeared to be of the semi-derelict variety. Frankly, we only suggest this anchorage if the havens farther to the south are chock-full, and even then, it's strictly for smaller, shallow vessels.

So much for the side channels. Back on the main Boca Chica Channel, this cut comes to an end immediately northeast of unlighted daybeacon #17. There is a large mooring field in the basin, just south of #17 (near 24 34.530 North/081 42.616 West), but only active and retired military personnel need apply. There is also a marina to the east of #17, but it also is reserved for the exclusive use of military members. No facilities or services are to be had for civilians.

Boca Chica Key

Boca Chica Key is dominated by the United States Navy, which established a permanent presence there in 1945. During World War II, German submarines had been sinking allied shipping along the coast of Florida at an alarming rate. Ships hugging the shore were often silhouetted against bright shore lights after sunset, making them sitting ducks for night submarine attacks. In May of 1943, German subs sunk 49 ships off Florida. By September the losses had dropped to one vessel. The airplanes that flew and patrolled from Key West Naval Air Station (NAS) were partially responsible for keeping the Germans

at bay and keeping their heads (and periscopes) down.

At the end of hostilities in 1945, a lot of retrenchment went on in the military, but NAS Key West—located on Boca Chica Key—stayed open as a training base. Today, naval fighter jets sortie from Boca Chica to train in the skies over the Gulf of Mexico. It is not unusual to see several distinctly different types of jet aircraft flying in loose formation as pilots come and go from NAS Key West for practice dogfights out over the Gulf.

Of course, the facility's proximity to Cuba gives it added worth as a defensive and offensive base. The psychological value isn't paltry either.

Stock Island Channel and Associated Facilities
(Various Lat/Lons—see below)

The southerly entrance to the wide, deep, well-marked Stock Island Channel cuts to the north past its outermost marker, flashing daybeacon #2, a short hop southwest of the southerly genesis of the Boca Chica Channel. Large, oceangoing freighters use the Stock Island cut, and you can bet there won't be any depth problems for pleasure craft in this channel. It is also well marked with a host of flashing daybeacons. Navigation in the Keys doesn't get much clearer than this.

Northeast of unlighted daybeacon #5, another marked cut leaves the main Stock Island Channel and leads to the best facility for pleasure craft on Stock Island. This passage carries 15+ feet of water.

Notice the three charted coves, east of unlighted daybeacon #9, on this side channel. This triple basin is the home of Oceanside Marina (24 33.835 North/081 43.833 West). You can't miss the huge name

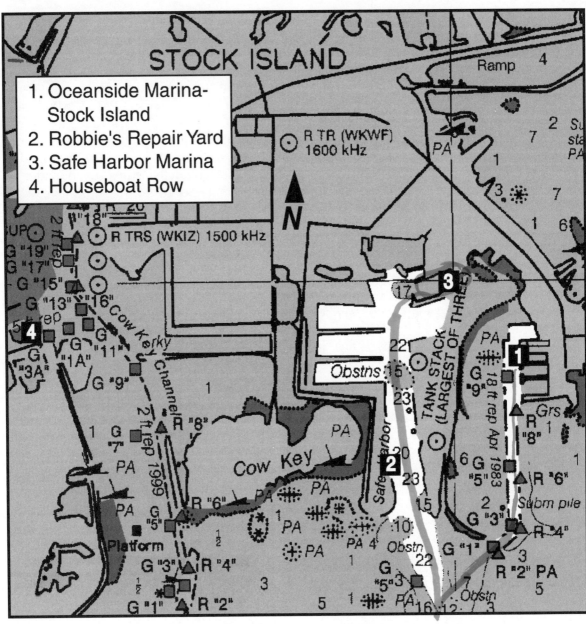

on the roof of their mammoth dry-stack storage building, just north of the docks. The outer fuel dock and dockmaster's office is found just north of the northernmost dockage basin, at the western tip of the point of land, backed by the dry-stack building. Depths alongside run from 9 feet to 24 feet (in front of the fuel dock). Anyone need more depth than that?

Oceanside Marina, Stock Island appears

well run and on the ball, and the grounds are clean. We can recommend this marina without reservation, particularly to larger powercraft, and of course, to those captains needing dry storage for smaller power vessels.

Oceanside is spacious and has a volume of dry storage that must be seen to be believed and numerous slips for cruising visitors. All berths are found at fixed concrete finger piers, with some alongside docking for larger craft. The dockside power connections are 30- and 50-amp and both fresh water and cable television hookups are also in the offing.

Look for all the shoreside amenities—rest rooms, showers, a Laundromat. These are all excellent, but alas, they are not air-conditioned.

Gas and diesel are available at the fuel pier mentioned above, as are mechanical repairs and waste pump-out. Oceanside does not have a ship's store here, per se, but there are marine supplies close by. The staff would be happy to direct you where you can get your basket filled.

The nearby Hickory House Restaurant (305-292-2211) has all the ambiance of a blimp hangar, but it is very popular with the local crowd. The menu is extensive.

Oceanside Marina, Stock Island (305) 294-4676
http://oceansidemarina.com

Approach depth—15+ feet
Dockside depth—9 feet minimum
Accepts transients—yes
Type of docking—concrete finger piers and
   some alongside docking
Dockside power connections—30 and 50 amp
Dockside water connections—yes

Oceanside Marina (Stock Island)

Showers—yes
Laundromat—yes
Waste pump-out—yes
Fuel available—gas and diesel
Mechanical repairs—yes
Restaurant—just off the property

Let us now return to the main Stock Island Channel and continue north to the well-sheltered commercial harbor, north of unlighted daybeacon #5. This basin is charted as "Safe Harbor." Besides making for some interesting sights from the water, Safe Harbor offers some repair and marina facilities that cater to pleasure craft.

First up is Robbie's Repair Yard (24 33.605 North/081 44.161 West, 305-294-1124), lining the westerly banks, just a stone's throw north of Safe Harbor's entrance. This yard has the equipment to get heavy stuff out of the water. There are three Travelifts here, the smallest of which is a 40-ton lift. The other two are an 85-ton job and a 150-ton monster. There is no transient dockage, but if you pilot a big boat and need below-waterline repairs, this has to be the place to come. Full mechanical repairs for both gasoline and diesel-power plants are also available here.

On the other hand, do not expect useable amenities. When we stopped by, the primitive showers were in sorry shape and neither rest room was operating.

Scattered on dry land nearby were what was left of maritime dreams . . . boats that hadn't seen the water in decades and a fiberglass fishing boat that had caught fire. Nothing burns faster or more furiously than a fiberglass boat that has gotten a good start.

Farther to the north, not too far from the harbor's northerly terminus, Safe Harbor Marina (24 33.998 North/081 44.004 West) makes its home on the second of the two charted coves, cutting into the easterly banks north of the charted "Tank Stack—Largest of Three." This facility accepts transients on a space-available basis. Some of the people who either live aboard in the marina or hang out in the bar, which is on the property, are seriously Keys gnarly. If your background is elite Junior League, you will never meet people like this again. Ever. That's a solemn promise.

Tucked inside a breakwater, Safe Harbor Marina offers protection from waves and breezes. With a 10-foot approach depth and a minimum of 6 feet at the dock, you should have plenty of water.

The dockage is a hodgepodge . . . about half alongside a concrete sea wall (with wooden pilings) and some floating wooden docks, and alongside a few fixed wooden finger piers. There is 30- and 50-amp electrical service, plus fresh water hookups available at all berths. Waste pump-out service is also at hand. Repairs to diesel-power plants are offered, and there are on-site (average) showers, rest rooms, and a Laundromat.

There is an on-site bar called the Nobody Knows Pub (305-292-0057), and it is open from 8 A.M. to midnight. Built out of bits and pieces of things—signs, water skis, boats—which others got rid of or which washed ashore, the Nobody Knows Pub is a one-of-a-kind operation. It has world-class cheeseburgers, owners who are amiable as long-term friends, and a clientele which is, to say the least, diverse.

Safe Harbor Marina (305) 294-9797

Approach depth—10 feet
Dockside depth—6 feet (minimum)
Accepts transients—yes
Type of docking—fixed and floating wooden piers—some face docking against a concrete sea wall buffered by wooden pilings

Dockside power connections—30 and 50 amp
Dockside water connections—yes
Waste pump-out—yes
Showers—yes
Laundromat—yes, laundry service also available
Mechanical repairs—diesel repairs
Restaurant—on site

Stock Island

Stock Island is probably the thorniest of the Keys. It is, shall we say, commercial. We are not talking commercial in a retail sense. Rather is it commercial in an industrial sense. The name Stock Island, by the way, was put on this key for practical reasons; it was where livestock was kept to delight the appetites of Key West citizens who had all the "surf" they could stand and wanted some "turf" to go with it.

Stock Island is also a study in contrasts. The Florida Keys Hospital is on Stock Island, as is the jail. The Tennessee Williams Fine Arts Center is also located here, as is Mount Trashmore, a sanitary landfill and the highest point in the lower keys. The Key West Resort Golf Course is on Stock Island, as are trailer parks and bars that, after the sun goes down, would give even a martial arts expert a case of the heebie-jeebies.

It was outside the golf course on Stock Island that several entrepreneurial homeless guys set up shop, finding lost and sunken golf balls and selling them for 25 cents each to golfers whose concept of a round of par golf was finding exactly as many golf balls as they lost. One golfer, who had played the course in the summer, stopped by to stock up before he played on a recent winter visit. He ordered up eight golf balls and gave the vendor two dollars. "That's not enough," explained the vendor. "That's what I paid last time," said the golfer. "Yeah, well now it's the season," explained the vendor, "and it's eight bucks."

Stock Islanders, many of whom are commercial fishermen, seem to live by their own set of rules and the local police seem content to let them do so. It was to Stock Island's busy

Modest pleasure craft on Safe Harbor (Stock Island)

docks that boats carrying cocaine (also known as Inca Pep Rally and Peruvian Marching Powder) tied up, back in the bad old days, when smugglers were the power elite in Key West and a serious head cold could pass for a simple case of overindulgence.

Cow Key Channel

The watery separator between Stock Island and Key West is known as Cow Key Channel. Even though the seaward side of this cut is marked, it carries only a bare 3 feet of water, or maybe slightly less in places, at low tide. We do NOT suggest that cruising-sized craft, of any draft, attempt to explore Cow Key Channel.

That's too bad, as this small channel has a claim to fame. From unlighted daybeacon #16 north to the fixed 9-foot bridge, there is a collection of houseboats moored (really sitting in the mud) along the westerly banks. This motley but colorful collection of "water craft" has become known as "Houseboat Row."

Controversy has swirled around the "row" for quite a few years, with city leaders expressing a desire to "move the vagrants out," while many Key West citizens have supported the right of those living aboard the houseboats to stay put. The authors of this guide would not presume to comment on this mess, but we will say that if Houseboat Row should ever be done away with entirely, a colorful and unique segment of Key West life will fade into the past.

For some time now, there have been noises made about removing the houseboats to Garrison Bight (see next chapter), but at least as of January 2001, there were still quite a collection lining Cow Key Channel. Just remember our word to the wise, do your Houseboat Row sightseeing by automobile, not by trying to ply this channel.

HAWK CHANNEL—MOSER CHANNEL TO KEY WEST NAVIGATION

If you have been following our account of Hawk Channel from Miami to Marathon, you will undoubtedly have already picked up on the fact that long runs between aids to navigation are *de rigueur* on this passage. Well, there is an awful lot of open water between markers along this stretch as well.

Okay, you are going to get to hear it one more time. This is yet another cruising ground where it is really a splendiferous idea to have a GPS interfaced with a laptop computer aboard and up and operating. It's ever so nice to be able to simply glance at the screen and immediately ascertain your position, rather than squinting at that apparition in the hazy distance, wondering whether it really is a marker and just what its number might be. Failing this modern-age setup, we suggest at least having a GPS.

Of course, no mariner should become too dependent on these new-age marvels. Woe be to the navigator who becomes so intoxicated by electronic position finders that he or she has no idea how to keep a DR track. What happens (as it has twice happened to us) if a rogue wave swamps the laptop and GPS? If you don't already have an understanding of the art and science of good, old, coastal navigation, you should acquire these skills

BEFORE tackling the waters of the Florida Keys.

As noted in the previous section of this chapter, another aspect that sets this portion of Hawk Channel apart from its eastern and northern counterparts is the wide collection of channels that cut to the north between the various keys and provide a multitude of overnight anchorage opportunities. These cuts run the gamut from easily navigated to the hair-pulling variety. Read the various accounts below and decide which of these side waters is right for your vessel's size and draft.

Charting Confusion Several charts, beginning with 11451, show the ICW magenta line passing south through the Seven Mile Bridge and Moser Channel then turning west on Hawk Channel. They have even continued the "Standard Mile" notations along the way. This indicates that the chart makers at NOAA have somehow gotten it into their heads that west of Moser Channel, Hawk Channel becomes a part of the Waterway or at least an alternate ICW route. This is probably caused by the fact that a vast majority of pleasure captains do indeed abandon the inside, ICW route at Moser Channel and continue on their way to Key West via Hawk Channel.

As we have stated many times in this chapter, it is our believe that the true ICW runs west to Big Spanish Channel, then northwest through that passage, until again turning to the west and following the northern edge of the keys to Key West.

With this judgment in mind, we have

chosen to ignore this extension of the magenta line AND its corresponding standard mile notations. We will treat these waters just like we have treated those portions of Hawk Channel already detailed earlier in this guide. We hope this explanation will help to avoid any confusion for our readers.

On Hawk Channel Cruisers on Hawk Channel, abeam of Knight Key Channel and Seven Mile Bridge to the north, will almost certainly spot the huge 142-foot Sombrero Key Light some 2.6 nautical miles south of their course line. Don't get anywhere near this huge aid to navigation. It is surrounded by shoal water.

Take a good look at the Sombrero Light (from a distance). It is the last aid to navigation anywhere near Hawk Channel for the next 6.4 nautical miles. As you are making this 6+ nautical mile run, the various markers of Moser Channel and the central, raised section of the fixed Seven Mile Bridge will be passed north of your course line.

Eventually (and it can seem like forever), captains using their binoculars will spot flashing daybeacon #49A. This aid marks an underwater reef and rock, but at least according to chart 11445, depths are never less than 12 feet. Unless you are in scuba diving mode, you will not want to make a close approach to #49A anyway.

Then, it's another little cruise of 8.7 nautical miles or so to come abeam of flashing daybeacon #50. Stay about .6 nautical miles south of #50. Several 2-foot shoals lie just north and northeast of this marker.

Along the way, cruisers might choose to cut north, about 3 nautical miles past Sombrero Light, and make use of the excellent anchorage and small marina between the two bridges crossing Bahia Honda Channel.

Bahia Honda Channel and Bahia Honda State Park Marina The southerly Bahia Honda Channel Bridge is the older span, and its extreme easterly section has been removed to allow easy passage by all pleasure craft, particularly sailboats. The newer bridge to the north is a fixed 20-foot structure that will bar further passage for most sailors and larger powercraft. Fortunately, the waters between the bridges can serve as a good anchorage, and the entrance to the small marina at Bahia Honda State Park makes into the easterly banks.

There are two cautions when entering these waters. First, note the long, long shoal running south-southwest from the southwesterly tip of Bahia Honda Key. Captains making for the easterly pass-through of the old Bahia Honda Bridge have been known to cut this corner and wind up hard aground. It is essential that you approach the open span from the deep waters lying southwest of this pass-through.

Commercial Harbor on Stock Island

Secondly, the tidal currents that boil through the seaward mouth of the Bahia Honda Channel are some of the fiercest in all of the Florida Keys. All mariners must be ready to take instant action if their vessel is caught in these swiftly moving waters.

Once the old bridge is in your wake, things get easier. Good depths are held to within 200 yards of the easterly banks between the new and old Bahia Honda bridges. Simply select a spot to your liking and drop the hook. Closer to shore, depths rise markedly.

Skippers bound for the marina at Bahia Honda State Park might want to make use of their binoculars to help pick out the small entrance cut, piercing the easterly shoreline. The approach canal is unmarked.

Cruise straight into the marina entrance canal on its centerline. Soon, the dockage harbor will open out to the north.

Newfound Harbor Channel and Associated Marinas and Anchorages The entrance to the Newfound Harbor Channel will be discovered some .9 nautical miles west-northwest of flashing daybeacon #50. Stay well south of #50 as you look for the outermost channel marker, flashing daybeacon #2. This aid to navigation denotes the westerly edge of a huge shoal and reef running out from the western banks of Munson Island (also known, but not charted, as Little Palm Island) and Big Munson Island. Come abeam of #2 by a good 250 yards to its westerly quarter.

From a position abeam of #2, the Newfound Harbor Channel cuts back to the east-northeast, while the Niles Channel strikes to the northwest. We'll check out the Niles Channel below.

From #2, take a lazy turn to the east-northeast and set course to eventually come abeam of unlighted daybeacon #3 by about 50 to 75 yards off its southerly side. Along the way, you will pass the ultraritzy Little Palm Island Resort docks south of your course. Feel free to take a look, but don't dare stop here unless your blood is blue. Don't allow leeway to ease you to the north between #2 and #3. The channel's northerly flank is very shallow, with depths of 2 to 4 feet as the norm.

At #3, the Newfound Harbor Channel begins a very gradual turn to the north. Point to come abeam and pass unlighted daybeacon #4 by about 25 yards to its northwesterly side. Next up are unlighted daybeacons #5 and #6. Simply point for the centerline of the wide gap between #5 and #6. Between #4 and #6, cruisers can break off to the east for a good anchorage.

To access this haven, depart the main cut about half way between #4 and #6 and turn east. Feel your way along with the sounder for up to .3 nautical miles. Pick any likely looking spot to drop the hook.

North of #5, an alternate channel cuts back to the west and leads to Newfound Harbor. If you choose to explore or anchor on this cut, turn to the west 150 yards north of unlighted daybeacon #5. Use your binoculars to pick out unlighted daybeacon #2 to the west. Point to come abeam and pass #2 by a good 200 yards to its southerly side.

While the channel is quite broad

between #5 and #2, shallow water does flank the cut to the north and south. Be mindful of these nearby shoals.

Cruising craft can anchor in the channel between #5 and #2. For safety's sake, it might be a good idea to drop the hook just a bit north or south of the centerline, in case some waterborne traffic happens along during the night.

Captains can also anchor west of #2 in the main body of Newfound Harbor. Some 5-foot soundings will be encountered on these waters. Watch out for the blunt finger of 2-foot depths to the north.

Don't attempt to enter the marked and charted channel to the west of Newfound Harbor. This cut leads to a collection of private docks with questionable depths and no room to anchor.

Back on the main Newfound Harbor Channel, skippers continuing on to the north should point to come abeam of unlighted daybeacon #8 by about 50 yards (or a bit more) to its westerly side. You can then cruise north for another .3 nautical miles in good water. Closer to the bridge, soundings rise to 3- and 4-foot levels.

Captains bound for Keys Sea Center will have to pick out this facility's entrance canal along the easterly banks. Turn straight into the canal from the wider waters to the west. Don't cut either corner. Soon the first charted northward-running canal will come abeam to port. Turn to port up this stream. Keys Sea Center will be spotted at the northerly tip of this side water.

Mariners in search of Dolphin Marina should ease to the northwest, toward the 15-foot fixed bridge. Watch the easterly banks for the entrance cut. As this stream comes directly abeam to port, turn 90 degrees to the west and enter the entrance canal, favoring the southern side slightly.

Smaller powercraft whose captains choose to explore the waters north of the 15-foot fixed bridge, known and charted as the Pine Channel, should approach the span from the southeast. This maneuver will help to avoid the finger of shallows east of the Dolphin Marina entrance.

Once the bridge is in your wake, cut to the north-northeast just a bit to bypass the broad shelf of shallows making out from the westerly shoreline. Of course, you must also stay west of the "Subm piling" and the very shallow water to the east.

By the way, we twice eased our research craft gingerly over the charted line of these underwater pilings, west of the charted "Micro Tr." We did not find any of these underwater obstructions. Maybe they have been removed, but maybe we were just lucky. Cautious mariners will stay west of these potential hazards.

After cruising north of the west-side point, opposite the "Tide Sta," begin a very slow, lazy turn to the west. Stay north and northeast of the charted 2-foot shoal. Eventually, if you're lucky, the anchor can go down about .2 nautical miles off the westerly banks. Remember, depths in this anchorage run up to 4 feet at low tide.

Niles Channel The southerly mouth of this north-northwestward-running cut is found just west of the southern entrance to Newfound Harbor Channel, reviewed above. Cruisers making for the Niles cut should also come abeam of flashing day-beacon #2, west of Munson Island, by at least 250 yards to its westerly side. However, instead of cutting to the east-northeast in the Newfound Harbor passage, turn to the northwest and point for the mid-line of the broad channel between unlighted daybeacons #4 and #5.

Don't get too close to #5. Notice the correctly charted shoal running southeast from this marker.

Northwest of #5 (and south of unlighted daybeacon #6), during fair weather only, skippers might choose to anchor northeast of the charted "M Grs" shallows.

Continuing upstream on Niles Channel, pass unlighted daybeacon #6 by at least 50 yards to its southwesterly side. The channel now begins a turn to the north, but navigators must take care not to swing to the north too quickly. Such a maneuver could land your craft square on the shallower water north of #6.

Northwest of #6, cruisers can anchor 450 yards off Pye Key's northeasterly shoreline. Feel your way along with the sounder and don't try a closer approach unless you pilot a truly shallow-draft boat.

As mentioned above, Niles Channel turns slowly to the north, upstream of unlighted daybeacon #6. Unfortunately, #6 is the last navigational marker on this cut. This means you are on your own to avoid the 4-foot, "rky" (rocky) shoal that thrusts into the channel's easterly flank, well north of #6. Favor the western side of the channel and keep a close watch on the sounder.

After coming abeam and passing the Mangrove Point to the east, a broad swath of deep water opens out to the north. This is an easily navigated portion of Niles Channel. Just favor the westerly shoreline slightly all the way to the 40-foot fixed bridge and all should be well.

Cruisers wishing to anchor south of the bridge can drop the hook about 200 yards off the westerly banks, 250 yards south of the span.

There is one SERIOUS caveat to this overnight haven. To the north, a seemingly low-lying power line crosses Niles Channel just south of the fixed bridge. We have been unable to find any published over-head clearance for these high-tension lines, but it's a safe bet that the mast of even a medium-sized sailcraft would encounter these shocking obstructions should such a vessel drag anchor to the north. For this reason, we do not recommend this anchorage for any sailcraft if there is even a hint of foul weather in the forecast. Even during fair weather, sailors be VERY SURE their anchor is well set before heading below.

On Hawk Channel From a position abeam of flashing daybeacon #50 to its southerly side, it's a straightforward run of approximately 3.5 nautical miles to the Hawk's next marker, flashing daybeacon #50A. Come abeam of #50A by some .5 nautical miles to its southerly side.

Kemp Channel North of #50A, cruisers could, but shouldn't, run the marked Kemp Channel. Low-water depths are only 3½ to 4 feet, and this cut does not allow access to any good anchorages or marina facilities. Our advice, keep on trucking!

On Hawk Channel An open-water stretch encompassing some 5.4 nautical miles separates flashing daybeacon #50A from the next westward marker on Hawk Channel. This aid to navigation is an 18-foot unnumbered daybeacon that marks the charted "Nine-foot Shoal." Pass about 200 yards north of the unnumbered Nine-foot Shoal daybeacon for best depths.

Between #50A and the Nine-foot Shoal marker, cruisers can break off to the north and run the twists and turns of Bow Channel.

Bow Channel The southernmost pair of markers on the Bow Channel are unlighted daybeacons #1 and #2. Pass between #1 and #2, then turn to the north-northeast, and pick out the next aid to navigation, unlighted daybeacon #3. Moving upstream from this point (north) on Bow Channel, take all subsequent red, even-numbered aids to navigation to your starboard side, pass green markers to port.

It would serve no purpose here to verbally describe all the many turns, twists, and swerves in the Bow Channel from its southerly entrance to the 8-foot fixed bridge. Not only would it add several pages to this guide, but navigators would still have to correctly identify all the various markers when on the water. So, our best advice is to take your time, carefully pick out the next daybeacon once abeam of the preceding marker, and make course adjustments accordingly. Clearly this is NOT a channel suited to larger, deeper-draft cruising vessels anyway, not only for its many ins and outs, but also due to its low-water

minimum depths of 4½ feet.

Just before coming abeam of unlighted daybeacon #10, passing cruisers will spy two additional unlighted daybeacons, #1 and #2, to the west. IGNORE these markers. They denote an extremely shallow cut that leads to the even shallower (if that's possible) waters of Sugarloaf Sound. Leave these cruising grounds to the small, flat-bottom skiffs that regular try their luck at fishing on these waters.

At unlighted daybeacon #20, a charted side channel breaks off first to the north and then cuts east into a canal, which eventually leads to Cudjoe Gardens Marina and Dive Center. Pass all the initial green markers fairly close to your port side, and then cut sharply east and pass between unlighted daybeacons #6A and #7A. Continue dead ahead into the canal's westerly mouth.

Cruise upstream on this canal, until the first stream on the northwesterly shore (port side) comes abeam. Turn to port and enter this side canal. The marina will be discovered in a sheltered basin at the northwesterly tip of this stream.

Other skippers will chose to continue north-northwest on the main Bow Channel and anchor south of the 8-foot fixed bridge. Navigation of this uppermost section of the channel is complicated by its misrepresentation of several daybeacons on chart 11445. Study this chart, and note that two markers, unlighted daybeacons #2B and #4B, are shown outlining a shallow patch along the easterly edge of the channel, north of unlighted daybeacon #24. Both #2B and #4B were absent during our several visits to these waters, and it seems likely that they have been deleted entirely.

So, slightly favor the western side of the channel, north of #24 for best depths. Anchor 350 yards south of the low (8-foot) fixed bridge. Be sure to set the hook so as to swing well clear of the now unmarked shallows to the east.

On Hawk Channel A run of about 1.85 nautical miles west of the unnumbered Nine-foot Shoal flashing daybeacon will bring cruisers abeam of unlighted daybeacon #53. This aid will come abeam some .7 nautical miles south of your course line. You may need binoculars to help spot it.

Daybeacon #53 marks an extensive underwater reef known as "West Washerwoman." Unless you are visiting these waters for their excellent scuba diving, we suggest that you give #53 a very wide berth.

Wow, things get a little closer together here. Would you believe that it's only a paltry 2 nautical miles west to the next Hawk Channel aid to navigation, unlighted daybeacon #55? Come abeam and pass #55 by some 200 to 300 yards off its northerly side.

North of #55, mariners might choose to tuck their craft snugly into the marvelous anchorage in Saddlebunch Harbor.

Saddlebunch Harbor-Similar Sound Anchorages The markers on the Saddlebunch Harbor channel have been changed since the current edition of chart 11445 was printed. The outermost pair of daybeacons are now located farther to the north than their position pictured on the chart. This is not really a cause for concern; it's just a bit different on the water than what 11445 would lead you to believe.

Pass between #1 and #2, and pick out unlighted daybeacon #3 to the north. Come abeam and pass #3 fairly close to its easterly side.

The channel now bends just a bit to the north-northeast. Pick up unlighted daybeacon #8, and point to pass to its fairly immediate westerly quarter. North of #8, cruisers can turn their craft east toward the shoreline. Good depths hold to within a surprisingly short distance of the shoreline. Drop the hook anywhere along this cove that strikes your fancy, and settle back for an evening of peace and security.

The vast majority of cruising skippers will want to discontinue their exploration of the Saddlebunch Harbor channel at the anchorage described above. Farther to the north, the channel becomes far shallower, particularly as it enters Similar Sound. To reach the Similar Sound anchorage we described earlier, you must negotiate the unmarked passage between the two lines of charted submerged pilings.

If you choose to make the attempt anyway, cut northwest once abeam of unlighted daybeacon #8, and set course to pass some 20 yards west of unlighted daybeacon #10. Continue cruising upstream on the marked cut to Similar Sound by passing all subsequent red markers to your starboard side and taking green makers off your port side.

North-northwest of unlighted daybeacon #18, there are no further markers.

Use your binoculars to pick out a small, public, launching ramp on the causeway to the north. While we did not find any of the "Subm pilings" that are charted east and west of the channel, some of these scary obstructions may very well still be there. Try to stay between the two lines of submerged pilings. Our best advice is to head for the tiny ramp and drop anchor several hundred yards short of the northerly banks. Good luck, you may need it.

On Hawk Channel A cruise of slightly better than 3.6 nautical miles west from a position abeam of unlighted daybeacon #55 will bring you abeam of flashing daybeacon #56. This marker sits hard by a broad shelf of shallows making out from the northerly shoreline. Pass .5 nautical miles south of #56.

Another 4 nautical miles will bring your vessel abeam of flashing daybeacon #57. Daybeacon #57 marks a patch of slightly shallower water. Come abeam and pass #57 by some 300 yards to its southerly side.

Between #56 and #57, captains might well decide to cut north and explore the many anchorages and marinas off Boca Chica and Stock Island channels.

Boca Chica Channel, Alternate Channels, Anchorages, and Repair Facilities Please allow us to repeat our earlier words about these waters. All the various crisscrossing channels and alternate passages can be more that a little confusing. PLEASE keep chart 11441 close to hand and follow along marker-to-marker as we present our account of these waters below. Believe us when we say, you will soon become lost amidst all the confusion without the help of this cartographic aid.

Navigators making for the Boca Chica Channel must be sure not to mistake the southernmost marker on the Stock Island Channel, flashing daybeacon #2, for the southerly genesis of the Boca Chica cut. Flashing daybeacon #1 is the first (southernmost) aid to navigation on the Boca Chica Channel. Come abeam and pass #1 fairly close to its easterly side.

Continue upstream on the Boca Chica cut by passing all subsequent red, even-numbered aids to navigation to your starboard side and take green markers to port. Did you remember your good, old, "red, right, returning" rule?

Navigation of the Boca Chica Channel is a fairly simple proposition, until one begins an approach to unlighted daybeacons #6 and #7. Just short of #7, an alternate channel breaks off to the north-northwest. Let's pause to explore this side passage.

As if our on-the-water lives were not complicated enough, this side channel splits north of its first marker, unlighted daybeacon #1A. Come abeam and pass #1A to its easterly side and cruise on to the north-northwest, as if you were going to pass between the next set of aids to navigation, unlighted daybeacons #3A and #4A. Just short of this pair, captains can alternately break off to the north and cruise between the charted mangroves and small islands. Hold to the centerline and drop anchor at any likely spot.

You can continue following this side cut of the side channel north and curl east around the northern tip of the small island to the east, rejoining the main Boca Chica Channel by passing between unlighted daybeacons #1B and #2B. Head straight toward Boca Chica's flashing daybeacon #8 and swing to port or starboard (depending on whether you want to cruise upstream or downstream on the Boca Chica Channel) some 20 yards short of #8.

You can also cut to the north, away from the Boca Chica Channel and head for unlighted daybeacon #3B. This (yet another) channel leads to the upper anchorages, which we shall review a little later in this section.

Okay, now back to the main side channel, running north-northwest from unlighted daybeacons #3A and #4A. In spite of the 2-foot bubble that chart 11441 shows in the middle of the channel along this stretch, we found nothing less than 5 feet of water, even at low tide.

Soon, the entrance to Peninsular Marine will come abeam to the west. Cruise into the entrance, favoring the northerly banks. A wide pool of moderately shallow water will open out to the south. We saw a few boats anchored here during our visit, but we suggest you keep clear. Soon, a canal will break off to the northwest. Turn into this short creek and track your way upstream to the repair yard.

Mariners who continue past the entrance to Peninsular Marine on their way to the anchorages, just to the north, we recommended in the previous section of this chapter, must begin to take greater care. A

charted, but mostly unmarked, shoal lines the easterly flank of the channel along this stretch. When we were last here, someone has placed a floating orange ball buoy to mark this hazard, but it was still hard to tell its exact position. Boats were anchored all over the place, some seemingly just behind the shoal in question. We soon came to understand that several of these craft were resting on the bottom. Be SURE to stay west of these shallows and west of the orange ball, if it's still there by the time of your arrival.

Once past the east-side shoal, the channel turns slightly to the north-northeast (really just slightly east of north). Here, you will find many fellow craft comfortably anchored. Pick out a likely spot. Don't continue cruising too far to the north. Just as suggested on chart 11441, depths eventually rise to 2-foot levels.

Now, wasn't that just a walk in the navigational park? Are your eyes dancing as much as ours trying to keep up with all of this? Well, hold on. There's more.

Let's skirt back to the main Boca Chica Channel and flashing daybeacon #8. Yet another side channel cuts north and then northwest from #8 and leads to one fair and one not so good anchorage. To enter this side cut, cruise between unlighted daybeacons #1B and #2B. Continue on to the north, pointing to pass between the next pair of markers, unlighted daybeacons #3B and #4B.

This channel now begins to pass through a very lazy turn to the northwest. Set course to come abeam of the next marker, unlighted daybeacon #5B, fairly close to its northeasterly side. You can anchor on the waters north of #5B.

Between #5B and the last marker on this channel, unlighted daybeacon #7B, shallow-draft vessels (only) can cut west through 4-foot depths and anchor in the midsection of the baylike body of water that will open out before you. Well, you can do that, but as said earlier, why would you want to?

Back on the main Boca Chica Channel once again, this track runs along on a straight, well-marked track, north-northeast of flashing daybeacon #8. Just above unlighted daybeacon #15, visiting cruisers will spy a large mooring field, with an adjoining marina east of unlighted daybeacon #17. Sorry gang, the moorings and the marina are for the exclusive use of military personnel.

Stock Island Channels and Marinas The Stock Island Channel is broad, deep, and easily navigated, as is the side cut that leads to Oceanside Marina. The main passage's southernmost marker is flashing daybeacon #2. What a surprise! Pass it to your starboard side, and continue north, pass all subsequent green, odd-numbered aids to navigation to your port side, while taking red markers to starboard.

Northeast of unlighted daybeacon #5, a side channel cuts first northeast then north to Oceanside Marina. Pass between the outermost markers, unlighted daybeacons #1 and #2, and then pick out the next pair of aids, unlighted daybeacons #3 and #4,

to the northeast. Cruise to a position between #3 and #4, then swing immediately and sharply north. You will then spot unlighted daybeacons #5 and #6. Come abeam and pass #6 to its westerly quarter, followed shortly by #5, which should be passed to its easterly side.

North of unlighted daybeacon #8, the several dockage basins of Oceanside Marina will come abeam to the east. The fuel dock and dockmaster's office will be spotted on the point of land just north of the northernmost dockage basin. Check in here to gas up and get your slip assignment.

Back on the main Stock Island Channel, at unlighted daybeacon #5, cruisers can continue following the wide channel north through the southerly mouth of Safe Harbor. Soon after leaving the harbor's entrance behind your stern, Robbie's Repair Yard will come abeam along the westerly banks. Remember, there is no transient dockage available here, but extensive repair service is available.

Skippers bound for Safe Harbor Marina should continue cruising north on the centerline of the commercial harbor. The marina's entrance will come abeam by way of the second east-side cove, north of the "Tank Stack—Largest of Three." Cruise straight into the cove. The marina will be spied at the rear of this water body.

Cow Key Channel The southern entrance to Cow Key Channel lies just about .5 nautical miles west of Stock Island Channel's unlighted daybeacon # 5. In three words,

DON'T GO HERE! Depths on the marked channel are all but nil at low water. Visit famous Houseboat Row from the land side.

On Hawk Channel Once abeam of flashing daybeacon #57, cruisers have only 3 nautical miles left on Hawk Channel. Set course to meet up with flashing buoy #12, south of Whitehead Spit and charted Fort Taylor. This marker is part of the Key West Main Ship Channel. A turn to the north soon leads to this historic port of call. Both Key West and the Main Ship Channel will be exhaustively reviewed in the next chapter.

Between #57 and #12, a series of small, unlighted daybeacons will be passed well north of your course line. These markers lie southwest of the charted "Aero R Bn." Frankly, we don't know what these aids to navigation are supposed to mark, but we suggest that cruising-sized craft, particularly those piloted by visitors, stay clear.

Audubon House interior

CHAPTER 6

Key West

"It's a strange, strange world we live in Master Jack,
It's a very strange world,
And I thank you Master Jack."

Whenever we contemplate the community that is Key West, these three lines from a late 1960s song by the South African group, Four Jacks and a Jill, never fail to come to mind. To be sure, at times Key West can be a strange place, with just about as many alternate lifestyles as one is ever likely to witness anywhere, anytime and some street scenes that can only be described as a "carnival."

But then again, Key West is also a place to be thankful for: thankful that it turns a friendly

Caroline Street (Key West)

eye to all who are willing to live and let live and thankful for all its color, romance, tropical breezes, fine dining, and shimmering waters that disappear into the spectacular sunsets. Key West is all these and much more, and cruisers have the opportunity to experience this city, which stands apart from all the rest, as it should be experienced, from the water.

Key West is, literally, the end of the line. When you hit Key West, you have gone about as far as you can go on the southeastern landmass of this United States. The "Southernmost Point" in the continental USA is well marked, and you can stand in front of it and have your picture taken for posterity.

For some people, Key West is the end of the line in a different sense. The city has—as many cities with a tourist-based economy also have—a visible collection of homeless people. Living is easy in Key West. It doesn't ever get really cold. There are fruits that can be eaten hanging from trees at different times of the year. The fishing is good. If you are living out of a rucksack or a plastic bag, you don't need much in Key West. Well, maybe you need a sense of humor. There is plenty that is amusing in this city.

For example, when you take the bus, you can be shocked to hear two people actually carrying on a conversation in English. Finding a really good parking space can move you to tears and be the starting point of your conversation for days on end. Gas costs only about $1.00 more per gallon than it does anywhere else in the United States. You can go to a baby shower that has two mothers and a sperm

Southernmost point in the United States (Key West)

donor. Your kid's third grade teacher has green hair, a nose ring, and goes by the name of "Spike."

This is not to say that Key West is totally weird. It is, however, different.

That is its charm. When you stroll the streets of Key West—and everybody does—you will see store windows with nearly every conceivable garish piece of touro-trash in evidence. Not much of it is in gracious, good taste, but it is unique. You will see people who make a living as street models; for a price, you can have your picture taken with them. You will see tourists like yourselves in every imaginable size and shape. You will pass by bars of every persuasion. You will talk to locals in street-corner booths who are hawking dive trips, fishing trips, airplane rides, condo time-shares, and about anything else that the law approves of. Key West is a carnival ride in perpetual motion. Climb aboard. Catch the brass ring.

As a tourist in Key West, you are in the majority. Tourists outnumber locals by a factor of 4:1. The townies, however, know their way around. They have seen it all before. It is better and wiser to get along with the people who serve the tourist industry than to assert your independence by demanding special service or creating a fuss. If you have a problem, get it solved in a low-key manner. Everyone, including you, will be happier.

You, like nearly everybody else, will be on vacation in Key West. There are, however, people in Key West who are not on vacation, people whose profession it is to "lighten the load" of folks who do not take proper security precautions with their belongings.

If you have your boat tied up to a dock, be smart and put obviously valuable fishing gear away so that it cannot be carried off. If you

leave your boat open while you are away for dinner, you could come back to find you had "visitors" while you were absent. Thefts in Key West, we have been informed, are generally targets of opportunity. If you put temptation out of sight, you will also put it out of mind. And that will go a long way to making your vacation there a lot more fun.

Numbers to know in Key West include:

West Marine—725 Carolina Street, 305-295-0999
Boater's World—3022 N. Roosevelt Blvd., 305-295-9232
Key West Marine Hardware—818 Caroline Street, 305-294-3519
All Key Transport —305-872-0577
Sunset Taxi —305-872-4233
Island Coaches—3052-296-4800
5 Sixes Cab Co.—305-296-6666
Friendly Cab Co.—305-295-5555
Florida Keys Taxi Dispatch—305-296-1800
Avis—305-296-8744
Dollar Rent A Car—305-296-9921
Publix Supermarket—3316 N. Roosevelt Center, 305-296-2225
Winn-Dixie Supermarket—2778 N. Roosevelt Blvd., 305-294-0491
Fausto's Food Palace—522 Fleming Street, 305-296-5663
Key West Airport—305-296-5439
Chamber of Commerce—305-294-2587
U.S. Coast Guard (marine emergency)—305-295-9700
U.S. Customs—305-294-3877
Lower Keys Medical Center—305-294-5531
Audubon House—305-294-2116
Duval Street Wreckers' Museum—305-294-9502
The Hemingway Home Museum—907 Whitehead Street, 305-294-1136
Geslin Sailmakers—305-294-5854
Meloy Sailmakers—305-296-4351

Charts 11441—perhaps the single-most-important Key West chart—covers all the approach channels, providing full details for the Main Ship Channel, the Northwest Channel, and the Southwest Channel

11447 ultradetailed chart of the Key West waterfront—very useful in navigating your way to the marinas on both Key West Bight and Garrison Bight, plus the various Key West anchorages and mooring fields

11445—useful chart when approaching Key West via either Hawk Channel or the ICW-inside route

11439—needed for navigation of the extreme westerly section of West Channel—really far more useful for those cruisers headed to the Dry Tortugas

Bridges

There is but a single bridge for Key West captains to worry with, and as it is a low, fixed structure, few will ever pass under it.

Fleming Key Cut Bridge—crosses Fleming Key Cut well east of the Key West Turning Basin and unlighted daybeacon #31—fixed—18 feet of vertical clearance

Key West Geography and Approaches

Key West is not only a city and a vibrant community, it is really a key as well. In fact, it is an oblong island, separated from Stock Island to the east by Cow Key Channel, with nothing more to the west but a few small isles, the chief groups of these being the Dry Tortugas and the Marquesas. Fleming Key, Sigsbee Park, Tank Island, and Wisteria Island lie just offshore and are generally considered part of Key West.

Key West's port facilities overlook the island's westerly shores. There is another set of facilities and a mooring field off the northern banks at Garrison Bight.

The southerly Key West shoreline is quite shoal, with 2-foot waters running as much as .2 nautical miles offshore. Stay well away from the southerly banks unless you are up for a most unpleasant grounding.

Key West has two primary approach channels and three also runs. The best marked, deepest, and most reliable passage is the Main Ship Channel. All those huge cruise ships you may well spot perched on the Key

West waterfront enter and exit the port by way of this cut. Need we say more? It is always well maintained and lit up like a proverbial Christmas tree.

Another big-time advantage of the Main Ship Channel is that our old and trusted friend, Hawk Channel, dead-ends at the former passage's flashing buoy #12. A 90-degree turn to the north will soon carry cruisers past the Whitehead Spit shallows, past historic Fort Taylor, and soon into the port itself. The Main Ship Channel is *the* passage of choice for mariners arriving from points east and north by way of Hawk Channel.

The other primary Key West approach passage is known as the Northwest Channel. We met this cut in the last chapter as part of our ICW to Key West discussion. Much as Hawk Channel dead-ends into the Main Ship Channel, the ICW passage, skirting along the northern face of the keys, west of Big Spanish Channel, comes face-to-face with Northwest Channel's outermost marker, flashing buoy #1.

The interior reaches of the Northwest Channel stretch southeast to Key West.

Cooling it on Key West Bight

Southeast of flashing daybeacons #18 and #19, captains can take a lazy turn to the east and find their way quickly to the principal Key West waterfront and all its many facilities and anchorages.

Aids to navigation are more widely spaced on Northwest Channel, as opposed to the Main Ship Channel, but it is still a well-marked cut. Good navigators will want to tick off the various markers as they work their way southeast on Northwest Channel. It would also be a good idea to have compass/GPS courses plotted and set up ahead of time.

Northwest Channel also provides what may well be the most reliable means to leave Key West behind and begin a passage to the Dry Tortugas (at least for those cruisers who decide to bypass Boca Grande Key and the

Marquesas Keys). This set of islands will comprise the southernmost and westernmost points of coverage for this guide and will be addressed in the last chapter.

The best of Key West's secondary channels is known as the Southwest Channel. This adequately marked passage begins well south of Woman Key and runs northeast to a meeting with the Main Ship Channel at flashing buoy #13. Southwest Channel skirts near some shallower water, but none of these underwater shoals are really shallow enough to worry pleasure craft.

Southwest Channel is most useful for those hardy souls approaching Key West from the offshore waters to the west and southwest. Of course, captains might alternately choose to continue east, pick up the Main Ship

Channel, and then turn north to Key West. With daylight and fair weather in the offing, we would not hesitate to use Southwest Channel. After all, this passage does cut the corner nicely, as opposed to continuing east to the Main Ship Channel. However, at night or with bad weather in the forecast, you will always find this guide's authors cruising on to the east and only then approaching Key West by way of the ultrareliable Main Ship Channel.

The so-called West Channel follows the wide swath of deep water south of Boca Grande Key and Woman Key and finally intersects the just-reviewed Southwest Channel at flashing buoy #D. This cut is very useful for cruisers leaving Key West on their way to a visit with Boca Grande Key, the Marquesas Keys, and perhaps afterward, the Dry Tortugas.

The down side (and it's a significant one) is that West Channel lacks much in the way of navigational markings. We suggest that you only make use of this passage on clear, calm days, and even then, you will need to keep an accurate DR and/or GPS track. Don't even think about trying this at night or with the winds whistling through the shrouds!

Then, there is the Calda Channel. This errant cut runs north from Key West, through Man of War Harbor (west of Fleming Key), and then skirts its way past a series of shoals and mangroves. It finally comes to a very uncertain northerly terminus at flashing day-beacon #1. While the Calda boasts prolific markings, low-tide minimum depths are only 3 feet (maybe just slightly less in a spot or two). North and west of #1, depths can run to 4 feet before finding your way into the deeper waters near the ICW passage. While it is theoretically possible to make use of the Calda

Channel to access Key West from the ICW route (and vice versa), and this passage is certainly shorter than cruising all the way to Northwest Channel, the shallow, controlling depths relegate this passage to the exclusive use of our outboard and I/O brethren. We strongly recommend that cruising-sized vessels keep clear of the Calda Channel.

Key West Marina Facilities

There are two groups of pleasure-craft-oriented marinas in Key West. The largest guards the island's westerly banks and is centered around Key West Bight (east of flashing buoy #24). The second makes its collective home on Garrison Bight, cutting into Key West's northerly shores.

We will begin our review of Key West marinas moving south to north across Key West's westerly shoreline. North of flashing buoy #14, cruisers will soon come abeam of Mallory Pier to the east. The cruise ships that regularly visit Key West dock here. You can often ogle any number of these oceangoing giants of the trade as you pass. It's always an impressive sight from the water.

By the way, Mallory Pier is the site of the daily "sundown activity." Key West celebrates the sinking of the sun daily with much hoopla and a sideshow of attractions, which will amaze, please, or bore you to tears. If you don't like what you are seeing or hearing, shuffle on. There is something that will simply knock your socks off nearby. The "people-watching" on Mallory Pier has to be sampled to be believed.

Hilton Key West Marina
(24 33.386 North/081 48.499 West)
Immediately north of the cruise-ship docks, cruisers can cut into the charted basin (which

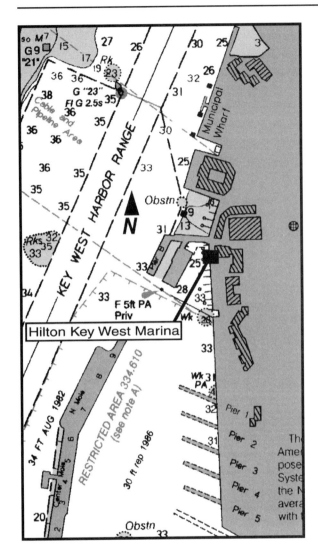

Hilton Key West Marina

once served as a submarine base) to the east. Here, on the extreme northerly corner of this harbor, Hilton Key West Marina makes its home.

Because of the waterfront activity—cruise ships, large as mountains, dock here and disgorge their loads of tourists—you won't get the privacy here you might in other marinas, which are slightly more off the beaten path. However, the Hilton name means something,

and the marina has the extras that mariners like when they are hooked up to land.

Transients are accepted at this marina's mixed collection of fixed wooden and floating concrete piers. Depths alongside run 12 feet or better, and the approach depths are, well, probably enough for the *Queen Mary*. Power hookups run from 30- to 100-amp service, and there is water on the docks, plus telephone and cable television hookups. For waste pump-out, you'll need to go elsewhere, the most convenient of which appears to be Conch Marina in Key West Bight.

The showers at Hilton Key West Marina are large, clean, and in excellent shape. There are four of them, unisex types. There's a Laundromat here, too.

There are a couple of restaurants on site that have good reputations. The high-end facility is Latitudes. The other, not quite as pricey, is Bistro 245.

Though no fuel is available, mechanical repairs can be arranged through local, independent technicians. The marina monitors Channel 16. If you need directions to the old, sub-base dockage basin, call and ask . . . but do that on a working channel.

Hilton Key West Marina (305) 294-4375
http://www.keywestresort.hilton.com

Approach depth—30 feet
Dockside depth—13-66 feet
Accepts transients—yes
Type of docking—fixed wooden and concrete
    floating piers
Dockside power connections—30/50/100 amps
Dockside water connections—yes
Showers—yes
Laundromat—yes
Mechanical repairs—independent contractors
Restaurant—two on site and many more close by

Hilton Key West Marina

Key West Bight Facilities
(Many Lat/Lons—see below)

Cruisers making for the (as the late Howard Cosell would have said) plethora of marinas housed in Key West Bight should continue north past Mallory Pier on the Key West Harbor Range. Just short of flashing buoy #24, cut to the east and track your way to the Key West Bight entrance, marked by flashing daybeacon #4.

Look to the northeast as you come abeam of #4. You may spot an old submarine tied up against the sea wall.

Key West Bight teems with marinas, bars, restaurants, retail shops, and just about anything else you might think of. Let's begin our review at the harbor's northwestern tip and work our way around the shoreline moving south and then northeast.

The Galleon Marina occupies the bight's northwestern corner near 24 33.740 North/081 48.220 West. This has been the primo transient stopping-off place in Key West for years. People come here again and again. The docks are modern, wooden-decked, floating structures and are always in topnotch repair. All berths feature full-power, fresh water, cable television, and telephone connections. You can expect to get a helping hand in your docking without asking for it, provided, of course, they know you are coming and you have a slip assigned. The dockmaster monitors

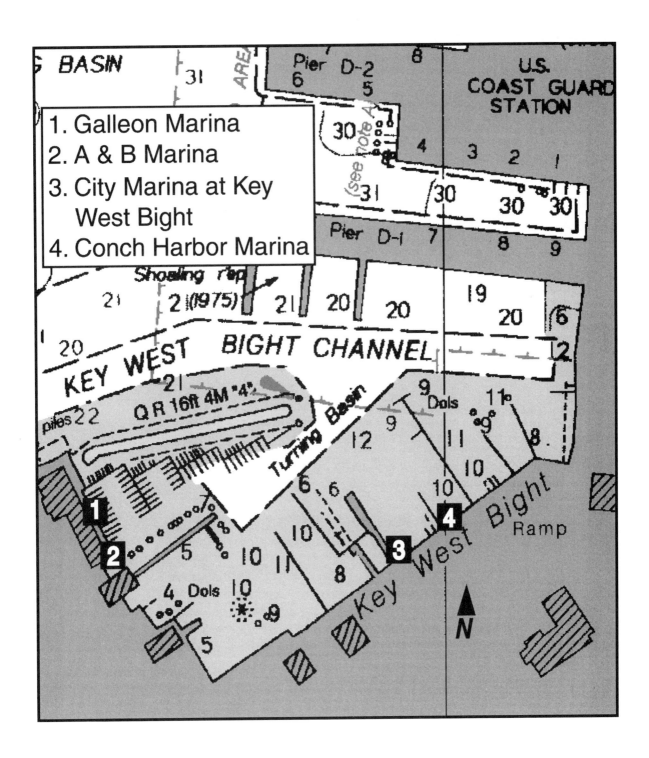

Entrance to Key West Bight

Galleon Marina (Key West Bight)

Channel 16 and switches you over to 17. The office is open from 6:30 A.M. until 9 P.M.

Dockside soundings run 9 to 11 feet, even at low water. Approach depths are in the 20-foot range.

The Galleon features a row of shops along its waterfront. You can get deli food, simple supplies, chat with the dockmaster, or rent a boat at one of the facilities along the board-walk.

Inside the main building, on the ground floor, are a health club, sauna, Jacuzzi, show-ers, and the rest rooms, all of which are air-conditioned and open to transients. The rest rooms and showers get a lot of use here, but you can expect them to be generally clean and well maintained. There's an on-site swim-ming pool (8 A.M. to 10 P.M.) with a bar right nearby. Want salt water? Try the private beach.

The Galleon used to be where you had to go if you came by boat and wanted to be close to all the exciting Key West nightlife, but there are additional choices now. Still, the Galleon is a magnet and has not suffered by the turning of the pages of time. You get a lot for the buck here, and the operation has been around enough to have eliminated all the serious glitches.

This is an amazingly busy place, so have your lines ready when you dock. You will be one of the many whom the marina serves simultaneously.

Galleon Marina (305) 292-1292
(800) 6-MARINA

Approach depth—20 feet
Dockside depth—9-11 feet
Accepts transients—yes
Type of docking—floating wooden docks, with
    slips, some alongside docking, all first-rate
Dockside power connections—30 and 50 amp

Dockside water connections—yes
Waste pump-out—yes
Showers—yes, three stalls for each gender, in
    the rest rooms
Laundromat—yes
Fuel available—no, but nearby at Conch Marina
Mechanical repairs—no
Below-waterline repairs—no
Ship's and variety store—no
Restaurant—next door and many others close by

Next up is A & B Marina (24 33.715 North/081 48.208 West), just south of the Galleon docks. This facility was once kind of an extension of the A&B Lobster House, a dock where you came when you didn't want to pay the full load, which they charged next door at Galleon Marina. Has this ever changed, and for the better, too!

A & B Marina is now overwhelmingly attractive, diverse, and convenient. The rest rooms, laundry, and showers here are absolutely topnotch. For example, the bath-room floor is black-and-white tile, and it's spotless. The showers are large and luxurious. There are four coin ops in the laundry, two dryers and two washers. There's a cruisers' library and even a StairMaster exercise machine.

Transients are readily accepted at A&B's floating, concrete, finger piers. Depths along-side run at least 7 to 12 feet. Power connec-tions up to 100 amps are in the offing as are fresh water and cable television connections. Diesel fuel (but strangely, NO gasoline) can be purchased at the marina fuel pier.

Also on the premises is the 24-hour deli with the unusual moniker of Damn Good Food To Go (305-294-0011), which has, well, damn good food. The deli monitors VHF Channel 16; the possibilities are limitless. There's a slick upscale grocery and wine store next door.

Galleon Marina (Key West Bight)

The Commodore Steakhouse (305-294-9191) is also located adjacent to A&B's docks. This fine dining attraction is a two-story affair with a large, attractive, sophisticated bar downstairs, along with a smaller ground-floor dining facility.

Upstairs, which is where we had dinner, guests overlook Key West Bight. The coming and going of water traffic after dark, with green, red, and white running lights illuminated, reminds one of Christmas. The upstairs dining room is finished in natural wood, with exposed rafters in the ceiling and the combination windows/doors open to let the breezes in when the weather is right. It all feels good.

After a day of hiking around Key West, we were hungry when we stopped here, and our eyes were bigger than our stomachs. We opened with Oysters Commodore—oysters fried in cornmeal, laid on a pallet of spinach, and topped with a spicy remoulade sauce. They were delicious.

The New York strip with béarnaise sauce was excellent. We asked why the steak was so extraordinarily tasty and were told that all the beef served here is prime. The béarnaise added a tasty extra dimension. We had mashed potatoes and asparagus with hollandaise. The asparagus was crispy and cooked just right, though we thought the hollandaise a tad "thin" in the taste department. The house Merlot was full-bodied and more interesting the longer we let it breathe.

The staff at the Commodore seems to have an international flavor. In the course of one meal, we spoke Russian, French, Spanish, and some Roaring Fork Valley (Colorado) English.

This is not an economy restaurant, but you always seem to get what you pay for anywhere you go.

A & B Marina (305) 294-2535
(800) 223-8352
http://www.ABmarina.com

Approach depth—16 feet
Dockside depth—7-12 feet
Accepts transients—yes
Type of docking—floating concrete docks
Dockside power connections—30/50/100 amps
Dockside water connections—yes
Waste pump-out—yes
Showers—yes, marvelous
Laundromat—yes
Fuel available—diesel only
Restaurant—yes, see above

The City Marina at Key West Bight (also known as Historic Seaport at Key West Bight) occupies a good portion of the rear (southeasterly shores) of Key West Bight. The dockmaster's office is found near 24 33.753 North/081 48.069 West.

This is a large city-owned marina with lots of traffic. There are 200 berths here and plenty of commercial boats that come and go, working the phenomenal tourist business that primes the commercial Key West pump in better fashion every year. Years ago, the business of Key West used to be "wrecking," salvaging boats and cargoes that foundered on the nearby reefs. Now, tourism reigns. There is something in this town for everyone, townie or tourist.

The dockmaster's office here is in a houseboat tied up to the southwestern side of an

City Marina at Key West Bight

old warehouse out on a pier. It can be more than slightly confusing for newcomers to enter Key West Bight for the first time, so have your wits about you. There are several different marinas in here, and you want to be certain that the one you are about to tie up to is the one you contacted on the VHF radio. If you aren't sure, ask for directions.

The City Marina at Key West Bight (CMAKWB) monitors VHF Channel 16. Call on 16, and they will switch you over to a working channel.

Approach depths here are plenty deep. You'll get 30 feet into the turning basin and 10 feet minimum after that. During our last visit, there were oceangoing sailboats and oceangoing yachts tied up alongside the main pier, which is also where the fuel dock (gasoline and diesel) is located.

Because of the size of this facility, you can expect full services and all the amenities. The dinghy dock, close ashore, is virtually a city unto itself. Of course there are many liveaboards who anchor out, and this is where many come in to make their shoreside connection. Daily or monthly dinghy fees are available here.

Transients are accepted here, naturally. Most dockage is found alongside a rugged, fixed, wooden pier, but there are also some finger slips. All berths feature power service up to 100 amps, plus fresh water and cable television hookups. Waste pump-out is also offered at the City Marina.

There are showers and rest room facilities, which are locked, just off the dock. Admission is gained by an electronic swipe card for which, to obtain, you will put down a $100 returnable deposit. If that seems like a lot of money to put down for admittance to the rest rooms, keep in mind that Key West is the end of the line for a lot of homeless people who have no place to stay and no place to clean up. To them, a rest room is like the Ritz Carlton, so they covet entry, which the city powers that be are determined to deny them by being penurious with their access cards.

The Laundromat and the showers here will last a lifetime, encased, as they are, by cement block. Cinder block may be the choice of builders for the outside of a building, but when you see the same on the inside, there is a definite lack of warmth. You could as well be in a bunker. Upon entering the showers, via "the card," one finds a hallway to the right, which leads to the men's and women's showers and toilets. Ahead and slightly to the left are the laundry facilities, with three coin-op washers and four coin-op dryers and a cruisers' library.

The men's shower/rest room had two sinks, three showers, a couple of urinals, and one enclosed sit-downer. The room was a bit battered, but clean. We were unable to check out the ladies' room because there was a lady in there. She may have been a tramp, but we assumed that she was a lady. It is always best to err on the side of generosity when it comes to women's moral fiber and age.

There is no ship's store here, because Key West has everything that a mariner might need, and much of it is sold within walking distance. There's a nearby restaurant, one of about a million, called Half Shell Raw Bar (305-294-4902, 231 Margaret St.), that dishes up some mighty tasty conch chowder. Served piping hot, it will take the chill off on a cold Key West day, when the wind is blowing 20 knots from the north. The burgers are good here, too.

City Marina at Key West Bight (305) 293-8309
http://www.keywesthistoricseaport.com OR
http://www.kwhistoricseaport.com

Approach depth—30 feet
Dockside depth—10 feet (minimum)
Accepts transients—yes
Type of docking—mostly alongside a rugged,
fixed wooden pier, but there are some
wooden finger piers here, also
Dockside power connections—up to 100-amp
service
Dockside water connections—yes
Waste pump-out—yes
Showers—yes
Laundromat—yes
Fuel available—gas and diesel
Restaurants—more than you can imagine within
walking distance

The easternmost facility on Key West Bight goes under the name of Conch Harbor Marina (24 33.753 North/081 48.013 West). This is a very large and classy facility, with little left to wish for.

Some truly huge yachts visit Conch Harbor for fuel or to tie up, so standard cruising craft will have no problem getting here in terms of finding the place. The dockmaster's office is at the seaward end of the pier, underneath the large Texaco sign. But because marinas change their affiliation with oil companies from time to time, it would be best to raise the dockmaster on VHF 16 before coming in. It would also be wise to have a reservation. There are times when Key West is full of boats participating in sanctioned events, and there could be no room in the inn.

City Marina at Key West Bight dinghy dock

Transients are readily accepted at Conch Harbor. The marina features fixed wooden finger piers and some alongside docking for larger craft. All berths offer electrical service up to 100 amps, plus fresh water connections and cable television and telephone hookups. Depths alongside run 10 feet or better. Waste pump-out service is also available, as is gasoline and two grades of diesel fuel.

Like the other facilities in Key West Bight—which is where the marine activity in Key West is unequivocally centered—Conch Harbor is within walking distance of all the "happening" places in Key West. The water-front in the bight is encrusted with restaurants of every stripe. Upscale, downscale, and in between, you can get it in Key West Bight. Don't like that? Walk a few blocks to downtown Key West, Florida's answer to Sodom and Gomorrah, or Alice's Restaurant. ("You can find anything you want in Alice's Rest-au-rant . . ." songwriter Arlo Guthrie, circa 1966).

Currently, Conch Harbor's showers and rest rooms (two each, both unisex but clean) are located in a temporary building at the end of the dock, on shore. A completely new shower facility, plus Laundromat, is slated for completion in September of 2002.

Key West Bight

Conch Harbor Marina (305) 294-2933
http://www.conchharbor.com

Approach depth—30 feet
Dockside depth—10+ feet
Accepts transients—yes
Type of docking—fixed wooden finger piers and
    some alongside docking
Dockside power connections—30/50/100 amp
Dockside water connections—yes
Cable TV and phone hookup—yes
Waste pump-out—yes
Showers—yes
Laundromat—to be completed in September
    2002
Fuel available—gas and diesel
Restaurant—a plethora nearby

Garrison Bight Facilities
(Many Lat/Lons-see below)

To access the Key West marinas on Garrison Bight, most cruising craft will need to cruise north through the deep water of Man of War Harbor and then follow the marked Garrison Bight Channel around the northerly tip of Fleming Key. This cut then leads back south to Key West. It's then only a short hop east to Garrison Bight.

A few, small, low-lying vessels might be able to short-cut this long voyage by way of Fleming Key Cut. This narrow passage plays host to some really wicked tidal currents, and it runs under an 18-foot fixed bridge. Smaller powercraft, with good maneuverability, may be able to make use of this channel, but all other cruising craft should choose the Man of War Harbor-Garrison Bight Channel route described above.

The entrance to Garrison Bight will come up south of flashing daybeacon #21. Entry into Garrison Bight is severely limited (at least for sailcraft) by the charted 50-foot power line that spans the harbor's entrance. If you have any questions about the height of your mast, don't come in here.

Conch Harbor Marina (Key West Bight)

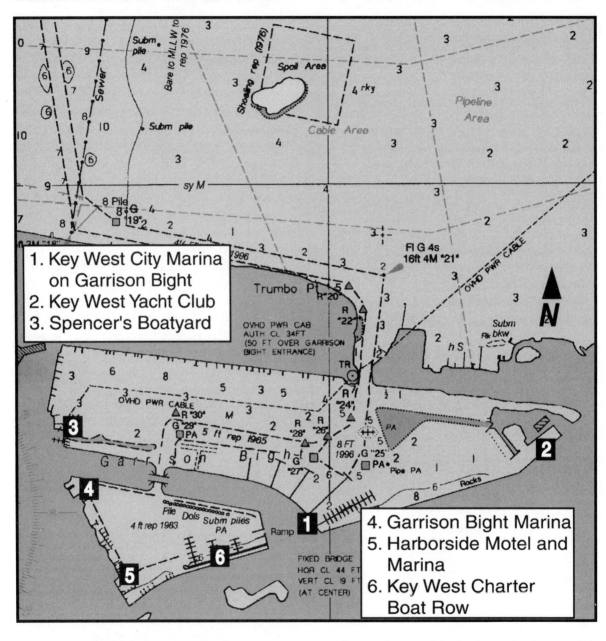

1. Key West City Marina on Garrison Bight
2. Key West Yacht Club
3. Spencer's Boatyard
4. Garrison Bight Marina
5. Harborside Motel and Marina
6. Key West Charter Boat Row

Garrison Bight is composed of two separate harbors linked by a narrow stream. This connector creek is crossed by a 17-foot fixed bridge. Large vessels will be relegated to the outer harbor, courtesy of this span, while smaller craft can visit the inner basin.

There is plenty of shallow water in Garrison Bight, with some soundings rising to 3-foot levels. Be sure to follow the various markers to maintain minimum 6½-foot depths. Outside of the defined channel, captains are in imminent risk of a most embarrassing grounding.

After passing through Garrison Bight's northerly entrance and under the 50-foot power line, the outer dockage basin of the City Marina on Garrison Bight will come up dead ahead. There are actually two distinct sections to this marina, or three if you count the Garrison Bight Mooring Field, which is managed through the Garrison Bight City Marina. The live-aboard and transient docks will be discovered in the outer portion of Garrison Bight, south of unlighted daybeacons #27 and #25 (near 24 33.648 North/081 46.964 West). The southern section (inner basin) is occupied mostly by illustrious Charter Boat Row, a Key West phenomenon

for decades. As mentioned above, your craft must be able to clear the 17-foot fixed bridge to access the inner harbor.

Transients are accepted here. Some 50 spaces are set aside for visitors, so adequate slip space should seldom be a problem. Berths consist of floating, concrete-decked, finger piers, with 30-amp (NO 50-amp) power connections and fresh water hookups. Depths alongside vary widely, though most dockside soundings are in the 6- to 8-foot range. A few slips have depths running to only 4 feet. No fuel is available at this facility, but waste pump-out service is offered.

When we first took a look at the transient showers at this marina (they are on the inner basin side), they were the most appallingly bad shower facilities we had ever seen.

Houseboat Row

Morgan wrote up a review of the showers based on his impression. It went like this:

"The existing transient showers at City Marina at Garrison Bight are some of the least attractive we have seen. Ever. Imagine what you might find at the end of the cell-block in a Cuban jail, and you can get an inkling of what you'll find here. This writer has seen the shower facilities available on Florida's Death Row, and we can state unequivocally that guys under the sentence of death in Florida have more attractive bathing accommodations than the City Marina at Garrison Bight. By a factor of four. There's a combination lock on the shower door to keep the 'unwashed' out, but if you go in here to shower, you had better pray to your god that the lock never jams. This would be an awful place to have to spend any extra time at all."

Happily, when we expressed our reservations about the showers to the management at City Marina at Garrison Bight, they saw the light and informed us that they would henceforth (and immediately) allow transients to use the nice, clean, modern facilities on the outer basin side, which had heretofore been available only to live-aboards. This was a huge break.

The concrete-block shower and rest room building is new and there are modern rest rooms and two unisex showers, which are also new. Also in this facility is a Laundromat. Access is gained by using a magnetic key. The difference between what was and what is (now) is heartwarming. If you want to take a look at what you might have been exposed to, ask to see the "old" showers. Then thank your lucky stars you won't have to use them.

Well, that's the good news. The bad news is that eight months after hearing that transients would not be subjected to the awful showers, we found out—from a City Marina at Garrison Bight employee—that the showers were back in use. People using the Fleming Key mooring field (see below) were also directed to use those terrible showers, we were informed. In the department of personal hygiene, this a monumental step backwards.

The marina hums with all kinds of traffic, but it is also a good hike from this marina to where the action is in downtown Key West. It would be a far longer and more arduous hike home, should you manage to get yourself overserved in any one of the watering holes that line Duvall Street.

Key West City Marina on Garrison Bight (305) 292-8167
http://www.keywestcity.com

Approach depth—6½+ feet
Dockside depth—4-8 feet, depending on location
Accepts transients—yes
Type of docking—floating, concrete, finger piers
Dockside power connections—30 amp only
Dockside water connections—yes
Waste pump-out—yes
Showers—yes (see above)
Restaurant—nearby, four within three blocks

Key West Yacht Club overlooks the east end of Garrison Bight's outer basin, near 24 33.689 North/081 46.725 West. This is a private club, open only to those visitors who have reciprocal privileges through the Florida Council of Yacht Clubs or some other sanctioned yacht club.

In spite of the soundings shown on chart 11447, we were able to maintain minimum 6-foot depths by cruising east from unlighted daybeacon #25 to the club's dockage basin. Depths alongside run 6 to 8 feet.

Garrison Bight Marina

Key West Yacht Club's piers are of the fixed, concrete variety and look very sturdy. However, members take up nearly all of the 65 slips and only a couple of slots are kept open for visitors. Be sure to call ahead to see if there is any room at the inn before committing to a plan which calls for an overnight stay at this facility.

The KWYC has a fixed waste pump-out system on the dock, plus water and electric service up to 50 amps. Some of the usual yacht club amenities—swimming pool and tennis courts—appear to be absent here.

The rest rooms and showers set aside for visitors are older but clean . . . and air-conditioned. They are in a small building about 100 feet southeast of the dock.

What one needs to know best are the opening and closing times of the Key West Yacht Club dining room, a sort of interlocking jigsaw puzzle of times and days. On Mondays and Tuesdays the club is closed. It is open for lunch and dinner on Wednesdays, Thursdays, and Fridays. On Saturdays it is open for lunch only. On Sundays it is open for dinner only.

For those who miss a meal here, there are lots of fast-food restaurants nearby.

Key West Yacht Club (305) 296-3446 (Dockmaster)
(305) 296-5389 (Office/Restaurant)

Approach depth—6 feet (minimum)
Dockside depth—6-8 feet
Accepts transients—limited to members of other yacht clubs with appropriate reciprocal privileges
Type of docking—fixed concrete finger piers

Dockside power connections—30/50 amp
Dockside water connections—yes
Showers—yes, old but clean and air-conditioned
Restaurant—on site, others nearby

West of unlighted daybeacons #29 and #30, a haphazard, white PVC-pipe-outlined channel leads to Spencer's Boatyard (305-296-8826) in the southwestern corner of Garrison Bight's outer basin (near 24 33.708 North/081 47.328 West). This little cut carries some 5 feet at low water (with similar soundings alongside), but it is quite easy to wander outside of the track into 3 and 4 feet of water.

Spencer's is a mostly haul-out repair yard, advertised as "the only full-service boatyard in Key West." While transients are not accepted here, because there is truly no place for them, this appears to be *the* place to be in Key West if one has below-waterline repairs in mind or just onboard service problems that require the attention of a skilled craftsman. Some light mechanical repairs are also offered, but we were politely informed that the yard "does not tear into engines."

Spencer's isn't pretty, but then what boatyard in the world is actually a garden spot? It has that cluttered air of purpose in it. There's a 25-ton Travelift on site and haul-out and bottom jobs appear to be a routine item here.

This is a busy facility, and it would be a good idea to call ahead to schedule the work you need done, as opposed to just showing up at the haul-out slip.

Moving to Garrison Bight's inner basin, cruisers can expect depths of 5 to 9 feet, in spite of the "4 ft rep 1983" notation on chart 11447.

Garrison Bight Marina (305-294-3093) guards the harbor's northwesterly corner (24

Key West Yacht Club

Sunset Marina (Stock Island)

33.650 North/081 47.324 West). This is a fuel dock (gasoline only) and dry-stack facility only. They do not accept transients. To get here for fuel, you must be able to get under the bridge, which has a clearance of about 17 feet. Look for the Chevron sign.

Pelican Landing makes its home in the very southwesternmost corner of Garrison Bight's inner basin (24 33.530 North/81 47.250 West). This private condominium facility consists of a four-story building with parking underneath. While this condo complex has its own docks, they are not open to the public.

Harborside Motel and Marina (305-294-2780) (24 33.541 North/081 47.267 West) is just a couple of doors down from Pelican Landing, and slightly to the northwest. Much like Pelican Landing, this is a false trail. Unless one stays in the motel, one cannot use the docks. So, staying aboard here is not an option.

Sunset Marina
(24 34.729 North/081 45.038 West)

We have one final Key West facility to review, but guess what? This one's really on Stock Island. However, the only way to access Sunset Marina is by way of the various Key West channels, so we'll place our account of this marina here (for lack of anything better to do with it).

To visit Sunset Marina, cruisers must journey north through the Garrison Bight Mooring Field (see below) and then cruise carefully around the northern shores of Sigsbee Park. Here you will pick up the northwesterly genesis of the Cow Key Channel. Do you remember this useless cut (from the Hawk Channel side) that we met in the last chapter? Well, the marked channel actually continues north through the 9-foot fixed bridge and eventually wanders across the charted basin known as the Salt Pond.

Cruisers can follow this extreme upper por-tion of the Cow Key Channel and make their way to Sunset Marina but not without some serious navigational headaches. We will cover this confusing passage in the naviga-tional account at the end of this chapter, but for now, let's just say the "red, right, return-ing" rule does NOT apply in this instance.

Well, to get back to Sunset Marina, this facility overlooks the Stock Island shoreline, west-southwest of unlighted daybeacon #28. Sunset Marina is part of a large condominium project being built on the property between the Monroe County Detention Center and the county's Mount Trashmore. This facility seems to have been under construction for quite some time, and as we will see just below, it's still not complete.

Approach depth is 7 feet and dockside soundings run 8 to 10 feet. Standing on the floating concrete docks, you can see where the marina was hewn from rock.

Transients are accepted at Sunset Marina. The docks are mostly floating, concrete, fin-ger piers, with some alongside docking. There is 30- and 50-amp electrical service on the docks and water, cable television, and phone hookups, too. Gas and diesel are both avail-able, as are on-site mechanical repairs and waste pump-out.

The ship's store is full of things to buy. It occupies a niche between BB&T and a indus-trial ship's store. It is neat, well stocked, and clean.

This is a Stock Island marina, so it would require a cab ride to get to town, which is sev-eral miles away. Unique among marinas we have visited in the Keys, Sunset Harbor offers nighttime security.

A new shower building is now in place adjacent to the dockage basin. The rest rooms and showers are located on the second floor, three showers per gender and a couple of sit-downer stalls in each. The men's showers were not clean when we inspected them, and this was in the morning when such facilities are usually at their best.

A Laundromat is coming, we were told. Eight months after we were told that, we were informed that this facility had not yet been installed. When (and if) the Laundromat does arrive, it will be located on the first floor of the shower building reviewed above.

We can only conclude that Sunset Marina, at least when we visited, was in a state of tran-sition. Only the future will tell whether this marina ever really fulfills its promise. Judging from the less than helpful attitude during our last call here, the future may not be all that rosey.

Sunset Marina (305) 296-7101
http://www.sunsetmarina-keywest.com

Approach depth—7 feet
Dockside depth—8-10 feet
Accepts transients—yes
Type of docking—mostly fixed concrete finger piers
Dockside power connections—30 and 50 amp
Dockside water connections—yes
Waste pump-out—yes
Showers—yes
Laundromat—yes
Fuel available—gas and diesel
Mechanical repairs—yes
Ship's and variety store—yes, complete
Restaurant—The Rusty Anchor (305-294-5369) is closest, but requires a cab ride

Key West Anchorages and Mooring Fields (Various Lat/Lons—see below)

Key West boasts a nice selection of anchor-ages, though one of these havens has recently been converted to a fee-paid mooring field.

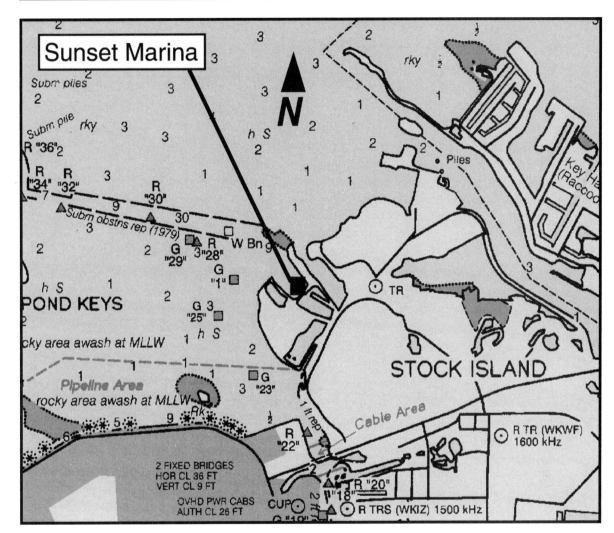

All these various overnight stops are VERY popular, and even in high summer, you will find each and every Key West anchorage crowded with fellow pleasure craft. It can sometimes be quite a challenge to find enough swinging room between your craft and neighboring vessels.

None of the various Key West anchorages (or the mooring field) is sheltered from every quarter. In fact, we do not consider any of these overnight stops to be truly foul-weather capable. Of course, there are lees in one or several directions, but just let the wind clock around and start to blow directly into the anchorage and you may find out what a Mexican jumping bean feels like. If a really nasty blow is in the forecast, we suggest moving to one of Key West's sheltered marinas.

As we did with our review of the city's marina facilities, we will begin with the anchorages off Key West's westerly shoreline

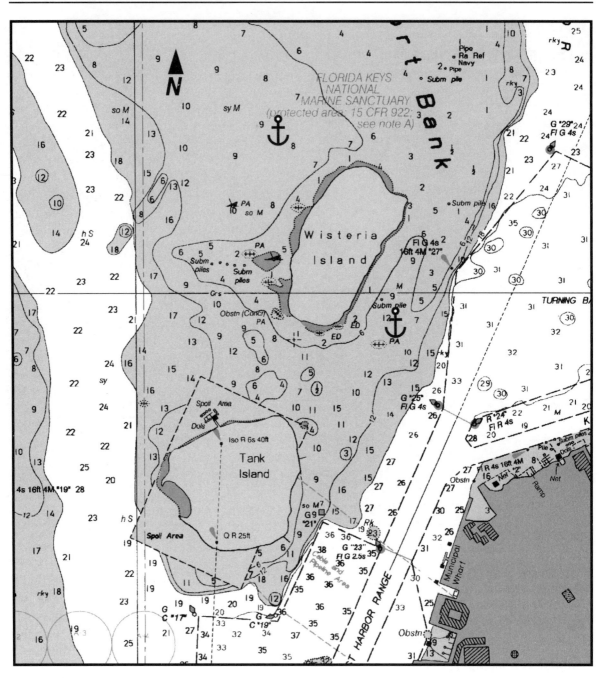

(west of Key West Bight) and work our way around to the northerly banks, near Garrison Bight.

Two anchorages are found off the shores of Wisteria Island (also known as Christmas Tree Island), west of flashing daybeacon

#27. The most sheltered stop lies off the island's southeasterly banks, near 24 33.945 North/081 48.557 West (northwest of flashing buoy #25). Minimum 8- to 10-foot depths are held on these waters, but be sure to stay at least 75 to 100 yards offshore. Also, be on guard against the correctly charted tongue of shallower water stretching south from flashing daybeacon #27.

This haven, which we shall dub the eastern Wisteria Island anchorage, has shelter to the west and northwest, and Key West gives some lee to the east and southeast, but you don't want to be here if strong winds are blowing from the north, northwest, or the south.

The boat population of this anchorage is pure Key West. Multimillion-dollar sailing yachts practically rub elbows with craft that make you wonder how they stay afloat. We have been told there is quite a sense of community among the live-aboards in this anchorage, but we did not get to experience this phenomenon for ourselves.

Many, many other visiting cruisers anchor off the northwesterly Wisteria Island shoreline, near 24 34.228 North/081 48.756 West. Good depths of 6 to as much as 10 feet run to within 75 yards of the isle's northwesterly shoreline, though you must take great care to avoid the long, charted shoal to the south.

This anchorage is sheltered from southern, southeastern, and eastern breezes, but it is wide open to winds for all other directions. Check the forecast and make your decision accordingly.

Northeast of Wisteria Island, a wide swath of deep water parallels the westerly shoreline of Fleming Key. This area is known and charted as Man of War Harbor. When we first perused chart 11447, it seemed as if the best anchorage would be found on the large cove northeast of flashing buoy #29. However, upon actually cruising these waters, we learned that this cove is U.S. Navy property and very much off-limits to pleasure craft.

So, a whole host of cruisers regularly anchor north of the cove, about 225 yards offshore, near 24 34.658 North/081 48.083 West. This haven has a lot going for it. Depths are in the 12+-foot range, and there is a good lee to the east-northeast and southeast. Strong blows from the north, south, or west call for another selection.

Next up is the Garrison Bight Mooring Field. To access this spot, cruisers must round the northern tip of Fleming Key by way of the Garrison Bight Channel. This passage then turns to the south. South of flashing daybeacon #17, the new mooring field spreads out before you, on both sides of the charted Garrison Bight Channel. The heart of the field will be found near 24 34.240 North/081 47.416 West. Its boundaries are denoted by a series of uncharted, diamond-shaped signs.

Currently, the Key West, city-owned, Garrison Bight-Fleming Key Mooring Field consists of 72 buoys. The field is licensed for 149 moorings, but they are not all in. In fact, the support facilities are still very much in the building stages. For example, a dinghy dock was not finished when last we checked in early August of 2001, but was supposed to be up and running by the following September. In the meantime, we were told, dinghies were coming into Garrison Bight Marina (see above).

This mooring field has clearly been designed with live-aboards in mind. You will

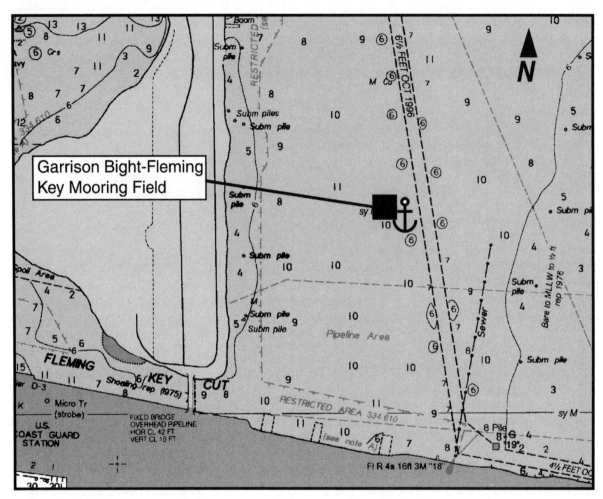

Garrison Bight-Fleming Key Mooring Field

note that the fees we quote below are "monthly." You can call (305) 292-8167 for more information or to check on the latest status of shoreside support facilities.

According to the manager of the City Marina at Garrison Bight, boats without holding tanks are not permitted to use the mooring field. Also, there is a maximum 40-foot size limitation. As one of the dockmasters explained it to us, this requirement is necessitated by the placement of the various mooring buoys.

Cruising craft moored in the field also have pump-outs included as part of their mooring fee. Waste removal is accomplished by a pump-out vessel that makes the rounds four times a week. However, each individual craft is only entitled to three pump-outs a month.

Captains can register and pay their fee for a mooring buoy in one of two ways. Craft that can clear the 50-foot power lines, which cross the entrance to Garrison Bight, can take care of their paperwork at the Key West City Marina on Garrison Bight (see above). You may also call the Garrison Bight City Marina on VHF Channel 16 (they will then switch your to Channel 9 as a working channel) BEFORE picking up a buoy. Skippers will then be directed to an appropriate mooring, and a tender will come out to register your vessels and pick up the field usage charge.

After checking in and paying a fee, cruisers will receive a pennant to fly from their boat to show that they are legal. Doubtless, you will also get a sticker to put on your dink, so you can use the new dinghy dock, when it opens.

The monthly fee for using the Garrison Bight Mooring Field is $120, plus tax. For that rate, skippers receive dinghy mooring privileges, a parking space, the use of the most unattractive showers in this hemisphere (see above) and pump-out service three times a month.

The mooring field boasts good shelter to the west, northwest, and southwest, courtesy of nearby Fleming Key. There is also some protection to the south, from Key West itself, and to the east, from Sigsbee Park. This is NOT a good place to be in a strong northerly wind.

Finally, captains who don't relish the idea of forking over a monthly fee for the Garrison Bight Mooring Field can anchor off the northwestern shores of Sigsbee Park, near 24 35.127 North/081 46.673 West. Stay at least 150 yards off the banks and enjoy minimum soundings of 8 feet, with typical 10-foot depths.

Frankly, this is an open, minimal anchorage with protection only to the south and southeast. Winds above 10 knots from any other direction would make for a very uncomfortable stay.

Key West Shoreside Attractions

There are many, many characteristics which make Key West a very special community. Undoubtedly one of its most unique features is a list of very special, second-to-none, shoreside attractions. In the paragraphs below, we will explore a good collection of these many fascinating, sometimes a little seedy, but always interesting points of interest. To learn a bit more about the true character of Key West, read on.

If Ernest Hemingway himself hadn't been the real deal, someone or some entity in Key West would have invented him and tied him into the town. Hemingway's image as a hell raiser, drinker, partier nonpariel, writer, macho guy, warrior, boxer, swimmer, and fisherman has been co-opted by the entire city of Key West. It fits, of course, but it is also possible that Key West itself shaped Hemingway as much as his legacy has defined modern Key West.

Hemingway, then twenty-nine years old, moved to Key West with his second wife Pauline in 1928, after having lived in Paris. Pauline had supplanted first wife Hadley. Hemingway would have two more wives after Pauline: Martha and Mary. Mary was his spouse in 1961 when he shot himself in the head with a double-barreled Boss shotgun out in Idaho.

After renting a winter manse for three years, the Hemingways were presented with a lovely home at 907 Whitehead Street by Pauline's rich uncle, Gus, who coughed up the $8,000 to buy the residence. It was (and is) charmingly situated in the middle of an acre of gardens. Back then, it was a grand house, maybe one of the grandest on the entire island. In 1963, when the house was

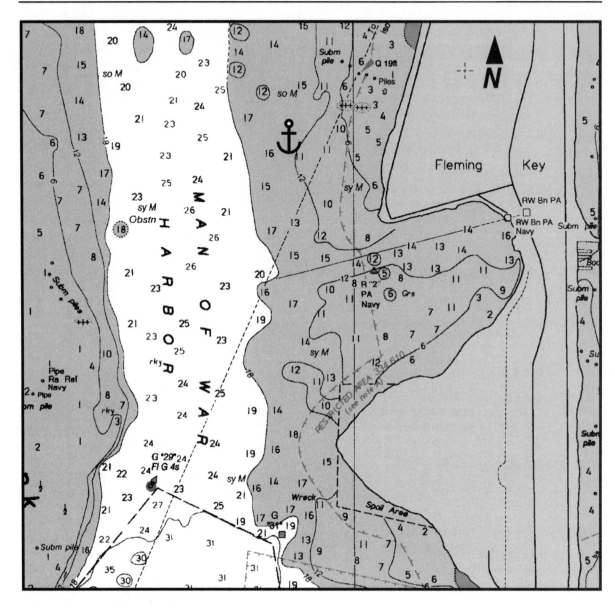

sold—Pauline had predeceased Hemingway by 10 years—it went for $80,000, a ten-fold increase over the original purchase price. Today, $8 million would seem like a bargain.

Hemingway wrote in a second-story studio, which he adapted from a carriage house adjoining the main building, and he had a

catwalk built to connect his studio with the house. It was while he was living in Key West that he wrote *A Farewell to Arms* and *To Have And Have Not,* the only novel he penned that was set in Key West. In fact, it was the only novel he wrote that was set in the United States.

The Hemingway House is a huge tourist attraction in Key West, maybe the biggest. There are legends attached to the house. Some are true. Many are just so much bunk. They are all fun. Anyway, the Hemingway House, with its ties to the man, is a must-stop on anyone's Key West trip.

The Hemingway House and Museum is open from 9 A.M. until 5 P.M. daily. There is an admission charge for both adults and children. Call (305) 294-1136 for further information.

The structure now known as the Little White House Museum was unoccupied in 1946 when Pres. Harry Truman came to Key West, on doctor's orders, to get away from the stress of living and working at 1600 Pennsylvania Avenue. He loved the house and he also loved Key West, as many people do. Better yet, he carried to Key West presidential clout. Government people were soon doing their all to make sure that the two-story, wooden, frame house, which had been officers' residences on the navy base, was up to the wants of Truman, whose needs were actually quite uncomplicated.

Truman was a simple man with an iron will and an outstanding knowledge of history. He had been, at one time in his life, back in Missouri, in the men's clothing business. Opponents used to refer to him in a putative way as a former haberdasher. As it turns out, today that would be like calling Georgio Armani a "suit salesman."

While he was president, Truman spent eleven working vacations in Key West. They

Sleeping cat in Hemingway House (Key West)

numbered nearly half a year, when tied together.

Truman loved to walk the streets of Key West. Back then, in simpler times, the president of the United States could actually stop and get a cup of coffee in the land which he helped rule. Truman played the piano in the Little White House, Chopin mostly. He and his cronies played poker there as well. It is said that while at the Little White House, Truman made his decision to fire Gen. Douglas MacArthur for his mishandling of what was then euphemistically called "The Korean Conflict."

Today the Little White House, located in what came to be called the Truman Naval Base (deactivated in 1974) and is now called Truman Annex, has been restored to nearly what it looked like when Truman was in residence. His piano is there, as well as his actual poker table and his personal briefcase. Truman, of course, is not, but his tenure in Key West gave this southernmost city something that will never die, worldwide attention. Over the years, that attention has transmogrified into something just as good . . . notoriety.

The Little White House (305-294-9911) is open for tours 9 A.M. to 5 P.M. There is an admission charge and all tours are guided.

Back in 1973, while on a trip from the western coast of Florida to the Florida Keys in a 22-foot Aquasport (the trip from Cape Sable to Marathon had a severe pucker factor in it and will always be remembered), one of this guide's authors rented a car and drove to Key West for a stay of a couple of days. We talked

Aboard the historic *Western Union* Schooner

to some people who were in the treasure-diving business. They were looking for investors. "Who do they think we are, farmers who just fell off the back of the turnip truck?" we said smugly to ourselves.

We were talking to Mel Fisher and another person. We were, as time would prove, definitely a couple of farmers who had fallen off the back of the turnip truck. Fisher went on to find the wreck of the Spanish galleon, *Atocha,* and about $200 million in treasure. The *Atocha* sank in 1622. It went to the bottom with gold, silver, and jewels. Fisher hit the mother lode in 1985, twelve years after we had spurned a chance to strike it rich.

What Fisher did in recovering the booty of bygone generations is testimony to vision, hard work, the tenacity of a leech, and the agony of personal loss. His own son and his daughter-in-law drowned during a freak boating accident out at the treasure site when the boat on which they were sleeping rolled over in a storm.

Much of what Mel Fisher and his legion of dedicated salvagers found is on display at the Mel Fisher Maritime Museum at 200 Green Street. The displays are static, so they might not be terribly exciting for young children, but adults can marvel at the exquisite riches the Spaniards were shipping home, loot that they had plundered from the New World. Interestingly, there was a lot more on the bottom where the *Atocha* lay than had been listed in the ship's manifest, showing that smuggling is probably the world's *second* oldest profession.

Mel Fisher died at the age of seventy-six on December 20, 1998. He'd had a full and satisfying life, and the tangibility of his dreams are on display for anyone to see.

The museum (305-294-2633) is open daily from 9:30 A.M. until 5 P.M. There is an admission fee.

The Audubon House and Tropical Gardens at 205 Whitehead Street (305-294-2116) is dedicated to the works of ornithologist John James Audubon. It is open for tours daily between the hours of 9:30 A.M. and 5:30 P.M.

It seems ironic that Audubon, the man whom people look to as the consummate ornithologist, may have also been one of this country's ablest killers of birds. He sketched the birds he drew, you see, from specimens he had shot himself and had posed for sketching by arranging them on stiff wires so that they would "hold" the pose.

Audubon was from France. He arrived in this country in 1803 and settled in Louisville, Kentucky, where he opened a general store. It is an age-old story, repeated often today in a more modern syntax—immigrant arrives in United States and works in convenience store until his English is bad enough so that he can become a big-city taxi driver. Anyway, Audubon didn't make a go of it in the world of commerce, but he made an everlasting name for himself in the world of birds.

Audubon was in the Florida Keys in 1832, and he left Key West that same year after acquiring eighteen new birds for his "Bird of America" folio.

The Audubon House had originally belonged to Capt. John H. Geiger, a Key West wrecker who had occupied this homeplace with his wife and nine children in the Key West heydays as a "wrecking" town. (Geiger Key is named after Captain Geiger.) The house had fallen into disrepair, a continuing Key West phenomenon, and was going to be torn down in 1958, when the Mitchell Wolfson Family Foundation bought it and restored it. It was the first, but certainly not the last, significant Key West restoration.

Geiger furnished his home with furniture

George Patterson House—Caroline Street

that he had salvaged from the ships he helped, and the antiques in the home today are representative of the time, and to some degree, faithfully reflect the opulence which came to Key West wreckers who knew their stuff.

It is, certainly, ironic that the society and the house which bears the name of the man who shot countless thousands of birds in the furtherance of his "art" should be so committed to preservation of the species, because Audubon himself never was. He was an artist and dedicated observer who produced the definitive work on birds. He was not even a sportsman, but he was a damn good shot.

John James Audubon, by the way, never lived in the house that bears his name and probably never visited it either.

The Key West Aquarium (305-296-2051), at the foot of Whitehead Street—1 Whitehead for you readers who are obsessed with exact locations—was originally built as a Works Projects Administration (WPA) endeavor. The WPA was a government-operated business that employed untold thousands during the Great Depression to give people jobs when no jobs in the private industry were available. It was make-work, to be sure, but some of the most venerable landmarks in the country—Timberline Lodge on Mount Hood, Oregon, among them—were WPA projects. This country writhed in agony during the Depression, but begat some of its most enduring treasures, too.

Aquariums are great fun, and the Key West variety is no different. If Mel Fisher's Museum is the kid-weary type, then the aquarium is kid-excitement personified. The sea critters move. You can see all the things that you have only read about, up close and personal. You can touch a shark and feel the roughness of its hide—the hide is actually sort of an extension of its teeth. This may be more than you will ever want to know about the subject, but *dermal denticles* (shark skin) are small, hard, toothlike forms which have the same structure as a tooth. They have an outer layer of enamel, dentine in the middle, and a center of pulp. When rubbed the wrong way— against the grain—shark skin is abrasive, enough so that it is used in putting the finishing sanding touches on fine furniture. At that stage, it is called *shagreen*. The shark is not attached to its skin during such an operation.

Kids will love the "touch tank," where they can pick up and observe conchs (the sea life, not the Keys natives, who are not nearly so compliant), starfish, horseshoe crabs, and other critters that will not bite nor wiggle free.

There are grouper, turtles, sharks, reef fish, and eels here, too. You can wander around on your own or you can take a tour. Tours start at 11:00, 1:00, 3:00, and 4:30. The Key West Aquarium is open from 10 A.M. until 6 P.M. Admission charged.

A visit to the Key West Lighthouse Museum at 938 Whitehead Street will allow you to see Key West from a perspective usually only appreciated by sea gulls, frigate birds, and navy fighter pilots. You can get *up* there.

A vantage point from on high, over a city whose height above sea level is in the single

Key West Treasure Museum

digits, is meaningful. You are the king of all you survey, or at least you can feel that way. If you have ever been to the top of the Washington Monument and looked out or down ("God, Mildred, we are so high up, it makes our uncles look like ants"), you know the feeling.

Down below lies the Atlantic Ocean and the blue-green of the gin-clear water. You can look out and see freighters, and possibly, ocean liners making their stately way along the horizon. You can look north into the Gulf of Mexico. Bring your camera. The views are stunning and being able to show the folks back home much of Key West in one shot will always be a thrill.

The lighthouse, by the way, was taken out of service in 1969, after 121 years of warning mariners that danger lurked in the shallows. We are not sure if anyone has ever tried it, but it might be a project worth telling your grandchildren about: to watch the sunset from Mallory Pier, and then race for the lighthouse, go to the top, and see the same sunset all over again. The Lighthouse Museum (305-294-0012) is open from 9:30 A.M. until 5 P.M. every day except Christmas. There's an admission charge, but kids under seven years of age get in for free.

There is a huge wooden schooner tied up in Key West Bight, a boat which is living history. The 130-foot *Western Union* (305-292-9830, http://www.schoonerwesternunion.com) was built in Key West in 1939. It is the flagship of Key West. Going out for a two-hour trip on this boat gives one a chance to see what it was all about before fiberglass, when sails were hoisted by strong men who had not heard of winches . . . though they well might have been acquainted with wenches.

Western Union was the last working schooner built at Key West, and its working life was devoted to laying undersea cable . . . 30,000 miles in all. It laid cable in the Atlantic, in the Caribbean, and in the Gulf of Mexico.

In 1998, *Western Union* came home. She now sails several times a day, weather and wind permitting. On the National Register of Historic Places, she is the last working schooner that is an original American ship design.

If you go out on her, you'll get to help sail her. The main sail, its gaff and boom, which you may be asked to help hoist, weighs 5,000 pounds. It's heavy work, made easier—but not easy—by the use of blocks, which give some mechanical advantage. When the first mate yells "Heave!" you respond with "Ho!"

Key West Lighthouse

The "Ho" tenses your stomach muscles and makes you into a better machine. Really.

The crew serves complimentary soft drinks, beer, wine, and champagne on the trip. Bring your own snacks, if you need some. And by all means, bring a camera. You'll be on a vessel the likes of which you might not ever be on again, and missing out on recording some of the visual treats would be criminal.

Don't forget to listen to the creaking of the main mast. You've heard the sound in movies or perhaps your dreams, but this is the real thing.

While the *Western Union* only draws eight feet—it was designed with a shallow draft so that it could work in shallow water—it's a heavy vessel and it takes some good winds to get it going. If you think 20 knots sustained are a bit much for your own craft, be advised that 20 knots on *Western Union* would be a walk in the park. You'd hardly feel the sea.

The Hog's Breath Saloon (400 Front Street, 305-292-2032) is one of those must-see places in Key West. The tourist traffic flows through here relentlessly, like the tide. "People watching" is first-rate.

It is hard to determine just what you will see at the Hog's Breath Saloon, but one time we saw a Harley Davidson motorcycle parked outside with two chrome cylinders next to the front shock absorbers. We asked the owner what they were for. He said that they provided an on-demand, nitrous oxide boost to the fuel system but that he had never had the courage to use them. Injecting nitrous oxide into the cylinders of an exotic Harley is

Key West street scene

akin to putting a JATO bottle on the back of 16-foot runabout and touching it off. The results are guaranteed to be dramatic. Scary, too.

The big attraction at the Hog's Breath for us has always been Dan Mobley, a singer of songs whose repertory is vast. Mobley delivers in a rich baritone and knows so many songs with seafaring themes that one can sink under the weight of them. He can also play "Classical Gas" like no one we have ever heard. He's fun to listen to, and he connects with his audience beautifully.

Mobley, a singer, songwriter, entertainer, sailor, father, husband and fisherman who is in his fifties, has been singing and recording music for more than thirty years. He has been playing at the Hog's Breath since 1988.

"From an entertainer's standpoint," Mobley said, "because there is a different crowd every week, it is like going on the road and never leaving home."

Mobley said his favorite spot in the Keys are the Maquesas. "Out there it is shallow and you can see everything that you are doing. You can watch the fish come up to hit your bait and see the whole fight."

One of Mobley's closest friends in Key West was Shel Silverstein, author, artist, and songwriter. Silverstein died unexpectedly in the year 2000.

"I have never been around a writer who worked so hard," Mobley said. "He loved what he did and his view of life in general was what made him magical, making the world just a little more fun, a little more silly. We wrote a lot of songs together. He wrote the lyrics and I wrote the music."

When asked if Key West was different without Shel Silverstein, Mobley paused a second, thought back over the alchemy that Silverstein had generated, gulped once, and softly said, "Yes."

Sunset the world over is an accepted fact of life. Everyone expects it. Just as sure as the sun will rise, it will also set. In the Florida Keys—and most particularly in Key West—sunset is a reason for almost anything, much of it having to do with alcohol. Battalions of Key West natives and legions of tourists are attracted every evening to the place to be when the sun sinks below the western horizon, Mallory Pier.

Nothing in Key West so typifies the carnival atmosphere prevalent in the entire chain of islands as the sunset celebration on Mallory Pier. Vendors set up shop a couple of hours early. You can buy jewelry, junk, palm hats, scarves, something cool to drink (nonalcoholic), T-shirts, and anything else you find attractive. The panoply of goods is as changing, day-to-day, as a teenage girl's moods.

The performers who you see on Mallory Pier are a direct link to the long-ago sideshows of touring carnivals, though the real freaks are absent. You can find a contortionist able to fit his entire body through small spheres. Listen to a drummer or two, or three. There is a man with a small armada of trained cats who can get them to do things no other human experienced in the insouciance of felines can believe. A man in a kilt marches stoically back and forth playing the bagpipe. He is so impassive that one is not certain that he enjoys what he does. There are fortune tellers, card readers, magicians and genial fakes. People who apparently have a direct pipeline to God will tell you how it is and how it will be, for now and ever more, amen.

Mallory Pier is the place to be at sunset in Key West. It is like a lot of other things in life, to be experienced to be believed. Suffice it to say that a visit to Key West without a stop at a Mallory Pier sunset doesn't really count. Mallory Pier is a way station on the highway of life.

Parking nearby is precious, but it is available in a city-owned parking lot for an hourly fee. However, Key West is a walking kind of town and most people leave their cars where they are and amble down on foot. You would do well to follow their example.

Like a sunset at Mallory Pier, a trip to Key West would be incomplete without a Conch Train Tour (305-294-5161). The Conch Train Tour leaves from Mallory Square and allows patrons to sample the highlights of Key West in about ninety minutes. It also allows everyone in Key West to have a look at you. The difference is that you are paying for your view—$19 for adults, $10 for kids 4-12—and theirs is free.

The Conch Train is not actually a train; it is a series of covered cars with bench seats coupled together and towed by a Jeep disguised as an engine. Also connecting the cars is a public address system operated by the "engineer," who keeps up a running commentary on what you are seeing (or missing).

The Conch Train takes you by all the high spots in Key West, and this allows you to make mental notes of what or where you might like to spend more time on your own.

While adults may feel a little goofy riding around Key West in such a hokey conveyance, kids absolutely adore it. Swallow your stuffiness, if it pains you, and get on board. You will only be about the zillionth person who has done it in the last forty or so years, so you will be in good company. If you still need convincing, probably your favorite movie star or political figure has made the Conch Train Tour; set your mind on that.

The Conch Republic

The Conch Republic was established in late April of 1982, after U.S. Border Patrol, on April 18th—a day which will live in infamy in the Florida Keys—inaugurated a public relations fiasco of gigantic proportions when it sealed off the Florida Keys from the rest of the country by establishing a roadblock at Florida City, on the mainland. The Border Patrol, it said, was trying to stop illegal drugs and illegal aliens from getting a foothold on the mainland. No matter that they were already on the mainland in profusion. The resultant traffic jam stretched back some twenty miles down the Keys, as agents searched every car for drugs and illegals.

"They are treating us like a foreign country," said the mayor of Key West, Dennis Wardlow. "We may as well become one."

Rebellion followed, as did succession from the Union. The new entity became the Conch Republic, after a blast from a conch shell, a shot that was heard, oh, a half-block down the street. The rebellion, succession, declaration of war, and surrender followed immediately thereafter . . . at warp speed. No stranger to seizing the moment, Wardlow then requested $1 billion in federal aid money.

Today, you can buy Conch Republic passports, visas, dollars, coffee mugs, and other such stuff, which has been produced to separate tourists from the United States dollars they bring to the Keys. The Conch Republic courtesy flag, which visiting yachtsmen can fly from the flag halyard on starboard spreader of the sailboat, is a pricey $35, plus tax.

It is a known fact, however, that vessels which fly the Conch Republic courtesy flag while in the Keys have never been boarded by Conch Republic customs inspectors, agricultural inspectors, or immigration officials. So maybe there is something to it.

Key West Events

There are so many different events in Key West that to list them all would nearly take a book of its own. We have been picky and subjective about the many Key West goings-on and decided to list only the most interesting ones per month. There is much more, of course, but these are the highlights.

January—Key West Race Week: Sponsored by *Yachting* magazine and Mount Gay Rum, this is where the entire focus of competitive sailing on this planet is for a few days every January. The winds are (usually) brisk and the weather cooperative. The streets are full of sailors; the circus is in town. Some locals complain that sailors are cheap ("the wind is free, so everything else should be") and demanding, but they drop money by the bucketload and generally have a good time sailing hard and drinking the same way.

February—Civil War Days: Fort Zachary Taylor in Key West was, oh shall we say, used sparingly during the War of Northern Aggression. The Federals held it for the entire time and no Confederate ship got close enough for the fort and its soldiers to spring into action and defend the city . . . and the virtue of the ladies in town. During Civil War days, locals and guests dress up like Civil War folks and mingle in friendship, perform reenactments of what life was like back then and generally have a most civil time together.

March—Conch Shell Blowing Contest: This contest started out years ago as something simple, but it has grown into a big deal. There

are probably more people who turn out for this—to either blow into a conch shell or listen to those who do—than there are conchs around Key West. The conch which one eats here comes from other places anyway, because local conch is protected. Real "salts" used to be able to use a conch shell in place of a horn, and some still do. But now there are virtuosos of the conch shell who can play melodies on the things. Could there be a Conch Symphony in the offing?

April—Conch Republic Independence Days and Celebration: After the United States Border Patrol, ignoring the international sieve along the Mexican border, blockaded the Florida Keys in April of 1982, Key West and the rest of the Florida Keys seceded from the rest of the country in a ceremony that took place at Mallory Square. It was witnessed by the media, to give it authenticity and publicity, and sanctified by press coverage the world over. The Border Patrol was embarrassed. The Conchs were thrilled. Not only that, but Conch Republic "stuff" has been available for sale in the Keys ever since, to the just enrichment of the people who had the wherewithal to get it started. There is a parade, races with all kinds of vehicles, a car show, a pig roast . . . you name it. It is just general craziness, but no one said that Key West was like Sutton Place or Greenwich.

May—Queen Mother Pageant: This is a send up of beauty pageants around the world, the ones which women like to watch on television while their other halves stalk out of the house to go see what is happening on ESPN2 down at the corner tavern. The contestants are all guys who dress up in campy outfits and compete for the title. The money raised from this event goes toward AIDS research and assistance. The winner gets a crown that she (he?) gets to keep and wear for a year.

June—Take the month off; there isn't a festival or event or contest scheduled. Maybe even Key West needs a break now and then.

July—Hemingway Days Festival: Ernest Hemingway's birthday was July 21, so Key West stages this festival during the week of July 21. It's the biggie of the year. There is a short-story contest, a storytelling contest, a Hemingway look-alike contest, an arm wrestling championship, golf and fishing tournaments, and lots of drinking. There is a social to-do at the Hemingway House. One thing that is not present is a "Get Married As Many Times As Pappa" contest. He went down the aisle four times. Thousands of people show up for this event each year. There must be a good reason.

August—Coral Reef Spawning: This is for divers only. You won't see this from a glass-bottomed tourist boat. You have to get down there to see the release of eggs and sperm by the coral polyps, and you have to do it at night. The occasion happens several days after the full moon in August. We have heard that the people who have seen it say that it is spectacular. We do not know if anyone asked if it was "good for you."

September—Womenfest Key West: This September happening is a week of seminars,

Hemingway's office—Hemingway House

wine tasting, sunset watching and cruising, film watching, bike tours, street fairs, and about anything else that involves women . . . and yes, even lesbian comedy. There is something for the boys, too, a wet T-shirt contest—by the ladies. Ain't life grand?

October—Fantasy Fest: Mix in Key West's reputation for being a bit outrageous, a chance for a huge party that lasts for days, costumed men, women, and pets, parades and what-have-you, and you have Fantasy Fest, an event that draws thousand and thousands of people from all over each year. The streets are full of crazies; the circus is in town. Nothing quite portrays the flip side of reality the way Fantasy Fest does. It is the Mount Everest of scandalous goings-on . . . and great fun to boot.

November—Offshore Power Boat Week: This is a week-long event which caps the powerboat racing season around the country. If you have never been to an offshore powerboat event, bring your camera. Though the races fairly reek of testosterone, the women are also something to see. Many have their own built-in flotation devices, should they fall off the dock. The boats race through Key West Harbor and also out in the Atlantic, where chop can send boats through the air as much as they are on the surface of the water. The "World Champeen" is crowned at this event. If you are into chamber music and abstemious behavior, do NOT come to Key West for this event. You will be sorely taxed.

December—Images by the Sea: This is an art exhibit wherein all the items on display are created by Keys artists and only Keys artists. It's a fundraiser, but it is also just this side of

sensational. The Keys have always attracted unusual people, and unusual people produce extraordinary art. The media is varied and eclectic. The only limit is human imagination.

Key West Dining

You can eat well in Key West. Sometimes it is expensive, sometimes not. But there is so much variety evident that doing the same old thing that you did for dinner back home is practically a capital offense. Key West is the place to try culinary experiences you never had the guts to try before. Or maybe you never had the opportunity. We would suggest strolling along the street and stopping where the ambiance and the menu (many bills of fare are displayed right on the street for easy perusal) connect with your mindset in a way that triggers an "Ummmmm" in your stomach. Dining in this city can best be enjoyed, we think, al fresco. "People watching" over a drink and dinner is a way to pass an evening, as a kaleidoscope of humanity spins past your point of view.

As usual, we have already reviewed several dining attractions as part of the various Key West marina accounts above. There are several other restaurants that we believe deserve a mention in this section. Be advised that this list is by NO means exhaustive. These are just a few spots that happened to tickle our collective taste buds. For a more complete account of Key West dining, may we once again recommend Joy Williams' excellent guidebook, *The Florida Keys.*

Kelly's Caribbean Bar, Grill, and Brewery (301 Whitehead Street, 305-293-8484) is a couple of blocks from Duval Street, the main drag of Key West nightlife. That gives you a few minutes, if you are walking, which is what everyone seems to do in Key West, to

Key West homeplace

get into a more relaxed, urbane mood. One does not eat at Kelly's; one dines.

The name of Kelly's comes from actress Kelly McGillis, who, along with her husband, Fred Tillman, owns and operate this unique restaurant. Situated in a large wooden building, which once housed the local offices of Pan Am Airlines when Pan Am was making the first ever international airplane flight—to Havana—Kelly's has enough ambiance in its interior and exterior dining to sweep you away, rhetorically speaking. The outside courtyard is protected and simply lovely. If one does not dine al fresco at Kelly's, it will be because of the weather or a lack of personal imagination.

Kelly's offers superb dining because the selections delight in unexpected ways. Think of opening Christmas presents when you were a kid to get a feeling of what could be coming to your taste buds at Kelly's.

We had coconut shrimp that were out of this world; the reason seems to be that the shrimp had been marinated for a day in coconut milk. Then there was egg roll with wasabi sauce, another treat before the entrée.

If you like seafood with some real interesting taste-twists, you'll love Kelly's. Yellowtail snapper is a must-try entrée. But don't overlook the perfectly cooked and crunchy shrimp, which are covered with a reduction of peanut butter sauce, with a touch of Cajun heat added for spice. Then there is blackened fish topped with a barbecue sauce with a mango finish. Are you getting the idea?

We do not usually participate in desserts,

preferring instead a postprandial cup of coffee. However, if you skip dessert at Kelly's, you will go home without a total experience. You've heard of Key lime pie, of course. Kelly's serves up Key lime *cake*. We've never had anything quite so delicious. And don't miss the peanut butter pie or the mango cobbler.

Kelly's has its own microbrewery and full bar service. If you get dehydrated here, it's your own fault.

Reservations at Kelly's are a great idea. There are others who already well know what you are about to enjoy.

Across the street from Kelly's entrance, stop and look at the gate on the road into Truman Annex. It is locked most of the time. It opens only for presidents. The last time was for John F. Kennedy.

Mangoe's (700 Duval Street, 305-292-4606) is our favorite lunch spot in town. Most of the tables are set in a delightful courtyard, with an unimpeded view of the colorful traffic along Duval Street. The black-bean burgers are the best we have ever enjoyed anytime, anywhere. Period! Trust us on this one. Those who have not visited Mangoe's for lunch have missed one of the great midday gastronomical delights that Key West has to offer.

What would a visit to Key West be without a stop at Jimmy Buffet's Margaritaville Café (500 Duval Street, 305-292-1435)? This is headquarters for the so-called "Cheeseburgers in Paradise," and some of the nighttime pasta entrées can be simply wonderful.

We have enjoyed any number of wonderful meals at the Rooftop Café (310 Front Street,

Kelly's Restaurant (Key West)

Rooftop Café (Key West)

305-294-2042). As its name implies, this dining spot is located on the second floor above the teeming crowds on Front Street. So, not only is the food good, but the view isn't bad either.

The Turtle Kraals Waterfront Seafood Grill and Bar (1 Lands End Village, 305-294-2640) is found hard by the Key West City Marina, overlooking the shores of Key West Bight. This is a semi-open-air dining spot, where you can enjoy the superb conch fritters with a roof over your head, while looking out on Key West Bight. This is one place where we disagree with fellow author Joy Williams. Seldom have we had a seafood dish at Turtle Kraals that was not good-to-memorable.

Do you want to "Hang with the Big Dogs"?

Well then, beat your way to the Schooner's Wharf Bar (202 William Street, 305-292-9520). This drinking establishment (mostly) exhibits some serious Keys gnarliness, but it is part and parcel of Key West. A whole passel of the local sailing crowd hangs out here, particularly on Sunday afternoons. Its headquarters guards Key West Bight's southeasterly shores and provides a superb view of the harbor. Schooner's Wharf is yet another semi-open-air spot which offers just about everything alcoholic that has ever been imagined by the mind of man. Don't miss the T-shirts, which not only have the "Hang With the Big Dogs" slogan, but also proclaim that Schooner's Wharf Bar is the "last little piece of Old Key West."

Schooner's Wharf Bar (Key West Bight)

Key West History

Key West, and presumably much of the rest of the Florida Keys, was first occupied by Indians, whose sovereignty came to an end when they were moved to Cuba by the Spanish some time after England took possession of Florida in 1763. These Native Americans had been living and hunting and fishing in the Keys for nearly one thousand years. Ponce de Leon discovered the Keys in 1513. He called the Keys *Los Martires*—The Martyrs—possibly after the Spanish sailors who had been shipwrecked on them and died there.

In 1822, John W. Simonton bought the entire island of Key West for $2,000 from one Juan P. Salas, who had acquired it via a Spanish land grant in 1815. The island was called Cayo Hueso—Bone Island—when Simonton bought it.

Florida was not yet a state; it was a territory, much like Guam is today. In fact, Florida had gone from Spanish rule to British rule to Spanish rule again (1784) to United States rule in the period from 1763 to 1821, only 58 years. It was seemingly the Yugo of real estate, shuttling from one owner to another like a used car, an outcast peninsular parcel, with no nation wanting to take the trouble to do anything with it.

While $2,000 was a sizeable chunk of money in 1822, you could spend at least that much money for a posh dinner for a dozen or so friends in Key West today. And that wouldn't include the tip.

Key West had a marvelous deep-water port, which today accommodates cruise ships. It made a perfect transshipment point for trade between western Florida and Cuba, where Simonton had business interests. He also had keen foresight, capable of measuring the commercial worth of Key West before others did. Not only could Key West give him a base of operations, but Simonton also could see the advantage of having a military base in Key West. A military presence would protect his investments and also provide a market for goods at the same time.

Simonton had contacts in Washington, D. C., good contacts. Two months after closing on his property, he had divided it into four equal portions and sold off three of the portions (to John Whitehead, John Fleeming [later Fleming], and Pardon Greene). Simonton had additionally gotten the United States Navy to consider Key West for a naval station. Just a little more than a year later, Key West had an established naval depot, which was under the command of Comdr. David Porter.

Porter's job was to keep law and order in the Keys and stop pirates from preying on shipping in the Caribbean. He did both jobs well. He was also a bit high-handed. He put Key West under military law and appropriated what he needed, disappointing local merchants, who had hoped to make a killing off the military. As far as chasing pirates was concerned, Porter saw that the deep-draft frigates, which the navy had assigned him were worthless in apprehending these brigands, who headed for shallow water when pursued. He procured eight shallow-draft schooners and obtained an old steam ferryboat from New York and used it to tow oared barges into battle. If the pirates went into shallow water, the schooners and the barges were able to continue pursuit.

Porter even chased some pirates into Fajardo, Puerto Rico, which was Spanish territory. When he sent one of his officers ashore to find the pirates, the officer was grabbed by local authorities. The locals had not counted on Porter's grit. He sent an armed party ashore, captured the local fort, freed his officer, and got an apology from Spanish authorities.

The Spanish, however, lodged a complaint with American authorities. Porter was called back to Washington and court-martialed. He resigned his commission and went on to found the Mexican Navy. Later, in an attempt to right the wrongs done to Porter, the United States made amends by appointing him to diplomatic posts in the Middle East. He died in Turkey in 1843.

Back on the civilian side, Whitehead, Fleming, and Greene built homes and shops along the natural harbor in Key West.

By 1828 Simonton was able to get the government to establish a federal court with admiralty jurisdiction in Key West. It was this court who determined who was awarded how much from shipwrecks and who, to some measure, brought order to the chaos which was the wrecking business. Wreckers were the people who, under license, salvaged cargoes and rescued people from ships which had gone aground on the treacherous reefs all around Key West.

Simonton tried (and failed) to produce commercial salt from the evaporation ponds on Key West, but in general, he succeeded at most of his endeavors in Key West. He died a rich man in 1854 in Washington, D. C. Key West has never slowed down since he got it started. It runs on perpetual momentum,

Key West dock watcher

Sloppy Joe's Bar (Key West)

fueled simultaneously by federal dollars and hard cash brought in by hordes of tourists.

In 1845, the federal government started construction on two forts in the Keys. One was Fort Jefferson, seventy miles west of Key West on Garden Key in the Dry Tortugas. The other, Fort Zachary Taylor, was in Key West proper. The forts were both masonry forts, made with brick and mortar. Unfortunately, the days of masonry forts were short, though no one knew it at the time. During the Civil War, outside of Savannah, Union forces laid siege to Fort Pulaski, which was located on Tybee Knoll Spit, right on the Savannah River, and protected the approaches to Savannah some eighteen miles southeast of the city. Fort Pulaski was a large fortress, buttressed by thick walls and protected from overland invasion by moats. But when the Union army fired rifled cannons at it, the projectiles went through the fort's walls like they were made of peanut butter.

Fort Pulaski's usefulness in the great War of Northern Aggression disappeared with one shot. The repercussions of the success of rifled cannon fire also were felt all the way to Fort Jefferson, which was never entirely finished, even though the masonry work which went into it was (and is) a marvel to behold.

Fort Zachary Taylor was built on the most western part of Key West as part of the nation's coastal defense system. Three stories tall, it was modified several times. In 1898, the year in which the United States went to war with Spain, the third tier of the fort was removed, possibly to make it a less easy target for naval gunfire. As it was technically obsolete from a military standpoint, an assignment to Fort Zachary Taylor must have given pause to those stationed there. The fort never figured militarily in any significant way, and in 1976, it was

declared surplus by the government and given to the state of Florida. The old fort was subsequently taken over by the Florida Park Service as a state historical site.

Shortly before the Civil War began, Key West was ravaged by fire. The structures in town were mostly wooden, and a number of them became torches.

During the War Between the States, Key West remained in the Union and was the headquarters for the Eastern Gulf Blockading Fleet, which was responsible for keeping munitions and other supplies from reaching the Confederacy. The many shallow inlets along the western coast of Florida provided shoal-draft vessels of Southern sympathizers access to inland bays and rivers. Running the blockade became an art form. The ships and crews that the blockading fleet caught were brought to Key West.

Hand-rolled cigars started coming out of Key West in 1867, and by 1880, Key West cigars were bringing in big money. Cuban refugees, who were the best cigar makers in the world, had arrived in Key West because of unrest back home, and they provided the labor for the growing industry.

Despite another large and ruinous fire in 1886, Key West was a prosperous city, and by 1890, it was the largest and wealthiest community in the state of Florida. Sponges alone were bringing in $1 million a year. However, labor troubles in the cigar industry convinced some owners that they could find a better labor market in Tampa, and much of the cigar-making business moved north.

As lighthouses went in along the Keys to warn ships of the impending danger, wrecking as an industry waned in Key West. But its maritime tradition did not. Shipping and boats remained a viable interest in Key West and the business of ship chandlers stayed healthy. They still are.

In 1898 the battleship *Maine* exploded in Havana Harbor, sparking (flames fanned by lurid newspaper stories) the Spanish-American War. The existing naval station was enlarged to meet the perceived threat. The military presence in Key West increased again during World War I.

In 1912 the Key West Extension of the Florida East Coast Railway was completed and dedicated by Henry Morrison Flagler. A year later, a Key West pilot was successful in flying from Key West to Cuba. Though no one knew it at the time, the airplane flight a year after the arrival of the railroad foretold of things to come.

After the end of World War I and with the enactment of the Volstead Act, which made the United States "dry," smugglers worked out of Key West to help bring relief to thirsty Americans. The city's maritime heritage and its proximity to Cuba made smuggling of alcoholic spirits a natural, and the smuggling brought new wealth to the city.

It may have been pure coincidence, but the same year that Prohibition ended (1934) the city of Key West declared bankruptcy. By now, Ernest Hemingway had discovered Key West and had purchased a house on Whitehead Street. In the following year, the infamous 1935 Hurricane wiped out the rail link to Key West by destroying the tracks. The numerous railroad bridges withstood the storm, however.

World War II brought a much larger naval

Hemingway House (Key West)

presence to Key West; antisubmarine patrols called it their home base. More importantly, the years after the war also brought the president of the United States, Harry S Truman, who used Key West and the naval base there as a winter getaway from the dreary Washington D. C. weather.

Truman's presence gave Key West all the publicity it could ever want. He often appeared in public wearing bright, floral-designed shirts that have been a Key West hallmark ever since. They said, "Key West is unusual, fun, colorful." Back then, Pecksniffian fashion experts, trapped in the drab of their wintry lairs, turned up their collective noses at Truman's alleged excess in casual dress. Harry S was just decades ahead of his time.

During the Cuban Missile Crisis, Key West saw another military build-up, but in 1974, the naval base closed for good. The ships and the submarines departed for other bases and the military payroll, which had almost always kept Key West healthy, shrunk markedly.

During this time period, fishermen, who had been just getting by plying the waters for snapper and grouper, found another more lucrative source of income, drug smuggling. Pot—and later cocaine—started to come into the Keys on boats and planes. Jimmy Buffet sang about the trade and other hedonistic Keys diversions in his inimitable style and made millions. Singing about it was far safer than doing it. Singing carries no risk of a few years in Club Fed at Eglin Air Force Base, up in the Florida Panhandle.

Key West—the nation's Southernmost City—is the end of the line, but its colorful history is still being written. The economy now is tourist-based and robust. Unusual people seem to wind up here. Unusual people do

Dan Mobley performing at Hog's Breath Saloon

unusual things. Some of these deeds make the crime report in *The Key West Citizen* the most popular read in the newspaper. Given the cushion of time, some of these deeds could also become part of Key West history.

In general, but particularly in Key West, it's hard to forecast just what the future will bring. Hold your breath.

KEY WEST NAVIGATION

Happy are the navigators who contemplate a cruise of the waters lapping about the margins of Keys West. The two primary approach channels are extremely well marked, and the inner cruising grounds are also expansively delineated by aids to navigation.

There are exceptions. Man of War Harbor has a noticeable lack of beacons, and the passage to Sunshine Marina on Stock Island is a mininavigational nightmare. There are also some shallows to concern oneself with around Tank Island, Wisteria Island, Fleming Key, and Sigsbee Park. In spite of these potential difficulties, our guess is that captains will emerge from their visit to Key West waters with good memories.

Key West's three secondary approach channels are another matter. While a sparse series of markers helps skippers find their way through Southwest Channel, West Channel is virtually without markers of any sort, and Calda Channel is quite shallow.

We will begin our Key West navigational coverage by taking a look at the various approach channels, followed by an account of the city's waterfront, and finishing off with a look at the passage to Stock Island and Sunset Marina.

Main Ship Channel The southerly genesis of the Main Ship Channel begins well south of Key West, out into the briny blue of the Straits of Florida and well east of the charted Eastern Dry Rocks. The outermost marker is flashing buoy #KW. You can pass this marker on either side and cut north, pointing to pass between the next pair of aids to navigation, flashing buoys #2 and #3. In spite of some patches of charted blue water east of #2 and west of #3, there are no depths here shallow enough to worry pleasure-craft skippers.

The Main Ship Channel remains straightforward until reaching the wide gap between flashing buoys #7 and #8. Here, the cut swerves to the northwest and begins following the "Cut A Range."

After coming abeam of flashing buoy #9 to its easterly side, the channel turns again, this time to the north, and begins a passage of the Cut B Range. Now it's time to pay a little closer attention. Between #9 and flashing buoys #14 and #15, the shallows associated with Whitehead Spit (the southwestern corner of Key West) will be passed east of your course line. Come abeam and pass flashing buoy #12 by 200 to 300 yards to its westerly side, and then set a careful compass/GPS course to come abeam of flashing buoy #13 to its fairly immediate easterly quarter. Then, point for the gap between flashing buoys #14 and #15.

Between #12 and #14, Whitehead Spit will lie to the east, and north of #13, the southwesterly tip of Key West will begin to come abeam. Use your binoculars for a good view of historic Fort Taylor.

Cruisers who have been following Hawk Channel west (and south) to Key West will meet up with the Main Ship Channel at flashing buoy #12. Take a turn around #12, south of its position, and come to a northerly heading. You can then follow the instructions laid out just above to track your way to a position between flashing buoys #14 and #15.

North of #14 and #15, the primary Key West waterfront, fronted by the old submarine base, will soon begin slipping by your craft's easterly side. At this point, we are going to leave these waters and go on to a consideration of Key West's other approach channels. We will return to take a detailed look at successful navigation of the waterfront later in this section.

Northwest Channel Break out your binoculars, and use your GPS if you have one, to locate flashing buoy #1 and the northwestern head of (guess what) Northwest Channel. It is important for you to come abeam of #1 to its northern side. Cruisers who arrive south of #1 might meet up with the "East Jetty," described below.

Be careful not to mistake the very prominent flashing daybeacon #A, which marks the northwestern end of the "East Jetty," as flashing buoy #1. For one thing, #1 is a buoy; and for another, it has a bell.

Round #1 and turn to the south. Set course to pass some 25 yards east of unlighted nun buoy #2, and then between unlighted nun buoy #4 and flashing buoy #3. From this point, vessels proceeding south to Key West should pass all subsequent red, even-numbered aids to navigation to their (the cruisers') starboard side and take green markers to port.

South and southeast of #2, a portion of Northwest Channel is protected by twin underwater jetties to the northeast and southwest respectively. Chart 11445 would lead you to believe that a portion of "East Jetty" is "Awash at MHW" (mean high water). Maybe so, but we couldn't see it during our last traversal of this channel. In any case, don't go anywhere near either jetty.

Northwest Channel is reasonably easy to follow as far as the gap between flashing daybeacon #10 and unlighted daybeacon #11. As always, keep your old, reliable binoculars close at hand to help identify the various markers along the way.

Southeast of #10 and #11, the markers spread out, and it's a much longer run between aids to navigation. You must pass through a little better than 1 nautical mile of open waters before sighting flashing daybeacon #12. Stay a couple hundred yards northeast of #12.

Then, another nautical mile will bring you abeam of unlighted daybeacon #14 to its northeasterly side, followed closely by unlighted daybeacon #15. There is a wide passage between #14 and #15. Wise mariners will run the centerline of the gap between these two markers.

The channel now shifts farther south. Point to come abeam of flashing daybeacon #15A by several hundred yards to its westerly quarter. Now, things get a little more interesting. An oblong shoal charted as "Middle Ground" flanks Northwest Channel to the east and northeast, south of #15A. Switch to chart 11447 for a more detailed depiction of the waters south of #15A.

Come abeam and pass unlighted daybeacon #16 by 500 yards or so to its easterly side. Daybeacon #16 sits hard by the shallows abutting the southwesterly side of Northwest Channel, and obviously, cruisers need to give this marker a wide berth. On the other hand, don't pass so far to the east of #16 that you begin to encroach on the "Middle Ground" shoal. Your eventual goal is to come abeam of the next Northwest Channel marker, flashing daybeacon #17, by about .25 nautical miles to its southwesterly quarter. This will put you smack in the middle of Northwest Channel and well away from any shallow-water problems.

Study chart 11447 for a moment, and notice unlighted daybeacons #1 and #2, south of unlighted daybeacon #16. These aids apparently mark some sort of local channel and are best avoided entirely.

Once abeam of #17, its only a short hop to the wide gap between flashing daybeacons #18 and #19. After passing #19 well to its southwesterly side, turn east and point to intersect the Main Ship Channel 300 yards south of flashing buoy #17 (itself hard by the southerly shores of Tank Island).

Southwest Channel The southwesterly tip of (appropriately named) Southwest Channel is marked by a flashing red-and-white buoy, #SW. Buoy #SW lies east of charted Vestal Shoal and west of Satan Shoal. Don't worry, none of these so-called shoals have anything less than 15 feet of water over the bottom.

The remainder of Southwest Channel is (mostly) outlined by a continuing series of red-and-white fairway markers. You can pass to either side of these aids to navigation, but be advised that they are widely spaced on certain portions of the channel, and the next one can be hard to spot.

From #SW, cut to the northeast and point to pass on either side of the next marker, buoy #A. It's then just a matter of picking out one fairway marker to the next, until coming abeam of buoy #C.

Northeast of #C, several nun and can buoys denote the southeastern and northwestern edges of the channel. Pass about 50 yards to the northwest of unlighted nun buoy #2 and 75 to 100 yards southeast of unlighted can buoy #3.

Don't wander too far to the southeast of #3. A really gross navigational error might land you in the shallower waters of charted "Middle Ground." There is even a portion of Middle Ground that is so shoaly it has its own marker, unlighted daybeacon #3. Fortunately, this hazard lies 1.2 nautical miles east of Southwest Channel's unlighted can buoy #3.

Once abeam of #3, point to pass northwest of unlighted nun buoy #4. Farther to the northeast, the fairway markers resume their outlining of Southwest Channel. The next one is buoy #D.

Northeast of #D, switch to chart 11447 for an expanded view of your approach to Key West. It's a fairly lengthy trek of 1.45 nautical miles from #D to the next fairway marker, buoy #E. A similar run is in the offing to the buoy #F.

Once #F is behind your stern, set a compass course for the Main Ship Channel's flashing buoy #13. A cruise of slightly better than .9 nautical miles will bring your craft face-to-face with #13. Pass just south of #13 and then immediately cut to the north on the Main Ship Channel, passing #13 to its easterly side. It's then a quick hop to the gap between flashing buoys #14 and #15, harbingers of the Key West waterfront.

Be careful not to mistake flashing buoy #WR5 for #13 as you are running the gap between #F and #13. Buoy #WR5 marks a sunken wreck, and skippers want to be very sure to pass well southeast of this marker.

West Channel West Channel is a useful cut for those cruisers returning from a visit to the Dry Tortugas, the Marquesas Keys, or Boca Grande Key. We will meet all these west-of-Key-West, cruising locations in the last chapter of this guide. For now, we need note that West Channel is a wide passage that runs south of the just-mentioned islands and a series of shoals and smaller keys nearer Key West.

Unfortunately, there are very few aids to navigation that outline the flanks of West Channel. And there is plenty of shallow water to worry with, particularly off West Channel's northerly flank. A few markers do denote some of the shoals south of the

channel, off the Marquesas Keys, but that's it.

Without the benefit of electronic navigation, running West Channel, even during fair weather in daylight, can be a real DR navigational challenge. Our best advice is, as always, to take your time and keep up with your position at all times.

To enter West Channel from points west, you must pass south of the unbelievably huge shoal striking west from the Marquesas Keys, known (and charted) as "The Quicksands." To the south, a 53-foot light denotes the westerly tip of a series of underwater reefs and rocks stretching to the east. The trick is to run the centerline of the broad swath of deep waters between The Quicksands and the southerly reefs.

Eventually, westbound craft will work their way to a position with the Marquesas Keys to the north and a continuing series of reefs to the south. These southerly hazards have some markings. Unlighted nun buoy #MR denotes "Marquesas Rock," while a 54-foot light marks the position of Cosgrove Shoal. Obviously, you want to stay well north of these markers and at least 2 nautical miles south of the Marquesas. These islands are surrounded by very shallow water.

Continue cruising to the east, passing Boca Grande Key by a least 2 nautical miles off its southerly banks and staying at least that far south of Woman Key, Man Key, Crawfish Key, and the extensive network of shoals and shallows that connect these small isles.

Eventually, captains running the West Channel will intersect the already reviewed

Southwest Channel between unlighted nun buoy #4 and buoy #D. At this point, follow the Southwest Channel northeast to Key West, as described above.

Calda Channel The northwesterly entrance to the Calda Channel lies north of Calda Bank and off the southerly flank of the ICW's approach to Northwest Channel. The Calda's southerly reaches intersect the Garrison Bight Channel, north of Man of War Harbor and west of Fleming Key's northerly tip.

As described earlier in this chapter, Calda Channel is outlined by a profuse collection of aids to navigation, but it is also quite shallow, too shallow for cruising-sized craft, no less. So, we will not present any sort of detailed account of this cut here.

For those small-craft skippers who do choose to run Calda Channel, be very careful to follow all the many twist, turns, and swerves in this errant passage. Even your shallow-draft vessel can find the bottom outside of the marked cut. Depths can run to inches.

Key West Waterfront All the approach passages outlined above (except shallow Calda Channel) lead to an intersection with the Main Ship Channel near Key West's southwesternmost point. North of flashing buoys #14 and #15, the channel shifts a bit to the north-northeast and soon begins to pass by the western face of Mallory Pier. If you happen to arrive near sunset, no, all those people are not out there just to greet you. As we described this daily event earlier, they are there to watch the sun sink below the horizon.

Mallory Pier is found just north of what was once a U.S. submarine base. Cruisers bound for the Hilton Key West Marina should turn to the east and pass just north of the breakwater's northerly tip. This route will take you into the old base's basin. The Hilton Marina occupies the northern corner of this harbor.

A bit farther to the north, captains should point their vessels to pass well east of flashing buoy #19 and about 100 yards east of both flashing buoys #23 and #25. Between #19 and #25, the channel parallels the shores of Tank Island to the west.

After passing Tank Island, the Main Ship Channel runs between flashing buoys #24 and #25. The deep water now spreads out into a wide "Turning Basin." A turn to the northwest will carry your craft to the anchorage off the southeasterly shore of Wisteria Island, while an easterly track leads to Key West Bight and its many facilities.

Wisteria Island Anchorages The anchorages off the southeasterly banks of Wisteria Island can be accessed directly from flashing buoy #25. Simply cruise to the northwest from #25, and drop anchor amidst the collection of fellow pleasure craft you will find swinging tranquilly on the waters southeast of the island. Stay 75 to 100 yards off the island banks.

Be sure to stay well away from the charted shallows southwest of flashing daybeacon #27. All but shallow-draft vessels should be very sure to anchor south of this shoal.

Captains intent on making their way to the anchorage off Wisteria Island's north-westerly shoreline should probably follow the deep-water path west of Tank Island. While it's possible to short-cut this route by passing between Tank and Wisteria Islands, the small, charted half-foot shoal is for real, and some other 4- to 5-foot patches can be expected.

Instead, leave the Main Ship Channel and cut to the north, well south of flashing buoy #19. Flashing buoy #17 marks the northerly edge of the deep water south of Tank Island. Stay south and west of #17.

Point to pass flashing daybeacon #19 by some 300 yards to its easterly side. Soon, the midwidth of Tank Island's north-to-south axis will come abeam to the east.

The next task is to avoid the long, long, charted shoal stretching west from Wisteria Island. These shallows run a surprising .20 nautical miles to the west of the isle's banks. Continue following the deep water north, staying well west of Wisteria Island's westerly shoreline to avoid this hazard.

Once north of these shallows, you can cut back to the northeast and find a place to drop the hook among the legions of boats you will find ensconced on these waters. Set your anchor so your craft will not swing to within less than 75 yards of Wisteria Island.

This northwesterly Wisteria Island shore-line can also be entered by way of the broad but completely unmarked channel that runs southeast from Northwest Channel's unlighted daybeacon #15. We do not particularly recommend this route to strangers, as it borders on shallow water to the northeast and southwest in places, but many locals who know the various ins and outs of this cut use this passage on a regular basis.

Key West Bight Mariners bound for the many marinas on Key West Bight should turn to the east at flashing buoy #24 and follow the Key West Bight Channel. Soon, the breakwater that fronts and protects Key West Bight will begin to slip on by, south of your course line. Watch for flashing day-beacon #4, which marks the breakwater's easterly tip. Be SURE to round #4 and pass this marker to its easterly side as you cut south into the bight's interior reaches.

Once into Key West Bight, Galleon Marina and A & B Marina will be spied to the west, while the City Marina at Key West Bight lies to the southeast, at the rear of the harbor. Conch Harbor Marina flanks the northeasterly side of the bight.

On to Man of War Harbor Cruisers headed for the anchorage on Man of War Harbor or the Garrison Bight facilities (including the mooring field and Sunshine Marina on Stock Island) should cruise on through the heart of the Key West Turning Basin, keeping well east of flashing daybeacon #27. Shallow water is found just west of #27 and may be building around this marker.

Flashing buoy #29 and unlighted day-beacon #31 mark the northeasterly side of the turning basin. Cruise between #29 and #31 and turn almost due north into the southerly entrance of Man of War Harbor.

There are no aids to navigation for quite a spell moving north on this body of water.

Very shallow water flanks the western side of Man of War Harbor (northwest of flashing buoy #29). Favor the easterly, Fleming Key side of this passage slightly to avoid these potentially grounding depths.

Man of War Harbor Anchorage Don't attempt to anchor on the protected cove making into Fleming Key's westerly banks, east-northeast of flashing buoy #29. These waters are military property and off-limits to pleasure craft.

Instead, drop anchor on the waters north of the restricted cove, keeping a good 225 yards west of Fleming Key. Again, you will find plenty of fellow cruising craft swinging at anchor here. Just pick a spot with plenty of room between your craft and the neighbors.

Garrison Bight Channel Moving north on Man of War Harbor, the channel begins to narrow. Switch to chart 11441 for coverage of the northerly portion of Man of War Harbor and Garrison Bight Channel.

Use your binoculars to pick out flashing daybeacon #2. Pass #2 by about 200 yards to its westerly quarter. Shoal water has encroached on #2 and the waters east of this aid to navigation. Similarly, the westerly flank of the channel along this section of Man of War Harbor borders on shallow depths. All these unhappy patches can be avoided by staying west (but not more than 200 yards west) of #2.

Next up is a pair of markers, flashing daybeacon #3 and unlighted daybeacon #4. All but shallow-draft vessels should point to pass between #3 and #4.

Those few smaller craft who choose to explore the shallow reaches of Calda Channel should pass west of #3 and cut to the northwest. The first set of markers you will meet are unlighted daybeacons #24 and #25. You're on your own thereafter—good luck!

Back on the Garrison Bight Channel, this passage turns to the north-northeast and begins to round the northern tip of Fleming Key. A whole series of red daybeacons, some lighted and some not, denote the channel's southeastern and southern edges. Be sure to pass all these even-numbered aids to your starboard side.

There is also one green marker along this stretch, flashing daybeacon #13. Pass south of #13. At this point the Garrison Bight Channel beings a semilazy turn to the south. Set course to pass unlighted daybeacon #14 and flashing daybeacon #16 by some 20 yards to their northeasterly sides.

By the time #16 is in your wake, the channel's turn to the south will be just about complete. Next up is flashing daybeacon #17. Point to pass #17 fairly close by its westerly quarter.

South of #17, a huge expanse of deep water opens out before you. Just stay at least 150 yards east of Fleming Key and all should be well until coming abeam of the southwesterly corner of Sigsbee Park Island, well east of your course line.

Switch back to chart 11447 after cruising .75 nautical miles south of flashing daybeacon #17. As noted earlier, this chart gives a much more detailed picture of Key West's inner waters.

At this point, a large expanse of shallow

water begins to flank the charted path of Garrison Bight Channel to the east. Try to stay in the charted track of the channel, a process that can be a bit difficult, as some of the craft in the Garrison Bight Mooring Field (see below) are to be found directly on the centerline of this passage. So, perhaps your best bet is to favor the westerly, Fleming Island side of these wide waters. Of course, continue to stay a least 150 yards east of Fleming Key.

Another good tip to help avoid the easterly shallows is to note where boats are NOT stationed in the mooring field. It's a safe bet that the waters east of the easternmost vessels swinging on the mooring buoys are shallow.

Garrison Bight-Fleming Key Mooring Field No trick to this one. As your cruise south on the Garrison Bight Channel, the expanse of vessels making use of the Garrison Bight Mooring Field will be more that slightly obvious. Call the Key West City Marina on Garrison Bight on VHF Channel 16, and you will be directed to an open mooring buoy. Later, a tender will come out to register your vessel and collect the monthly fee. Alternately, captains piloting vessels that can clear the 50-foot power line crossing the entrance to Garrison Bight (see below) can register and pay at the Key West City Marina on Garrison Bight. You will then have to retrace your steps to the assigned mooring buoy.

Fleming Key Cut Small powercraft that can clear an 18-foot fixed bridge can take a shortcut from the Key West Turning Basin to the Garrison Bight Mooring Field, and thereafter, the marinas on Garrison Bight. This small passage is known as Fleming Key Cut, and it skirts just south of Fleming's southerly tip. Its western entrance comes up east of unlighted daybeacon #31.

One other caveat to this route is the vicious tidal currents that regularly scour this cut. At times, the rapid water movement under the fixed bridge must be seen to be believed.

Be SURE, very SURE, your boat can easily clear the bridge before committing to this route. If the tidal current is running with you, there will be NO turning around should you discover that your vessel can't clear this span.

If you decide to take this shortcut anyway, favor the southerly shoreline. Shallower water lies to the north, particularly along the cut's westerly reaches.

Cruise carefully under the 18-foot bridge and continue out into the wide waters to the east. Now, the Garrison Bight Mooring Field will come abeam to the north, and the entrance to Garrison Bight will lie just to the east.

On to Garrison Bight Cruisers headed for the marinas on Garrison Bight should continue south through the Garrison Bight Mooring Field. Pick up flashing daybeacon #18, a scant stone's throw off the southerly banks. Turn east about 25 yards north of #18 and point to pass south of unlighted daybeacon #19.

The Garrison Bight approach channel hugs the southerly shoreline. Stay about 25 yards north of these banks. Very shallow water lines this passage to the north. If depths start to rise on your sounder, ease a bit more to the south and see if soundings improve.

Eventually, you will sight flashing daybeacon #21 ahead. Set course as if you intended to come abeam of #21 by some 25 yards to its southerly side. Some 50 yards short of #21, the entrance to Garrison Bight will open out to the south. Turn south well short of #21 and pass northeast of unlighted daybeacon #20 and east of unlighted daybeacon #22. Now, the entrance to Garrison Bight will be obvious, dead ahead.

Garrison Bight and its Shocking Obstructions Okay all you sailors out there, if you haven't paid attention to anything else in this guidebook, listen up now. Not only is the entrance to Garrison Bight crossed by a 50-foot high-tension power line, but this same line borders the inner harbor channel just to the north. What is often not appreciated is that this inner portion of the power line has only a 34-foot vertical clearance, NOT a 50-foot clearance.

So, suppose you pilot a small sailboat and decide you can make it under the 50-foot line at the entrance without problems. That's fine, but what if your vessel loses power (and you can't get the sails up in time) once into the inner reaches of Garrison Bight? If the prevailing winds start pushing you to the north, those 34-foot power lines can suddenly start looking very ominous indeed. So, PLEASE take these power lines into account as you plan a possible entry into Garrison Bight.

Well, would you believe that we are not yet through with cataloguing all of Garrison Bight's navigational worries? Take a look at chart 11441, and note that there is a marked channel in the bight. These markers are not just here for show. Depths outside of the various channels run to 3 and 4 feet. The motto is to stay within the markers.

So, back to how to navigate Garrison Bight. Cruise through the entrance and under the 50-foot portion of the power lines. Soon the harbor will open out before you, but as indicated above, don't think that all these waters are deep. Pass unlighted daybeacons #24 and #26 fairly close by their easterly sides, and then continue south toward the piers associated with the Key West City Marina on Garrison Bight. If this is your destination, you're there.

Captains and crews bound for the Key West Yacht Club have a bit more difficult passage. Continue cruising south until you are just off the city docks. Then, turn to the southeast, and staying just off the city piers, work your way around until you are some 35 yards off the southerly shoreline. Be sure to pass south of unlighted daybeacon #25 along the way.

Favor the southerly banks as you cruise east to the yacht club dockage basin. Of course, you don't want to get too close to the southern shoreline, but be advised that just north of this unmarked channel, depths rise to 1-foot levels.

Cruisers headed for the inner harbor or Spencer's Boatyard should cut west just short of the city docks and pass south of unlighted daybeacon #28. As you might have guessed, the channel takes a 90-degree turn to the west at #28.

Cruise to the west, pointing for the gap between unlighted daybeacons #29 and #30. At this point, the main channel turns south and passes under a 19-foot fixed bridge on its way to Garrison Bight's inner basin.

Skippers bound for Spencer's Boatyard should leave the main cut at #29 and #30 and cruise carefully to the west. You will have to pick out a channel marked by a few white PVC pipes. And you must find this channel, as depths outside of the cut rise markedly. It might be a good idea for first-timers to call the boatyard ahead of time and ask for the latest entry instructions. Anyway, the white pipe-lined channel eventually runs to the outer basin's southwesterly corner, where Spencer's Travelift will be spotted.

Cruising craft headed to the inner basin should pass under the 19-foot fixed bridge. Soon, the inner basin will open out before you. The city "charter row" docks will then be spotted along the southeasterly banks, while Garrison Bight Marina can be accessed in the harbor's northwesterly corner. Pelican Landing and the Harborside Motel docks line the basin's southwesterly shores.

Sigsbee Park Anchorage Those few cruisers who choose to anchor off the northwesterly corner of the island known as Sigsbee Park should abandon the Garrison Bight Channel about .45 nautical miles south of flashing daybeacon #17. Cruise east for about .75 nautical miles, and anchor off Sigsbee Park's northwesterly corner. Stay AT LEAST 150 yards offshore. We actually suggest that you do not approach to within less than 200 yards of the banks.

Sunset Marina Captains bound for Sunset Marina should follow the same path to the little-used Sigsbee Park Anchorage, outlined just above. However, instead of anchoring off the isle's northwesterly banks, continue paralleling the shoreline as it cuts to the east. Stay a good 200 yards north of these banks.

Don't stray more than 200 to 300 yards north of Sigsbee Park, or you could find your keel stuck in the charted 3- and 4-foot waters farther to the north. The chart also indicates some submerged piles in this region. We've always thought avoiding submerged piles is a truly inspired idea.

As you begin to come abeam of Sigsbee Park's northeasternmost point of land, look south to catch sight of unlighted daybeacon #36. Slow to idle speed. You are about to enter the "Twilight Zone" of Key West navigation!

Daybeacon #36 is actually the northern and westernmost marker of the Cow Key Channel. We met this useless cut in the last chapter. It divides Stock Island from Key West. For reasons that will remain forever known only to the U.S. Coast Guard, the markings on Cow Key Channel extend north and then west of the 9-foot fixed bridge, south of unlighted daybeacon #22. Obviously, no cruising-sized craft is going to be able to navigate its way under this span. However, at least the upper (northern and western) extension of this channel does

Leaving Sunset Marina (Stock Island)

provide a means to visit Sunset Marina, but ONLY if you know which markers are which, and on which side you should pass them. This is one spot where the usually ultrareliable, "red, right, returning" rule does NOT seemingly apply!

Basically what's going on here is that the channel lying before you is NOT laid out as an entrance passage leading to Sunset Marina. Rather, as indicated above, it is a westerly extension of the Cow Key Channel. So, as you are working your way south and then west between unlighted daybeacons #36 and #28, the Coast Guard considers that you are headed "toward" the open sea. So, in a way, "red, right, returning" does

apply, as you need to pass red beacons off your port side and take green markers to starboard between #36 and #28. Now that we have informed you, gentle reader, it is up to you to pass #36 to your port side and take #35 to starboard.

South of #35, the channel cuts sharply west. Pass unlighted daybeacons #34, #32, and #30 to their fairly immediate southerly sides.

After passing #30, you will spot a pair of markers ahead, unlighted daybeacons #28 and #29. These aids to navigation mark a southerly turn in the Cow Key Channel. You don't want to turn south, as the marina lies just to the east-southeast. So, crazy as it sounds, pass BOTH #28 and #29 to their northerly side and continue cruising east-southeast. The harbor entrance will be in sight by this time. Cruise directly for the opening.

Trying to run this channel at night, or in really foul weather, is a decidedly bad idea, particularly for newcomers. It might also be a very, very good practice to call the marina ahead of time and get some up close and personal navigational advice on the approach route. There's nothing easy or intuitive about this one!

Fort Jefferson (Garden Key)

CHAPTER 7

Key West to the Dry Tortugas

Seventy nautical miles west of Key West lie the Dry Tortugas, a group of islands whose historical significance far outshines their collective size. Many a cruising skipper has mused upon a trip to these storied isles, with perhaps a stop along the way at Boca Grande Key or the Marquesas Keys. To be sure, those who do undertake this cruise and actually go ashore and visit old Fort Jefferson on Garden Key will have a historic visit unlike anything else in the Florida Keys.

Several factors weigh in against such a cruise, however. First and foremost, your craft will be plowing through serious blue water on the way to and returning from the Dry Tortugas. While this may be an almost childishly simple proposition to true blue-water sailors, mariners used to more sheltered coastal cruising grounds may justifiably pause before undertaking such a voyage. Couple this offshore concept with a total lack of marina and fueling facilities, plus a miniscule selection of sheltered anchorages short of the

Dry Tortugas, and many will readily understand why a cruise to these isles demands contemplation, and if the decision is taken to go, careful preparation and execution.

We suggest that you review the account below with an open mind. Check out all the good points and the cautions. Access the size of your vessel, its fuel requirements, and its ability to handle ocean-size waves in foul weather. Set this against thoughts of walking in the footsteps of prisoners who were exiled to the most feared federal prison of the 1800s and make up your mind accordingly.

There are those who will opine that cruisers who have not seen the sun setting behind Loggerhead Key have not really experienced the best that the Florida Keys have to offer. Maybe, but then again, if you are retching your guts out over the lee rail, or wondering just where those damn islands have gotten to, with nothing but blue water all around you, it's ever so difficult to appreciate a sunset.

Charts Cruisers will need a number of charts to provide complete coverage of all the waters between Key West and the Dry Tortugas. We suggest that you acquire ALL the charts listed below. You simply can't have too many aces up your sleeve when it comes to navigation of these wide waters.

11441—covers the initial departure from Key West, including the Northwest Channel, the Main Ship Channel, the Southwest Channel, and West Channel—also provides good detail of the anchorages near Boca Grande Key

11439—details both the northern and

southern routes to the Dry Tortugas (see below) past Boca Grande Key, the Marquesas Keys, The Quicksands, New Ground, and Half-moon Shoal

11434—a large coverage chart that spans the gap between the western limits of 11439 and the easterly beginnings of the specialized Dry Tortugas chart, 11438

11438—detailed map of the Dry Tortugas, including a special inset for "Tortugas Harbor"—a MUST for anyone planning a visit to this collection of islands

Routes to the Dry Tortugas

There are basically two fundamentally different plans of attack when contemplating a visit to the Dry Tortugas. The most straightforward, but also the least sheltered, approach, which we shall henceforth dub the "northern route," is to run well-marked Northwest Channel from Key West to its northwesterly terminus. You can then turn to the west and skip along the southerly edge of the deep water that fronts a large shelf of shallows to the south. This shoaly water runs north for as much as 7.5 nautical miles from the likes of Man Key, Woman Key, and Boca Grande Key. There are even a few (read that with a capital *F*) aids to navigation along the way, which can help to fix your position. No promises, though.

The good news is that all the shoals described above do give some shelter from southern, southeastern, and southwestern, winds, at least until your track takes you west of New Ground Shoal. There's another 24 nautical miles of thoroughly open water to negotiate before the Dry Tortugas will be within striking distance.

All in all, it is a trek of about 53 nautical miles from the tip of Northwest Channel to a point where captains can safely cut to the south and make their way to the anchorage abeam of Garden Key (see below). Not exactly a 2.3 nautical mile run between daybeacons is it?

The other plan (our "southerly route") calls for leaving Key West by way of scantily marked Southwest Channel, then turning due west once, between buoy #D and unlighted nun buoy #4, and running unmarked West Channel. The first ⅔ of this passage are an almost mirror image to the northern route described above. Here, cruisers will work to

stay just south of the same sea of shallows. And again, the shoals give a bit of a lee, this time to the north, northeast, and northwest.

This questionable protection comes to an abrupt end as you move west of Half-moon Shoal. Then, you're on your own for the next 24 nautical miles. All in all, the southern route encompasses a voyage of at least 56 nautical miles from the point where your vessel leaves Southwest Channel to the Dry Tortugas' Garden Key.

The southerly route has two advantages over its northern counterpart. First, there are a few more navigational aids along the way, at least on the waters east of Half-moon Shoal. More importantly, captains and crews plying this route can find reasonably secure anchorage near Boca Grande Key. Very shoal-draft boats might even be able to visit the enchanting Marquesas Keys, but you couldn't tell that by us.

So, either way, it's a long trek with precious few marks and amenities to help you along your way. Check out our navigational account of both routes at the end of this chapter before deciding on your plan of action.

By the way, both Boca Grande Key and the Marquesas will be considered separately below. If you would like an advance peep, we hit a rock trying to access the inner reaches of the Marquesas. Think we're going to have much good to say about this cruising ground?

Boca Grande Key and the Marquesas Keys

As mentioned above, both Boca Grande Key and the Marquesas Keys line the southerly route's northern flank. Moving east to west, first up is Boca Grande, followed some 7.7 miles later by the Marquesas. Let's get the Marquesas out of the way first. As idyllic as this group of mangrove islands may look from

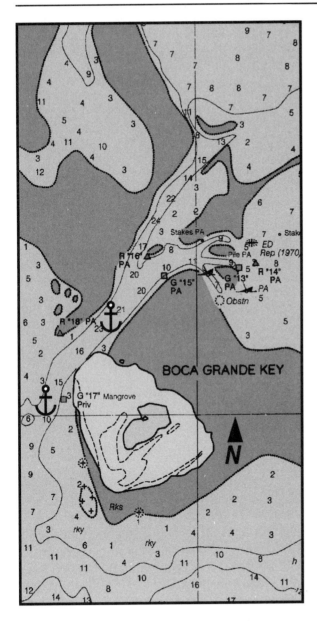

charted rock that was, apparently, right where the chart said it was.

If you absolutely must go here—and we do not recommend it—then the way to do it is anchor off and send a dinghy ahead to hand sound, with a lead line, the best approach in. You can find starting points on the NOAA chart 11439-1. If that sounds arduous, it is. It isn't that it is impossible to get into the inner reaches of the Marquesas; it is just that it is a huge nuisance. There are other, easier, and more pleasant stops to make—the Dry Tortugas, to name one and nearby Boca Grande Key, to name another.

The only person we know who has been to the Marquesas was a friend who was on a sightseeing airplane flight out to the Dry Tortugas and back with his wife and a buddy, who was flying the *Cessna 172*. On the way back to Key West, the plane had serious engine problems and ditched in the lagoon at the Marquesas. No one was hurt. The navy showed up with a chopper to bring them all back to Key West. Anyway, our friend has seen it all up close and personal, and he doesn't think there is any reason to go back.

Conversely, Boca Grande Key is a good stopping-off place. The water is deep between the key and the sand bars on its northern side. Normally, one would make the approach into this anchorage from the southwest. The beginning of the channel is not well defined and the water on either side is shallow. With caution, it is possible, however, to carry six feet up into the interior reaches of the anchorage, where the bottom drops off to the high teens in depth. Eyeball navigation is probably the best way to get in here. There are white sand banks where the water is skinny, and they are easy to see. Cross winds can make the job a little more ticklish.

the chart—twisting entrances to be explored, serenity, far from the madding crowd and all that—they are not. What may look like a dead-certain approach may not be that way at all when you try it. We tried it. Nothing doing. The only thing that we found for sure was a

There are at least two anchor-down spots to consider on the waters adjacent to Boca Grande Key. We like to drop the hook east of unlighted daybeacon #18, near 24 32.411 North/082 00.442 West. Depths run 18+ feet, and there is good protection to the south and southeast, with some lee also to the north and northwest.

Be advised that tidal currents pass through this inner Boca Grande Key anchorage with some force. It might be a good idea to consider a Bahamian moor here, to keep your boat in one place.

While there is nothing to do at Boca Grande Key except take life easy—fishing, swimming, relaxing—those endeavors and the fact that you will not likely run into others here lend this anchorage particular charm.

With strong easterlies in the offing, you might also consider anchoring 350 yards west of Boca Grande Key, southwest of unlighted daybeacon #17. Depths run 7 to 10 feet. Let's be clear about this one, you should ONLY anchor here if (and only if) strong winds are predicted from the east and are not likely to clock around to any other direction during your stay. Check the NOAA weather forecast carefully!

Boca Grande Channel

The Boca Grande Channel is a wide swath of deep water that runs between Boca Grande Key and the Marquesas Keys. There are even two navigational markers to help you along the way, though a few more would certainly be appreciated. Are you listening USCG?

Minimum depths run around 8 feet, with typical soundings in the 10+-foot region. The channel does abut some shoal water to the east and west, however, and care must be taken to bypass these mostly unmarked shallows.

This passage is a good means to travel from the southern route (to the Dry Tortugas) to the northern route or vice versa. Cruisers who want to make this transition will find this channel very useful, courtesy of the long, long shoal that runs west from the Marquesas Keys. This mammoth patch of shallows, known as "The Quicksands," obliges captains to cruise some 18 nautical miles farther to the west before cutting north or south and journeying to the alternate passage. The Boca Grande Channel is located well east of The Quicksands and bypasses this obstruction nicely.

Approaching the Dry Tortugas

We suggest that captains approaching the Dry Tortugas via either the southerly or northerly routes make use of the charted "Southeast Channel." This is by far the best marked of the various charted passages leading to the interior reaches of the Dry Tortugas, and we believe it to be the safest approach. Navigational details of this passage will be presented at the end of this chapter.

The Dry Tortugas

Though some guidebook writers say differently, there are seven islands (not six) in the Dry Tortugas. This entire region is now the Fort Jefferson National Monument. The individual isles are Loggerhead Key, Garden Key, Bush Key, Long Key, East Key, Middle Key, and Hospital Key.

Loggerhead Key has a highly visible lighthouse. Garden Key is taken up by Fort Jefferson, named after Pres. Thomas Jefferson. Adjacent to Garden Key are Bush Key and Long Key. (Bush Key is not named for any presidents, but for its shrubbery, a democratic concept.) As the islands are rookeries for

Fort Jefferson with Loggerhead Key in the background

sooty terns, they are off-limits to humans most of the time. The other three keys are small—Middle Key is awash in the summer—and there is nothing on them. When yellow fever was prevalent here in the 1860s, it is possible that sufferers were sent to Hospital Key to recover, so they would not infect other men. If that is so, it was an ignoble punishment for men already deathly sick.

For mariners visiting the Dry Tortugas, the main requisite is that you bring everything you need with you and take everything that you have used back home. Fresh water is not available in the Dry Tortugas. Pumping heads overboard is not allowed; you must have a holding tank. You may not leave your trash behind. And if you are going to fish within park boundaries, you will need a Florida fishing license. Out in the deep, you are in international waters.

While reefs abound in the Dry Tortugas, much of the water is plenty deep enough for pleasure craft, and the channels are well marked. The only exception to that—and it's a big one—is the channel on the east side of Garden Key. Most, if not all, charts show that channel having 30 feet of water. *The channel is now closed, having filled in between Garden Key and Bush Key.* The silting in had been going on for years, but it closed for good around Christmas 2000. Now, there is a land bridge, albeit thready, between Garden Key and Bush Key. Foot access to Bush Key along the spit is closed, roped off. Wonder when the NOAA charting division will catch on.

Fishing in the Dry Tortugas is nearly a sure

thing. However, one needs to consider that when one hooks up with something that will be tasty on the dinner table—Spanish mackerel, kingfish, dolphin, wahoo—there are also barracudas and sharks around which can relieve you of much of your dinner before you get it in the boat. They know a sure thing when they see one.

Recently, two patches of water OUTSIDE of the national monument boundaries (not within the park as reported in some newspaper articles) have been declared "no fishing" zones. There has also been discussion about making some of the park's water off-limits to anglers as well, but these plans have not been finalized as of this writing.

It should also be noted that spearfishing within the bounds of Fort Jefferson National Monument is a real no-no. Upon visiting Garden Key anchorage for the first time, many years ago, we noticed behind the desk in the Park Service office a "Hawaiian Slingshot" spear with a trident head on it. The spear was tagged. We asked what that was all about. The spear, we were told, had been confiscated by a ranger from a person or persons spearfishing in the anchorage. It was tagged as evidence that would be presented in a hearing before a federal magistrate. And how could they detect something so easily disguised? we asked. The ranger on duty told us that the Park Service had (and still does) a spotting scope in the black lighthouse tower on top of Fort Jefferson. We checked. He wasn't kidding.

There is no reason not to believe that the Park Service is as vigilant today as it was those many years ago. When you come up against the federal government, win or lose, it will be an expensive experience.

There is a large, fixed, wooden dock at Garden Key, abutting its southeasterly shores,

open to all comers and convenient to the nearby anchorage (see below). There is, however, a two-hour limit for mooring to this pier. Overnight stays are no longer permitted, though there was a time, decades removed, when several boats could get together at the dock at night for an ongoing party that moved from vessel to vessel and seemed to never stop.

It was during one of those parties that we watched an attractive woman from Arkansas, wearing a rather formal-looking long dress, hitch up her garment, plop her bottom onto the taffrail of a sailing vessel by the name of *Miracle of God*, and relieve herself over the side whilst never breaking—or even wavering in—the conversational yarn she was so assiduously knitting. There are some images that stay with you forever.

Primitive camping is allowed in a designated area on Garden Key, but again, you must bring everything with you, including water, and leave nothing behind. There are toilet facilities on the dock at Garden Key, but that is the only "extra" you can expect while camping.

Snorkeling is available just off Garden Key. For the more adventurous, there is a large, sunken, steel-hulled sailing vessel on the reef to the south of Loggerhead Key, its mast still visible and whole on the bottom. The trip from the Garden Key anchorage to where you can dive off Loggerhead is several miles and probably not wise in an inflatable. A breakdown out where no one could see you and in water so deep that you couldn't get a dinghy anchor to touch bottom might launch you on a trip of life-or-death significance.

Loggerhead Key, by the way, is not closed during daylight hours, but you must come ashore in a small boat, such as a dinghy. Boats are not permitted to tie up to the Loggerhead Key dock.

Garden Key anchorage (off Fort Jefferson)

Dry Tortugas-Garden Key Anchorage

While most mariners anchor quite close to Fort Jefferson, on the southeast side of Garden Key, there are other anchorages—principally Bird Key Harbor, to the southwest of the fort—that work very well. Protected by reefs, Bird Key Harbor offers privacy that one will not get closer to Garden Key, where the action is.

The approaches to both anchorages are well marked and reasonably easy to navigate, at least during daylight and in fair weather. Depths in the Garden Key haven run from 18 to as much as 35 feet, while depths in Bird Key are in the 25+-foot range. Obviously, you will need a long anchor rode to maintain a proper 6 to 1 (or 7 to 1 in foul weather) scope.

From personal experience, we can say that

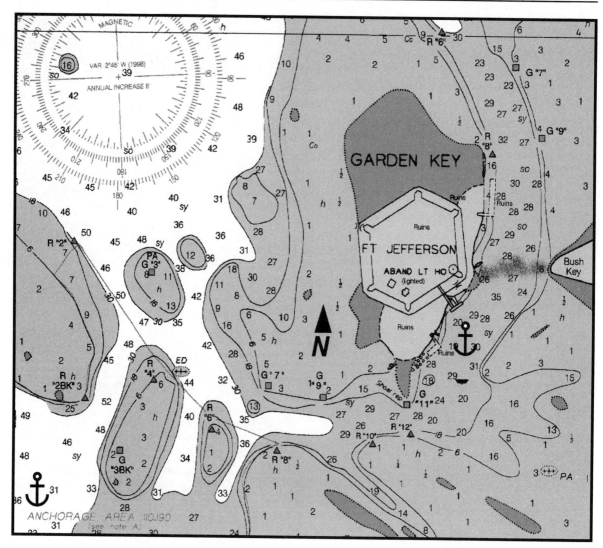

the closer one anchors to other boats, the more reliant you become upon the efficacy of others' seamanship skills. For example, in doing research for this book, we arrived at the anchorage late in the afternoon. Winds had been blowing from the east-northeast at 15 to 20 knots for days, and the anchorage was full. Upon dropping the hook, we noticed a sailboat that was not arranged in the anchorage like the other boats. It was

aground. The water in the Dry Tortugas is gin clear, and the yacht in question was large enough and expensive enough to have a depth sounder. We assumed that the owner had made a mistake. Not wanting him to make a mistake that impacted upon us, we anchored a good ways away from him. As luck would have it, though, his anchor dragged the next day and he drifted down on a boat in front of us, dislodging that vessel's anchor. That boat then drifted down on us, but our anchor was hooked solidly. We stayed put and stopped the drifting boat until the skipper could get things sorted out.

Anchoring regulations in the park are simple. Vessels must anchor within one mile of Fort Jefferson after dark. That's it. Failure to obey park regulations, it is fair to note, can result in an appearance before a federal magistrate. That would be a major inconvenience.

With a dinghy, the world of the Dry Tortugas is yours to explore. An inflatable with a small kicker on the back is ideal. Some people tow small sailing boats out so that they will have some sailing fun. Large luxury yachts can (and do) carry out small sportfishing boats, usually on deck.

Garden Key-Fort Jefferson Ashore

After tying off your dinghy and coming ashore on Garden Key, it is possible—recommended even—to take a self-guided tour of Fort Jefferson; it is well worth the effort. Start by turning right as you come through the main sally port of Fort Jefferson. You will see signs directing you to a small museum, which is in an air-conditioned room, a blessing of immense proportions in the summer. Artifacts from the days when Fort Jefferson was part of this country's arsenal are on display, and one can also view a short movie about the fort. With a little bit of historical knowledge stashed away, you may take the tour at your own speed. It leads you along gun galleries, up spiral granite stairs whose craftsmanship is only perfect, and up onto the top of the fort, where you will have a magnificent view of both Loggerhead Key and the Garden Key Anchorage. To go to the Dry Tortugas without touring the fort is a serious omission. There is much to see, much to learn.

Pay particular attention to the "hot shot" furnace on the ground level, next to the powder magazine. Gunners could heat up cannonballs to cherry red in this furnace and fire them at ships. A hit would set a wooden ship on fire, even if the cannonball skipped across the water before the strike. If you ever wondered why cannonballs had holes in either side, a stop here will clear up the mystery.

Next to the museum is a store where you can purchase NOAA charts and books about what life was like out here, in the olden days. A modern device in the store is a satellite phone. You can call home from the phone, if you want. It works, we were told, "much of the time." The charges are around $15 a minute, a fact that speeds up one's adrenaline production and rate of speech. Teenage daughters with a host of boyfriends back home are best not advised of this connection.

Take you time on this tour. There is no rush. You are a century and a half late anyway.

Dry Tortugas History

It was Spanish explorer Ponce de Leon who discovered these islands in 1513. He called them *Las Tortugas,* after the numerous turtles he also found here, doubtless the main course of many a meal for the captain and his sailors and soldiers. Later, mariners began calling the island group the Dry Tortugas, to signify that there was no fresh water there. Some things never change. There is still no fresh water available in the Dry Tortugas; the people who live there now—National Park Service employees and a smattering of volunteers—get theirs from cisterns, devices that trap and store rainwater.

After Florida became a state in 1821, a lighthouse was built on Garden Key in 1825 to warn shipping of the shoals and the reefs.

In 1886, the lighthouse that now stands and operates on Loggerhead Key was erected.

Fort Jefferson is the principle structure in the Dry Tortugas. The islands were surveyed for their defensive possibilities in 1829. If an enemy controlled the islands, it was postulated, it could control entrance to the Gulf of Mexico. Work was started in 1846 on the fort, which was to be the biggest in a series of fortified coastal defensive seacoast structures. The walls, eight feet thick, tower fifty feet high. The fort could hold four hundred fifty guns and fifteen hundred defenders. But it never did.

Fort Jefferson was doomed to military obsolescence by rifled cannon fire—the Union type—up at Fort Pulaski, on the entrance to the Savannah River in Georgia.

During the Civil War when Union forces laid siege to Fort Pulaski, they used guns that hurled a shell through the sides of the masonry fort like a 44-magnum bullet going though a tub of lard. Though construction on Fort Jefferson—it was being managed by the Army Corps of Engineers—went on for another thirty years, the fort was never completed.

The men who garrisoned the fort never numbered much more than five hundred. They spent most of their time working on building the fort. In 1864, engineers found out, the fort was being constructed not on solid coral reef, as had been originally thought, but on sand and coral rubble, which would not support its foundation. It was slowly settling; the walls began to crack.

During the Civil War, Fort Jefferson served as a military prison for Union deserters who had the bad fortune to be captured. They were sent to the Dry Tortugas, which had about as much charm and ambiance back then as Devil's Island, the notorious outpost of the French penal system in what is now Guyana.

The most famous prisoners ever sent to Fort Jefferson were Michael O'Loughlin, Samuel Arnold, Edward Spangler, and Dr. Samuel Mudd, the so-called "Lincoln Conspirators." Mudd, anyone with a smattering of historical knowledge should remember, was the Maryland physician who set the broken leg of John Wilkes Booth, Lincoln's killer.

Mudd was tried by a military tribunal in Washington, D. C. and escaped being hung for his involvement in the Lincoln affair by one single vote. Four others, including a woman—the first ever executed by the federal government—were not so fortunate. On June 29, 1865, Mudd was found guilty of conspiracy to murder Lincoln and summarily shipped off to Fort Jefferson, about as distant and forlorn a prison as the government could muster.

He was there when yellow fever came to the Dry Tortugas in 1867. The fort's doctor was killed by the mosquito-borne disease, and Mudd filled in for him, even though he got yellow fever himself. Michael O'Loughlin fared less well. He died from the disease. His remains may still be in the Dry Tortugas, but it is more likely—given the small amount of real estate available—that his body, as well as the bodies of others who died from disease, was disposed of "at sea."

In 1869, Pres. Andrew Johnson pardoned Samuel Mudd, Spangler, and Arnold. The latter two disappeared into history. Mudd returned to his home state, Maryland, and was elected to the state legislature in 1876. Mudd died of pneumonia in 1883. The first-story cell that Dr. Mudd occupied is part of the self-guided tour of Fort Jefferson today.

In 1874, the United States Army gave up on

Fort Jefferson and left. Yellow fever was a problem at the fort, and a hurricane had come through and done significant damage. The navy later built a coaling station adjacent to Fort Jefferson, and the battleship *Maine* took on coal there before sailing to Cuba and its cataclysmic rendezvous with history a month later.

In 1935, Pres. Franklin Roosevelt named the region a national monument. Since then, the Dry Tortugas—but principally the fort—have become vastly more popular. For decades, the only effective way to get out to the Dry Tortugas was by sailboat. Privately owned motorboats couldn't carry the fuel to make the 140-mile round trip from Key West, the closest point on the mainland with services. Nowadays, all kinds of watercraft visit the Dry Tortugas. The biggest are a couple of daytrip boats that make the trip out in, we guess, a couple of hours. For people with more money and less time, seaplanes can get them out and back in about an hour's travel time.

DRY TORTUGAS NAVIGATION

As we have already mentioned several times previously in this chapter, there are two routes out from Key West to the Dry Tortugas, south of the shallows that encompass Boca Grande Key and the Marquesas or north of same. In good weather, take either route. In weather with a northerly component, the southern route would be preferred. When the opposite is true, then the northerly route would work best.

Marks are few and far between out in these reaches, so keeping a close eye on your current location makes sense. Even in good weather, it is easy to lose track of where you are, if you are not paying attention. A GPS will help you get a fix on where you are in a hurry, but if you have not invested in such a luxury, then a running plot is absolutely necessary. Be aware, also, that strong currents sweep past these islands. If you should mistakenly run aground out in this area, far removed from quick help, and need commercial assistance, you had best have a huge insurance policy and a radio that will reach more than the customary 25-mile range attributed to a VHF radio.

For sailing vessels, it is easily a daytrip from Key West to the Dry Tortugas, and an early start is recommended if one wants to be in safe harbor when the sun comes down. For motor vessels the same caveat applies.

Northerly Route To begin your passage to the Dry Tortugas via the northerly route, depart Key West by way of the Northwest Channel. This cut was well outlined in the preceding chapter. Please refer to that section for navigational detail.

The outermost marker on Northwest Channel is flashing buoy #1. Come abeam of this marker to its westerly side, and then continue north for another 1 nautical mile. Now, it's time to turn west and head for the Dry Tortugas.

Let the fun begin. Bid a fond goodbye to all those markers on Northwest Channel.

You won't see many more like them short of the Dry Tortugas.

Switch from chart 11441 to 11439 for continued coverage of the waters moving to the west. Now, you have about 15.3 nautical miles to cross before reaching your first recognizable on-the-water marker. This aid to navigation is the unnumbered 16-foot flashing daybeacon marking "Ellis Rock." Stay at least 1 nautical mile north of this daybeacon. It marks a large rock and shoal, which lie mostly north of its position.

There isn't a whole lot to worry with between Northwest Channel's flashing buoy #1 and the Ellis Rock daybeacon. Don't allow an unfavorable current to ease you to the south. A gross southerly navigational error could land you in the charted shoals shelving out from both Boca Grande Key and the Marquesas Keys. Your vessel would have to be a long way from the ideal course line, however, to impinge upon these shallows.

After proceeding west from a position 1 nautical mile north of flashing buoy #1 for some 9.4 nautical miles, captains could choose to turn south and run the Boca Grande Channel. This route allows relatively simple access to the southerly passage and the anchorages off Boca Grande Key, both outlined separately below.

Once abeam of the Ellis Rock marker, things become a bit more exacting. The shortest route to the Dry Tortugas calls for a course line running between New Ground Shoal to the north, and the huge patch of shoals running west from the Marquesas for many miles. These latter shallows are known by the ominous moniker, "The Quicksands." By the way, it was in The Quicksands that a famous treasure salvage expert, Mel Fisher, found his mother lode, the *Atocha*.

This is yet another really good spot to employ a GPS, or better yet, a GPS interfaced with a laptop computer. Believe in us when we say, all that open water can look, well, pretty open, without having a definite idea of where you are.

Fortunately, the westerly tip of New Ground has an unnumbered 19-foot flashing daybeacon. This aid to navigation is invaluable to help navigators fix their positions, particularly if you are tracking your path by way of DR navigation only.

Come abeam of the New Ground daybeacon by about 1 nautical mile to its southerly side. Do not attempt a closer approach. This aid is surrounded by very shoal water.

Set course for flashing buoy #O, east of charted Southeast Channel. It is a long run of 19.5 nautical miles from the New Ground marker to #O. Fortunately, this passage does not really stray near any shallow water.

Also, between New Ground and #O, navigators will need to switch briefly to chart 11434. As you approach #O, switch again, this time to chart 11438. This cartographic aid is the dedicated Dry Tortugas chart, and it is a must for mariners trying to navigate their way to the park's inner reaches.

Flashing buoy #O is one of the boundary markers for the Fort Jefferson National Monument Park. We'll pick up a continuing account of the passage to the anchorages near Garden Key and the interior reaches of the park below, after taking a look at the southerly route to the Dry Tortugas.

Southerly Route Depart Key West by heading south on the Main Ship Channel. At flashing buoy #13, break off to the southwest and begin running the Southwest Channel. Again, this passage was thoroughly covered in the last chapter. Please refer to that account for full navigational details.

Cut due west off Southwest Channel about halfway between buoy #D and unlighted nun buoy #4. You are now on the waters of scantily marked "West Channel," and your craft will follow this passage all the way west to the Marquesas Keys.

You must now cross 7.3 nautical miles of open water. Guard against slipping too far to the north. While West Channel is quite broad, those who really get off course to the north could say hello to the shoals around Man Key and Woman Key.

At the end of your 7.3-nautical-mile sojourn, Boca Grande Key will lie to the north. Let's pause in our westward trek to consider the routes to these havens.

Boca Grande Key Anchorages Your first task is to make sure you are indeed approaching Boca Grande Key and not one of its imitators farther to the east. Use your binoculars to pick out unlighted daybeacon #17 off the island's westerly banks. Then, you can be sure you have the right place.

Stay at least .35 nautical miles west of Boca Grande Key's westerly shoreline. Closer in, soundings deteriorate rapidly.

With easterly winds in the offing, you can anchor southwest of #17, 350 yards or so offshore. Most captains will want to cut northeast and cruise to the inner haven.

Pass #17 by about 25 yards to its northwesterly side and continue cruising to the northeast, pointing to come abeam and pass unlighted daybeacon #18 by about 150 yards to its southeasterly quarter. We suggest anchoring in the channel about 200 to 300 yards east of #18. While the markers continue upstream for a bit, depths become far more questionable and not reliable enough for larger craft.

Boca Grande Channel All you really need do to successfully navigate the Boca Grande Channel is to cruise along the centerline of the wide swath of water between Boca Grande Key and the Marquesas Keys. Be sure to stay well east of unlighted daybeacon #2, which warns vessels away from the shallows stretching east from the Marquesas. Then, all you need do is successfully spot unlighted daybeacon #1 at the northern head of the Boca Grande Channel. Using your binoculars here would be a wise notion.

Pass about 50 yards west of #1, and presto chango, you've found your way to the northern Dry Tortugas passage.

On to the Dry Tortugas West of Boca Grande, West Channel remains quite wide, but now there are shallows lying to the north and south. Of course, these shoals are a good ways off, so if you can maintain your track in any way, shape, or form, they will hopefully be bypassed without difficulty.

It is a very lengthy cruise of 25 nautical

miles from a position south of Boca Grande Key to a position well south of the 19-foot, flashing daybeacon #WR2, marking a wreck just west of Half-moon Shoal. Don't get anywhere near #WR2. We suggest coming abeam of this aid to navigation by a healthy 3.5 nautical miles to its southerly side.

After crossing the first 7.2 nautical miles of the run between Boca Grande and the Half-moon Shoal wreck marker, the Marquesas Keys will lie to the north. As described earlier in this chapter, we don't suggest that any cruising-sized craft attempt to access these interesting islands. Sigghhhh, well maybe we can come back in a small craft some time later.

A mammoth bank of shallows, known as "The Quicksands" extends west from the Marquesas Keys for better than 17 nautical miles. We're not just talking about a little ribbon of shoals either. At its westerly end, these shallows have a north-to-south breadth of 3.5 nautical miles. Quite obviously, you need to make sure your craft stays well south of this gargantuan shoal.

As if that weren't enough to watch for between Boca Grande Key and Half-moon Shoal, there are also a series of reefs flanking the channel's southerly side. Several low-key markers denote a portion of these shoals. Moving east to west they are, in order, unlighted nun buoy #CB, the 54-foot Cosgrove Shoal light, and unlighted nun buoy #MR, marking the Marquesas Rock. Stay a good 2 nautical miles or better north of all these aids to navigation.

Okay, with all that out of the way, let's finally return to our position 3.5 nautical miles south of Half-moon Shoal and flashing daybeacon #WR2. We now suggest that you cut to the northwest and set course to come abeam of the 66-foot Rebecca Shoal light by about 1.3 nautical miles to its southerly side.

Once abeam of the 66-foot marker, things are looking up. All you need do now is to run a careful compass course for the next 12.25 nautical miles to flashing buoy #O (near 24 37.002 North/082 47.997 West), without losing your way, of course. Buoy #O denotes the boundary of the Dry Tortugas and the Fort Jefferson National Monument.

Between your position south of Rebecca Shoal and #O, you will need to briefly switch to chart 11434. As you begin a close approach to #O, switch to 11438. This is the detailed chart of the Dry Tortugas, and it is mandatory for good navigation in and around this collection of islands.

Dry Tortugas-Garden Key-Bird Key Harbor Navigation Navigation in the Dry Tortugas is not hard. On the other hand, sloppy work could leave you on a reef, which will cost you more money in salvage fees and fines than you would care to calculate in the dark of your unremembered dreams. Most likely, it would cost you your boat. Be careful out there.

As mentioned twice above, use chart 11438 for all navigation within the Dry Tortugas. This chart has a special inset that gives a really detailed look at the waters near historic Fort Jefferson and Garden Key.

Allow us to remind you once again that the NOAA charting folks are definitely asleep at the switch on this one. In spite of the 25+-foot soundings noted on 11438 off the eastern shores of Garden Key, this channel has now closed in completely. A tenuous spit of land now connects Garden Key and Bush Key.

With the closure of the channel east of Garden Key, the only viable approach to the Garden Key-Fort Jefferson and its adjoining anchorage is now from the south. The entire route is, happily, extremely well marked and the water is deep.

The perimeter of the entire national monument is marked by large yellow buoys, each carrying an alphabetical designation, starting with "A," several miles south-southwest of Garden Key and proceeding clockwise in an irregular pattern to "Q" almost due south of Garden Key. Nine of these buoys are lit; the rest are not. The lights are flashing yellow.

From flashing buoy #O, cruise to the west-northwest, pointing to come abeam of flashing buoy #2 by some .2 nautical miles to its southerly side. Take a very lazy turn around #2, and then turn to the north, following the midwidth of charted Southeast Channel.

Watch to the northwest for both flashing daybeacon #3 and unlighted daybeacon #4. Turn to the northwest and pass between #3 and #4. There is a wide gap of better than .5 nautical miles between #3 and #4, so your vessel shouldn't be too cramped.

Be advised that #3 lies hard by Iowa Rock. It makes very good sense to stay well

away from this aid to navigation.

From a position between #3 and #4, cruise to the west-southwest for about 1.3 nautical miles. Garden Key and Fort Jefferson will be passed well off your southerly side as you are making this run. Be sure to stay a good .5 nautical miles north of Garden Key to avoid the long tongue of shoals that strike north from this isle.

Once these shallows are well behind you, turn south and use your binoculars to help pick out the approach channel's first aid to navigation, unlighted daybeacon #2. Switch to the Garden Key inset of chart 11438 for a more detailed account of these waters. Come abeam of #2 by about 25 yards to its easterly side.

Southeast of #2, the marked channel takes a lazy turn around the southerly tip of Garden Key. Pass all subsequent red, even-numbered aids to navigation to your starboard side and take green markers to port.

Northwest of unlighted daybeacon #4, cruisers bound for the anchorage on Bird Key Harbor should break off to the south-southwest and point to pass between unlighted daybeacons #2BK and #3BK. Don't approach either marker closely. Both are founded in shallow water. Fortunately, there is a broad, deep path between #2BK and #3BK. Stick to the centerline of this passage.

South of #3BK, the wide pool of deep water known as Bird Key Harbor will open out before you. Unlighted daybeacon #5BK marks the southeasterly extreme of the deep water. Be sure to stay well northwest of #5BK. Otherwise, just select a spot to your liking, set the anchor, and prepare for a well-earned toddy.

Captains continuing on to the popular anchorage southeast of Garden Key should follow the main channel as it moves southeast from #4. Soon the cut turns farther to the east and passes northeast of unlighted daybeacon #6. Next, point to pass unlighted daybeacon #7 to its southerly side, then north of unlighted daybeacon #8, and south of unlighted daybeacon #9. Again, stay to the centerline.

East of #9, the channel narrows. Be SURE to pick out the next three markers, unlighted daybeacons #10, #11, and #12. Pass 50 yards north of #10, and then directly between #11 and #12. Very shallow water flanks the channel south of both #10 and #12, and a tongue of shoals making south from Garden Key lies north of #11.

After passing between #11 and #12, turn to the north. Stay about 100 yards or so off the southeastern and eastern banks of Garden Key. Unmarked shallows are found off the channel farther to the southeast. By staying within the specified distance of Garden Key, these shallows can be avoided.

The anchorage will soon be more than obvious, courtesy of the many other vessels you would undoubtedly spy at anchor. Pick out a likely spot with enough elbowroom and set the anchor. Remember our earlier admonition that some of the vessels you see might have made a mistake and actually be aground. So, watch the sounder as you pick the way to your intended spot.

The fort and the visitors' dock will be easily visible to the northwest. Break out the dinghy and get ready for some historic explorations.

Bibliography

Bethel, Rodman J. *Flagler's Folly: The Railroad That Went to Sea & Was Blown Away.* Key West: Rods Books, 1990.

Eyster, Irving R., and Jeane Eyster. *Islamorada and More.* Marathon, FL: Pigeon Key Foundation, n.d.

Gallagher, Dan, ed. *The Florida Keys Environmental Story: A Panorama of the Environment, Culture, and History of Monroe County, Florida.* N.p.: Seacamp Association, 1997

Grace, Nick. *Radio Marti.* via Internet download: 1998

Keith, June. *Key West and the Florida Keys.* Key West: Palm Island Press, 1997.

Norman, Walter. *Nicknames and Conch Tales.* Tavernier, FL: W. H. Norman, 1979.

Parks, Pat. *The Railroad That Died at Sea.* Brattleboro, VT: The Stephen Greene Press, 1968.

Ripoli, Carlos. *Jose Marti.* via Internet download

Stevenson, George B. *Key Guide to Key West and the Florida Keys.* Tavernier, FL: N.p., 1970.

Williams, Joy. *The Florida Keys: A History & Guide, Eight Edition.* New York: Random House, 1997.

Index

CRUISING GUIDE TO NEW YORK
  WATERWAYS AND LAKE CHAMPLAIN
By Chris W. Brown III
Edited by Claiborne S. Young
480 pp. 8 x 9¼ b/w photos Maps
Appendixes Biblio. Index
ISBN: 1-56554-250-9 pb original

CRUISING GUIDE FROM LAKE
  MICHIGAN TO KENTUCKY LAKE
  The Heartland Rivers Route
By Captain Rick Rhodes
208 pp. 8 x 9¼ 70 b/w photos 26 maps
Index Appendixes Biblio.
ISBN: 1-56554-995-3 pb original

POWER CRUISING
  The Complete Guide to Selecting,
  Outfitting, and Maintaining Your Power
  Boat, Second Edition
By Claiborne S. Young
240 pp. 6 x 9
Illus. b/w photos Glossary Index
ISBN: 1-56554-635-0 pb original

Future Publications:

COASTAL CHARTS FOR CRUISING GUIDE
  TO EASTERN FLORIDA
By Claiborne S. Young

COASTAL CHARTS FOR CRUISING GUIDE
  TO COASTAL SOUTH CAROLINA AND
  GEORGIA
By Claiborne S. Young

Available at better bookstores,
1-888-5-PELICAN, or www.epelican.com